The New York Times

Guide to
New York City
2002

The New York Times
New York, New York

Please send all comments to:
The New York Times Guide to New York City
122 E. 42nd St., 14th Floor
New York, NY 10168

Published by:
The New York Times
229 W. 43rd St.
New York, NY 10036

ISBN 1-930881-04-5
First Printing 2001
10 9 8 7 6 5 4 3 2 1

For the New York Times: Mitchel Levitas, Editorial Director, Book Development;
Thomas K. Carley, President, News Services Division; Nancy Lee, Director of Business
Development.

Correspondents: Randy Archibold, James Barron, Ben Brantley, Barbara Crossette, David W.
Dunlap, Leslie Eaton, Grace Glueck, Abby Goodnough, Laurel Graeber, Clyde Haberman,
Anemona Hartocollis, Amanda Hesser, Bernard Holland, Leslie Kaufman, Randy Kennedy,
Michael Kimmelman, Anna Kisselgoff, Douglas Martin, Herbert Muschamp, Robin Pogrebin,
Rita Reif, Tracie Rozhon, Susan Sachs, Jennifer Steinhauer, Anthony Tommasini, Amy
Waldman, Claire Wilson.

Maps: Charles Blow, Natasha Perkel

Prepared by Elizabeth Publishing: *General Editor:* John W. Wright. *Senior Editors and
Writers:* Alice Finer, Alan Joyce, Cheryl Farr Leas, Richard Mooney, John Rosenthal.
Writers: Kurt Hettler, Jerold Kappes, Gloria Levitas, Elda Rotor, Vivien Watts.

Design and Production: G&H SOHO, Inc., Hoboken, N.J.: Jim Harris, Gerry Burstein,
Ian Wright, Mary Jo Rhodes, Christina Viera, Gerald Wolfe.

Cover Design: Barbara Chilenskas, Bishop Books

Distributed by St. Martin's Press

Table of Contents

PHOTOS

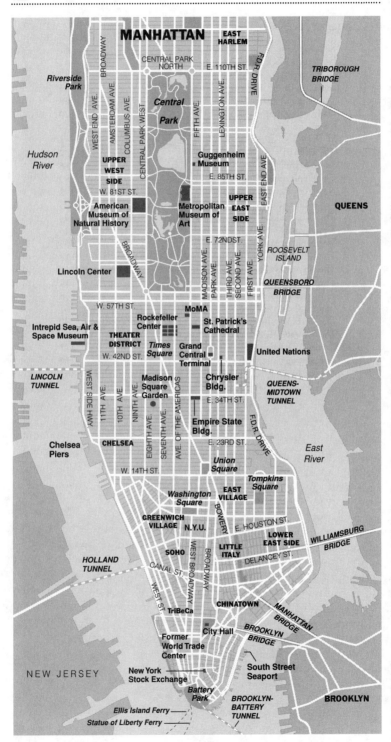

Manhattan Highlights

GETTING IN AND OUT
By Car

Before you decide to bring your car into Manhattan consider these simple facts: tolls for turnpikes, bridges and tunnels are the highest in the nation, traffic is horrendous in the daylight hours and parking fees are four or five times what they are anywhere else. If you need to drive, call your hotel beforehand and find out how much they'll charge you for parking so there are no surprises.

Directions from the South and West: From the New Jersey Turnpike (I-95) to midtown Manhattan take exit 16E to the Lincoln Tunnel, which will bring you to 42nd St. and Ninth Ave. If you are staying downtown, you can go to exit 15W and take the Holland Tunnel, which will leave you on or near Canal St. You can also use exit 13 and take the Goethals Bridge onto the Staten Island Expressway, which goes to the Verrazano Bridge. From here you follow the signs to the Shore Parkway to the Gowanus Expressway to the Brooklyn Battery Tunnel which, will bring you out downtown.

Directions from the West: I-80 is the major highway leading to the George Washington Bridge, which will take you onto the Cross Bronx Expressway unless you exit almost immediately. For the east side of Manhattan, look for the exit to the Harlem River Drive (this leads to the FDR Drive); for the west side take the Henry Hudson Parkway or Riverside Drive (south).

Directions from the North: The New York State Thruway (I-87) becomes the Major Deegan Expressway as you enter the Bronx. If you wish to go to Manhattan's west side, exit at the Cross Bronx Expressway (west) and quickly exit at the Henry Hudson Parkway (south); this turns into the West Side Highway. If you want the east side of Manhattan, stay on 87, go past Yankee Stadium to the Third Ave. Bridge, or a little farther to the Triborough Bridge. Both lead to the FDR Drive.

Directions from New England: Take I-95 to the Bruckner Expressway (I-278) to the Triborough Bridge to the FDR Drive (for the east side); for the west side take the Bruckner to the Cross Bronx Expressway (west) to the Henry Hudson Parkway.

By Train or Bus

Major Terminals

Grand Central Terminal
42nd St. at Park Ave.
www.grandcentralterminal.com
Schedules: (212) 532-4900

Penn Station
32nd St. at Seventh Ave.

Port Authority Bus Terminal
Between Eighth and Ninth Aves., 40th to 42nd St.
Schedules: (212) 564-8484

Rail Lines

Amtrak
www.amtrak.com
Departs from: Penn Station
Major areas served: In addition to service to Florida and nationwide, there are
frequent trains to Washington, D.C. and Boston—including the new high-
speed (extra fare) Acela.
Phone: (800) 872-7245

Long Island Rail Road (LIRR)
www.mta.nyc.ny.us/lirr
Departs from: Penn Station, Jamaica Center Station, Flatbush Avenue Station
Major areas served: Points throughout Long Island
Phone: (718) 217-LIRR (5477), (718) 558-3022 (TTY), (516) 822-LIRR
(5477) or (516) 231-LIRR (5477)

Metro North
www.mta.nyc.ny.us/mnr
Departs from: Grand Central Terminal and 125th Street Station (all lines);
Fordham (Fordham Rd. at Webster Ave.—New Haven and Harlem lines only);
other stations in the Bronx serve individual lines.
Major areas served: Westchester, Putnam and Dutchess Counties in New York
State; Fairfield and New Haven Counties in Connecticut with connections to
the rest of the state.
Phone: (212) 532-4900), (800) METRO-INFO, (800) 724-3322 (TTY)

New Jersey Transit
www.njtransit.state.nj.us
Departs from: Penn Station
Major areas served: Points throughout New Jersey, including Atlantic City;
Philadelphia
Phone: (800) 626-7433, (973) 762-5100

Bus Lines

Greyhound
www.greyhound.com
Departs from: Port Authority (Eighth Ave. at W. 42nd St.), Queens Village
(219–17 Hillside Ave.)
Major areas served: United States (points throughout the country); Canada;
Mexico
Phone: (800) 231-2222

Peter Pan Trailways
www.peterpan-bus.com
Departs from: Port Authority (Eighth Ave. at W. 42nd St.)
Major areas served: Points between Boston and Washington, D.C., including all
of New England.
Phone: (800) 343-9999

Regional Buses
Depart from: Port Authority (Eighth Ave. at W. 42nd St.)
Phone: (212) 564-8484

New Jersey Transit
www.njtransit.state.nj.us
Departs from: Port Authority (Eighth Ave. at W. 42nd St.), George Washington
Bridge Bus Station (at 179th St., between Broadway and Ft. Washington Ave.)
Major areas served: Points throughout New Jersey, including Atlantic City and
the Jersey Shore; Philadelphia; Wilmington, Delaware and Washington, D.C.
Phone: (800) 626-7433, (973) 762-5100

MTA Long Island
www.mta.nyc.ny.us/libus
Departs from: Flushing (at Main St. and Roosevelt Ave.), Jamaica
Center, 179th St. (at Hillside Ave., Jamaica)
Major areas served: Points in Nassau and Suffolk Counties, including Jones
Beach, Roosevelt Field and Walt Whitman Mall.
Note: Free transfer with MetroCard
Phone: (516) 766-6722, (516) 228-4000 (Paratransit)

Hampton Jitney
www.hamptonjitney.com
Departs from: 86th St. (between Lexington and Third Aves); 69th St. (at Lexington Ave.); 59th St. (at Lexington Ave); 40th St. (between Lexington and
Third Aves.)
Major areas served: Points between Manhattan and Montauk, including the
Hamptons.
Phone: (800) 936-0440, (516) 283-4600

Navigating the Airports

Traveling to the metropolitan area's three major airports continues to require patience and lots of extra time. Here are some suggestions for getting to La Guardia Airport, Kennedy International Airport and Newark International Airport—some ways are cheaper. Limousines are more expensive—and more convenient (*see section* "Limousine and Car Services" *in this chapter*).

By Public Transportation

To La Guardia: Take the E, F, G or R subway to the Roosevelt Avenue–Jackson Heights subway station or the No. 7 to the 74th Street–Broadway stop; then get the Q-33 at the bus terminal located at street level or jump in a cab (estimated time from midtown, 50 minutes). Or take the A, B, C, D or No. 2, 3, 4, 5 or 6 subway to 125th Street, or the No. 1 or 9 trains to Adam Clayton Powell Jr. Blvd. and 116th Street; then take the M-60 bus, which runs every half hour and stops at most avenues along 125th Street. Or take the N train to Astoria Boulevard, where you can catch the M-60 bus.

To Kennedy (JFK): Take the A train marked Far Rockaway to the Howard Beach–JFK Airport station, then get the free shuttle bus to JFK terminals (estimated time from midtown, 70 minutes). Or take the E or F train to Union Turnpike, then get the Q-10 Green Bus . Or take the F train to 179th Street–Jamaica, where you can get the Q-3 bus . Or take the No. 3 train to New Lots Avenue, where you get the B-15 bus to Kennedy. MetroCards allow you free transfer to the buses in Queens. For more information call the M.T.A. at (718) 330-1234.

To Newark Airport: Take NJ Transit train from New York's Penn Station to Newark Penn Station. It costs $2.50. In Newark, take the Air Link bus (No. 302) run by NJ Transit. It runs every 20 minutes or so and costs $4. (NJ Transit: 973-762-5100 or 800-626-7433.) The trip takes about 40 minutes (22 on the train, 20 on the bus).

It is advisable to leave extra time when traveling by any bus or rail connection to the airport, especially if you expect to be traveling during morning or evening rush hours. Transportation agencies in the metropolitan area offer lots of additional route and schedule information on the Web to help you get to the airports using their transit systems.

By Private Bus or Van

To Newark Airport: Olympia Airport Express (212-964-6233) leaves from three places in Manhattan and charges $11 for the trip to Newark Airport. From Penn Station (at the northwest corner of 34th Street and Eighth Avenue), buses leave every half hour from 5:10 to 7:10 A.M., then every 20 minutes until 11:10 P.M. Travel time is approximately 35 minutes. From the Grand Central Terminal area (at 120 E. 41st St., between Park and Lexington Aves.), every half hour from 5 A.M. to 7 A.M., then every 20 minutes until 11 P.M. Approximate travel time is 45 minutes.

At the Port Authority Bus Terminal (212-564-8484), purchase your ticket at the Airport Bus Center on the 42nd Street side of the building. Service starts at 4:15 A.M., then every half hour from 5 to 7 A.M, then every 20 minutes until midnight, then at 1 A.M. and 2:45 A.M. Approximate travel time is 35 minutes. Even with express bus lanes, leave extra time in rush hours.

To La Guardia and Kennedy: New York Airport Service (718-706-9658) has service from the Port Authority Bus Terminal, Grand Central and Penn Station, and you can make arrangements to be picked up at some midtown hotels. Approximate travel time is 45 minutes to one hour. It costs $10 to La Guardia and $13 to Kennedy.

To All Airports: Gray Line NY (212-315-3006). Call 24 hours ahead to reserve a pickup at some midtown hotels between 23rd and 63rd Streets from 5 to 7 P.M. La Guardia ($16); Kennedy and Newark Airports ($19). Call the blue Super Shuttle (212-209-7000) vans a day ahead to arrange for the service to pick you up at your home or office and take you to the airport. A van may make up to three pick-ups. La Guardia ($14–$15); Kennedy ($15–$24); Newark Airport ($17–$28). The least expensive fares are from the Battery and the most expensive are from the northern end of Manhattan. Fares can be even more expensive depending on the request; if the price is over $30 a yellow cab or car service may be cheaper. You can also arrange to meet the shuttle at the airport for the trip home. Super Shuttle service is available in Manhattan only.

By Helicopter

To All Airports: Helicopter Flight Services (212-355-0801) charges $595— more outside of normal business hours—for a helicopter trip to the three airports. It carries four people with one bag to check and one carry-on each. Once there, a van transfers you to the airline terminals. Make arrangements at least a day in advance. Approximate travel time is 10 minutes. Helicopters leave from West 30th Street, East 34th Street and the Wall Street heliport (which is three blocks south of where Wall Street meets the East River).

Renting a Car

Renting a car in New York can be an expensive hassle if you're not careful. You'll need to decipher a dizzying, somewhat confusing collection of rules and rates. Your age, your driving record and where you live may all factor into how much it will cost you to rent a car.

Age: It is illegal in New York State to discriminate against young drivers (25 and under), according to the New York State Bureau of Consumer Fraud and Protection. But car rental companies are allowed to tack on a steep surcharge that covers the cost of the additional insurance they must provide for younger drivers.

Driving record: In New York State, a car's owner (in this case the car rental company)—not the driver—is financially and legally liable in the event of an accident. Many national chains now check your driving record with the New York State Department of Motor Vehicles when you give them your license at the counter. If you've had serious driving violations, they may decide not to rent to you; however, rules vary by company.

GETTING AROUND

New York has quite a few places that can help you find your way. There are two visitor information centers, one in Times Square and the other nearby. Both centers have bus and subway maps, and much more. Also, the agency that runs the city buses and subways—the Metropolitan Transportation Authority (MTA)—has a 24-hour Travel Information Center where you can get directions by telephone at (718) 330-1234. Subway toll booths have subway maps, too; some buses have bus maps.

New York Today, *The New York Times'* online service, offers a wealth of information about New York City events, arts and entertainment, restaurant reviews, shopping, sports, news, weather, traffic conditions and a customizable calendar of city activities and events. The site is updated daily, giving users access to the latest news and reviews from the respected writers of *The New York Times*. Features of the site include the **Around Town** section, with overviews, attractions and current events listings for specific neighborhoods in all five boroughs; comprehensive, searchable databases of *New York Times* restaurant, hotel and movie reviews; and *newyork.urbanbaby.com*, with helpful information on living in or visiting New York with children. **Note:** Visitors with some brands of handheld computers can also download **Vindigo** (*www.vindigo.com*), which gives users access to descriptions and walking directions for thousands of restaurants, bars and stores, plus current movie listings and showtimes, all drawn from New York Today's online database.

The Times Square Visitors Center
Broadway at 47th St. (212) 869-1890. The center has an information desk where help is available in five languages, racks and racks of brochures, an MTA booth for MetroCards and information, a row of computer terminals where you can spend 10 free minutes on the Internet and send e-mail, an out-of-town newspaper stand with U.S. and foreign publications, a full-price theater ticket desk, Times Square's history on closed-circuit TV, a free video game, a sightseeing tour desk, a New York City souvenir counter, an Automatic Teller Machine (ATM), a machine that exchanges 10 foreign currencies for dollars, discount coupons and clean bathrooms. A free tour of Times Square begins at the center every Friday at noon.

New York City & Co.
810 Seventh Ave. (between 52nd and 53rd Sts.) (212) 484-1222 or (800) 692-8474. This center, operated by the New York Convention and Visitors Bureau, has an information desk where they speak seven languages, several

touch screens for the day's events and tickets to Broadway shows, info on museums and tours, racks of brochures, an ATM, a MetroCard machine, a one-hour
photo developer and discount coupons. You can also call or visit the bureau
online (*www.nycvisit.com*) to order the bureau's Official NYC Visitor Kit, which
includes a pocket-size guide to New York, a fold-out map, a newsletter about
upcoming events and brochures from various New York attractions. Delivery is
$9.95 for rush delivery, $5.95 for non-rush or free for the city guide only.

Useful Web Sites

www.nyc.gov
Official New York City Web site.

www.mta.nyc.ny.us
Official site of the Metropolitan Transit Authority for info on buses, subways
and trips out of town.

www.nycvisit.com
Web site of the New York City Convention and Visitors Bureau.

www.aaccessmaps.com/show/map/us/ny/nyc_area_hwy
www.cmap.nypirg.org/webmaps/MyGovernmentNYC.htm
For detailed local maps.

www.nytoday.com   *www.newyork.citysearch.com*
www.timeoutny.com   *www.metronewyork.com*
www.villagevoice.com

For arts and entertainment, restaurant reviews, shopping, sports, news,
weather, traffic conditions, info on city activities and events, and more.

Transportation

There are three modes of transportation to get you around the city—not counting your own two feet.

1. Subways are usually the fastest way to get you where you're going, which is
why the natives use them. They are relatively safe, but you should always be
alert to what is going on around you. A $1.50 fare will take you to the far ends
of the city. (*See section "MetroCards" in this chapter for best fare deals.*)

2. Buses tend to be slow, but they have advantages. There are no stairs to climb
and bus stops are closer together than subway stations. Buses also allow you to
take in the street scene as you go. Buses also cost $1.50.

3. Taxis are better than buses at weaving through sticky traffic and more convenient. There are taxi stands at La Guardia and Kennedy airports, and at Penn
Station, Grand Central Terminal and the Port Authority Bus Terminal. Other-

wise, taxis cruise the streets looking for customers. Yellow cabs are regulated by
the city, which makes them a safer bet than unmarked gypsy cabs for tourists.
The gypsies usually charge lower fares, but may fleece the unsuspecting. There
are also dozens of **Limousine** services *(see section* "Limousine and Car Services"
in this chapter).

The Subway System

The New York subway system may be one of the oldest in the world, but it is
also one of the most efficient. It runs 24 hours a day, 365 days a year and covers
every area of the city except Staten Island. There are over 722 miles of track
and 469 stations.

While it is true that parts of the subway are a bit run down, and the screech-
ing noise from the few remaining older trains can cause jangled nerves, one look
at the traffic jams in midtown and at the bridges and tunnels leading to the outer
boroughs will tell you why millions of New Yorkers ride the subway every day.

Manhattan
West Side: served by the A, B, C, D, 1, 2, 3 and 9 trains. The A, 2 and 3 are
express lines. The C, 1 and 9 are local trains, which stop more frequently. E and
F lines run local north–south service south of 50th St., then head east for
crosstown stops on 53rd. The N and R run north–south below 57th St., then
head east for crosstown stops on 60th St.

Note: Because of construction the B and D lines have been replaced by the Q
and W lines making express stops in Manhattan along the N/R Broadway line
to 57th Street. The B and D resume their normal routes from 34th uptown.

East Side: served by the 4, 5 and 6 trains. Trains run along Lexington Ave.
north of 42nd St., and along Park Ave. to the south. The 4 and 5 are express
trains; the 6 is local. They all have interchanges with the E, F, N, R, the 42nd
St. Shuttle (S) and the 7 line.

Bronx:
Served by the B, D, 1, 2, 4, 5, 6 and 9 trains *(see* "The Bronx"*)*.

Brooklyn:
Served by the A, C, F, G, M, Q, R, W, 2, 3, 4 and 5 trains *(see* "Brooklyn"*)*.

Queens:
Served by the B, E, F, G, J, M, N, R, Z and 7 trains *(see* "Queens"*)*.

The Bus System

Note well: you **must** have a token, a MetroCard or $1.50 in coins when you
board a bus. The driver does not handle money. You pay your fare with coins or
a token, or by dipping a MetroCard in the fare box. If you are paying cash and
do not have the right coins, you may find someone on the bus who can make
change for your paper money or pay for you with his MetroCard and take your
cash—or you may not, in which case you must get off.

Some Advice from the Natives About Subways

Subways are safe, but visitors to New York City are advised to **be alert**, especially when packed tight on a crowded train. **Beware of pickpockets**, a crafty lot. Keep your hands on your purse and your wallet. Don't wear flashy jewelry. At night, **don't ride in the last car**, which tends to be the emptiest and riskiest. If you are nervous, seek out the middle car where the operator is positioned to open and close the doors.

Take note of posted signs that tell you if trains will not be running or be re-routed (often on the weekends) because of construction. Loudspeaker announcements are almost always unintelligible. **Don't hesitate to ask someone for directions**—you'll be amazed at how much New Yorkers like to show off their knowledge of the subway system.

The Metropolitan Transportation Authority has a 24-hour Travel Information Center, which you can telephone at (718) 330-1234, but it is not always completely informed about weekend service. It can, however, give directions. The MTA also posts weekly service notices on its Web site, *www.mta.nyc.ny.us*.

City bus lines run the length and breadth of Manhattan. They are especially useful for getting across town. The route numbers for all routes within Manhattan begin with the letter M. Many of the crosstown routes have the same number as the street on which they cross. Traffic on the principal crosstown streets runs in both directions; all the rest are one-way. As a general rule, even-numbered streets are one-way from west to east, and odd-numbered streets run east to west.

Here are the crosstown routes:

M-8 runs on 8th and 9th Sts. from Avenue D and 10th St. to Christopher St.
M-14 operates on 14th St.
M-16 and **M-34** operate on 34th St.
M-23 operates on 23rd St.
M-27 and **M-50** operate on 49th St.; the **27** goes to Penn Station.
M-31 crosses 57th St., then up Madison Ave. and across E. 72nd St.
M-42 operates on 42nd St.
M-66 operates on E. 67th St. westbound and crosses Central Park at 66th St.; eastbound it operates on W. 65th St. until it crosses Central Park, then continues on E. 68th St.
M-72 operates on W. 72nd St. and E. 72nd St., crossing Central Park at 65th St. eastbound and 66th St. westbound.
M-79 operates on E. 79th St. east of Central Park and W. 81st St. west of the park.
M-86 operates on 86th St. and crosses Central Park on that street.
M-96 operates on 96th St. and crosses Central Park on that street.
M-106 operates on 106th St. east of Central Park, and 96th St. west of the park.
M-100, **M-101** and **Bx-15** operate on 125th St.
M-116 runs across 116th St. to Manhattan Ave., then down to W. 106th St.

METROCARDS

MetroCards are the smart way to pay for riding subways and buses. They are always convenient and often a bargain. You can buy them in subway stations and at 3,000 other locations—newsstands, restaurants, hotels, pharmacies and wherever an orange-and-blue MetroCard sign is posted.

A "Funpass" MetroCard for $4 permits unlimited rides on buses and subways for one day. Funpasses may be purchased from machines in subway stations—not from token clerks—and at both of the two tourist information centers mentioned earlier in this chapter.

A $17 weekly MetroCard permits unlimited rides during the seven days after you first use it. A monthly $63 card permits unlimited rides for 30 days after the first use. Otherwise, you can buy a MetroCard for $3 (two rides) or any higher amount you want. If you buy one for $15 (10 rides) you automatically get an 11th ride free.

The use of a MetroCard is usually simple, just swipe it through the slot at a subway turnstile or dip it into a bus fare box. But sometimes a turnstile will tell you to swipe the card again . . . and again . . . and again. The key is to place the card all the way down in the slot, hold it firmly and run it all the way through quickly and smoothly. If all else fails, go to the token clerk, who should then let you through the "special entry" turnstile.

Transfers: A MetroCard permits transfers between subways and buses and vice versa, and between buses and buses, so long as you do not transfer to the same route you started on. After you use your card at the start of a trip, you have two hours to transfer to another route, not necessarily connecting with the first leg of your trip, at no extra charge. (The card "knows" when your two hours has expired.) Note: When you pay a bus fare with cash or a token the fare box will give you a transfer for another bus ride within two hours. It will not work for the subway.

Taxis

A taxi's roof light will tell you if it is available. Look for cabs with the center section of the light lit. They are empty, looking for customers. If the center section is off and the two ends are lit, they say "OFF DUTY" and the driver is not interested in you. If the entire light is off, don't bother with frantic waving—the cab has a passenger. Unlike some other cities, cabs with passengers do not stop to pick up more. (Hailing taxis in the rain is maximum frustration. Consider some other way to go.)

Hailing a cab: There is a knack to this that you can learn by watching how experienced taxi riders do it: stick your arm out and all the way up, and don't be shy. Yell "taxi" if necessary—no one in New York will look strangely at you for yelling. Get off the sidewalk if there is a lot of traffic or if parked cars will prevent the taxis from seeing you. Remember to be watchful of cars and trucks swerving into the lane where you may be standing.

Rules and Traditions: First of all, you should always remember that a New York taxi driver is *required* by law to take you anywhere within the city—even to the far ends of Brooklyn or Staten Island—as well as to Newark Airport and Westchester or Nassau Counties. Most drivers today are natives of India, Pakistan and the Middle East and many are religious Muslims. While a small percentage have less than adequate skills with English, most New Yorkers will tell you that they are far more courteous and respectful than drivers of earlier periods. Unfortunately, like their predecessors, the long hours and low pay often lead to aggressive and reckless driving, so:

- Buckle your seat belt.
- Tell the driver to slow down if you become fearful (he knows his tip is dependent on your satisfaction and that you can file a complaint if you are unhappy).
- Take a fare receipt from the cab driver when you get out. It gives the trip number and the taxi's official medallion number—information you need if you want to make a complaint or trace something you may have left in the cab. It also shows the 24-hour consumer hotline, (212) NYC-TAXI.

Fares: Yellow cab fares start with an initial charge of $2. The fare rises by 30 cents for every 1/5 mile traveled, and by 20 cents for every 90 seconds in stopped or slow traffic. From 8 P.M. to 6 A.M. there is a surcharge of 50 cents per trip.

On trips to Westchester and Nassau Counties you pay the metered amount to the city line plus double the metered amount from the city line to your destination, as well as round-trip tolls. Cabs are required to pick you up if you have a Seeing Eye dog or are in a collapsible wheelchair.

Airports: From JFK Airport there is a flat fee of $30 to any point in Manhattan, plus bridge or tunnel tolls. This is the only one of the three major airports in the metropolitan area for which a flat rate is charged. Fares to and from La Guardia are on the meter, and may hit $20 or more. Fares to and from Newark Airport are higher—the metered amount and another $10, plus the driver's round-trip tolls.

Limousine and Car Services

There are dozens of limousine and car services, from long white Lincolns and Cadillacs equipped with bars and TVs to regular sedans. They often cost more than taxis, but will come when you want them. You must arrange for them in advance. Here are a few, but there are also local companies serving virtually every New York neighborhood (check the phone book):

Tel Aviv (212) 777-7777 and 1-800-222-9888
Carmel (212) 666-6666
Sabra (212) 777-7171 and 1-800-722-7122
Allstate (212) 333-3333 and 1-800-453-4099

Tips on Tipping

Many visitors to New York City—as well as many long-time residents—are unclear on who should be tipped and how much. Below are some general guidelines. Visit the Web site of the New York City Department of Consumer Affairs for more information, *www.nyc.gov/consumers*.

Restaurants: The server should get 15 to 20 percent of the cost of food and beverages before tax, according to quality of service. (Note: an easy way to calculate a reasonable tip is to double the 8.5 percent tax on the bill.) In more upscale restaurants that have a sommelier or wine steward, tip 8 to 10 percent of the cost of wine (cost of wine is subtracted from the bill when calculating the server's tip).

Some restaurants automatically add a gratuity for large parties (usually 15 to 20 percent for parties of eight or more). Customers should be informed in advance, but some restaurants are less forthcoming than others. Be careful not to tip twice when dining with larger groups.

Hotels: Below is the *minimum* appropriate tip for each hotel staff member. In more expensive hotels, the average tip is often more.
Shuttle bus driver: $1. *Bellhop:* $2 per bag. *Maid:* $2 per person per night. (Leave it at the end of your stay.) *Room service:* 15 percent of the bill. *Bellman:* $2 for each visit to the room. *Parking attendant:* $2 or more.

Taxis: Compared with many other cities, New York's taxi charges are not out of line. So we urge visitors to tip generously if the ride is satisfactory since drivers depend on this to raise their pay to a decent level. Some rules of thumb: never tip less than a dollar. Tip $2 when the fare is over $6, $3 if over $10. For trips to the airports tip $6 to $10, more if the driver helps with your luggage.

Beauty Salons: A beautician, barber or manicurist should receive anywhere from 10 to 20 percent of the cost of the service, depending on how long it takes and how labor-intensive. Never tip less than $2.

Exploring New York

Like all the great cities of the world, New York opens up much more of its inner self to those visitors who take the time to walk its streets. There is no other city, at least not in America, that is more inviting to see on foot because no other place has New York's variety of buildings, shops and people.

Only by taking long, leisurely (if still purposeful) strolls can you begin to sense that energy and drive so many visitors to New York have written about for over 200 years. It may not be a tangible thing but it *is* palpable—you will feel it. Even people born and raised here acknowledge its existence, if only because they feel its absence when they travel elsewhere.

So if you can do it, plan to walk somewhere at least once a day; if you can take the time to walk for five or six hours one day you won't regret it and you will learn much more about New York than you will from the top of a tour bus.

Helpful Hint: Don't stand in the middle of the sidewalk while you are talking, studying a map or looking up at a tall building. Always step back toward the buildings.

Be Careful: Most first-time visitors have never experienced the hazardous traffic conditions found in New York. Cars, trucks, busses and bicycle messengers all compete for a favored place on the road and people on foot are seen as just another impediment to their halting progress through the city.

The traditional pedestrian's right of way is, as Shakespeare says, "more honored in the breach than the observance." So walk defensively: assume that a taxi will jump the red light, or a truck or van will turn rapidly into the crosswalk in an attempt to beat you into the center of the street so he doesn't have to wait for all the pedestrians to cross.

You will notice almost immediately that New Yorkers pay no attention whatsoever to "Walk" "Don't Walk" signs (it is just a part of that New York "state of mind," the part that stresses independent thinking, self-reliance, and asks: why trust a sign? I have eyes!). But if you are new here you should obey them at least for a few days, until you get the hang of crossing when it's safe.

Crime Safety

New York is much safer now than it was only a few years ago, but crime does still exist so err on the side of caution. Here are some common-sense rules:
- Avoid desolate areas at night.
- Don't walk in Central Park at night unless there is a major event or you've attended a play at the Delacorte Theater.
- Always try to walk in groups.
- Keep your money in an inconspicuous place; women should grasp their

pocketbooks or wear them across the body; men should be sure a wad of
money is not bulging conspicuously in their pants pocket.

- Don't wear valuable necklaces (especially in the warm weather months)
that can be ripped off with ease.

Public Bathrooms

New York City is notorious for its lack of public bathrooms. Though there are
always plans in the works to improve the situation, it hasn't happened yet. Here
are a few places where you will surely find relief as you stroll around the city:

- Department stores
- Hotels (commonly on the same floor as the ballroom)
- Bryant Park (behind the Public Library on the 42nd St. side)
- Mid-Manhattan Library (across Fifth Ave. from the Public Library)
- Donnell Library (across 53rd St. from the Museum of Modern Art)
- Grand Central Terminal
- Pennsylvania Station
- Port Authority Bus Terminal
- Central Park Boathouse

Finding Your Way

Although New York City proper is made up of five boroughs and stretches for 10
to 20 miles in several directions, the focal point of virtually every new visitor is
the island of Manhattan. If you can plan to spend more than a few days in New
York by all means take the time to visit such wonderful places as the Bronx Zoo
(especially if you are traveling as a family) or the Brooklyn Botanic Garden.
These are world famous institutions and should not be regarded as inferior by reason of location. You will find descriptions, directions, hours and prices for these as
well as other wonderful sites in the specific borough entries later in this chapter.

As the accompanying maps make clear, Manhattan—or "the city" as the
natives call it—is one of the easiest places in the world to visit. The island is
only 13 1/2 miles long and 2 1/3 miles wide at the center (not even a mile at
the southern tip). The basic facts to keep in mind are:

Avenues: run north to south

Streets: run east to west

East Side-West Side: the dividing line is Fifth Avenue. All addresses on the
east side of Fifth begin at 1 East; on the west side of Fifth they begin 1 West.

Streets are for the most part numbered consecutively and laid out in a grid.
From 8th Street north to 181 Street (and beyond) you will always know where
you are relative to, say, 42nd Street. South of 8th Street the streets have names
and you will need to consult the maps for each neighborhood to keep your bear-
ings. (In Greenwich Village, be forewarned, even a map can be confusing especially in the area where W. 4th St. crosses W. 10th St.!).

Avenues (again these run north–south) are also mostly numbered with First,
Second, Third being on the East Side (Lexington, Park and Madison follow);

after Fifth Avenue comes Avenue of the Americas (still called Sixth Ave. by almost everyone), then Seventh Avenue and Broadway (which heads east at 34th St.); in midtown you'll find Eighth, Ninth, 10th, 11th and 12th Avenues but uptown they assume new identities as Central Park West, Amsterdam, Columbus, West End and Riverside Drive.

NEW YORK'S
TOP 25 ATTRACTIONS

American Museum of Natural History
Brooklyn Bridge
Bronx Zoo
Brooklyn Botanic Garden
Central Park
Chrysler Building
Columbia University
Ellis Island
Empire State Building
Grand Central Terminal
Grant's Tomb
Guggenheim Museum
Lincoln Center
Metropolitan Museum of Art
Museum of Modern Art
New York Botanical Garden (Bronx)
New York Public Library
Radio City Music Hall
Rockefeller Center
Saint Patrick's Cathedral
Statue of Liberty
Times Square
United Nations
Yankee Stadium
Wall Street (The Stock Exchange)

SUGGESTED WALKING TOURS

Below are four short walks you can easily fit into your schedule. Each begins at one of New York's premier attractions: Battery Park, Lincoln Center, the Empire State Building or the Metropolitan Museum of Art.

Lower Broadway: Battery Park north to City Hall Park

A trip to the Statue of Liberty lands you back at Battery Park, the natural starting point for a walk up historic lower Broadway, the canyon of ticker tape parades. Along the way you will pass No. 39, site of the house where George and Martha Washington lived in his first year as President. You will also see where Alexander Hamilton was buried after his fateful duel with Aaron Burr, and the offices where John D. Rockefeller ran Standard Oil.

In Washington's time Manhattan Island began at what is now the northern edge of Battery Park. No. 1 Broadway is the building with blue awnings across the street. One entrance says "Cabin Class," and the other "First Class." Now a Citibank branch, this was where travelers of an earlier day booked passage on the United States Lines. The bank has preserved the hall as it was, a grand space befitting a great steamship company.

Across Broadway the massive building with four sculptures out front is the **Alexander Hamilton U.S. Customs House**, a national landmark. It houses the Museum of the American Indian now, but the building itself is remarkable. The large oval in the cavernous rotunda is where importers declared their wares, back when most government revenue came from customs collected in New York. Overhead is a gallery of maritime murals commissioned as a WPA project during the Depression.

The Customs House faces on **Bowling Green**, the city's oldest park. In colonial times it had a gilded equestrian statue of King George III, toppled by a mob in 1776 when the colonies were in revolt. The fence, erected in 1771, is still there.

No. 26 Broadway is the **Standard Oil Building**. Across Broadway, the **Post Office** at No. 25 was the booking office of the Cunard Lines, and pre-Cunard the site of the famously fashionable Delmonico's Hotel. Cunard's great vaulted hall is one of the grandest. Now cluttered with postal paraphernalia, it is worth viewing anyhow. They don't build them like that anymore.

A few blocks uptown is historic **Trinity Church**, once the tallest building in the city. The first Trinity Church was wooden, built in 1697 and destroyed in the great fire that leveled much of the city in 1776. A map inside the church, behind the last pews on the left, shows where Hamilton, Robert Fulton and others are buried. Directly across Broadway at 1 Wall Street is the **Bank of New York** with an eye-popping Art Deco lobby of red and gold mosaic.

Up four blocks is **St. Paul's Chapel**, where Washington worshiped on the day of his inauguration in 1789. He continued to attend during the months when New York was the capital. His pew is to the right as you enter.

You are now at the foot of **City Hall Park**. Branching to your right is **Park Row**, where Greeley, Pulitzer, Hearst, Ochs and other newspaper titans held forth for most of the 19th and some of the 20th century. No. 41 was the original *New York Times* building, now part of **Pace University**. Messrs. Currier and Ives made their prints behind it at 152 Nassau Street.

Finally, take in the **Woolworth Building** on Broadway facing City Hall Park. This, too, was tallest for a while, and the view from the top was a magnet for tourists. The critic Brendan Gill called it "a romantic confection," and described the lobby as "one of the most sumptuous in the country . . . a bedazzlement of marble walls and gilt bronze doors with a vaulted ceiling of blue and gold mosaics." Don't miss it, and while inside don't miss the architect's jest, a whimsical carving of Woolworth counting his money.

Midtown: 34th Street–59th Street

Fifth Avenue, walking north from 34th Street: This walk is only a little more than a mile and could be done after a visit to the **Empire State Building**. Diagonally across the street from the Empire State Building is the new branch of the **City University** (formerly a famous department store, B. Altman, built in 1906). As you walk north there are small stores, coffee shops, a Yankees store and the popular department store **Lord & Taylor** (on the west side of the avenue at 37th St.). Just across the street is the former **Tiffany Building** (409 Fifth Ave.), designed in 1906 by Stanford White, who based it on a 16th-century Venetian palazzo.

At 42nd Street you'll reach the magnificent **New York Public Library** *(see section* "Midtown West"*)*. Weather permitting, you could stop for lunch in beautiful **Bryant Park** right behind the library. There are two outdoor restaurants and an upscale indoor one called the **Bryant Park Grill**.

Heading north you will find many more stores and several interesting buildings especially the **Fred F. French Building** (at the northeast corner of 45th St.). Built in 1927, its arcade and lobby are wonderful examples of the Art Deco style. Only a few blocks north are two of the most popular attractions in New York: **St. Patrick's Cathedral** and **Rockefeller Center**. All through the 40's and 50's you'll find the heart of New York's fanciest shopping district with such stores as **Saks Fifth Avenue** (which dates from 1924), **Tiffany's**, **Bergdorf Goodman**, **Henri Bendel** and at 59th Street **F.A.O. Schwartz**, reported to be the nation's largest toy store. *(See chapter* **Shopping** *for details.)*

Upper West Side:
Lincoln Center to 86th Street

Broadway, walking north from 65th Street: This short walk will take you through an interesting cross section of Manhattan. The Upper West Side is an area where young professionals, families and older New Yorkers reside and commingle with ease, strolling broad sidewalks that run past a wide variety of stores including the dazzling food emporia **Fairway Market** (74th St., west side of Broadway), **Citarella** (next door) and **Zabar's** (81st St., also the west side). *(See chapter* **Shopping** *for details.)*

When you reach the busy intersection of 72nd Street and Broadway (where Amsterdam Ave. crosses Broadway) you can enjoy a well-known New York treat, a couple of franks and a drink for only $1.95 at **Gray's Papaya**. At 73rd Street on the east side of Broadway, the wonderful **Apple Bank** building, erected in 1928, is a great favorite of architects. At 74th Street on the west side of Broadway is the old **Ansonia Hotel,** which was built by a French firm in 1904. Recently cleaned, restored and converted to apartments, its ornamental facade will dazzle you from every angle. Only four blocks up the street is the 1908 **Apthorp,** a huge apartment house that occupies a full city block; midblock between 78th and 79th is a huge arched entrance leading to a vast interior courtyard.

To get a true sense of this community you should walk down any of the side streets for a few blocks. If you head west you'll pass West End Avenue and then Riverside Drive. The park that runs along the Drive is one of the highlights of the neighborhood and well worth a visit. You'll find views of the Hudson River, wonderful flower gardens and, quite often, families, dogs and picnickers. At 87th Street and Riverside Drive the impressive **Soldiers and Sailors Monument** is a terrific place to sit and relax. At 79th Street you can walk down by the river to the outdoor **Boat Basin Cafe** for a delightful snack while watching the boats and barges pass by.

If you head east from Broadway you'll be heading toward Central Park. At 72nd Street and Central Park West you'll find the famous **Dakota** apartment building, built in 1884. It has always been a symbol of New York opulence but it became world famous in 1980 when John Lennon, a resident of the building, was shot to death in the entryway. A well-visited memorial to Lennon, **Strawberry Fields**, is located just across the street at the entrance to Central Park.

To return to Midtown you can take an enjoyable walk through the park or stay on Central Park West and see some of the finest apartment houses in the city.

Upper East Side: Fifth Avenue

The Metropolitan Museum Neighborhood: As you leave the **Metropolitan Museum of Art**, look straight across Fifth Avenue to the southeast corner of East 82nd Street and the former mansion home of Benjamin Duke. Born to a tobacco farming family in North Carolina, Duke and his younger brother James were founders of the American Tobacco Company and the principal benefactors of a little college that became Duke University. With this elegant home as a starting point, you are on your way to a revealing walk up or down what was once called "millionaire's row," the stretch of Fifth Avenue first settled a century ago by such legendary men as Vanderbilt, Carnegie and Whitney. Most of their homes are now museums, schools and charitable organizations, or offices of foreign embassies. A few are subdivided as apartments. Many are city landmarks. If you head downtown, you will see the block-long **Frick Mansion**, as well as the immodest digs of the publisher Joseph Pulitzer and the double town house Sara Delano Roosevelt built for herself and her son, Franklin—a closeness that made FDR's wife, Eleanor, understandably uncomfortable. If you head uptown, you will see Andrew Carnegie's mansion, Frank Lloyd Wright's **Guggenheim Museum** and the homes of bankers Otto Kahn and Felix Warburg. Here are the highlights.

Walking downtown from the museum: The Benjamin Dukes bought their place from a developer who built it on spec in 1901. They later sold it to his brother James, who lived there until he built his own nearby. Members of the Duke family and their relatives the Biddles lived in the Benjamin Duke house until recently.

The French Gothic palace on the southeast corner of 79th Street, property of several millionaires at different times, belongs now to the **Ukrainian Institute of America**. The onetime home of the millionaire financier Payne Whitney between 78th and 79th Streets now serves as the French Embassy's cultural offices.

James Duke's place, modeled on a chateau in Bordeaux, rose on the northeast corner of 78th Street in 1912. A leading critic calls it "one of the most magnificent mansions in New York." Duke's widow and their daughter, Doris Duke, lived there until the late 1950's when they gave it to New York University. It is now **NYU's Graduate School of Art History**.

At 75th Street on the northeast corner, the **Commonwealth Fund** occupies the home of Edward Harkness, son of one of John D. Rockefeller's original partners in the Standard Oil Company. Edward Harkness built most of the undergraduate dorms at Harvard and Yale. The Commonwealth Fund, founded by his mother, devotes Harkness millions to health and medical research.

Halfway into the first block of East 73rd Street is the house Joseph Pulitzer built—No. 11, the one with lots of columns—now subdivided by 13 less affluent tenants. Pulitzer, German-born publisher of the *New York World* and the *St. Louis Post-Dispatch*, had lived briefly at 9 East 72nd Street, which he bought from Henry Sloane, son of one of the founders of the W. and J. Sloane furniture stores.

The mansion of coke and steel tycoon Henry Clay Frick stretches from 70th Street to 71st Street. Frick, once chairman of Carnegie Steel, was an avid collector of art, especially of the Italian Renaissance. The mansion was designed by the same architects who designed the New York Public Library, and planned from the start as both home and gallery. Frick left the house and the art to the city (*see section* "Museums").

The Roosevelts' twin town house is worth a final two-block walk from Fifth Avenue to No. 47–49 East 65th Street. It has just one front door. Inside the vestibule were separate entrances to FDR's domineering mother's quarters on the left, and her son's on the right. Small wonder that Eleanor didn't like it. The Roosevelts lived there in 1920–21 when FDR was convalescing from polio and stayed there when they were in the city. The house is now a student center for **Hunter College**, which is nearby on Park Avenue.

Walking uptown from the museum: Two blocks north of Benjamin Duke's place on 82nd Street is the **Marymount School** at 84th Street, spread through three houses—the house at the southeast corner and two adjacent on Fifth Avenue—once owned by three different families. At the southeast corner of 86th Street is a former Vanderbilt mansion, now home to the **Serge Sabarsky Foundation**, which exhibits the art collection of a noted dealer-collector who died in 1996.

The **Guggenheim Museum** at 88th Street is Frank Lloyd Wright's major
work in New York City, as notable for its architecture as for its art. Even if you're
not up for another museum today, step inside for a moment to see what the
American Institute of Architects calls "one of the greatest Modern interiors in
the world."

Andrew Carnegie's mansion at 91st Street reflects his grand style and great
wealth. While his peers were clustered farther down the avenue, he bought a
large piece of empty acreage uptown so he could decide who his neighbors
would be. After putting up his 64-room house with its large garden, he built
something smaller next door at 9 East 90th Street for his daughter and sold land
across 91st Street to Otto Kahn.

Carnegie gave away millions of his fortune in steel for thousands of public
libraries, Carnegie Hall, various Carnegie foundations and many other good
causes. His mansion is now the Smithsonian Institution's **Cooper-Hewitt
Museum of National Design**. Kahn, a partner in the Kuhn, Loeb investment
house, was a leader in philanthropic promotion of the arts and chairman of the
Metropolitan Opera for a quarter century. His mansion at No. 1 East 91st Street
copied the 15th-century Palazzo della Cancellaria in Rome. It is now a school
and faculty housing for the **Convent of the Sacred Heart**.

No. 7 and No. 9 East 91st Street were built by William Sloane and his wife,
Emily—a Vanderbilt—for their daughters. The founder of the Vanderbilt fortune, Commodore Cornelius Vanderbilt, was a notorious tightwad, but he left a
bundle for generations of his descendants to build impressive shelter for their
children. There is another Vanderbilt place at 56 East 93rd Street.

Two more neighborhood mansions are distinguished museums. The Gothic
chateau that houses the **Jewish Museum** at the northeast corner of 92nd Street
was the home of Felix Warburg, another Kuhn, Loeb partner, and his wife,
Frieda, a Schiff, who donated it to the museum. The museum doubled its size in
the 1990's. The **International Center of Photography** (which will be moving
downtown soon) at the northeast corner of 94th Street was originally the home
of Willard Straight, a diplomat and financier, and his wife Dorothy, a Whitney.
The Straights founded the *New Republic* magazine.

GUIDED SIGHTSEEING TOURS

The Department of Consumer Affairs estimates the current number of sightseeing licensees, including bus, boat, building and walking guides, at well over a
thousand. Tour-takers range from native New Yorkers and empty-nest suburban-
ites reconnecting with the city to out-of-towners of every description. The people leading the tours include historians, entrepreneurs, nonprofit institutions,
licensed guides, unlicensed guides and rank amateurs who are pretty much talking through their hats. The best guides blend the skills of historian, teacher,
showman and safety guard as they shepherd their charges through streets teem-
ing with traffic.

There are John Lennon walks, Jacqueline Kennedy Onassis itineraries, pub
crawls, celebrity and movie-location jaunts, *Seinfeld* tours and "gourmet" visits to

neighborhood restaurants. There are self-guided tours that include rented compact disk players. Unlike bus tours, walking excursions allow for greater interaction with people in the neighborhoods.

"New York is a city of small villages, and there is an infinite number of possible tours because New York is endlessly fascinating," says tour guide Joyce Gold, who has a library of 500 books on New York and has read 500 more. "Right at the corner of Wall Street and Broadway, you could talk for three hours and you wouldn't need to take a single step."

Boat, bus and other vehicular tours tend to have reasonably regular schedules, but some seasonal change can occur. Schedules, prices and meeting places for most of the walking tours listed here can vary wildly throughout the year, so call well in advance or check Web sites to avoid surprises. Do-it-yourselfers can have a wealth of self-guided tour books to choose from, or they can contact Talk-a-Walk Sound Publishers (212-686-0356), a publisher of audiotaped, self-guided tours of Manhattan. *The New York Times* also carries a list of tours every Friday, and nytoday.com's "Around Town" section offers more listings.

Walking Tours

Adventure on a Shoestring (212) 265-2663. This group offers 90-minute tours of New York and the surrounding areas. Most trips focus on areas in lower Manhattan, but tours of Astoria, Hoboken and Roosevelt Island are also available. Special tours also take place each year on the "birthdays" of the Brooklyn and George Washington Bridges. Tours include chats with members of the community when possible, and some walks are followed by luncheons at local restaurants. **Prices:** $5, cash only (luncheons not included). **Schedule:** 90-minute tours, most on Sat. and Sun.

Architecture City Tours (800) 557-2176 *www.artandarchitecture.com*. Architectural historians and local writers lead these easy, educational tours. No previous knowledge of architecture is expected, and highlights include the Chrysler Building, the United Nations and Rockefeller Center. **Prices:** $18 ($15 per person for more than 50 participants).

Big Apple Greeter (212) 669-2896 *www.bigapplegreeter.org*. Offers very personal tours for very small groups, such as a family or two. The itinerary can be set by the group if they want, and tour guides are volunteers who love to show off their city. **Prices:** Free. Reservations required.

Big Onion Walking Tours (212) 439-1090 *www.bigonion.com*. Big Onion offers two-hour tours every weekend and holiday. Themes range from neighborhood tours and in-depth historical and ethnic surveys to special holiday and eating tours. All guides are licensed by the city and hold advanced degrees in American history. **Prices:** $12, adults; $10, students and seniors; special tours, $13–$18. **Features:** Group tours for 1 to 200 participants available year-round.

Central Park Conservancy (212) 360-2727 *www.centralparknyc.org*. The Central Park Conservancy sponsors one-hour tours that explore the history, ecology, design or simple beauty of Central Park. Routes vary, and some tours require registration. Guides are New York City Park Rangers, skilled birders and other park experts. **Prices:** Free. **Features:** Group tours (call 212-360-2726).

Citywalks (212) 989-2456. Citywalks offers private, historical and architectural tours of lower Manhattan, especially Chelsea, Greenwich Village, the Lower East Side and the Financial District. **Prices:** $50-$100 per hour.

Discover Harlem (917) 763-8051. Four tours of upper Manhattan are available through this group, exploring everything from jazz clubs to churches to the Morris-Jumel Mansion, Washington's headquarters in 1776. Some tours are expensive, but they include some great extras, like an evening of jazz or a meal at Sylvia's restaurant. **Prices:** Vary, up to $77.

Greenwich Village: Food & Culture Off the Beaten Path (212) 334-5070 *www.imar.com*. Over the course of this three-hour tour of the food, landmarks, music and culture of Greenwich Village, you'll visit 15 eating establishments and sample food from six of them. **Price:** $35 (max. 16 people per tour), includes food. **Schedule:** Tours Tue.–Sun., reservations required. Credit card only.

Grand Central Terminal (212) 818-1777. Free tours of Grand Central Terminal are held every Friday at 12:30 P.M. Participants meet on 42nd Street at the Philip Morris/Whitney Museum, across the street from the terminal.

Harlem Spirituals Gospel and Jazz Tours (212) 391-0900 *www.harlemspirituals.com*. Despite the name, Harlem Spirituals offers tours in every New York borough. But the Harlem walking tours make it stand out, featuring everything from Sunday church services to Saturday night soul food and jazz tours. **Prices:** $30–$95, adults; $22.50–$95, children.

iMar (Insiders Marketplace) (212) 334-5070 *www.imar.com*. This group offers literally hundreds of New York tours and experiences. Tour the city streets with a retired NYPD officer, shop with a fashion model or ride shotgun with a New York City cabbie. Check the Web site for more unique experiences. **Price:** $22–$150. Reservations required. Credit card only.

Joyce Gold History Tours (212) 242-5762 *www.nyctours.com*. All of these tours are conducted by Joyce Gold herself, an instructor of Manhattan History at the New School University and New York University and author of several walking guides to New York City. Ms. Gold boasts an extensive list of neighborhood tours heavy on history, with titles like "East Village—Culture and Counter-Culture" and "The New Meat Market—Butchers, Bakers and Art Scene Makers." **Price:** $12, no reservations needed. **Schedule:** Sat.–Sun., 1 P.M. (2–3 hours).

Municipal Art Society Tours (212) 935-3960 *www.mas.org*. The MAS program "Discover New York" sponsors these diverse, year-round tours of New York's neighborhoods, history and culture. Some special tours, like "Cast in Iron: Manhole and Chute Covers" have companion lectures and slide shows. **Prices:** Weekdays: $12; $10, students, seniors and MAS members. Weekends: $15; $12, MAS members. Lecture fees vary.

New York City Cultural Walking Tours (212) 979-2388 *www.nycwalk.com*. Alfred Pommer has been researching and conducting a wide array of tours for over 15 years. Featured walks include multi-ethnic "heritage" tours, as well as staples like the "Bohemian Walking Tour of Greenwich Village" and the unusual "Gargoyles in Manhattan." There is a different tour each month, March-December. **Prices:** Public tours: $10. Private tours: $30 per hour, groups of four or more; $20 per hour, groups of three or fewer.

New York Talks and Walks (888) 377-4455 *www.newyorktalksandwalks.com*. Dr. Philip Schoenberg offers a multitude of seasonal, ethnic and historical tours, including the "Hidden Treasures of Chinatown" and the "Jewish Gangster Tour." **Prices:** Most tours, $12–$15.

92nd Street Y Tours (212) 996-1100 *www.92ndsty.org/tours/tours.asp*. There are hundreds of walks to choose from here, covering aspects of the city from arts and architecture to history. **Prices:** $15–$70. **Schedule:** Weekends, times vary.

NYC Discovery Tours (212) 465-3331. NYC Discovery offers over 60 different historical tours. The group covers major attractions as well as lesser known, but equally important sites in the city. Themes include "Historic Taverns," "The Civil War" and "John Lennon's New York." **Prices:** $12–$15. **Schedule:** Year-round; tours last two hours (days and times vary).

Radical Walking Tours (718) 492-0069 *www.he.net/~radtours*. These tours are led by historian Bruce Kayton. Walks explore significant sites in New York's history of political activism, with special attention to topics like civil rights and gay and lesbian rights. Kayton also offers special private group tours focusing on these topics and others such as labor, black history and women's history. **Prices:** $10; children 12 and under free. Private group tours, $150. Cash only. **Schedule:** Tours Sat.–Sun., Mar.-Dec.

Savory Sojourns (212) 691-7314 *www.savorysojourns.com*. These tours can be expensive, but for your money you get a five- to six-hour eating tour of one of the city's neighborhoods, complete with cooking demonstrations, kitchen tours, food, beer and wine. **Prices:** Vary according to neighborhood, $120 and up. $50 deposit is required at time of reservation. **Schedule:** By reservation only. Customized tours available.

Urban Explorations (718) 721-5254. Patricia Olmstead's operation covers many neighborhoods and themes, including trips through gay and lesbian Greenwich Village and tours of private artists' lofts. **Prices:** $12, adults; $10, students and seniors; $5, children. Discounts for repeat customers.

Wildman Steve Brill's Food and Ecology Tours (718) 291-6825 *www.accesshub.net/~wildmansteve*. Steve Brill, once arrested for eating dandelions in Central Park, now offers four-hour tours of city parks teaching identification and applications of a variety of wild plants. Walkers are encouraged to bring bags and containers to carry home wild herbs, mushrooms and berries. **Prices:** $10, adults; $5, children. Checks accepted. **Schedule:** Mar.-Dec.

Bus Tours

On Location Tours (212) 935-0168 *www.sceneontv.com*. This tour shuttles visitors to sites used as exterior settings for a number of TV shows. All tours depart from the Times Square Visitors Center on Broadway (between 46th and 47th Sts.). A *Sopranos* tour is also available ($30) complete with free cannoli. Also ask about the *Sex and the City* tour. **Prices:** $20, adults; $10, children 10 and under.

Gray Line (212) 397-2600. Hop-on, hop-off tours of Manhattan, the boroughs and beyond. "Total New York" tour includes a two-day bus ticket and free admission to the Statue of Liberty, plus the Empire State Building observation deck. **Prices:** $26–$75. Packages outside New York are more expensive.

Hassidic Tours (718) 953-5244. This group "hopes to educate, inspire, and familiarize people with the ideals of Hassidic Jewry," as seen in the Crown Heights area. Bus tours leave from Midtown every Sunday, and women are advised to dress "modestly" in keeping with the community's standards.

Kramer's Reality Tour (800) KRAMERS *www.kennykramer.com*. Kenny Kramer, the real-life inspiration for the Kramer character on TV's *Seinfeld*, hosts these three-hour "multi-media" tours of the Seinfeld universe. See locations like the "Soup Nazi" shop, Joe's Produce Store and Monk's Restaurant, and feast on the "Real Kramer's Original Famous Pizza." **Prices:** $37.50, reservations required. **Schedule:** Sat.–Sun., 12:00–3:00 P.M.

Cruises

Circle Line (212) 563-3200 *www.circleline.com*. Tours leave from Pier 83 at the west end of 42nd St. and Pier 16 at the South Street Seaport. The three-hour "Full Island" cruise draws the most people here, but be warned: complete circumnavigation of Manhattan may be a novel idea, but you'll see just as many major sights on the shorter cruises. Stick with the one-hour "Liberty Cruise," the Beast speedboat ride or one of the themed trips. Arrive 45 minutes before departure time. **Prices:** $13–$24, adults; $7–$12, seniors; $11–$20, children. **Schedule:** Cruises seven days, times vary. Closed Tue.–Wed. in Jan. and Feb., Dec. 24–25, or Jan. 1. **Services:** Group tours; snack bar on all cruises.

New York Waterways (800) 533-3779 *www.nywaterway.com*. Tours depart from Pier 78 at the west end of 38th St. and Pier 17 at the South Street Seaport. This is the Circle Line's biggest competitor, offering a similar variety of cruises on their new, clean boats. Besides the standard harbor cruises, they also run special baseball cruises to Yankees and Mets games and a number of cruises to destinations up the Hudson. **Prices:** Harbor Cruises: $19–$24, adults; $9–$12, children. Other cruises: $10–$66. **Schedule:** Cruises seven days, times vary. No cruises Mon.–Wed. from Jan. to mid-March., Dec. 24–25, or Jan. 1.

Seaport Liberty Cruises (212) 630-8888. Jazz and dance cruises depart from Pier 16 at the South Street Seaport every evening. **Prices:** $25–$35. **Schedule:** 7 P.M., 9:30 P.M.

Spirit Cruises (212) 727-2789. Another catch-all cruise operator, offering a variety of packages that take in the major sites of New York's harbor and rivers. Tours depart from Chelsea Piers on the Hudson at W. 23rd St. **Prices:** $28–$78, depending on day and time of cruise.

Helicopter Tours

Liberty Helicopter Tours (212) 967-6464 *www.libertyhelicopters.com*. These are expensive and brief tours, but they do offer a unique perspective on the city. Trips tend to range from five to 20 minutes and take in most of the major sights, from the Statue of Liberty to Central Park. **Prices:** $55–$162. Same-day reservations available at (212) 967-4550.

Other Transportation
(See also **Sports & Recreation**, *section* "Biking.")

Carriage Rides
(See section "Central Park" *later in this chapter.)*

Central Park Bicycle Tours
(See section "Central Park" *later in this chapter.)*

Crypt Keeper Tours (888) EXHUMED *www.cryptkeepertours.com*. Visit sites of famous people's deaths (including John Lennon, Sid Vicious, Jackie Onassis, Andy Warhol and Typhoid Mary) in a vintage hearse. **Price:** $45, reservations required.

NEW YORK CITY SEASONAL EVENTS

Winter
The Nutcracker New York State Theater at Lincoln Center (212) 870-5570 *www.nycballet.com*. The New York City Ballet performs this famous work each year with students from the School of American Ballet. It's a special treat for the kids.   *November-December*

Christmas Spectacular Radio City Music Hall, 1260 Sixth Ave. (at 50th St.) (212) 247-4777 *www.radiocity.com*. The Radio City Christmas Spectacular features the famed Rockettes in Santa hats kicking alongside larger-than-life Nutcracker soldiers.   *November-early January*

Christmas Window Displays Along Fifth Avenue in Midtown marvel at the tiny winter scenes in department store windows. (Lord & Taylor and Saks Fifth Avenue are the most popular). Check out the Cartier building wrapped for

Christmas in an enormous red bow and the doormen at FAO Schwarz dressed as wooden soldiers.   *December*

Christmas Tree Lighting Ceremony Rockefeller Center, Fifth Ave. (between 49th and 50th Sts.) (212) 632-3975. One of the tallest Christmas trees in the country is mounted in Rockefeller Center, where it is strung with five miles of lights and lit by the mayor in a ceremony that includes an ice-skating show and other entertainment.   *Early December*

Lighting of the Hanukkah Menorah Grand Army Plaza, 59th St. and Fifth Ave. (718) 778-6000. Just a few blocks from one of the country's largest Christmas trees in Rockefeller Center is a 32-foot-tall Menorah, reportedly the world's largest. An electric candle is lit for each day of Hanukkah.   *December*

Kwanza Holiday Expo Jacob K. Javits Convention Center, 655 W. 34th St. (at 11th Ave.) (212) 216-2000. To celebrate this African-American holiday 300 vendors from around the country gather at the convention center to sell crafts, jewelry and food. There is dancing and musical entertainment, as well as storytelling in the youth pavilion. It's a multicultural celebration that is open to all.   *Third weekend in December*

Messiah Sing-In Avery Fisher Hall, Lincoln Center (212) 333-5333 *www.lincolncenter.org*. The National Chorale Counsel organizes this sing-a-long of Handel's "Messiah" led by 20 conductors with an audience of up to 3,000 including four trained soloists to rescue the arias. No experience is necessary and lyrics sheets are provided. Amateurs, professionals, even high school choirs participate.
                                                                    Mid-late December

New Year's Eve Ball Drop Times Square (212) 768-1560. It's not the New Year until the ball drops over Times Square. The new and improved ball is now adorned with a stunning 12,000 rhinestones and 180 75-watt bulbs. The ball drop is televised all over the world, but if you want the folks back home to see you, arrive early. The area is packed with revelers hours before midnight.

New Year's Eve Fireworks Central Park. Spectators gather at Tavern on the Green and other spots throughout the park for views of the annual fireworks display. Festivities begin at 11:30 P.M.

New York National Boat Show Jacob K. Javits Convention Center, 655 W. 34th St. (at 11th Ave.) (212) 216-2000. 100,000 people show up each year to see 400 of the world's leading manufacturers show off 1,000 of the latest powerboats—from small craft to yachts—and marine accessories. Seminars on fishing and boating are also offered.   *Nine days in early January*

Winter Antiques Show Seventh Regiment Armory, Park Ave. (at 67th St.) (718) 292-7392 *www.winterantiquesshow.comy*. The city's premier antiques fair—featuring collections ranging from ancient to Art Nouveau—is also a benefit for East Side House Settlement.   *Mid-late January*

Outsider Art Fair The Puck Building, 295 Lafayette St. (at Houston St.)
(212) 777-5218. This three-day event draws an international crowd of dealers,
collectors and art aficionados. Thirty-five dealers exhibit self-taught, visionary
and art brut pieces to crowds in the thousands. It's a good place for celebrity
sightings and the occasional star-studded seminar. Prices range from about $300
to $75,000.   *Last Thursday of January*

Chinese New Year Chinese Cultural Center, (212) 373-1800, Tourist Info,
(212) 484-1222. Celebrate the year of the snake in 2002 in Chinatown, on and
around Mott Street. Five days of celebrating culminate in a lively and colorful
procession of lions and dragons made from wood and silk that wind their way
through the narrow and festively decorated streets. Fireworks were banned in
1997, which has taken some of the bang out of the festivities, but the colors,
lights, dancing and food still make it quite an experience.
                                        Begins first full moon after January 21

Valentine's Day Marriage Marathon Empire State Building, 350 Fifth Ave.
(at 34th St.) (212) 736-3100, ext. 377 *www.esbnyc.com*. Fifteen couples marry
atop the Empire State Building in back-to-back 15-minute ceremonies every
Valentine's Day. Couples vie for the honor each year. The deadline for entry is
December 31 and each couple is limited to 10 guests who then gather in the Sky
Lobby on the 80th floor for champagne and photographs.   *February 14*

Westminster Kennel Club Dog Show Madison Square Garden, Seventh
Ave. (at 33rd St.) *www.westminsterkennelclub.org*. The nation's oldest and second largest animal event after the Kentucky Derby features 3,000 dogs that are
pared down to seven finalists and then a single winner. About 30,000 spectators
show up for the two-day event.   *Mid-February*

The Art Show Seventh Regiment Armory, Park Ave. (at 67th St.)
(212) 766-9200 *www.artdealers.org*. Sponsored by the Art Dealers Association
of America, this is New York's foremost art fair. Seventy of the nation's leading
galleries gather to exhibit works that span five centuries from 17th-century masters to contemporary artists in a range of media that includes painting, drawing,
print, sculpture, photography and video. Proceeds benefit the Henry Street Settlement, a longstanding social service agency in the Lower East Side.
                                                             Mid-late February

Empire State Building Run-Up 350 Fifth Ave. (at 34th St.) (212) 860-4455
www.esbnyc.com. On a Wednesday in February 150 runners race up the 1,576
steps of the Empire State Building from the lobby to the observation deck on
the 86th floor, all vying for the record-breaking time. The current time to beat
is 10:49 for the men and 12:19 for the women. Afterward the runners and their
families gather on the 80th floor for an awards ceremony and refreshments.
                                                             Late February

Manhattan Antiques and Collectibles Triple Pier Expo 12th Ave.
(between 48th and 51st Sts.) (212) 255-0020 *www.antiqnet.com/stella*. Nine

hundred dealers take over Piers 88, 90 and 92 along the Hudson River to sell everything from posters, toys, textiles, fashions and furniture to silver, porcelain, fine china, paintings, jewelry and glassware. The prices range anywhere from $2 to $75,000.   *Last two weekends of February, and Mid-November*

Spring

International Cat Show Madison Square Garden, Seventh Ave. (at 33rd St.) (212) 465-6741. This event draws 35,000 people to the Garden, where they can watch as 800 felines covering 40 breeds compete for the Best of Show award with all the composure for which cats are famous. After, you can shop for cat accessories at the cat supermarket or listen to cat-related lectures on topics like cat acupuncture, massage and feline aerobics.   *March*

St. Patrick's Day Parade Fifth Ave. (from 44th to 86th St.) (212) 484-1222. In one of the city's oldest annual events, over 150,000 Irish Americans and other revelers draped in green join the festivities along Fifth Avenue (starting at 11 A.M.) and fill the city's bars well into the night. You can find green beer, green bagels and virtually everything in the shape of shamrock, as New York goes Hibernian for a day. For best views of the parade, line up early.   *March 17*

International Asian Art Fair Seventh Regiment Armory, Park Ave. (at 67th St.) (212) 642-8572 *www.haughton.com*. Top dealers from around the world gather at the Armory to sell art from Southeast Asia and the Middle and Far East. The art, sculpture, ceramics and textiles typify the talent and skills of Eastern Artists over the centuries. Fourteen thousand people come to browse and buy items that range anywhere from $200 to hundreds of thousands of dollars.
Late March

New Directors/New Films Museum of Modern Art, 11 W. 53rd St. (between Fifth and Sixth Aves.) (212) 875-5610 *www.filmlinc.com*. This film festival, sponsored by the Museum of Modern Art and the Film Society of Lincoln Center, features works by emerging, overlooked and new directors. Such notables as Wim Wenders, Spike Lee and Steven Spielberg have screened films in past years.   *Late March-early April*

Ringling Bros. and Barnum & Bailey Circus Madison Square Garden, Seventh Avenue (at 33rd Street) (212) 465-6741 *www.ringling.com*. Kicking off its New York run each spring the circus's lions, tigers and bears (and elephants) parade along 34th Street to Madison Square Garden at midnight on the night before the first performance. The spectacular procession of animals is a great way to get a free peek at "The Greatest Show on Earth."   *Late March-early May*

Whitney Biennial Whitney Museum of American Art, 945 Madison Ave. (at 75th St.) (212) 570-3600 *www.whitney.org*. Every two years since 1932, the Whitney has presented an exhibition of what it regards as the most influential contemporary American art, often highlighting works by innovative and vanguard artists.   *Late March-early June*

Easter Parade Fifth Avenue (44th-57th Sts.) (212) 484-1222. One of the older New York traditions that dates back to the Civil War era, the Easter Parade draws crowds of bonneted spectators sporting everything from the classic bowler to the more extravagant flowering bonnets. The best perch is the platform at St. Patrick's Cathedral, if you can get near it.   *Easter Sunday*

New York International Auto Show Jacob K. Javits Convention Center, 655 W. 34th St. (at 11th Ave.) (800) 282-3336 *www.autoshowny.com*. North America's first and largest auto show features hundreds of the newest cars, trucks and SUV's as well as classics from automotive history.   *Mid-April*

New York Antiquarian Book Fair Seventh Regiment Armory, Park Ave. (at 67th St.) (212) 777-5218. About 180 international book dealers offer rare books, manuscripts, autographs, fine bindings, maps, modern firsts, illustrated books, children's books and more. Prices range from $25 to $25,000.   *Mid-April*

Macy's Flower Show 34th St. (at Broadway) (212) 494-2922. Celebrate the arrival of spring when Macy's department store turns into a botanical paradise with over 30,000 varieties of flowers, plants and trees from around the world. If you're too rushed to go inside, walk on by and glimpse the floral window displays along Broadway.   *Last two weeks of April (not coinciding with Easter)*

The Cherry Blossom Festival Brooklyn Botanic Garden (718) 622-4433 *www.bbg.org*. To celebrate the blooming of the Garden's 200 cherry trees in 40 varieties, this festival features classical Japanese dance performances accompanied by bamboo flutes and taiko drums. There is storytelling as well as lessons in calligraphy, flower arranging, oriental brush painting, block painting and origami.   *Late April or Early May*

You Gotta Have Park Parks throughout the five boroughs (212) 360-3456 *www.ci.nyc.ny.us/html/dpr*. Look for free activities and events in city parks throughout May during the Parks Department's kickoff to summer. Check the Department's Web site for details.   *May*

Bike New York: The Great Five Boro Bike Tour (212) 932-BIKE. America's largest bicycling event includes 30,000 riders who traverse 42 miles (68k) and five boroughs. The tour starts in Battery Park with a sendoff by the mayor and ends with a ride across the Verrazano-Narrows Bridge to Staten Island. A post-ride festival and picnic given by sponsors features food, concessions and activities.   *Early May*

Lower East Side Festival of the Arts Theater for the New City, 155 First Ave. (at 10th St.) (212) 245-1109. This annual festival featuring more than 20 theatrical troupes and local notables celebrates the culture of the Lower East Side, where such iconoclasts as Allen Ginsberg and Andy Warhol drew inspiration.   *First weekend of May*

Ninth Avenue International Food Festival Ninth Ave. (37th-57th St.) (212) 581-7029. Hundreds of stalls are set up along Ninth Avenue for two days to serve every type of ethic food you can imagine—from Thai to Italian. Musicians and vendors hawking plants, crafts and T-shirts join in the festivities while over a million people sample the gamut of New York's ethnic cuisines. *Mid-May*

Bird Watching in Central Park Central Park (212) 427-4040. With 275 species sighted at last count, Central Park is one of the 14 best bird watching places in North America. From parrots to bald eagles to the red-tailed hawks that nest along Fifth Avenue, all manner of birds show up for springtime in the Park. Many of the more exotic species arrive en route from southern states, Mexico and even the tropical rain forests. *May-June*

Fleet Week Sea, Air and Space Museum, *U.S.S. Intrepid* (46th St. at 12th Ave.) (212) 245-0072. Fifteen to 20 battleships, aircraft carriers and other ships from the U.S. Navy and Coast Guard as well as foreign fleets sail up the Hudson, past the Statue of Liberty, and dock at Pier 86 where 10,000 uniformed personnel disembark and make room for curious New Yorkers to go on for free. During the week there are also parachute drops and air displays that are sure to impress the kids. *Late May*

Washington Square Outdoor Art Exhibition Washington Square Park (212) 982-6255. For nearly 70 years, the 20 blocks in and around the park have been transformed into an arts and crafts fairground on Memorial Day and continuing for the three following weekends. Around 600 exhibitors participate each day of the fair from noon until sundown. *Starts Memorial Day*

Summer

Metropolitan Opera Parks Concerts Various locations (212) 362-6000. Each year the Met presents free performances of two operas in Central Park and other locations throughout the city. Bring a picnic and grab a patch of grass early if you want to get a good view. *June*

Bryant Park Free Summer Season Sixth Ave. (at 42nd St.) (212) 922-9393. Lunchtime concerts and performances are a favorite of Midtown workers throughout the summer. The free classic movies under the stars on Monday evenings are a New York City summertime must. Bring a blanket and a picnic and be sure to arrive early for some prime lawn space. *June-August*

Celebrate Brooklyn! Performing Arts Festival Prospect Park Bandshell, 9th St. (at Prospect Park West), Park Slope (718) 855-7882 *www.bkny.net/celebrate*. Around 25 free outdoor performances in music, dance, film and theater are offered for nine weeks in this Prospect Park venue. The city's longest-running free performing arts festival attracts top-notch acts from around the country and the world. Check the Web site for a schedule of events. *June-August*

Central Park SummerStage Rumsey Playfield, Central Park (at 72nd St.) (212) 360-2777 *www.summerstage.com*. Since its founding in 1986, SummerStage has presented over 500 free weekend afternoon concerts and performances for over 5 million people. Everyone from the latest pop stars to up-and-coming artists have graced the stage. Occasional benefit shows charge admission to help fund the program. *June-August*

Hudson River Festival World Financial Center, West St. (at Vesey St.) (212) 945-0505 *www.worldfinancialcenter.com*. The World Financial Center's Winter Garden presents free outdoor performances as the sun sets over the Hudson, as well as indoor arts events. *June-August*

New York Shakespeare Festival Delacorte Theater, Central Park (at 81st St.) (212) 539-8750, (212) 539-8500. Sponsored by the Joseph Papp Public Theater, this is the quintessential summer activity in New York. Celebrity performers often join the cast for free outdoor performances of two plays each summer—one by Shakespeare and one by another famous dramatist. Available at the Public Theater and the Delacorte Theater, tickets can be difficult to come by when the cast is particularly star-studded. *June-August*

Puerto Rican Day Parade Fifth Avenue (44th-86th St.) (212) 484-1222, (718) 401-0404. With lively music and an enthusiastic crowd, this is one of New York's most festive parades. *First Sunday in June*

New York Jazz Festival Various locations (212) 343-8805 *www.jazfest.com*. Taking the name of its corporate sponsor each year, this festival presents hundreds of acts running the gamut of jazz styles from classic to avant-garde. The two-week series run by the Knitting Factory occupies 10 of the city's smaller venues as an alternative to the more mainstream JVC Jazz Festival. *Early June*

Toyota Comedy Festival Various locations (800) 331-4331. Thirty venues throughout the city host over a hundred acts. *Early-mid June*

Museum Mile Festival Various locations (212) 606-2296. For one day a year you can get into nine of the city's major museums for free. Coupled with the entertainment along Fifth Avenue (82nd-104th St.), it's quite a bargain. *Second Tuesday in June*

JVC Jazz Festival Various locations (212) 501-1390 *www.festivalproductions.net/jvc/ny*. From small clubs to Carnegie Hall and Lincoln Center, jazz takes over most of the city's major music venues for two weeks each year. World-class jazz musicians and lesser-known artists take to New York's stages for performances and jam sessions. *Mid-late June*

Mermaid Parade Boardwalk at Coney Island (W. 10th-16th St.) (718) 372-5159 *www.coneyisland.brooklyn.ny.us*. To kick off the summer, hundreds of mermaids, as well as mermen, merchildren and other sea creatures march down the boardwalk in a colorful display. Elaborate floats and outlandish costumes make this one of the city's most unique parades. *Saturday after summer solstice*

Gay and Lesbian Pride Parade Fifth Ave. (Columbus Circle-Christopher St.)
(212) 807-7433. To commemorate the 1969 Stonewall riots, thousands take to
the streets to celebrate the birth of the gay liberation movement in the world's
largest gay pride parade. A week of events surrounds the parade with an outdoor
dance party at the West Side Piers, a film festival, club events throughout the
city and many other activities.   *Late June*

Restaurant Week *www.restaurantweek.com*. A prix-fixe lunch at over 100 of
the city's top restaurants is only $20 for a week in June. For a list of participating
restaurants send a self-addressed stamped envelope to NYCVB, 810 Seventh
Avenue, New York, NY 10019 or check local papers.   *Late June*

Midsummer Night Swing Lincoln Center Plaza (212) 875-5766. Nothing
can quite compare to dancing under the stars with Lincoln Center's famed fountain as a backdrop while top dance bands play everything from swing to salsa.
Dance lessons, which are included in the price of admission, begin at 6:30 P.M.
and the featured band goes on at 8:15 P.M. (Tue.–Sat.).   *Late June-late July*

Lincoln Center Festival Lincoln Center (212) 875-5928
www.lincolncenter.org/festival. This relatively new program, begun in 1996, showcases dance, theater, music and opera in and around Lincoln Center's several
venues, with performances by the Center's regular companies and other artists from
around the world. Tickets to special symposia about and inspired by the festival's
performances are also available.   *July*

Summergarden Museum of Modern Art, 11 W. 53rd St. (between Fifth and
Sixth Aves.) (212) 708-9491 *www.moma.org/programs/summergarden*. This free
concert series in the museum's sculpture garden features classical performances
by graduate students and alumni of the Juilliard School of Music. (Concerts
may be suspended for the museums renovation. Call first)   *July-August*

Macy's Fireworks Display East River (212) 494-4495. The FDR Drive is
closed to traffic for a few hours so pedestrians can get a better look at the 30-
minute display launched from two points on the East River beginning at 9 P.M.
                                                                            July 4

New York Philharmonic Concerts in the Parks Various locations
(212) 875-5656. For 10 days the Philharmonic presents evening concerts in
parks throughout the city.   *Late July-early August*

Mostly Mozart Avery Fisher Hall, Lincoln Center (212) 875-5030. The
Mostly Mozart Festival Orchestra—along with world-class soloists and guest
performers—presents around 30 concerts in a four-week period each summer.
                                                            Late July-late August

Lincoln Center Out-of-Doors Lincoln Center (212) 875-5108 *www.lincoln-
center.org/outofdoors*. Everything from classical music and dancing to children's
puppet shows can be found at this popular festival on the plazas of Lincoln Center.   *August*

Harlem Week Throughout Harlem (212) 862-8477. The Taste of Harlem food festival, the Black Film Festival and a lively street fair along Fifth Avenue (125th-135th St.) are highlights of the largest Black and Latino festival in the world. Look for museum open houses, block parties, outdoor concerts and special events at area jazz clubs during this festival which lasts two to three weeks.

Starts early August

Hong Kong Dragon Boat Festival The Lake at Flushing Meadows-Corona Park, Queens (718) 539-8974 *www.hkdbf-ny.org*. Local teams race these traditional 39-foot boats decorated like Chinese dragons in a spectacular display.

Mid-August

Greenwich Village Jazz Festival Throughout Greenwich Village (212) 929-5149. Most of the Village's jazz venues participate in 10 days of performances topped off by a free concert in Washington Square Park. *Late August*

Wigstock Pier 54 (12th-13th St.) (800) 494-8497 *www.wigstock.nu*. With up to 10,000 bewigged spectators and around 60 performers, this drag festival may be the city's most colorful. The festival benefits the Gay Men's Health Crisis.

Labor Day weekend

West Indian Day Carnival Eastern Parkway (Utica Ave.-Grand Army Plaza), Brooklyn (212) 484-1222, (718) 625-1515. A crowd of nearly 2 million revelers turns out to celebrate Caribbean culture in New York's biggest and most energetic parade. The parade of extravagant costumes and colorful floats caps a weekend of festivities beginning Friday evening with reggae, salsa and calypso at the Brooklyn Museum. *Labor Day*

Autumn

Broadway on Broadway 43rd and Broadway (212) 768-1560. For a couple of hours each year Broadway is accessible to everyone. On a stage erected in the middle of Times Square, a free concert of highlights from the season's biggest shows gives a taste of what Broadway has to offer. *Mid-September*

Brooklyn BeerFest Brooklyn Brewery, 79 N. 11th St. (between Berry and Wythe Sts.) (718) 486-7422 *www.craftbrewers.com*. This outdoor festival in Williamsburg offers food, music and, of course, a whole lot of beer. Each year nearly 100 brews from around the world are there for the tasting to celebrate the first day of Oktoberfest. *Mid-September*

Downtown Arts Festival Various locations (212) 243-5050. What better place for an arts festival than SoHo? Art lovers come from far and wide for three days of exhibitions, performances and lectures at dozens of SoHo locations.

Mid-September

Atlantic Antic Atlantic Ave. (Flatbush Ave.–East River) (718) 875-8993 *www.atlanticave.org*. With music, food, arts and crafts, a children's circus and over 450 vendors the Antic is one of Brooklyn's largest street fairs drawing nearly 1 million people each year. *Last Sunday in September*

Columbus Day Parade Fifth Ave. (44th-86th St.) (212) 484-1222. Columbus may have landed far from New York on a Spanish ship, but he was born in Italy. That's enough for the city's Italian-Americans who are front and center for this parade up Fifth Avenue.   *Columbus Day, second Monday in October*

Big Apple Circus Damrosch Park, Lincoln Center (212) 268-2500, (800) 922-3772 *www.bigapplecircus.org*. With its local roots, intimate one-ring big top and kid-friendly mission, the Big Apple Circus has staked out its own ground between the glitz of the Ringling Brothers circus and the adults-only artistry of the Cirque du Soleil.   *November-January*

Feast of San Gennaro Mulberry St. (Houston-Worth St.) (212) 764-6330 *www.nyclittleitaly.com*. Since 1926 Little Italy's main drag, Mulberry Street, is transformed into a fairground for 11 days in September. Three million people turn out each year for food and fun at this festival honoring the patron saint of Naples.   *Third week of September*

New York Film Festival Alice Tully Hall, Lincoln Center (212) 875-5610 *www.filmlinc.com/nyff*. Approximately 20 independent, foreign and big studio films are screened in a two-week run at Lincoln Center's Alice Tully Hall. Held annually since 1965, the festival has premiered films by directors such as Martin Scorsese, Jean-Luc Godard and Robert Altman.   *Late September-early October*

Next Wave Festival Brooklyn Academy of Music, (718) 636-4100 *www.bam.org*. BAM showcases experimental works by both established and lesser-known contemporary artists from around the world in music, theater and dance.   *October-December*

Halloween Parade Sixth Ave. (Spring-23rd St.) (212) 475-3333, ext. 4044 *www.halloween-nyc.com*. Over 25,000 participants take to the streets of Greenwich Village for the most famous Halloween parade in the country. Join the crowd of elaborately costumed revelers or have nearly as much fun watching from the sidelines.   *October 31*

New York City Marathon Starts Staten Island side of the Verrazano-Narrows Bridge (212) 860-4455 *www.nycmarathon.org*. The 26.2-mile race finishes at Tavern on the Green in Central Park at West 67th Street as a crowd cheers on the 35,000 participants each year. Spectators line the streets handing out drinks all along the course, which hits each of the five boroughs.
                              Last Sunday in October or first Sunday in November

Macy's Parade Central Park West (at 77th St.) to Macy's (Broadway and 34th St.) (212) 494-4495 *www.macyparade.com*. From 9 A.M. to 12 P.M. on Thanksgiving a procession of floats and huge cartoon character balloons marches to Macy's in this children's favorite. Catch the inflating of the balloons the night before at Central Park West and 77th Street (6–11 P.M.). *Thanksgiving Day*

MANHATTAN NEIGHBORHOODS
World Trade Center/Battery Park

On September 11, 2001, two hijacked commercial airplanes crashed into and destroyed both towers of the World Trade Center, killing everybody aboard the planes and thousands more inside the two 110-story buildings. Another building at 7 World Trade Center collapsed later that day, and several other buildings in the surrounding area were severely damaged. As this book went to press, rescue workers were still sifting through the wreckage for survivors and for clues as to who was responsible for plotting this disaster.

Much of the neighborhood formerly known as the World Trade Center area (including the subway lines that pass through it) was ravaged by the attack, and will be in various states of repair or reconstruction for the next few years. If your plans take you through this part of New York, call ahead.

Across the West Side Highway is the **World Financial Center**, which was also damaged as a result of the attacks.

Subway: 2, 3 to Park Pl.; N, R, 1, 9 to Cortlandt St.; N, R to Whitehall St.; 1, 9 to South Ferry; 4, 5 to Bowling Green.

HIGHLIGHTS OF THE NEIGHBORHOOD

Battery Park Battery Place (212) 732-0756. Need a reminder that Manhattan is an island? Try windswept Battery Park. Wedged between skyscrapers and New York Harbor, the park reminds visitors that the city's history is based on commerce and seafaring. Built entirely on landfill, the park is filled with historic landmarks, including **Castle Clinton**, (212) 344-7220, designed in 1811 as a fort to protect against British invasion, and later converted into an opera house, an immigration center and the New York Aquarium (*see "Coney Island"*). It's now the ticket center for boat trips to Ellis Island and the Statue of Liberty.

Bowling Green Broadway and Whitehall Sts. Bowling Green, a small triangle at the foot of Broadway, was Manhattan's first park—no small claim to fame in a city with more than 1,500 parks. It was once used as a cattle market and later as a bowling lawn. A statue of King George III stood in the park until 1776, when it was destroyed as a symbol of oppressive British rule. The statue's remains were then melted down and turned into ammunition, but some pieces remain in historic collections. At the south end is the elegant **U.S. Customs House**, which houses the **National Museum of the American Indian**. A farmers' market operates here daily.

Museum of Jewish Heritage—A Living Memorial to the Holocaust
18 First Pl., Battery Park City (at West St.) (212) 968-1800.
(*See section* "Institutes of World Culture" *in chapter* **The Arts** *for full listing.*)

National Museum of the American Indian 1 Bowling Green (between Whitehall and State Sts.) (212) 668-6624 *www.si.edu/nmai*. The basis of the museum's permanent collection is the unsurpassed collection assembled by

George Gustav Heye. Now located in the former **U.S. Customs House**, a spectacular domed Beaux-Arts landmark at the foot of Broadway, this branch of the Smithsonian Institution is the model for a new national museum, scheduled to open in 2002 on the Mall in Washington, D.C.

New York City Police Museum 100 Old Slip (at the East River) (212) 301-4440. Moving in late 2001 to the headquarters of the city's first police precinct, the New York City Police Museum is finally back where it belongs. With interactive exhibits, computer simulations, vintage uniforms and antique badges, the museum presents a multifaceted view of the rigorous, clearly dangerous, at times political and often tedious life of a police officer.

Shrine of St. Elizabeth Ann Seton 7 State St. (between Whitehall and Pearl Sts.) (212) 269-6865. This 1793 Federal-style building is dedicated to Elizabeth Ann Seton, the first American-born Catholic saint. Seton, who founded the American Sisters of Charity, the first order of nuns in the U.S., lived here from 1801 to 1803. The building is one of the few surviving mansions in lower Manhattan. The adjoining church was built at the same time.

Staten Island Ferry southeast end of Battery Park (212) 225-5368. Historically, there have been few better bargains in New York than a ride on the Staten Island Ferry. For decades, it cost only a nickel. That changed in the mid-1970's, when the first of several fare increases took effect, inching the price up eventually to $.50 for the round trip between Battery Park in Manhattan and St. George, Staten Island. But these days a ferry ride is absolutely the best deal in town. It costs nothing, part of a new system of free mass-transit transfers.

The ferry is a lifeline to the city for many Staten Islanders; some 30,000 people ride it each midweek day. But it also provides as romantic a journey as the city can offer. The ferry operates 24 hours a day—every 15 minutes during rush hours, every 30 minutes the rest of the day and evening, and once an hour at night. To truly appreciate the grandeur of New York, ride the ferry at sunrise, starting with the 25-minute trip from Manhattan to Staten Island and then reversing the journey on the next boat back. At dawn, the first rays of the sun strike the glass towers of lower Manhattan, while off to the left, the Statue of Liberty's torch still burns bright in the vanishing darkness.   —*Clyde Haberman*

World Financial Center and Winter Garden 1 World Financial Center (between Albany and Liberty Sts.) (212) 945-0505. Note: The World Financial Center and Winter Garden were seriously damaged by the September 11, 2001 plane crashes that destroyed the World Trade Center. At press time, it was impossible to discern exactly how extensive the destruction was.

Built on landfill along the Hudson River, this commercial development includes shops, restaurants, gallery space, a yacht harbor and the Winter Garden performance space. The Winter Garden is a gigantic, glass-vaulted public space, complete with a monumental arced staircase and tall desert palm trees. Outside, a promenade circles the yacht harbor, and the proximity of the water reminds visitors and residents alike that they are indeed on an island.

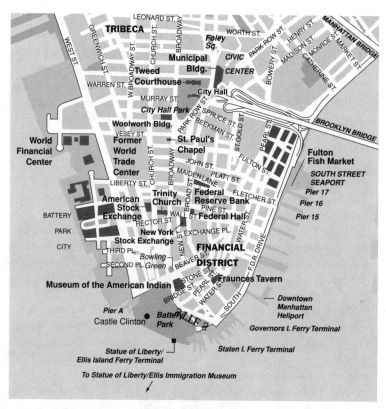

Lower Manhattan

Wall Street/Financial District

The Wall Street denizens of film and fiction—brash stockbrokers, icy invest-ment bankers and hair-trigger traders—really do exist. But catching a glimpse of them is hard, even when you are strolling on Wall Street itself.

That's partly because many of the big stock and bond firms have aban-doned the traditional financial district and opened offices all over Manhattan. Those that remain tend to keep odd hours. Most financial types like to be at their desks at dawn. Some flee as soon as the stock market closes at 4 P.M. Others work till all hours of the night and take private taxis home. If you are out late enough, you can see the "black cars" lined up outside **Goldman Sachs** (85 Broad Street).

Most who work on Wall Street think they are far too important to take a break for lunch, except when celebrating a deal. Still, there are a few good spots for Wall Street watching. Outside the **New York Stock Exchange** build-ing on both Wall and Broad Streets, you will see men and the occasional woman (this is still a male-dominated business), wearing brightly colored jack-ets and smoking. These are the brokers and traders who work on the floor of the

Statue of Liberty & Ellis Island

These days, nothing more inspiring than the baggage claim area at John F. Kennedy International Airport greets most visitors and immigrants to the United States. But a century ago, the exhilarating sight of the towering Statue of Liberty at the entrance to New York Harbor signaled to shiploads of travelers, both the bedraggled and the bejeweled, that they had reached the shores of a new land.

At Ellis Island, only paperwork was processed for first-class and second-class passengers; the passengers themselves were inspected on their ships and dispatched directly to Manhattan. But each day saw up to 5,000 immigrants, fresh from a two-week ocean voyage in steerage, herded inside and inspected for disease, deformities and destitution.

Inspired by the colossal monuments of Egypt and an outsized 19th-century French fascination with American egalitarian ideals, the **Statue of Liberty** still has the power to take your breath away, just as it thrilled the 12 million immigrants who passed it on their way to Ellis Island in the first decades of the 20th century.

Resolute and stern, the massive female figure, 151 feet high from her toes to the top of her torch of freedom, rests on a 150-foot-high pedestal at the tip of a tiny landscaped island in New York Bay. Gardens around the base, dotted with dozens of white wrought-iron chairs, offer a sumptuous view of the skyscrapers of Lower Manhattan.

The idea for a grand statue to celebrate friendship between France and the United States, originated in 1865 around the Parisian dinner table of Edouard de Laboulaye, a scholar of the American Constitution. (A great-grandson of de Laboulaye spearheaded fundraising in France for restoration of the statue 100 years after it opened). Alexis de Tocqueville, another admirer of American democracy, is said to have been a guest at the dinner. So was the sculptor who would design the statue, Frédéric-Auguste Bartholdi.

For many visitors, no trip to Liberty Island is complete without a 354-step climb up a narrow twisting staircase to the statue's crown, where glimpses of the New York and New Jersey coasts are visible on clear days through small-ish Plexiglas windows. Because of overheated conditions in the stairwell, only passengers on the first morning ferries during the summer are allowed in the crown.

But there is a better view from the skinny outdoor walkway around the base of the statue. It can be reached by an elevator, or up four flights of steps.

Inside the pedestal, an informative museum shows the evolution of Bartholdi's vision of what the statue should look like, the engineering used to keep it stable in the tricky harbor winds, and the lasting impressions it made on generations of immigrants. Visitors also can gaze on a full-scale copper replica of one of Miss Liberty's feet, which sports toenails the size of truck tires. A delightful collection of old Statue of Liberty kitsch, as opposed to the new collection in the gift shop downstairs, concludes the exhibit, demonstrating the monument's enduring role as both icon and huckster.

At **Ellis Island**, renovations of the long abandoned site, completed in 1992, recreated the processing center as it looked in the first decades of the 20th century.

Even if you do not trace your roots to an ancestor who arrived in the United States through Ellis Island—and these days, fewer than 40 percent of Americans do—you may well feel a kinship with the 12 million anxious immigrants who shuffled through the echoing halls of this red-brick way station between 1892 and 1954 on their way to a new life in a new land. All through the impressively restored building, there are bigger-than-life sepia photos of the evocative faces that passed through Ellis Island to become symbols of the American experience. Among them: a young boy in a jauntily angled embroidered cap, his lips pursed as if he is trying to suppress a grin of pure exultation. Two Dutch brothers, each with a processing number pinned to his shirt and each with a determined gaze already directed far beyond New York Harbor. A pair of dignified young black women coming from Guadeloupe in 1911, both in ankle-length lace-trimmed dresses and tiny hats shaped like a handful of rose petals.

The main processing center is the only part of the original compound that is open to the public. Displays on its three floors use film, photos, turn-of-the-century posters and the voices of reminiscing immigrants to show a broader story of immigration. You hear immigrants tell their stories of adjustment, discrimination, poverty and success. You learn about the nativist movements that feared immigrants; a 1902 political cartoon shows them as the personification of "filth" and "disease." And you see how popular culture was enriched by immigrants—as in the old song, "Hello Wisconsin, Won't You Find My Yonnie Yonson?"

A few rooms on the third floor give a taste of what the dormitories and detention cells were like. But, other than the thoughtful museum exhibits, there is little left in the second-floor Registry Room to recall the millions of human dramas that it witnessed.

The long-awaited Family History Center opened in 2001, where visitors can look up the immigration records of anyone who arrived by way of Ellis Island up to 1924.

—Susan Sachs

Information, (212) 363-32009, Ferry Schedule, (212) 269-5755, *www.nps.gov.stli*. **Hours:** 8:45 A.M.–5:45 P.M. daily, extended summer hours. **Price:** Admission is free. Round-trip ferry tickets: $8, adults; $3, children under 17; $6, senior citizens.

Statue of Liberty

exchange. To see them in action, go to 20 Broad Street for a ticket to the visitors' gallery overlooking the trading floor (stop by early, because tickets are often gone by noon).

Some traders still swill martinis at **Harry's Hanover Square** (downstairs at 1 Hanover Square between Stone and Pearl Sts.), though the younger crowd seems to opt for the **Wall Street Kitchen and Bar** (70 Broad St.). And as long as they can put the meal on an expense account, executives eat lunch at **Delmonico's** (56 Beaver St. between William and Broad Sts.).

The cliché that Wall Street guys love cigars turns out to be true; you can see them buying 'em by the box at **Barclay Rex** (7 Maiden Lane) and **JR Cigars** (corner of Wall and Pearl).

For a sense of what Wall Street used to be like before the days of skyscrapers, take a stroll through the twisty little streets just north of Broad: Stone Street, Mill Lane and South William Street, which intersects with William Street.

The **Museum of American Financial History** (28 Broadway), is more interesting than it may sound. Nearby, two wonderful old buildings that housed steamship companies have been put to other uses but still bear traces of their glory days. At 1 Broadway, just west of **Bowling Green**, the door for first-class passengers now leads to a Citibank branch. Up the block, the old **Cunard Line Building** (25 Broadway) now serves as an ugly Post Office, but it's almost worth standing in line for stamps when you can gaze at the amazing original ceiling.

There are three places that Wall Street regulars seldom visit, but that are worth a quick stop: the statue of the charging bull by Arturo di Modica at the north end of Bowling Green (great place for photos); **Federal Hall** (dull exhibits, nice view) and **Trinity Church**. If you think a church makes an odd symbol for an area long associated with Mammon, think again. Trinity once owned most of lower Manhattan, made big bucks from the island's development, and remains a major commercial landlord to this day. St. Paul's Chapel, a short distance up Broadway, is linked to Trinity Church. Washington worshiped there as President and his pew has been preserved. — *Leslie Eaton*

Subway: 2, 3, 4, 5 to Wall St. or Fulton Street; J, M, Z to Broad St. or Fulton St.; A, C to Broadway–Nassau St.

HIGHLIGHTS OF THE NEIGHBORHOOD

Federal Hall National Memorial Wall St. at Nassau St. (212) 825-6888. Wall Street's version of the Parthenon, Federal Hall stands on the site of George Washington's inauguration in 1789, which explains his statue on the front steps. One of the finest Greek Revival buildings in the city, the former U.S. Customs House and early Federal Reserve branch was designed in 1834 and built in 1842. Behind its portico of severe Doric columns and five-foot walls, the building houses a museum of constitutional history.

Federal Reserve Bank 33 Liberty Place (between Nassau and William Sts.) (212) 720-5000. Five stories below Liberty Street, the Federal Reserve's New York branch houses a substantial share of the world's gold reserves behind jail-like bars. The bank offers tours of the underground vaults, which store approximately $100 billion worth of gold ingots for some 60 countries. A government bank for banks, the Federal Reserve regulates U.S. currency, supervises commercial banks and has considerable impact on the economy through its influence on the money supply and interest rates. The New York branch, which domi-

nates the other 11, covers a trapezoidal city block. Its rusticated limestone
building is reminiscent of a Florentine Renaissance palazzo.

Fraunces Tavern Museum 54 Pearl St. (at Broad St.) (212) 425 1778.
The 18th-century Fraunces Tavern has been substantially rebuilt since it was
the haunt of George Washington and the Sons of Liberty. It is now a small
museum of American history. The Long Room, where Washington made his
farewell address to his Revolutionary War officers, is one of the several period
rooms where displays are located. The Museum offers tours, lectures and performances coordinated with current exhibitions, as well as special events on Washington's Birthday and Independence Day. **Prices:** $2.50, adults; $1, children,
students and seniors.

New York Stock Exchange 11 Wall St. (between New and Broad Sts.)
(212) 656-3000. On a good day—a day when the stock market is soaring—you
can almost smell the money in the air outside the New York Stock Exchange. If
you go inside, you can see it being made (or lost). To visit the exchange, go to
the little booth on Broad Street and pick up a free ticket. You will be sent
around to the back of the building, through a lobby, up an elevator to the third
floor, and into the "Interactive Education Center." You can skip all the propa-
gan . . . er, educational exhibits . . . though there is a lively video clip that helps
to explain exactly what it happening on the floor of the exchange.

From the glassed-in visitors' gallery, you can gaze at the main trading floor.
The effect is rather like watching a really fancy ant farm. Hundreds of strangely
dressed people bustle about, bark at each other, gab on phones, peer at computer screens and drop little bits of paper all over the floor. Most of them are

New York Stock Exchange

Fred R. Conrad/The New York Times

Ruby Washington/ The New York Times

Wall Street

brokers carrying big buy and sell orders to the specialists, auctioneers of a sort. Each specialist handles trading in several stocks.

Peer past the web of wires and pipes and cables to see the turn-of-the-century ceiling, all carved ivory and gold. In a few years, the exchange is slated to leave this old building for a new complex to be built across the street. But some seers predict that before that happens, the whole kit-and-caboodle will have moved to cyberspace.   *—Leslie Eaton*

St. Paul's Chapel 211 Broadway (between Fulton and Vesey Sts.) (212) 602-0874. New York City's oldest church building, the chapel served uptown parishioners of Trinity Church as the colonial city expanded northward. Completed in 1766, the church is a New York brownstone version of London's St. Martin-in-the-Fields, a marble Georgian church that greatly influenced American ecclesiastic architecture. George Washington worshiped here on the day of his inauguration and during the 18 months New York was the nation's capital. The tree-filled graveyard behind the church preserves a parcel of the 18th-century countryside. In conjunction with Trinity Church, St. Paul's offers a well-attended lunchtime concert series.

Trinity Church and Museum Broadway (at Wall St.) (212) 602-0872. At the foot of Wall Street in downtown Manhattan stands Trinity Church, once the tallest structure in Manhattan. The first Episcopal church in New York, the parish was chartered in 1697. The Gothic-style church on the site now was built in 1846 by Richard Upjohn. Two earlier churches on the site were destroyed by fire. Many prominent New Yorkers, including Alexander Hamilton and William Bradford, are buried in the graveyard next to the church. During the summer months, they share the spot with office workers on their lunch breaks, enjoying the sun in this rare downtown patch of open space. The church hosts a popular lunchtime concert series and houses a museum featuring changing exhibitions and a permanent collection of artifacts.

Highly Recommended Neighborhood Restaurants
(*See chapter* **Restaurants** *for reviews.*)

Bayard's	☆☆	$$$	NEW AMERICAN
Delmonico's	☆	$$$	ITALIAN/NEW AMERICAN
Grill Room	☆☆	$$$	NEW AMERICAN/SEAFOOD

South Street Seaport/City Hall

For several hundred years, the **South Street Seaport** was a thriving commercial dockland of warehouses and markets handling great ships from all points: China clippers, schooners, ferries and fishing boats. Barges floated down from the Erie Canal bearing cargo from middle America. This busy East River port became obsolete in the late 19th century, however, as bigger ships powered by steam docked at new and larger piers on the Hudson River.

When restoration of the area began in the 1960's, a jewel of a neighborhood was recreated to evoke a great age in New York's maritime history. There were cobbled streets free of traffic and piers open to wind and water. Alas, over recent years the seaport has turned into something of a theme-park shopping mall, where busloads of tourists clamber over each other on their way to boutiques and vast restaurants bearing no relationship to a seafaring life. Still, it remains an unusual corner of the city, and a pleasant place to spend a sunny day away from skyscrapers and stark, perpendicular avenues.

The restoration of the South Street district has included the construction of a large new pier, too, but one built for pleasure, where a stroll offers a bracing breeze and a view across to Brooklyn. Nearby is the original **Fulton Fish Market** with a restaurant and other facilities in a dockside building once known for its fish and produce. The fish market is still the place where restaurants and retail fish markets buy their daily fare in the wee hours of the morning. Moored at the port is a four-masted sailing barque, the **Peking**, part of the **South Street Seaport Museum**. The *Peking*, launched in 1911 even as its breed was doomed, is one of the largest sailing vessels ever built. Visitors can board her and go below decks to learn her history.

At the Water Street entrance to the Seaport is the **Titanic Memorial Lighthouse** built in 1913 to commemorate the disaster. On Fulton Street between South and Front Streets is **Schermerhorn Row**, a series of early 19th-century Georgian-Federal-style buildings once used as warehouses by leading merchants.

To the west where Fulton Street meets Broadway is **Park Row**, the street that borders the east side of **City Hall Park** and leads to the entrance of the **Brooklyn Bridge**. Among the sights in and around the park are **City Hall**, the **Woolworth Building** and the **Municipal Building** (*see* "Highlights of the Neighborhood") as well as the **African Burial Ground** (Duane St. at Elk St.) where approximately 20,000 African Americans were laid to rest during the

Brooklyn Bridge pedestrian walkway

18th century. The site was uncovered in 1991 during construction of the Federal office tower across the street. The **Tweed Courthouse**, just north of City Hall, was the old New York County Courthouse made famous by the corrupt dealings of politician William "Boss" Tweed in the late 1800's. With its Italianate design and stunning interiors the building is worth a visit.

Farther north along Centre Street are today's active court buildings. At 40 Centre Street is the **United States Courthouse**, a mid-1930's Classical Revival skyscraper topped with a golden pyramid. The **New York County Courthouse** moved to its current location at 60 Centre Street in 1927. This hexagonal, Roman classical building is a frequent backdrop for *Law & Order* and countless other television shows and films. At the **Criminal Courts Building** (100 Centre Street) arraignments are held 24 hours a day, seven days a week. The 5:30 P.M. to 1 A.M. shift ("night court") is real-life theater. It is mostly pantomime, robbed of its dialogue by bad acoustics, but it offers the curious visitor a hard look at New York life.

South Street Seaport: Fulton St. at South St. on the East River (212) 748-8600 *www.southstseaport.org.* **Subway:** J, M, Z, 2, 3, 4, 5, to Fulton St.; A, C to Broadway–Nassau; 4, 5, 6 to Brooklyn Bridge–City Hall; N, R to City Hall; J, M, Z to Chambers St.

HIGHLIGHTS OF THE NEIGHBORHOOD

Brooklyn Bridge Manhattan entrance: Park Row at Centre St. Brooklyn entrance: Washington St. at Adams St. One of the grandest and most potent symbols of New York City since the day it opened in 1883, the Brooklyn Bridge still provides probably the best free tourist activity in the whole city— walking across it toward the Manhattan skyline.

A Cultural Hub Takes Shape Downtown

Never mind the Met, the Frick, the Guggenheim. New York's new Museum Mile is taking shape from Chambers Street to State Street.

With little fanfare, Lower Manhattan has become a cultural destination in its own right, coming out of a strong economy and capitalizing on the growing popular interest in heritage and history. A dozen museums are now operating, and several important ones will be arriving in the next few years. In fact, keep the Guggenheim in mind. It may end up as the 800-pound, titanium-skinned gorilla on the downtown museum scene.

It seems almost inevitable that the oldest quarter of New York should emerge as a museum nexus, something more than a stopping-off point on the way over to Liberty and Ellis Islands. Though no one seriously proposes that Lower Manhattan will soon overtake the Upper East Side as a destination for cultural tourism, it has some special advantages.

A distinct characteristic is that almost every museum downtown is historically connected in some way to the building it occupies or the land on which it stands.

"New Yorkers are coming to understand and appreciate that they do have a history," said Robert R. Macdonald, director of the **Museum of the City of New York**, which is planning to move from Uptown to the Tweed Courthouse behind City Hall in two years (*see* "Upper East Side" *for listing*).

The **Heye Center** (pronounced "high") in the **National Museum of the American Indian** (*see* "World Trade Center and Battery Park" *for listing*) is a branch of the Smithsonian Institution that sprawls through the Beaux-Arts chambers of the former United States Custom House on Bowling Green. As it happens, this marks the end of what was once the Wiechquaekeck Trail, an important Algonquian trading route.

The museum moved in 1994 from Audubon Terrace at 155th Street, which will soon be losing another institution, the **American Numismatic Society**, to Lower Manhattan (*see* "Washington Heights/Inwood" *for listing*).

In 2002, the society will move into the seven-story former Fidelity and

To start on the Brooklyn side, climb the three flights of stairs on Washington Street. (The closest subway stop is the High Street station on the A line). You will be following in the steps of President Chester A. Arthur, who led the first group of pedestrians across. And you will thank John A. Roebling, who designed the bridge in 1867 and put the elevated walkway in the center, above other traffic, so that pedestrians could "enjoy the beautiful views and the pure air."

From end to end, it is more than a mile—6,016 feet. The portion over the East River soars 135 feet above mean high water.

But long before you thread through the massive keyholes of the bridge's Gothic-arched towers (at the time they were built, the towers were taller than

Deposit Company Building at 140 William Street, on the corner of Fulton Street, where it plans to build its own museum. For the next five years, the society will present "Drachmas, Doubloons and Dollars: The History of Money" in a 5,000-square-foot exhibition space at the Federal Reserve Bank of New York, at 33 Liberty Street.

By December 2001, the **New York City Police Museum** (*see* "World Trade Center and Battery Park" *for listing*) will have moved out of the former Cunard Building at 25 Broadway and into its own home in the former First Precinct station house at 100 Old Slip, on the East River, where it will have 8,000 square feet of exhibition space.

Also by the end of 2001, a designer may have been chosen for the **Museum of Women: the Leadership Center**, cater-corner from the **Museum of Jewish Heritage** (*see* "Institutes of World Culture" *in chapter* **The Arts** *for listing*), said Timothy S. Carey, president of the Battery Park City Authority.

In March 2002, the **Irish Hunger Memorial** will open in Battery Park City. Though not strictly a museum, the 96-by-170-foot installation will have a real 19th-century stone cottage from Attymass, Ireland, as the centerpiece of a landscape meant to evoke the Irish countryside.

Later in 2002, the **Skyscraper Museum** will open at the base of the Ritz-Carlton Downtown, on the third corner of Battery Park City's museum crossroads.

The year 2003 should prove to be a cultural watershed for downtown. In addition to the relocation of the Museum of the City of New York, in September 2003, the Museum of Jewish Heritage plans to open a $60 million, 70,000-square-foot east wing to its existing museum. Toward the end of 2003, the **South Street Seaport Museum** plans to complete a $20 million renovation of **Schermerhorn Row** on Fulton Street and the adjacent **A. A. Low Building**. Also in 2003, the Heye Center will open a $3 million education center in a 6,400-square-foot space under the grand rotunda.

—*David W. Dunlap*

anything on either shore, besides the Trinity Church spire), you will easily understand why the bridge has loomed so large in the nation's imagination.

Over the years, it has loomed indeed. It has been painted by everyone from George Bellows to Georgia O'Keeffe. Its glories have been sung in poetry and prose by thousands, including Hart Crane, the poet who asked: "How could mere toil align thy choiring strings!"   —*Randy Kennedy*

City Hall Broadway and Chambers St. (212) 788-6865. Topped by a cupola that once offered commanding views of the countryside, City Hall is now dwarfed by office towers. An amalgamation of French Renaissance and Federal design completed between 1802 and 1812, it houses the offices of the mayor and the City Council. Official receptions for winning teams, astronauts and other dignitaries take place on the steps outside. The interior has a remarkable pair of cantilevered stairs under a central rotunda.

Fulton Fish Market South St. and Fulton St. (212) 748-8590. The nation's largest fish market becomes hectic around 4 A.M., but is largely deserted during the day. Still, a fishy odor lingers in the air long after the pandemonium of fork-lifts and trucks has delivered the day's catch to wholesalers, retailers and chefs from the city's finest restaurants. As a federal prosecutor in the 1980's, Rudolph Giuliani began a crackdown against Mafia influence and, in 1995, the city stepped in to take control of the market. Nearby, the renovated 19th-century Fulton Market holds upscale food stalls, but it has been overtaken in popularity by neighboring Pier 17, which juts into the East River. One of the last working areas of the Manhattan waterfront, the fish market adjoins bars and restaurants that guarantee a lively snack break in the middle of the night.

Municipal Building 1 Centre St. (at Chambers St.). Best known as the place where thousands of couples get married every year, the Municipal Building is coincidentally crowned by a round, colonnaded tower that resembles a wedding cake. Instead of two colossal newlyweds, however, the top of the building houses a monumental gilt sculpture called "Civic Flame." Roughly a decade after the merger of the five boroughs in 1898, the city held a competition for an office building to house various city agencies under one roof. The resulting Beaux-Arts skyscraper—designed by McKim, Mead & White and completed in 1914—stands guard over the approach to the Brooklyn Bridge. The building's entrance, which incorporates a Roman triumphal arch, boldly straddles Chambers Street.

Surrogates Court Hall of Records 31 Chambers St. (at Reade St.) (212) 374-8286. One of the most impressive downtown monuments, the Hall of Records was constructed in 1899 at a time when civic monuments were inten-tionally grandiose. Built by John R. Thomas and the firm of Hogan & Slattery, it possesses a particularly beautiful central hall. Whether or not citizens' records merited such splendor is another matter altogether, but the building itself is def-initely worth the visit.

Woolworth Building Broadway opposite City Hall Park. View this dramatic structure from a distance far enough to take in the Gothic flourishes of intri-cately carved buttresses capped by a summit that sits like a medieval castle 792 feet above lower Broadway. The building is truly from another era, when corpo-rate barons like F.W. Woolworth, of five-and-dime fame, battled for skyscraper supremacy. Designed by the celebrated architect Cass Gilbert, the Woolworth Building was the tallest skyscraper until the Chrysler Building (and countless others subsequently) conquered it in 1930. It remains a standout among the more contemporary glass-and-steel boxes of the nearby financial district. Some-where inside are a swimming pool and a storeroom of Gothic ornaments to replace the ones adorning the exterior. The only area open for casual visitors is the lobby, a sight itself to behold with its vaulted ceilings of tiled mosaics, murals, marble splendor and, on a windy day, a moaning, eerie whistle befitting the building's style. —*Randy Archibold*

Chinatown

Geography, New York style: China shares a border with Italy, and has for more than a century. The boundary is fluid, to be sure, and Chinatown's expansion in recent years across the traditional demarcation line of Canal Street has whittled Little Italy down to Tiny Italy. The area has Vietnamese, Cambodian and Hispanic communities too, and some traces of a once vibrant Jewish culture.

The Chinese population grew slowly from about 150 residents in the mid 1800's to around 4,000 just before the repeal of the Chinese Exclusion Act in 1943. Since 1965 the population has exploded and it is now the largest Chinese community in the Western Hemisphere. With about 150,000 documented residents (and many more undocumented), this is one of the most densely populated sections of the city.

A self-sufficient community with a large population of non-English speakers, many residents never have to leave the area. On narrow streets, fishmongers and greengrocers spill onto the sidewalks. In late January or early February the **Chinese New Year** is marked by a raucous street festival (former mayor Giuliani took some of the sizzle out of the celebration in the year 4695, that's 1997, when he banned firecrackers). The **Museum of Chinese in the Americas** (70 Mulberry St.) offers exhibits celebrating Chinese-American culture and history.

To the outsider searching for the perfect egg roll, Chinatown may seem changeless. Yet along with the infusion of Hong Kong capital has come a shift in the economic center from Mott Street to the **Bowery** and **East Broadway**, while the traditional dominance of immigrants from China's Guangdong Province is being ceded to those from Fujian.

There are an estimated 300 restaurants in the area focusing on any of several Chinese cuisines. After dinner or dim sum (traditional lunch of dumplings and other specialties) try the **Chinatown Ice Cream Factory** (65 Bayard St. between Mott and Elizabeth Sts.) for a scoop of green-tea ice cream. The **Pearl River Mart** at Canal St. and Broadway carries a huge selection of Chinese imports—dishes, traditional costumes and decorations, housewares and food. Along with smaller import shops, most Chinatown streets (particularly Canal Street) are lined with little storefronts and sidewalk stands selling everything from cheap electronics and batteries to Rolex knockoffs and discount luggage.

Just south of the **Manhattan Bridge** entrance (at Bowery and Canal St.) past **Confucius Plaza**, one of the area's newer housing developments, is **Chatham Square**. Here the **Kimlau Arch** honors Chinese soldiers killed in American wars. Where Catherine Street meets East Broadway is the **Republic National Bank**, the quintessential Chinatown building designed with the flourishes of a pagoda.

Subway: J, M, N, Q, R, W, Z, 6 to Canal St.; F to East Broadway.

HIGHLIGHTS OF THE NEIGHBORHOOD

Asian American Arts Center 26 Bowery (between Bayard and Pell Sts.) (212) 233-2154. The Asian American Arts Center, founded in 1974, presents exhibits of both traditional and contemporary Asian and Asian-American art. The center examines the historical and cultural context of Asian arts, and supports contemporary Asian artists working in traditional media.

Columbus Park Mulberry St. at Bayard St. This mostly concrete plaza in the heart of Chinatown seems like a lush oasis when you enter it from some of the narrowest and most congested streets in the city. The park's benches and stone chess tables are usually occupied, from dawn to dusk, by elderly Chinese women and men playing cards and mah-jongg. The park is located on the site of the Mulberry Bend, an infamous tenement slum of the 1800's, and one of the most dangerous places in the city. The buildings were torn down at the urging of the reformer Jacob Riis, who wrote a scathing report on the area's disgraceful condition.

Museum of the Chinese in the Americas 70 Mulberry St. (at Bayard St.) (212) 619-4785. This is the only professionally staffed American museum focused on Chinese-American history. Located on the second floor of a century-old school building in the heart of Chinatown, it offers educational and community programs and facilities for research on Chinese/Asian American studies.

Recommended Inexpensive Neighborhood Restaurants
*(See chapter **Restaurants** for reviews.)*

Big Wong	CHINESE
Evergreen Shanghai	CHINESE
Goody's	CHINESE
Joe's Shanghai	CHINESE
New York Noodle Town	CHINESE
New Green Bo	CHINESE
Nha Trang	VIETNAMESE
Sweet-N-Tart Café	CHINESE

Lower East Side

The Lower East Side has a charm that much of Manhattan has lost. Though the area has seen its share of rent hikes and gentrification in recent years, it remains a tapestry of cultures and a celebration of New York's diversity. Since the mid-19th century it has been the gateway to America for countless generations of immigrants. Waves of families from Eastern Europe, Italy, Ireland, Germany, and more recently China, Puerto Rico and the Dominican Republic, have passed through here leaving their stamp on the neighborhood's cultural landscape. In the last two decades an influx of artists and young people have made the Lower East Side not only a cross-cultural mecca, but also a thriving center for art, fashion and nightlife.

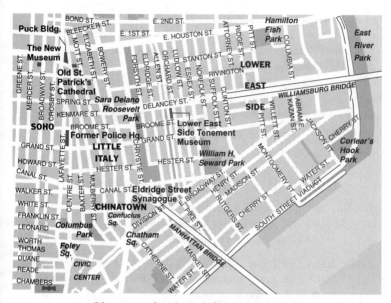

Chinatown/Little Italy/Lower East Side

In the storefronts on blocks like **Essex Street** (between Canal and Grand Sts.) the Lower East Side of the past and present converge. Asian-owned electronics stores abut old Jewish businesses like **Guss' Pickles**. Guss', with its open front and barrels lining the sidewalk, has been scooping pickles by hand for 90 years. (The green tomatoes are excellent). Signs in Yiddish alternate with signs in Chinese along this stretch; locals pack **Kossar's Bagelry** (some of the best bagels in the city), as others settle down for a Sichuan lunch a few doors away.

To the north **Delancey Street** bisects the area, beyond which residents are largely Hispanic with a strong showing of younger newcomers. This thoroughfare offers mostly discount goods and cheap knock-offs, and an occasional shaved-ice snow cone vendor. **Ratner's**, a Delancey Street relic, has been serving Jewish dairy food since 1905—only now it's a fraction of its former size and shares a building with **Lansky Lounge**, a hot spot for nostalgic hipsters (*see chapter* **Nightlife**).

Rivington Street, one block north of Delancey, is dotted with Puerto Rican and Dominican businesses and home to **ABC No Rio**, one of several area cultural centers. It's also home to **Schapiro's Kosher Wines**, the last functioning winery in the city, family-run since 1899, and **Streit's Matzos**, one of the premier suppliers of matzo and other Jewish staples for over 75 years.

Just west of Rivington is the **Orchard Street Bargain District** (*see chapter* **Shopping**), where peddlers with pushcarts once crowded the streets. Shoppers still come to the area for discount leather goods, luggage and clothing.

Orchard and **Ludlow Streets** are home to some of the most fashionable shops and a slew of chic bars and lounges (*see chapter* **Nightlife**). A few paces away are some of the Lower East Side's longest standing eateries. **Katz's Deli-**

catessen, an area artifact and originator of the World War II slogan, "Send a salami to your boy in the Army," still carves pastrami and corned beef by hand. The kitschy Borscht Belt party atmosphere of **Sammy's Roumanian**, the enormous garlic-rubbed beef tenderloins and the bowls of schmaltz (rendered chicken fat) on every table are a nostalgic paean to the days before cholesterol consciousness. Also don't miss **Russ and Daughters** for smoked fish and other deli specialties and **Yonah Shimmel**, supplying the neighborhood with knishes since 1910.

Subway: F to Second Ave. or Delancey St.; J, M, Z to Essex St.

HIGHLIGHTS OF THE NEIGHBORHOOD

ABC No Rio 156 Rivington St. (between Clinton and Suffolk Sts.) (212) 254-3697. This cultural center has sponsored punk rock concerts, political discussions, film showings and poetry readings as well as art exhibitions.

Eldridge Street Synagogue 12 Eldridge St. (between Canal and Division Sts.) (212) 219-0888. Even in a state of disrepair, the Eldridge Street Synagogue's intricate carved facade and stained-glass windows stand out amid the tenements. Built in the late 1800's by immigrants from Eastern Europe, it was the first large-scale Orthodox synagogue in New York. It is being restored under the stewardship of the Eldridge Street Project, which offers tours of the building, lectures, and educational programs including rugelach baking lessons and genealogy workshops.

First Shearith Israel Graveyard 55–57 St. James Pl. (between Oliver and James Sts.). Located in Chinatown, this small cemetery is the oldest surviving burial ground for the first Jewish congregation in North America. The congregation was mostly comprised of Spanish and Portuguese Jews. The oldest stone dates from 1683.

Henry Street Settlement—Abrons Arts Center 466 Grand St. (at Pitt St.) (212) 598-0400. In its century or so of existence, the Henry Street Settlement has been unsurpassed in bringing a multitude of cultural and community-related activities—including opera, music, dance, theater, talks and workshops—to the residents of the Lower East Side. The hub of the Settlement, which occupies a row of handsome Greek Revival town houses, is the Abrons Arts Center. The majority of performances take place in the 350-seat Harry De Jur Playhouse, a national historic landmark. There is also a smaller theater, a recital hall, an outdoor amphitheater, classrooms, studios and art galleries.

Lower East Side Tenement Museum 90 Orchard St. (at Broome St.) (212) 431-0233. If a museum is meant to be a place where things are displayed to teach us who we are and where we've come from, then the grimy and dank building at 90 Orchard Street may prove to be more intimately meaningful for many than the Louvre or the Metropolitan. From beneath the floorboards of this 130-year-old house and between many layers of wallpaper have come notes

and artifacts to illuminate the experiences of more than 1,300 people who
passed through the building's 22 units.
Admission: $9, general; $7, students and seniors. **Credit cards:** All major.
Hours: Tue., Wed., Fri., noon–5 P.M.; Thu., noon–9 P.M.; Sat.–Sun., 11
A.M.–5 P.M. **Services:** Tours, gift shop, lectures.

Schapiro's Wine Company 126 Rivington St. (between Essex and Norfolk
Sts.) (212) 674-4404. The grapes are grown upstate, where much of the wine is
now fermented and bottled, but some is still produced in ancient barrels on the
premises. On Sundays from 11 A.M. to 5 P.M., Norman Schapiro, a real old-
time character, offers free tours of the winery and tastes of his wines, ranging
from the treacly sweet to the dry. For more information, visit their Web site:
www.schapiro-wine.com.

Williamsburg Bridge Delancey St. and the East River. The Williamsburg
Bridge was born of a dare. Could Leffert Lefferts Buck, the city's chief engineer,
build a bridge that was longer than the Brooklyn Bridge in half the time and
with less money? He could, and did. When it opened in 1903, the Williamsburg
was the world's longest suspension bridge at 7,308 feet with a main span of 1,600
feet, five feet more than the Brooklyn Bridge. At a cost of $24,188,090, it was
$906,487 under its rival. And it was built in seven years; the Brooklyn took 13.

Selected Restaurants and Food Shops

Congee Village
100 Orchard St. (between Delancey and Broome Sts.)   (212) 941-1818

Guss' Pickles
35 Essex Street (between Hester and Grand Sts.)   (212) 254-4477

Katz's Delicatessen
205 E. Houston St. (at Ludlow St.)   (212) 254-2246

Kossar's Bagelry
39 Essex St. (between Hester and Grand Sts.)   (212) 387-9940

Ratner's
138 Delancey St. (between Norfolk and Suffolk Sts.)   (212) 677-5588

Russ and Daughters
179 E. Houston St. (between Orchard and Allen Sts.)   (212) 475-4880

Sammy's Roumanian
157 Chrystie St. (between Delancey and Houston Sts.)   (212) 673-0330

Streit's Matzos
150 Rivington St. (at Suffolk St.)   (212) 475-7000

Yonah Shimmel Knishes
175 E. Houston St. (between Eldridge and Forsythe Sts.)   (212) 477-2858

Little Italy/NoLIta

Historically, Little Italy was a family neighborhood, home to several waves of immigrants who settled in its five- and six-story tenement buildings. Some of them moved up and out, but others turned into the gray-haired grandmothers who still sit out on the stoops in pleasant weather.

The Italians moved in during the 1850's. In the first half of the 20th century nearly everyone was of Italian descent. Since the late 1960's, when the United States opened its doors to Chinese immigrants, Chinatown has been creeping northward, crossing over its traditional Canal Street boundary. Although many Italian restaurants and stores remain, much of Little Italy proper—the blocks between Canal and Kenmare Streets—has the feel of Chinatown.

Along **Mulberry Street** there are still dozens of Italian restaurants and cafes serving such specialties as coal-oven pizza and chocolate cannoli. **Ferrara Pastries** (195 Grand St.) has been producing traditional Italian desserts for over 100 years. Try **Puglia** (189 Hester St.) for a unique, family-style dining experience. **Mare Chiaro** (176 1/2 Mulberry St.), with its Sinatra photos and authentic feel, is the place to go for a drink (*see chapter* **Nightlife**). For a taste of the area's Mafia past, go to the former site of **Umberto's Clam House** (149 Mulberry St.) where mobster Joey Gallo was gunned down in 1972. A couple of blocks north was the **Ravenite Social Club** (247 Mulberry St.), now a boutique, which served as John Gotti's unofficial headquarters until he was arrested there in 1990.

The big annual event is the **Feast of San Gennaro**, which starts the Thursday after Labor Day. For 10 days several streets are open to pedestrians only.

Old St. Patrick's Cathedral on Prince Street (at Mulberry St.) was founded by Irish immigrants in 1809. The cathedral became a parish church in 1879 when it was eclipsed by the new St. Patrick's Cathedral on Fifth Avenue. The old church achieved a measure of cinematic fame as the childhood parish of Martin Scorsese and as a backdrop for several movies, including two in Francis Ford Coppola's *Godfather* series. Another area building worth seeing is the **New York City Police Headquarters** (240 Centre St. between Broome and Grand Sts.). This domed Edwardian Baroque building completed in 1909 was converted into a luxury apartment building in 1988.

NoLIta (which stands for **N**orth **o**f **Little Ita**ly) is the extension of Little Italy north to Houston Street. It attracts a young and trend-setting clientele of artists and professionals. As they set up shop and home, they are recasting the neighborhood with an up-to-the-minute mix of retailing and nightlife. Boutiques, galleries, cafes and nightclubs have sprouted in once-vacant storefronts (*see also chapters* **Shopping** *and* **Nightlife**).

Subway: F, S to Broadway–Laffayette St.; N, R to Prince St.; 6 to Spring St.

Recommended Inexpensive Restaurant

Lombardi's   PIZZA

TriBeCa

At night and on weekends, TriBeCa can look and feel rather desolate. There is little activity on the streets, compared with SoHo and other trendy downtown neighborhoods. It's hard to tell which of the many cast-iron loft buildings have apartments tucked inside and which are commercial spaces.

But if you look hard enough, you can find signs of life no matter when you visit TriBeCa, a patch of lower Manhattan bounded to the north by Canal Street, to the east by Broadway, to the south by Chambers Street and to the west by the Hudson River.

TriBeCa was a bustling commercial and manufacturing center in the 19th century. Since the neighborhood was near the river and several shipping piers, wealthy merchants built warehouses there to hold agricultural goods, as well as spices, nuts and coffee. Factories and warehouses dominated the neighborhood well into the 20th century, but most were abandoned by 1970. That's when artists began trickling in, transforming space in many empty lofts into studios, galleries and living quarters.

Savvy real estate developers came up with the name TriBeCa, from **Tri**angle **Be**low **Ca**nal Street. By the early 80's, the neighborhood was drawing investment bankers who liked its proximity to Wall Street, celebrities who liked its relative privacy, and anyone else who could afford the vast loft apartments whose values were shooting up.

A well-known landmark is **Odeon**, the sleek and cavernous restaurant that played a leading role in *Bright Lights, Big City*, Jay McInerny's novel about the hedonistic nightlife of young New Yorkers in the 80's. Odeon still serves American and French bistro food and stays open until 2 A.M. on weekdays, 3 on weekends. TriBeCa is also home to several hip eateries owned by Robert De Niro and Drew Nieporent, including **Nobu**, a sushi restaurant, and **Layla**, a Middle Eastern restaurant complete with belly dancers (*see* **Restaurants**).

Mr. De Niro, who opened the **TriBeCa Film Center** (375 Greenwich Street), is one of the area's most famous residents. John F. Kennedy Jr. was another. After he and his wife died in a plane crash in 1999, hundreds of mourners placed flowers and notes in front of 20 North Moore Street, where they lived.

Reade Street between Broadway and Church has some fine examples of the marble and cast-iron buildings that the neighborhood is known for, as does Duane Street between Church and West Broadway. Franklin, White and Walker Streets are also good places to check out the local architecture.

For green space, TriBeCa has **Duane Park**, a triangular patch of land that was a formal garden in the early 1800's. An overpass leads pedestrians across the West Side Highway at Chambers Street, past the prestigious **Stuyvesant High School**, to **Hudson River Park**. Starting just north of the World Financial Center, the riverside park is eventually supposed to stretch all the way to Midtown. For now, you can walk along the river from just north of Chambers Street, up to Gansevoort Street in Greenwich Village.

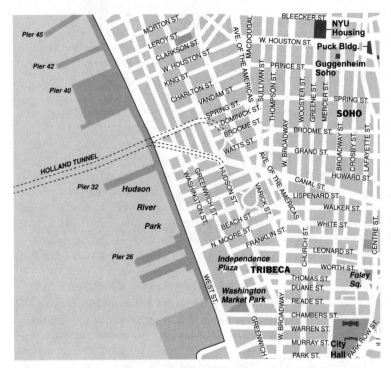

TriBeCa/SoHo

TriBeCa's eastern fringes are its most commercial, particularly along Church Street, where coffee shops, discount stores and fast food restaurants abound. One worth checking out is **Pakistan Tea House** (176 Church Street), a crowded but cozy little place that serves generous portions of tasty and surprisingly inexpensive food, drawing equal numbers of cab drivers, office workers and hip TriBeCa residents.   —*Abby Goodnough*

Subway: A, C, 1, 2, 3, 9 to Chambers St.; A, C, E, 1, 9 to Canal St.; 1, 9 to Franklin St.

Highly Recommended Neighborhood Restaurants
(*See chapter* **Restaurants** *for reviews.*)

Bouley Bakery	☆☆☆☆	$ $ $ $	FRENCH
Chanterelle	☆☆☆	$ $ $ $	FRENCH
Danube	☆☆☆	$ $ $ $	EAST EUROPEAN/GERMAN
F.illi Ponte	☆☆	$ $ $ $	ITALIAN
Layla	☆☆	$ $ $	MIDDLE EASTERN
Montrachet	☆☆☆	$ $ $ $	FRENCH
Next Door Nobu	☆☆☆	$ $ $ $	JAPANESE
Nobu	☆☆☆	$ $ $ $	JAPANESE
Odeon	☆☆	$ $	BISTRO/NEW AMERICAN
Salaam Bombay	☆☆	$ $	INDIAN

SoHo

Art and commerce coexist in SoHo (for **South of Houston** St.) more fiercely, perhaps, than anywhere else in New York City, yet still haven't driven each other out. (Artists who can't afford million-dollar lofts are a different matter.) There is impromptu art, like the fetchingly arranged baskets of unbelievably yellow tomatoes at **Dean & DeLuca** (*see chapter* **Shopping**) or the plumage of an elegant woman stepping down restaurant row on West Broadway. And then there is the more institutional art: the 200-odd galleries that have colonized the neighborhood since four prominent uptown dealers, **Leo Castelli, Ileana Sonnabend, John Weber** and **Andre Emmerick** settled in the big loft building at 420 West Broadway in 1971 (*see section* "Galleries" *in chapter* **The Arts**).

The arrival of the big-four dealers signalled the transformation of the once gritty warehouse neighborhood populated, often illegally, by penniless artists into the chic scene it is today, with limousines idling outside stores where a deceptively minimalist esthetic—lots of space, little merchandise—telegraphs old-money taste to new-money patrons. Many galleries have moved to Chelsea.

Mr. Castelli, who used to put artists on a payroll whether they produced or not, introduced Andy Warhol's Campbell's Soup cans to SoHo. The neighborhood went on to nurture the wiggly post-graffiti art of Keith Haring and Jean Michel Basquiat. Mary Boone, a Castelli protégée who promoted Julian Schnabel and David Salle, has since moved her gallery north of 58th Street, where she was arrested for handing out nine-millimeter cartridges to visitors the way coffee shops offer mints. She may have gotten away with it downtown.

In SoHo, almost nothing is ordinary, from the gorgeous art and architecture books of **Rizzoli** (454 West Broadway) to the ornate brackets at upscale hardware store **Anthropologie** (375 West Broadway), to the handmade note papers at **Kate's Paperie** (561 Broadway), to the french fries with lemony mayonnaise at **Balthazar** (80 Spring St.). Trendy clothing and accessory designers like **Anna Sui** (113 Greene St.), **kate spade** (454 Broome St.) and **Agnes B.** (79 Greene St.) also have shops here. To the south is Canal Street, on the border with Chinatown, where jeans are both hip and functional, Lucite is still cool and a bit of haggling will get you the cheapest watch in town.

But cheap rents are as quaint in SoHo these days as the sweatshops that once occupied the 26 blocks of the historic cast-iron district, when it was called Hell's Hundred Acres, because of the frequent fires fueled by cloth and chemicals. Since Jill Clayburgh became a painter and drank at the **Spring Street Bar** (corner of Spring and Mulberry Sts.) in Paul Mazursky's 1978 movie, *An Unmarried Woman*, the anonymous artist homesteaders have been replaced at various times by celebrity denizens like *Maus* cartoonist Art Spiegelman, sculptor Claes Oldenburg, art critic Robert Hughes, actor Willem Dafoe, paleontologist Stephen Jay Gould and monologuist Spalding Gray.

Would they, let alone the original artists, have discovered SoHo without its architecture? From the **Puck Building** (295 Lafayette St.), with its gilded homage to *A Midsummer Night's Dream* on East Houston, SoHo's northern border, to the **Haughwout Building** (488–492 Broadway), to the **Marble House** (southern edge of Mercer and Canal), the area is filled with distinctive buildings. The most famous, of course, are the post-Civil War cast-iron buildings, their Italianate elegance belying their seminal role as the grandfather of prefab architecture, the Sears catalog of building design, with owners choosing a Doric capital from column A and a Corinthian from column B. The bottle-glass sidewalks once allowed sunlight to illuminate the storage vaults below. Some streets are still paved with Belgian brick (not cobblestone) brought over as ship's ballast.

On Sullivan Street there are still some remnants of the Italian population that once called this area home. **Joe's Dairy** (156 Sullivan Street) and **Pino's Prime Meats** (149 Sullivan Street) are classics.

For children, a cast-iron tour can be almost as much fun as the **New York City Fire Museum**, with its collection of old firefighting equipment. Just buy a pack of cheap magnets; they'll help you tell the authentic cast-iron facades from the ringers.   —*Anemona Hartocollis*

Subway: F, S to Broadway–Lafayette St.; N, R to Prince St.; C, E, 6 to Spring St. or Bleecker St.

HIGHLIGHTS OF THE NEIGHBORHOOD

(*For* **Alternative Museum of the Arts, Guggenheim SoHo, Museum for African Art** *and* **New Museum of Contemporary Art**, *see section* "Museums" *in chapter* **The Arts**; *for* **Children's Museum of the Arts** *see chapter* **New York for Children**.)

New York City Fire Museum 278 Spring St. (between Hudson and Varick Sts.) (212) 691-1303. Located in a 1904 firehouse, the New York City Fire Museum displays historic firefighting equipment and traces the history of New York's bravest from the 1600's to the present. The permanent collection includes a horse-drawn firefighting carriage and an exhibit on the "bucket brigade." In addition to all the items related to putting out fires, the museum focuses on what secretly interests many of the museum's visitors: big fires. An exhibit of photographs records the nation's most serious fires, including New York's Triangle Shirtwaist fire of 1911 and the Chicago fire of 1871.

Highly Recommended Neighborhood Restaurants
(*See chapter* **Restaurants** *for reviews.*)

Alison on Dominick	☆☆	$$$	FRENCH
Balthazar	☆☆	$$	BISTRO/FRENCH
Honmura An	☆☆☆	$$$	JAPANESE/NOODLES
Provence	☆	$$$	FRENCH

Recommended Inexpensive Restaurants

Jean Claude	BISTRO/FRENCH
Pão	PORTUGUESE
Soho Steak	BISTRO/STEAK

NoHo

It's easy to forget that NoHo, wedged between the West Village, the East Village and SoHo, is a neighborhood in its own right. But while it shares many qualities with its better-known neighbors, NoHo—which stretches from Houston Street to Astor Place, and from Mercer Street to the Bowery—has its own quirky history.

Some of the city's glitziest families, including the Astors and the Vanderbilts, were drawn to the neighborhood in the 1830's. They lived in the Greek Revival town houses known collectively as **Colonnade Row** (Lafayette St. between Astor Pl. and Great Jones St.). Only four of the nine mansions remain, and although the city has designated them landmarks, they are in shabby shape.

One of them houses the **Astor Place Theater** (434 Lafayette St.) where the ever-popular performance troupe called Blue Man Group has been putting on a wacky show involving Twinkies and marshmallows since 1991. But NoHo's most venerable performance venue is the **Joseph Papp Public Theater** (425 Lafayette St.). The big old Italian Renaissance-style building originally belonged to John Jacob Astor, the city's first multimillionaire and one of NoHo's most famous residents. He donated the building to the city in 1854, and it became New York's first free public library.

The building was set to be demolished in the 1960's, but at the last minute it was renovated and reopened by Joseph Papp, founder of the New York Shakespeare Festival. There are actually six theaters inside, and altogether they seat more than 2,500 people. *Hair* and *A Chorus Line* opened there, and the theater now stages about 25 productions a year.

The city designated much of NoHo a historic district in 1999, after a three-year crusade by residents to preserve the largely intact rows of 19th-century loft buildings scattered throughout the neighborhood. The buildings, with facades of marble, cast iron, limestone and terra cotta, once housed retail stores topped by manufacturing spaces or warehouses.

Artists began moving into the area in the early 1970's, trickling north from SoHo in search of cheaper rents. They adopted the name NoHo—for North of Houston—and in 1976 got the city to rezone the neighborhood similarly to SoHo, allowing artists to live and work in the same space.

NoHo has no park, school or library, but trendy bars and restaurants abound. One popular dinner spot is the **Time Café** (380 Lafayette St.), an 1888 building designed by Henry J. Hardenburgh, architect of the Plaza Hotel and the Dakota apartment house on Central Park West. In the basement is **Fez**, a neo-Moroccan lounge with Persian rugs, plenty of couches and performances that range from folk music to poetry readings.

Marion's Continental (354 Bowery) is a retro-chic supper club with good cocktails and 50's décor. And **NoHo Star** (330 Lafayette St.), a laid-back neighborhood favorite, offers a mix of Asian and American fare.

—Abby Goodnough

Subway: F, S to Broadway–Lafayette St.; 6 to Bleecker St.

East Village

Almost since it stopped being Peter Stuyvesant's "bouwerie" (Dutch for "farm") and grew up into a neighborhood, the East Village has been the city's place for bold statements.

It was there, at **Cooper Union**, in what is now the city's oldest auditorium, that Abraham Lincoln delivered the famous anti-slavery speech that helped him win the Republican nomination in 1860. It was on St. Marks Place that Leon Trotsky started talking about revolution and later went to join one in Russia. And it was in the smoky music clubs around the Bowery, most notably **CBGB** (*see section* "Rock Clubs" *in* **Nightlife**), many decades later, that punk rock got its deafening start.

Now, with skyrocketing rents and new $12-a-drink bars opening on every other corner, the only apparent rebellion happening near St. Marks Place is the kind practiced by youngsters with dated mohawks and pink spiked hair.

But the East Village—stretching from the East River to the Bowery, and from 14th Street to Houston Street—has not completely lost the rough edges it acquired back in the early 1960s, when radicals, musicians and artists flocked there when they were priced out of Greenwich Village. Stroll, for example, past the **Hell's Angels'** headquarters on East 3rd Street, where most of the members are middle-aged now, but the plaque near the door still offers this youthful advice: "When in doubt, knock 'em out." Or get a mug of beer at **McSorley's** (E. 7th St. near Third Ave.), which was male-only until just 30 years ago and looks as if no one has mopped since the first mugs were filled there in 1854 (or 1862, depending on whose version of New York bar history you believe).

There are also still a few traces left of the neighborhood's multifarious ethnic past. Beginning after World War II, the East Village—back then it was known, less glamorously, as the Lower East Side—became the center of the city's Ukrainian community, as immigrants fleeing Soviet oppression joined others who had settled in the neighborhood around the turn of the century.

On Second Avenue you can still spot old men reading *Svoboda*, the Ukrainian-American newspaper. You can also grab a blintz or a bowl of borscht at **Veselka**, the recently renovated Ukrainian diner at the corner of 9th Street.

Practically all evidence has disappeared of the days when a stretch of Second Avenue was known as the Jewish Rialto, the Broadway of Yiddish theater. But a quick side trip on East 10th Street takes you to the **Russian and Turkish Baths**, a cavernous, tiled throwback to a time when the neighborhood was filled with "shvitzes," Yiddish slang for sweat or steambath. For $20, there's an endless supply of steam and for a little more, a vigorous oak-leaf scrub is available, designed to draw out the body's toxins.

Little India (E. 6th St. between First and Second Aves.) offers a cluster of little Indian restaurants with nearly identical menus and décor. These are great places to stop for a cheap tasty meal. For dessert grab a cannoli at **Veniero's** (342 E. 11th St.) or **De Roberti's** (176 First Ave.) around the corner. These turn-of-the-century shops are two of the city's oldest Italian pasticcerias.

The best example of the East Village's bohemian credentials can be found on **St. Marks Place**, which—despite the arrival of a Gap and a Subway sandwich shop and the recent loss of a popular rock club, Coney Island High—still manages to attract nightly crowds of the heavily pierced and the colorfully coifed to its scrappy stores, bars and cafes. The street is not, however, quite as scrappy as it used to be: If you decide you would like a tattoo, there are places to get one while you sip a cappuccino.

St. Marks dead-ends at another of the neighborhood's raucous landmarks, **Tompkins Square Park**, where in 1988 riots erupted when the police moved in impose a curfew. Three years later, the police cleared out homeless people and self-styled anarchists and closed the park for extensive renovations and clean-up. Today, the loudest place in the park is usually near the concrete chess tables, where speed players shout to throw off their opponents' concentration.

The easternmost part of the East Village, from Avenues A to Avenue D, was known until only a decade ago mostly for its abundance of drug dealers and crime. But this area—called **Alphabet City** by some and **Loisaida** (Low-ee-SIDE-ah) by others because of its identification as the Hispanic center of the Lower East Side—has been undoubtedly the most changed by the neighborhood's rapid gentrification.

On the same corner where heroin sales were once the main commercial activity, upscale bakeries are doing a brisk business in blackberry scones. Buildings once called tenements now offer $1,500-a-month, closet-sized studios with superfast Internet connections. So what about all the radicals, musicians and artists who came to the neighborhood in search of lower rents? They are searching elsewhere. —*Randy Kennedy*

Subway: F to Second Ave. or Broadway–Lafayette St.; 6 to Astor Pl. or Bleecker St.; N, R to 8th St.; L, N, Q, R, W, 4, 5, 6 to Union Sq.

HIGHLIGHTS OF THE NEIGHBORHOOD
(*For the* **Ukrainian Museum** *see chapter* **The Arts**.)

Cooper Union 30 Cooper Square, E. 8th St. and Fourth Ave. (212) 254-6300. Cooper Union, New York's first free nonsectarian college, housed in the city's first steel-frame building, was founded in 1859 by Peter Cooper, the industrialist who built the first U.S. locomotive. Cooper wanted to offer students the technical education that he himself had never received and to create a center for open discussion. The school's Great Hall is just that. Inaugurated in 1859 by Mark Twain, it served as the site for Lincoln's "right makes might" speech in 1860. Today you can still attend lectures and concerts there. In the triangle south of the building is a statue of Peter Cooper by Augustus Saint-Gaudens. The gallery features exhibitions of fine art, architecture and graphic design. Very competetive, the school offers a college degree in engineering, architecture and the graphic arts, and tuition is still free.

Grace Church 802 Broadway (at 10th St.) (212) 254-2000. This Gothic-style Episcopalian church, built in 1846, was designed by James Renwick, later the architect of St. Patrick's Cathedral. Later in the century, a marble spire was added to the white limestone church, as were several adjacent Gothic Revival buildings. A longtime center for the evangelical Low Church movement, Grace Church in recent years has operated overseas missions and a shelter for the homeless.

Merchant's House Museum 29 E. 4th St. (between Lafayette St. and Bowery) (212) 777-1089. If you get a charge out of looking at *Architectural Digest* and seeing how the other half lives, you'll enjoy this small town house museum in the East Village. It provides a historically accurate glimpse of the lifestyle of an affluent 19th-century family, with original furnishings and exhibitions related to the period. Lectures and readings are held throughout the year.
Admission: $5, general; $3, students and seniors.

Nuyorican Poets Cafe 236 E. 3rd St. (between Aves. B and C) (212) 505-8183. Since the 1970's, the Nuyorican Poets Cafe has been a veritable warehouse of Lower East Side culture. A product of the black and Latino liberation movements, the Cafe spawned the spoken-word poetry slams popularized by MTV in the early 1990's. The slams, contests in which the audience judges poets in game show fashion, still take place in the high-ceilinged space, as do featured reader nights, Latin big-band music blowouts and occasional theater productions. The black and Latino liberation movements' notion of street poetry—full of humor and sass, a little rough around the edges, but honest and perceptive—still holds forth at the Nuyorican, though the poets now come from a wide range of backgrounds.

Russian and Turkish Baths 268 E. 10th St. (between First Ave. and Ave. A) (212) 473-8806 *www.russianturkishbaths.com*. There is nothing particularly remote or serene about these baths, housed in a timeworn tenement on East 10th Street. But a visit there offers a voyage to an era when the Lower East Side bustled with peddlers and Yiddish-speaking immigrants. Before the arrival of sushi and $10 martinis, the neighborhood's dozen or so public bathhouses were basic amenities for people deprived of indoor plumbing. Today, only the 10th Street Baths remain. Aside from the steep $22 admission charge and a juice bar—which still serves pierogen and pickled herring—little seems to have changed at what regulars still call "the shvitz," a temple to the art of sweating. And most of the clientele is refreshingly oblivious to late 20th-century notions of fitness.

St. Marks Church in the Bowery 131 E. 10th St. (between Second and Third Aves.) (212) 674-6377. Tilted on a true east-west axis, this Episcopal church sits on land that was the farm of New Amsterdam's Governor Peter Stuyvesant. A Federal-style fieldstone building completed in 1799, the city's second-oldest church (after St. Paul's Chapel) was later outfitted with a Greek Revival steeple and a cast-iron portico. Following a devastating fire in 1978, the interior was restructured into a versatile open space that functions as a venue for the performing arts as well as religious services. In addition to its

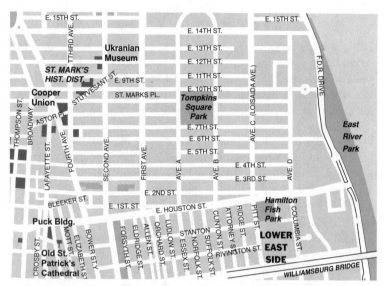

East Village/Lower East Side

ongoing Poetry Project, the socially progressive East Village church hosts an outdoor pop music series. Stuyvesant and his wife are buried under the church.

Highly Recommended Neighborhood Restaurants
(See chapter Restaurants *for reviews.)*

Bambou	☆☆	$ $ $	CARIBBEAN
Tappo	☆	$ $ $	MEDITERRANEAN

Recommended Inexpensive Restaurants

Acquario	MEDITERRANEAN
Boca Chica	LATIN AMERICAN
Cyclo	VIETNAMESE
First	NEW AMERICAN
Flor's Kitchen	LATIN AMERICAN
Frank	ITALIAN
Holy Basil	THAI
Lavagna	MEDITERRANEAN
Le Tableau	MEDITERRANEAN
Mama's Food Shop	AMERICAN
Moustache	MIDDLE EASTERN
National Cafe	CUBAN/LATIN AMERICAN
Soba-Ya	JAPANESE/NOODLES
Xunta	SPANISH/TAPAS

Greenwich Village

This neighborhood is compelling not only for its curving side streets and quaint charm, but because it embodies both New York City's historic past and its hip present. On the one hand, there are the regal Greek Revival row houses that line **Washington Square**, built in the mid-1800's. But there are also the lively coffee houses and music clubs filled with New York University students and other locals.

Bounded to the north by 14th Street, to the east by Fourth Avenue and the Bowery, to the west by the Hudson River, and to the south by Houston Street, the Village is one of the city's oldest and most diverse residential neighborhoods. Originally laid out in the late 18th century, the neighborhood began to be urbanized in the 1820's. By the early 19th century, people moved to the Village to escape crowding and epidemics in the more densely populated areas to the south. Federal-style row houses were built of brick or wood with brick facades for middle-class households.

In the 1830's, wealthy New Yorkers began moving to the Village, particularly the area between Fifth Avenue and Sixth Avenue north of Washington Square. Later, the population changed as middle-class families moved to newer neighborhoods uptown, and poor immigrants crowded into single-family row houses that were converted into multiple dwellings. Then Italian and German immigrants moved in. Apartment buildings went up. And, in the early 20th century, the neighborhood's low rents and heterogeneous population began to attract artists and political and social radicals. The nontraditional character of the Village also began to draw a large number of gay men and lesbians, establishing Greenwich Village as a center of gay life in New York.

Among the sites to see are **St. Luke's Episcopal Church** (485 Hudson St.), one of most active and diverse congregations in the neighborhood; the former **Stonewall Inn** (53 Christopher St.)—now just called The Stonewall—the gay bar that was raided by the police in 1969, setting off events that resulted in the birth of the modern gay and lesbian rights movement; **Jefferson Market Courthouse** (425 Sixth Ave.), now a branch of the New York Public Library; and the Beaux-Arts **Washington Memorial Arch** at Washington Square, completed in 1895. The arch was designed by Stanford White as part of the centennial anniversary of George Washington's inauguration.

Among the better places to grab a bite are **John's Pizzeria** (278 Bleecker St.) for thin-crusted pizza from a brick oven; **Bruno Bakery** (West Broadway between Bleecker and Houston Sts.) for renowned cannoli and the **White Horse Tavern** (567 Hudson St.) for burgers and beer *(see chapter* **Nightlife***)*.

To have a cappuccino and people-watch, stop in at **Café Reggio** (119 Macdougal St.) or **Cafe Borgia** (185 Bleecker St.), where Allen Ginsberg and Jack Kerouac gave poetry readings during the 60's.   *—Robin Pogrebin*

Subway: A, C, E, F to W. 4th St.–Washington Sq.; A, C, E, F, 1, 2, 3, 9 to 14th St.; 1, 9 to Christopher St.

HIGHLIGHTS OF THE NEIGHBORHOOD

Church of St. Luke in the Fields 487 Hudson St. (between Grove and Christopher Sts.) (212) 924-0562. "Twas the night before Christmas," the opening line of Clement Clarke Moore's famous Yuletide poem, has special meaning for parishioners at this enchanting Federal-style landmark church in the West Village. Moore was a founding warden of the church, which was built in 1822 as a satellite of Trinity Church. Strolling through the delightful gardens behind St. Luke in the Fields adds to the sense of being in a remote village. In 1981, a devastating fire (the second in the church's history) destroyed the structure and it was restored to capture its original simplicity. The church is extremely active in local neighborhood life and maintains a high musical profile. It's where the St. Luke's Chamber Ensemble was born, and where the West Village Chorale regularly performs.

Church of the Ascension Fifth Ave. and 10th St. (212) 254-8620. Among Richard Upjohn's legacy to New York City are several wonderful churches, among them the Church of the Ascension. Completed in 1841, the church was the first built on Fifth Avenue, which was then an unpaved track ending in a wooden fence at 23rd Street. A Gothic Revival-style brownstone structure, the church relates closely to Upjohn's earlier (and better-known) Trinity Church in lower Manhattan. The beautiful interior is famous for its John LaFarge mural and stained-glass windows, and exquisite marble statuary by Louis Saint-Gaudens. Music plays a particularly important role at the Church of the Ascension. Its 81-rank Holtkamp organ, installed in 1967, is a decent if not distinguished instrument. The extraordinary Voices of Ascension, a professional choir and orchestra, presents some of the finest choral concerts in town.

Forbes Magazine Galleries Fifth Ave. at 12th St. (212) 620-2200. Malcolm Forbes, millionaire publisher, collected glamorous friends, Fabergé eggs, toy soldiers, toy boats, old Monopoly games, autographs and presidential papers. It's all here—except the glamorous friends—tastefully exhibited on the ground floor of the Forbes magazine building, and it's free.

Judson Memorial Church 55 Washington Sq. South (between Thompson and Sullivan Sts.) (212) 477-0351. A Romanesque Revival building designed by McKim, Mead and White, this landmark Baptist church has long served as a center for social activism. In the 1960's and 70's, it served as a meeting place for antiwar and abortion-rights activists. Later, in response to the AIDS crisis, it offered space for drug trials. The yellow brick and limestone church, built in 1892 on the southern edge of Washington Square Park, is decorated with ornate details, including marble reliefs patterned on plans by Saint-Gaudens.

Meatpacking District The meatpacking district, a curious mix of commerce and community, is finally living down its reputation as a seamy, threatening segment of the far West Village, a place where trade was in human flesh as well as animal. Certainly, some indelicate elements remain. But a crackdown on crime and the expansion of housing and small businesses have combined to make the area more desirable. The meat market itself, extending north from Gansevoort Street to West 15th Street, is zoned for light manufacturing. Because of this, few people live there. But the area is changing quickly, with a boom in restaurants, bars, art galleries, antiques stores and dance clubs.

New York Public Library—Jefferson Market Library 425 Sixth Ave. (between Ninth and 10th Sts.) (212) 243-4334. If you go anywhere near this building you'll notice it, and chances are you'll also like it. It's an eyeful of bright red stone and ornate pinnacles, towers, carvings and stained-glass windows, all topped off with a clock tower that still keeps perfect time. These days it houses a branch of the New York Public Library, but it was originally built in 1877 as a courthouse, on the site of a public meat-and-produce market. The courthouse was part of a complex including a firehouse and a jail, which stood in the area now occupied by a lush community garden.

New York University Information Center, 40 Washington Sq. South (at Wooster St.) (212) 998-4636. Sometimes it seems as if everywhere you turn in Greenwich Village, you see a violet flag on a building telling you that you are looking at another part of New York University's sprawling campus. Washington Square Park is the de facto center of the campus, surrounded by university offices, student centers, dorms and libraries. Founded in 1831, NYU was designed to cater not only to the 19th-century penchant for the study of Greek and Latin, but also to feed the more practical needs of students wishing to pursue careers in science, business, industry, the arts, law and medicine. The school now hosts some 17,000 undergraduate and 18,000 graduate students, and boasts the nation's largest open-stack library. The university sponsors performance events at several of its auditoriums including the Loewe Auditorium, the NYU Theater and the Loeb Student Center.

Salmagundi Museum of American Art 47 Fifth Ave. (between 11th and 12th Sts.) (212) 255-7740. Also known as the Salmagundi Club, the museum is the oldest artists' club in the U.S. Founded in 1870, it was moved to its current site when the club purchased the Irving Hawley residence in 1917. Members of this private club have included famed artists Childe Hassam, William Merritt Chase and Louis C. Tiffany, as well as architect Stanford White. Painting exhibitions are held in a beautiful downstairs parlor. The museum is open to the public. The conference room and art reference library are open to members only. Whether you're interested in joining the club or simply viewing an exhibition, the Salmagundi is a charming, little-known jewel in Greenwich Village.

75 1/2 Bedford Street (at Commerce St.). Only 9.5 feet wide and dating from 1893, this house is said to be the narrowest in the city. Edna St. Vincent Millay, Margaret Mead, William Steig and Cary Grant all lived in this tiny place at one time or another. The house fell into disrepair for several years, but it recently attracted a new owner who restored the place, named it the Millay House and rented it out for an astounding amount of money. Around the corner at 38

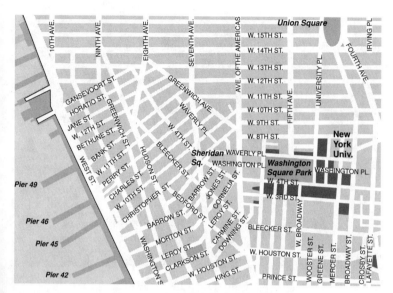

Greenwich Village/West Village

Commerce Street you can also visit the **Cherry Lane Theater**, opened by Millay and friends in 1924 in an old barn and still in operation.

Washington Mews Fifth Ave., between Washington Sq. North and E. 8th St. This private street of two-story houses in Greenwich Village once functioned as stables and service quarters for the residents of the Greek Revival row houses along Washington Square North. These 19th-century structures were converted into private residences during the early 1900's, and were leased to New York University in 1949. Today, some of the buildings contain NYU offices, but this cobblestone street maintains its quiet charm.

Washington Square Park W. 4th St. (at Macdougal St.) (212) 387-7676. One of lower Manhattan's few large public spaces, Washington Square Park brings together downtown's diverse population. Musicians jam near the central fountain as skateboarders jump park benches. Students from nearby New York University lounge or shoot films, gay and straight singles swap canine tales as their dogs frolic and children swing in the fenced playground. The southwestern corner is also the proving ground for the city's most serious chess players. The park's identifying landmark is a large marble arch, constructed in 1895, which commemorates George Washington's inauguration. In the early part of the 20th century, the artists Marcel Duchamp and John Sloan climbed onto the arch to declare the secession of the neighborhood from the United States. A generation earlier, Henry James named a novel for the square. But as a public gathering place, the park also has its dark history, having served in the early 19th century as a graveyard and the site of public hangings. You would be excused for thinking it's haunted, as the gallows tree remains standing and many of the graves were left undisturbed when the park was established in 1827.

Washington Square Park

Highly Recommended Neighborhood Restaurants

(See chapter **Restaurants** *for reviews.)*

Babbo	☆☆☆	$$$$	ITALIAN
Blue Hill	☆☆	$$$	FRENCH
Clementine	☆☆	$$$	NEW AMERICAN
Gotham Bar and Grill	☆☆☆	$$$$	NEW AMERICAN
Surya	☆☆	$$	INDIAN

Recommended Inexpensive Restaurants

Bar Pitti	ITALIAN
Cookies and Couscous	MOROCCAN
Do Hwa	KOREAN
Good	LATIN AMERICAN
Grange Hall	AMERICAN
Home	AMERICAN
Le Gigot	FRENCH
Little Basil	THAI
Marumi	JAPANESE/SUSHI
Mexicana Mama	MEXICAN
Moustache	MIDDLE EASTERN
Pearl Oyster Bar	SEAFOOD
Pepe Verde	ITALIAN
Velli	NEW AMERICAN

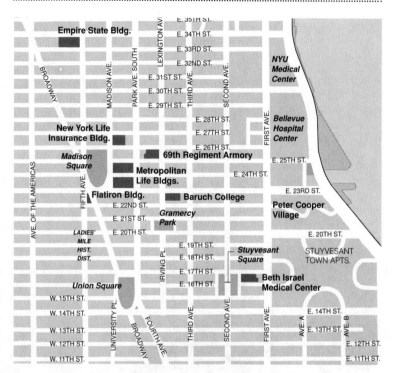

Flatiron/Union Square/ Gramercy Park

Flatiron/Union Square/Gramercy Park

The neighborhoods that make up the broad swath of Manhattan between Sixth Avenue and the East River, from 14th to 27th Streets, contain some of the best preserved historical districts and landmarks in the city, as well as many of today's most fashionable spots for shopping, dining and nightlife. The area is dotted with little emerald oases—five parks whose importance far exceeds their acreage.

Madison Square (Fifth Ave. and 23rd St.), opened in 1847, was once home to a depot of the New York and Harlem Rail Road and two earlier incarnations of Madison Square Garden. It offers a front row view of two quintessential New York buildings: the **Flatiron Building** (175 Fifth Ave.) and the **Metropolitan Life Insurance Building** (1 Madison Ave.) whose 1909 tower with its four-faced clock and lantern is still intact despite substantial renovations. Also in the area are the exquisite **Appellate Division Courthouse** (27 Madison Ave.), the head-quarters of the **New York Life Insurance Company** since 1928 (51 Madison Ave.) and high-tech enterprises in **Silicon Alley** along Broadway and Fifth Avenue.

Union Square (14th-17th St. and Broadway) was once a rallying place for the organized labor movement, but it got its name as the union of the Bloom-ingdale Road (now Broadway) and the Bowery Road (now Fourth Ave.). By

The Flatiron Building

turns the province of aristocrats, anarchists and addicts, it has in recent decades felt more like a village green, thanks to the big **farmers' market** established there in 1977 (*see section* "Food Markets" *in* **Shopping**) and to a cleansing renovation that was completed in 1992. Between Madison Square and Union Square from Broadway to Sixth Avenue is **Ladies' Mile**, the post-Civil War shopping district that was the former home of Lord & Taylor (901 Broadway) and B. Altman & Co. (615–629 Sixth Ave.) until department stores began to migrate uptown in the early decades of the 20th century. The recent rebound of

The City as a Gallery: New York's Public Art

Walking around Manhattan, you'll probably inadvertently wander past some of the hundreds of examples of public sculpture that constitute the city's urban gallery. Intended for a large audience, these works often engender controversy at their installation but in time become part of the public landscape, serving as landmarks, honoring their patrons, and providing relief from the straight lines of the city's skyscrapers and gridded streets.

Because most streets leave little room for crowds, let alone sculpture, you'll find the majority of public art in parks and plazas. **Battery Park** contains several examples, including "The Immigrants" (Luis Sanguino, 1981). Located in front of Castle Clinton, the sculpture depicts six immigrants of varying ethnicities, arriving in America. With its rough surface and unconventional subject matter, this piece stands in contrast with the traditional hero-on-a horse statuary. Also in Battery Park, overlooking the water, is the "American Merchant Mariner's Memorial" (Marisol Escobar, 1991), a sculpture depicting the victims of a German U-boat attack. Escobar used actual pictures taken by the German perpetrators to design the work.

In the windy **Financial District**, you'll find "The Red Cube" (Isamu Noguchi, 1967) in front of the Marine Midland Building (140 Broadway). The 28-foot-tall red cube balances precariously on its corner. Nearby, Manhattan Chase Plaza (at Pine and William Sts.) is home to "Group of Four Trees" (Jean Dubuffet, 1972). The curvy tree canopies rest at the top of 42-foot-tall crooked trunks. The whimsical sculpture is striking in its corporate surroundings and well worth a look.

Battery Park City is the site of many recent works of public art, including Tony Cragg's "Resonating Bodies" (1996), a giant lute and trumpet with a layered relief meant to depict unseen energy forces.

In **Union Square**, passersby are often initially baffled by "Metronome" (Kristin Jones and Andrew Ginzel, 2000), a $3 million, 100-foot-tall work located on the facade of the Virgin Megastore; but most can't help noticing the giant digital clock simultaneously counting down and up to midnight, a red and gold brick wall of concentric circles emanating from a hole out of which steam is expelled, and a five-foot-tall spherical "moon-phase indicator." A hand, called the "relic," reaching from the top of the wall, parts the steam sputtering from below and responds to the Union Square statue of George Washington (1855) with its similarly outstretched hand.

Lincoln Center boasts famous abstract works such as "Reclining Figures" (Henry Moore, 1965), located in a reflecting pool (currently dry) on Lincoln Center Plaza North. Famous for his abstractions of the human figure, Moore intended the curved shapes to contrast with the geometric angles of the setting. Nearby, you will find Alexander Calder's "Le Guichet" (1963).

There are countless examples of public art ranging from the traditional to the abstract throughout the city. For more information visit, the Municipal Art Society's Web site at *www.mas.org*, or for information on temporary outdoor installations, visit *www.publicartfund.org*.

the area extends throughout this district where the buildings that housed the dry-goods emporiums of the Gilded Age have been restored to retail life as home furnishing stores, like **ABC Carpet and Home** on Broadway and **Bed, Bath & Beyond** on Sixth Avenue. Among Fifth Avenue's many shopping offerings are **Banana Republic**, the **Gap** and **Kenneth Cole**. Park Avenue South and other streets in the vicinity are lined with upscale restaurants such as **Tabla**, **Gramercy Tavern** and **Veritas**.

Gramercy Park (Lexington Ave. and 21st St.), a fenced and locked enclave reserved for those who live on its perimeter, remains one of the most genteel squares in urban America, as it has been since 1831. The park is open to the public just three days each year: one Saturday in May (for the Clean and Green celebration), Christmas Eve and the first night of Hannukah. A more expensive way to visit is to stay at the **Gramercy Park Hotel** (*see chapter* **Hotels**), which allows guests to use its keys to the park. One of the city's earliest high-rise apartment buildings stands on the park's southeast corner, while several town houses with ornate wrought iron porches endure on the western side. Nearby is the **69th Regiment Armory** (68 Lexington Ave.), which hosted the celebrated 1913 "Armory Show" that introduced America to modern art and continues to host various arts and antiques shows. Also in the area are several of the liveliest nightspots in town, like the concert hall **Irving Plaza** (*see chapter* **Nightlife**).

Straddling Second Avenue, **Stuyvesant Square** is home to a number of vital institutions, including Beth Israel Medical Center (one of many hospitals and infirmaries in the area, irreverently known along First Avenue as "Bedpan Alley"). The fifth area park is the gracious **Stuyvesant Oval**—a gathering place surrounded by the vast **Stuyvesant Town** housing project. Built to accommodate servicemen returning from World War II, this well-maintained complex and neighboring **Peter Cooper Village** have more than 11,000 apartments and remain among the more sought after addresses in a city starved for affordable housing.

Subway: L, N, R, Q, W, 4, 5, 6 to Union Sq.; N, R, 6 to 23rd St. or 28th St.

HIGHLIGHTS OF THE NEIGHBORHOOD

Flatiron Building 175 Fifth Ave. (at 23rd St.). Originally known as the Fuller Building, the Flatiron Building took its nickname from its shape on a triangular block of land. The architect, Daniel H. Burnham, designed this early skyscraper, built in 1902, by overlaying an Italian Renaissance terra-cotta facade on a modern steel frame. The tall, wedge-shaped office building looks like a ship sailing uptown. Today the revitalized surrounding Flatiron District has taken on the building's name.

Friends Meeting House 15 Rutherford Pl. (between Second and Third Aves.) (212) 777-8866. Reflecting the Quaker love of simplicity, the Friends Meeting House, an 1860 landmark building, is beautiful in its austerity. It is a plain, red-brick structure in the Federalist style. Inside, the room is filled with rows of simple gray benches, with red cushions adding the only splash of color. On sunny days light pours through the tall windows, enhancing the room's subtle beauty. In addition to being used for Quaker meetings, the Friends Meeting House is often a venue of choice for concerts by small chamber ensembles.

National Arts Club 15 Gramercy Park South (between Park Ave. and Irving Pl.) (212) 477-2389. Established in 1898, the National Arts Club promotes various forms of American art. Over the past century, its membership has included notable painters, sculptors, architects, writers, musicians and philanthropists. The club's headquarters is a Gramercy Park brownstone, which Calvert Vaux— Frederick Law Olmstead's partner in the design of Central Park—renovated in a Victorian Gothic style for Governor Samuel J. Tilden. Behind the sumptuous clubhouse, which is a national landmark, stands a 13-story building containing members' studios. The organization awards art prizes and scholarships, hosts an assortment of public events and maintains several galleries open to the public.

School of Visual Arts Museum 209 E. 23rd St. (between Third and Fourth Aves.) (212) 592-2144. The School of Visual Arts was established in 1947 to train students as professional graphic and fine artists. The school's museum features changing exhibitions by students and established artists. Most of the work is contemporary, but shows span an array of mediums including illustration, fine art, sculpture, animation and photography. The school hosts film, music and lecture events throughout the year.

Theodore Roosevelt Birthplace 28 E. 20th St. (between Park Ave. South and Broadway) (212) 260-1616. This brownstone, which includes period rooms from 1865 and 1872, is a reconstruction of the four-story house where Theodore Roosevelt was born and lived until he was a teenager. During much of his childhood, Roosevelt was confined to the house with a variety of illnesses, including chronic asthma. There are 250,000 objects in the permanent collection, including T.R.'s christening gown and the stuffed Teddy bears that take his name. The site boasts the largest collection of the president's memorabilia anywhere, narrowly ahead of the collection at his home, Sagamore Hill, in Oyster Bay, Long Island. Displays from the permanent collection change regularly, and the museum hosts concerts and lectures throughout the year.

Highly Recommended Neighborhood Restaurants
(*See chapter* **Restaurants** *for reviews.*)

Blue Water Grill	☆	$ $	SEAFOOD
Campagna	☆ ☆	$ $ $	ITALIAN
Eleven Madison Park	☆ ☆	$ $ $	NEW AMERICAN
Gramercy Tavern	☆ ☆ ☆	$ $ $ $	NEW AMERICAN
I Trulli	☆ ☆	$ $ $	ITALIAN
Mesa Grill	☆ ☆	$ $ $ $	SOUTHWESTERN
Patria	☆ ☆ ☆	$ $ $	LATIN AMERICAN
Tabla	☆ ☆ ☆	$ $ $ $	PAN ASIAN
Veritas	☆ ☆ ☆	$ $ $ $	NEW AMERICAN

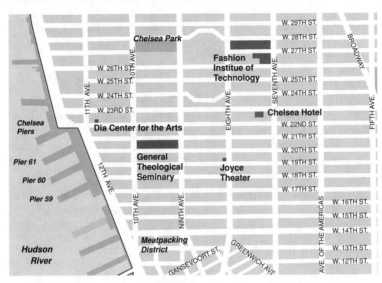

Chelsea

Recommended Inexpensive Restaurants

Chat 'n Chew   NEW AMERICAN
Mavalli Palace   INDIAN/VEGETARIAN

Chelsea

The formerly gritty neighborhood of Chelsea is better known these days for
high rents, up-and-coming art galleries, a sprawling riverside sports complex and
the hip clubs and restaurants springing up in the meatpacking district (*see chapters* **Restaurants** *and* **Nightlife**).

Chelsea stretches from Sixth Avenue to the Hudson River, roughly between
West 14th and West 28th Streets. Clement Clarke Moore, the scholar-poet who
wrote "A Visit From St. Nicholas," developed the neighborhood in the early
1800's. His grandfather had bought the land in 1750 and named it after the
Chelsea Royal Hospital in London.

These days, Chelsea's eastern end, along Sixth Avenue, is increasingly dominated by big-box stores like **Bed, Bath & Beyond** and **Old Navy**. For an outdoor shopping alternative, try the weekend **flea market** at the corner of Sixth
Avenue and West 26th Street. It's a fun place to troll for kitschy treasures,
although true bargain hunters will scoff at the prices. If you're looking for any
sort of plant or blossom, the nearby **flower district** (around 27th St. and Sixth
Ave.) is the place to find it.

For more breathing room, wander over to the residential cross streets
between Seventh and 10th Avenues, where 19th-century brownstones proliferate and river breezes often take wanderers by surprise. West 20th, 21st and 22nd
Streets between Eighth and 10th Avenues are especially winsome blocks, per-

fect for meditative strolls. **Cushman Row** (408–18 W. 20th St., between Ninth and 10th Aves.) contains some particularly notable Greek Revival row houses (1839–40). One landmark worth glimpsing is the **General Theological Seminary**, which occupies the block between Ninth and 10th Avenues, from 20th to 21st Street. The ivy-covered, Gothic-style buildings have a soothing effect on harried passersby.

Eighth Avenue in Chelsea is another heavily trafficked retail strip, where quirky boutiques mix with restaurants whose tables spill onto the sidewalks in the warmer months. There are also many bars and clubs catering to the area's large gay community (*see chapter* **Nightlife**).

One of Chelsea's most lively thoroughfares is West 23rd Street, whose best known landmark is probably the **Chelsea Hotel** (222 W. 23rd St. between Seventh and Eighth Aves.). In the past it was a beloved, if verging on decrepit, way station for artists, poets and rock musicians. You can still stay here, but a crop of new boutique hotels are providing stiff competition (*see chapter* **Hotels**). If you're hungry, grab a chocolate-frosted doughnut from the **Krispy Kreme** shop down the block, a New York favorite.

Athletic types would say that no tour of Chelsea is complete without a stop at the **Chelsea Piers** sports complex, which has taken over four piers on the Hudson River from 17th to 23rd Street (*see chapter* **Sports & Recreation**). There are ice and roller skating rinks, a health club, a fieldhouse for soccer and other sports, batting cages, a driving range and a bowling alley.

For those not inclined to exert themselves, Chelsea Piers also has benches on which to loaf an afternoon away, with views across the river to Jersey City and, if you linger long enough, the setting sun.   —*Abby Goodnough*

Subway: C, E, F, 1, 9 to 23rd St.

HIGHLIGHTS OF THE NEIGHBORHOOD
(*See chapter* **The Arts** *for the* **Bessie Schonberg Theater**, **Dia Center for the Arts**, **Joyce Theater** *and* **The Kitchen**.)

Fashion Institute of Technology Seventh Ave. and 27th St. (212) 217-5779. The alma mater of superstars like Calvin Klein and Norma Kamali, the Fashion Institute of Technology (FIT) is the training ground for many of the players, and even more of the workers, in New York's garment industry. The school was founded in 1944 as the Central Needle Trades High School to meet the industry's demand for skilled workers. It has since expanded to become a community college campus of the State University of New York for students in all areas of design, fine arts, business and technology. The maze of buildings that make up the campus occupies a full block. You'll notice a proliferation of fashion-forward students in the neighborhood sporting their own exotic designs. The museum at FIT boasts one of the world's largest collections of costumes, textiles and accessories of dress from the 18th to the 20th century, and it presents inventive fashion-related exhibitions. The institute's functional auditorium serves as home base to the Village Light Opera Group.

Highly Recommended Neighborhood Restaurants
(*See chapter* **Restaurants** *for reviews.*)

Chelsea Bistro & Bar	☆☆	$ $ $	BISTRO/FRENCH
Frank's	☆	$ $ $	STEAKHOUSE
Periyali	☆ ☆ ☆	$ $ $	GREEK
The Red Cat	☆	$ $	NEW AMERICAN
The Tonic	☆ ☆	$ $ $	NEW AMERICAN

Recommended Inexpensive Restaurants

Bright Food Shop	NEW AMERICAN
El Cid	SPANISH
Grand Sichuan	CHINESE
Gus's Figs Bistro & Bar	MEDITERRANEAN
Le Zie	ITALIAN
Royal Siam	THAI

Murray Hill

When the British landed in 1776 near importer Robert Murray's country estate (which stood near where E. 37th St. crosses Park Ave.), Murray's wife and daughters are said to have invited British General Sir William Howe to tea, a respite that diverted Howe's forces long enough to allow George Washington's exhausted American troops to escape to Harlem.

The core of old Murray Hill—which stretches along the middle to upper 30's between Madison and Third Avenues—includes landmarks like the **Pierpont Morgan Library** and the renovated carriage houses of **Sniffen Court** (150–158 E. 36th St.). Side streets are lined with diplomatic missions, social and cultural clubs and mid-range hotels.

Murray Hill residents have long been wary of commercial development. When Benjamin Altman opened what was among the first luxury department stores on Fifth Avenue and 34th Street in 1906, he disguised it as an Italian palazzo in an effort to allay those fears. The landmark **B. Altman & Co.** building now houses the Public Library's high-tech Science, Industry and Business Library (188 Madison Ave. at 34th St.), the Graduate Center of the City University of New York (365 Fifth Ave. at 34th St.) and Oxford University Press. The west side of Fifth Avenue bustles with small retail stores, while a number of Asian, Indian and Middle Eastern restaurants line Third Avenue. On the northern edge of Murray Hill is **Tudor City**, completed in 1928, a middle-class "city within a city."

Anchoring the area on the south is the picturesque **Church of the Transfiguration** on 29th Street (between Madison and Fifth Aves.). It earned a place in the hearts of actors in 1870 when the minister at a nearby church refused to bury actor George Holland, and suggested instead "the little church around the corner."

Subway: 6 to 33rd St.; S, 4, 5, 6, 7 to Grand Central.

HIGHLIGHT OF THE NEIGHBORHOOD

The Pierpont Morgan Library 29 E. 36th St. (at Madison Ave.)
(212) 685-0008 *www.morganlibrary.org*. The world's most powerful financier in his day, J. P. Morgan started collecting medieval and Renaissance manuscripts, rare books, and English and American authors' manuscripts in 1890. Within a decade, his collection had grown to such an extent that he needed an entire building to house it. Designed by Charles McKim and completed in 1906, the neoclassical building that houses the library opened to the public in 1924. The library serves as both a museum and a center for scholarly research. In addition to drawings by Dürer, Blake and Degas, and the country's largest collection of Rembrandt etchings, the Morgan owns 1,300 manuscripts. The library's literary holdings include three copies of the Gutenberg Bible, letters by Jane Austen, Charles Dickens's manuscript of *A Christmas Carol* and Henry David Thoreau's journals. Musical texts include handwritten works by Bach, Mozart, Schubert and Stravinsky.
Admission: $8, general; $6, students and seniors; children under 12, free.

Highly Recommended Neighborhood Restaurants
(See chapter **Restaurants** *for reviews.)*

Asia de Cuba	☆	$ $ $	ASIAN/LATIN
Hangawi	☆ ☆	$ $	KOREAN/VEGETARIAN
Icon	☆ ☆	$ $	NEW AMERICAN

Recommended Inexpensive Restaurants

Da Ciro	ITALIAN
Evergreen Shanghai	CHINESE
Wu Liang Ye	CHINESE

Midtown East

From the European jet set who browse posh shops along its affluent avenues, to the diplomatic polyglot that is the **United Nations**, Midtown East is one of New York City's most cosmopolitan areas. The annual tribute to St. Patrick and a succession of parades that pass the Fifth Avenue cathedral named in his honor, reflect the strong connection many New Yorkers have to places like Ireland, Puerto Rico, Israel and Greece.

After the Civil War, New York society settled along Fifth Avenue from 34th to 59th Streets, then moved north as businesses arrived in the early 1900's. Today, the neighborhood is one of the city's largest business districts and hosts corporate headquarters filled each day by commuters who pass through the cavernous Beaux Arts concourse of **Grand Central Terminal**. Park Avenue and other neighborhood thoroughfares are lined with "glass boxes" like **Lever House** completed in 1952 (390 Park Ave. between 53rd and 54th Sts.) and Art Deco marvels like the **Chrysler Building**, the **Waldorf-Astoria Hotel** (Park Ave. at 49th St.), a favorite stopover for U.S. presidents and other visiting dignitaries, and the **Chanin Building** on the southwest corner of 42nd Street and Lexington Avenue.

Saks Fifth Avenue, Henri Bendel and **Takashimaya New York** are among the several stylish stores in the area (*see chapter* **Shopping**). Neighborhood streets and avenues are dotted with grand hotels and cultural institutions like the **Japan Society** and the **Dahesh Museum** (*see chapter* **The Arts**).

At rush hour, pedestrians and drivers battle for control of the asphalt. It is hard to imagine Midtown East ever being the tranquil place it once was when turtles thrived near the quiet cove from which the **Turtle Bay** area takes its name. The most serene spots left are the affluent cul-de-sacs of **Beekman** and **Sutton Places**.

Second Avenue between 43rd and 53rd Streets is the commercial hub of Turtle Bay, lined with shops, businesses and a variety of eating establishments. The area is known for its steakhouses, such as **Sparks, Smith and Wollensky, Palm** and **Palm Too,** and a number of elegant restaurants, such as **Lutéce**. The **Amish Market** on 45th Street just off Second Avenue stocks a wide variety of produce, cheese and specialty items.

Turtle Bay's most charming side-street enclave is **Turtle Bay Gardens Historic District,** a stretch of 10 town houses on the north side of East 48th Street and 10 on the south side of East 49th Street between Second and Third Avenues. Gardens residents have included Katharine Hepburn, Stephen Sondheim and E.B. White, who wrote about the neighborhood for *The New Yorker*.

Subway: S, 4, 5, 6, 7 to Grand Central; E, F, N, R, W to Fifth Ave. or Lexington Ave.; 6 to 51st St.; 4, 5, 6 to 59th St.

HIGHLIGHTS OF THE NEIGHBORHOOD

Chrysler Building 405 Lexington Ave. (between 42nd and 43rd Sts.) (212) 682-3070. In late 1929 New Yorkers gawked as the Chrysler Building emerged from its construction scaffolding. The brilliant steel ornament and spire were unlike anything in New York, and at 1,046 feet, 4.75 inches high it was the tallest building in the world. The Chrysler Building is still unique, but until the recent cleaning of the metalwork, passers-by had become blasé about this Art Deco masterpiece. Now, people are again looking up.

Kenneth Murchison, an architect and critic of the time, admired the steel crown and "the astonishing plays of light which nature alone can furnish." While other buildings had been put up with distinctive spires, they were all in traditional materials: copper, terra cotta, iron, stone, brick. But on the Chrysler Building the entire upper section above the 61st floor—and much of the ornament below—is gleaming chrome-nickel steel, which reflects sunlight with dazzling brilliance.

From a distance the Chrysler Building seems like near kin to the Empire State Building, which took away its height record in 1931. But unlike the Empire State, which was proudly hailed by one of its architects as a building where "hand work was done away with," the Chrysler Building is like a giant craft project. The metal is generally soldered or crimped—all by hand—and the thick, wavy solder lines and the irregular bends all betray individual craftsman-ship. The broad surfaces of metal, almost all stamped to form on the site, are wavy and bumpy, like giant pieces of hand-finished silver jewelry.

Just as surprising is the section just below the spire. So solid-looking from the outside, this part has no occupants and only intermittent flooring; only a few of the triangular openings have glazing. Inside, the wind rushes through what seems like a high, thin gazebo-shell of steel, at striking variance with the otherwise modernistic solidity of this continually fascinating building.

—Christopher Gray

The Chrysler Building

Citicorp Center 153 E. 53rd St. (between Lexington and Third Aves.). The wedge-shaped spire of Citicorp Center, designed by Hugh Stubbins and Emery Roth, was designed to hold penthouse apartments, but residential zoning was denied. The aluminum and glass tower is headquarters for the Citigroup conglomerate, but it also has commercial, retail, mass-transit and even religious functions. The 915-foot building, supported entirely by four massive pillars, hovers over a sunken plaza that connects a multi-layered shopping mall, a subway crossroads and a church. St. Peter's, a starkly modernist replacement of the church that stood on the building site, holds Sunday jazz vespers and weekday concerts.

Grand Central Terminal 42nd St. at Park Ave. *www.grandcentralterminal.com*. On its physical merits alone, Grand Central Terminal is one of New York's great treasures. Its main concourse is an immense, bustling space with a blue-green ceiling painted to resemble a starlit sky. But Grand Central is vastly important also as a historical and political symbol, for it lies at the heart of court decisions affirming the city's right to protect its architectural heritage. Opened in 1913, the Beaux-Arts monument was threatened in the 1960's by developers wanting to demolish the concourse and build office towers all around it. Preservationists took their case to court and to the public, with high-profile assistance from Jacqueline Kennedy Onassis. They won. In 1978, the United States Supreme Court ruled that the city had a right to protect Grand Central—and, by extension, other landmarks—from destruction. After falling into disrepair, the station got an expensive cleanup in the 1990's that restored much of its original grandeur. Above all, Grand Central remains what it has always been: one of the world's busiest train stations, with half a million people passing through it each day.

Trains serve suburban New York and Connecticut commuters, upstate New York and points west. The Municipal Arts Society conducts tours of the building, departing from the station's information booth every Wednesday at 12:30 P.M. Call (212) 935-3960 for tour information.   —*Clyde Haberman*

MetLife Building 200 Park Ave. (between 43rd and 45th Sts.) (212) 922-9100. Pan Am's former headquarters was the world's largest commercial office building when it was completed in 1963—its mammoth bulk effectively blocking the vista up and down Park Avenue. A team that included Emery Roth and Sons, Pietro Belluschi and Walter Gropius used concrete curtain walls to frame the building's structure. The lobby doubles as a concourse leading to Grand Central. Until a helicopter accident claimed five lives in 1977, a rooftop helipad provided quick airport access. In the 1980's Metropolitan Life Insurance bought the building from the financially troubled airline, and the MetLife logo supplanted Pan Am's globe as a landmark of Manhattan's skyline.

St. Patrick's Cathedral Fifth Ave. (at 50th St.) (212) 753-2261 *www.ny-archdiocese.org/pastoral*. St. Pat's is the Roman Catholic cathedral for the Dioceses of New York, Brooklyn and several upstate regions and is generally recognized as a center of Catholic life in America. Constructed of granite, its design by James Renwick was based on the great cathedral in Cologne, Germany. The nave was opened in 1877, almost 20 years after the start of construction; the 330-foot twin spires were completed in 1888. At the time it stood on the northern edge of the city, visible from miles around. Architectural purists deride its mixed forms and the lack of flying buttresses, but it is a grand and elaborate statement nonetheless, surrounded now by city skyscrapers.

A magnificent rose window over the central portal measures 26 feet in diam-

St. Patrick's Cathedral

eter. The cathedral's 70 stained-glass windows were crafted in studios in Chartres and Nantes in France, Birmingham, England, and Boston—and not finally completed until the 1930's. The 14 stations of the cross were carved in Holland. The Pieta is three times larger than the Pieta in St. Peter's in Rome. There are three organs.

The Fifth Avenue cathedral replaced the original and much smaller St. Patrick's Cathedral that was founded in 1809. Restored after a fire in 1866 and now called Old St. Patrick's Cathedral, it still functions downtown as a parish church in Chinatown at the corner of Mott and Prince Streets.

United Nations First Ave. at 42nd St. Tours: (212) 963-4440. *www.un.org.* Literally in a world of its own, United Nations headquarters and its grounds occupy a strip of international territory on the edge of Manhattan, running between First Avenue and the East River from 42nd to 48th Street. The site was donated to the U.N. in 1946, a year after the organization's birth, by John D. Rockefeller, Jr. Three connected buildings—the boxy Dag Hammarskjold Library, the glass-walled Secretariat tower and the low-slung General Assembly—dominate the site. Erected between 1947 and 1953, they frame a central fountain crowned with a 21-foot-high bronze sculpture, "Single Form" by Barbara Hepworth, dedicated to the memory of Hammarskjold. He is the only Secretary General to have been killed in office, on a peace mission to the Congo in 1961. Daily public tours take in the most famous indoor chambers, including the Security Council and General Assembly halls. An eclectic collection of artwork donated by many countries is scattered throughout corridors and lounges. In the basement, shops sell jewelry and handicrafts from around the world, international books for adults and children and souvenirs of the U.N. itself. There are also outdoor attractions, especially when the weather is warm. Visitors stop to see the colorful array of flags from 188

Chester Higgins, Jr./The New York times

The United Nations

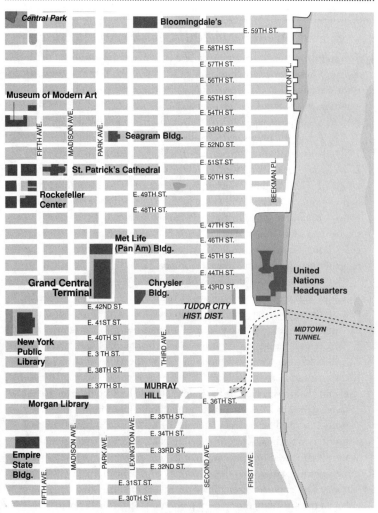

Midtown East/Murray Hill

nations flying along First Avenue or to enjoy walking on the riverside promenade and through the quiet formal gardens that form a two-block oasis of
serenity north of the 46th Street visitors' entrance. The gardens form a backdrop for several other monumental sculptures dedicated to the ideal of peace
among nations.   —Barbara Crossette

Visitors can also eat at the Delegates' Dining Room Monday through Friday
between 11:30 A.M. and 2 P.M., as tables become available. Reservations are a
good idea and should be made in advance at (212) 963-7625.

Tour prices: $7.50, adults; $6, senior citizens; $5, high school and college
students; $4, students in grades 1–8. 20 percent discount for persons with
disabilities.

Park Avenue and 20th-Century Architecture

To a surprising number of architects and city-lovers, the so-called Park Avenue Corridor is the architectural heart of the 20th century. The corridor is the crystallization of the New York myth, the soaring city of work and ambition, where the sky is the limit and dreams are fulfilled. It symbolizes New York's displacement of Paris as the century's most vibrant City of Light.

The corridor contains several individual buildings of distinction from the 1950's to 60's, including the **Seagram Building** *(discussed in detail below)*, **Lever House, 500 Park Avenue** and the **Chase Building** (originally the Union Carbide Building), the last three designed by the New York firm Skidmore, Owings & Merrill, and Philip Johnson's Russell Sage Foundation (originally Asia House). James Ingo Freed's **Park Tower**, completed in 1981, is a somber late addition to the group, while Frank Lloyd Wright's 1958 **Mercedes-Benz Showroom** (originally Jaguar) offers a quirky footnote to the ramp of the Guggenheim Museum's rotunda.

But much of the corridor's power lies in the aggregate, in the mix of lesser buildings with well-known landmarks. At the century's outset, long before the first curtain wall was actually hung, architects used to dream about the gleaming cities that glass would enable them to build. Here, the dream was realized.

The term International Style was coined by Philip Johnson and Henry Russell Hitchcock for an exhibition in 1932 at the Museum of Modern Art. In the postwar decades, the International Style became shorthand for the steel and glass towers like the Seagram Building, the supreme example of the genre, designed by Mies van der Rohe and Philip Johnson in 1957–58.

Mies described his own aesthetic as one of "almost nothing," a paring down of form to the discreet articulation of construction and enclosure. Walls were reduced to the transparent membrane of the glass curtain wall. Structure was expressed on the exterior by the application of nonstructural I-beams. This approach exemplified the architect's belief that less is more. It enlarged the artistic significance of proportion, scale, quality of materials and refinement of detail.

Not long ago, it was said that these buildings represented a rejection of history. In fact, the International Style was grounded in 19th-century historicism: the view that each epoch should produce a distinctive architectural style.

In the early 1960's, the International Style was a symbol of urban sophistication in many Hollywood movies, as accurate a barometer as we have of popular desires. In *Breakfast at Tiffany's*, *The Best of Everything* and even several Doris Day comedies, the glass tower epitomized worldly aspiration and success. In the reflections of the crystal canyon, the world of external reality merges with the subjective realm of ambition, fantasy and desire.

No design in recent years has given firmer shape to this idea than Christian de Portzamparc's **LVMH Tower** at 19–21 East 57th Street. Described by Mr. Portzamparc as an homage to the city of glass, the 23-story tower features a faceted glass skin that unfolds like a crystal flower. While the tower can't possibly be mistaken for an International Style skyscraper, LVMH responds to the context of the mythical New York where modernity took root. And it is the first blossom that this root has sent forth in many years.

Seagram Building and Plaza 375 Park Ave. (between 52nd and 53rd Sts.) (212) 572-7000. For much of the past thousand years, the pendulum of Western architectural taste has swung between two esthetic poles: Gothic and classical, they eventually came to be called. Because it fuses elements of both positions in a supremely elegant whole, the Seagram Building is my choice as the millennium's most important building.

The 38-story Manhattan office tower was designed in 1958 by Ludwig Mies van der Rohe in association with Philip Johnson and is the most refined version of the modern glass skyscraper. It faces Park Avenue across a broad plaza of pink Vermont granite, bordered on either side by reflecting pools and ledges of verd antique marble. The tower itself is a steel-framed structure wrapped in a curtain wall of pink-gray glass. Spandrels, mullions and I-beams, used to modulate the surface of the glass skin, are made of bronze. The walls and elevator banks are lined with travertine.

Mies once defined architecture as the will of an epoch translated into space. For architects of his generation, this meant reckoning with the reality of the industrial age and the transforming power of machine technology. But it also meant overcoming the war of the styles, which had fragmented architecture into battling ideological camps.

In the Seagram Building, the classical elements are more obvious: the symmetry of its massing on the raised plaza; the tripartite division of the tower into base, shaft and capital; the rhythmic regularity of its columns and bays; the antique associations borne by bronze.

The building's Gothicism is subtler. It is evident in the tower's soaring 516 feet, the lightness and transparency of the curtain wall, the vertical emphasis conveyed by the I-beams attached to the glass skin and the cruciform plan of the tall shaft and the lower rear extension. Indeed, the Gothic cathedral was the prelude to the whole of modern glass architecture.

Today we recognize that Gothic and classical represent more than two architectural styles. They stand for two views of the world, neurologists have determined, that correspond to functions located in the left and right sides of the brain. The classical is rational, logical, analytic. The Gothic is intuitive, exploratory, synthetic. In hindsight, we recognize, too, that there's little to be gained by embracing one side at the other's expense. The business of civilization is to hold opposites together. That goal, often reached through conflict, has been rendered here by Mies with a serenity unsurpassed in modern times.

—Herbert Muschamp

The Seagram Building

Highly Recommended Neighborhood Restaurants
(See chapter Restaurants for reviews.)

An American Place	☆☆	$ $ $ $	NEW AMERICAN
Bouterin	☆	$ $ $ $	FRENCH

Brasserie	☆ ☆	$ $ $	BISTRO/FRENCH
Chola	☆ ☆	$ $	INDIAN
Della Femina	☆	$ $ $ $	NEW AMERICAN
Felidia	☆ ☆ ☆	$ $ $ $	NORTHERN ITALIAN
Fifty Seven Fifty Seven	☆ ☆ ☆	$ $ $ $	AMERICAN
The Four Seasons	☆ ☆ ☆	$ $ $ $	NEW AMERICAN
Guastavino's	☆ ☆	$ $ $ $	ENGLISH/FRENCH
Heartbeat	☆ ☆	$ $	NEW AMERICAN
Il Valentino	☆ ☆	$ $	ITALIAN
Kuruma Zushi	☆ ☆ ☆	$ $ $ $	JAPANESE
La Grenouille	☆ ☆ ☆	$ $ $ $	FRENCH
Le Cirque 2000	☆ ☆ ☆ ☆	$ $ $ $	NEW AMERICAN
Le Colonial	☆ ☆	$ $	VIETNAMESE
Lespinasse	☆ ☆ ☆ ☆	$ $ $ $	FRENCH
Lutéce	☆ ☆ ☆	$ $ $ $	FRENCH
March	☆ ☆ ☆	$ $ $ $	NEW AMERICAN
Michael Jordan's	☆ ☆	$ $ $ $	STEAKHOUSE
Oceana	☆ ☆ ☆	$ $ $ $	SEAFOOD
Patroon	☆ ☆ ☆	$ $ $ $	NEW AMERICAN
Peacock Alley	☆ ☆ ☆	$ $ $ $	FRENCH
Rosa Mexicano	☆ ☆	$ $ $ $	MEXICAN/TEX-MEX
Shun Lee Palace	☆ ☆	$ $ $ $	CHINESE
Smith & Wollensky	☆ ☆	$ $ $ $	STEAKHOUSE
Solera	☆ ☆	$ $ $ $	SPANISH
Sushi Yasuda	☆ ☆ ☆	$ $ $ $	JAPANESE/SUSHI
Zarela	☆ ☆	$ $	MEXICAN/TEX-MEX

Recommended Inexpensive Restaurants

Jubilee	FRENCH
Katsu-Hama	JAPANESE
Meltemi	GREEK/SEAFOOD

Midtown West

There is probably more to see and do in Midtown in the West 30's, 40's and 50's than anywhere else in the city—not least the sizzling wattage of the newly booming **Times Square**. Long touted as "the crossroads of the world," it is fast becoming America's carnival midway. But Midtown is also the tonier gleam of **Rockefeller Center**, the breathtaking pinnacle of the **Empire State Building**, the vigilant marble lions—Patience and Fortitude—guarding the Fifth Avenue entrance to the **New York Public Library**. Everything seems outsized.

Did someone mention shopping? **Saks Fifth Avenue, Tiffany, Bergdorf Goodman, Brooks Brothers** and more. Accommodations? Most of the city's most elegant hotels—**The Plaza, St. Regis, Four Seasons**, etc.—and any number of lesser establishments around **Penn Station** and the **Port Authority Bus**

Terminal. By the way, "the world's most famous store"—**Macy's**—is just one block from Penn Station in **Herald Square**. *(See chapters* **Shopping** *and* **Hotels***.)*

If you're a fan of the *Today* show or *Good Morning America* on the little screen, see them live and full-size through the plate glass of their street-level studios—in Rockefeller Center and Times Square, respectively. *(For tickets to other TV shows see feature later in this section.)*

MTV has studios behind glass in Times Square, too, not so easy to view because they are on the second floor; to find them, listen for squealing teeny-boppers. For music of a somehat finer calibre, there is **Carnegie Hall** on 57th Street *(see chapter* **The Arts***.)* For a corned beef sandwich that feeds two, there is the **Carnegie Deli** just two blocks away.

Broadway and Seventh Avenue south of 42nd Street have been the main arteries of the **Garment District** for more than 100 years, home to the ware-houses and workshops of the fashion industry. The **Theater District** runs north from 42nd Street—so-called "Broadway" theater on side streets east and west of Broadway, and a half-dozen "off-Broadway" houses on 42nd Street west of Ninth Avenue.

West of the Theater District is a residential neighborhood famed as **Hell's Kitchen**, the rough-and-tumble home of immigrant Irish in the second half of the 19th century—former Senator Daniel Patrick Moynihan grew up there. Greeks, Eastern Europeans, Puerto Ricans and other groups moved in later. The politically sanitized name for the area now is **Clinton** (for DeWitt, not Bill) and its residents are young professionals, theater people and remnants of the old immigrant groups. **Restaurant Row** (46th St. between Eighth and Ninth Aves.) is a long block of restaurants side-by-side, all packed with the-ater-goers before curtain time—and half-empty after 8 P.M. New restaurants and bars along Ninth Ave., often with lower prices, cater to the rapidly grow-ing younger population.

Subway: A, B, C, D, E, F, N, Q, R, S, W, 1, 2, 3, 9 to 34th St.; A, B, C, D, E, F, N, Q, R, S, W, 1, 2, 3, 7, 9 to 42nd St.; B, D, F, S to 47th-50th St.–Rockefeller Center; N, R, W to 49th St.; C, E, to 50th St.; N, R, Q, S, W to 57th St.; A, B, C, D, 1, 9 to 59th St.

HIGHLIGHTS OF THE NEIGHBORHOOD

Bryant Park Sixth Ave., 40th St. to 42nd St. (212) 983-4142. On warm weekdays, Midtown workers descend on Bryant Park to shed ties and heels for some lunchtime relaxation. They arrange the park's folding chairs to gossip, or stretch out on the luxurious lawn for catnaps. Regulars play chess near a statue honoring the park's namesake, William Cullen Bryant, longtime editor of the *New York Post* and an early advocate of radical ideas such as abolition and public parks. Dotting its tree-lined boundaries are statues commemorating literary figures ranging from Goethe to Gertrude Stein, making the park a great place to read a chapter or two before heading back to the office. Probably the best time to go, though, is Monday nights in the summer, when HBO, headquartered across the street, presents movie classics on a huge screen.

Carnegie Hall Seventh Ave. and 57th St. (212) 247-7800.
(See section "Classical Music Centers" *in chapter* **The Arts** *for full listing.)*

Empire State Building 350 Fifth Ave. (between 33rd and 34th Sts.) (212) 736-3100. Known as the "Empty State" after it was completed in 1931, the Empire State Building remained half-rented during the Depression. Designed by Shreve, Lamb and Harmon, the Empire State was constructed at breakneck speed on the former site of the original Waldorf-Astoria Hotel. The Art Deco tower won a three-way competition with the Chrysler Building and 40 Wall Street to become the world's tallest skyscraper, a title it kept for more than half a century. The building's spire, immortalized as King Kong's perch, was designed—but used only once—as a mooring mast for dirigibles. Metal detectors were installed following a shooting spree in 1997 on the building's observation deck.

The Empire State Building

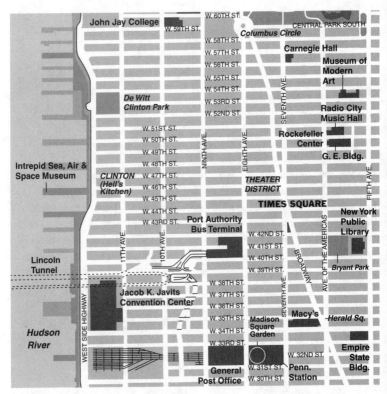

Midtown West

General Post Office 421 Eighth Ave. (between 32nd and 33rd Sts.)
(212) 330-3601. When you're running to get a package postmarked before midnight, the main post office's staircase feels as monumental as it looks. The facility is open 24 hours a day. (Check out the scene on the night of April 15, when late tax filers race to meet the midnight deadline.) Built in 1914 and designed by McKim, Mead and White as a complement to the first Pennsylvania Station—a landmark that was demolished in the 1960's—the Classical Revival building stretches across two city blocks.

The post office's unofficial motto is spelled out above a parade of Corinthian columns: "Neither snow nor rain nor heat nor gloom of night stays these couriers from the swift completion of their appointed rounds." After a campaign by former Senator Daniel Patrick Moynihan, plans are now being developed to turn a large part of the building into a new train station to replace the current, uninspiring incarnation of Penn Station.

Herald Square Broadway and Sixth Ave. (at 34th St.). This Midtown shopping district is named for the headquarters of the defunct *New York Herald*, which was torn down in 1921. (A statue of Horace Greeley, the newspaper's founder, still stands in Greeley Square on the south side of 34th St.) R. H. Macy opened the world's largest department store on the square in 1902. Others followed but eventually departed. By 1925, Saks had already moved uptown to Fifth Avenue. Gimbels gave way to a multilevel mall in the 1980's, and the district partially adapted to more suburban modes of shopping.

Jacob K. Javits Convention Center 655 W. 34th St. (between 11th and 12th Aves.) (212) 216-2000. The convention complex, completed in 1986 at a cost of half a billion dollars, boasts over 17 acres of floor space. Named after the late New York senator, the center was designed by the world-famous architectural firm of I. M. Pei. The New York International Auto Show, held here each April, alone draws more than one million visitors.

Madison Square Garden 2 Penn Plaza (at 33rd St. and Seventh Ave.) (212) 465-6741 *www.thegarden.com*. Few other sports arenas provide drama quite like Madison Square Garden. Unfortunately, to see the Knicks or the Rangers, you'll either need to know someone with season tickets, shell out your weekly paycheck to a ticket broker, or simply be extremely lucky. However, tickets to see the New York Liberty women's basketball team, the New York Cityhawks arena football team, or college basketball are much easier to come by. Visitors can also take a tour of the 20,000-seat arena for $15 ($12, children 12 and under). (*See also* **Sports & Recreation**).

The Museum of Television and Radio 25 W. 52nd St. (between Fifth and Sixth Aves.) (212) 621-6600. This plain, Midtown museum houses the some of the city's most fascinating and unlikely exhibits. Although the theaters show specials on TV and radio's most notable figures and events, the treasure of the museum is the archives in which you'll find a copy of almost anything from broadcast's past—old Jack Paar shows, Edward R. Murrow radio reports and even classic episodes of *Taxi* and other programs. Note: closed Monday. Prices: $6, general; $4, students and seniors; $3, children under 13.

New York Public Library Fifth Ave. and 42nd St. (212) 661-7220 *www.nypl.org*. One of the world's greatest libraries, this two-block-long Beaux-Arts palace of books has long been thought of as the main branch of the New York Public Library system, which includes 85 branches in the Bronx, Manhattan and Staten Island. But the building is actually the biggest of the system's four research libraries. Formally known as the Humanities and Social Sciences Library, no books are allowed to leave the building. Its 15 million items, from rare illuminated manuscripts to pulp fiction to Cherokee literature, may be checked out and read in the library.

It is a place where leafing through a book takes on a whole new meaning. The Main Reading Room on the third floor, open again after a $15 million renovation stretches the length of a football field. Beneath its soaring ceiling murals of bright blue skies and clouds, readers can plug in a laptop, peruse a newspaper or just daydream.

Anyone can ask for a book to be fetched from seven floors of stacks underneath the room or two more floors concealed under the lawn of Bryant Park

New York Public Library

next door. There are about 132 miles of shelves in the stacks, not open to the public. (In order to maintain the proper hush, tourists are encouraged to take scheduled tours of the Reading Room.)

The library came along relatively late in the city's history—it is just 100 years old. A little-known architecture firm, Carrere and Hastings, won a competition to build what was then the largest marble structure ever attempted in the country.

And the famous marble lions? They have stood guard at the Fifth Avenue entrance since the beginning. Mayor Fiorello La Guardia's administration dubbed the one to the south Patience and the one to the north—you guessed it—Fortitude.

—*Randy Kennedy*

Radio City Music Hall 1260 Ave. of the Americas (at 50th St.) (212) 307-1000. Radio City Music Hall is Manhattan's version of a natural wonder. It's our Rainbow Arch, our Old Faithful, our Niagara Falls. After a $70 million restoration in 1999, the great hall's awesome beauty can be seen once again in the genius of its original conception.

Completed in 1932, the Music Hall is a tribute to the Rockefeller family's spirit of culturally progressive enterprise. Like Rockefeller Center, which surrounds it in Midtown, the theater countered the Great Depression with a great infusion of hope in the city's future. Radio City! Live from Radio City!

Always seen as a place for families, the Music Hall opened at a time when family entertainment might include ballet, symphony and opera, along with comedy, popular song, acrobatics and the Rockettes. The vaudeville mix was recognizably of the radio age, when folks gathered round the Bakelite console to hear their favorite shows. The Music Hall gave them tunes and great visuals besides.

Three New York architectural firms are credited with the design of the theater. These firms brought to harmonious realization the unlikely alliance between the patrician Rockefellers and the plebeian Samuel L. Rothafel, known as Roxy, an impresario of movie palaces for the masses.

The building is a triumph of processional design. Its most dramatic aspect is an expanded version of an effect common in theater architecture: the disarming contrast between a small-scale exterior and an interior of epic proportions. The entrance and ticket lobby are lodged on the ground floor of an office tower that gives little sign of the grandiose space inside.

The ticket lobby is in keeping with the scale of the building's exterior, but the box offices anticipate the amplitude within. There are so many of them, and all for one theater: a soloplex. The box offices may remind some of passport-control counters. The comparison is apt, for from here we proceed to a grand ocean liner of a space, the Grand Foyer. Moderne rather than modern, the foyer is one of the world's great Art Deco interiors, its length and height amplified by mirrors of gold-backed glass.

Entering the auditorium, we find ourselves on the deck of the ocean liner, gazing out to sea, precisely the image Roxy Rothafel wanted his architects to capture for his new 6,000-seat show palace. In time the showman's wish was conveyed to the young Edward Durell Stone, a draftsman in one of the three architectural firms responsible for the design. In later life Stone made his mark with Manhattan buildings like the Museum of Modern Art and the General Motors Building. At age 30 Stone found himself designing the most stupendous arch this side of Rome.

The auditorium's formal power is derived from the plain, unadorned half-circle of the proscenium, and from the projection of that shape from the front to the rear of the house. Like a dome, the design eliminates both walls and ceiling.

Fred R. Conrad/The New York Times

Radio City Music Hall

The New York Times

The G.E. Building at Rockefeller Center

This is why the auditorium is psychologically so overwhelming. No matter where you sit, you have the sensation of tumbling through the sky. This feeling is heightened by the broad strips of air-conditioning grilles, also used for lighting, that radiate longitudinally from the proscenium. These bands further diminish the orientation that walls and ceiling usually provide. It's a cinematic effect, the architectural equivalent of the simultaneous reverse track and forward zoom in Hitchcock's *Vertigo*.

For design historians the Music Hall is forever linked to Donald Deskey, responsible for the theater's iconic Art Deco interiors. Plate-glass vanity tables, metal tube chairs, mohair sofas, round mirrors, balustrades, light fixtures, theater seats: these are some of the classic pieces Deskey created for the Hall.

—*Herbert Muschamp*

Rockefeller Center Between 48th and 52nd Streets, Fifth to Seventh Avenue. This impressive complex in the heart of Manhattan includes some of New York's best-known landmarks, including Radio City Music Hall and a sunken plaza that becomes an ice skating rink with a Christmas tree in wintertime. The Rainbow Room has dinner and dancing on the 65th floor of the G.E. Building (30 Rockefeller Plaza, between 49th and 50th Sts.), the sleek centerpiece of Rockefeller Center, but new owners are limiting public access to a few days a month.

The brainchild of John D. Rockefeller, the center is noteworthy for incorporating office buildings, stores, theaters and open space—including NBC Studios, where people can come to watch the live telecasts of the *Today* show and tapings of *Conan O'Brien* and *Saturday Night Live*. (*For ticket info see feature later in this section.*)

Rockefeller Center was the largest privately sponsored real estate venture ever undertaken in New York City when construction began in 1929. Originally intended to include a new Metropolitan Opera House, those plans were scrapped after the stock market crash that October. Mr. Rockefeller then reconceived the project as an entirely commercial complex. Rockefeller Center is home to over 100 works of art all chosen along one theme: "The Progress of Man." The Center houses "Prometheus" (Paul Manship, 1934) at the end of the lower plaza and "Atlas" (Lee Laurie, 1937) in front of the International Building (630 Fifth Ave.), as well as famous facades, including "News" (Isamu Noguchi, 1940). The impressively dynamic stainless steel relief adorns the Associated Press Building, at 50 Rockefeller Plaza, and depicts five news reporters. —*Robin Pogrebin*

St. Thomas Church 1 W. 53rd St. (at Fifth Ave.) (212) 757-7013. Fifth Avenue's Easter Parade first began at St. Thomas's in the 19th century, when congregants carried flowers to a nearby hospital. The church's current incarnation—a French Gothic building designed by Cram, Goodhue and Ferguson and completed in 1914—juxtaposes detailed sculptures and austere volumes on the tight corner site. The Episcopal parish maintains a boarding school for members of its renowned boys' choir and accommodates a medley of musical events.

Times Square Broadway and Seventh Ave., from 42nd St. to 47th St. New Yorkers insist on calling it the Crossroads of the World. Of course, New Yorkers like to think of their city as the center of the cosmos, so it is hardly surprising that they attach mere global import to the dot on the hometown map where Broadway and 42nd Street collide. For once, however, the New York penchant for overstatement happens to be fact.

Times Square is, without a doubt, the most recognized intersection on the planet, and never is that more true than on New Year's Eve. Hundreds of thou-

Ozier Muhammad/The New York Times

Times Square

sands of people jam the square and tens of millions more watch on television as a glittering ball slowly descends, ticking off the final seconds of the dying year (the special ball manufactured to mark the year 2000 was made by Waterford Crystal, covered with 144 strobe lights and 12,000 rhinestones). By now, some are willing to believe that there would not be a new year, a new century, a new millennium without this communal gathering in the heart of New York.

It wasn't always like that. At the turn of the last century, the area was a humble place called Long Acre Square. The name was changed in 1904 when *The New York Times* moved there; the cachet of the Times Square name attracted people to the surrounding blocks, and the square became a neighborhood. For decades to come, Times Square would provide the country with some of its most enduring images, from the finger-snap pace of the crowds outside Jack Dempsey's restaurant to the strangers exultantly embracing on VJ Day. All it took was an overhead shot of the neon-bathed square to tell moviegoers that they were entering a world of sophistication.

Decay set in with the Great Depression; by the 1970's, Times Square had become synonymous with sleazy arcades and tawdry sex shows. The menace and sheer creepiness of the place, almost a vision of hell, was memorably captured by Martin Scorsese in his 1976 film, *Taxi Driver*. Historic theaters and hotels were sacrificed for office space, the *Times* moved around the corner and the building's terra-cotta facade was replaced with faceless white marble.

But the 90's brought rebirth, with porno houses giving way to the likes of Disney and Warner Brothers stores. Some find the new attractions a tad too sanitized, but few truly mourn the passing of the dope dealers and pimps.

Today, there is no better place to people-watch than Times Square. Street performers, gawking tourists and get-out-of-my-way New Yorkers—they are all

If You'd Like to Be Part of the Studio Audience . . .

From sitcoms to talk shows, New York has an abundance of programs that are taped before a live (and eager) audience. Here's your chance to take part, but take notice of the fine print. Some of these programs require commitments up to a year in advance. In most cases the lucky winners who can plan that far in advance—or are fortunate enough to win a lottery—will receive their tickets through the mail. For more show tapings in the area check *www.nytoday.com*.

The Daily Show With Jon Stewart Mon.–Thurs., 5:45–7:30 P.M. No one under 18 admitted. Call (212) 586-2477 or send a postcard with your preferred dates to The Daily Show, 513 W. 54th St., New York, NY 10019. Requests must be made four to six weeks in advance.

Late Night With Conan O'Brien Tues.–Thurs., 5:30–6:30 P.M. No one under 16 admitted. Arrive at 4 P.M. at the 49th Street entrance. Call (212) 664-3056/7, 664–3055 for groups, or send a postcard to Late Night with Conan O'Brien, 30 Rockefeller Plaza, Suite 9W, New York, NY 10112. Ticket reservations should be made four to five months in advance. Standby tickets are available at 9 A.M. at the page desk in the NBC Studios lobby.

The Late Show with David Letterman Mon.–Wed., 5:30 P.M.; Thurs., 5:30 and 8 P.M. Arrive at 4:15 for 5:30 tapings and 6:45 for tapings at 8. Call (212) 975-5853, order them through the CBS Web site or write to Late Show Tickets, Ed Sullivan Theater, 1697 Broadway, New York, NY 10019. Include your preferred date. For standby tickets, call (212) 247-6497 at 11 A.M. on taping days.

Live With Regis and Kelly Mon.–Fri., 9 A.M. No one under 10 admitted. Send a postcard to LIVE Tickets, P.O. Box 777, Ansonia Station, New York, NY 10023. For information, call (212) 456-3054. Requests should be made one year in advance. Standby seats are available before 8 A.M. daily.

Saturday Night Live Sat., 11:30 P.M. No one under 16 admitted. Tickets are decided by lottery based on postcards received during August. Winners are notified one to two weeks in advance with tickets for the dress rehearsal or the live show. Postcards can be sent to SNL, 30 Rockefeller Plaza, New York, NY 10112. Call (212) 664-3056 for more information. Standby tickets (one per person) are distributed at 9:15 A.M. on the mezzanine of Rockefeller Plaza (49th Street side). These tickets do not guarantee admission.

The View Mon.–Fri., 11 A.M. No one under 18 admitted. Arrive at 10 A.M. Send ticket requests to The View, Tickets, 320 W. 66th St., New York, NY 10023 or visit the ABC Web site. Requests should be made three to four months in advance. Standby tickets are available before 10 A.M.

here, and are easily the most fascinating thing about the place. For show business, there's also no place like Times Square. In the early years of the century, a big show could earn an average of a million dollars in its first year. In the final year of the century, Broadway was still packing them in, with attendance a record 11.6 million and a box-office take of $588 million, also a record. There are also about 1,500 businesses and organizations here; 21 million square feet of office space and 2.4 million more being built; one-fifth of all New York City hotel rooms; 3.9 million overnight visitors each year, and 26 million day-trippers; more than 251 restaurants, 10 movie theaters and 22 landmarked Broadway theaters. And believe it or not, nearly 27,000 people actually live in the Times Square area; 231,000 folks go to work there every day.

Through the years, Times Square has evolved and is still evolving. Yet it remains the place to gather, whether to watch a televised space shot or protest a war or celebrate triumph over tyranny. It is far more than a neighborhood. It is America's town square.   —*Clyde Haberman*

U.S.S. Intrepid Sea-Air-Space Museum 46th St. at 12th Ave. (212) 245-2533 *www.intrepidmuseum.org.* Launched in 1943 and decommissioned in 1974, the *Intrepid* once had more than 100 aircraft and a crew of over 3,000. The aircraft carrier was deployed in the Second World War, the Korean and Vietnam Wars and served as a recovery vessel for NASA capsules. There are jets and prop planes on the flight and hangar decks, and exhibits relating to the ship's history and undersea exploration. A flight simulator recreates the feeling of being inside an F-18 fighter during the Gulf War. The open-air flight deck allows access to the navigation bridge and wheelhouse, and close examination of planes, helicopters and gun galleries. The destroyer *Edison* and the submarine *Growler* lie alongside. All three vessels are open to visitors, but the 900-foot *Intrepid*, which occupies an area greater than a Midtown Manhattan block, is the most impressive.
Admission: $12, general; $9, students and seniors; $6, children (6–11); $2, children (2-5); children under 2 free.

Highly Recommended Neighborhood Restaurants
(*See chapter* **Restaurants** *for reviews.*)

Aquavit	☆☆☆	$$$$	SCANDINAVIAN
Chez Josephine	☆☆	$$$	BISTRO/FRENCH
Cho Dang Gol	☆☆	$$$	KOREAN
Christer's	☆☆	$$$	SCANDINAVIAN
Churrascaria Plataforma	☆☆	$$$	BRAZILIAN
Estiatorio Milos	☆☆	$$$$	GREEK/SEAFOOD
Firebird	☆☆	$$$	RUSSIAN
Joe's Shanghai	☆☆	$	CHINESE
Judson Grill	☆☆☆	$$$	NEW AMERICAN
Kang Suh	☆☆	$$	KOREAN
La Caravelle	☆☆☆	$$$$	FRENCH
La Côte Basque	☆☆☆	$$$$	FRENCH

Le Bernardin	☆☆☆☆	$ $ $ $	FRENCH/SEAFOOD
Molyvos	☆☆☆	$ $ $	GREEK
Osteria Del Circo	☆☆	$ $ $	ITALIAN
Petrossian	☆☆	$ $ $ $	RUSSIAN
Remi	☆☆	$ $ $	ITALIAN
San Domenico	☆☆☆	$ $ $ $	ITALIAN
Sea Grill	☆☆	$ $ $	SEAFOOD
Thalia	☆☆	$ $ $	NEW AMERICAN
"21" Club	☆☆	$ $ $ $	NEW AMERICAN
Viceversa	☆	$ $	ITALIAN

Recommended Inexpensive Restaurants

Carnegie Deli	DELI
Chimichurri Grill	LATIN AMERICAN
Han Bat	KOREAN
Havana NY	LATIN AMERICAN
Island Spice	CARIBBEAN
Los Dos Rancheros	MEXICAN
McHale's	BAR SNACKS/BURGERS
Rinconcito Peruano	PERUVIAN
Topaz Thai	THAI
Wu Liang Ye	CHINESE

Upper East Side

From the stately homes and manicured flower beds along **Park Avenue** to the art galleries and pricey boutiques on **Madison Avenue**, the Upper East Side has all the trappings of power and privilege (as well as 10021, the nation's wealthiest ZIP code in 1990). Walk along Park Avenue or its side streets on a weekday morning and you're likely to see professional dog walkers being tugged along in a tangle of pedigree pooches, or uniformed children traipsing off to Spence, Chapin and other exclusive private schools.

Historically the Upper East Side has been a place of privilege. Until the 1840's, it was primarily pastureland. That changed with the opening of Central Park in 1860. In the late 19th century, mansions rose on Fifth Avenue and brownstones lined the side streets. In 1906, when the New York Central Railroad converted from steam to electricity, the Park Avenue tracks were moved underground. In the 1950's the Third Avenue El was demolished, and within a few years that artery's tenements were vanishing, too.

But the Upper East Side has a more diverse population than its reputation suggests. On Lexington Avenue, neighborhood institutions such as **Bloomingdale's** department store, **Hunter College** and the **92nd Street Y** lure shoppers, students and culture lovers from across the city. Farther east, middle-class families and young professionals who snagged rent-stabilized apartments in the early 1990's fill high-rise apartments that sprang up after World War II.

This area hosts some of the best-known cultural institutions in the world. **Museum Mile** along Fifth Avenue has the **Metropolitan Museum of Art**, the **Solomon R. Guggenheim Museum**, the **Jewish Museum**, the **Museum of the City of New York** and **El Museo del Barrio**. The Frick and Carnegie mansions house the **Frick Collection** and the **Cooper-Hewitt National Design Museum**, respectively (*see chapter* **The Arts**). The mansions are two remnants of **Millionaire's Row**, where European-style grand residences overlooking Central Park were built in the early 1900s by super-rich industrialists competing to outdo each other. Several institutions dedicated to world societies and cultures are also located here including the **Asia Society** and the **China Institute in America** (*see section* "Institutes of World Culture" *in* **The Arts**).

Farther south is the **Seventh Regiment Armory** (Park Ave. and 66th St.), an 1879 medieval-style building that became the model for armories throughout the country. With its Tiffany interiors and enormous drill room, the armory hosts frequent art and antiques shows. Also at the southern end of the neighborhood are several private clubs that are housed in historic buildings. Worth seeing are the **Metropolitan Club** (1–11 E. 60th St.), designed by Stanford White in the 1890's, the **Knickerbocker Club** (2 E. 62nd St.) and the **Lotos Club** (5 E. 66th St.). Other historical town houses and carriage houses line the streets east of Park Avenue, particularly on 69th Street (between Third and Lexington Aves.) and in the **Treadwell Farm Historic District** on 61st and 62nd Streets (between Second and Third Aves.).

In **Yorkville** (70th-96th St., east of Lexington Ave.), the Old World flavor of this once German and Hungarian (also Irish and Czech) enclave is fading. There are remnants such as **Schaller and Weber** (1654 Second Ave. between 85th and 86th Sts.) which has been selling authentic German sausage and other specialties since 1937. The **Heidelberg** (1648 Second Ave. near 86th St.) is the last authentic German restaurant in a neighborhood that was once home to more than two dozen of them. For the most part, the old groceries and bakeries have been replaced by a more youthful spirit found in the cafes along Second and Third Avenues and bars that fill with exuberant drinkers on weekends. Joggers and the less harried take to the East River esplanade and **Carl Schurz Park** outside **Gracie Mansion**, the mayor's official residence.

Across the East River, just minutes away by aerial tram, lies tranquil **Roosevelt Island**, the site of a prison, an almshouse and an insane asylum from the early 1800's through the early 1900's. Today, the island is a mixed-income residential community that offers an escape from Manhattan's frenzy.

Subway: 4 (express), 5 (express) and 6 (local) make stops along Lexington Ave. from 59th St. to 125th St.

HIGHLIGHTS OF THE NEIGHBORHOOD

Abigail Adams Smith Museum 421 E. 61st St. (between First and York Aves.) (212) 838-6878. This small museum sits well within earshot of the FDR Drive and in the shadow the Queensboro Bridge. You might find it hard to

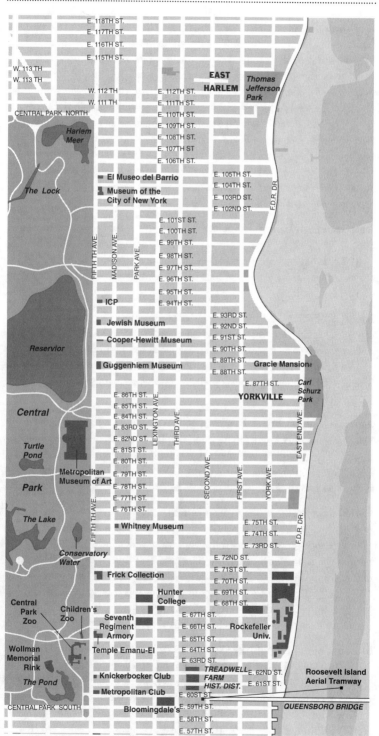

E. 118TH ST.
E. 117TH ST.
E. 116TH ST.
E. 115TH ST.

W. 113TH
W. 113TH

W. 112 TH
W. 111 TH

EAST HARLEM

Thomas Jefferson Park

E. 112TH ST.
E. 111TH ST.
E. 110TH ST.
E. 109TH ST.
E. 108TH ST.
E. 107TH ST.
E. 106TH ST.

CENTRAL PARK NORTH

Harlem Meer

The Lock

El Museo del Barrio
Museum of the City of New York

E. 105TH ST.
E. 104TH ST.
E. 103RD ST.
E. 102ND ST.

F.D.R. DR.

E. 101ST ST.
E. 100TH ST.
E. 99TH ST.
E. 98TH ST.
E. 97TH ST.
E. 96TH ST.
E. 95TH ST.
E. 94TH ST.

FIFTH AVE.
MADISON AVE.
PARK AVE.

ICP

Reservior

Jewish Museum
Cooper-Hewitt Museum
Guggenhiem Museum

E. 93RD ST.
E. 92ND ST.
E. 91ST ST.
E. 90TH ST.
E. 89TH ST.
E. 88TH ST.

Gracie Mansion

Carl Schurz Park

E. 87TH ST.

YORKVILLE

E. 86TH ST.
E. 85TH ST.
E. 84TH ST.
E. 83RD ST.
E. 82ND ST.
E. 81ST ST.
E. 80TH ST.
E. 79TH ST.
E. 78TH ST.
E. 77TH ST.
E. 76TH ST.

LEXINGTON AVE.
THIRD AVE.
SECOND AVE.
FIRST AVE.
YORK AVE.
EAST END AVE.
F.D.R. DR.

Central

Turtle Pond

Metropolitan Museum of Art

FIFTH AVE.

Park

The Lake

Conservatory Water

Whitney Museum

E. 75TH ST.
E. 74TH ST.
E. 73RD ST.

Frick Collection

E. 72ND ST.
E. 71ST ST.
E. 70TH ST.
E. 69TH ST.
E. 68TH ST.

Hunter College

Central Park Zoo

Children's Zoo

Seventh Regiment Armory

Temple Emanu-El

Rockefeller Univ.

E. 67TH ST.
E. 66TH ST.
E. 65TH ST.
E. 64TH ST.
E. 63RD ST.

Wollman Memorial Rink

The Pond

Knickerbocker Club

Metropolitan Club

TREADWELL FARM HIST. DIST.

E. 62ND ST.
E. 61ST ST.

Roosevelt Island Aerial Tramway

E. 60ST ST.

CENTRAL PARK SOUTH

Bloomingdale's

E. 59TH ST.
E. 58TH ST.
E. 57TH ST.

QUEENSBORO BRIDGE

Upper East Side

imagine that people used to flock to this setting for a peaceful escape from the hustle and bustle of downtown. But after an hour or so wandering through the museum's nine richly appointed period rooms and relaxing on a stone bench in the 18th-century-style gardens, it starts to seem more plausible. In the 1830's, wealthy New Yorkers would retreat to what was then called the Mount Vernon Hotel for the weekend. The Federal-style structure, built in 1799, is the only remaining building of its kind in Manhattan. The museum is named for Abigail Adams Smith, daughter of President John Adams, who originally built it as part of a planned 23-acre estate modeled after Mount Vernon. It was never completed. The museum offers guided tours, dramatic programs and lectures. **Admission:** $3, general; $2, students and seniors; museum members and children under 12, free.

American Irish Historical Society 991 Fifth Ave. (between 80th and 81st Sts.) (212) 288-2263. The society features a substantial library and a gallery in its 100-year-old building, which offers small temporary exhibits that highlight Irish contributions to American society. There are frequent readings, lectures and concerts.

American Society of Illustrators 128 E. 63rd St. (between Park and Lexington Aves.) (212) 838-2560. You'll come away from this museum with a new respect for everyday images, from soup-can labels to CD covers. The society has existed since 1901 to preserve the past and promote the future of illustration. The museum's permanent collection includes work by Norman Rockwell and J.C. Lyendecker.

Americas Society 680 Park Ave. (at 68th St.) (212) 249-8950. Founded in 1967 by Nelson Rockefeller to heighten economic, social and cultural awareness of all countries in the Western Hemisphere, the Americas Society features exhibitions, lectures and concerts. The neo-Federal building housing the Society was designed by McKim, Mead and White in 1909.

Carl Schurz Park East End Ave. at 84th St. (212) 360-1311. Named after a newspaper editor and reform politician who exercised great influence upon 19th-century elections, Carl Schurz Park is the site of Gracie Mansion, the mayor's official residence. Stretching along the East River, the park is also one of the city's quietest. Benches line a relaxing promenade that offers views of tugboats, Hell's Gate Bridge and the Roosevelt Island lighthouse. To the delight of loungers, the brick paths make the park a terrible place for in-line skating. The park has a basketball court and children's playground.

Museum of the City of New York 1220 Fifth Ave. (between 103rd and 104th Sts.) (212) 534-1672 *www.mcny.org*. If you accept the premise that New York is the world's greatest city, you will be at home at the Museum of the City of New York. Created in 1923 to collect and preserve the history of the city, the museum's intimate galleries are filled with a rich trove of artifacts from the 19th and 20th centuries. Its collections trace the development of the modern city

Fred R. Conrad/The New York Times

Metropolitan Museum of Art

and its people, from the skating ponds portrayed on Currier & Ives prints to the skyscrapers photographed by Berenice Abbott. Visitors can count on exhibits about the history of Broadway theater and American decorative arts. Kids will be drawn to the historic fire pumps and a gallery stuffed with toys. The museumm will be moving downtown to the Tweed Courthouse within two years. **Admission** (suggested): $7; $4, students, children and seniors. **Credit cards:** All major; checks. **Hours:** Wed.–Sat., 10 A.M.–5 P.M.; Sun., noon–5 P.M.

New York Society Library 53 E. 79th St. (between Madison and Park Aves.) (212) 288-6900 *www.nysoclib.org*. The Society Library is the city's oldest library, dating from 1754. It has moved several times, but for 60 years it has been at its current location. It is a membership library with nearly 200,000 volumes. (Annual family membership is $150.) Nonmembers can use the ground floor for reference or reading without charge. It feels and smells like an old-fashioned library with a wonderful reading room filled with Audubon sketches.

Temple Emanu-El 1 E. 65th St. (at Fifth Ave.) (212) 744-1400. The Temple Emanu-El is said to be the largest Jewish congregation in the world. The impressive limestone Moorish-Romanesque structure was completed in 1929 on the site of an Astor mansion. In size and beauty it rivals some of Europe's cathedrals.

The sanctuary, which seats 2,500, has an extraordinary bronze ark in the shape of a Torah and is decorated with marvelous mosaics by Hildreth Meiere. The temple regularly hosts recitals and concerts, and, surprisingly enough (given its size), music sounds rather good here.

Highly Recommended Neighborhood Restaurants
(*See chapter* **Restaurants** *for reviews.*)

Aureole	☆☆	$ $ $ $	NEW AMERICAN
Café Boulud	☆☆☆	$ $ $ $	FRENCH
Cello	☆☆☆	$ $ $	BISTRO/FRENCH
Circus	☆☆	$ $ $	BRAZILIAN
Daniel	☆☆☆	$ $ $ $	FRENCH
Destinee	☆☆	$ $ $ $	FRENCH
Etats-Unis	☆☆	$ $ $	NEW AMERICAN
Jo Jo	☆☆☆	$ $ $ $	FRENCH
Little Dove	☆☆	$ $ $	NEW AMERICAN
Mark's	☆☆	$ $ $	AMERICAN
Maya	☆☆	$ $ $	MEXICAN/TEX-MEX
Paola's	☆☆	$ $	ITALIAN
Parioli Romanissimo	☆☆	$ $ $ $	ITALIAN
Payard Pâtisserie	☆☆	$ $ $	BISTRO/FRENCH
Sushi Hatsu	☆☆☆	$ $ $ $	JAPANESE/SUSHI

Recommended Inexpensive Restaurants

Bandol	FRENCH
Bistro Le Steak	BISTRO/STEAK
Congee Village	CHINESE
John's Pizzeria	ITALIAN/PIZZA
La Fonda Boricua	LATIN AMERICAN
L'Ardoise	FRENCH
Luca	ITALIAN
Pig Heaven	CHINESE
The Sultan	TURKISH
Taco Taco	MEXICAN/TEX-MEX

Upper West Side

How to explain the Upper West Side? It has Columbus Circle at one end and
Columbia University at the other. In between is a rectangle four miles long and
one mile wide that is unlike any other neighborhood in the United States.
Politicians who know the city by its ZIP codes know that 10023, 10024 and
10025—the Upper West Side—are three of the most liberal anywhere. But the
rectangle is really a place of contrasts. It is a place of rich and poor, sometimes
on the same block, of ethnic and religious variety, of churches and synagogues,
and of culture that ranges from **Lincoln Center** to small neighborhood stages.

Where to begin an exploration? Not with a place but an idea: the Upper
West Side is not old New York. It was farmland until well after the Civil
War—the city, such as it was, covered only the lower third of the island of
Manhattan. Before the proud apartment buildings began marching up Central
Park West, Central Park's 843 acres were penciled off as a big green rectangle— "the grand-daddy of all American landscaped parks," an American Institute of Architects guide called it. But Frederick Law Olmsted, principal
designer of the park, did not want New Yorkers to think of the park as architecture. "What we want to gain is tranquility and rest to the mind," he said.
The park is full of places where one can gain both. Runners circle the reservoir
in endless laps. Rowers ply the lake in bulky rented boats. Zelda Fitzgerald, the
wife of Jazz Age novelist F. Scott Fitzgerald, painted the bridge that bisects the
lake. (*See section* "Central Park" *later in this chapter.*)

From there, one can see the Dakota, an apartment building so spacious that
Leonard Bernstein had no trouble fitting two grand pianos into his living room.
The Dakota was also home to John Lennon, who was shot to death just outside
the archway that leads to the building's elegant courtyard. His widow, Yoko
Ono, still lives in the Dakota, only a short walk from **Strawberry Fields**, an area
inside the park honoring his memory.

Up Central Park West, past the twin-towered San Remo apartments, are
the museums. **The New-York Historical Society** has kept the hyphen that
the rest of the city dropped more than a century ago. Next door is the **American Museum of Natural History**. The oldest section of the museum was
designed by Calvert Vaux, Olmsted's collaborator on the design of the park
just across the street. The museum's newest addition is the sleek glass box that
encloses the **Hayden Planetarium** in the **Rose Center for Earth and Space**.
Three blocks west is Broadway; between 72nd Street and 96th Streets is a
food shopper's paradise, with markets like **Fairway, Citarella** and **Zabar's**—
and a sleek new **Balducci's** (*see chapter* **Shopping**). Three stops beyond 96th
Street on the No. 1 local is **Columbia University**. The campus was laid out
by Charles Follen McKim, a partner in McKim, Mead & White, the legendary
firm that satisfied the city's lust for carefully proportioned neoclassical creations at the beginning of the 20th century. The newest building on the

Columbia campus is an $85 million student center, a gleaming glass box that opened in 1999, completing McKim's master plan.   —*James Barron*

Subway: 1 (local), 2 (express), 3 (express), 9 (local) make stops along Broadway from 59th St. to 96th St. (1, 9 continue uptown on the West Side); B, C make stops along Central Park West.

HIGHLIGHTS OF THE NEIGHBORHOOD
(*See chapter* **The Arts** *for* **Lincoln Center**)

The American Museum of Natural History Central Park West and 79th St. (212) 769-5100 *www.amnh.org*. Holden Caulfield reported in *The Catcher in the Rye* that he loved this huge, hushed museum because "everything always stayed right where it was."

But over the last several years, the Natural History Museum—the largest of its kind in the world, with about three-quarters of a million square feet of public exhibition space—has actually moved a lot of things around. The world-famous dinosaur halls were expanded and spruced up in the late 1990's, and the fossils themselves were rearranged to conform with new anthropological research. The towering Tyrannosaurus Rex was completely reshaped into a low stalking pose with its tail in the air. The Barosaurus, probably the first thing you will see when you walk in, still towers; at five stories, it is the world's tallest free-standing dinosaur exhibit.

In February 2000, the museum opened the new **Rose Center for Earth and Space**, which encloses the rebuilt **Hayden Planetarium**, now the most technologically advanced planetarium in the world. The Rose Center includes a recreation of the birth of the universe in the Big Bang Theater, and a dazzling variety of exhibits relating to Mother Earth and outer space (*see* **Rose Center** *description below*).

But if you get tired of flash, the museum still has many reliable standbys to remind you of its origins. There's Akeley Hall, with its silent herds of stuffed elephants; the famous Star of India sapphire, the world's largest; and the 94-foot model of the Blue Whale, in whose shadow you might want to enjoy a smoked salmon sandwich in the Ocean Life Food Court.   —*Randy Kennedy*

Admission (suggested): $10, adults; $7.50, students and seniors; $6, children.

The Ansonia 2109 Broadway (between 73rd and 74th Sts.) (212) 724-2600. The thick, soundproof walls of the Ansonia have long harbored musicians. Enrico Caruso and Igor Stravinsky once lived upstairs in the Beaux-Arts apartment building, which dates from 1904, and Bette Midler launched her career singing downstairs in the Continental Baths, a gay spa that doubled as a cabaret in the 1970's. In more recent years, the building has been the site of fierce battles between the landlord and rent-regulated tenants, some of whom operate music rehearsal studios in their apartments. A confection of balconies, turrets and dormer windows, the restored 17-story facade gives its block of upper Broadway the look of a Parisian boulevard exaggerated on a New York scale.

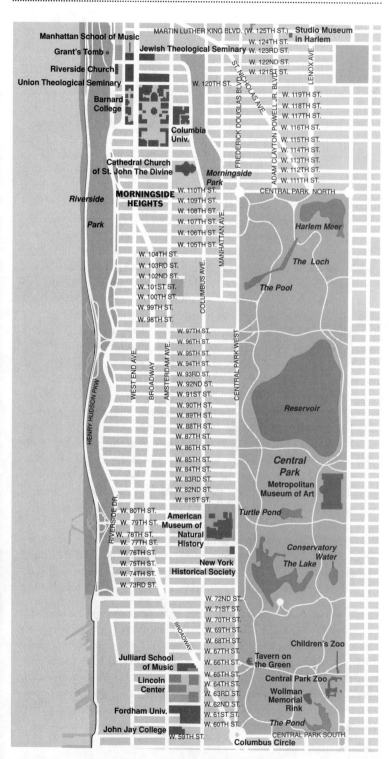

Upper West Side/Morningside Heights

Cathedral Church of St. John the Divine 1047 Amsterdam Ave. (at 112th St.) (212) 316-7540 *www.stjohndivine.org.* The clerics at the Cathedral Church of St. John the Divine like to call it a medieval cathedral for New York City, not just in architectural style but in spirit and commitment. The cathedral is the seat of the Episcopal Diocese in New York; its bishop once said it combines all the life and struggle of the city. Peacocks strut across the bucolic 13-acre grounds, delighting the children who chase after them for tail feathers. Artists in residence haunt the basement vaults, rehearsing their pieces, then perform them in the eclectic splendor of the Gothic, Romanesque and Byzantine sanctuary. The cathedral tends to New York's forgotten homeless, as well as holds memorial services for many of the city's most famous citizens. About the only time you might see an elephant on Amsterdam Avenue is early fall, when St. John's clergy bless animals large and small in honor of St. Francis.

Neighborhood residents have affectionately nicknamed the cathedral, with its soaring Gothic arches, two luminous rose windows and carved stone figures, St. John the Unfinished. When its cornerstone was laid in 1892, on the site of a former orphan asylum, it was envisioned as a great acropolis on a hill, the rocky schist of upper Manhattan. Indeed, it is second in size only to St. Peter's Basilica in Rome, with more floor area than Notre Dame and Chartres combined, and still growing, mainly upward. Construction ceased during the iron and steel shortages of World War II. During the civil rights struggles of the late 1960's, the Diocese hesitated to lavish money on a building in an area filled with poverty, and dedicated itself to good works instead. Work has slowly resumed.

On the vertiginous vertical tour, you can peer down from the crossway more than 100 feet above the floor—the real excitement of the cathedral for visiting schoolchildren. A guided tour through the interior helps uncover details from the whimsical (the prayer bay dedicated to sports, from polo to baseball) to the sobering (the bay dedicated to the healing arts, now dominated by a memorial to those who have suffered and died from AIDS). Among the profusion of icons, both sacred and mundane, are an ostrich egg, a symbol of meditation, donated by P.L. Travers, the author of *Mary Poppins,* and a prominently displayed pair of menorahs donated by Adolph Ochs, former publisher of *The New York Times.* The bronze lights in front were salvaged from the demolished Penn Station. The bronze doors were fabricated in Paris by Ferdinand Barbedienne, who also cast the Statue of Liberty. St. John's is truly, as its founders hoped, a house of prayer for all nations.   —*Anemona Hartocollis*

Christ and St. Stephen's Church 122 W. 69th St. (between Broadway and Columbus Ave.) (212) 787-2755. Nestled mid-block on a tree-lined street near Lincoln Center, behind a well-manicured patch of lawn (a rare sight in these parts), is Christ and St. Stephen's Episcopal Church, a cozy brick chapel with some pretty turn-of-the-century stained glass. Built in 1880, the small church is a popular performance venue for musicians of all types. On any given day you might catch a recital, a chamber-music group, an orchestra or a choral concert. Thanks to the church's unusually low ceiling, the sound here is good.

Church of St. Michael Amsterdam Ave. and 100th St. (212) 222-2700. St. Michael's Church has a beautiful refurbished interior, with mosaics and Tiffany glass. The seven chancel windows, depicting St. Michael's victory over Lucifer, are among Tiffany's most notable works.

St. Michael's, an Episcopal church is also a wonderful place for music, and groups who perform here regularly, like the acclaimed early-music vocal quartet Anonymous 4, provide a compelling reason to venture this far uptown. The church is also home to an unusually fine organ, built by Rudolf von Beckerath in 1967, which, like the building itself, was recently restored and is considered to be one of the best in town.

Columbia University 116th St. and Broadway (212) 854-1754. Built on the site of a former insane asylum, Columbia University's main campus represents one of the most balanced expressions of Beaux-Arts urban design in America. Chartered as King's College before the American Revolution, New York's Ivy League university moved from Madison Avenue and 49th Street to Morningside Heights at the turn of the last century. McKim, Mead & White designed a symmetrical quadrangle of Italian Renaissance-style buildings around the classical Low Library, whose monumental stone staircase has become a favorite warm-weather hangout for students. As Columbia expanded into a major research university, it overflowed its original four-block plan, creating tensions with the surrounding community. A stage for beatniks in the 1950's and student protests during the Vietnam War, Columbia has in recent years become a quieter place, both politically and culturally. Despite gentrification moving up the Upper West Side, the university's neighborhood—with its academic bookstores and antiquated coffee shops—maintains a certain detachment from the rest of the city. (*See chapter* **The Arts** *for Columbia University's* **Miriam and Ira Wallach Art Gallery** *and the* **Miller Theater**.)

Columbus Circle Broadway at Central Park South. At the southwest corner of Central Park, defined by wide avenues, open sky and the park, the traffic circle is well situated for civic grandeur. Yet it is filled with memorials to past schemes driven by self-interest. In the 1890's the city's growing Italian-American community outmaneuvered Spaniards to dedicate the statue of Christopher Columbus, which celebrates the 400th anniversary of the explorer's arrival in the New World. William Randolph Hearst financed the Maine Monument at the entrance to the park to commemorate the sinking of the ship that precipitated the Spanish-American War. As traffic increased, the circle began to look more like Times Square, with its large billboards and neon advertisements, than a Beaux-Arts pedestrian plaza. More recently, Donald Trump turned the former Gulf and Western building into a glitzy residential and hotel tower. The New York Coliseum was torn down in 2000.

Corpus Christi Church 529 W. 121st St. (between Broadway and Amsterdam Ave.) (212) 666-9266. Located in the heart of seminary country (Union Theological and Jewish Theological Seminaries are nearby) is Corpus Christi

Church, one of the many beautiful small churches that dot New York's neighborhoods. Built in the 1930's, this Roman Catholic church is the home of Music Before 1800, a highly acclaimed early-music series established in 1975, just before the period-instrument craze took the classical music world by storm. With its decorated ceiling and side galleries, intimate atmosphere and almost flawless acoustics, the 525-seat church is a wonderful setting for medieval, Renaissance and Baroque music.

The Dakota 1 W. 72nd St. (at Central Park West) (212) 874-8671. Located far uptown amid largely vacant lots when it was completed in 1884, the Dakota was said to be as remote as the Dakota Territory. An early luxury building in an era when rich New Yorkers had only just begun to move from town houses into apartments, the Dakota came equipped with steam-pumped elevators and ceilings that soar as high as 15 feet. In addition to John Lennon, who was fatally shot here in 1980, the building has housed a flock of arts and entertainment figures, including Leonard Bernstein and Lauren Bacall, and provided the setting for the movie *Rosemary's Baby*. During the building's recent restoration, the mute yellow brick lost its brown patina. With its steeply gabled roof and massive structures—features that Henry J. Hardenbergh, the architect, deployed in his later design for the Plaza Hotel—the Dakota stands like a fortress guarding the 72nd Street entrance to Central Park.

Grant's Tomb Riverside Dr. at 122nd St. (212) 666-1640 *www.nps.gov*. Quick! Who's buried in Grant's Tomb? Don't groan at the old joke. It is asked only because most people give the wrong answer, or at least an incomplete one.

Of course, the tomb contains the remains of Ulysses S. Grant, the great Civil War general and perhaps not-so-great 18th president. But many are unaware that next to him, in a matching sarcophagus of red granite, lies his wife, Julia Dent Grant. Grant, who died in 1885, had wanted to be buried at West Point, but his wife would not have been allowed to join him there. Thus he became the only president buried in New York City, in a neoclassical granite monument overlooking the Hudson.

For decades after its dedication in 1897, the tomb was among the most celebrated buildings in the country. Time dimmed its popularity. Over the years, the memorial deteriorated into a graffiti-scarred drug hangout, until finally in the 1990's the National Park Service gave it a much deserved face-lift. The cost was $1.8 million—three times what it took to build it.

Visitors are few. That is good news for anyone interested in a tranquil refuge, embodying Grant's epitaph, chiseled above the entrance: "Let us have peace."

—*Clyde Haberman*

Morningside Park Morningside Ave. (at 110th St.) (212) 360-1311. Morningside Park was built in 1887 atop the cliffs just to the east of the site, now occupied by Barnard College, where the Battle of Harlem Heights was fought in 1776. (A later battle over Columbia University's plans to build a gym in the park led to the student demonstrations and takeover of the campus in 1968.) The thin 31-acre park, which lies between Harlem and the Columbia campus, includes a concourse at the top of a tall stone wall built along Morningside Drive. The promontories on the concourse offer commanding views of spirited basketball and handball games in the courts below.

New-York Historical Society 2 W. 77th St. (between Columbus Ave. and Central Park West) (212) 873-3400 *www.nyhistory.org*. New York City's oldest museum in continuous operation, the society is an important institution for the study and preservation of the city's history and culture. The society's art collection includes landscape paintings by major artists from the Hudson River school of painters, 135 Tiffany lamps and one of the largest collections of miniature portraits in the country. The building also houses a highly regarded print collection with thousands of photographs, architectural drawings and ephemera (available by appointment only) and a research library with over two million manuscripts, 10,000 maps, and hundreds of photographs, prints and other materials. **Admission** (suggested): $5, adults; $3, students and seniors; children 12 and under, free.

Riverside Church Riverside Drive and 120th St. (Claremont Ave. and 121st St.) (212) 870-6700. Built in 1930 and modeled after the cathedral in Chartres, France, this mammoth Gothic-style church bordering Riverside Park has magnificent stonework and stained-glass windows. The church's nearly 400-foot tower has an observation deck affording spectacular views of the city and the Palisades across the Hudson. At $1 to ascend, it's a true bargain. Aside from vistas of the landscape, there are unique views inside of the peregrine falcons that have taken up residence, as well as a close-up look at the innards of the famous carillon, a gift of the Rockefeller family. (It has 74 bells—one weighing 20 tons—making it the world's largest.) You can hear it played every Sunday at 3 P.M. And though 120th Street is not on the maps of most theatergoers, the resident Melting Pot Theater is worth a visit. It seats about 270, has great sightlines, an ample stage and first-rate lighting and sound systems. The theater used to present dance and music events, but now focuses on plays and musicals generally geared toward a family audience.

Rose Center for Earth and Space 79th St. and Central Park West (212) 769-5100 *www.amnh.org/rose*. The $210 million Rose Center for Earth and Space opened in February 2000, offering visitors a virtual journey through time, space and the mysteries of the cosmos. The 333,500-square-foot, seven-floor, 120-foot-high exhibition and research facility includes the new Hayden Planetarium, the Cullman Hall of the Universe and the Gottesman Hall of Planet Earth. The Hayden Planetarium contains the Space Theater, presenting *Passport to the Universe*, and the Big Bang Theater, featuring narrated visual and audio effects simulating how the universe began. The Cullman Hall of the Universe is a 7,000-square-foot permanent exhibition hall on the bottom level of the Rose Center, divided into four zones that illustrate the processes that led to the creation of the planets, stars, galaxies and universe.

The domed Space Theater offers synthetic views of the cosmos far more detailed than the most elaborate Hollywood productions. With the help of a supercomputer, a state-of-the-art Zeiss star projector, an advanced laser system, a gigantic database and, of course, the hemispheric Space Theater itself, the builders have created a marvelous celestial playhouse. The Space Theater show is a spectacular virtual ride through the universe. The audience seated under the dome whizzes past Mars, Jupiter and Saturn and on toward the constellation Orion. The voice of Tom Hanks narrates along the way.

The sky show occupies the upper half of the center's 87-foot diameter sphere; the lower half is devoted to a very brief light and sound show depicting the Big Bang. Between the upper and lower levels of the Rose Center is a spiral walkway (reminiscent of the Guggenheim Museum) with a splendid gallery of 220 astronomical photographs.

The spiral ramp itself is one of many devices incorporated in the Rose Center to impart a sense of scale—in particular, an appreciation of the staggering dimensions of the universe. The length of the walkway, nearly 100 yards, represents a span of about 13 billion years, at the end of which is a single hair, the thickness of which represents the duration of human history. Some of the most interesting photographs along the walkway show the results of gravitational lensing, an effect not explained until we reach a little enclosure called the Black Hole Theater on the lowest level of the center, which gives viewers the flavor of relativity theory, of the genius of Einstein and of the bizarre distortions enormous masses cause in nearby space-time.

The Rose Center also contains curiosities, including a sealed ecosphere in which little crustaceans and various plants live isolated from the outer world, thriving on each other and the light that shines on their transparent globe, and the 15.5-ton Willamette Meteorite. Interactive television monitors are everywhere, and a remote-controlled robot entertains young visitors.

Hours: Sun.–Thu., 10 A.M.–5:45 P.M.; Fri. and Sat. until 8:45 P.M. Space shows run throughout the day. **Admission** (suggested): $10; for students and the elderly, $7.50; children 12 and under, $6; under 2 free. Admission to the museum, the Rose Center and the new Hayden Planetarium Space Show: $19; for students and the elderly, $14; children 12 and under, $11.50.

Highly Recommended Neighborhood Restaurants
(*See chapter* **Restaurants** *for reviews.*)

Calle Ocho	☆	$ $	PAN-LATIN
Gabriel's	☆ ☆	$ $ $	ITALIAN
Jean Georges	☆ ☆ ☆ ☆	$ $ $ $	NEW AMERICAN
Nick and Toni's	☆ ☆	$ $ $	MEDITERRANEAN
Picholine	☆ ☆ ☆	$ $ $ $	MEDITERRANEAN/ FRENCH
Ruby Foo's	☆ ☆	$ $	PAN-ASIAN

Recommended Inexpensive Restaurants

Alouette	BISTRO/FRENCH
Artie's	DELI

Hayden Planetarium/The New York Times

The Rose Center for Earth and Space

Avenue	BISTRO/FRENCH
Gabriela's	MEXICAN
Gennaro	ITALIAN/MEDITERRANEAN
Isola	ITALIAN
Josie's	NEW AMERICAN
Luzia's	PORTUGUESE
Metsovo	GREEK
Mughlai	INDIAN
Turkuaz	TURKISH/MIDDLE EASTERN

Harlem

The Harlem Renaissance of the 1920's brought the world the likes of
Langston Hughes, Countee Cullen, Dorothy West and Zora Neale Hurston.
The Harlem renaissance now under way is bringing the community the likes
of the Gap, a Disney store, Starbucks and ... Bill Clinton. It is an economic
blooming as sure as the literary one of generations ago. And visitors will find
plenty to satisfy their interest in both.

Harlem emerged in the 18th century as an upper Manhattan getaway for
wealthy downtowners, who gave way to a succession of immigrants—Jews,
Irish and, in the early 1900's, blacks, who turned it into the capital of black
America. Its exact boundaries are disputed; geography and emotion don't
always mix. But Harlem's history and legend indisputably resonate today, particularly among black Americans. In its heydey in the 1920's and 30's, jazz and

blues luminaries such as Ella Fitzgerald and Duke Ellington played long into the night at places like the Savoy and Cotton Club, now long gone. Langston Hughes gave poetry readings at the Harlem YMCA, one of the early cultural centers, and 125th Street bustled with the energy of any village main street.

Eventually, with the flight of the middle class and the scourge of drugs and crime, Harlem slid into a decay from which it is only now emerging. The middle and upper classes are moving back into its elegant brownstones and newer housing, and the neighborhood once again is growing into a popular tourist attraction.

The decision by Mr. Clinton to locate his post-presidential offices on the 14th floor of 55 West 125th St.—after causing an outcry by initially choosing more expensive digs near Carnegie Hall—was seen by many in the community as an affirmation of Harlem's rebirth. Mr. Clinton has already drawn throngs in his walks through the neighborhood, and has dined at Bayou, one of Harlem's newest, fine restaurants.

Indeed, other popular new restaurants such as Jimmy's Uptown, Sugar Shack and Amy Ruth's are drawing a racially mixed clientele, joining legendary mainstays like Charles' Southern Style Kitchen, offering what many consider the best soul food in the city. The **Lenox Lounge**, more than a half-century old and recently renovated, offers jazz, along with more intimate settings like **St. Nick's Pub** (see section "Popular Music Venues" in chapter **Nightlife**.)

All the change suits many residents just fine, but it has irked others who scoff at the rising rents and worry that gentrification will diminish Harlem's status as the capital of black America.

The most popular destination remains **125th Street**, the thriving main shopping strip. The **Apollo Theater** is the 86-year-old showplace where Billie Holiday, Aretha Franklin, Count Basie and many others graced the stage—and many more got the "hook" for disappointing feisty audiences. A weekly television variety program It's Showtime at the Apollo is produced there.

Famous places such as the Audubon Ballroom, where Malcolm X was assassinated in 1965, have disappeared. But many cultural and historic spots remain. The **Schomburg Center for Research on Black Culture**, the **Studio Museum** (see chapter **The Arts**) and the **National Black Theater** (212-722-3800) all have deep roots in the community and offer frequent exhibitions and shows that testify to the importance of black culture.

New development on 125th Street includes a 285,000-square-foot shopping mall called Harlem U.S.A., a nine-screen cinema, a Disney store, Old Navy and a branch of the New York Sports Club. One of the largest black booksellers in the nation plans to open Hue Man, a 4,000-square-foot store, on the street in the fall of 2001.

The new development has not reached much into nearby East Harlem, also worth a trek. **El Museo del Barrio**, a 30-year-old institution on Fifth Avenue at 104th Street (see chapter **The Arts**), is among the many finds. Its focus is the Hispanic culture that defines East Harlem.   —Randy Archibold

Subway: A, B, C, D, 2, 3 to 125th St.; B, C, 2, 3 to 135th St.; A, B, C, D, 3 to 145th St.

HIGHLIGHTS OF THE NEIGHBORHOOD

Abyssinian Baptist Church 132 W. 138th St. (between Adam Clayton Powell and Malcolm X Blvds.) (212) 862-7474. The Abysinnian Baptist Church has become such a popular attraction that it has had to turn away tourists on Easter. Known for its rousing gospel choir, this 1923 Gothic church was home for many years to rousing sermons by Adam Clayton Powell, the charismatic preacher and congressman. A memorial room displays artifacts from his life. Visit during Sunday services if you can, and afterward head over for a soul food lunch at Sylvia's nearby.

Hamilton Grange National Memorial 287 Convent Ave. (between. 141st and 142nd Sts.) (212) 283-5154. A quaint country house built in 1802 that was once the country home of Alexander Hamilton—the first U.S. Secretary of the Treasury. Hamilton lived in Hamilton Grange with his family for only two years until he was killed in his duel with Aaron Burr in 1804. Given landmark status decades ago, the Grange now stands amid busy streets near the City College campus. The house features an interpretative program planned around themes of drama, music and colonial craft, and activities for children.

The Project 427 W. 126th St. (bet. Morningside and Amsterdam Aves.) (212) 662-8610. This interesting new development in the Harlem contemporary art scene was started by the writer Christian Haye in 1999. The Project has brought an international roster of young artists from Europe, Asia, Africa and the United States to a cosmopolitan section of Manhattan. Recent exhibits have included work by Paul Pfeiffer, Tom Gidley and Martín Weber.

Schomburg Center for Research on Black Culture 515 Malcolm X Blvd. (at 135th St.) (212) 491-2200. The Schomburg Center's holdings are built on the personal collection of Arturo Alfonso Schomburg, a Puerto Rican black scholar and bibliophile who died in Brooklyn in 1938 at the age of 64. Schomburg's personal collection of materials was added to the Division of Negro Literature, History and Prints of the 135th Street branch of the New York Public Library in 1926. It became a research library of the Public Library system in 1972. The collection has grown to include more than five million items—books, manuscripts, art objects, audio, video and even sheet music—documenting the history and culture of people of African descent throughout the world.

Recommended Inexpensive Restaurants

*(See chapter **Restaurants** for reviews.)*

Amy Ruth's	SOUTHERN
Bayou	CAJUN/SOUTHERN
El Fogon	SPANISH
Emily's	SOUTHERN
Sylvia's	SOUTHERN

Washington Heights/Inwood

Dominican immigrants are only the latest arrivals in Washington Heights, an area that has been the first stop for many new Americans. In the early 1900's, the Irish poured into the area, especially to Inwood. In the period around World War II a large contingent of German Jews—including a young Henry Kissinger—made a home in the northern section near Fort Tryon Park.

Before the surge of immigration, Washington Heights was a rural retreat where the wealthy had country estates. It was this spaciousness that first attracted two major institutions: **Columbia-Presbyterian Hospital**, which opened in 1928, and **Yeshiva University**, which came in 1929. Other landmarks include the **Cloisters**, the Metropolitan Museum of Art's showcase for medieval art, which sits atop a hill in **Fort Tryon Park** and creates a sense of tranquility amid a noisy city. Long gone is the Polo Grounds, the former home of the baseball and football Giants, which overlooked the Harlem River at 157th Street.

At Manhattan Island's northernmost tip, the **Inwood** section lies between the Harlem River and **Inwood Hill Park**, where the borough's last stands of primeval forest remain. This neighborhood's newest arrivals are young professionals seeking affordable apartments in the Art Deco apartment buildings. On the banks of the Harlem River near Broadway, another dream lives on at **Baker Field**, where Columbia University's football team continues its often quixotic quest for glory.

Subway: A, C, 1, 9 make stops from 168th St.–Washington Heights uptown into Inwood.

HIGHLIGHTS OF THE NEIGHBORHOOD

American Academy of Arts and Letters 633 W. 155th St. (at Broadway) (212) 368-5900. Though often criticized for elitism, the American Academy of Arts and Letters has honored an impressive and unarguably free-thinking group of architects, artists, writers and composers since its founding in 1904. Located in adjacent Beaux-Arts buildings, the Academy's activities for nonmembers are limited, but you can visit the galleries, featuring works by honorees, members and others.

American Numismatic Society Broadway (at 156th St.) (212) 234-3130. Filthy lucre looks wholesome and interesting in "The World of Coins," a permanent exhibition chronicling the history of units of exchange, including cowrie shells, beads, paper money and credit cards. Some of the earliest coins ever found are here: crudely shaped knife pieces dating to 1000 B.C., from China. Among the many oddities on view are a bronze coin struck with an unflattering portrait of Cleopatra and a 1,000,000,000,000,000,000-pengo bill from the inflation-ridden Hungary of 1946.

Dyckman Farmhouse 4881 Broadway (at 204th St.) (212) 304-9422 One of the few reminders that Manhattan was once farmland is standing its

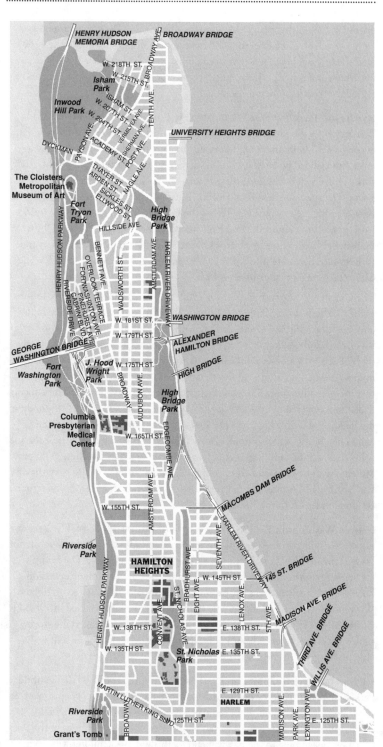

Upper Manhattan

ground at the northern tip of Manhattan. The existing Dyckman Farmhouse, with a Dutch-style gambrel roof and field stone walls, was rebuilt in the 1780's after the original house was destroyed during the Revolutionary War. The museum features five period rooms, a reconstructed German military hut and a reproduction of a kitchen smokehouse.

Fort Tryon Park 741 Fort Washington Ave. (at 193rd St.) (212) 360-1311. Best known as the site of the Metropolitan Museum's Cloisters, Fort Tryon Park encompasses Manhattan's highest point, Linden Terrace, 268 feet above sea level. Surrounded by 66 hilly, wooded acres north of Washington Heights, the park's promenades offer unsurpassed views of the Hudson River and the Palisades. The site once held Fort Tryon, a Revolutionary War fort captured by the British and named for William Tryon, the last British governor of New York. During the 19th century, several large mansions were built in the area. John D. Rockefeller Jr. hired Frederick Law Olmsted Jr., son of the designer of Central Park, to turn his estate into a park, which he donated to the city in 1930. The Cloisters opened there eight years later.

The Cloisters Fort Tryon Park (near 190th St.) (212) 923-3700. The Cloisters at the northern tip of Manhattan is one of New York's most remarkable museums. Set atop a hill in Fort Tryon Park with stunning views of the Hudson River, the Cloisters houses much of the Metropolitan Museum of Art's extensive collection of medieval art. The building combines architectural elements from medieval monasteries, cloisters and secular buildings, with a collection that includes illuminated manuscripts, stained glass and tapestries. The Unicorn Tapestries, woven around 1500, depict a popular medieval legend. Surrounding the building are sprawling gardens filled with plants with medieval-sounding names like bistort and mandrake. Opened in 1938, the majority of the Cloisters collection and the buildings themselves were purchased by the Metropolitan Museum with money donated by John D. Rockefeller Jr., who also gave the city Fort Tryon Park. **Admission** (suggested): $10, general; $5, students and seniors; children under 12, free. Closed Mondays.

George Washington Bridge Fort Washington Ave. at 178th St. The longest suspension bridge in the world when it opened in 1931, the George Washington Bridge remains New York City's only bridge across the Hudson. The bridge's towers were supposed to be sheathed in granite; as a result of the Depression, however, the steelwork was left exposed. They are now illuminated on holidays. With the postwar rise in automobile traffic, a lower level was added in 1962. Le Corbusier, the French proponent of modernist architecture, called the steel-cabled structure the most beautiful bridge in the world. "It is blessed. It is the only seat of grace in the disordered city," he said.

Highbridge Park 172nd St. and Amsterdam Ave. (212) 691-9510. Highbridge Park, designed in 1888 by Samuel Parsons Jr. and Calvert Vaux, begins in a thin spit called Coogan's Bluff that rises abruptly at West 155th Street and Edgecombe Avenue. In the swamps below, abutting the Harlem River, were the Polo Grounds, once home to the baseball and football Giants. Children who didn't have the price of admission could perch on the bluff and see part of the field. The southern zone of the park, stretching roughly 20 blocks uptown to the grand old High Bridge itself, was long impassable. But in 1997 the Parks Department began the arduous work of opening a trail along the route of the buried Croton Aqueduct. Three bridges—the Washington, the Hamilton and the pedestrian High Bridge—traverse the midpoint of the park within seven blocks. Rather than being a fatal incursion, the spans with their warren of access ramps lend to this stretch of park beneath them an extra dimension of drama.

If you build up an appetite during a Highbridge hike, a dining opportunity beckons at the south end of the park, below Coogan's Bluff on the Harlem River Drive at 158th Street: **Guagua Amarilla** (or **Yellow Bus**), a school bus transformed into a restaurant specializing in down-home Dominican fare.

Hispanic Society of America Broadway at 155th St. (212) 926-2234 *www.hispanicsociety.org.* The Hispanic Society of America, in its atmospheric shabby-genteel Beaux-Arts setting on Audubon Terrace, is filled with fabulous paintings by El Greco, Goya and Velásquez, as well as fine examples of decorative arts, sculpture and textiles. There are some amazing pieces, like a breathtaking 10th-century Hispano-Mooresque ivory box; the only comparable pieces of this kind locally are a few precious examples in the Met's collection. The Society also maintains a 250,000-volume research library (open to the public with photo ID) on all aspects of history and culture in Spain, Portugal, Latin America and the Philippines, as well as an extensive collection of rare books (contact the Society for viewing information).

Inwood Hill Park Seaman Ave. at 207th St. (212) 304-2381. The most dramatic approach to the park is from the north, along 218th Street, a five-minute walk from the 215th Street subway station on the No. 1 or 9 local. You will come upon a complex vista unlike any other in Manhattan. To the north, on your right, is the Harlem River on its final leg before joining the Hudson in the swirl of Spuyten Duyvil. The sheer cliff on the far side, threaded at its base by Metro North tracks, defines Marble Hill, its heights studded with ungainly apartment buildings. Straight ahead is a tidal lagoon. Bordered by swamp grasses, it is the only accessible salt marsh in Manhattan and a magnet for water birds. Off to the left are low rolling athletic fields where soccer is the favored sport. Straight ahead, Inwood Hill itself juts into Spuyten Duyvil, which is spanned by the Henry Hudson Bridge to the Bronx, its steel gridwork painted bright blue. Beyond that is the low-slung Amtrak bridge, part of the shoreline route to Albany. The final piece of this complex tableau is the noble New Jersey Palisades, looming up a mile away across the Hudson. Before heading into the forest, stop first at the park's ecology center on the lagoon. You can pick up a map and a schedule of tours led by urban park rangers all year. They even offer canoe expeditions.

Morris-Jumel Mansion 65 Jumel Terrace (at 161st St.) (212) 923-8008. In the midst of a citified neighborhood scenically situated on a high bluff, a delightful enclave suddenly opens up to the wanderer. In its center is a columned, white, two-story house, all peaks and gables, in a verdant acre-and-a-

The George Washington Bridge

half setting of greenery. The Georgian-Federal mansion was built in the 1760's as a summer home by Roger Morris, a Tory who left during the Revolution. George Washington made it his headquarters in 1776 as his troops were being driven from the city. During that retreat he made the troops bite back in the Battle of Harlem Heights, in July 1776, when the British actually gave ground to the Americans. The mansion's name also recognizes a later occupant, Stephen Jumel, a wine merchant whose widow, Eliza, married Aaron Burr in the front parlor in 1833. The mansion's eight rooms, furnished in old-style elegance, are open for public visits.

Admission: $3, general; $2, students. **Hours:** Wed.–Sun., 10 A.M.–4 P.M.

Trinity Cemetery Amsterdam Ave. (at W. 153rd St.). Spread across a sloping hillside between Amsterdam Avenue and Riverside Drive from West 153rd to West 155th Streets, Trinity Cemetery was opened in 1843 after a series of epidemics left the congregation's Wall Street churchyard dangerously overcrowded. Many of New York's most prominent citizens ended up on this rocky promontory, which overlooks the Hudson River and the New Jersey Palisades. As soon as you pass through the tall, wrought-iron gates on West 153rd Street, the roar of Broadway is eclipsed by the cawing of ravens. A century-old canopy of ash and oak trees keeps the grounds appropriately shaded and somber. Trinity's monuments are richly varied in material, form and symbolism. Look for broken columns (died in the prime of life), sheaves of wheat (lived to a ripe old age), polished spheres and shrouded urns (symbols of the soul). There are Gothic-style marble mausoleums, towering steles of brownstone and simple slabs that conceal spacious subterranean vaults. Among those buried at Trinity are John Jacob Astor, the philanthropist; John Audubon, the naturalist, and Clement Clarke Moore, who wrote "A Visit From St. Nicholas."

Yeshiva University Museum 2520 Amsterdam Ave. (between 185th and 186th Sts.) (212) 960-5390. Begun in 1886 as an elementary yeshiva for Orthodox Jewish boys, the school expanded during the early 1900's to include a theological seminary and the first Orthodox Jewish high school in the United States. Yeshiva College, with its campus in Washington Heights, was formed in 1929, and in 1946 it was incorporated as a university. The museum features exhibits and cultural artifacts relating to Jewish history as well as some secular art. **Admission:** $6, general; $4, seniors and students; children under 5 free.

Recommended Inexpensive Restaurant

El Presidente   CARIBBEAN/PAN-LATIN

CENTRAL PARK

The miracle of Central Park is partly that it exists at all, but even more that it exists smack in the middle of a huge, throbbing city. The very incongruity of its charms—rolling meadows, jagged cliffs, graceful bridges and more than 26,000 trees—is what takes your breath away.

Central Park almost didn't happen. If the land had not been snapped up by City Fathers in the early 1850's, Manhattan would have quickly and inexorably become a single rectilinear street grid. Central Park was America's first major public park to be designed and built, as opposed to simply preserving nature. Frederick Law Olmsted and Calvert Vaux planned each square foot of the 843-acre park to create the effects of nature. A fake waterfowl here. A shrub placed there for almost painterly reasons. The goal was *rus in urb,* country in the city.

Olmsted and Vaux created an illusion of immense size by curving paths, carefully composed vistas and other landscaping techniques. From no point in the park can one see side to side or end to end. Illusion becomes reality. Not for nothing are the park's founders sometimes called precursors to Disney.

For the visitor, the best place to get an idea of the designers' intent is to go to the **Ramble**, a 38-acre "wild garden" in Olmsted's words. The Ramble is located in the middle of the park between 73rd and 79th Streets and except for the underlying bedrock is a completely artificial creation. Paths twist and turn through the brush and there are scenic overlooks and rustic log structures. A tumbling stream called the Gill gurgles coolly by.

The Ramble is one of the many great places for birdwatching in Central Park, a major stop along the Atlantic flyway. More than 275 species, from rare owls to hummingbirds have been spotted there. One of the park's more fascinating curiosities is located at the **Loeb Boathouse**, on the east side of the park between 74th and 75th Streets, where birders record their sightings in a loose-leaf notebook that visitors are welcome to examine or add to. The Boathouse is located at the eastern entrance to the Ramble, where volunteers raise wildflowers to attract butterflies. So far 26 species have been spotted.

The Boathouse is on a 20-acre lake, the largest of seven bodies of water in the park. You can rent rowboats for $10 an hour ($30 deposit); a gondola for $30 an hour (seats six) or bikes for $14 for a tandem or $6 for a children's bike. It is one of the real pleasures of New York City to row in the shimmering duck-filled lake, marveling at the graceful cast iron Bow Bridge used in many movies, in the shadow of grand apartment buildings and skyscrapers.

But the best things in Central Park are free, and not just the obvious ones. One of the visual delights of the park, **Belvedere Castle**, a Gothic fantasy, contains a nature center where would-be naturalists can borrow backpacks that contain binoculars, a bird guide and other reference material and notepaper. At the **Charles A. Dana Discovery Center**, a beautifully restored nature center on **Harlem Meer** at the northeast corner of the park, 50 bamboo fishing rods are lent out free of charge to fish for (and release) catfish, bluegills and other fish. Bait is also provided, either night crawlers or biscuit dough.

Central Park is a fabulous place for kids. The zoo in the southeast corner, with its underwater view of swimming polar bears—and adjacent children's zoo where kids can pet a Vietnamese pot-bellied pig—is worth a leisurely couple of hours. The **carousel** (mid-park at 64th St.) is the fourth generation of its genre—the first was turned by a blind mule and a horse—and whirls at a briskly invigorating pace. Nearby at 66th Street and the East Drive, the statue of Balto, the sled dog who took medicine to Nome, Alaska, to squelch a diphtheria epidemic, has been polished by generations of loving, fascinated hands.

But there are also elements clearly for adults, and not just the **Tavern on the Green** restaurant with its fabulous Harvest Wild Mushroom Soup, among other treats. (You can also sip wine and dine elegantly in a restaurant at Loeb Boathouse, or go to the well-appointed snack bar there—or, more likely grab a hot dog for $1.50 from any of scores of vendors in the park.) Adults will also be drawn to the **Mall** on the east side between 66th and 69th Streets, where the elegant elm trees and lines of benches feel like Paris, especially in winter. The rougher terrain in the northern reaches of the park, with its pond and waterfall and outcroppings of 450-million-year-old Manhattan schist rock, are also best traversed by adults, or perhaps adults accompanied by children.

There is so much else of interest in Central Park: the elegant **Conservatory Garden** at Fifth Avenue and 105th Street with its French, Italian and English floral treatments; the **Shakespeare Garden** on the west side between 79th and 80th Streets composed entirely of plant species mentioned by the Bard, including a red mulberry said to be taken from Shakespeare's mother's garden; and, of course, **Strawberry Fields** on the west side between 71st and 74th Streets, built in memory of John Lennon by Yoko Ono. At its center is a mosaic, impressed with the world "Imagine," from a Lennon song. There are always fresh flowers and personal notes.

And don't forget the **Naturalist's Walk**, a walk along the park's west side that celebrates biodiversity. Or the **Egyptian Obelisk** (east side at 81st St.), a 71-foot-tall stone needle that dates back to 1500 B.C. Or the **Pond** at the southeastern entrance, where J.D. Salinger's Holden Caulfield watched the ducks.

But the heart and soul of the park lay in the large places where people can come together and play ball, picnic and sunbathe—all kinds of people from all kinds of circumstances, exercising the democratic vision of parks so audaciously pioneered by Olmsted and Vaux. These are the **Sheep Meadow** on the west side of the park between 66th and 69th Streets, and the **Great Lawn** in mid-park between 79th and 86th Streets. You can fly kites, throw Frisbees, stare into a lover's eyes and sip from a bottle of wine. Just be prepared for these pristine areas being at least partly closed, if there has been recent rain. These are the true backyards of New York City.

A last thought, which might well be a visitor's first. **The Central Park Conservancy**, which since 1980 has raised millions to restore and improve the park, runs a visitor's center in what was once the **Dairy**, which originally dispensed glasses of free milk. It is on the East Side at 65th Street. You can get directions, brochures and see exhibits that include a flip map showing how the park was built from the original landforms. —*Douglas Martin*

Transportation: West side of park: A, B, C, D, 1, 9 to 59th St.-Columbus Circle or any B/C subway stop or M10 bus stop between 59th and 110th Sts. East side of park: N, R, W to Fifth Ave. at 59th St.; any 4, 5, 6 subway or M1, 2, 3, 4 bus stop between 59th and 110th Sts.

Tours

Carriage Rides Central Park South (212) 246-0520. These rides are a romantic idea, but the reality—high prices, itchy blankets and the smell of manure—is rarely so perfect. Still, for some, this is an essential New York experience. Buggy rides are available year round, with fewer carriages operating in very cold and very hot weather. **Prices:** $35, 20 minutes; $10 each additional 15 minutes.

Central Park Bicycle Tour (212) 541-8759. These guided tours hit major park locations like Belvedere Castle, Jacqueline Kennedy Onassis Reservoir, and Strawberry Fields. Prices include bicycle rental. The Central Park Movie Scenes Bike Tour is also available at 2 P.M., weekends. **Prices:** $35 adults, $20 children. **Schedule:** Tours depart every day at 10 A.M., 1 P.M., and 4 P.M.

Park Attractions

The Arsenal 64th St. and Fifth Ave. Originally built in 1848, the Arsenal is one of only two buildings in Central Park that were built before the park existed. This imposing structure resembles a medieval castle, with many architectural and artistic touches added over the years inside and out. It's worth visiting for its Depression-era murals and art exhibits focused on New York or Central Park. It also houses Olmsted and Vaux's original "Greensward Plan" for the park. This landmark building is now the headquarters of New York City's Dept. of Parks and Recreation and the Central Park Wildlife Conservation Center. **Hours:** Mon.–Fri., 9 A.M.–5 P.M.

Balto East Drive at 66th St. This is one of the most sought-out sites in the park, and is the only park statue commemorating an animal. Balto was a heroic Siberian husky who braved a blizzard to bring diptheria antitoxin to Nome, Alaska; he was also the subject of a popular animated film. Created by Frederick George Richard Roth in 1925, Balto sports a golden back and snout, the patina and outer layer of bronze rubbed off by fingers, noses and backsides of thousands of worshipful children.

Belvedere Castle Mid-park at 79th St. This impressive Victorian structure, perched atop the highest natural point in the park, was occupied by the U.S. Weather Bureau from 1919 to the early 1960's, then fell into disrepair until the new Conservancy restored and reopened it in 1982. The site now offers good views of the park—especially Delacorte Theater, the Great Lawn, and the Turtle Pond—as well as excellent bird-watching. It also houses the Henry Luce Nature Observatory, where visitors can explore the plants and animals of the park through interactive exhibits. Also available are backpacks with information and binoculars to help budding scientists study the nearby Ramble or Turtle Pond (available Tue.–Sun., 10 A.M.–5 P.M.).

Bethesda Terrace and Fountain Mid-park at 72nd St. Olmsted and Vaux wanted nature to dominate the scene, but they did propose an architectural "heart of the park" overlooking the Lake. The split-level Terrace, decorated with detailed carvings of plants and animals, is one of the most popular areas of the park, affording gorgeous views of the Mall, the Lake, the Ramble, and all the human activity around the plaza. Bethesda Fountain itself, possibly the most-photographed monument in Central Park, commemorates the opening the Croton Aqueduct in 1842. It was the only sculpture called for in the original park plan, and its creator, Emma Stebbins, was the first woman to be commissioned to produce a major piece of public art in the city.

Central Park Wildlife Center East Side, 63rd-66th St. (212) 861-6030. Generations of New Yorkers have grown up with the Central Park Zoo. The oldest zoo in the city began in the 1860's as a menagerie to house animals given to the park, but has since been renovated many times and rechristened as the Central Park Wildlife Conservation Center. Divided into three zones—Arctic, rain forest and temperate—the center features animals in naturalistic settings. Its emphasis on public education is evident in the newly remodeled **Tisch Children's Zoo**, in which interactive nature exhibits have replaced kitschy storybook characters. Admission to the children's zoo is included in the general admission price, but make sure you bring along an extra pocketful of quarters for the feed dispensers. Kids love to feed the goats, cows and potbellied pigs. Parents will also want to check on sea lion, polar bear and penguin feeding times—all of which provide a fascinating spectacle for kids and adults. The beloved **George Delacorte Musical Clock**, between the Wildlife Center and the Children's Zoo, draws crowds on the hour and half-hour when a menagerie of motorized animals circle the clock to nursery-rhyme tunes.

Admission: $3.50, adults; $1.25, seniors; $.50, children 3–12; children under 3, free. There are no group rates. **Hours:** Open 365 days a year, 10 A.M. until 5 P.M. on weekdays and 10:30 A.M.–5:30 P.M. weekends and holidays April-Oct; 10 A.M. until 4:30 P.M.. daily Nov-March. **Services:** Cafeteria, gift shop, handicapped accessible.

Chess and Checkers House East Side at 65th St. This is the park's largest and most ornate wooden summer house. Playing pieces for the 24 indoor and outdoor tables here can be borrowed from the Dairy, and children's chess lessons are offered by the Central Park Conservancy in the summer.

The Concert Ground Mid-park, 69th-72nd St. (212) 360-2756. Music, theater, and dance performances are occasionally held at the neoclassical limestone **Naumberg Bandshell**, but strict regulations keep the number of shows down. Behind the shady Wisteria Pergola to the east of the bandshell, **Rumsey Playfield** plays host to **SummerStage**, a series of free rock concerts and opera performances, held June-August each year.

Conservatory Garden East Side, 104th-106th Sts. One of Central Park's best-kept secrets, these six acres of horticultural magnificence are tucked away behind the wrought iron gates that once served as the entrance to the Vanderbilt mansion at Fifth Avenue and 58th Street. This is the only formal garden in the park, with trees, flowers, statues and fountains spread throughout three very different sub-gardens. To the north is a French-style garden, with concentric rings of flowers around a central fountain. Favorite sights here are the massive displays of tulips in the spring, chrysanthemums in the fall, and white roses in the summer. The central area is done in an Italian style, with a carefully tended central lawn and a simple fountain. The southern portion of the garden was created in an English style, and may be the most popular of the three. This may be due to the statuary fountain here, featuring characters from the children's book, *The Secret Garden*.

Conservatory Water East Side,72nd–75th St. The name of this popular pond comes from the conservatory, or greenhouse, that was meant to be built nearby. Most park patrons know it as the boat pond, because of the numerous model ships floating in it on most good days. The **Kerbs Memorial Boathouse**, on the east side of the pond, rents out boats and sells refreshments beside a large patio. Other popular attractions are the red-tailed hawk watchers on the southwest edge of the pond and several statues along the pathways around the pond. In the summer, storytellers can often be found near the statue of **Hans Christian Andersen** to the west of the pond, and children love to climb on the **Alice in Wonderland** statue to the north.

The Andersen statue is also the best vantage point for one of the park's most remarkable wildlife dramas. For years, a pair of red-tailed hawks have been nesting on the 12th-floor ledge of a building just across from the pond, at Fifth Avenue and 74th Street. One most weekends, hawk watchers bring in telescopes and offer all passersby close-up views of the nest.

The Dairy East Side at 65th St. During 19th-century "milk scandals" and diphtheria outbreaks, this Swiss-Gothic hybrid cottage served as a distribution center for fresh milk brought in from farms outside New York. It now serves as Central Park's Visitor Information Center and Recreation Building. The Dairy houses exhibits and information about the park, including an excellent flip map documenting the changes wrought on the landscape during park construction, as well as before-and-after photographs of the area.

Hours: Tue.–Sun. 10 A.M.–5 P.M. (Closes 4 P.M. in winter.)

Charles A. Dana Discovery Center Mid-park at 110th St. Central Park's newest building, on the north shore of Harlem Meer at the top of the park, offers general park information, conducts nature classes, showcases community projects and art, and loans out poles for catch-and-release fishing in the Meer (available Tue.–Sun., 10 A.M.–4 P.M. from April-Oct.). A deck outside the Center looks out over the Meer to the south, and an outdoor plaza, bordered by trees, hosts concerts and special public events throughout the year. Call for dates and times of the Harlem Meer Performance Festival (May-Sept.) or Dancing on the Plaza (Thursday evenings in August).

Hours: Tue.–Sun. 10 A.M.–5 P.M. (until 4 P.M. in winter).

Delacorte Theatre Mid-park at 80th St. (SW corner of Great Lawn) (212) 539-8655. For over 30 years, the Delacorte has offered free "Shakespeare in the Park" performances in July and August. With Belvedere Castle looming nearby, the Turtle Pond to the east, and the Great Lawn across a path to the north, an evening at the theater in Central Park can be unforgettable. New Yorkers and tourists line up for hours to get tickets, which are distributed at 1 P.M. the day of the performance (limit two per person). Tickets are also available from the Joseph Papp Public Theater at 425 Lafayette Street, near Astor Place.

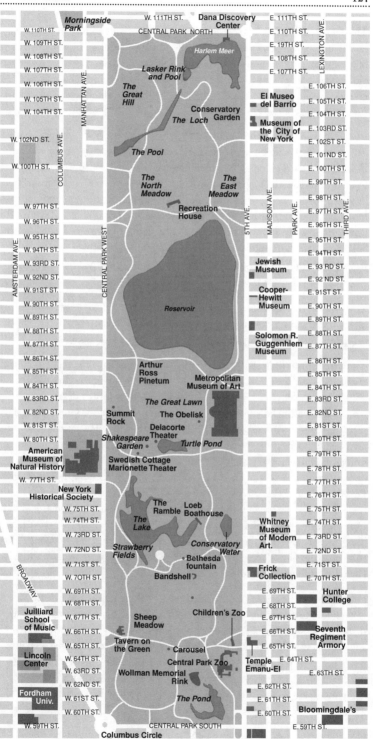

Central Park

The Dene East Side, 66th-72nd St. Running between the Zoo and Conservatory Water, the Dene (which means "valley") is a peaceful, rolling landscape lined with shady trees and flowers. At the southern end, visitors can explore an old wooden shelter known as the Summerhouse. To the north of the Dene, a meadow called the East Green has been restored to its original, pristine condition, after years of use as a cricket field.

The Friedsam Memorial Carousel 65th St. Transverse and Central Drive. This is one of the largest merry-go-rounds in America, with 58 horses and two chariots. It's not the original carousel, however: the first was supposedly driven by a horse and a blind mule; this was replaced by a steam-powered carousel that burned down, as did its replacement in 1950. The present historic carousel was rescued from Coney Island by the Parks Department. It was built in 1908 by the firm of Stein and Goldstein, respected carvers from Brooklyn. Today the quaint building and calliope music draw over 250,000 riders per year.
Price: $.90, adults; $.50, children. **Hours:** Apr.-Nov. 10 A.M.–6 P.M.; Nov.-Apr. 10 A.M.–4:30 P.M., weather permitting.

The Great Hill West Side, 103rd-107th St. This green field offers picnic tables, a soft-surface walking or jogging path, and, in August, the "Great Jazz on the Great Hill" concert organized by the Central Park Conservancy.

The Great Lawn Mid-park, 79th–86th St. Today the Lawn is one of the most popular areas of the Park, but until 1934 this was the site of the Croton Reservoir. When the city's water supply changed, the reservoir became obsolete. It was filled in with rubble from city construction to become the Great Lawn, a pond and two playgrounds. These 13 acres of grass, with eight softball fields, are used for all manner of private and public functions, especially after a massive restoration project in the mid-1990's. The Great Lawn has been the site of some of New York's largest outdoor events, including Paul Simon's 1991 concert and Pope John Paul II's 1995 Mass (which drew 600,000 and 350,000 people, respectively); it also plays host to annual summer concerts by the Metropolitan Opera and the New York Philharmonic. All this use takes its toll, however, so the rules here are strict these days: no dogs, no bicycles, permits are required for ball games, and it is open only when the Keeper of the Great Lawn feels the lawn can handle public use.

Harlem Meer East Side, 106th–110th St. A walking tour of the 11-acre Meer (Dutch for "small sea") takes in an impressive array of plants and wildlife, including some impressive oak, beech and gingko trees. The formerly fenced-off edge of the Meer has been restored to a more natural state, including a small sandy beach near the Charles A. Dana Discovery Center. At the southeast corner of the Meer, follow some steps to the water, where you will find yourself completely surrounded by flowers, with a private view of the water.

The Lake Mid-park, 71st-78th St. After the Reservoir, this is the largest body of water in Central Park. Its meandering shoreline offers many sights and attractions, from the wisteria arbor in the south and Bow Bridge, the beautiful span in the center of the Lake, to the ornate Ladies' Pavilion on its northwest shore. Some of these sights may be best viewed from one of the rowboats available for rental at the Loeb Boathouse, at the northeastern edge of the Lake.

Hernshead West Side, 75th–76th St. Hernshead Landing, located just to the south along the Lake's edge, is a rocky promontory that is supposed to resemble a heron's head—hence the name, from an old English pronunciation of "heron." The Ladies' Pavilion, a cast iron structure originally built to shelter horsecar passengers, sits in the middle of Hernshead, and a mass of rocks at the eastern end offers good views of the lake and opportunities for climbing.

Loeb Boathouse East Side, 74th–75th Sts. The original Vaux-designed wooden building burned down long ago, but the current Loeb Boathouse has become a hub of park activity. The restaurant, **Park View at the Boathouse**, is a romantic, two-star favorite; more casual dining is possible at an outside cafe. Energetic visitors can rent bicycles and rowboats, while those in search of more relaxation can take a ride in a genuine Venetian gondola. Bird watchers come here to enter their sightings in the Bird Register, a large notebook stored in the Boathouse. And the Conservancy has installed a small wildflower garden, meant to attract butterflies, to the west of the Boathouse entrance.

Bike Rental: (212) 861-4137. Hourly rates from $6 for children to $14 for tandem bikes. March-Oct., 9 A.M.–5 P.M. **Rowboat Rental:** (212) 517-2233. $10 per hour with $30 refundable deposit. mid-April-mid-October 10 A.M.-one hour before dusk. **Gondola Rental:** (212) 517-2233. $30 per half hour (gondolas seat six). March-mid-Oct. 5:30–10 P.M.

Lasker Rink and Pool Mid-park, 108th–109th St. (212) 534-7639. As the name suggests, this facility offers skating in the winter on two oval rinks and free swimming in the summer. It occupies an area that was once part of the Harlem Meer. In fact, nearby Duck Island was created to replace an island formerly on the Lasker site, serving as a protected home to some of the Meer's flora and fauna.

Skating rinks: Admission: $3, adults; $1.50, children and seniors. **Skate rental:** $3.50. **Dates:** Nov.-Apr. **Hours:** Mon-Thurs 10 A.M.–3 P.M.; Fri 10 A.M.–2 P.M., 5 P.M.–9 P.M.; Sat 11 A.M.–10 P.M.; Sun. 11 A.M.–6 P.M.

Pool: Admission: Free. **Dates:** July 1-Labor Day. **Hours:** seven days a week, 11 A.M.–7 P.M.

Lawn Sports Center West Side at 69th St. (North of Sheep Meadow). Visitors can play croquet or lawn bowling on two tiny lawns from May 1st to October 1st. The New York Croquet Club (212-369-7949) offers free clinics on Tuesday nights and tournaments on weekends; the New York Lawn Bowling club (212-289-3245) also offers free lessons and regular club games.

The Mall (Literary Walk) Mid-park, 69th–72nd St. Four long rows of American elms, often the first park stop for spring warblers, form a cathedral-like canopy over the Mall. This grand promenade is one of only two formal elements remaining from Olmsted and Vaux's original park design (the other is Bethesda Fountain), and it contains many of the park's best-known sculptures. Among them are William Shakespeare, Robert Burns, Victor Herbert, Beethoven and Christopher Columbus. At the southern end of the walk is a nonsculptural tribute to Frederick Law Olmsted—a memorial flower garden surrounded by American elms.

Merchants' Gate and Maine Monument Southeast Park Entrance (Columbus Circle). Most of the original entrances to the park were dedicated to different professions, and Olmsted and Vaux insisted on very modest designs for the gates. Over time, however, the city added striking military monuments to the entrances along Central Park South, including this massive pylon commemorating the sinking of the battleship *Maine* in 1898. The monument honors the Americans killed in the Spanish-American War, and was partially funded with pennies and nickels collected from schoolchildren after the war. The Conservancy renovated the area around the gate in 1997, creating a well-lit public plaza with decorative paving and a seating wall.

Naturalists' Walk West Side, 77th–81st St. This landscape was restored with the nearby American Museum of Natural History in mind: a dramatic variety of flowers, plants and trees have been introduced to this area, attracting birds and butterflies and making it a natural destination after exploring the museum's Hall of Biodiversity and other exhibits.

The North Meadow Mid-Park, 97th–102nd St. This is the largest grassy space in Central Park, divided only by 12 fields for baseball, softball and soccer. Inside the landmark **North Meadow Recreation Center**, the park Conservancy offers a wide range of programs for children, from computer-based education to more physical activities. Any visitor with a photo ID can borrow one of the Center's Field Day kits, containing play items like balls, Frisbees and jump ropes (available Mon.–Fri., 9 A.M.–7 P.M., Sat.–Sun., 10 A.M.–6 P.M.).

The Obelisk (Cleopatra's Needle) East Side at 81st St. This 3,500-year-old stone obelisk was erected behind the Metropolitan Museum on January 22, 1881 after being uprooted from the city of Heliopolis, making a tumultuous ocean crossing, and crawling through the streets of Manhattan for four months. It remains the oldest man-made object in the park. Each corner is supported by a several hundred pound bronze replica of a sea crab—the originals of which are in the Met's Sackler Wing.

The Jacqueline Kennedy Onassis Reservoir Mid-park, 85th–96th St. Until 1991, this 106-acre body of water still provided water to parts of Manhattan and the Bronx; now three huge tunnels bring water from upstate New York, but the Reservoir remains a good spot for jogging, bird watching and observing the city skyline. The New York Road Runners Club (which organizes the New York City Marathon) holds weekly races on the 1.58-mile track, which is especially beautiful when the ornamental cherry trees bloom in the spring. Also worth a look are three elegant cast-iron pedestrian bridges that span the Bridle Trail, and three Vaux-designed gatehouses containing water-flow controlling and treatment equipment.

The Pond Southeast corner of park. Once an area of foul swampland, this is now one of the most attractive parts of Central Park, well shielded from street noise by trees and rocks. The small fenced-in area here is the Hallett Nature Sanctuary—four acres of park left untended, creating a haven for animals (like woodchucks, rabbits and raccoons) and plants (including Black Cherry trees and many wildflowers). An excellent view of the Pond is available from Gapstow Bridge at the northern end of the Pond, or from the Cop Cot (Scottish for "little house on the crest of the hill"), near the Sixth Avenue park entrance.

The Pool West Side, 100th–103rd St. This body of water is a romantic place, sheltered by weeping willows and an impressive assortment of other tree species. A small peninsula on the south shore is a good spot for duck feeding or for viewing the Pool's foliage.

The Ramble Mid-park, 73rd–79th St. It's hard to believe that this 38-acre sprawl of pathways, streams, cliffs and trees is entirely man-made—meticulously designed by Frederick Law Olmsted and carved out of a natural hillside. This may be the easiest place to get lost in Central Park, so entering with a map is advised. But the opportunity to lose yourself and escape from the crush of city life has also made it one of the most popular destinations in the park, a fact that has in turn led to an ongoing need for restoration. What many people don't know is that this is also one of the best sites for bird watching in the country, ranked among the top 15 by the Audubon Society. Over 200 different species of birds have been seen here; the best time for birding is during spring and fall migration, in April and May and again in September and October.

The Ravine Mid-park, 102nd–106th St. Stretching from the southern end of Lasker Rink to the Pool just above West 100th St., the Ravine is a peaceful destination filled with wildflowers, bird watching trails, and odd and beautiful bridges. One of the most impressive of these is Huddlestone Arch, a careful assemblage of rough boulders fitted together without any mortar or other binding material.

Arthur Ross Pinetum Mid-park, 84th–86th St. This collection of 20 species of pine tree (plus elms and oaks) is the largest collection of evergreens in Central Park. Walking tours of the Pinetum are available starting at nearby Belvedere Castle, including a popular seasonal tour in early December. Birdwatchers also come here to spot owls in the pines, and there is a small playground that finds more use as a quiet picnic spot.

Shakespeare Garden West Side, 79th–80th St. Once an extension of the Ramble, this area was dedicated to Shakespeare on the tricentennial of his death in 1916. This meandering, four-acre garden showcases about half of the 200 plants mentioned in the Bard's works, including a mulberry tree said to be grown from a cutting from Shakespeare's mother's garden. Bronze plaques provide the quotations relevant to each plant.

Sheep Meadow Mid-park, 66th–69th St. This 15-acre meadow was an actual grazing field for sheep until the 1930's, when the sheep were shipped out and their building became the Tavern on the Green restaurant. In the 1960's and 70's the field suffered severe damage from sporting activities, concerts and hippie be-ins. But since the 1980's, the Park Conservancy has exercised strict control over meadow visitors. On warm summer days, this rolling lawn still attracts thousands of walkers, sunbathers and people-watchers. Radios, team sports and dogs are prohibited, but often show up anyway. Just outside the northern fence is Lilac Walk, lined with 23 varieties of lilac. The Meadow is open mid-April to mid-October, dawn to dusk in fair weather.

Strawberry Fields West Side, 72nd St. The landscaping of this area was made possible by Yoko Ono, who presented it to the city in memory of John Lennon, who was murdered outside the nearby Dakota apartment house in 1980. There aren't many strawberries here, but there is an incredible variety of plants and trees, all donated by countries around the world, forming what a plaque calls a "Garden of Peace." Over 161 species of plants, representing the countries of the United Nations, have been introduced to the park here, but most visitors come to view a gift from the city of Naples, Italy: a mosaic with the word "Imagine" at its center.

Summit Rock West Side, 81st–85th St. At 137.5 feet, this is the highest point in Central Park. An ampitheater overlooks the south and east slopes, and a path leads up the southern slope to a beautiful green lawn that affords good views of the park and the Upper West Side. This and adjacent areas of Central Park were home to 5,000 New Yorkers before the city purchased the land and began park construction. At the time, there were nearly a thousand buildings on the land, including factories and churches. Seneca Village occupied this territory in the mid-1800s; this was one of the best-known African-American communities in New York, composed mostly of free, black, land-owning families.

Swedish Cottage Marionette Theater West Side at 79th St.
(212) 988-9093. Originally built for the 1876 Centennial Exposition in Philadelphia and used variously over the years as a storage shed, public toilets, an entomological laboratory and a Civil Defense headquarters, this replica of a 19th-century Swedish schoolhouse now hosts performances of children's stories, birthday parties and other events year-round. The theater seats 100 children and features central air-conditioning and a state-of-the-art stage. This is also the headquarters of the Citywide Puppets in the Parks program.
Suggested donation: Adults, $5; children, $4.

Turtle Pond Mid-park, 79th–80th St. When the old Croton Reservoir was filled in with construction debris in the 1930's, becoming the Great Lawn, the southern end became Belvedere Lake. It quickly attracted a wide range of aquatic life and the site was rechristened in honor of some of its more popular inhabitants in 1987. A 1997 renovation altered the pond's shoreline, added new plants and introduced Turtle Island, a new habitat for the turtles and birds that make their home here. A dock and nature blind offer great views of the pond and its denizens sunning themselves on dead tree trunks.

Wollman Memorial Skating Rink East Side at 62nd St. To appreciate the beauty and calm of Central Park, head to the 33,000-square-foot Wollman Rink, near the park entrance at Sixth Avenue and Central Park South. Wollman also offers classes and guided tours around the park. After ice skating in the winter or rollerblading in the summer, you can relax on the terrace, patio or at the rink's cafe. During the spring and summer months, most patrons are tourists and novice skaters. Compared to the lanes in the park, the rink is fairly uncrowded, leaving plenty of skating room for New Yorkers.

Sports in Central Park
(*See also chapter* **Sports & Recreation**.)

Baseball/Softball. The North Meadow has baseball diamonds. The Great Lawn has seven softball fields; five more are at the Heckscher Ballfields. Arsenal West (16 W. 61st St.) is the place to go for permits, or call (212) 408-0226 for information.

Biking. Stick to the roads: park security may confiscate your bike if you ride on walkways or trails. Rental bikes are available near Loeb Boathouse, at 74th St. and the East Drive. Call (212) 861-4137.

Boating. Rowboats and gondolas can be rented at the Loeb Boathouse (call 212-517-2233 or see above for details).

Fishing. The Dana Discovery Center loans out poles and bait for catch-and-release fishing; fishing in the Lake is permitted, but may become more restricted in the future following the poisoning of some birds.

Horseback Riding. Horse rentals and riding lessons are available at the Claremont Riding Academy at 175 W. 89th St.; call (212) 724-5100 for information. The park's bridle path runs around the Reservoir and northern quadrant of the park, and down the west side to 60th St.

Ice Skating. Available November through March at Wollman (212-396-1010) and Lasker (212-534-7639) rinks. See above for more information.

Inline Skating. The park drives are popular with skaters, but some prefer the area at the north end of the Mall and the driveway to the west of the Mall. From April to September, Wollman Rink is also open for inline skating. Call (212) 396-1010.

Running. There are designated running lanes on all park drives, and the entire road is closed to automobile traffic between 10 A.M. and 3 P.M. and after 7 P.M. on weekdays, and from 7 P.M. Friday to 6 A.M. Monday.

Lonnie Schlein/The New York Times

The Sheep Meadow in Central Park

Swimming. Swimming is forbidden in all open bodies of water in the park, but the Lasker Rink becomes a free swimming pool in July and August. Call (212) 534-7639.

Tennis. The tennis center to the northwest of the Reservoir houses 30 courts; permits are required most of the time and are available at the Arsenal. Call (212) 360-8131 for details.

THE BOROUGHS

THE BRONX

"The Bronx is up" in more ways than one. Geographically, this is the northernmost part of the city and the only borough attached to the U.S. mainland. More important is the Bronx's rise from the ashes of burning buildings and crime-ridden streets of the 1970's. Renewed vibrancy and pride have come to the borough that was a collection of rural villages—Mott Haven, Kingsbridge, Morrisania, et al.—in the 1890's, before being annexed into the expanding city. Throughout the early decades of the 20th century the Bronx was mainly populated by waves of Irish and German immigrants seeking the open, green space of the borough made available by the growth of the subway system. Early Bronxites could watch D.W. Griffith making movies in a local studio and some spent their summers living in tents on a rocky shoreline, where Robert Moses later hauled in sand for **Orchard Beach** in the 1930's.

Perhaps best known as the home of the **Bronx Zoo** and **Yankee Stadium**, the Bronx also features the green spaces of the **New York Botanical Garden**, Van Cortlandt and Pelham Bay Parks, as well as **Wave Hill** in Riverdale. **City Island** is a virtual New England village.

The Bronx is home to several colleges and universities: Fordham University and Manhattan College; Bronx Community College, once the uptown campus of NYU, with its Hall of Fame for Great Americans; and Lehman College, formerly Hunter College.

Many visitors to the Bronx travel to **Woodlawn Cemetery** to view its grandiose mausoleums and especially the grave of Herman Melville. The man at the gate is happy to tell you where to find it. Bronx visitors and residents more interested in the living travel to **Arthur Avenue** in the Belmont section of the borough. There they find lively food shopping and excellent Italian dining just down the street from the Zoo and opposite Fordham University's Rose Hill campus.

How did the Bronx get its name? Yes, the Bronx River flows through the borough, but the name probably goes back to the early Dutch settlers of the city that was originally called New Amsterdam. The first Dutch inhabitants of the area were Dutch farmer Jonas Bronck and his family, who owned a 500-acre farm near what is now Morrisania. According to legend people would say they were going to visit "the Broncks," thereby establishing the use of the definite article in the borough's name, the only one of the five with that distinction.

HIGHLIGHTS OF THE BRONX

Bartow-Pell Mansion Museum 895 Shore Rd. (718) 885-1461. A 150-year-old Federal-style mansion with formal gardens, the Bartow-Pell house is all but hidden in foliage several yards off the heavily traveled road to Orchard Beach. The neo-classical stone mansion with a Greek Revival interior sits on property purchased from the Indians by Thomas Pell in 1654, in a nine-acre setting consonant with its original surroundings.

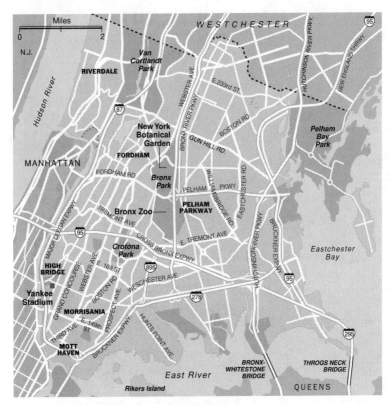

The Bronx

Admission: $2.50; $1.25, seniors and students. **Subway:** 6 to Pelham Bay Park (about a mile from the station).

Bronx Museum of the Arts 1040 Grand Concourse (at 165th St.), Bronx (718) 681-6000. The only arts museum in the Bronx was established in 1961 and exhibits contemporary and historical art, particularly by Bronx artists or artists related in some way to the borough. Known for its high-quality, well-curated exhibitions, it's considered one of the many well-kept secrets in the Bronx. The permanent collection includes a strong collection of work by artists of African, Asian and Latin-American ancestry.

Admission: $3; $2, students with I.D.; free, children under 12. Free Wednesdays. **Credit cards:** All major; checks. **Hours:** Wed., 3–9 P.M.; Thu.–Fri., 10 A.M.–5 P.M.; Sat.–Sun., 12–6 P.M. Closed Monday and major holidays. **Programs for Children:** Workshops for families and groups. Phone the Education Department at the Museum for a calendar of events and additional information. **Services:** Tours, lectures, concerts. **Subway:** C, D, 4 to 161st St.; D to 167th St.-Grand Concourse

City Island Just off the northeastern edge of the Bronx, City Island is a quiet (except in summer) year-round virtual village of some 4,000 permanent residents, with one main drag, many boatyards and marinas, several newish condominium colonies and some dozen and a half mostly seafood restaurants. A mile and a half long and no more than half a mile wide, the island blends the forlorn mystery of a Hopper dreamscape with a cheerful blue-collar brawn and flashes of intriguing wealth: Sports cars behind gated walls; a gleaming black Mercedes convertible outside the bait shop.

Le Refuge Inn on City Island is a charming French provincial bed-and-breakfast that presents a weekly noontime series of chamber-music concerts in a setting reminiscent of the European salons of bygone days. The island's **North Wind Undersea Institute**, founded by a deep-sea diver to raise awareness of the serious plight of marine life surrounding City Island, is housed in a 125-year-old sea-captain's mansion and on a nearby tugboat. The **Boat Livery** is one of the best ways to explore City Island and nearby High Island. The Boat Livery rents small motorboats by the day ($45, weekdays; $55, weekends and holidays).

Directions: 6 train to Pelham Bay Park, then take the Bx 29 bus.

Edgar Allan Poe Cottage 2640 Grand Concourse (between 192nd and 193rd Sts.) (718) 881-8900. Edgar Allan Poe moved to this cottage in Kingsbridge, the Bronx, from Manhattan in 1846, hoping that the country air would help his wife recover from tuberculosis. For three years, he lived in the tiny house, where he wrote "Annabel Lee." Three period rooms—a kitchen, parlor and bedroom—are filled with furniture from the 1840's, including Poe's own rocking chair and bed and the bed where his wife died not long after the move. At the museum you can watch a 20-minute film on Poe's life and the history of the house. A small gallery houses paintings, photographs and drawings from the 1840's.

Admission: $2. **Subway:** B, D, 4 to Kingsbridge Rd.

Hall of Fame for Great Americans University Ave. at W. 181st St. (718) 289-5162. This landmark institution was founded in 1900 as part of the uptown campus of New York University (now Bronx Community College). The main attraction here is the 630-foot open air Colonnade, honoring Americans who have played a significant role in the nation's history—including Alexander Graham Bell, Eli Whitney and George Westinghouse.

Admission: Free. **Hours:** 10 A.M.–5 P.M. daily. **Subway:** 4 to Burnside Ave.

New York Botanical Garden Opposite the Bronx Zoo (718) 817-8700 *www.nybg.org*. Located at the northern end of Bronx Park along East Fordham Road, this elegant expansive garden was created in 1891, inspired by the success of the Royal Botanic Garden at Kew, England. The 250-acre garden was planted between 1895 and 1896, the landscape and construction work began in 1899. One highlight of the garden is the Enid A. Haupt Conservatory, a beautiful Victorian greenhouse, but the main attraction is of course the 47 gardens and plant collections and thousands of shrubs and trees. The Bronx River flows through the site, next to a stone mill dating from 1840. The rose garden was planned by Beatrix Farrand, the first American female landscape designer. There are 40 acres of the forest that once covered all of New York.

The garden runs hands-on discovery, craft and gardening activities for everyone on weekends. There are special events throughout the year, such as a holiday

Bronx Zoo

Sprawled over 265 acres, the Bronx Zoo is the largest urban zoo in the United States. With paths winding through lush greenery shaded by canopies of trees, it can feel as much like a park as an animal repository. But turn any corner, and you will be reminded exactly where you are. The zoo has more than 7,000 animals, of over 700 species, enough to make any skeptic marvel at nature's prolific creativity. There are the exotic—cassowaries (flightless birds capable of killing a person with their toenails); Mongolian wild horses, completely extinct in the wild; a 24-foot-long reticulated python; black-necked swans. And there are the routine but lovable—massive, placid elephants, vanilla-colored polar bears, docile zebras.

The zoo has contrived all sorts of settings to let nature do its thing, and let you watch. The "World of Darkness," for example, takes you through a darkened building so you can see how nocturnal animals behave—bats spread their wings, a gopher snake resolutely devours a mouse (conveniently delivered by a zoo keeper). And some of the outdoor settings are lovely, such as the steep, grassy hill that is home to gelada baboons and nubian ibex, with their baroquely curled horns.

The zoo brings not just the wild, but the world, to the city. JungleWorld, housed in a 37,000 square foot building, recreates four Asian habitats. One of them is a mangrove forest, which most of us will never see, stocked with animal inhabitants like bear cats, the black leopard and the Asian small-clawed otter, the world's smallest otter species. The Bengali Express Monorail crosses the Bronx River to take you on a leisurely, photo-friendly journey though Wild Asia. There are antelopes, deer, wild cattle with their white-stockinged

feet, Indian rhinoceros—the largest land animal on earth—Asian elephant and the Siberian tiger.

Championed by, among others, Theodore Roosevelt, the Bronx Zoo opened in 1899, and has not stopped growing since. The newest addition—and the highlight of the zoo—is the Congo Gorilla Forest, which opened in 1999. It is 6.5 acres of a green playland, or homeland, for African rain forest animals, with 11 waterfalls, 55 artificial rain forest trees, misting machines and even jungle sounds. The animals range from tiny, scampering colobus monkeys to brilliantly vareigated mandrills to massive, lolling silverbacks. Some of the gorillas, who group around male leaders, are lazy, some bawdy, some familially inclined, but all are fascinating to watch. Only a layer of glass separates the masses from the apes—close enough, it seems, to touch them.

The gorilla exhibit includes a film on their threatened habitats, which is in keeping with the larger mission of the Wildlife Conservation Society, which runs the zoo: to preserve species and habitats around the world. The conservation message is ubiquitous, and effective. The diversity of species on display generates amazement—but also alarm, given the number that are on the edge of extinction. The zoo's educational mission succeeds as well, managing to teach, for example, about stork breeding habits. The zoo also does its part to promote procreation: more than 300 animals were born there in 1998.

But the best thing about any zoo—and certainly the Bronx Zoo—is serendipity: turning a corner to catch a glimpse of a giraffe's awkward beauty as it nibbles grass from a sun-bathed plain. Making a wrong turn that introduces you to the primeval-looking marabou stork. Looking up as you trudge toward the exit to see a North American brown bear standing atop a boulder.

Throughout, of course, there are ample opportunities to consume food, drink and souvenirs. Be warned that a day at the zoo will not necessarily come cheap, particularly for a family, given the extra charges for the Children's Zoo, the Bengali Express Monorail and the Congo Gorilla exhibit.

The crowds can be overwhelming as well, sometimes giving the zoo the feel of an amusement park. Be prepared, for example, to wait 45 minutes or more for Congo Gorilla Forest on a summer weekend.

But those gripes aside, it is a remarkably pleasant way to spend a day. That is not least because you get to see New Yorkers in nature themselves—for once, unhurried, and perhaps only mildly more aggressive than many of the animals they are contemplating.   —*Amy Waldman*

Fordham Rd. and Bronx River Pkwy. (718) 367-1010 *www.wcs.org*. **Hours:** Mon.–Fri., 10 A.M.–5 P.M.; Sat., Sun. and holidays, 10 A.M.–5:30 P.M. **Admission:** $9, adults; $5, children 2–12 and seniors. Wed. admission free (suggested donation), except during Holiday Lights. **Special Admission Costs:** Congo Gorilla Forest, $3; Holiday Lights, (evenings, Nov.26-Jan. 2), $6; Children's Theater, $2; Bengali Express Monorail, Skyfari Aerial Tramway and Zoo Shuttle, $2 each; camel rides, $3. **Services:** Baby stroller rental at entrances (except Rainey Gate); adult strollers available by reservation at (718) 220-5188. **Subway:** 2, 5 to Bronx Park East.

model train show and the Everett Children's Adventure Garden, with attractions like topiary bunnies. For live animals—including apes, elephants and monkeys—the Bronx Zoo is right next-door. For events info, call (718) 817-817-8777.

Directions: Metro North from Grand Central to Botanical Garden.

Van Cortlandt Park Broadway and W. 240th St. (at Birchhall Ave.) (718) 430-1890. Frederick Van Cortlandt's stone mansion, built in 1748 and today the Bronx's oldest building, served as Revolutionary War headquarters for both George Washington and a British general. In the late 19th century, the Van Cortlandt family donated the house and the surrounding 1,146 acres to the city. The park's southern portion houses the **Van Cortlandt House Museum**, a lake, a golf course and playing fields for soccer, cricket, rugby, baseball and hurling. Meanwhile, the northern end of the park remains largely pastoral; along with a nationally renowned cross-country track, it features nature trails that wind through a 100-year-old hardwood forest populated by foxes, raccoons and pheasant. (*See chapter* **Sports & Recreation** *for details on activities.*)
Subway: 1, 9 to 242nd St.–Van Cortlandt Park.

Wave Hill House W. 249 St. and Independence Ave. (near Palisade Ave.) (718) 549-3200. Established in 1960 as a center for the arts and environmental studies, Wave Hill comprises 28 acres of land atop a hill overlooking the Hudson. The estate's mansion was built in 1843 of local stone. Theodore Roosevelt, Mark Twain and Arturo Toscanini all stayed at the Riverdale compound. Today, visitors can stroll through gardens and greenhouses, picnic in an enclosed courtyard, attend special events and concerts and view art exhibitions.
Directions: Metro North from Grand Central to Riverdale.

Yankee Stadium 161st St. (at River Ave.), Bronx (718) 293-4300. (*See chapter* **Sports & Recreation**.)
Subway: B, D, 4 to 161st St.–Yankee Stadium.

BROOKLYN

If you're not a native, all you might know about Brooklyn is this: the Brooklyn Bridge is at one end, Coney Island the other, and the Dodgers used to play ball somewhere in between. Historically, though, Brooklyn has given more to the world than Jackie Robinson and Nathan's Famous hot dogs. The borough has been (and still is) a home to millions who were drawn to New York but found Manhattan life too hectic or expensive—and has been an inspiration to everyone from Walt Whitman to Spike Lee.

The original town of Breuckelen was chartered by the Dutch West India Company in 1646 and incorporated into Kings County in 1683. Despite British occupation during the Revolutionary War, the resident population continued to grow, reaching over 4,500 by 1800. By then, more than 30 percent of the county's residents were of African descent. During the Civil War, Brooklyn found itself at the center of the abolitionist movement in America. The area was home to some of the first black landowners in America, as well as one of the first towns (Weeksville) settled by freed slaves.

At the start of the war, Brooklyn ranked as the third largest city in the U.S., and its dynamic population and proximity to New York had already sparked a major cultural renaissance. In 1855, a Brooklyn resident named Walt Whitman published *Leaves of Grass*; the next decade saw the creation of the Philharmonic Society of Brooklyn, the Brooklyn Academy of Music and the National Association of Baseball Players—the first such centralized organization in the country. In 1867, Olmsted and Vaux completed work on **Prospect Park**, thought by some to rival Central Park in the beauty and genius of its design and execution. Eastern Parkway, another of the duo's designs, opened a year later, becoming the nation's first six-lane parkway.

The second major wave of immigrants began to arrive from eastern and southern Europe around 1880; the increased labor force helped Brooklyn to become the country's fourth largest producer of manufactured goods. In 1883 the **Brooklyn Bridge** opened, followed soon after by an elevated railroad and electric trolley service. Brooklynites had fought hard for years to retain the borough's identity and political independence, but in 1898, a close vote finally consolidated Brooklyn into Greater New York City. Brooklyn entered the 20th century as a borough of New York, with a population of over one million.

The Williamsburg and Manhattan bridges (as well as the IRT, New York's first subway line) made the Manhattan-Brooklyn commute even easier, and funneled more arrivals across the East River. The "Great Migration" of African-Americans to Brooklyn began around 1915, adding to the steady influx of European immigrants. By 1930, half of the borough's residents were foreign born, and a substantial percentage remained African-American—but the Depression was tough on these immigrants and poor families from the rural South, and some of Brooklyn's beautiful neighborhoods turned into slums.

Lately, things are looking up. Business is growing again in the downtown Brooklyn area, especially the business district around **Borough Hall** and the **Metrotech Center**. The **Brooklyn Academy of Music**'s Next Wave Festival, begun in 1983, has consistently drawn cutting-edge artists—as well as crowds from Manhattan. And as Manhattan rents creep skyward, more young professionals are drifting across the river, bringing new life (and money) to old neighborhoods, and making areas like Brooklyn Heights and Park Slope some of the more desirable addresses in New York. Brooklyn's population of nearly 2.5 million makes it (unofficially, of course) the fourth largest city in the U.S., and it seems poised for many more changes in the century ahead.

Coney Island

A seemingly endless stretch of sand, a boardwalk offering every imaginable variety of greasy food item, water-squirt games, a roller coaster that defines the term death-defying, a Ferris wheel you can see from miles away at night, carnival music, the world's best hot dog, cheap beer—no wonder Coney Island became the most famous beach in America. If you pay a visit today, however, be prepared

to see an entirely different "Coney"—as the natives once called it—from the one
of story and fable. The old bathhouses are crumbling, many buildings are run
down and the Boardwalk vastly diminished from the days when crowds jammed
the shops or huddled near the now silent Parachute Jump to marvel at the brav-
ery of the men and women who soared 250 feet into the sky in an open seat.

Still, most out-of-towners report very positively about their journeys to the
far reaches of Brooklyn. There's just enough left, it seems, to capture the spirit
of one of New York's most recognizable symbols of a bygone era. The Boardwalk
stretches from the community of Brighton Beach through Coney Island to Sea
Gate, a strip that has known better and worse days. At the turn of the century,
the eastern end was a high-society preserve, with oceanfront luxury hotels,
restaurants, theaters and a racetrack. But anti-gambling sentiment closed the
track in 1910, and by 1920 all the hotels were gone. To the west around Coney
Island, more popular attractions developed, with the great amusement parks of
Dreamland, Luna Park and George C. Tilyou's Steeplechase.

The arrival of the subway in 1920 created what was known as "a poor people's paradise" and soon hundreds of thousands of working class New Yorkers
were spending weekends at the beach. Decline set in during the social disloca-
tions of the 1960's. Changing populations and a series of fires in the flimsily
built fun parks brought decaying buildings, poverty and crime. In more recent
years, Russian and Ukrainian immigrants have established a thriving beachhead
in the area.

Baseball recently returned to Brooklyn in a stadium on Surf Avenue, with a
view of the beach and the boardwalk from the grandstand. The Cyclones, a
publicly subsidized Mets minor-league affiliate arrived in 2001 to much enthusiasm from Brooklynites, many of whom never recovered from the departure of
the Dodgers nearly a half century ago (*see chapter* **Sports & Recreation**).
Although a promised Coney Island renaissance has not entirely materialized,
The advent of the Cyclones promises further economic growth.

Subway: F, N, Q, W to Coney Island—Stillwell Ave. (about an hour from
Manhattan).

Amusement Park Rides:

B & B Carousel Surf Ave. at W. 12th St. Complete with painted horses carved
around 1920 in the renowned workshop of Marcus Illions, a Polish immigrant
who established the fancifully flamboyant Coney Island style of carousel horses.

Cyclone Surf Ave. at W. 8th St. Fans scream their way through the 1927 roller
coaster's 100-second ride in cars that plunge from nine thrill-packed hills. Like
the Parachute Jump, this is on the National Register of Historic Places and is
landmarked by the state and the city.

Wonder Wheel W. 12th St. (between Surf Ave. and the Boardwalk). The
orange and green frame of the 78-year-old landmark Ferris wheel is 150 feet in
diameter. A leisurely ride, day or night, affords terrific views of the Brooklyn
landscape.

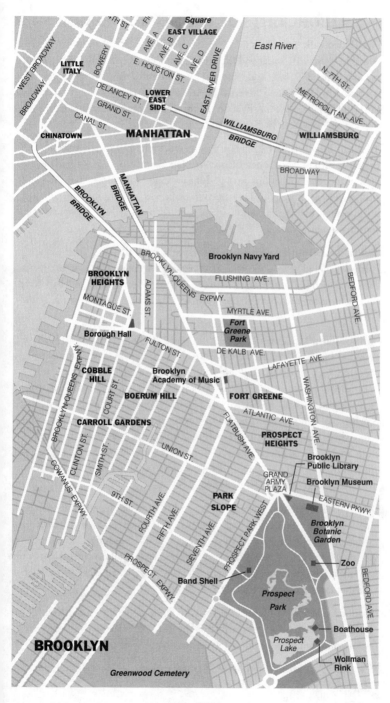

Brooklyn

HIGHLIGHTS OF THE NEIGHBORHOOD

The Boardwalk From Brighton 15th St. and Brightwater Ave. in Brighton Beach to West 37th Street and the private residential community of Sea Gate in Coney Island. Rebuilt and extended intermittently, this inviting promenade is now 2.5 miles long and 80 feet wide. It is also the starting point of the annual **Mermaid Parade**, generally held on the first Saturday after the summer solstice (*see section* "New York By Season" *earlier in this chapter*).

Brighton Beach Baths Brighton Beach Ave. to the Boardwalk, between Brighton 12th St. and Coney Island Ave. The Boardwalk affords a bird's-eye view of the remnants of this once posh beach club, which opened in 1907 and closed a few years ago. Until it is razed to make way for housing, its swimming pools, playing courts and bandstand are nostalgic landmarks to those who spent youthful summers there.

Childs' Restaurant Boardwalk at W. 21st St. Coney Island's answer to the Parthenon could be this ruin of a once splendid restaurant. Terra-cotta tiles embossed with sea motifs are set into the Spanish yellow facade, and two florid ceramic urns top twin turrets. Opened in 1923, it is now a graffiti-marred candy factory.

Coney Island Museum 1208 Surf Ave. (at 12th St.) (718) 372-5159. This museum is stocked with mementos from the great pay-one-price amusement centers of Coney Island, like Luna Park, Dreamland and Steeplechase, that once ruled the shore. Chief among the antic artifacts are a fun-house mirror, an original wicker Boardwalk Rolling Chair and one of the rare wooden Steeplechase Horses. The museum has a video loop of rare Coney Island film clips, which includes a bizarre 1904 film of an elephant being electrocuted, a stunt apparently engineered by Thomas Edison to persuade the public that the electric chair would be the most humane form of capital punishment. **Hours:** Sat., Sun. Noon-Sundown. **Admission:** $.99

Flea Market Surf Ave. between W. 8th and W. 10th Sts. Open-front shops and alley stalls under the moving frieze of elevated trains display all sorts of new and used merchandise: kitchen utensils, tools, bric-a-brac, clothing, electronics, videotapes and CD's, a few genuine antiques and a lot of dusty junk. Most of the vendors are Russian immigrants who sometimes feign a language barrier when it suits them, but all bargain handily in English.

Handball Courts Boardwalk at W. 5th St. These are said to be the busiest handball courts in New York, attracting the city's best players. Even midweek, the six courts will host vigorous doubles matches, always with kibitzers.

New York Aquarium for Wildlife Conservation
(*See chapter* **New York for Children**.)

Parachute Jump Boardwalk at W. 17th St. Suggesting a miniature Eiffel Tower, this landmark 250-foot-high structure looks remarkably intact, leading to optimistic rumors of its restoration. Originally a ride at the 1939–40 New York World's Fair, it was moved here in 1941.

Steeplechase Pier Boardwalk at W. 17th St. Off-season, you can walk 1,000 feet out into the Atlantic Ocean as tides lap beneath you. Gaze out to sea, picnic on benches and watch fishermen hook herring.

Brooklyn Heights/Cobble Hill/ Carroll Gardens

In 1965, **Brooklyn Heights** was designated the city's first historic district, assuring protection for brick and brownstone row houses on streets sometimes little altered since the Civil War. The area is now one of Brooklyn's most desirable (and expensive) residential areas, and remains a popular destination for architecture-lovers. Montague Street, the commercial core, is lined with shops, chain stores and restaurants and it is clogged with midday traffic.

Brooklyn Heights has played host to some impressive literary figures over the years, including Walt Whitman, who wrote *Leaves of Grass* while living here. Truman Capote, Arthur Miller and W.H. Auden all lived here for a time, and Thomas Wolfe completed *You Can't Go Home Again* in a house on Montague Terrace. Today, Norman Mailer lives in one of the elegant brownstones on Columbia Heights.

One of the best reasons to visit, however, has to be the Brooklyn Heights Promenade. Stretching from Montague to Middagh Street, it offers striking views of the lower Manhattan skyline and the Brooklyn Bridge. Lined by the lush gardens of picturesque town houses, the walkway and benches draw runners, families and—at night—romancing couples. The view of Manhattan is startling: You're far enough away to take it all in, but close enough that the buildings still loom large. If you lean over the railing a bit, you'll realize that the peaceful esplanade juts over the Brooklyn-Queens Expressway.

The best ending to a visit here is a stroll back across the Brooklyn Bridge. The footpath is accessible from Cadman Plaza Park, and the trip toward Manhattan offers the best views and photo opportunities.

If you want to venture a little deeper into Brooklyn, head south to the quiet neighborhood of **Cobble Hill**, most of which is part of a New York City Historic District designated in 1969 and slightly extended in 1988. In the 1930's, Thomas Wolfe lived here on Verandah Place. Jenny Jerome, the mother of Winston Churchill, was born on Amity Street in 1854. And Louis Comfort Tiffany in 1917 designed the windows, high altar and other appointments of the Episcopal Christ Church and Holy Family at 326 Clinton Street, a Greek Revival structure built in 1842.

Among merchants are a handful each of butchers, greengrocers and bakeries. Arabic restaurants and specialty food shops dot Atlantic Avenue in a section known as Little Arabia, offering Middle Eastern delicacies, particularly from Egypt, Yemen and Morocco. Atlantic Avenue is also well known for its antiques stores.

Carroll Gardens, slightly farther to the south, has long had a strong Italian-American flavor, and that flavor is still very much in evidence. Court Street, the area's commercial district, has a high density of Italian restaurants and pizza stores. Part of the neighborhood was designated the Carroll Gardens Historic District by the New York City Landmarks Preservation Commission in 1973. The district, which contains more than 160 buildings, includes houses on President and Carroll Streets between Smith and Hoyt Streets as well as adjacent parts of the four streets and a bit of First Street east of Hoyt. All the district's brownstone row houses were erected between 1869 and 1884.

Smith Street has been experiencing something of a renaissance over the past few years as young professionals and artists have been populating the area. New restaurants, cafes and bars now line this street which recently had virtually no nightlife at all. The street is also home to several hip boutiques.

Subway: Brooklyn Heights: 2, 3 to Clark St. or Borough Hall; 4, 5 Borough Hall; N, R, to Court St. Cobble Hill: 2, 3, 4, 5 to Nevins St. Carroll Gardens: F to Bergen St.

HIGHLIGHTS OF THE AREA

Borough Hall Court St. (at Joralemon St.) (718) 875-4047. This historic building won a Municipal Art Society award after its renovation around 1990. The plaza between Borough Hall and the nearby Supreme Court is the site of a large greenmarket on Fridays and Saturdays, and is a popular spot for rollerbladers and local office workers on their lunch breaks. Tours of the building are available on Tuesdays.

Brooklyn Historical Society 128 Pierrepont St. (between Clinton and Montague Sts.) (718) 624-0890. Founded in 1863 as the Long Island Historical Society, the society has long housed the world's most extensive collection of Brooklynalia in its landmark building. Its collections range from fine paintings and sculpture to archeological artifacts, including an outstanding collection of ephemera on the lamented Brooklyn Dodgers. The building is closed for rennovation until mid-2002 at the earliest. The society's temporary location is 2 Metrotech Center, suite 4200 (718-254-9830).
Hours: Mon., Thu., Fri., Sat., noon–5 P.M. **Price** : $2.50, general; $1, children under 12; Mondays admission is free. **Credit cards:** All major. **Services:** Tours.

New York Transit Museum Boerum Pl. and Schermerhorn St. (718) 243-3060. The entrance to the Transit Museum looks like that of any subway station, from the green-painted railing to the cement stairway. And as you head inside you go through the standard subway entry routine, paying your admission at a token booth (although there's an audible and eager-to-please staff member inside) and passing through a turnstile. But when you reach the lower platforms of this former subway station, you start exploring the past. Some of the old turnstiles are made of wood and ask for just five cents; the subway cars include magnificent wooden carriages from the early 1900's, with big windows and narrow wicker benches. And, unlike in so many museums, you and the kids can touch and play with nearly everything—you can even sit in a motorman's seat and operate a signal tower.

Hours: Tue.–Fri., 10 A.M.–4 P.M.; Sat., Sun., noon–5 P.M. **Admission:** $3, general; $1.50, seniors and children under 17; MTA employees, free.

Plymouth Church of the Pilgrims 75 Hicks St. (near Henry St.) (718) 624-4743. This historic church was founded by Henry Ward Beecher, the famous 19th-century abolitionist, and is sometimes referred to as the Grand Central Terminal of the Underground Railroad. Plymouth Church also features windows designed by Louis Comfort Tiffany.

Park Slope

At the turn of the century, Park Slope was one of the wealthiest neighborhoods in the country. But by the 1920's, mansions were being razed for apartment houses, and brownstones were going out of fashion. By the end of World War II, many had been carved up into rooming houses. Through the 50's, middle-class families moved to the suburbs and urban decay set in. In the early 60's, brown-stone pioneers, recognizing bargains, arrived to renovate and restore fading brownstones and eventually reverse the area's precipitous decline. Park Slope has been on the rise ever since. Today, a stroll down Eighth Avenue takes you past some of the finest brownstones in New York; start near **Grand Army Plaza** at the historic Montauk Club (at Eighth Ave. and Lincoln Pl.), and follow Eighth Avenue south, exploring the homes on President Street, Carroll Street, and Montgomery Place.

In few other parts of Brooklyn does the past so enrich the present. The 526-acre **Prospect Park** on the neighborhood's eastern edge is thronged on weekends by parents and children. The Soldiers' and Sailors' Memorial at Grand Army Plaza, with its twin Doric columns, grand arch and crowning statue of Victory in her horse-drawn chariot, is modeled after the Arc de Tri-omphe. And every Labor Day weekend the massive West Indian American Day Parade rolls along nearby Eastern Parkway, the first six-lane parkway in the world (*for parade info see section* "New York by Season" *in this chapter.*)

With its exquisite churches, stellar brownstone row houses, thriving Sev-enth and Fifth Avenue shops and restaurants, and the eclectic spirit of both its people and its neo-Renaissance and neo-Classical architectural styles, Park Slope is one of Brooklyn's most popular neighborhoods. Its proximity to the park, the **Brooklyn Public Library**, the **Brooklyn Museum** and the **Brooklyn Botanic Garden** adds to its desirability, and subway links to Man-hattan are numerous. With that desirability came rising rents that have pushed many of the area's younger and less affluent residents into nearby **Prospect Heights**, a neighborhood due a renaissance of its own.

Residents invariably speak of the small-town feeling and social cohesion of Park Slope, a tree-lined, nearly all-residential area especially attractive to fami-lies. It is a place where activities for children are unending, shopkeepers know

Brooklyn Academy of Music

It's the oldest performing arts center in the United States, yet the Brooklyn Academy of Music (or BAM as it is commonly called) is practically synonymous with the avant-garde. The main building houses the **BAM Opera House**, which hosts programs like the innovative **Next Wave Festival**, bringing the best in new music, dance, opera and theater to New York each year (festival regulars include Laurie Anderson, Philip Glass and Robert Wilson). Other annual Opera House performers include the Brooklyn Philharmonic and BAM Opera.

The neighborhood around BAM, **Fort Greene**, is a friendly, multicultural community with quite a few interesting shops and restaurants along Fulton Street.

BAM Rose Cinemas Also housed in the main BAM building, the Rose Cinemas shows first-run independent and foreign films in four theaters with good sightlines and good-size screens. One of those screens is devoted exclusively to a program featuring classic American and foreign films, documentaries, retrospectives and special festivals.

BAMcafé A good place for food and drinks before and after BAM performances. The café also hosts BAMcafé Live every Thursday, Friday and Saturday night, featuring a wide range of musical and spoken-word performances (no cover, $10 food and drink minimum).

BAM Harvey Theater Built in 1904 as a legitimate theater and later used to show movies, the Harvey Theater (formerly known as the Majestic but renamed in 1999 for Harvey Lichtenstein, BAM's former president and executive producer) was abandoned in 1968 and lay dark until its renovation in 1987. But don't be fooled by the term "renovation": The building's shell, with exposed brick, crumbling paint, chipped friezes and exposed ducts, was deliberately left more or less intact. The theater has 900 seats and practically no obstructed views. BAM uses it as a showcase for a variety of performing arts, including dance, jazz and opera.

30 Lafayette Ave. (at Ashland Pl.), Brooklyn (718) 636-4100
Tickets: Box office; Ticketmaster. **Credit cards:** All major. **Subway:** Q, 2, 3, 4, 5 to Atlantic Ave.; M, N, R, W to Pacific St. or take the BAMbus from Manhattan (call for prices and reservations).

their customers and people stop in the street to chat. The population mix is all-encompassing—whites, blacks, Hispanics and Asians, and a sizable lesbian and gay community as well.

Subway: F, Q to Seventh Ave.; 2, 3 to Grand Army Plaza; R to Union or 9th St.

HIGHLIGHTS OF THE AREA

Brooklyn Botanic Garden 1000 Washington Ave. (at Eastern Parkway) (718) 622-4433 *www.bbg.org*. A stunningly beautiful and tranquil place to help you forget you're anywhere near a city, the best time to visit the garden is late March through mid-May. This is when the Oriental cherry trees flower in all their glory. And if you go on Tuesdays, you can see them—and the roses and lilacs and daffodils, too—for free.

But there's plenty more to see year-round. Wander through the famous collection of bonsai trees or steam yourself in a fern grotto in the Warm Temperate Pavilion. Admire a great reproduction of a Kyoto temple or visit the orchids in the Aquatic House.

In all, more than 12,000 kinds of plants from around the world fill the intricate, multilevel gardens and the insides of soaring greenhouses in the Steinhardt Conservatory. And you might catch a wedding party spilling out of the glass-and-steel Palm House, the conservatory's Victorian centerpiece.

It's hard to imagine that the whole 52-acre spread was, in the late 1800's, mostly an ash dump. By the mid-1920's, the bonsai collection had already begun and the famous rose garden was being built. In the garden now, you can find a hybrid tea rose named for Audrey Hepburn and another variety called Elizabeth Taylors. In 1955, the Fragrance Garden was built, the first in the country to be designed for sight impaired people. By the late 1970's, the garden was even granted its own patent—for developing the first yellow magnolia.

—*Randy Kennedy*

Admission: $3, adults; $1.50, seniors; children under 16 free. **Hours:** Tue.–Fri., 8 A.M.–6 P.M.; Sat.–Sun., 10 A.M.–6 P.M.

Brooklyn Children's Museum
(*See chapter **New York for Children** for full description.*)

Brooklyn Museum of Art 200 Eastern Parkway (at Washington Ave.) (718) 638-5000 *www.brooklynart.org*. As Brooklyn's population skyrocketed in the 19th century, the Brooklyn Museum grew out of a library for apprentices into a full-fledged museum with an encyclopedic scope. Its monumental Beaux-Arts building, designed by McKim, Mead and White in 1893, is just one pavilion of a larger plan that was never completed. Having divested its science and natural history exhibits in the 1930's, the museum now concentrates upon the fine arts.

For most visitors, the major draw is the museum's far-reaching exhibition program, which in recent years has presented not only blockbusters (such as "Monet and the Mediterrenean"), but also smaller, highly innovative shows (on topics such as the relationship between hip-hop and fashion). From its inception, the museum has sought to serve as more than a repository of high culture. In fact, the monumental staircase that once faced Eastern Parkway was removed in the 1930's partly with the aim of making the museum more accessible to the public. In addition to its many educational activities, the museum also hosts thematic series of films.

Permanent Collection: The museum's more than 1.5 million objects of art exemplify a comprehensive range of cultures—from classical antiquity to Asia to colonial America—and constitute the second-largest collection in the U.S. after the Metropolitan's. The museum's Egyptian art section, which is housed in ultramodern galleries designed by the Japanese architect Arata Isozaki, is considered to be one of the finest in the world. Other highlights include a Gilbert Stuart portrait of George Washington and an array of sculptures by Rodin.

Admission (suggested)**:** $6, adults; $3, students and seniors; children under 12 free. **Hours:** Wed.–Fri., 10 A.M.–5 P.M.; Sat., Sun. 11 A.M.–6 P.M. First Saturday of each month, open until 11 P.M.; free admission from 5 P.M., drinks and live music available from 6 P.M. Closed Mon., Tue. **Programs for Children:** storytelling, studio classes and performances. Call for details. **Tours:** Docent-led tours for groups and special exhibitions. Groups, call: (718) 638-5000, ext. 234.

Grand Army Plaza Arch Intersection of Prospect Park West, Flatbush Ave. and Eastern Pkwy. This triumphal arch commemorates the soldiers and sailors who fought for the Union Army during the Civil War (which interrupted the construction of the park). The Arch was designed by John H. Duncan, the designer of Grant's Tomb, and sculpted by Frederick William MacMonnies. Art exhibits and tours are held in the spring and fall (call 718-965-8999 for information on seeing the top of the arch). Nearby Bailey Fountain is the site of the second-largest greenmarket in New York, after Union Square.

Prospect Park

As a destination in itself or as a starting point for exploring Brooklyn's artistic and cultural treasures, Prospect Park is well worth the trip. This 526-acre triangle is considered by many to be the crowning achievement of Olmsted and Vaux, who also designed Central Park a decade earlier. Unfortunately, many Brooklyn visitors never venture into the park, coming instead to explore the nearby **Brooklyn Museum of Art**, **Brooklyn Botanic Garden** and **Brooklyn Public Library**, or to visit **Park Slope**, one of Brooklyn's most beautiful neighborhoods, just outside the park across Prospect Park West.

But the park itself has many formal attractions, starting with its grand main entrance: the 72-foot-tall Memorial Arch in **Grand Army Plaza** with its bronze sculptures honoring the soldiers and sailors of the Union forces in the Civil War. The park offers **Wollman Rink** for skating and **Lefferts Homestead**, a historic farmhouse with a children's museum. There's a **zoo**, a **carousel** and many fine examples of architecture from the late 19th and early 20th centuries such as the whimsical Oriental Pavilion and neighboring formal garden. And don't miss the elegant Italian-style boathouse with its romantic setting along the Lullwater, a fingerlike extension of **Prospect Lake**, and its view of the graceful arched **Lullwater Bridge** designed by McKim, Mead & White. At the lake, people feed ducks, fish for striped bass or pedal a boat into one of the many small inlets that make this body of water feel much larger than its 60 acres.

Twenty years ago the park was run-down and somewhat menacing: every building was closed and visitors had dwindled to 1.5 million annually. But with low crime rates, renewed confidence in public safety and numerous restoration projects, the park is undergoing a renaissance. Bit by bit, the park has begun once again to serve as an urban oasis for its visitors.

Tours: The Prospect Park Alliance offers free tours of the park every Saturday and Sunday at 1 P.M. and 3 P.M. (*www.prospectpark.org*, 718-965-6988). The free *Heart of Brooklyn* trolley leaves theWollman Rink on the hour and makes a complete loop around the park, with stops near the carousel, the zoo, Grand Army Plaza (at about 15 and 40 minutes past the hour), Brooklyn Museum of Art, Brooklyn Botanic Garden, the Picnic House, Bandshell and other locations on the park's perimeter. **Parking:** Available at Wollman Rink, Bartel-Pritchard Circle, Litchfield Villa and the Picnic House. **Subway:** 2, 3 to Grand Army Plaza; F, Q to Seventh Ave.

Sites of Interest in Prospect Park

Lefferts Historic House Flatbush Ave. and Empire Blvd. (in Prospect Park) (718) 965-6505. Peter Lefferts was an affluent farmer, a delegate to the New York State Constitutional Convention in 1788 and head of the largest slave-holding family in Kings County. One of the few surviving Dutch-American farmhouses in Brooklyn, the homestead, which couples Dutch colonial architecture with Federal details, was built in 1783 to replace the earlier family home, destroyed by fire in the Battle of Long Island in 1776. The period rooms reflect daily life in the 1820's, with changing exhibitions detailing the concerns of the day, including slave emancipation and the opening of the Erie Canal. The museum offers tours, demonstrations of early American crafts, family workshops and other educational events.
Hours: Mon.–Fri., 9 A.M.–5 P.M. **Price:** Free.

Litchfield Villa 95 Prospect Park West (between 4th and 5th Sts.) (718) 965-8951. Built in 1857 by prominent Brooklyn businessman Edwin Litchfield, this building is now the headquarters for City of New York/Parks & Recreation, as well as the office of the Prospect Park Administrator and the Prospect Park Alliance. It offers a dramatic hillside view of Park Slope.

The Long Meadow off Prospect Park West, 15th to Union St. This 90-acre expanse of grass stretches nearly a mile down the west side of Prospect Park, and may be the most visited and familiar site in the park. Many of the park's six million annual visitors end up here at some point to play ball, fly kites or just lie on the grass. The Metropolitan Opera also performs in the meadow once each June, and the New York Philharmonic Orchestra plays one evening concert each July, complete with fireworks.

The Music Pagoda Lincoln Rd. and Ocean Blvd. This century-old structure, resembling a Chinese city gate, is the site of numerous concerts, religious ceremonies, and other activities throughout the year. Contact the Prospect Park Alliance for schedules.

The Nethermead Mid-park, on Center Drive. Somewhat smaller than the Long Meadow, this central, open field is nevertheless a popular spot for large group events.

Playgrounds The **Tot Spot** (Garfield Pl. entrance) is designed specifically for the three-and-under set. **Imagination Playground** (Ocean Ave. entrance) features safe, modern play equipment, as well as a storytelling area with an array of statues of characters from the books of Brooklyn-born author Ezra Jack Keats.The Prospect Park Alliance has directed extensive playground renovations over the last decade, making the park's major play areas safer and more entertaining for kids. In addition to the two areas highlighted above, there are renovated playgrounds near the Lincoln Rd., 3rd St. and Vanderbilt St. street park entrances.

Prospect Lake Southeast edge of the park. Swimming is prohibited in this 60-acre lake, but it hosts all kinds of other activities throughout the year. Visitors are welcome to fish on a catch-and-release basis, and each July kids 14 and under can compete in the annual Macy's Fishing Contest. Same-day registration is available, but groups of 10 or more should contact Urban Park Rangers at (718) 438-0100. Fishing poles are provided or kids can bring their own. Pedal boats are also available for rental at the Wollman Center and Rink; for information, call (718) 282-7789.

Prospect Park Band Shell 9th St. and Prospect Park West (718) 855-7882. This amphitheater on the edge of Park Slope is one of the city's most pleasant venues for a summer afternoon or evening concert, particularly when it is part of the eclectic "Celebrate Brooklyn!" series. The world music concerts—from African to Brazilian to Asian—are some of the best in the city. Readings, children's shows, rock and folk music and occasional opera and classical performances round out the offerings. Most concerts are free to the public.

Prospect Park Carousel Enter at Empire Blvd. and Flatbush Ave. (718) 965-6512. This is one of only 12 remaining carousels designed by renowned horse carver Charles Carmel. The carousel features 51 horses and an assortment of other animals.
Admission: $.50. **Hours:** Open Apr.–Oct., hours vary. **Features:** Party rentals.

Prospect Park Picnic House Enter at Prospect Park West and 5th St. (718) 965-6512. The Picnic House pavilion can accommodate 175–200 guests for parties, concerts or lectures. It offers excellent views of the Long Meadow, as well as a stage, fireplace, piano and free tables and chairs for renters.

Prospect Park Tennis Center
(*See chapter* **Sports & Recreation**.)

Prospect Park Wildlife Center
(*See chapter* **New York for Children**.)

Wollman Center and Rink
(*See chapter* **Sports & Recreation**.)

Activities in Prospect Park

Baseball Permits are required to play baseball or softball on the 9th Street ball-fields at the southwest end of the Long Meadow. Call (718) 965-8943 for permits or (718) 965-8969 for more information on playing ball in Prospect Park.

Bicycling Cycling is permitted only on designated bicycle and runner lanes around the edge of the park. The Kissena Cycling Club (718-343-7343) and the Metropolitan Cycling Association (718-522-7390) can offer information on bicycle races.

Birding The Urban Park Rangers (718-438-0100) and the Brooklyn Bird Watchers Club (718-875-1151) run bird-watching tours in the park.

Festivals Prospect Park festival information is available at (718) 965-8999 and on the sandwich boards at Park entrances. One of the largest festivals is the Celebrate Brooklyn! Performing Arts Festival, running annually from June through August at the Band Shell. See *www.brooklynx.org/celebrate* or call (718) 855-7882 for details.

Horseback Riding Prospect Park's bridle path runs from Park Circle to the end of the Long Meadow. Contact Kensington Stables for horse rental information (718-972-4588).

Nature Walks Park visitors can join the Prospect Park Alliance and the Urban Park Rangers (718-438-0100) from April through November to explore the Prospect Park Ravine, Brooklyn's last remaining forest. Guides and maps for self-guided walking tours are available at the Prospect Park Alliance office in Litchfield Villa and at the Wollman Rink.

Picnics Permits are required for groups of more than 25; information is available at (718) 965-8969.

Running Running is permitted only on the 3.35-mile running lane along Park Drive, and on other sidewalks and paved surfaces in the park.

Williamsburg

Over the past several years, Williamsburg's well-established Hasidic, Puerto Rican, Dominican and Polish communities have made way for a newer group of residents—artists and other homesteaders seeking affordable space close to Manhattan.

In the mid-1800's, Williamsburg was a fashionable resort area, with hotels, clubs and beer gardens near the Brooklyn ferry attracting wealthy industrialists and professionals. The neighborhood's nature changed with the 1903 opening of the Williamsburg Bridge and the 1905 inauguration of trolley service over the bridge. Working-class Jews and other Eastern European immigrants flooded in from the crowded Lower East Side; they were followed by various groups of working-class immigrants, including Puerto Ricans working in the factories. In 1957, the Brooklyn-Queens Expressway opened, slicing through the neighborhood.

As recently as 1990, it was hard to find even basic services in Williamsburg. There is still a shortage of banks and ATM machines but the area now abounds with coin laundries and convenience stores; Bedford Avenue even features Sarkana Discount Art Supplies (the name means red in Latvian). So far, chain stores are nonexistent. But fresh food and well-regarded restaurants flourish including the landmark Peter Luger Steak House, in its original 1887 location.

Ground zero for the artistic renaissance of Williamsburg is Bedford Avenue and surrounding side streets, where Polish delicatessens are sandwiched in between galleries, shops, restaurants and bars. A day or night in this part of Williamsburg, can include everything from cinema to fusion food to avant-garde circus performances.

Subway: L train to Bedford Avenue.

HIGHLIGHTS OF THE NEIGHBORHOOD

McCarren Park Northern end of Bedford Ave. (between N. 12th St. and Leonard Ave.). The park is a spiffier spot these days after the New York City Parks department gave it some long-overdue repairs. From spring through fall, this is a great place to take in the local scene. It's a conflagration of ethnic groups: older Polish men and women dance to live polka music; Latino families play fierce games of soccer and volleyball and stage huge festive barbecues; artist/hipster residents lie on the grass or play Frisbee, and occasionally, Hasidic men toss baseballs in games of catch.

Metropolitan Pool and Bathhouse 261 Bedford Ave. (718) 965-6576. This historic site was reopened in the fall of 1997 after a $4.88 million renovation. The 1922 building, which includes a 30-by-75-foot swimming pool, two new locker rooms, a community room and a fitness area, was originally designed by Henry Bacon, architect of the Lincoln Memorial in Washington.

Williamsburg Bridge
(See section "Lower East Side" *earlier in this chapter.)*

Art in Williamsburg

Galapagos 70 N. 6th St. (between Wythe and Kent Aves.) (718) 782-5188. This Williamsburg bar and arts center is hard to find but worth the hunt for its expansive cathedral-like interior, brilliantly spotlit with candles on the walls, bare I-beams and a stark, minimal bar ringed with tables. Ocularis is Galapagos' screening room, run by Donal O'Ceille, a young Irishman who started showing old movies on the roof one summer and quickly attracted a local following. The space seats about 100 people.

Holland Tunnel 61 S. 3rd St. (between Berry St. and Wythe Ave.) (718) 384-5738. One of the quirkiest art spaces in Williamsburg, Holland Tunnel is run by Pauline Lethen, an energetic Dutch woman who sees it partly as a conduit for Dutch art (hence the title). It occupies a small pre-fab gardener's shed set in a pretty little yard behind an old apartment building.

Art Moving 166 N. 12th St. (between Berry St. and Bedford Ave.) (718) 486-8366. Art Moving is the accidental gallery of the artist Aaron Namenwirth, who in 1992 moved into a storefront that had been occupied by one of Williamsburg's first galleries. Passersby regularly inquired about the next show, and the previous tenant's mail, including many artists' slides, continued unabated. Finally Mr. Namenwirth began holding sporadic shows of neighborhood artists.

Pierogi 2000 177 N. 9th St. (at Bedford Ave.) (718) 599-2144. Joe Amrhein decided to promote the work of Williamsburg artists by filling a flat file with their drawing portfolios, creating a remarkably efficient and mobile way to let interested parties see the work of hundreds of artists. Mr. Amrhein also mounts ambitious exhibitions in the space.

RECOMMENDED BROOKLYN RESTAURANTS

Brooklyn Heights

Gage & Tollner   **$$**   SEAFOOD/SOUTHERN
372 Fulton St. (between Adams and Jay Sts.)   (718) 875-5181
Gage & Tollner opened in 1879 and moved to its current downtown Brooklyn location in 1892. It is a wonderfully old-fashioned room. The beautiful old gas-fired lights have been retrofitted and acoustic tiles have been removed, exposing the original vaulted ceiling. Unlike the room, the menu has barely changed in a century, with old favorites like soft clam bellies, lobster Newburg, she-crab soup and "blooming onions," which are cunningly fried whole. **Price range:** Entrees, $15–$27. Closed Sun.

Grimaldi's   **$$**   PIZZA
19 Old Fulton St. (under Brooklyn Bridge)   (718) 858-4300
This stellar pizzeria overshadowed by the Brooklyn Bridge makes classic, coal-oven New York pizza. Crusts are thin and crisp in the center, blackened and blistered around the dense and bready edges. The mozzarella is fresh, the tomato sauce is fragrant and made at the restaurant, as are roasted peppers. Expect a wait and expect to hear Sinatra playing in the background. Cash only.

River Café   ☆☆   **$$$$**   NEW AMERICAN
1 Water St. (at the Brooklyn Bridge)   (718) 522-5200
Is this New York City's most romantic restaurant? With waterside seating, a spectacular view of downtown Manhattan, dim lighting, heaps of flowers and live piano music, it certainly must be. Such a view might have made the food irrelevant, but this has been a seminal restaurant in the annals of New American food. The food is excellent and innovative and brunch is a special pleasure. So too is the dessert made of chocolate and shaped like the Brooklyn Bridge. **Price range:** Prix fixe, $70; tasting menu, $90.

Tinto $25 & Under   TAPAS
60 Henry St. (at Cranberry St.)   (718) 243-2010
Tinto looks the part of a Spanish tapas bar, with leather banquettes, dim chandeliers and candles. The menu changes nightly and includes excellent cold tapas like roasted marinated red peppers or mellow and flavorful scallops ceviche. Among the hot tapas, try bacon-wrapped dates, served pierced with a toothpick like 1950's canapes. Lobster tacos, served with a sweet mango-and-pepper sauce, are quite good. **Price range:** Entrees, $12–$17.

Carroll Gardens

Banania Café $25 & Under   FRENCH
241 Smith St. (between Butler and Douglass Sts.)   (718) 237-9100
Banania, named for a French children's drink, has an enticing menu of reasonably priced bistro dishes. There are Asian and Middle Eastern touches, so that though it feels French, it falls into that catchall international category that might be called contemporary. Calamari rings, for example, are dusted with cumin, roasted and served with carrot purée, a happy match of power and pungency. Among main courses, braised lamb shank and moist roasted cod are delicious. **Price range:** Entrees, $12–$15. Cash only.

Ferdinando's Focacceria $25 & Under   ITALIAN
151 Union St. (between Columbia Pl. and Hicks St.)   (718) 855-1545
They filmed *Moonstruck* on this street, and you can see why. Ferdinando's is a throwback to turn-of-the-century Brooklyn, before Ebbets Field had even been built. The menu offers old Sicilian dishes, like chickpea-flour fritters; vasteddi, a focaccia made with calf's spleen; and pasta topped with sardines canned by the owner. **Price range:** Entrees, $10–$13. Cash only. Closed Sun.

Mignon $25 & Under   FRENCH
394 Court St. (between Carroll St. and 1st Pl.)   (718) 222-8383
Even when it's very busy, service in Mignon's lace-curtained dining room is friendly, courteous and efficient, food arrives at an acceptable pace, and best of all, it's delicious. Chilled seafood bisque, with the intense, rich flavors of shrimp and lobster reduced to their essences, is a great appetizer. Cod coated with ground almonds is terrifically moist and flavorful, while both sautéed monkfish and grilled red snapper are also perfectly cooked. Desserts include a wonderful fruit tart. **Price range:** Entrees, $13–$18.50. Cash only. Closed Mon.

Patois $25 & Under   BISTRO/FRENCH
255 Smith St. (between Douglass and Degraw Sts.)   (718) 855-1535
This small storefront restaurant offers rich, gutsy bistro fare that can range from authentically French tripe stew—a mellow, wonderful dish, if not destined for popularity—to juicy pork chops and satisfying casseroles. Dishes don't always work, but it's nice that Patois is trying. **Price range:** Entrees, $10–$17. Closed Mon.

Saul $25 & Under   NEW AMERICAN
140 Smith St. (between Dean and Bergen Sts.)   (718) 935-9844
The small menu in this sweet little brick storefront offers strong, clear flavors,
bolstered by background harmonies that augment without overshadowing. The
main courses seem familiar—salmon, chicken, pork loin—but they are beautifully handled and surprisingly good. Desserts are wonderful, like lush baked
alaska with a chocolate cookie crust. **Price range:** Entrees, $15–$20.

Smith Street Kitchen $25 & Under   SEAFOOD/NEW AMERICAN
174 Smith St. (between Warren and Wycoff Sts.)   (718) 858-5359
The small dining room here has an inviting lived-in look, service is solicitous
without being overfriendly, and the restaurant takes its obligations seriously.
Perhaps best of all, the restaurant offers excellent value. The menu is small, but
the appetizers include some exceptional selections, like a small tart filled with
sweet lobster and smoky chorizo along with mushrooms, spinach and tomato
confit. The main courses are less consistent, but thick slices of grilled tuna left
rosy in the middle and flavored with sesame oil are excellent, as is sautéed cod.
The pear bread pudding can take its place among the bread pudding elite. **Price
range:** Entrees, $15–$22.

Sur $25 & Under   ARGENTINE
232 Smith St. (between Butler and Douglass Sts.)   (718) 875-1716
This brick-walled, candlelit Argentine restaurant is warm and inviting without
any of the usual gaucho clichés. The focus, naturally, is on beef. Try the lean,
almost grassy Argentine sirloin, served with a mound of crisp, salty french fries.
Alternatives to beef include juicy and flavorful roast chicken and several pasta
dishes. For dessert, try the crepes filled with dulce de leche, a sublime caramel-
like confection of cream and sugar. **Price range:** Entrees, $12–$19.

Cobble Hill/Boerum Hill

Brawta $25 & Under   CARIBBEAN
347 Atlantic Ave. (between Hoyt and Bond Sts.)   (718) 855-5515
Brawta, Jamaican patois for "something extra," offers top-flight Jamaican food
in a relaxed, colorful dining room. Rotis—peppery stews of chicken or mellow
goat rolled up in huge, soft flatbreads—are superb, as is the spicy jerk chicken.
Coco shrimp is an unusual and generous shrimp curry made with coconut milk.
Don't miss the traditional Caribbean beverages, like sweet-and-spicy sorrel and
the thick sea moss, a legendary boon to male virility. For dessert, try the bread
pudding. **Price range:** $9.50–$18

Harvest $25 & Under   AMERICAN
218 Court St. (at First Pl.)   (718) 624-9267
A lively, appealing neighborhood restaurant that is plagued by inconsistency.
Harvest feels like the best restaurant in a small college town, and the menu of
American regional food like roasted beet salad, gumbo and meatloaf whets the
appetite. **Price range:** Entrees, $9–$14. Closed Mon.

Coney Island

Gargiulo's $$$ ITALIAN
2911 W. 15th St. (between Surf and Mermaid Aves.)   (718) 266-4891
In business since 1907 and at this location since 1928, Gargiulo's is a longtime
favorite, especially for the kind of subtle, freshly prepared Neapolitan specialties
that are hard to find these days. You won't go wrong with roasted peppers, fried
calamari with a delicate tomato sauce dip, baked clams, mussels in tomato
broth, all of the southern pastas and lobster oreganato (here called racanati).

Nathan's Famous $ FAST FOOD
1310 Surf Ave. (between Stillwell Ave. and W. 16th St.)   (718) 946-2202
Famous is the word for this 1916 original, opened to compete with the long-
gone Feltman's, where Charles Feltman, a German immigrant, is believed to
have invented the hot dog by slipping a frankfurter into a long heated roll. One
of his waiters, Nathan Handwerker, spun off his own version, and the rest is
hot-dog history. It is said that these juicy all-beef franks are still made according
to the meat and spice recipes developed by Nathan and his wife, Ida.

Totonno Pizzeria $$ PIZZA
1524 Neptune Ave. (between W. 15th and W. 16th Sts.)   (718) 372-8606.
Just three blocks off the Boardwalk, in the heart of what's left of Coney Island's
Little Italy, this is a highly touted 74-year-old pizzeria, more interesting for its
history than for its pizzas, which can be fine or fair.

Fort Greene and vicinity

Cambodian Cuisine $25 & Under   CAMBODIAN
87 S. Elliott Pl. (between Fulton St. and Lafayette Ave.)   (718) 858-3262
This may be the only Cambodian restaurant in New York City and is worth
checking out for that reason alone. Most dishes are similar to Thai and Vietnamese foods but some of the preparations are unusual. In the signature dish,
chicken ahmok, chicken breast is marinated in coconut milk, lemongrass,
galangal and kaffir lime and steamed until it achieves a soft, pudding-like texture. **Price range:** Entrees, $3.50–$14.95.

Junior's $$ DINER
386 Flatbush Ave. (at DeKalb Ave.)   (718) 852-5257
There's a full menu of meat, fish and pan-ethnic dishes, but the real house specials are the superb cheese blintzes (minus strawberry sauce), hefty egg dishes,
corned beef or tongue (rather than pastrami) sandwiches and gloriously creamy
but firm cheesecake, best when plain. **Price range:** Main courses, $6–$10.

Locanda Vini & Olii $25 & Under   ITALIAN
129 Gates Ave. (between Cambridge Pl. and Grand Ave.)   (718) 622-9202
This mom-and-pop trattoria was a pharmacy for 130 years. The woodwork has
been lovingly restored, and many old features have been left intact. But
Locanda's menu is full of surprising dishes. Superb choices abound among the

pastas, especially the maltagliati, fat strands of carrot-colored pasta in a light ricotta sauce with soft fava beans, diced prosciutto and plenty of sage. **Price range:** Entrees, $6–$16. Cash only. Closed Mon.

Park Slope

Al di la $25 & Under   ITALIAN
248 Fifth Ave (at Carroll St.)   (718) 783-4555
The food at Al di la is soulful and gutsy, with profound flavors. This neighborhood restaurant serves on bare wooden tables, but hints at a more sensual attitude with such luxurious touches as velvet drapes and chandeliers. The chef coaxes deep flavors out of simple dishes, and all the pastas are wonderful. **Price range:** Main courses, $9–$17.

Blue Ribbon $$ NEW AMERICAN
280 Fifth Ave. (at First St.)   (718) 840-0404
The Brooklyn outpost of the Blue Ribbon empire feels like many things at once. It's part saloon, part oyster bar, part bistro, part diner and part Jewish deli, if matzo ball soup is anything to go by. The extensive menu hops and skips from herring to clam stew to hummus to a fried catfish hero. This is home cooking no matter where home happens to be. **Price range:** Main courses, $8–$25.

Chip Shop $25 & Under   ENGLISH
383 Fifth Ave. (at 6th St.)   (718) 832-7701
At this small, extremely English fish and chips restaurant, much of the food is honest and forthright, filling and satisfying. With music at high volume, the pitch is clearly toward a younger crowd, but the yellow dining room is cheerful and pleasant. The mushy pea fritter is a wonderful dish. You can also try some of England's greatest pub hits, like fine bangers and mash, plump pork-and-cereal sausages over mashed potatoes. For dessert, try the deep-fried Mars bar. **Price range:** Entrees, $6–$11. Cash only.

Coco Roco $25 & Under   LATIN AMERICAN
392 Fifth Ave. (near 6th St.)   (718) 965-3376
This bright, pleasant restaurant offers some of the best Peruvian food in New York. The menu ranges from tender, delicious ceviches from Peru's coast to Andean dishes that have been enjoyed since the days of the Incan empire. Roast chicken is excellent, and desserts like rice pudding and lucuma ice cream, made with a Peruvian fruit, are wonderful. **Price range:** Entrees, $8.95–$16.95.

Rose Water $25 & Under   NEW AMERICAN
787 Union St. (between Fifth and Sixth Aves.)   (718) 783-3800
Rose Water's innovative cooking, moderate prices and relaxed ambience would be exciting anywhere. Try a brik, a crisp North African turnover filled with ground lamb, caraway and mint and surrounded with a pungent parsley sauce. Rose Water offers a pork chop with a fabulous flavor as well as a thin-sliced rump steak, flavored with cloves that works very well. **Price range:** Entrees, $12.50–$16.50.

Prospect Heights

Bistro St. Mark's $25 & Under   BISTRO
76 St. Mark's Ave. (between Flatbush and Sixth Aves.)   (718) 857-8600
Bistro St. Mark's blends so inconspicuously with the surroundings that you
might walk right by. A look at the menu provokes a double take, because this is
no simple bistro fare. Try the glistening mackerel tartar topped with a luscious
smidgen of caviar and dressed in capers and a bracing sauce gribiche, or the
moist and delicious skate wing, dusted with ground walnuts. **Price range:**
Entrees, $14–$19.

Garden Café $25 & Under   NEW AMERICAN
620 Vanderbilt Ave. (at Prospect Pl.)   (718) 857-8863
This family-run operation near the Brooklyn Academy of Music serves an ever-
changing menu of artful American food that is always satisfying. Standards like
grilled veal chops and steaks are superb, and the chef occasionally comes up
with dishes like jambalaya with Middle Eastern spicing. It's the kind of place
you wish was in your neighborhood. **Price range:** Entrees, $17.50–$20. Closed
Sun., Mon.

Tom's Restaurant $ DINER
782 Washington Ave. (at Sterling Pl.) (718) 636-9738
Around the corner from the Brooklyn Museum is Tom's, a 65-year-old Brooklyn
institution offering the best in diner food for ludicrously low prices. With a classic diner menu (they still serve cherry lime rickeys) and the warmest atmosphere (and kitschiest décor) in town, Tom's alone is worth a trip to Prospect
Heights. Closes daily at 4 P.M. Closed Sunday. **Price range:** Entrees, $4 and up.

Williamsburg

Bahia $25 & Under   SALVADORAN
690 Grand St. (near Manhattan Ave.)   (718) 218-9592
Although the extensive menu includes hamburgers and Buffalo wings, the specialties are typical Salvadoran dishes like pupusas, corn pancakes with small
amounts of meats and vegetables stuffed into the center. If you pile a side of
coleslaw on the pupusa and eat them together, tangy, rich magic occurs. Don't
pass up horchata, a sweet iced rice drink with cinnamon and cocoa. **Price
range:** Entrees, $6.50–$15.

Diner $25 & Under   DINER
85 Broadway (at Berry St.)   (718) 486-3077
Diner brings the diner idea up to date, offering the sort of everyday food that
appeals to the local art crowd. The basics are fine, and other dishes can be
superb, like skirt steak, perfectly cooked whole trout, black bean soup and eggs
scrambled with grilled trout. The atmosphere is bustling and smoky. **Price
range:** Entrees, $6.50–$15. Cash only.

Oznot's Dish $25 & Under   MEDITERRANEAN
79 Berry St. (at N. 9th St.)   (718) 599-6596
Oznot's is truly unusual, a veritable flea market of mosaics, mismatched furniture and artwork set on a rickety, uneven wood floor. The blend of Mediterranean food is just as interesting, with dishes like grilled shrimp served over tab-
bouleh with fennel chutney. Main courses include fish and seafood stew served
in a tomato-saffron broth and fennel-dusted tuna with hummus and tapenade.
Price range: Entrees, $10–$18.

Peter Luger   ☆☆☆ $$$$ STEAKHOUSE
178 Broadway (at Driggs Ave.)   (718) 387-7400
Peter Luger serves no lobsters, takes no major credit cards and lacks a great wine
list. Service, though professional and often humorous, can sometimes be
brusque. So why is it packed night and day, seven days a week? Simple: Peter
Luger has the best steak in New York City. The family that runs the restaurant
buys fresh shortloins and dry-ages them on the premises. You know the steak is
great from the fine, funky aroma that wafts across the table. An occasional diner
will choose the thick and powerfully delicious lamb chops, or the fine salmon.
And even side dishes have their moments. But the steak's the thing here, and
they serve just one cut: an enormous porterhouse charred to perfection over
intense heat. **Price range:** Avg. price for three courses, $60. Cash only.

Plan-Eat Thailand $25 & Under   THAI
141 N. 7th St. (between Bedford and Berry Sts.)   (718) 599-5758
This unusual, much-applauded Thai restaurant serving Williamsburg has its ups
and downs, but more often than not serves spicy, meticulously prepared dishes
like ground pork salad, sautéed bean curd and striped bass with crunchy greens.
It is often crowded and loud. **Price range:** Entrees, $4.75–$12.95. Cash only.

Relish $25 & Under   NEW AMERICAN/DINER
225 Wythe Ave. (at N. 3rd St.)   (718) 963-4546
Relish is a diner of gleaming, embossed stainless steel. The chef is clearly at
home in the modern vernacular, and his menu is rarely pretentious and often
winning. It may be laughable for a diner to serve foie gras, but his version is
quite good. Among the main courses, juicy, flavorful chicken and fresh waffles
are served with a mound of garlic-imbued kale. **Price range:** Entrees, $11–$17.

Brooklyn Nightlife

Go out in Brooklyn? On the weekend? For New Yorkers in the know, that was
once an unbearably tepid proposition. Russian immigrants may drink vodka in
Brighton Beach leisure palaces, and Trinidadians let loose to soca near Nostrand
Avenue. But the students, artists and hipsters seeking the cultural edge started
their evenings on the subway to the Village and beyond.

Now the Brooklyn-Manhattan power balance is changing. Exiled trendsetters eventually found themselves loving their neighborhoods and dressed them up with shops, restaurants and bars. Younger residents tried spots that no one else had yet declared chic. Hot spots multiplied, some as buzz-filled as Manhattan, others retaining an air of simplicity, messiness, home.

Brooklyn Heights, Cobble Hill, Boerum Hill, Carroll Gardens

The Bar 280 Smith St. (at Sackett St.) (718) 246-9050. If you look closely, you'll notice details here like black-vinyl barstools, red holiday lights, glittery tables and mismatched chairs. But what it all adds up to is a no-nonsense place to throw back a few cold ones, filled not with throngs of decked-out posers but rather with real folk wearing ratty T-shirts and smoking borrowed cigarettes.

Boat 175 Smith St (between Warren and Wyckoff Sts.) (718) 254-0607. This neighborhood bar has a friendly, attentive staff and a pretty laid-back clientele. The bar features plenty of seating, with cafe-style tables in front, a long wooden bar and the lounge at the rear.

Brooklyn Inn 138 Bergen St. (at Hoyt St.). Believed to have opened in 1868, the Brooklyn Inn is a regal, historic bar where the residents of Boerum Hill still gather over drafts of beer. There is no sign out front, adding to the bar's mysterious allure. The high ceilings, woodwork and stained-glass panels are impressive.

Halcyon 227 Smith St. (between Butler and Douglass Sts.) (718) 260-9299. Halcyon, a hipster cafe/bar, is filled with couches, tables, books, board games, lamps and other items from the 1950's through the 70's—all for sale. There is also a rear patio and a record store with 6,000 new and used records. Every Saturday night there is a dance party with a DJ.

Last Exit 136 Atlantic Ave. (between Henry and Clinton Sts.) (718) 222-9198. With its brick walls, red track lighting, vintage couches, art on the walls and a full house of young, laid-back hipster types, you might think you're in the East Village. The lack of attitude will tell you otherwise.

Quench 282 Smith St. (at Sackett St.) (718) 875-1500. Behind its sleek, frosted-glass exterior, Quench—a highlight on the Smith Street scene—exudes an air of unpretentious sophistication. Illuminated orbs hang from the ceiling, while the rich wood floor and bar gives the place a relaxed elegance.

Pete's Waterfront Ale House 155 Atlantic Ave. (between Clinton and Henry Sts.) (718) 522-3794. Pete's is the epitome of the friendly neighborhood bar. Not too divey or too classy, it's all about decent beer in a nice, well-ventilated space that offers a kid- and dog-friendly environment.

Fort Greene

Alibi 242 DeKalb Ave. (between Vanderbilt and Clermont Aves.) (718) 783-8519. Alibi is a dive bar in the great tradition of East Village. This one, though, lives across the East River in Fort Greene, and for what it offers, it doesn't have much local competition. Pratt students pack in, joining a decent-sized crowd.

Frank's Lounge 660 Fulton Street (at S. Elliott Pl.). This old-school lounge is a Fort Greene gem. With Christmas lights, red vinyl seats and three-inch stucco spikes hanging from the ceiling over the bar, Frank's is a kitsch-lovers dream. Check local listings for DJs and other events both in the lounge and in the loft upstairs.

Park Slope, Prospect Heights
(See also section "Gay & Lesbian" *in chapter* **Nightlife**.*)*

Freddy's Sixth Ave. (at Dean St.). With a neighborhood feel, cheap drinks and a backroom with a pool table, Freddy's is the ultimate dive. Everyone is welcome here where the crowd is a mix of older regulars, younger locals and everything in between.

The Gate 321 Fifth Ave. (at 3rd St.) (718) 768-4329. The Gate is a textbook example of low-key charm in every detail, from the attractive, distressed wood benches and tables to the amiable Irish bartender. This place provides a welcome antidote to the cutesiness of Park Slope.

Great Lakes 284 Fifth Ave. (at 1st St.) (718) 499-3710. Great Lakes on a busy Friday night would not surprise many Manhattanites. It is dimly lighted, smoky and filled with nicely dressed young professionals chatting about their day, sitting on couches and listening to the house DJ's funky sounds.

Loki 304 Fifth Ave. (at 2nd St.) (718) 965-9600. Dark and cavernous with something for everyone, Loki's front room is dominated by a long, dark-wood bar lined with candles—perfect for a quiet after-work read in the room's cafe-style ambiance. Loki's middle space is its rumpus room, with a pool table, jukebox and a dart board. And finally, tucked behind a cascade of heavy, red-velvet curtains, is a back room filled with a lavish, haphazard assortment of plush couches.

O'Connor's 39 Fifth Ave. (between Bergen and Dean Sts.) (718) 783-9721. Although O'Connor's might look scary from the outside, it's actually a delightful neighborhood bar where a mix of Park Slope residents socializes with ease. A second-generation Irish bar that was a speakeasy during Prohibition, O'Connor's is a beer-and-smoke-worn watering hole with rickety old wooden booths.

Williamsburg, Greenpoint

The Abbey 536 Driggs Ave. (between N. 7th and N. 8th Sts.) (718) 599-4400. Seeking a cozy cloister on a chilly night? Take refuge in the monastic intimacy of the Abbey. Exposed brick and a red felt pool table exude warmth, while torch-like wall candles dripping big blobs of wax enhance the medieval feel. Within, talkative, dressed-down twenty-somethings cluster in booths, perch on stools, and circle the pinball machine.

Black Betty 366 Metropolitan Ave. (at Havemeyer St.) (718) 599-0243. Although Black Betty is popular with locals, it's easy to miss. The only sign out front says Don Diego's (a remnant from the previous tenant, a divey nightclub). The transition from divey club to divey bar seems to have been pretty smooth. The space's new décor is more sleazy than anything else, but not unpleasantly so.

Blu Lounge 197 N. 8th St. (at Driggs St.) (718) 782-8005. This spot has the kind of cozy, friendly atmosphere that appeals to a variety of bar-goers. Blu's décor (with little of the expected color) consists of the kind of black-and-white checkered floor one finds in a diner, Crayola-orange walls and a mismatched array of vintage furniture and hanging lamps. A pleasantly mellow mix of electronica and other grooves enhances Blu's low-lit vibe.

Brooklyn Brewery 79 N. 11th St (between Berry St. and Wise Ave.) (718) 486-7422. You wouldn't spot the entrance to the Brooklyn Brewery's "tasting room" if it weren't for the dejected smokers pacing around after not being let in. Once inside the cavernous, brick-and-cinder-block-walled warehouse room, you'll feel like you're at the county fair: Brooklyn label brews are your only option here—unless you're interested in the Pepsi machine just inside the entrance.

Enid's 560 Manhattan Ave. (at Driggs Ave.) (718) 349-3859. This spot has struck the perfect formula for hipster cachet. Once a raw loft space, Enid's has been transformed into a comfortable SoHo-style living room, complete with amber lighting and—with its plastic-covered couches and "Revenge from Mars" pinball machine—just the right touch of a suburban rec room.

Galapagos 70 N. 6th St. (between Wythe and Kent Aves.) (718) 782-5188. The species may be less varied here than on the original Galapagos Islands— Williamsburg and Manhattan creative types, mostly—but the scenery is lush and the competition for mates is no less fierce. Better drown your dating sorrows in drink and take some Miyako sushi down with you. The music is international, but tends towards Electronica, intensifying as the night progresses.

Mug's Ale House 125 Bedford Ave. (between N. 10th and N. 11th Sts.) (718) 384-8494. The name of this traditional bar and grill derives from the beer steins strung along the top of wall—they range from a simple glass to a monstrous, elaborate German tankard. Though it has a full bar, Mug's is, of course, all about beer, with over 20 varieties on tap for $3 to $5 a pint.

Pete's Candy Store 709 Lorimer St. (between Frost and Richardson Sts.) (718) 302-3770 As its name suggests, Pete's Candy Store is full of treats. The small, comfortable space is at once eclectic and traditional, a cross between a hip bar and a genuine sweets shop. Its appeal is in the details: tables covered in Japanese newspaper, a menu of various "toasted sandwiches," plastic chickens roosting in a bale of hay in the storefront window.

Sweet Water Tavern 105 N. 6th St. (between Berry and Wythe Sts.) (718) 963-0608. The steamed-up windows on the facade of this longtime

Williamsburg joint seem to advertise a wanton world behind the glass. People hang out at the bar, mill around the pool table, or crowd into the small back room with its punk-and-metal jukebox, pinball machine and Sweet Water Tavern's take of local art, a wall full of playfully obnoxious graffiti.

Teddy's 96 Berry St. (at N. 8th St.) (718) 384-9787. Teddy's is a homey tavern, where mouthwatering pub fare, drinks and good spirits are served up nightly to a diverse bunch of locals. The ornate, dark wood furnishings don't just look old: They once inhabited a brewery, which opened the space in the 1890's. Performers appear every other Thursday; on Saturday nights, DJ's are featured.

QUEENS

There is more to Queens than two airports and Archie Bunker. Ethnically diverse and mostly residential, it is the second most populous borough (over 2 million residents) after Brooklyn, but far and away the largest, occupying one-third of the city's total area. Its neighborhoods are still identified by their names as villages before they were merged into New York City in 1898—Flushing, Jamaica, Astoria (named for John Jacob Astor), Little Neck (where the clams got their name), the Rockaways with their Atlantic Ocean beaches, and the upper-class enclaves of Forest Hills and Douglaston. Industry is concentrated in Long Island City on the East River facing Manhattan and in neighborhoods nearby—Steinway where William Steinway made pianos and his heirs still do, and Astoria where Gloria Swanson, Rudolph Valentino and the Marx Brothers made movies in the Kaufman Astoria studios, still the largest film and TV studios in the East.

Named in 1683 for Queen Catherine, wife of King Charles II of England, the borough was mostly farmland until the Queensboro Bridge to Manhattan was built in 1909—and there is still a working farm museum. But the population today is decidedly nonagrarian and increasingly foreign-born or born of immigrants—more than 100,000 Chinese and Koreans in Flushing, Indian immigrants in Jackson Heights, Greeks in Astoria, Irish in Sunnyside and Latinos in Elmhurst. To see for yourself, take "the international express"—the No. 7 subway line from Times Square. That line is also how to get to a Mets game in Shea Stadium, the U.S. Open in the National Tennis Center, and the New York Hall of Science. (Take the A train to get to Aqueduct racetrack near Jamaica Bay—or stay on the train for two more stops to the Jamaica Bay Wildlife Refuge, a renowned bird sanctuary.)

Astoria/Long Island City

Although Astoria has long been known as a Greek neighborhood, the area is extraordinarily diverse, with large numbers of Italians, Brazilians, Indians and Koreans making the Queens enclave their home. It's an anomaly, a wind-swept industrial district along the East River that is home—along with the waterfront section of nearby **Long Island City**—to some of the city's most exciting art institutions.

A visit to the **P.S. 1 Contemporary Art Center**, the **Isamu Noguchi Sculpture Museum**, the **American Museum of the Moving Image** and the **Socrates Sculpture Park** are all worth the trip across the river. But while you're there, city sites ranging from the **Steinway Piano Factory** (built in the 1880's) to **Gantry Plaza park** (built in the 1990's) offer a glimpse of the area's past and future.

HIGHLIGHTS OF THE NEIGHBORHOOD

American Museum of the Moving Image 35th Ave. at 36th St. (718) 784-0077 *www.ammi.org*. Before Hollywood drew much of the film industry west, Long Island City was the heart of American film production. Now, appropriately, it is the location of this museum devoted to the art and history of film. The exhibits here skillfully demonstrate the science of moving images as well as provide interesting collections of artifacts and set pieces from familiar movies and television shows. The museum also offers screenings of avant-garde films. Closed Monday.
Admission: $8.50, general; $5.50, students and seniors; $4.50, children 5-18; children under 5 free. **Subway:** R, G to Steinway St.; N to Broadway.

Gantry Plaza State Park 49th Ave. on the East River (718) 786-6385. The miracle of Gantry Park is that it takes risks in a city that has long been frightened of them. The payoff is spectacular. With the Manhattan skyline as a backdrop and gorgeous light bouncing off the river, the site itself is magnificent. The park takes its name from two giant, hulking structures of blackened iron on the site, which used to lift freight trains onto river barges. The gantries are as powerful as the triumphal arches and classical monuments built by the City Beautiful Movement a century ago. So is the brick power station, with its quartet of de Chirico stacks, that looms nearby. Visitors are greeted by a circular area that encloses a fog fountain, a shallow cauldron of seething mist that in summer cools the air. Beyond is a large, hemispherical plaza for performances.

The plaza connects to two of four piers that project into the river. Each is different in length, shape and furnishings. One has a circular lunch bar, with stools and awning. Another, the Star Gazing Pier, is outfitted with overscaled wooden chaises. On the Fishing Pier, there's a large, free-form table complete with running water, for dressing the catch of the day. But the best thing about the piers is the views they afford of each other and the people using them. Or you can proceed along one of the paths that lead away from the plaza's southern edge. The widest path, paved with stone, defines the water's edge in a series of graceful, serpentine arcs. Along the way, it passes over a bridge that looks down on a small river inlet. From there, you can make your way down almost to the water. A second path, lined with gravel, takes you on an inland ramble, through vegetation and stone blocks clustered in crystalline formations. The blocks echo the Manhattan skyline and partly take the place of benches. The overall effect is of a Cubist rock garden.   —*Herbert Muschamp*
Subway: 7 to Vernon Blvd.

Thomas Balsey Associates/Slowinski Sullivan Architects

Gantry Plaza State Park

Isamu Noguchi Garden Museum 32–37 Vernon Blvd. (at 33rd Rd.)
(718) 721-1932 *www.noguchi.org*. One of the most serene places in the city,
the Isamu Noguchi Garden Museum in Long Island City is a great spot for
lovers of the Japanese-American sculptor, or anyone who wants to get away
from the city without ever leaving it. Noguchi is best known for melding Eastern and Western influences in his stark, beautiful abstract sculptures and for
designing the world-famous Akari lamps, the multishaped paper lanterns that
have become a staple of SoHo lofts and anyone with a taste for Japanese
design. Visitors can stroll in the Japanese garden, buy Noguchi items in the
gift shop or just admire the haunting beauty of the artist's work. Designed by
Shogi Shizao, the museum is steps away from the Socrates Sculpture Garden.
Admission (suggested): $4, adults; $2, students and seniors. Two-thirds of the
collection is handicapped accessible. **Hours:** April-Oct.: Wed.–Fri., 10 A.M.–5
P.M.; Sat.–Sun., 11 A.M.–6 P.M. **Subway:** N to Broadway.

P.S. 1 Contemporary Art Center 22–25 Jackson Ave. (at 46th Ave. and 46th
Rd.) (718) 784-2084 *www.ps1.org*. Across the East River in Long Island City,
the P.S. 1 Contemporary Art Center is far from SoHo and the Museum Mile.
But its outer-borough location is an apt metaphor for the center's focus on mar-
ginal artists and art that isn't often exhibited in more traditional museums.
P.S. 1 has presented over 2,000 exhibitions since 1976. It occupies a
Romanesque Revival school building, built from 1893 to 1906 and renovated by
Frederick Fisher with the addition of a 20,000-square-foot outdoor courtyard
that serves as a sculpture garden, a dramatic front entry and a two-story project
space. A branch, the Clocktower Gallery at 108 Leonard Street in the TriBeCa
section of Manhattan, is open for special shows and events.
Permanent Collection: P.S.1 is a non-collecting institution but maintains many
long-term, site-specific installations throughout its 125,000 square feet of gallery

space by artists including James Turrell, Pipilotti Rist, Richard Serra, Lucio
Pozzi, Julian Schnabel and Richard Artschwager
Admission (suggested): $5, general; $2, artists, students and seniors. **Credit cards:** All major. **Hours:** Wed.–Sun., noon–6 P.M. Closed Mon., Tue. **Services:** Food, tours, lectures, concerts. **Programs for Children:** "Art Camp" for elementary-school children throughout the year; "High School to Art School" preparation courses, and family events. **Tours:** Docent-guided tours for groups and individuals, by appointment only. Prices vary. **Subway:** E, F to 23rd St.–Ely Ave.; 7 to 45th Rd.–Court House Sq.; G to Court Sq.

The Queensboro Bridge (59th Street Bridge). Silhouetted against a darkening sky, this elaborate expanse looks like a work of crochet. Once known as the Blackwells Island Bridge, it is still known commonly as the 59th Street Bridge. Walking across on the south side, look through the lacy structure to appreciate the skyscraper panorama and the river opening wide. From the north walk, you will see river currents rushing over rocks, and get a good close-up of Roosevelt Island (formerly Blackwells Island, then Welfare Island) and the red Roosevelt Island tram mechanism that suggests a Calder mobile.

Socrates Sculpture Park Broadway and Vernon Blvd. (718) 956-1819. This 4.5-acre jewel on the banks of the East River in Long Island City was once a ship yard, then for 20 years an illegal dump site. Through the efforts of sculptor Mark di Suvero, the site was converted in the mid-1980's to an outdoor sculpture park. Leased from the New York City Department of Ports and Trade for $1 a year, the site features semi-annual exhibitions of public sculpture in a variety of media. Among the sculptures are subtle and pleasing artistic touches: winding paths, marble benches, and stones carved to resemble a child's letter blocks. The park hosts dance, film and video presentations.
Subway: N to Broadway.

Steinway and Sons Piano Factory 19th Ave. and 38th St. (718) 721-2600. Steinway's 440,000-square-foot factory in Astoria, built in the 1880's, still produces great pianos. A tour of the factory affords a close-up view of some 300 craftsmen who saw, bend and sand the wood, put on the strings and voice the instruments. Visitors are also allowed to enter the factory's "pounder" room, where a machine tests the integrity of each instrument by banging on all 88 keys at once, 10,000 times.
Subway: N to Ditmars Blvd.

AREA RESTAURANTS

Christos Hasapo-Taverna   **$25 & Under**   GREEK/STEAK
41–08 23rd Ave. (at 41st St.)   (718) 726-5195
This cheerful, handsome Greek steakhouse recreates the traditional Greek pairing of a butcher shop and a restaurant. Meals begin with fresh tzatziki, a combination of yogurt, garlic and cucumber, and tarama, the wonderful fish roe purée. Appetizer portions are big and easily shared, and there is a large selection of

grilled offal if you like to precede your meat with more meat. Richly flavored steaks and chops dominate the menu, and some nights more traditional fare, like piglet and baby lamb, is turned on the rotisserie. Best desserts include baklava, a wonderful apple cake and a plate of prunes and figs marinated in sweet wine. **Price range:** Entrees, $20–$25.

Churrascaria Girassol $25 & Under   BRAZILIAN
33-18 28th Ave.   (718) 545-8250

If you are excited by the idea of juicy, salt-edged steaks, rich sauces mellowed with palm oil and the prospect of unlimited meat courses, then Girassol can be a little bit of paradise. The chef and owner, Lilian Fagundes, prepares almost everything from scratch, like an excellent feijoada, a richly flavorful black bean stew filling an iron kettle, thick with all manner of pork. **Price range:** Entrees, $9–$16.

Elias Corner $25 & Under   GREEK/SEAFOOD
24–02 31st St. (at 24th Ave.)   (718) 932-1510

This bright, raucous Greek seafood specialist offers no menus. Regulars know to check the glass display case in front to select the freshest looking fish. Go in the off hours, before the crowd arrives. Otherwise the wait is interminable and the staff becomes harried. **Price range:** Entrees, $12–$17. Cash only.

Syros $25 and Under   GREEK/SEAFOOD
32–11 Broadway   (718) 278-1877

Syros is named after the Greek island on which the owner grew up. It is attractive enough, in a conventional kind of way, and the Greek dips are particularly good. The grilled fish is superb—perfectly cooked, moist and delicious. Spanakopita, crisp layers of phyllo encasing spinach and feta cheese, is fresh and savory. Lemony fish soup is excellent, and even a T-bone steak is beefy and winning. **Price range:** Entrees, $9.25–$22.

Ubol's Kitchen $25 & Under   THAI
24–42 Steinway St.   (718) 545-2874

This simply decorated but authentic (there's a Buddhist shrine in the rear) Thai restaurant does not stint on its spicing or seasoning. Dishes marked on the menu as hot and spicy can be counted on to be searing, while dishes traditionally rich in fish sauce are suitably pungent. Top dishes include spicy salads and curries. **Price range:** Entrees, $5.95–$14.95.

Uncle George's $25 & Under   GREEK
33–19 Broadway   (718) 626-0593

A cross between a giant diner that's always open and a boisterous family restaurant, Uncle George's is an Astoria Greek classic. Portions are big, service is speedy and the menu offers every kind of Greek dish, from great grilled fish to the ubiquitous spanakopita (spinach pie). You won't leave hungry. With bright

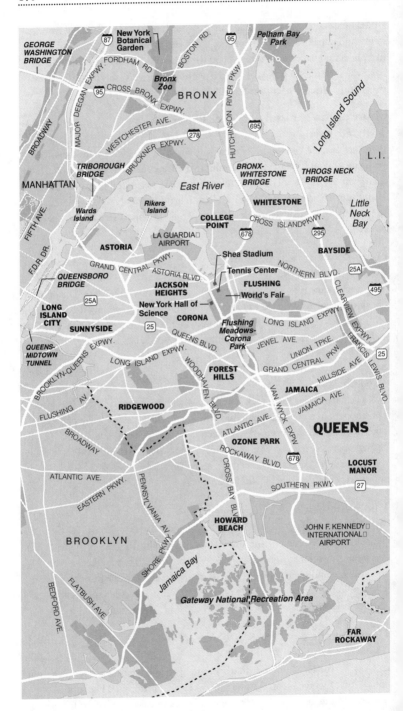

Queens

lights, plastic table covers and seats crowded into every available spot, it's fair to say that Uncle George's doesn't attract people for the décor. **Price range:** Entrees, $6–$12. Cash only.

Water's Edge   ☆ ☆   **$$$$**   NEW AMERICAN
44th Dr. at the East River   (718) 482-0033
The best thing about the whole event is the free ferry ride from 34th Street and the East River in Manhattan. The restaurant sits on a barge in the East River with a ship captain's view of Midtown Manhattan. The menu falls squarely in the mainstream, with all the trendy Asian touches and newly familiar ingredients. **Price range:** Prix-fixe dinner, $50–$80.

Flushing Meadows—Corona Park

Immortalized as the "Valley of the Ashes" in F. Scott Fitzgerald's *The Great Gatsby*, these former marshes were filled in long ago and became a park in 1939, when the site hosted the New York World's Fair. (It did so again in 1964). There's something for everyone at the park: You can catch a Mets game at **Shea Stadium** or watch the U.S. Open at the **U.S.T.A. National Tennis Center** (*see chapter* **Sports & Recreation**). You can also marvel at the 12-story-high **Unisphere**, visit the **New York Hall of Science** collection of American spacecraft (*see chapter* **New York for Children**) or walk around a scale model of New York at the **Queens Museum** —all of which were first built for the '64 fair.

HIGHLIGHTS OF THE NEIGHBORHOOD

Bowne House 37–01 Bowne St. (between 37th and 38th Aves.) (718) 359-0528. One of the city's oldest and most historic homes, this English-style farmhouse was built by John Bowne in 1661. He lived there and used it as New Amsterdam's first indoor Quaker meeting place, in defiance of the Dutch Reformed Church. Nine generations of Bownes lived here while a bustling Flushing neighborhood grew up around them. The house features restored rooms and changing exhibits. **Admission:** $4; $2, children and seniors. **Subway:** 7 to Main St.–Flushing.

Flushing Town Hall 137–35 Northern Blvd. at Linden Pl. (718) 463-7700. This two-story brick Romanesque Revival building served as Flushing's town hall until 1900, when the village was incorporated into New York City. Constructed in 1862 on what are believed to have been the Matinecock Indians' burial grounds, it is a veritable encyclopedia of American history. It served as a militia depot during the Civil War, a forum for speeches by Ulysses S. Grant and Teddy Roosevelt, a performance space for P.T. Barnum and Mark Twain, as well as a traffic court, jail, opera house, ballroom, police precinct and even a dinner theater. The Flushing Council on Culture and the Arts presents a variety of programs here. **Subway:** 7 to Main St.–Flushing.

Louis Armstrong's House 65–30 Kissena Blvd. (near Melbourne Ave.) (718) 478-8274. Louis and his wife, Lucille, lived here from 1943 until they died. It was built in 1910, and is today just as Lucille left it when she died in 1983. Now a museum, it contains the Louis Armstrong Archives.
Directions: E, F to Parsons Blvd., then take the Q 25 bus to Queens College.

Queens Museum of Art New York City Bldg. (111th St. and 49th Ave.) (718) 592-9700 www.queensmuse.org. If you go to the Queens Museum only to see the Panorama, an immense model of New York City, it would be well worth the trip. Originally built for the 1964 World's Fair, the model replicates in painstaking detail the geography, buildings, bridges and roads of all five boroughs at a scale of 1,200 to 1. The world's largest scale model, it fills a room the size of two basketball courts. The only art museum in Queens, it is housed in one of the few remaining buildings of the 1939 World's Fair. In addition to exhibiting contemporary art, the museum has an impressive collection of World's Fair memorabilia, an assortment of Tiffany lamps and a sculpture hall. The museum's satellite exhibition space at Bulova Corporate Center in Jackson Heights features a permanent sculpture exhibit as well as rotating shows of work by emerging artists.
Admission (suggested): $5; $2.50, students and seniors; children under 5 free. **Credit cards:** Cash only. **Hours:** Wed.–Fri., 10 A.M.–5 P.M.; Sat.–Sun., noon–5 P.M. **Services:** Gift shop, lectures. **Subway:** 7 to 11th St.

AREA RESTAURANTS

East Buffet & Restaurant $25 & Under   CHINESE
42-07 Main St., Flushing   (718) 353-6333
This huge, glossy Chinese eating hall seats 400 people in the buffet hall and 350 in another room for sit-down service. Three islands in the center of the buffet area hold more than 30 dim sum selections, a dozen soups, 40 dishes served cold and another 40 served hot. In the sit-down area try the extraordinary sticky rice, steamed in bamboo leaves and stuffed, tamale-like, with chopped pork.
Price range: Dinner, $20–$24.

Joe's Shanghai   ☆☆ $ CHINESE
136–21 37th Ave. (near Main St.), Flushing   (718) 539-3838
Joe's signature dish, "steamed buns," is alone worth the trip. The buns are wonderful soup dumplings that hold a lusty blend of pork or crab meat in a richly flavored broth. Among entrees, look for dishes like stewed mussels in black bean sauce; beef shank with bean curd Sichuan style; crabs, steamed and served over sweet sticky rice; tea-smoked duck; and braised pork shoulder in brown sauce. **Price range:** $9.50 and up. Cash only.

Kazan Turkish Cuisine $25 & Under   TURKISH
95–36 Queens Blvd., Rego Park   (718) 897-1509
Kazan's stone oven produces exceptional pide, soft football-shape loaves of bread dotted with sesame seeds, which are just right with any of the superb cold

appetizers. Eggplant is excellent, either charcoal grilled and puréed with garlic or left chunky and served with tomato and garlic. Kazan's short selection of main courses also includes some real winners like shish yogurtlu, juicy chunks of tender grilled lamb served over a sauce of yogurt blended with tomatoes. Kasarli kofte is another standout, made with chopped lamb blended with mild kasseri cheese, which gives the meat an unusual airiness. Desserts are good, but extremely sweet. **Price range:** Entrees, $8.50–$13.95.

La Esquina Criolla $25 & Under   SOUTH AMERICAN
94-67 Corona Blvd., Corona   (718) 699-5579
La Esquina Criolla is both meat market and restaurant. While some customers may take home one of the reasonably priced steaks, almost everybody in the throng on a Saturday night is filling up right there. It's hard to imagine a sweeter restaurant, despite a language barrier. And you can't get a better steak value than La Criolla's shell steak. Also good is the beefy skirt steak or the enormous mixed grill plate. Cap it off with an excellent flan topped with creamy dulce de leche. **Price range:** Entrees, $5.95-$18.95.

La Flor $25 & Under   MEXICAN/FRENCH/ITALIAN
53-02 Roosevelt Ave., Woodside   (718) 426-8023
La Flor stands out both for its looks and its food. The menu puts specialties from Mexico side by side with French and Italian dishes, or even fusion dishes like shrimp pastilla, shrimp wrapped with rice and almonds in crisp phyllo dough and served in a mole poblano sauce. The polyglot menu includes excellent individual pizzas. The Mexican pizza is a standout, and almost everything with pork is good. Breakfast and dessert are high points. **Price range:** Entrees, $6–$13.

Master Grill $25 & Under   BRAZILIAN
34–09 College Point Blvd., Flushing   (718) 762-0300
Possibly the most elaborate Brazilian rodizio in the city: Master Grill feels like an enormous banquet hall, with seating for 1,000 people and a samba band playing full tilt. It's all great fun if you're in the mood. The buffet itself is the size of a small restaurant, where you can fortify yourself with all manner of marinated vegetables, fruit, seafood, pasta, rolls, roasted potatoes and fried plantains. The parade of all-you-can-eat grilled meats, from chicken hearts to six kinds of beef, goes on as long as you can hold out. **Price range:** All you can eat, $18.95.

Pachas $25 & Under   LATIN AMERICAN
93–21 37th Ave., Flushing   (718) 397-0729
When a menu offers food from more than one land, the trick is knowing which way to go. Sometimes this is an easy call, but the Colombian-Venezuelan menu at Pachas presents problems. Order from the much bigger Colombian menu. A simple arepa con queso, fragrant with corn, is served steaming with a block of dense, salty cheese on top. Even better are the sublime arepa buche, a blend of tender tripe, tomato and onion, boiled down to a soulful essence. Pachas has no

liquor license but makes excellent batidos, or fruit shakes, in tropical flavors.
Price range: Entrees, $6–$13.

Pearson's Texas Barbecue $25 & Under   BARBECUE
71–04 35th Ave., Jackson Heights   (718) 779-7715

The only pit barbecue restaurant in New York City. In the rear, burnished slabs
of pork ribs glisten behind a counter next to piles of plump sausages and chickens turned almost chestnut by smoke. The glory of Pearson's is its brisket,
superb, tender and fully imbued with smoke from the rosy-brown, almost crisp
exterior through to the pink center. **Price range:** Sandwiches, $5.95; barbecue
by the pound, $4–$14. Cash only.

Penang $$ MALAYSIAN
38–04 Prince St., Flushing   (718) 321-2078

What started as a small Malaysian storefront in Flushing has turned into an
institution serving surprisingly authentic Malaysian flavors. The dish not to
miss is the roti canai, a seductive, savory crepe served with coconut milk sauce.
Price range: Avg. entree, $13.95.

Ping's   ☆☆ $$ CHINESE
83–02 Queens Blvd., Elmhurst   (718) 396-1238

Ping's looks like hundreds of other Chinese restaurants in New York City. Not
until you approach the fish tanks do you appreciate how extraordinary the food
is likely to be: in addition to the usual lobsters and sea bass, there may be several types of live shrimp, crab, both fresh-and salt-water eels and a number of
fish rarely seen swimming around in restaurants. Fried giant prawns filled with
roe and served with little sweet-potato dumplings are superb. For the best
options, ask for the translation of the Chinese menu. **Price range:** Entrees, from
$7.95 (all live seafood is market-priced).

Pio Pio $ PERUVIAN
84–13 Northern Blvd., Jackson Heights   (718) 426-1010

With brick walls, a pressed tin ceiling and big windows, this is an attractive
restaurant and a good place for a date. The menu is brief and the specialty is the
moist and beautifully spiced roast chicken. Tostones are excellent, as are the
pisco cocktails. Ceviche is served only on weekends. **Price range:** Combination
dinner, $20 for two people.

Rumi-Huasi $25 & Under   LATIN AMERICAN
44–10 48th Ave., Woodside   (718) 784-5111

If you're having a bad day, owner Donny Salas has a prescription for you: sopa
de pollo. The chicken soup speaks for itself, a rich, homey broth with a tender
chicken thigh and white rice sprinkled with parsley and cilantro. Order k'jallu,
a hominy salad, and she'll tell you not to worry, she'll serve it without the hot
peppers. Protest that you love hot peppers, and she looks very happy. The rest of
the menu is a carnivore's delight, particularly chicharrons, gnarled chunks of

fried pork on the bone, basted with a garlic sauce and served with hominy. **Price range:** Entrees, $7.95–$9.95. Cash only.

Sapori d'Ischia $25 & Under   ITALIAN
55-15 37th Ave., Woodside   (718) 446-1500
By day, this is a bright and thriving Italian specialty market. But at 5 P.M. candles are lit, soft music begins to play and a waiter takes over. The kitchen turns out fine individual pizzas, with thin, crisp, beautifully smooth crusts, but the small menu has other excellent choices, like budino di carciofi, or artichoke puree. Don't miss fettuccine al'Antonio, an excellent dish of fresh pasta with cream and prosciutto prepared at the table in a bowl carved out of a wheel of parmesan. **Price range:** Entrees, $7.50–$14. Cash only.

Shanghai Tang $25 & Under   CHINESE
135–20 40th Rd., Flushing   (718) 661-4234
This bright, handsome restaurant, one of the best Chinese places in Flushing, serves many excellent Shanghai specialties. You know you're in for an unusual meal when you enter and see fish tanks full of lively eels. Service is unusually friendly and helpful. **Price range:** Entrees, $6.95–$13.95 (specials to $24.95).

Sweet 'n' Tart Café $25 & Under   CHINESE
136–11 38th Ave., Flushing   (718) 661-3380
The specialty here is tong shui, a range of sweet tonics intended to benefit specific parts of the body or to balance one's yin and yang. But Sweet 'n' Tart's more typical dishes are terrific as well, like Chinese sausage and taro with rice, served in a tall bamboo steamer, and congee with beef, pork and squid. Little English is spoken here, but waitresses describe dishes as well as they can. **Price range:** $5–$14. Cash only.

OTHER ATTRACTIONS IN QUEENS

Gateway National Recreation Area—Jamaica Bay Wildlife Refuge Cross Bay Blvd., Broad Channel (718) 338-3338. The Jamaica Bay Wildlife Refuge near Kennedy Airport spans an area almost the size of Manhattan. Thousands of birds—including geese and ducks—stop here during their migration north and south along the Atlantic flyway. (The best time to visit is in the spring or fall, when birds fill the skies.) Over 300 species of birds and 65 species of butterflies have been found on the 9,000-acre preserve. Diverse habitats include salt marshland, upland fields, woods, ponds and an open expanse of bays and islands. **Subway:** A, S to Broad Channel.

Queens County Farm Museum 73–50 Little Neck Pkwy. at Union Tpke., Floral Park (718) 347-3276. This 47-acre, 200-year-old farm became such an anomaly that the city decided to turn it into a museum. But it's not what you'd expect. To this day it continues as a working farm with planted fields, orchards and livestock. The historic 1770's home features period rooms and changing

exhibitions on the history of agriculture. Special events include agricultural and
craft fairs, apple festivals and antique car shows, as well as quilting, candle making and other craft demonstrations and courses.
Directions: E, F to Kew Gardens, then take the Q 46 bus to Little Neck Pkwy.

STATEN ISLAND

The reaction to New York City's so-called forgotten borough is usually the
same: skepticism, sometimes tinged with a bit of disdain. "Staten Island? You
must be kidding." As if the only thing out there was the Fresh Kills landfill and
now that it has closed, the borough has nothing left to redeem it. Which could-
n't be more wrong. Staten Island is a wonderful place to explore—and to some,
it's so "out" it's "in." There are great little museums, three centuries of American
architecture, historic military sites, extensive gardens and lots of programs for
children. Nature lovers can meander through 7,500 acres of lush protected
parkland and along miles of uncrowded beaches, or discover wetlands that are
ripe for canoeing and communing with herons and cormorants.

All of this is easily accessible because the borough is well served by public
transportation, starting with the Staten Island Ferry. It can be surprisingly big to
first-time visitors, so a car can be an advantage. But with the Staten Island Railroad, many bus routes and efficient express bus service from Manhattan (all of
which take the MetroCard), you will never be stranded.

Cycling around the borough is especially fun in nice weather, and both the
ferry and the local trains are bike friendly. The City Department of Transportation publishes a free bike map, which can be picked up at the Staten Island Visitors Bureau in either ferry terminal. The ferry is the best way to get to Staten
Island. Once a bargain at a nickel a ride, it is now absolutely free and as breezy
and romantic as ever (the doughnuts and hot dogs aren't bad, either). Riding
one of those big orange boats at sunset on a summer evening is like a mini-
cruise and almost as restorative.

Boats leave from South Ferry in Manhattan and dock in St. George, the
county seat and transportation hub, which is also home to the borough's newest
landmark, the **Richmond County Bank Ballpark**, headquarters of the Staten
Island Yankees minor league baseball team. Since the first ball was thrown out
in June 2001, the Baby Bombers have drawn huge crowds to the home games, as
much for the sport—and the rivalry with the Brooklyn Cyclones—as for the
stadium's sweeping views of New York Harbor.

Another new landmark for St. George is the **National Lighthouse Museum**,
which will open in phases beginning in the summer of 2002. Housed in what
was most recently a Coast Guard base adjacent to the ferry terminal, it will
explore the science and lore of lighthouses. You can already tour the site, which
in the late 19th century was the United States Lighthouse Depot, the country's
main center for technological development and the manufacture of lighthouses.

Another proposal envisions adding a satellite of the **Staten Island Institute
of Arts and Sciences** along the leafy new port-side promenade. The institute,
the borough's main museum, is just a three-block walk from the ferry terminal.

It has a large cache of possessions, from bugs and botanicals to paintings and decorative objects, displayed in regular temporary exhibitions. Look for surprise gems such as paintings by the Staten Island native Jasper Cropsey, or works by Chagall, Warhol, Toulouse-Lautrec, Piranesi or Dürer.

The **Newhouse Center for Contemporary Art**, just a 10- to 15-minute ride west along Richmond Terrace by car, bus or bike, is the main exhibition space at the borough's best known art and performance site, the 83-acre **Snug Harbor Cultural Center**. Opened 200 years ago as a haven "for aged, decrepit and worn-out sailors"—or Snugs, as the retired seamen were called—Snug Harbor is a collection of 28 buildings in the Greek Revival, Italianate and Beaux-Arts styles, all of which are slowly being spruced up.

There is an 1892 music hall that is just a year younger than Carnegie Hall and a new museum, the **Noble Maritime Collection**. The museum opened in November 2000 in a three-story 1844 Greek Revival structure, which was renovated almost exclusively with volunteer labor. It focuses on the work of John A. Noble, the Paris-born lithographer, painter and seaman whose favorite subject was wooden sailing vessels.

You could spend a whole day at Snug Harbor, which offers an escape for every taste and age. If nature is what you crave, amble into the **Chinese Scholar's Garden** and you are instantly transported to China's Suzhou province, and maybe to another level of consciousness. The crown jewel of the **Staten Island Botanical Garden**, the Scholar's Garden was executed by 40 artisans from China and is the only garden of its kind in the United States. Seasonal changes in light and flora make it an oasis at any time of the year.

The **Jacques Marchais Museum of Tibetan Art**, on Lighthouse Hill in the middle of the island, has a wonderful garden, too, though a bit more intimate. Cyclists and hikers will find climbing the hill a bit daunting, but the surprise of finding a replica of a Himalayan monastery tucked in among the trees soon makes you forget your fatigue. The collection of Tibetan artifacts inside was assembled by Jacqueline Klauber, the late Manhattan dealer whose professional name was Jacques Marchais, and it was praised for its authenticity by the Dalai Lama, who visited in 1991.

Youngsters visiting Staten Island probably won't care about the deeper meaning of Moon Gates and mandalas, but they might go for the Botanical Garden's mazes. Through a clutch of screaming peacocks is the **Connie Gretz Secret Garden**, complete with circuitous paths, hedges and a turreted castle. Inspired by Frances Hodgson Burnett's book, it is a good place for the little ones to let loose.

And then there is always the **Carousel-for-All-Children** in Willowbrook Park, about 10 minutes by car. Its 51 old-fashioned wooden animals, hand-carved and hand-painted, revolve on a structure decorated with scenes of Staten Island. (*See* chapter **New York for Children** *for* **Staten Island Children's Museum** and **Staten Island Zoo**.)

A flood of development since the 1964 opening of the Verrazano-Narrows Bridge has robbed the island of much of its charm and character. But scattered among new houses and the kinds of elaborate lawn ornaments that make one long for the simpler days of petrified fawns, are some unusual things, both old and new, that add to the borough's appeal.

Doug Schwartz's rock installation is one. If you are driving or biking down Hylan Boulevard, stop by the beach at the end of Sharrots Road, at Mount Loretto, a former orphanage where some church scenes in *The Godfather* were filmed. A work in progress for 10 years, the installation is made up of rock circles and towers that are meant to evoke life, death, the sky and taking care of day-to-day affairs, says the artist, who is also the groundhog trainer and tropical forest keeper at the Staten Island Zoo.

On Lighthouse Hill near the Tibetan Museum, the **Crimson Beech**, a 1950's prefab house designed by Frank Lloyd Wright, is regarded as a piece of important mid-20th-century culture.

The same can be said for **Mandolin Brothers**, a bustling little shop-cum-museum close to the zoo, which is one of the world's foremost dealers in new and vintage guitars and other fretted instruments. The shop has been responsible for bringing some unlikely tourists to Staten Island: Joni Mitchell, for one, who immortalized the shop in a song, and George Harrison, who popped in one day unannounced and went on a 40-minute shopping spree.

If you love history, **Historic Richmond Town**, a village of 27 structures, offers not Disney-style reproductions but restorations of actual Staten Island buildings, some local and others moved to the 100-acre site from other island communities. The oldest is the red 17th-century Voorlezer's house, which is the oldest known school in the United States.

The collection of 18th-century Dutch Colonial farmhouses and workshops and a 19th-century country church are interesting for the tales that the village museum can reveal of the part they played in earlier community and family life. The County Fair here, with its pig races and do-wop concerts, is the borough's end-of-summer rendezvous of choice.

The **Conference House**, 15 minutes or so by bike from the Oakwood train station, is where one can begin to trace Staten Island's role in international politics. It was here in September 1776, with 32,000 British troops and Hessian mercenaries billeted among the island's 3,000 residents, that Lord Admiral Richard Howe met with Benjamin Franklin, John Adams and Edward Rutledge in a failed attempt to hammer out the finer points of the country's independence. The Conference House is in Tottenville, the end of the train line and Staten Island's southernmost tip. An unusual mix of Victorian houses and cottages, old mansions, odd urban and industrial ruins, beaches and tranquil wooded areas like **Blue Heron Pond** as well as relatively traffic-free streets, make this whole area a popular cycling destination.

The area also has lots of little green pockets, most of them too dense for cycling but great for hikes. The Urban Park Rangers offer canoeing lessons at **Wolfe's Pond Park**, but those with their own canoe or kayak can find out how unusual the **William T. Davis Wildlife Refuge** is. Part of the 2,800-acre **Green-belt**, a collection of six Staten Island parks and nature preserves, it has a network of navigable creeks whose grasses and banks are a habitat for native

Staten Island

wildlife and temporary quarters for many migratory birds. It also provides a
bird's-eye view of the old Fresh Kills Landfill.

For those interested in things military, **Battery Weed**, a multitiered fortress,
is a short bus or bike ride from the ferry. It is one of the oldest forts in the nation
and one of only three examples of its kind ever built. The site, **Fort
Wadsworth**, visible from the Verrazano-Narrows Bridge as one crosses from
Brooklyn, is the oldest continually staffed military post in the United States.

The 19th century might be considered Staten Island's Golden Age, when
the borough appealed even to international political exiles. The Italian patriot
Giuseppe Garibaldi forged the plan for his country's independence in the home
of Antonio Meucci, said to be the true inventor of the telephone. At the
Garibaldi-Meucci Museum, between the ferry and Fort Wadsworth, you can see
some of the first telephones and assorted Garibaldi memorabilia, including the
red shirt he wore defending Rome against the French in 1849.

In the 19th century, life was madcap for the privileged classes on Staten
Island, a playground for families like the Vanderbilts and the Cunards. You can

Barton Silverman/The New York Times

The Verrazano Bridge, at the start of the New York Marathon

see the busy life of the borough's comfortably wealthy as it was captured on film
by one of their own, **Alice Austen**, at her family's home, now a museum.
Austen was one of the first American women to take up photography.

Her vine-covered cottage, Clear Comfort, serves as a museum of the Victorian lifestyle as well as a photo gallery showing prints by Austen and other photographers. It is a poignant memorial to her and to a forgotten era in the forgotten borough.   —*Claire Wilson*

Verrazano-Narrows Bridge

With a main span of 4,260 feet, this is the longest suspension bridge in the
United States and the second longest in the world. Even so, the Verrazano-Narrows seems doomed to forever play second fiddle to the Brooklyn Bridge. It
lacks its elder sibling's pedestrian walkway, its close-up views of Manhattan and
its rich, romantic history. But there's no denying the Verazzano's grandeur, with
a total length (including the approaches) of over two and a half miles. The tops
of the 693-foot-high towers are 1⅝ inches farther apart than their bases, to
compensate for the earth's curvature. And due to seasonal expansion and con-
traction of the bridge's cables, the roadway can be 12 feet lower in the summer
than in the winter.

The Verrazano-Narrows opened to traffic in 1964, a project of Robert Moses
and the Triborough Bridge and Tunnel Authority, which he headed. It is the
youngest span in New York, but it is literally and figuratively linked to the past.
The name comes from Giovanni da Verrazano, the first European to sail into
New York Harbor, and the ends of the bridge lie in the historic guardians of the
harbor: Brooklyn's Fort Hamilton and Staten Island's Fort Wadsworth. Today,
the bridge is the only direct link between Brooklyn and Staten Island, and it
offers the shortest route between Long Island and the Middle Atlantic states.

ATTRACTIONS

(*For more on the* **Staten Island Ferry** *see chapter* **Exploring New York**; *for* **Staten Island Children's Museum** and **Staten Island Zoo** *see chapter* **New York for Children**; *for* **Staten Island Yankees** *see chapter* **Sports & Recreation**.)

Alice Austen House 2 Hylan Blvd., Rosebank (718) 816-4506. **Hours:** Thu–Sun., noon–5 P.M. **Admission:** $2; children under 6, free. **Bus:** S-51.

Carousel-for-All-Children Willowbrook Park, 1 Eaton Pl., Willowbrook (718) 477-0605, (718) 667-2165. **Hours:** Daily, 11 A.M.–5:45 P.M. **Tickets:** $1 a ride. **Bus:** S-62 to the park's gate on Victory Blvd.

Conference House waterfront at end of Hylan Blvd., Tottenville (718) 984-6046. **Hours:** Fri–Sun., 1–4 P.M. **Admission:** $2; $1, children and seniors. **Bus:** S-78 to Craig Ave.

Fort Wadsworth and Battery Weed Bay St. at Hylan Blvd. (718) 354-4500. Fort Wadsworth Visitors Center, Wed.–Sun., 10 A.M.–P.M. Free tours, Sat.–Sun., 10:30 A.M. and 2:30 P.M.; Wed.–Fri., 2:30 P.M. "Living History at Fort Wadsworth," with musket demonstrations and infantry drills, Sun., 11 A.M.–4 P.M.; free. **Bus:** S51 to Von Briesen Park.

Garibaldi-Meucci Museum 420 Tompkins Avenue, Rosebank (718) 442-1608. **Bus:** S52, S78 or S79, to the door.

Historic Richmond Town 441 Clarke Ave. (718) 351-1611. **Hours:** Wed.–Sat., 10 A.M.–5 P.M.; Sun., 1–5 P.M. **Admission:** $4; $2.50, students and seniors; children under 6, free. **Bus:** S-74 to Richmond Rd. and St. Patrick's Pl.

Mandolin Brothers 629 Forest Ave., West Brighton (718) 981-3226. **Hours:** Mon.–Sat., 10 A.M.–6 P.M. **Bus:** S-48 to Forest and Pelton Aves.

Jacques Marchais Museum of Tibetan Art 338 Lighthouse Ave., Richmond (718) 987-3500. **Hours:** Wed.–Sun., 1–5 P.M. **Admission:** $5; $3, students and seniors; $2, children under 12. **Bus:** S-74 to Richmond Rd. and Lighthouse Ave.

National Lighthouse Museum 1 Lighthouse Plaza, St. George (718) 556-1681. Tours, Wed. and Sat., 11 A.M. and 1, 2 and 3 P.M.; Sun., 1, 2 and 3 P.M. Reservations required. **Admission** (suggested): $2. **Directions:** Walk from ferry.

Staten Island Institute of Arts and Sciences 75 Stuyvesant Pl., St. George (718) 727-1135. **Hours:** Mon–Sat., 9 A.M.–P.M.; Sun., 1–5 P.M. **Admission** (suggested): $2.50; $1, children. **Directions:** Walk from ferry.

Snug Harbor Cultural Center 1000 Richmond Terrace, Livingston (718) 448-2500. Free. **Bus:** S-40.

Newhouse Center for Contemporary Art at the Center. **Hours:** Sun.–Fri., 11 A.M.–5 P.M.; Sat., 11 A.M.–7 P.M. **Admission** (suggested): $2.

Noble Maritime Collection at the Center (718) 447-6490. **Hours:** Thu.–Sun., 1–5 P.M. **Admission:** $3; $2, students and seniors; children under 10 and members, free.

Staten Island Botanical Garden at the Center (718) 273-8200. The park is open, free, dawn to dusk. The **Chinese Scholar's Garden** is open Tue.–Sun., 9 A.M.–5 P.M. **Admission:** $5; $4, children, students and visitors over 55. The **Connie Gretz Secret Garden** is open Tue.–Sun., 9 A.M.–5 P.M. **Admission:** $2, adults; $1, children; adults accompanied by a child enter free.

WHERE TO EAT

Aesop's Tables 1233 Bay St., Rosebank (718) 720-2005. Among the best, with a garden out back.

Adobe Blues 63 Lafayette Ave., New Brighton (718) 720-2583. Casual Mexican, not far from St. George.

American Grill 420 Forest Ave., West Brighton (718) 442-4742. Good bet for American fare.

Cargo Cafe 120 Bay St., St. George (718) 876-0539. Much better than it looks. Great fries, and a five-minute walk from the ferry.

Denino's Pizzeria Tavern 524 Port Richmond Ave., Port Richmond (718) 442-9401. Thin-crust pizza and a big line to get in. Try the white pizza.

Killmeyer's Old Bavarian Inn 4254 Arthur Kill Rd., Charleston (718) 984-1202. German food, great old bar and a beer garden out back.

Ralph's Ice Cream Store 501 Port Richmond Ave., Port Richmond (718) 273-3675. The authority—in the city, not just the borough—on Italian ice.

Getting There

By subway and ferry: 1, 9 to South Ferry; 4, 5 to Bowling Green; N, R to Whitehall Street. Then take the Staten Island Ferry to St. George.

By express bus: From Manhattan, there are 30 express buses (1X, 9X, 10X, for example) that go to various Staten Island destinations. Info: (718) 330-1234.

By Car: From Manhattan, take either the Brooklyn Bridge or the Brooklyn Battery Tunnel to Route 278, then head for the Verrazano-Narrows Bridge (toll is $7 from Brooklyn, no toll back to Brooklyn). This takes you to the Staten Island Expressway. From New Jersey, there are three bridges: from the Bayonne Bridge, Route 440 takes you to Route 278; from I-95, the Goethals Bridge takes you to Route 278; from the Outerbridge Crossing, Route 440 takes you to the West Shore Expressway and then to Route 278.

The Arts

If it is true, as many have observed, that the flesh and blood of New York are nourished by the financial and business communities, then surely its soul and spirit are sustained by the extraordinary art, music, theater and dance that pervade the entire city and lead so many people to spend their lives here. This has been so for over a century-and-a-half and in recent years an explosion of energy and talent, nourished by the city's great wealth, has made New York even more central to the nation's artistic well-being.

Like so many other aspects of New York, visitors can be slightly overwhelmed by the sheer depth of artistic possibilities available here. If you are bored in New York, you've lost the desire for finding the finest experiences life has to offer. If you love painting, there are not only five world-class museums featuring the work of every great artist, there are also literally hundreds of galleries spread throughout Manhattan, making available virtually every kind of work. For the devotee of music, where else can one find 10 or more classical music events on a single evening? Or five or six dance performances? And of course the city has been home to the best in American theater for generations.

So whatever your artistic interests, we guarantee you will not be disappointed in New York. If the experience of many others proves true, most likely you will be planning another trip here on the journey back home.

ART MUSEUMS AND GALLERIES

New York City has dozens of museums and hundreds of art galleries, and even cutting those numbers down by eliminating everything except the important sites, you would still be left with an impossible task if you tried to see all of what's going on at a given time. Art in the galleries changes more or less monthly, and the endless rounds of exhibitions in the museums means aficionados must practice triage. Geography is a factor. The city being spread out across five boroughs, and art being concentrated in pockets separated by long subway rides and formidable taxi fares, a visitor with limited time who, say, makes the (highly recommended) trip to the Brooklyn Museum may have to skip P.S. 1 in Long Island City, the contemporary art center now affiliated with the Museum of Modern Art. Or if one chooses to browse the galleries in Williamsburg, Brooklyn, he or she may not have time for the conglomeration of galleries in the converted factories and garages in Chelsea, the neighborhood that has replaced SoHo as the epicenter of new art.

How to make choices? Start with the basics. The Modern, more than any place else, defines the history of art in the 20th century through its permanent collection, which actually starts in the 19th century with Cézanne, Seurat, Gauguin and van Gogh. It's possible to list the greatest hits—van Gogh's

Museum Mile

The Met, being the country's, if not the world's, premier art museum, is naturally the locus of art in the city and, particularly, of Museum Mile, the city's catchphrase for a stretch of Fifth Avenue on the Upper East Side of Manhattan that also encompasses the Frick Collection, the Guggenheim Museum, the National Academy of Design, the Jewish Museum, part of the International Center of Photography and several other places that encapsulate the artistic diversity of New York.

A visit to the Met should include checking out the European paintings, Near Eastern and Egyptian rooms, and the ongoing renovations of the Greek and Roman galleries, which include the coffered, skylit, barrel-vaulted gallery beside the Great Hall at the entrance to the museum (one of the city's most splendid public spaces). But the smart visitor avoids, if possible, the inevitable crowds at the special exhibitions and in the Impressionist galleries and makes a beeline for less trammeled quarters. Examples include the Islamic galleries, with the burbling fountain in the Nur ad-Din Room; the Astor Court; a scholar's garden in the Chinese galleries, where you can approach Zen calm; the rooms of musical instruments, of arms and armor and of American pioneer and Colonial-era furniture, which are so obscure that you almost feel like a pioneer yourself going to see them.

Another must on Museum Mile, the Frick Collection, is almost everyone's favorite small museum, the finest private collection put together in America, even counting Isabella Stewart Gardner's collection in Boston. The Frick building, a mansion designed in 1913 by Thomas Hastings, the architect of the New York Public Library, is one of the last of the great former private houses on Fifth Avenue. Picture for picture (Bellini, Holbein, Rembrandt, Vermeer, Fragonard, the list goes on) the quality of the collection is unsurpassed in America.

Farther up Museum Mile, tourists ogle Frank Lloyd Wright's spiral Guggenheim often without bothering about the art in it, although the permanent collection, which includes the Justin K. Thannhauser Collection, is,

"Starry Night," Cézanne's "Male Bather," Picasso's "Demoiselles d'Avignon," Matisse's "Red Studio," Pollock's "One" (Number 1, 1950), Warhol's "Gold Marilyn"—but suffice it to say that, having begun in 1929 in a few modest rooms, the Modern has grown through several expansions to the point of needing yet another expansion that, when it's finished, will occupy most of the block between Fifth and Sixth Avenues and between 53rd and 54th Streets. The expansion means the museum will be shut at that site for several years starting in the spring of 2002, but is relocated in more modest temporary quarters near P.S. 1 in Queens, where there will always be a selection of the permanent collection on view along with changing exhibitions. Like the Metropolitan Museum, the Modern can, by itself, occupy an entire trip to New York.

—*Michael Kimmelman*

after the Modern's collection, the top overview of art from the first half of the 20th century regularly available in the city.

The Jewish Museum is the best institution of its kind in the country, with not only objects related to the history of Judaism but also a strong exhibition program emphasizing modern and contemporary art.

The Whitney Museum of American Art, a block off Fifth, on Madison Avenue, isn't technically on Museum Mile but should be on the itinerary, too. It has permanent galleries where visitors can see the Hoppers and Calders they expect to find there, and a lively program of changing exhibitions.

The savvy traveler along Museum Mile also makes sure to see the less-heralded stops at the north end of Fifth. The Museum of the City of New York is moving downtown (*see chapter* **Exploring New York**) in the fall of 2002, but until then is worth a look. El Museo del Barrio, a museum of the art and culture of Latin America and the city's expanding Latino community, might take over that building but is meanwhile still in its usual location nearby. Like the Studio Museum, El Museo del Barrio was founded during the late 1960's in a period of upheaval, when artists of many backgrounds clamored for places to show their work. The Museum of Modern Art, with its stress on high European modernism and big-name postwar Americans, wasn't paying them enough attention, they felt, and so they came up with the idea of community-based institutions, the result being a new breadth of collections and exhibitions—and renewed debate, as these young museums themselves turned into established institutions and faced criticism from within their own diversifying communities.

New York, they demonstrated, rejects the status quo, whatever it may be, which is of course the city's virtue. Its museums reflect this fact as well as anything else. To travel along Museum Mile from Frick's mansion to El Museo del Barrio is to see a fraction of what's going on in art, but it's to go a long distance toward understanding the essential nature of a place where culture, like the rest of life, remains a moving target.

—*Michael Kimmelman*

Major Art Museums

Metropolitan Museum of Art
Fifth Ave. at 82nd St. (212) 535-7710

UPPER EAST SIDE
www.metmuseum.org

The Met is a national treasure, one of the world's great museums, right up there with the Louvre. Some of its art is the best anywhere, and the collection as a whole is simply outstanding. From ancient cuneiforms, rare Greek vases and statuary to Monet, Jasper Johns and Ellsworth Kelly, its variety is breathtaking.

Altogether this magnificent museum has more than two million works of art—paintings, sculpture, decorative arts, artifacts from ancient cultures, arms and armor, elegant clothing and musical instruments. There are 53 galleries devoted solely to European painters, and another maze devoted to Americans.

In fact, two American artists and a German were indirectly responsible for the creation of the Met in the 1880's—the majestic landscapes of Alfred Bierstadt and Frederic Church, and the dramatic "Washington Crossing the Delaware" by Emanuel Leutze, a German-American. Partly to establish a place to exhibit these huge pieces, the Met was born. You will find all three in the American Wing at the north end of the first and second floors, close to the massive Temple of Dendur, an actual Egyptian burial place that every visitor must see. (*See section "Washington Heights/Inwood" for* **the Cloisters**, *the Met's showcase for medieval art.*)

NAVIGATING THE MET

There are so many highlights to see here, it is a good idea to plan ahead. Unfortunately, for all its grandeur, the Met does not make it easy to find your way around. There is a very general floor plan of the whole museum in English at both information desks as you enter the main lobby, and in several other languages if you ask. For detailed maps of where to find Rembrandt, van Gogh, et al. you also have to ask. There are two detailed maps for the European paintings and sculpture; none for other collections.

Some galleries are numbered, but many aren't. As you enter a gallery, you may see numbers on your right and on your left; as a general rule, the one on your right is the one you are entering.

Finding the daily tour schedule is another challenge. It is posted on a obscured wall at the southern end of the lobby, to your left as you enter, just before the long corridor of Greek and Roman statuary. The children's gift shop is hidden, too. It is at the top of the main stairway, to the right, but you wouldn't know it until you are at the door. Inside are T-shirts, games, erasers in the shape of a sphinx, etc. The escalator to the second floor isn't obvious either; look left as you approach the main stairs.

Best bet: Ask any uniformed guard where to find what you are looking for. They are walking, talking catalogs, and user friendly. If you hit upon one who doesn't have the answer, ask the next one.

Best bet beforehand: The Met's Web site (*www.metmuseum.org*) is excellent. Things that are hard to find in the museum itself are easy to find online, including daily schedules of tours and gallery talks, exact locations of the painting you're looking for, and everything else you might want to know before you mount the steps on Fifth Avenue.

Each of the Met's departments is a museum in itself. It would take more than an afternoon to fully explore the holdings of any one section. Wandering through the galleries, you will chance upon some wonderful surprises—a living room designed by Frank Lloyd Wright in the American Wing, a detailed scale model of the Parthenon at the street-level entrance to the museum, a tranquil Chinese scholar's garden in the Astor Court on the second floor and, in the music collection nearby, violins made by Nicolo Amati and his student Antonio Stradivari in the 17th century.

You may get more from your visit, however, by picking some objects or areas ahead of time, and searching them out. Or take a "highlights" tour to see what interests you and then go back and give it more time yourself.

Main Floor

As you enter the main lobby, **Egyptian Art** collections and the **Temple of Dendur** are to your right, **Greek and Roman Art** to your left.

At the entrance to the Egyptian section is a tomb you can walk into—fun for kids. The Met's own archeological explorations are responsible for more than half of the collection, which extends chronologically through 40 galleries. The Temple of Dendur was a gift from Egypt in recognition of U.S. aid in saving ancient monuments from the rising waters of the Nile behind the Aswan Dam.

The Greek and Roman works explore the full range of classical art, from jewelry and pottery to sculpture and painting, with prize examples of Greek vases and Roman portrait busts.

Beyond these galleries you will find a spacious **cafeteria** and a **restaurant.**

Straight through the main lobby from the entrance, passing to either side of the main stairway, you will find **Medieval Art** and a large spread of **European Sculpture and Decorative Arts.** This is one of the museum's largest collections. One of its gems is an ornate 15th-century "studiolo"—it means "little study"—with walls of inlaid woodwork that looks three-dimensional but is actually flat. There are only two such rooms in the world, this one and the one in the ducal palace in Urbino, Italy.

Continuing straight ahead to the back of the museum, don't miss the eclectic **Robert Lehman Collection** of Impressionists and Old Masters, paintings and drawings, and pieces of decorative art. The gallery space, on two floors, is designed to evoke Lehman's own stately home on East 54th Street in Manhattan. Highlights include an Annunciation by Botticelli, a Rembrandt sketch of Leonardo's "Last Supper," a Leonardo sketch of "A Bear Walking," paintings by Rembrandt, El Greco, Goya, Renoir, Seurat, van Gogh and some impressive pieces of Renaissance earthenware and Venetian glass.

The southern flank of the first floor houses the **Arts of Africa, Oceania and the Americas** and a series of galleries of **20th century art.** The third-world collections are based on entire museum that Nelson Rockefeller gave to the Met—the Museum of Primitive Art, which he founded. Highlights include royal decorative art from the Court of Benin in Nigeria, and the world's most comprehensive collection of gold objects from the Americas.

The 20th-century collection, on two floors in the southwest corner of the building, is where to find Jasper Johns, Picasso, Braque, Modigliani, O'Keeffe and Pollock.

In the northern flank of the first floor is the stunning **Arms and Armor** collection, as well as the **Temple of Dendur.** Another knockout at the same end of the museum is a grand wrap-around panorama of the palace and gardens at Versailles, from the early 1800's. Standing in the center of this large chamber you can imagine you are there on the palace steps. And while you are at the north end of the building, check out the Met's collection of classic baseball cards, exhibited in the hallway behind Dendur on the way to Versailles.

The Arms and Armor collection is unique among American museums, with elegantly etched armor and weaponry ranging from the fourth century B.C. to the 19th century A.D., and from ancient Egypt and Islam to the

Americas. The Japanese pieces are generally regarded as the finest anywhere outside Japan.

The American Wing, on two floors, is a magnet for tourists and New Yorkers alike. Everyone will recognize the epic "George Washington Crossing the Delaware," 21 feet wide, painted in Düsseldorf some 75 years after the fact by Emanuel Leutze. Note also the surrounding display of that particular gallery (no. 223). It has been arranged to resemble the museums of a century ago, crammed full of art, with three, four or five paintings hung one above the other.

Elsewhere in this wing are familiar Washington portraits by Gilbert Stuart and Charles Willson Peale, as well as John Singer Sargent's "Madame X," Frederic Church's "Heart of the Andes," Alfred Bierstadt's "Rocky Mountains: Lander's Peak," along with paintings by Winslow Homer, James McNeill Whistler and Mary Cassatt (whose brother, president of the Pennsylvania Railroad, told her she would never amount to anything as a painter), and sculptures by Frederic Remington and John Quincy Adams Ward.

Extraordinary features of the wing include 25 period rooms—furnished and decorated just as they were in years and centuries past—a renowned collection of stained glass, much of it by Louis Comfort Tiffany, and upstairs an "attic" of shelves where the museum displays things it doesn't have room to display out front. There you will see rows of antique chairs, Lincoln busts, crystal goblets and much, much more. This sort of display is especially useful to students and scholars, but made interesting for anyone by its sheer volume.

Second Floor

Straight ahead at the top of the central stairway from the lobby, push through a pair of glass doors and enter the wonderful world of **European Paintings**. This is one of the two collections for which there are detail maps if you ask for them at the information desk in the lobby. The works in this one are the Old Masters— starting with three enormous paintings by Tiepolo in the first gallery, past an remarkable diptych of "The Crucifixion" and "The Last Judgment" by Jan van Eyck, the most celebrated painter of 15th century Europe, to Bruegel, Rubens, El Greco, Raphael, Titian, Tintoretto, Vermeer, Rembrandt, Hals, Gainsborough, Velasquez, Fragonard, Goya and still more. The Met has more Vermeers than any other museum.

These galleries are not to be confused with **Nineteenth-Century European Paintings and Sculpture**—the second collection for which there is a detailed map. Reach this area by turning left at the top of the central stairs and walking through a long gallery hall of etchings and photographs. Don't hurry. The etchings are the work of great artists; they illustrate how an artist sketches out ideas for later paintings—whole scenes, or a torso, or maybe just an elbow or a nose.

In the 19th-century galleries you will find the popular works of the Impressionists, but first a large expanse of Rodin's sculptured marbles. Inside are the young Claude Monet's vibrantly colorful "Garden at Sainte-Adresse," daring for its time, a Cézanne still-life once owned by Monet, Edouard Manet's peaceful "Boating," van Gogh's "Cypresses," and room after room of Bonnard, Degas, Rousseau, Daumier, Toulouse-Lautrec, Renoir and more.

Adjacent to these galleries are, to the west, the second-floor space of the
20th-Century Art collection, and on the Fifth Avenue side to the east, **Islamic
Art** and **Ancient Near Eastern Art.** The long Fifth Avenue side of the second
floor proceeds geographically from the Near East at the southern end, through
the balcony over the lobby to a half-dozen sectors of **Asian Art—Chinese,
Japanese, Korean, South Asian** and **Southeast Asian**—at the northern end.

The Islamic collection may be the most comprehensive permanent Islamic
art installation anywhere. Items of note include miniature paintings and huge
16th- and 17th-century carpets, as well as glass and metalwork from Egypt and
Mesopotamia. Ancient and Near Eastern Art spans nearly 9,000 years, from
Mesopotamia to the Indian subcontinent. The Asian collections are reputed to
be the largest and most comprehensive in the West, best known for their Chinese calligraphy, folding screens and other decorative objects from Japan, sculpture from Southeast Asia and paintings from the Himalayan kingdoms. Here,
too, is the restful **Chinese Scholar's Garden** called **Astor Court,** behind a wall
with a round entryway symbolizing a full moon. Enter and sit a few minutes.
You will be almost alone.

Close by are the upper floor of the **American Wing** and the **Musical Instruments** collection, where you will find a piano made by the instrument's inventor,
Bartolomeo Cristofori, two guitars owned and used by Andres Segovia, and all sorts
of rare horns, harps and other music makers from distant lands and other times.

Ground Floor

Entering the museum through the street-level door to the south of the outside
steps, or through the parking garage, there is an information desk that will
accept your "suggested donation," a splendid model of the Acropolis, and a coat
check where the line moves faster than at the one upstairs in the main lobby.
The museum library is down here, too.

The galleries of **The Costume Institute** are also on the ground floor, but
they are entered from above, by stairs or an elevator from the main floor in the
middle of **Egyptian Art.** A little hard to find, the institute is a small three-
gallery treasure. Clothes dating from the 18th century and to the present are
exhibited on mannequins in glass showcases with informative descriptions, and
shows are organized around themes and particular designers.

Sculpture Garden

Last but not least, weather permiting, take yourself up to the **Sculpture Garden**
on the roof, not only for the sculpture but for a treetop view of Central Park.

Admission: (These are suggested donations, but you will not be challenged if
you give less. Many New Yorkers give $2 or $3.) $10, adults; $5, students and
seniors; children under 12 with an adult, free. **Hours:** Fri.–Sat., 9:30 A.M.–8:45
P.M.; Sun., Tue., Wed., Thu., 9:30 A.M.– 5:15 P.M.; Closed Mon. **Tours and
gallery talks:** Walking tours, gallery talks, lectures, films and workshops, call
(212) 570-3930. Tourist groups call (212) 570-3711; school groups call (212) 288-
7733; programs for children call (212) 570-3932. The basic tour is given by
Philippe de Montebello, the museum's director, and the choice of what you see is
his. It takes 2½ to 3 hours. **Subway:** 4, 5, 6 to 86th St.

The Guggenheim as Architecture

Frank Lloyd Wright's Guggenheim has always been like an explosion on Fifth Avenue. It is strident, it is loud, it defers not a whit to anything around it. It breaks every rule. It is so astonishing as a piece of architecture, of course, that it makes you feel that rules hardly matter. But the very way in which Wright's building breaks the rules of urban design becomes its own rule: the way it clashes with its surroundings is the way the Guggenheim communicates its architectural essence.

It has been a commonplace since this building opened in 1959 to speak of it as inhospitable to paintings, to talk of the long spiral ramp and slanted walls as Wright's way of forcing painting to be subservient to architecture. While this complaint has always been exaggerated—Wright's space can work wonderfully for the display of large Color Field abstractions, Calder mobiles, Pop Art and other postwar works—there is no question that the architecture fights the art a lot of the time. The building usually ends up in the foreground of one's consciousness, no matter what the paintings.

The rush of joy that Wright's great rotunda brings has always been worth its limitations as a gallery. There aren't a lot of cathedrals in New York—never mind that, there isn't a lot of architecture anywhere that is capable of making the heart beat faster, that so fills you with the sense that the making of enclosure can be an act of opening up, a discovery of noble possibilities. It is a wonderful paradox to find, in the act of enclosing, revelation. There is nowhere else in New York where the passion of architecture is more clearly there, set more directly in front of us for all to see and understand.

The north side addition (1992) contains double-height galleries, which give the Guggenheim the ability to display large contemporary canvases for the first time. While the galleries are not ideal display spaces—they are a bit narrow, and the elevator core intrudes partway into them—they are more versatile than anything the museum has had until now. This, then, is the great achievement: the building is now a better museum and a better work of architecture. If the Guggenheim's roles as a museum and as a piece of architecture have always been somewhat at odds, this renovation at least partly resolves them.

—Paul Goldberger

Solomon R. Guggenheim Museum

UPPER EAST SIDE

1071 Fifth Ave. (at 89th St.) (212) 423-3500   *www.guggenheim.org*

Long before it was completed in 1959, the Guggenheim—the strange round building in a city full of square boxes—was already suffering darts from critics. It was called everything from a washtub to an indigestible hot-cross bun. Robert

The Solomon R. Guggenheim Museum

Moses, the city's irascible master builder, said it looked like an inverted oatmeal dish.

But the museum's creator, Frank Lloyd Wright, called it nothing less than "the liberation of painting by architecture." And on the first Sunday it opened, 10,000 people lined up to get in for 50 cents a head. (Only 6,000 made it; bribes offered to guards did not work.)

Today, after a $24 million dollar renovation and the addition of a controversial 10-story annex in 1992, the landmarked museum, considered by some to be Wright's masterpiece, is celebrating its 40th anniversary. Along with one of the world's largest collections of Vasily Kandinsky, it has works by many major 20th-century artists—Constantin Brancusi, Alexander Calder, Marc Chagall, Robert Delaunay, Paul Klee, Joan Miro and Pablo Picasso. The museum itself is, of course, a major attraction. And worth the trip, despite its admission charge, which is one of the highest in the city.

Instead of moving from room to room, as in other museums, you take the elevator to the top, 92 feet up, then soak up the art as you descend a gently sloping circular ramp, glancing across the sweeping rotunda at other art lovers winding their way around you.   —*Randy Kennedy*

Admission: $12; $8, students and seniors; children 12 and under, free. **Hours:** Fri.–Sat., 9 A.M.–8 P.M.; Sun.–Wed., 9 A.M.–6 P.M. Closed Thu. **Programs for children:** Films, tours and workshops throughout the year. Call for information. **Tours:** Daily; call for information. **Subway:** 4, 5, 6 to 86th St.

The Museum of Modern Art   MIDTOWN WEST
11 W. 53rd St. (between Fifth and Sixth Aves.) (212) 708-9400
(212) 247-1230 for the deaf   *www.moma.org*

It is hard to imagine that this museum started with eight prints and one drawing
in 1929, because it now houses one the largest collections of 20th-century
painting, drawings, photographs and sculpture in the world. Its permanent collection of Pablo Picasso, Frida Kahlo, Henri Matisse, Jackson Pollock and
Robert Rauschenberg alone draws the crowds, especially on Friday nights, when
there is a pay-what-you-wish admissions policy from 4:40 to 8:15 P.M. While
perhaps not the best time to get a peek at van Gogh's "Starry Night," Friday
nights offer their own pleasures, including jazz music in the garden cafe and
"Conversations with Contemporary Artists," during which artists talk about
their work in the galleries. Like most of New York's museums, there are places
in "MoMA"—as the museum is commonly called—to escape the headphone-
set crowd and contemplate the time you just passed with, say, Dali and
Duchamp. There is a nice comfy bench in front of Monet's "Water Lilies." The
sculpture garden on a quiet afternoon can be a pleasant respite. Indoors, the
architecture and design collection is rarely as crowded as are certain rooms filled
with important painters, and its fur coffee cup and silicon chips are an amusing
diversion. MoMA claims to be the first art museum to embrace motion pictures
as an art form. It has an extensive collection of significant films, including silent
films of D.W. Griffith and Charlie Chaplin, and contemporary works from
Scorcese to Kubrick. The museum is a regular host to film festivals and video
screenings.   —*Jennifer Steinhauer*

Architecture and Design Established in 1932, this was the first curatorial
department of its kind. The work of specific architects and general architectural
topics are illustrated through a variety of models, drawings and photographs.
The design collection includes everything from hockey masks to helicopters,
with substantial display space devoted to furniture and decorative and functional items for the home. There is also a highly-regarded collection of typogra-
phy, posters and other examples of graphic design.

Drawing This department holds over 6,000 drawings, including works in
watercolor and mixed media, making it one of the world's most comprehensive
collections of modern drawing. Highlights include works by Ernst, Schiele,
Degas and Cézanne.

Painting and Sculpture This is the heart of the museum: 3,200 works making
up the world's largest collection of modern art, from the late 19th century to the
present. Some of the most famous works of modern art are here, including van
Gogh's "Starry Night," Cézanne's "The Bather," Rodin's "Monument to Balzac,"
Rousseau's "The Dream," and an impressive collection of Picassos.

Film and Video MoMA bills this as the strongest international film collection
in the United States, with over 14,000 films and four million film stills, ranging
from original Edison Company negatives to contemporary Hollywood movies,
television documentaries and video art.

Photography The photography collection extends as far back as the 1840's, and reaches outside the art world to include photographs by journalists, scientists and amateurs. The collection includes important works by Walker Evans, Ansel Adams and Robert Frank.

Prints and Illustrated Books 40,000 prints and books chart the history of techniques like lithography, screenprinting, woodcut and more contemporary forms of printmaking. Famous works here include Edvard Munch's "The Kiss" and van Gogh's "Sorrow."

Admission: $10; $6.50, students and seniors; children under 16 accompanied by an adult, free. Friday, 4:30–8:15 P.M., donation requested. Handicapped accessible. Cash or checks only. **Hours:** Sat.–Tue. and Thu., 10:30 A.M.–5:45 P.M.; Fri., 10:30 A.M.–8:15 P.M. Closed Wed. **Programs for children:** Workshops and family programs. **Tours:** Daily; call for information. **Subway:** E, F to Fifth Ave. **NOTE:** Starting in the spring of 2002, MoMA will be under construction and closed for several years. Displays will be moved to **P.S. 1** in Queens (see section "Queens" in chapter **Exploring New York** for details).

Frick Collection   UPPER EAST SIDE
1 E. 70th St. (between Fifth and Madison Aves.) (212) 288-0700 www.frick.org
As you walk through the rooms of this stately Upper East Side mansion, you almost expect to run into Henry Clay Frick himself. The house, completed in 1914, has been preserved much as it was when Frick (1849–1919), a steel magnate, lived there with the extraordinary art collection visitors see today. The experience is completely absorbing and transporting. The galleries are intimate and astoundingly quiet in every way, from the noise level to the lighting, allowing the unmatched collection to shine. The Frick hosts an excellent series of free concerts in the museum's music parlor and in the courtyard.

Permanent Collection: Highlights: Bellini, "Saint Francis in Ecstasy"; dell Francesca, "St. John the Evangelist"; van Eyck, "Virgin With Child, With Saints and Donor"; Vermeer, "Officer and Laughing Girl"; Holbein, "Sir Thomas More and Thomas Cromwell"; Rembrandt, "Self-Portrait"; Stuart, "George Washington."

Admission: $10; $5, seniors and students; children under 10 not allowed, those under 16 must be accompanied by an adult. Handicapped accessible. **Hours:** Tue.–Sat., 10 A.M.–6 P.M.; Sun., holidays, 1–6 P.M. Closed Mon. **Programs for children:** Free lectures and concerts. Call for information. **Tours:** Included in the price of admission is an audio tour of the permanent collection available in English, French, German, Italian, Japanese and Spanish. School groups by reservation. **Subway:** 6 to 68th St.

Whitney Museum of American Art   UPPER EAST SIDE
945 Madison Ave. (at 75th St.) (212) 570-3676   www.whitney.org
Founded in 1914 by Gertrude Vanderbilt Whitney, the Whitney opened in 1931 in three adjoining brownstones on West 8th Street—mostly as a response to a rebuff from the Metropolitan Museum, which refused the donation of the

500-work collection. The museum is now housed in a hulking building designed by a former Bauhaus teacher, Marcel Breuer. The Whitney includes among its programs the Biennial, a much-discussed and often controversial exhibition that surveys recent developments in American art. The museum's corporate-funded branches—including two in midtown and one in Stamford, Connecticut—also have exhibitions.

Permanent Collection: The museum has an excellent permanent collection of 20th-century art, which can be seen in several new galleries opened in 1998. Includes some 12,000 works of art representing more than 1,900 artists. Highlights: The entire artistic estate of Edward Hopper, as well as significant works by Marsh, Calder, Gorky, Hartley, O'Keeffe, Rauschenberg and Johns among other artists.

Admission: $10; $8, students and seniors; children under 12, free. Fri., 6–9 P.M., pay as you wish. Cash only. **Hours:** Tue.–Thu., Sat., Sun., 11 A.M.–6 P.M. Fri. 1 P.M.–9 P.M. Closed Mon. **Tours:** Call (212) 570-7722 for daily schedule; call (212) 570-7720 for group tours. **Subway:** 6 to 77th St.

Other Art Museums

(See section "The Boroughs" in chapter **Exploring New York** *for* **Bronx Museum of the Arts, Brooklyn Museum of Art, Isamu Noguchi Garden Museum, Jacques Marchais Museum of Tibetan Art, P.S. 1, Queens Museum of Art** *and the* **Socrates Sculpture Garden**. *For other types of museums and historic houses, many containing collections of art, see chapter* **Exploring New York**.*)*

Alternative Museum of the Arts SOHO 594 Broadway (between Houston and Prince Sts.) (212) 966-4444. Operated by artists since its founding in 1975, the Alternative Museum sponsors work that is outside the mainstream. Its 3,200-square-foot space exhibits work in a variety of media and often presents shows that address social and political issues. The museum's Annual National Showcase benefits artists who are members of the museum. It also has a history of supporting new American music. Don Cherry, Kronos Quartet and Terry Riley have performed here. In 1996, the museum decided to focus on media-based arts: photography, video, film, and electronic and computer-generated art. To explore the possibilities of the "virtual" museum, the "Alter-NET-ive" museum is developing interactive online forums, debates and panels, as well as exhibitions of the "electronic" collection. **Admission** (suggested): $3. Cash only. **Hours:** Wed.–Sat., 11 A.M.–6 P.M. **Subway:** F, S to Broadway–Lafayette St.; N, R to Prince St.

American Craft Museum MIDTOWN WEST 40 W. 53rd St. (between Fifth and Sixth Aves.) (212) 956-3535. Located directly across the street from the Museum of Modern Art, the American Craft Museum is the most significant museum in the country dedicated to exhibiting and supporting contemporary crafts. A visit will dispel anyone's notion that crafts aren't worthy of consideration as an art form. You'll see no macaroni necklaces on the museum's three floors of exhibition space. Instead, the work ranges from utilitarian objects with a strong aesthetic focus to sculptural pieces with a barely conceivable utility.

The exhibits tend to be carefully designed and thematic, exploring a single craft, material or artist. **Admission:** $7.50, adults; $4.50, seniors and students; children under 12, free; Thu., 6 P.M.–8 P.M., pay as you wish. **Hours:** Tue.–Sun., 10 A.M.–6 P.M.; Thu., 10 A.M.–8 P.M. Closed Mon. **Subway:** E, F to Fifth Ave.

Cooper-Hewitt National Design Museum UPPER EAST SIDE 2 E. 91st St. (at Fifth Ave.) (212) 849-8300 *www.si.edu/ndm/*. Peter Cooper would have been proud. The small museum he envisioned more than 100 years ago to support Cooper Union's instruction in the applied arts developed into what is now the country's best place to view and study design. In 1897 Sarah, Eleanor and Amy Hewitt, who were Cooper's granddaughters, opened a museum modeled after Paris's Musée des Arts Décoratifs in the Cooper Union Building. The museum has amassed a collection encompassing objects as diverse as radiators, gloves and 18th-century French furniture. Part of the Smithsonian Institution since 1969, it later moved to Andrew Carnegie's Fifth Avenue mansion. Recent shows have focused on everything from Alexander Calder's designs for everyday objects to architects' plans for doghouses. **Admission:** $8, general; $5, students and seniors; children under 12, free; Tue. 5 P.M.–9 P.M., free. Cash only. **Hours:** Tue., 10 A.M.–9 P.M.; Wed.–Sat., 10 A.M.–5 P.M.; Sun., noon–5 P.M. **Programs for Children:** Call (212) 849-8380 for information. **Tours:** Call (212) 849-8380 for information. **Subway:** 4, 5, 6 to 86th St.

Dahesh Museum MIDTOWN EAST 601 Fifth Ave. (between 48th and 49th Sts.) (212) 759-0606 *www.daheshmuseum.org*. The Dahesh Museum was opened in 1993 with the goal of collecting, preserving, exhibiting and interpreting 19th- and 20th-century European academic art. Modern art was founded in opposition to academic art, which was subsequently dismissed for over a century. As the word "academic" became derogatory, once influential artists and teachers like William-Adolphe Bouguereau, Jean-Léon Gérome and Alexandre Cabanel were derided as reactionaries. More recent scholarship has taken a less ideological view. Drawing from its own collection as well as others, the Dahesh allows the most popular art of its time to be seen on its own terms. **Admission:** Free. Handicapped accessible. **Hours:** Tue.–Sat., 11 A.M.–6 P.M. Closed Sun., Mon. **Tours:** Participates in the "Insider's Hour" through the New York Convention and Visitors Bureau. Special tours can also be arranged. **Subway:** B, D, F, S to 47th-50th St.–Rockefeller Center.

Dia Center for the Arts CHELSEA 545 and 548 W. 22nd St. (212) 989-5566 *www.diacenter.org*. Once an isolated arts center on the edge of the West Side Highway, the Dia Center is now seen as a pioneer on the art world's latest frontier, West Chelsea. The original purpose of the center over 20 years ago was to provide an exhibition space for large-scale works—particularly earth works and Minimalist sculpture—which conventional museums had trouble accommodating. Dia still supports long-term installations, including Walter De Maria's "Earth Room" and "Broken Kilometer." But since its move in 1987 to a 40,000-square-foot renovated warehouse on West 22nd Street, it has focused on single-artist exhibitions that last anywhere from a few months to several years. There are also monthly poetry readings, art lectures, music and art performances, and a bookstore. Dia operates a space across the street from the main building which hosts long-term exhibits and installations. The center is also one of Chelsea's best hangouts, including a rooftop coffee bar overlooking the Hudson River. Plan to be there at sunset. The permanent collection includes works by Joseph Beuys, John Chamberlain, Walter De Maria, Dan Flavin, Donald Judd, Imi Knoebel, Blinky Palermo, Fred Sandback, Cy Twombly and Andy Warhol. **Admission:** $6, adults; $3, students and seniors; children under 10, free. **Hours:** Wed.–Sun., noon–6 P.M. Closed Mon., Tue. **Subway:** C, E, 1, 9 to 23rd St.

Drawing Center SOHO 35 Wooster St. (between Broome and Grand Sts.) (212) 219-2166. Housed in an airy ground-floor space on Wooster Street, the Drawing Center is a small nonprofit museum dedicated to drawings, loosely defined as original works on paper. Past exhibits have included wall drawings, monoprints and computer-generated drawings. In addition to its four or five annual group shows, usually featuring emerging artists, the center mounts historical and special exhibitions. Across the street is the Drawing Room, an annex dedicated to site-specific projects by individual artists. The gallery also runs the "Nightlight" reading series featuring prominent authors, as well as children's programs. **Admission:** Free. **Hours:** Tue.–Fri., 10 A.M.–6 P.M.; Sat., 11 A.M.–6 P.M. **Subway:** N, R to Prince St.; J, M, N, Q, R, W, Z, 6 to Canal St.

El Museo del Barrio UPPER EAST SIDE 1230 Fifth Ave. (at 104th St.) (212) 831-7272 *www.elmuseo.org.* Located in Central Park's Heckscher Building and founded by a group of Puerto Rican educators, artists and activists in 1969, the museum originally aimed to serve the Puerto Rican community in nearby Spanish Harlem. Its mission has since expanded in response to the growth of New York's Latino population—particularly the Mexican, Central and South American, and Caribbean communities. The scope of art ranges from pre-Columbian to contemporary. Two or more exhibitions are in progress here at any given time, along with a rotating installation of the splendid collection of Puerto Rican religious figures, or santos. **Admission:** $4; $2, students and seniors; children under 12, free. Handicapped accessible. **Hours:** Wed.–Sun., 11 A.M.–5 P.M. **Subway:** 6 to 103rd St.

Guggenheim Museum SoHo 575 Broadway (at Prince St.) (212) 423-3500. In 1992, the Guggenheim took another bold step, opening this contemporary art center on lower Broadway with 30,000 square feet of exhibition space designed by Arata Isozaki. Free admission. **Hours:** Thu.–Mon., 11 A.M.–6 P.M. **Subway:** F, S to Broadway–Lafayette St.; N, R to Prince St.; 6 to Spring St.

International Center of Photography 1133 Sixth Ave. (between 43rd and 44th Sts.) (212) 768-4680; 130 Fifth Ave. (at 94th St.) (212) 860-1777 *www.icp.org.* Established in 1974, the center mounts approximately 20 exhibitions per year, covering everything from photojournalism to fashion photography. In addition to its exhibition program, the center shows films and hosts a lecture series. ICP also accommodates those who want to get behind the camera by offering extensive continuing-education courses, as well as three certificate

programs and an M.A. run jointly with New York University. **Admission:** $8;
$6, seniors and students; pay as you wish, Fri., 5 P.M.–8 P.M. Cash only. **Hours:**
Tue.–Thu., 10 A.M.–5 P.M.; Fri., 10 A.M.–8 P.M.; Sat.–Sun., 10 A.M.–6 P.M.
Closed Mon. **Tours:** Call (212) 860-1777 ext. 154. **Subway:** Midtown: B, D, F,
S to 42nd St.; Uptown: 6 to 96th St.

Jewish Museum UPPER EAST SIDE 1109 Fifth Ave. (at 92nd St.)
(212) 423-3200 *www.thejewishmuseum.org.* Located on Museum Mile, the Jewish Museum is dedicated to showing work that addresses issues related to Jewish
identity and art by Jewish artists. The museum is housed in the former Felix M.
Warburg residence, a Gothic chateau built in 1908. The museum has shown
work by individual artists such as Camille Pisarro and Lasar Segall and has
mounted thematic exhibitions, such as an exhibit of photographs taken during
the Holocaust. The permanent collection includes objects that span 4,000
years, from Israeli archaeological artifacts to prints by Marc Chagall and Max
Weber, as well as George Segal's sculpture, "The Holocaust." The museum also
hosts film screenings, lectures and classical and klezmer concerts. **Admission:**
$8; $5.50, students and seniors; children under 12, free; Tue., 5–8 P.M., free.
Hours: Sun.–Mon., Wed.–Thu., 11 A.M.–5:45 P.M.; Tue., 11 A.M.–8 P.M.
Closed Fri., Sat. **Programs for Children:** Art workshops, performances, film
and video screenings and family tours on Sundays from Oct.–May, and some
days during school vacation. **Tours:** Mon.–Thu., 12:15 P.M. and 2:15 P.M.;
Mon., Wed., Thu., 4:15 P.M.; Tue., 6:15 P.M. **Subway:** 6 to 96th St; 4, 5, 6 to
86th St.

Miriam and Ira D. Wallach Art Gallery UPPER WEST SIDE Columbia University, Schermerhorn Hall (between Broadway and Amsterdam Ave.)
(212) 854-7288. Miriam and Ira D. Wallach donated funds in 1986 for a gallery
at Columbia as both a resource for teaching and study, and a public exhibition
space. As its curators are often graduate students and faculty from the art history
department, the gallery's exhibitions tend to be well researched and often have
titles that require two sentences and a colon. They are nevertheless treasure
troves, drawing on Columbia's resources as well as public and private collections
to present issues, methods and art that are not often seen elsewhere. **Subway:** 1,
9 to 116th St.—Columbia University.

Museum for African Art SOHO 593 Broadway (between Houston and Prince
Sts.) (212) 966-1313 *www.africanart.org.* Until recently, you were more likely to
encounter sub-Saharan African sculpture in an anthropology textbook than in
an art museum. Today, African art is considered one of the most inventive art
forms of the past two centuries, and the Museum for African Art can take much
of the credit for this shift. Founded in 1984, the museum mounts provocative
changing exhibitions, which include historical surveys in addition to contemporary African art. Designed by Maya Lin, the museum includes a bookstore where
you can find basic introductions to African art alongside advanced scholarship
and reasonably priced art. **Admission:** $5; $2.50, students, seniors and children
(6–18). Handicapped accessible. **Hours:** Tue.–Fri., 10:30 A.M.–5:30 P.M.;

Sat.–Sun., noon–6 P.M. Closed Mon. **Tours:** Groups call ext. 117 or 118 at least two weeks in advance. **Subway:** F, S to Broadway–Lafayette St.; N, R to Prince St.; 6 to Spring St.

Museum of American Folk Art MIDTOWN WEST Columbus Ave. at 66th St. (212) 977-7298 *www.folkartmuseum.org.* If the term "folk art" makes you think of craft shows and grandma's quilts, then you are overdue for a visit to the Museum of American Folk Art. Folk art is very hot among collectors and scholars intrigued by vernacular American culture, and the museum has contributed to this reinvigoration of the field. Shedding new light on folk art standbys like cigar store Indians, the museum also mounts provocative exhibitions of "outsider art," or "untrained art." The fact that folk art eludes simple classifications is an indication of its complexity. The museum houses temporary exhibitions as well as selections from its permanent collection. It is currently building a new home next to the Museum of Modern Art on West 53rd Street, scheduled to open in 2002. **Admission:** Free. **Hours:** Tue.–Sun., 11:30 A.M.–7:30 P.M. **Subway:** 1, 9 to 66th St.—Lincoln Center.

National Museum of the American Indian LOWER MANHATTAN 1 Bowling Green (between Whitehall and State Sts.) (212) 668-6624. *(See chapter* **Exploring New York** *for full listing.)*

New Museum of Contemporary Art SOHO 583 Broadway (between Prince and Houston Sts.) (212) 219-1222 *www.newmuseum.org.* The New Museum celebrated the beginning of its third decade on art's cutting edge with a face lift that signaled other changes inside. Recent renovations expanded the museum's exhibition space, creating discrete galleries and a free public space with a bookstore, lounge and exhibits. Founded in 1977, the SoHo museum has a reputation for controversial exhibitions, edgy programs and a mixed critical reception. **Admission:** $6; $3, artists, students and seniors; children 18 and under, free. Thu., 6 P.M.–8 P.M, free. **Hours:** Tue.–Sun., noon–6 P.M.; Thu., noon–8 P.M. Closed Mon. **Subway:** F, S to Broadway–Lafayette St.; N, R to Prince St.; 6 to Spring St.

Nicholas Roerich Museum UPPER WEST SIDE 319 W. 107th St. (between Broadway and Riverside Dr.) (212) 864-7752. Nicholas Roerich, the Russian-American star of this one-man museum, was a true Renaissance man, involved in a vast range of artistic, philosophical and spiritual pursuits. He worked with Stravinsky to design sets and costumes, studied Russian archaeology, wrote, painted and traveled extensively. The museum features a permanent collection of Roerich's works and personal memorabilia, including numerous paintings inspired by his interest in Buddhism and the Tibetan highlands. The museum also hosts concerts and poetry readings. **Subway:** 1, 9 to 110th St.

Studio Museum in Harlem 144 W. 125th St. (between Lenox Ave. and Adam Clayton Powell Blvd.) (212) 864-4500 *www.studiomuseuminharlem.org.* Dedicated to African-American art, as well as work from Africa and throughout the diaspora, the Studio Museum was organized in 1967 for artists. Originally housed atop a liquor store on Fifth Avenue, the museum is now located on

125th Street in a building donated by the New York Bank for Savings. This
Harlem museum organizes thematic and single-artist exhibitions. The permanent collection includes works by Romare Bearden, Elizabeth Catlett, Jacob
Lawrence and Norman Lewis, and the James Van Der Zee photographic
archives.In addition, the building houses archives, studios, workshops and a
museum shop. **Admission:** $5; $3, students and seniors; $1, children under 12;
members, free. Free first Sat. each month. Cash and checks only. **Hours:**
Wed.–Fri., 10 A.M.–5 P.M.; Sat.–Sun., 1 P.M.–6 P.M. Closed Mon., Tue. Group
tours, call (212) 864-4500, ext. 230. **Subway:** 2, 3 to 125th St.

Whitney Museum of American Art—Philip Morris Branch
MIDTOWN EAST 120 Park Ave. (at 42nd St.) (917) 663-2453. Philip Morris's
headquarters building across the street from Grand Central Terminal houses a
midtown exhibition space for the Whitney Museum. The Sculpture Court
accommodates large sculptures that the museum cannot, while the gallery primarily shows contemporary painting and smaller sculptures. **Admission:** Free.
Hours: Gallery: Mon–Fri., 11 A.M.–6 P.M.; Thu. until 7:30 P.M. Sculpture
Court: Mon.–Sat., 7:30 A.M.–9:30 P.M.; Sun., 11 A.M.–7 P.M. **Subway:** 4, 5, 6
to 42nd St.

Art Galleries

There are probably more art galleries with active exhibition schedules in New
York than anywhere else—far too many to list them all here. But the names and
brief descriptions of the dealers below represent a hearty sampling. From paintings to ceramics, from photography and film to Conceptual art, from small decorative objects to massive installations, their exhibitions make up an art menu
unequalled in range and variety.

The criteria for the listed galleries are that they hold regular exhibitions and
they are open to the public during normal viewing hours (generally from 10
A.M. to 6 P.M. five days a week, closed Sundays and Mondays). But it is always
wise to call first, check *The New York Times* on Friday for art listings, or visit
"Art and Museums" on *www.nytoday.com*.

SoHo
ACE Gallery 275 Hudson St. (at Dominick St.) (212) 255-5599. The menu in
this large arena is Abstract Expressionist, Pop, Minimal and Conceptual art
from 1960 to the present, along with established and emerging U.S. and international art going back to 1980. The exhibition schedule is full of surprises,
from a huge suite of wall paintings by the Minimalist Sol LeWitt to an all-out
show of creations by the fashion designer Issey Miyake. Behind it all is a sharp
contemporary sensibility.

Howard Greenberg 120 Wooster St., 2nd Fl. (between Prince and Spring Sts.)
(212) 334-0010. With one of the biggest inventories in the trade, this gallery
focuses on classic 20th-century European and American photography. It handles the estates of such icons as Ruth Orkin, Roman Vishniac, James Van Der

Zee, Andre Kertesz and Ralph Eugene Meatyard, and represents well-known contemporaries like William Klein, Sarah Moon, Bill Owens, Ralph Gibson, Gordon Parks and Mary Ellen Mark. Theme shows have dealt with American car culture, the New York subway and civil rights, among other topics.

Nolan/Eckman 560 Broadway (at Prince St.) (212) 925-6190. This small, intimate and easy gallery specializes in works on paper by contemporary American and German artists. Shows range from the outrageous, no-holds-barred polemics of the cartoony Peter Saul to the less scandalous musings of German stars like Gerhard Richter, Martin Kippenberger and Sigmar Polke.

Phyllis Kind Gallery 136 Greene St. (between Prince and Houston Sts.) (212) 925-1200. The quirky, the odd and the offbeat are to be found at this SoHo gallery, whose offerings run from far-out folk art like the garrulous paintings of the preacher Howard Finster to the wacky renderings of Chicago School painters like Jim Nutt. The gallery's lively Chicago sensibility reveals its start in the Second City.

Chelsea

Barbara Gladstone Gallery 515 W. 24th St. (between 10th and 11th Aves.) (212) 206-0300. An émigré from SoHo (where it opened in the early 1980's) to Chelsea, this gallery represents all areas of the visual arts, with the emphasis on Conceptual, installation, video and photographic work. The rhapsodic filmmaker Matthew Barney is one of its stars, along with the painters Anish Kapoor and Lari Pittman, the photographers Richard Prince and Shirin Neshat, the German installation artist Gregor Schneider and the Italian Conceptual artists Mario and Marisa Merz.

Cheim and Read 521 W. 23rd St. (between 10th and 11th Aves.) (212) 242-7727. One of the wider ranging galleries in Chelsea, this spacious ground-floor showcase handles a variety of contemporary painters, sculptors, photographers, video and installation artists of different generations. The gallery emphasizes art involved with strong psychological themes, like that of the sculptor Louise Bourgeois, as well as work devoted to the language of painting, like the abstractions of Richmond Burton. Other high-profile artists represented by the gallery are the painters Joan Mitchell, Louise Fishman, Pat Steir and Juan Uslé; the sculptor Lynda Benglis; the photographers William Eggleston, Robert Mapplethorpe, Adam Fuss and Jack Pierson; and the installation artist Jenny Holzer.

Feigen Contemporary 535 W. 20th St. (between 10th and 11th Aves.) (212) 929-0500. The newest branch of the veteran Richard L. Feigen Gallery, which in its uptown headquarters focuses on Old Masters, Feigen Contemporary moved from Chicago to Chelsea in 1997. It represents emerging, mid-career and established contemporary artists, ranging from James Rosenquist and the estate of Ray Johnson to the young video artist Jeremy Blake.

Ileana Sonnabend 536 W. 22nd St. (between 10th and 11th Aves.)
(212) 627-1018. Noted for introducing 60's proto Pop pioneers like Rauschenberg and Johns to Europe, Sonnabend came to New York in 1970 and has assembled a stable of internationally known contemporary European and American painters, sculptors, photographers and installation artists. Some of its current stars are the English conceptualists Gilbert and George, kitsch-loving sculptor Jeff Koons, assemblagists Ashley Bickerton and Haim Steinbach from the East Village "Neo-Geo" movement of the mid-1980's, German photographers Bernd and Hilla Becher and site sculptors Anne and Patrick Poirier.

Leslie Tonkonow Artworks + Projects 535 W. 22th St. (between 10th and 11th Aves.) (212) 255-8450. The roster of this young gallery emphasizes photographers from all over the world, among them the Korean Nikki S. Lee, the Japanese Tokihiro Sato and the American team of Robbins and Becher. But a recent move into larger quarters allows the showing of other kinds of visual artists, too, like the sculptors Beverly Semmes and Robert Watts. The dealer's eye for lively talent makes the gallery a cool stop on the Chelsea trail.

Matthew Marks Gallery 523 W. 24th St. and 522 W. 22nd St. (between 10th and 11th Aves.) (212) 243-0200. It takes not one but two spacious galleries in Chelsea to display the work of the 20-odd artists on Matthew Marks' superstar roster, ranging from the English figure painter Lucian Freud and the estate of the Abstract Expressionist Willem deKooning to the very contemporary abstract painter Terry Winters and the much admired but widely differing photographers Nan Goldin and Andreas Gursky.

MetroPictures 519 W. 24th St. (between 10th and 11th Aves.)
(212) 206-7100. Receptive to the new and far-out, this gallery, which opened in SoHo in 1980 but now occupies a vast Chelsea space, carries on with a group of contemporaries that have become more established over the years. They include the painter, sculptor and filmmaker Robert Longon, the video installation artist Tony Oursler and the photographer Cindy Sherman.

Paula Cooper 534 W. 21st St. (between 10th and 11th Aves.) (212) 255-1105. Founded in 1968, this gallery was one of the very first to open in SoHo, establishing early on an agenda focused on (but not limited to) Conceptual and Minimalist sculpture. Sol LeWitt, Carl Andre, Donald Judd, Robert Grosvenor and Dan Flavin were among early exhibitors, but the gallery also has different breeds of artists in its stable, among them the painters Jennifer Bartlett and Michael Hurson, the sculptors Jonathan Borofsky and Jackie Winsor and the photographer Peter Campus.

Yancey-Richardson 535 W. 22nd St. (between 10th and 11th Aves.)
(212) 343-1225. Focusing on contemporary and vintage 20th century photography, this small gallery is known for excellent shows of the work of individual photographers, among them the Czech Josef Sudek, the Brazilians Sebastiao Selgado and Mario Cravo Netto, along with U.S. lensmen Julius Shulman, Lynn Geesaman, Andrew Moore and the Depression era's Marian Post Wolcott.

Midtown and Uptown

Barry Friedman, Ltd. 32 E. 67th St. (between Park and Madison Aves.) (212) 794-8950. European decorative arts of the 20th century dominate this sumptuous town house, including French furniture and objects of the 1930's and 40's, Wiener Werkstatte and Bauhaus productions and avant-garde paintings from the 20's and 30's, works on paper, sculpture and contemporary vintage photography. The gallery is also moving into the field of contemporary decorative arts with shows of studio glass, art furniture, ceramics and wood objects by artists from all over the world. A keenly discriminating taste prevails.

C & M Arts 45 E. 78th St. (between Park and Madison Aves.) (212) 861-0020. Distinguished presentations of European and American masters—from Impressionists through Matisse, Picasso, deKooning, Jackson Pollock and Joseph Cornell—are at home in this discriminating gallery, quartered in what was once a luxurious town house. The gallery, opened in 1992, does relatively few shows, but high standards prevail.

Edwynn Houk 745 Fifth Ave. (at 57th St.) (212) 750-7070. Specializing in masters of 20th-century photography, with an emphasis on the 1920's and 30's as well as the work of contemporary Americans, this elegantly understated gallery has a cavernous space in which to show them. It represents the estates of Brassai and Dorothea Lange, among others, and is the exclusive representative for such American contemporaries as Elliott Erwitt, Sally Mann, Lynn Davis and Andrea Modica.

Gagosian 980 Madison Ave. (at 76th St.) (212) 744-2313; 555 W. 24th St. (between 10th and 11th Sts.) (212) 741-1111. Big name contemporaries, as well as the work of Pop artists light up the big spaces of this two-location gallery. Large-scale installations by Richard Serra, Mark di Suvero, Damien Hirst and others appear in the huge Chelsea branch; the Madison Avenue gallery handles more conventionally-sized works. The sculptors Maya Lin and Elyn Zimmerman and the painters Ed Ruscha, Annette Messager, James Rosenquist and David Salle are also on the roster.

Galerie St. Etienne 24 W. 57th St. (between Fifth and Sixth Aves.) (212) 245-6734. Austrian and German Expressionism from the turn of the century through the 1920's are the house specialties at this gallery, along with the work of American folk artists. Founded in 1939 by Dr. Otto Kallir, St. Etienne was the first to show Grandma Moses. The gallery introduced major Expressionists like Gustav Klimt, Oskar Kokoschka and Egon Schiele to the United States, and deals with other Austrian and German modernists, including Kaethe Kollwitz, Lovis Corinth and Paula Modersohn-Becker. Its stable of classic American folk painters includes John Kane, Morris Hirshfield and Horace Pippin.

Garth Clark 24 W. 57th St. (between Fifth and Sixth Aves.) (212) 246-2205. This small but serious showcase for 20th-century ceramics handles a mix of artists spanning the century. Some come from the ceramics world, like George

Ohr, Beatrice Wood and Ron Nagle; others, better known as painters or sculptors, have turned their hands to ceramics, among them Lucio Fontana, Sir Anthony Caro, Joan Miró and Louise Nevelson.

Hirschl & Adler; Hirschl & Adler Modern 21 E. 70th St. (at Madison Ave.) (212) 535-8810. American and European paintings, watercolors, drawings and sculpture from the 18th through the early 20th century are the province of this active gallery, along with American prints of all periods and American decorative arts from 1810 to 1910. Established in 1952, it occupies a handsome landmark town house that is also home to a contemporary arm that deals with European and American art from post-World War II to the present.

Joan T. Washburn 20 W. 57th St. (between Fifth and Sixth Aves.) (212) 397-6780. American art from World War I to the present is the territory staked out by this long established gallery, which handles the estates of the painters Jackson Pollock and Myron Stout, Louise Nevelson's sculpture and drawings from the 1930's and '40's, and David Smith's paintings from the same period. Its contemporary stable includes the sculptors Jack Youngerman and Gwynn Murrill and the painter Richard Baker.

Kennedy Galleries 730 Fifth Ave. (at 56th St.) (212) 541-9600. Now celebrating its 126th year, Kennedy is one of the oldest dealers in American art. In its plush, carpeted quarters it shows paintings from an inventory that runs from the 18th to the 20th century, including the Hudson River School, American Impressionism, Social Realism and Modernism. On the 20th-century side, it handles exclusively the estates of Charles Burchfield and Rockwell Kent, and regularly exhibits the work of American classics like George Bellows, John Sloan, Stuart Davis, Charles Demuth, John Marin and Walt Kuhn.

Knoedler & Company 19 E. 70th St. (between Fifth and Madison Aves.) (212) 794-0550. The oldest art gallery in New York, Knoedler goes back to 1846, when its French founder immigrated to America. It became a leading international dealer in European and American art and in 1930 scored a coup by buying 21 masterpieces from the Hermitage in St. Petersburg for the American acquisitor Andrew Mellon. Always a champion of contemporary artists as well, it shows works today by Helen Frankenthaler, Milton Avery, Adolph Gottlieb, Richard Pousette-Dart and other established talents.

Marian Goodman 24 W. 57th St. (between Fifth and Sixth Aves.) (212) 977-7160. An international repertory distinguishes this long-established gallery, a quiet but important presence on the art scene that has recently added significantly to its space. To its schedule of shows by prominent European and American Conceptual artists like Jannis Kounellis, Rebecca Horn, members of the socially-conscious Italian Arte Povera group, along with the Conceptual artists Lawrence Weiner and Dan Graham, it has been adding the work of contemporary photographers, among them large-scale prints by Germany's Thomas Struth.

Marlborough 40 W. 57th St. (between Fifth and Sixth Aves.) (212) 541-4900 and **Marlborough Chelsea** 211 W. 19th St. (between Seventh and Eighth Aves.) (212) 463-8634. The emphasis in the spacious uptown branch of this gallery is on contemporary artists with established reputations. Larry Rivers, Marisol, Alex Katz, Red Grooms and the Colombian sculptor-painter Fernando Botero are regular exhibitors at Marlborough's glossy uptown headquarters. A graphics division there shows 19th- through 20th-century work, with occasional historical shows; the roomy Chelsea branch specializes in the work of contemporary sculptors like Anthony Caro, Magdalena Abakanowicz and Kenneth Snelson.

Mary Boone 745 Fifth Ave. (at 58th St.) (212) 752-2929; and in Chelsea, 541 W. 21st St. (between 10th and 11th Aves.). Not so "cutting edge" as it once was, this trendy, highly publicized gallery, a launching pad for rockets like Julian Schnabel and David Salle, is still going strong. The gallery continues to represent some of the older talents from its roster in the 1970's and 80's, like the painters Bill Jensen, Ross Bleckner, Eric Fischl and Barbara Kruger, and it continues to be a showcase for younger artists, among them Leonardo Drew, Damian Loeb, Peter Wegner and Karin Davie. The gallery recently opened additional space in Chelsea for large-scale works and installations.

McKee Gallery 745 Fifth Ave. (at 58th St.) (212) 688-5951. Established contemporaries and an outlook independent of fashions or trends are the strengths of this gallery, opened in 1974. Among its painters are Vija Celmins, Jake Berthot, Harvey Quaytman and the estate of Philip Guston; its sculptors include William Tucker, Martin Puryear and the young Spanish maestra Susanna Solano.

Michael Rosenfeld 24 W. 57th St. (between Fifth and Sixth Aves.) (212) 247-0082. Specializing in American art from 1910 to 1970, the gallery has mounted "movement" shows of early American abstraction and Abstract Expressionism; it also handles the estates of the Surrealist Alfonso Ossorio and the abstractionist Burgoyne Diller, and the work of contemporaries like Charles Seliger, Martha Madigan and Betye Saar. The gallery is particularly receptive to the work of minority artists, and has mounted a number of shows of African-American art.

PaceWildenstein 32 E. 57th St. (between Fifth and Sixth Aves.) (212) 421-3292 and 534 W. 25th St. (212) 929-7000; **Pace MacGill** 32 E. 57th St. (between Fifth and Sixth Aves.). Beautifully mounted shows in cool, elegant settings are the rule at PaceWildenstein, originally founded as the Pace Gallery in the 1960's. Not a hotbed of new talent, it's the place to see the work of contemporary "Old Masters," like Mark Rothko, Ad Reinhardt, Louise Nevelson and the satirist Saul Steinberg, as well as living icons like Julian Schnabel, Chuck Close and Alex Katz. Pace MacGill, in the same building, shows 20th-century American photography; the Chelsea branch of PaceWildenstein adds more space for larger-scale sculpture and installations.

Salander-O'Reilly Galleries 20 E. 79th St. (at Madison Ave.) (212) 879-6606.
With one of the most ambitious rosters in the art world, this gallery in an
impressive town house shows a broad range of American and European painting
and sculpture from the 18th to the 20th century. It has mounted more than 300
exhibitions, from work by the 18th-century English painters John Constable
and Joseph M.W. Turner to the American modernist Alfred Maurer and the late
abstractionist Stanley Boxer. It represents the estates of Stuart Davis, Gaston
Lachaise, Gerald Murphy and Elaine deKooning, as well as the work of living
artists like Paul Georges, Don Gummer, Graham Nickson, Larry Poons, Katherine Porter and Michael Steiner.

Zabriskie 41 E. 57th St. (between Fifth and Sixth Aves.) (212) 752-1223.
Opened in 1955, the Zabriskie Gallery is known for its strong emphasis on
American Modernism, Dada and Surrealism, showing works in all media. It is
also a stronghold of modern and contemporary French and American photography, from the Frenchman Eugene Atget to the American Nicholas Nixon. The
gallery represents the estates of the sculptors Richard Stankiewicz and William
Zorach as well as the work of contemporary painters such as Pat Adams and
Katherine Schmidt. Group shows of important movements and periods are also
part of the fare.

—*Grace Glueck*

PERFORMING ARTS
Theater in New York

Broadway, as a word, still has an enchanted sound to the stagestruck, summon-
ing an impossibly glamorous neighborhood of palatial theaters, stars of incan-
denscent wattage and plays and musicals of unmatchable wit and polish. That,
anyway, is the myth. In reality, such a Broadway—and by Broadway, one means
an area of roughly 40 square blocks around Times Square in midtown Manhattan—hasn't existed, if it ever did, for at least some 30 years and probably longer.
Broadway more than ever is a state of mind, albeit a state within the city of
New York. As a piece of nomenclature, it has never been exact, since most
"Broadway" theaters are found on other streets. And if you can stretch your
imagination—and your legs—to encompass at least a few hundred more blocks,
you'll discover that something very much like the Broadway that was still exists.
You just can't find it all in one place, anymore than all of the city's multistar
restaurants are within an oyster shell's throw of one another.

Finding what meets your tastes may require a little more research than it
might have in, say, the 1930's.

What is produced in the official Broadway area is still what gets the most
attention nationally. The plays put on there have bigger budgets and usually bigger names, with ticket prices to match. What it seldom offers is much in the
way of originality or daring. Investing in a Broadway production is a high-risk
gamble and producers are accordingly cautious. That is why the neighborhood
is dominated by revivals, shows based on successful movies and British imports

perfumed with class and flowery reviews from abroad. With the cleaning up and slicking up of Times Square in the 1990's, there has also arisen a new crop of shows directly targeted at tourists, trading on brand-name familiarity, most notably those of Disney, whose *The Lion King* (admittedly, a brilliantly rethought stage production of a cartoon movie) may well outlive us all.

There's still plenty to get excited about on Broadway. Revivals of dramas in recent seasons have been on an exceptionally high level. New musicals have tended to be either lost or leaden, with the blessed exception of Susan Stroman's multi-Tony-winning *Contact*. But cutting edge, or even nicking edge, is definitely not an attribute of midtown Manhattan theater. When a production with a cool quotient shows up on Broadway (*Rent*), you can safely assume that it started life in some other neighborhood. Indeed, since 1970 the overwhelming majority of Pulitzer Prizes for drama have gone to non-Broadway productions.

Finding what's hot Off-Broadway and in the increasingly less marginalized realm known as Off-Off-Broadway can take you as far from midtown as Brooklyn or as close as Theater Row—the stretch of 42nd Street west of Eighth Avenue. There's no strict rule of thumb for conducting your search: a theater, after all, is judged by what is on its stage, and that changes constantly.

In the glitzy block of 42nd Street between Seventh and Eighth Avenues, there is a most charming and innovative new theater for children, the restored little jewel box called the **New Victory**, right next door to the goliath **Ford Performing Arts Center**. If you're looking for literate, polished plays in thoroughly professional productions, there are several institutional theaters that have become bywords for just that: the **Manhattan Theater Club**, **Lincoln Center**, **Playwrights Horizons** and to a lesser extent, the **Joseph Papp Public Theater**. There are also younger, smaller and more vital companies that have already established a track record for putting on works that get people talking.

These include the **Vineyard Theater**, off Union Square (birthplace of Pulitzer winner Edward Albee's *Three Tall Women* and Paula Vogel's *How I Learned to Drive*), the **New York Theater Workshop** on 4th Street in the East Village (the cradle of the now fabled rock opera *Rent* and Claudia Shear's *Dirty Blonde*) and **MCC** (the Manhattan Class Company) on West 23rd Street, which brought Margaret Edson's brave, surprisingly popular *Wit* to New York. The **Drama Dept.** on East 9th Street, filled with some of the most vital young theater talents in the city, has in five years established itself as a company whose imaginative reinventions of classic plays are essential viewing.

If your tastes lean more toward the truly experimental—that is, without such conventions as plot and easily understood characters—there remains a host of fertile outlets for such work, mostly located south of 14th Street, from the legendary **LaMama** on 4th Street in the East Village to the more recently created **HERE** performing arts complex on Sixth Avenue in SoHo, where an underwater puppet show became the talk of the town several seasons ago. Two mighty bastions of the avant-garde remain indomitably in place and abidingly influential: Richard Foreman's **Ontological-Hysteric Theater** and the **Wooster Group**, both of which have hardcore cult followings, making tickets to their productions tough to come by.

For theatergoers with an international palate, there is the annual **Lincoln Center Festival**, which in recent years has brought major works from Ireland, South Africa and Eastern Europe. And just across the river from Manhattan is the **Brooklyn Academy of Music** (*see section* "Brooklyn" *in chapter* **Exploring New York**), unquestionably the city's most ambitious and adventurous importer of theater, regularly bringing in productions from titanic directors like Peter Brook and Ingmar Bergman. Indeed, some of the most electric theater seen in New York of late has been at the Academy. Even those who consider Brooklyn a foreign country must concede that it's closer than Stockholm.

— *Ben Brantley*

Broadway

Broadway theater has become rather pricey—and the seats in the older theaters aren't terribly comfortable—but those things cease to matter when the lights go down and the curtain goes up. You are in the right place.

There are 32 "Broadway" theaters, and even more Off-Broadway and Off-Off-Broadway. Off- and Off-Off are less expensive than Broadway, and the the-atrical quality can be superior, but the comfort level is no better. To find out what's playing and where, the fullest listings are in *Time Out New York*, *The New Yorker* and *The New York Times* (listings every day, but more on Friday and Sunday); *www.nytoday.com* also has everything you need.

Getting Tickets

If you want to see *The Lion King*, you should have written for tickets months ago. For everything else, there may be tickets available at the theater box office or through one of the telephone services that charge extra. Here are two: **Ticketmaster** at (212) 307-7171 and **Tele-Charge** at (212) 239-6200.

But many smart theatergoers don't pay full price: There are two ways to pay less. Best known is the half-price **TKTS** booth in Times Square. Also popular are the discount coupons distributed all over town by an organization that calls itself the **Hit Show Club**.

TKTS

The Times Square TKTS booth, on Broadway at 47th Street, has tickets to dozens of Broadway and Off-Broadway shows for half-price on the day of the performance.

Tickets to a few shows are discounted 25 percent at the TKTS booth, but most are 50 percent. There is also a $2.50 charge per ticket, to support the TKTS operation. You can't buy the best seats but there are often very good ones. **NOTE:** Credit cards are not accepted. Cash and travelers checks only.

TKTS was established in 1973 by the Theater Development Fund to fill seats that weren't selling at full price. Hundreds of people line up for tickets at the booth so the line can be long, but the savings are real. If the line is one block long, figure on waiting a half-hour; an hour in peak holiday seasons.

TIP #1: The line is longest when the booth opens and for the next hour or so. They are dramatically shorter at the end of the day—as short as a 10-minute wait after 5 P.M., and even less after 7 P.M. Some tickets that were available when the booth opened may have been sold out if you go late, but the selection is usually good at any hour. Also, some shows that were not offering discount tickets earlier in the day may have released some as curtain time approached.

TIP #2: Tickets available at the booth are listed every day after 4 P.M. at *www.newyork.citysearch.com*, which has a link to TKTS.

TIP #3: Do not buy tickets from hawkers along the waiting line. They offer deeper discounts, but you run the risk that they are counterfeit and the theater will turn you away.

Times Square TKTS Booth
The booth is technically in Duffy Square, an island between Broadway and Seventh Avenue at 47th Street. TKTS shares the island with statues of Father Francis Duffy, Roman Catholic chaplain of the Fighting 69th in World War I and pastor of a church on 42nd Street, and George M. ("I'm a Yankee Doodle Dandy") Cohan.
Hours: Mon–Sat., 3 P.M.–8 P.M. for evening performances; Wed., Sat.: 10 A.M.–2 P.M. for matinees; Sun., 11 A.M. to closing. **Subway:** N, Q, R, S, W, 1, 2, 3, 7, 9 to 42nd St.—Times Square.

Hit Show Club
630 Ninth Ave., Rm. 808 (between 44th and 45th Sts.). When you walk in, you'll see a rack with discount coupons for maybe a dozen shows. The choice is smaller than same-day tickets at TKTS, but there is a big advantage: You can use these coupons to buy tickets in advance. Another advantage: You don't have to stand on a long line outside in foul weather. Take (or mail) the coupon to the theater, present the coupon, and if they have what you want they will sell you two tickets (or one) at the discount. Most Hit Show Club discounts are about 40 percent, with no extra charge, compared to 50 percent plus $2.50 for most TKTS shows. The dollar difference is minor.

There are smaller selections of Hit Show and other discount coupons beside the cash register in some restaurants. Not all discounts are the same, and not all shows offer discounts for all performances. Some long-run shows offer seats anywhere in the house. Others will not offer seats in the first 10 or 12 rows of the orchestra or the front balcony.

As an unexpected bonus, a leading architectural critic calls the landmarked lobby "one of the most beautiful Art Deco interiors in New York," with a glistening mosaic on one wall and a pleated gold ceiling. It is worth a visit.
Hours: 9 A.M.–4 P.M. **Subway:** A, C, E to 42nd St.

Classical Music

Musical life in New York begins but by no means ends with two big institutions. **Carnegie Hall** and **Lincoln Center** generate concerts of every size and description and have halls big and small to put them in. Next to these giants is a ring of smaller organizations; they organize chamber music, new music ensembles and recitals. Though traditionally the season stretches from September until well into June, it's now possible to find worthwhile events in August as well as November.

Surrounding these major islands of activity is an ocean of free enterprise, and it is this mass of self-generated events and cottage industries that gives New York its energy. Experimental music groups, amateur choirs with big agendas, small opera companies doing new or esoteric repertory, self-financed and self-promoted debut performances fill downtown lofts and uptown churches in profusion. The quality will vary as much as the material, but the level of ambition is always high.

Carnegie Hall has no resident orchestras or ensembles; it is a presenter, gathering the best orchestras, singers and recitalists from this country and the world and fitting them into subscription series. Sign up for a season-long list, or choose individual events. In the main hall (seating 2,800) expect the Vienna and Berlin Philharmonics every year, as well as the orchestras of Cleveland, Philadelphia, Boston and Chicago. The Pittsburgh and Montreal Symphonies and many others will drop in, too, and there will be both familiar and exotic symphonic visitors from Europe and the East *(see section "Classical Music Centers" later in this chapter for full listing)*.

Lincoln Center's Avery Fisher Hall is Carnegie's equivalent in size and seating capacity, if not beauty. It produces series in the same way as well, but with a difference. For Fisher is also the home of the New York Philharmonic, and the smaller Alice Tully Hall next door houses the Chamber Music Society of Lincoln Center. The Philharmonic is at work steadily through the season, either under its music director Kurt Masur or guest conductors. Weekly programs are generally repeated three to four times, often with Friday morning performances for those less easy with nightlife in the city. *(See section "Lincoln Center" later in this chapter for full listings.)* NOTE: At the end of the 2002 season Avery Fisher Hall will be closed for renovation; the Philharmonic will perform elsewhere until the renovation is completed.

The Chamber Music Society is a permanent ensemble of 10 to 20 performers. They mix and match their instruments and skills to make all possible combinations. Sextets with bassoon are no problem, but conventional quartets and trios turn up as well. The Society's programs are usually repeated only once.

A major renovation a decade ago turned the dreary small theater at Carnegie Hall into a little gem called Weill Recital Hall. Formerly a rental operation for almost all comers, it is now the home of chamber music series, musical theater in concert, song recitals by good artists and, very important, debut recitals by beginning professionals. Deciding which new talent is worth a trip and the price of a ticket is a less haphazard procedure today. The performers are selected by Carnegie Hall in conjunction with several European concert halls, and the young people give their recitals in all of them.

Lincoln Center has several debut series as well, as does the **92nd Street Y.** And then there is the Young Concert Artists which has been presenting and preparing young musicians and singers for a generation. The **Juilliard School** is eager to put its best students before the public and sponsors a number of in-house competitions with major public recitals as rewards. Go to the box office at the school in Lincoln Center for schedules and tickets. Most performances are free. (*See section* "Classical Music Centers" *later in this chapter for full listing.*)

Indeed, the students of Juilliard and their companion schools, **Mannes** and **Manhattan,** often blur the distinction between amateur and professional (*see section* "Classical Music Centers"). All three schools teem with concerts and operas at which the public is welcome, usually for free. Opera productions at the Juilliard Theater (one of the city's best spaces) are often on a par if not superior to the professional efforts of companies in other cities. Manhattan regularly puts on skillful versions of out-of-the-way 20th-century operas, and Mannes has recently been in the midst of an extensive Handel project.

Although New York is often criticized for having only one major orchestra, the accusation is deceptive. Floating groups like the estimable Orchestra of St. Luke's have their own seasons. The New York Chamber Symphony and the conductorless Orpheus are well rated, and the American Symphony Orchestra is making strides as well. Under Robert Spano, the Brooklyn Philharmonic is giving some of the most interesting orchestra programs in town. The **Brooklyn Academy of Music** (*see section* "Brooklyn" *in chapter* **Exploring New York**) where it performs is a quick and easy subway ride across the East River from Manhattan.

Smaller venues are remarkably active. The **Miller Theater** at Columbia University has become the hotbed of choice for the serious new-music crowd. **Merkin Concert Hall** is plain to look at but night after night provides a place for every kind of music, new and old, provocative and conservative. The **Florence Gould Theater** and the **Kaye Playhouse** join the **92nd Street Y** as East Side presenters. **The Kitchen** downtown near the Hudson River is a clearinghouse for musical and theatrical experiment where electronic instruments and new sounds are the norm. The **World Music Institute** brings in ethnic performers from Tibet, Africa or, for that matter, down the street.

Summer is becoming busy, although Carnegie Hall usually closes in August. In June and July the Lincoln Center Festival brings operas, orchestra concerts and interesting exotica. It uses its own halls and a few others nearby. There is also the vastly popular Mostly Mozart Festival, which divides its frequent summer-long programs between Avery Fisher and Alice Tully Halls. The repertory is usually more comforting than challenging.

A lot of summer entertainment is free: the Met giving concert versions of operas in the parks of the five boroughs, the New York Philharmonic doing much the same, and then Lincoln Center's Damrosch Park offering concert brass bands, choruses and mostly lighthearted fare.

—Bernard Holland

Classical Music Centers

Below is a small list of places that offer concerts on a regular basis. The serious music lover should check listings every Sunday in *The New York Times* "Arts & Leisure" section (the next-to-last page) or *www.nytoday.com*. *(For* **Brooklyn Academy of Music** *see section* "Brooklyn" *in chapter* **Exploring New York***.)*

Bargemusic BROOKLYN Fulton Ferry Landing (between Water and River Sts.) (718) 624-4061. Olga Bloom, the driving force behind Bargemusic, deserves an award for creating a unique venue. "I wanted a place where musicians could escape the combat zone of the New York music scene," she said. So in 1974 Bloom, a violinist, purchased an old coffee barge, almost single-handedly refurbished it and turned it into a floating chamber music space where artists can perform in an informal atmosphere and actually enjoy making music. Moored in the East River under the Brooklyn Bridge, with the Manhattan skyline providing a breathtaking backdrop, Bargemusic is a cozy, wood-paneled room that seats about 125 people on folding chairs. Year-round, the finest chamber music performers play concerts of the highest caliber. It's a magical spot, well worth the trip to Brooklyn Heights and the occasionally choppy waters. Advance reservations are necessary, as performances sell out. **Subway:** A, C to High St.

CAMI Hall MIDTOWN WEST 165 W. 57th St. (between Sixth and Seventh Aves.) (212) 841-9500. It may be one of the city's most nondescript concert halls, but no matter. It serves its purpose, which is to give performers a decent, affordable place to peddle their art in Midtown. CAMI stands for Columbia Artists Management Inc., the prestigious firm that owns the pleasant 200-seat hall located directly across the street from Carnegie Hall (where Columbia's own artists are more likely to be appearing). Cash and checks only. **Subway:** N, Q, R, W to 57th St.; B, D, E to Seventh Ave.

Carnegie Hall MIDTOWN WEST Seventh Ave. and 57th St. (212) 247-7800. Can you imagine New York without Carnegie Hall? Probably not. But in 1960, its owners were ready to demolish Andrew Carnegie's shrine to music to make way for a new skyscraper. Violinist Isaac Stern almost single-handedly saved the world's most famous concert hall from becoming merely a fond memory. From the time it opened in 1891 (with Tchaikovsky conducting the inaugural concert) the 2,804-seat landmark has been synonymous with the greatest musicians of the 20th century, from Arturo Toscanini, Marian Anderson and Vladimir Horowitz to Ella Fitzgerald, Frank Sinatra and the Beatles.

Carnegie's acoustics are legendary, though some feel the sound was compromised after much-needed renovations were completed in 1986. (A concrete slab

Fred R. Conrad/The New York Times

Carnegie Hall

under the stage, discovered in 1995, didn't help matters and was later removed.) Once you get past the claustrophobic lobby, you're in for a visual and sonic treat. On the walls are photos and letters from famous composers, singers, instrumentalists and conductors. The seats are plush and the gilded décor ravishing. Even if a performance does not live up to your expectations, a visit to Carnegie always does.

During intermission, instead of squeezing into the lobby or the Cafe Carnegie, stop by the Rose Museum on the First Tier level, where interesting music-related exhibits give you a taste of the hall's illustrious history. On the same level are another cafe, the Rohatyn Room, and a gift shop. But beware: The shop is even more claustrophobic than the lobby.

Tickets: Carnegie Charge. **Subway:** N, Q, R, W to 57th St.; B, D, E to Seventh Ave.

Columbia University—Miller Theater UPPER WEST SIDE 2960 Broadway (at 116th St.) (212) 854-7799. Thanks to a $3 million reconstruction, a third of which came from the Kathryn and Gilbert Miller Fund, Columbia now has a state-of-the-art theater that brings the finest opera, music and dance, as well as theater, poetry readings and lectures, to Morningside Heights. One extremely popular event is the sensational Sonic Boom Festival, a new-music series. **Subway:** 1, 9 to 116th St.

Juilliard School—Juilliard Theater UPPER WEST SIDE 60 Lincoln Center Plaza (Broadway at 65th St.) (212) 799-5000. The Juilliard School enjoys a reputation as one of the world's leading music conservatories. Indeed, some of the world's best-known performers are graduates. The principal auditorium, the Juilliard Theater, is as impressive as the students who regularly appear on its stage. A steeply raked 933-seat hall with extremely comfortable seats, superior acoustics and excellent sightlines, it is most often used for opera and orchestral concerts, though chamber music, drama and dance are no strangers here. **Tickets:** Many performances are free. Others have relatively modest ticket prices, available at the box office or, for a fee, through Ticketmaster. Cash and checks only at box office. **Subway:** 1, 9 to 66th St.; A, B, C, D to 59th St.

Kosciuszko Foundation UPPER EAST SIDE 15 E. 65th St. (between Madison and Fifth Aves.) (212) 734-2130. On the second floor of the Kosciuszko Foundation's splendid three-story limestone town house, just off Central Park, is one of the loveliest recital spaces in town. An elegant wood-paneled parlor at the top of a red-carpeted spiral staircase, the room doubles as a gallery for 19th- and 20th-century Polish art and is dominated by a large portrait of Tadeusz Kosciuszko, a Polish-born military engineer who fought with colonial American forces, designed the fortress at West Point and achieved the rank of major general in the Polish army. The Foundation, founded in 1925, is a center for Polish culture and education, so naturally the focus of its excellent concert series is on Polish music and musicians. **Tickets:** Purchase at office during office hours. **Subway:** 6 to 68th St.; N, R to Fifth Ave,

Manhattan School of Music UPPER WEST SIDE 122 Claremont Ave. (at Broadway and 122nd St.) (212) 749-2802. One of the country's premier conservatories, the Manhattan School of Music is located just a few blocks from Grant's Tomb and Riverside Church in the less-than-glamorous building that was the Juilliard School before it moved to posher digs at Lincoln Center. The Manhattan School is bustling with all sorts of music, from student, faculty and professional recitals and chamber music to opera, orchestral and jazz presentations. The quality is usually high and the price of admission often free. There are several auditoriums at the school. The two principal spaces are Borden Auditorium, a long, narrow 1,000-seat hall with decent if not wonderful sound, and upstairs, the intimate, 380-seat Hubbard Recital Hall. **Tickets:** Call for prices (often free). **Subway:** 1, 9 to 125th St.

Mannes College of Music UPPER WEST SIDE 150 W. 85th St. (between Amsterdam and Columbus Aves.) (212) 580-0210. When Mannes moved in 1984 from the Upper East Side into new quarters on West 85th Street—a six-story,

Lincoln Center

Hardly beautiful, but stunning in its comprehensive cultural offerings, Lincoln Center for the Performing Arts is a great stop on any visitor's itinerary. Even if you don't take in the myriad programs, from opera to ballet to film to jazz, it is fun to sit and watch those who do. The winter season brings the fur coat crowd to the Metropolitan Opera, its building their spectacular, glittering backdrop. In September, when the New York Film Festival is on, die-hard film fans as well as directors and stars come here for everything from the first screening of Woody Allen's latest to obscure films from Iran *(see* **Walter Reade Theater** *in section* "Film"). Lincoln Center also houses the New York Philharmonic, the New York City Opera, the New York City Ballet and the Juilliard School. The fountain, located in the center's plaza, is a great place to sit and watch people meet their dates, and try to conjure the day that ground was broken for the center—May 14, 1959, when President Dwight Eisenhower wielded the shovel and Leonard Bernstein led the Philharmonic and Juilliard chorus in the "Hallelujah Chorus." In the summer, there is outdoor dancing in that plaza, where New Yorkers do everything from ballroom to square dancing under the stars.

—*Jennifer Steinhauer*

Broadway (West 62nd–66th St.) (212) 546-2656 *www.lincolncenter.org.* **Subway:** 1, 9 to 66th St.—Lincoln Center; A, B, C, D to 59th St.

Alice Tully Hall (212) 875-5050. Alice Tully Hall opened in September of 1969—the 67th birthday of its namesake, whose portrait dominates the large but underutilized lobby. The Chamber Music Society of Lincoln Center—which still calls the 1,096-seat hall home—played the inaugural concert of Bach, Schumann and Schubert, after which it was immediately apparent that, finally, after two acoustic failures, Lincoln Center had a concert hall it could be proud of. It's a wonderful stage for chamber music and recitals, as well as small-scale opera and orchestral concerts. Jazz and avant-garde artists play here, too, and there's even an occasional appearance by a pop star or two.

Avery Fisher Hall (212) 875-5030. When the New York Philharmonic relocated in 1962 from Carnegie Hall to Avery Fisher Hall (then called Philharmonic Hall), it found itself in a shiny new building with appalling acoustics. Enter Avery Fisher—the electronics mogul and an amateur violinist—who gave great sums to improve the hall and attach his already well-known name to its portals. The results of these—and subsequent—renovations proved far from perfect. Nevertheless, the 2,738-seat hall is one of the city's premier concert venues. It's where a generation of baby boomers learned about classical music thanks to Leonard Bernstein's Young People's Concerts, and where Kurt Masur now presides over the city's internationally acclaimed orchestra. Avery Fisher Hall also hosts the world's top visiting orchestras, instrumentalists, chamber groups and singers, as well as pop and jazz performers. NOTE: At the end of the 2002 season the hall will be closed for renovation; the Philharmonic will perform elsewhere until the renovation is completed.

Library for the Performing Arts at Lincoln Center (212) 870-1630. This branch of the New York Public Library is a treasure trove of invaluable materials, boasting the largest reference, archival and circulating arts-related collection in the world. It is closed for renovations until 2003, but will reopen with a new information center, measures to help speed material retrieval, centralized playback for the videotape archives and a central reading room. **Temporary location:** 521 West 43rd St. (between 10th and 11th Aves.)

Metropolitan Opera House (212) 362-6000. The second and current Metropolitan Opera House opened in September 1966 with the world premiere of Samuel Barber's *Antony and Cleopatra*. Leontyne Price sang. Thomas Schippers conducted. But the real star of the evening was the magnificent (some might say garish) theater that dominates the Lincoln Center plaza. It's the world's largest opera house, and even from a distance its grandeur is apparent. Five enormous glass arches overwhelm the eye. Behind them hang Marc Chagall's spectacular murals, "The Triumph of Music" on the south wall and "The Sources of Music" on the north.

Once inside the 3,900-seat house, the sweeping staircase ushers you into a glittering world of red velvet, gold leaf and gaudy crystal chandeliers that rise up to the ceiling at the beginning of each performance. Even in the nosebleed sections the sound is good, so it's not necessary to spend $150 or more for orchestra seats. Standing-room tickets are about $15, but they sell out fast.

Technically, the Met is a director's dream, equipped with a slew of mechanical wonders: Four huge stages with elevators and revolving platforms and a computerized lighting system. Every seat has a "Met Titles" screen, providing simultaneous translation. The orchestra pit accommodates more than 100 top-notch musicians. James Levine, the artistic director, has turned the Met Orchestra into one of the best orchestras in or out of a pit.

Intermissions are rather long, giving you time to explore the Met's nooks and crannies. There are costume and art exhibits that impart a sense of the company's history. If you prefer, have a drink or dessert, which in balmy weather you can take onto the terrace overlooking the plaza. (Or have dinner in the Grand Tier Restaurant, but you must ordere it in advance.)

Lest we forget, the Met is also the home of the American Ballet Theater in May, June and early July.

New York State Theater (212) 870-5570. It may not be as posh as its sister opera house across the plaza, but in some ways, the New York State Theater is the more interesting building. Designed by Philip Johnson as a home for the New York City Ballet and the New York City Opera, the 2,800-seat theater's most striking feature is the grand, four-story foyer, flanked by two marvelous white marble Elie Nadelman sculptures and surrounded by balconies. Hundreds of long chains serve as draperies for a glass wall that opens onto a large terrace facing Avery Fisher Hall. The seats are comfortable, the sightlines good. Because the theater was built with dance in mind, acoustics are often a problem here. But the addition of acoustical panels have improved matters considerably.

red-brick, Federal-style building that once belonged to the United Order of True Sisters—it became the third big-name music school, along with Juilliard and the Manhattan School of Music, on Manhattan's West Side. Like other conservatories, Mannes has an impressive student body and faculty and presents a wide array of high-quality events, from early music consorts to grand opera and beyond. Its two auditoriums—the 200-seat Concert Hall and the 60-seat Goldmark Auditorium, used mainly for recitals—are adequate if not luxurious. (For larger-scale events, Mannes often uses the nearby Symphony Space.) **Tickets:** Free. **Subway:** 1, 9, B, C to 86th St.

Merkin Concert Hall UPPER WEST SIDE 129 W. 67th St. (between Broadway and Amsterdam Ave.) (212) 362-8719. "Intimate" is a word that gets its share of use, or misuse, in describing mid-size concert venues. But in the case of Merkin, it applies. The 457-seat hall is an attractive space with superior acoustics, making it a favorite for chamber ensembles, recitalists and even mid-size orchestras and choral groups. A number of popular series are held here, including "Interpretations" and "New Sounds Live," both of which focus on avant-garde, jazz or ethnic music. Merkin is part of the Elaine Kaufman Cultural Center, which means that many programs here highlight Jewish roots and culture. It also means that the hall is dark on Friday nights, Saturdays and all Jewish holidays. **Subway:** 1, 9 to 66th St.

Metropolitan Museum of Art—Grace Rainey Rogers Auditorium UPPER EAST SIDE 1000 Fifth Ave. (between 81st and 82nd Sts.) (212) 570-3949. An excellent 708-seat hall, acoustically one of the best in town, it is particularly well suited for recitals and chamber music. One of its secrets is the warm-toned African korina wood paneling, a highly reflective material that helps magnify sound. Many of the world's prominent performers appreciate the merits of this hall, which is why you'll find the Juilliard and Guarneri String Quartets, the Beaux Arts Trio and other big-name artists gracing the stage. There's also a sporadic jazz concert, and many of the museum's popular lectures take place here. One of the best things about Grace Rainey Rogers is that to enter the auditorium you have to walk through the museum's spectacular Egyptian collection, which is always a thrill. Concerts are also regularly presented in other locations around the museum—call for times and locations. **Subway:** 4, 5, 6 to 86th St.

New School University GREENWICH VILLAGE 66 W. 12th St. (between Fifth and Sixth Aves.) (800) 709-4321. A rich array of lectures and concerts take place at the New School's varied venues: in the Orozco Room, at the Parsons School of Design (66 Fifth Ave.), at the Mannes College Jazz Performance Space and in the Tishman Auditorium. The Tishman is a cozy Art Deco auditorium designed by the architect Joseph Urban in 1930 and named an interior landmark in 1993. Urban's rounded ceiling of concentric rings inspired a similar design at Radio City Music Hall a few years later. Raked seating makes for clear views all around. **Subway:** F to 14th St.

Opera

Opera in New York means, first and foremost, the **Metropolitan Opera** at Lincoln Center. Sometimes it seems that opera in the whole world means, first and foremost, the Metropolitan Opera. The company essentially deserves its iconic status. Leading international singers regularly perform there; indeed, a Metropolitan Opera debut is still a benchmark of a singer's career. In over 25 years as artistic director, James Levine has built the Met orchestra into one of the finest anywhere. The musicians know they are good and play with palpable pride and confidence. The 3,900-seat opera house, which opened its doors in 1966, is looking a bit tattered these days, but the sound in the auditorium remains marvelous, and, if anything, the sound up in the cheaper balcony and family circle seats is better than the pricey orchestra section. *(See section "Lincoln Center" earlier in this chapter for full listing.)*

Which brings up price. The Met is expensive. But putting on international-level opera is an expensive enterprise. It's mostly worth it. Yes, there are off-nights at the Met, and ill-conceived productions, and automatic-pilot performances of the most popular bread-and-butter operas. And sometimes second-string casts fall too far below the level of the name singers who open a run of an opera and garner the reviews. Still, company officials assert that, night for night, the Met presents opera on a more consistently high level than any other company, and they are right.

A newcomer to opera or a visitor from out of town will be tempted to go to the crowd-pleasers, like *La Boheme, Tosca,* and *Aida.* These are good shows. But it would be wise to check out reviews and select something that is special, for the Met at its best is exhilarating. In recent seasons, for example, the presentations of Tchaikovsky's *Queen of Spades,* Mozart's *Marriage of Figaro,* Strauss's *Ariadne auf Naxos,* Wagner's *Meistersinger* and Berg's *Wozzeck* have been exceptionally produced and splendidly sung.

By the way, the Met's official guided tour is one of the best kept secrets in New York. It's fascinating to go backstage and see the rotating stage, the set shops, the rehearsal spaces. The costume builders also demonstrate how they must adapt outfits to singers with enormously varying sizes and shapes.

Across the plaza from the Met, in the New York State Theater, is the **New York City Opera,** and the biggest frustration of this enterprising company is its location. The mission of the company under its current leader, Paul Kellogg, is to create an identity that is distinct from its neighbor's. Why do what the Met can do better? So City Opera may not offer world-famous singers in the standard repertory, but it can offer young, eager artists who look and act like the characters they portray. Moreover, the City Opera tends to be more daring about repertory than the Met. The company regularly offers Baroque operas by Handel, neglected 20th-century works like Strauss' *Intermezzo,* Britten's *Paul Bunyan* (an entrancing production), and Carlisle Floyd's *Of Mice and Men* (a riveting musical and dramatic experience).

Ticket prices there are much more affordable than at the Met, as well. All this has made the company attractive to younger, hipper audiences.

The company's goal of distinguishing itself from the Met would be easier, however, if it performed in a different facility in a different neighborhood. With over 2,700 seats, the New York State Theater is somewhat too big for the type of involving musical theater experience the City Opera works have to offer. And the acoustics of the auditorium are far from ideal, though the company is currently experimenting with an electronic sound-enhancement system for the space, a move that has agitated many traditionalists but been largely unnoticed by most attendees. All in all, the City Opera is not just a cheaper alternative to the Met, but an interesting company in its own right.

There are many other smaller opera companies in the city, organizations that typically present two or three productions per season. **DiCapo Opera** is a scrappy company that performs in an appealing modest-sized theater on East 76th Street, and presents classics and occasionally contemporary works in effective productions with, by and large, talented young casts.

For 50 years the **Amato Opera** was a mom-and-pop outfit on a tight budget with a loyal following. Sadly, the mom half of the team, Sally Amato, died at 82 in the summer of 2000. But the pop, her husband Anthony Amato, carries on with productions of popular operas presented in a theater on the Bowery that gives new meaning to the term "intimate" drama.

The **Bronx Opera** usually presents just two productions a years (check local listings), in English translation, on two consecutive weekends, first at the Lehman Center in the Bronx, then at John Jay College Theater in Manhattan.

The **Juilliard Opera Center** is not, as its name implies, a company of students from the Juilliard School, but a training institute that offers singers in leading roles who are on the brink of, or already engaged in, professional careers. Students fill out the smaller roles and provide the orchestra and chorus. But Juilliard students are more accomplished than many professionals, and the Opera Center productions are often excellent. The **Manhattan School of Music** also presents some worthwhile productions in its commodious theater on Broadway and 122nd Street, for example, an important recent revival of Ned Rorem's stirring operatic adaptation of Strindberg's *Miss Julie*. Opera at the **Mannes College of Music** on West 85th Street is also worth checking out.

The estimable **L'Opera Francais de New York** presents stylish, semi-staged performances of French operas, often rarities, at Alice Tully Hall in Lincoln Center, though just two a year (check local listings). They are always first-rate.

If you can do without sets and costumes entirely the **Opera Orchestra of New York,** directed by the conductor Eve Queler, is a must. Ms. Queler seeks out inexplicably neglected operas and presents them in concert performances at Carnegie Hall with strong casts, sometimes including major singers. In recent seasons Renee Fleming, Ruth Ann Swenson, and Vesselina Kasarova, to cite just some illustrious artists, have scored triumphs with the Opera Orchestra. Ms. Queler's work reminds us that opera is, at its core, music, and can work quite effectively without its theatrical trimmings. (*See section* "Classical Music Centers" *earlier in this chapter for more information on venues.*)

—*Anthony Tommasini*

The Metropolitan Opera

Amato Opera Theater 319 Bowery (between 2nd and Bleecker Sts.)
(212) 228-8200. **Tickets:** Avg. $28. **Subway:** F to Second Ave.; 6 to Bleecker
St.; F, S to Broadway–Lafayette St.

DiCapo Opera Theater 184 E. 76th St. (between Lexington and Third Aves.)
(212) 288-9438. **Tickets:** $33. **Subway:** 6 to 77th St.

Juilliard Opera Center—Juilliard Theater 60 Lincoln Center Plaza (Columbus Ave. and 64th St.) (212) 799-5000. **Tickets:** Avg. $20. Cash only. **Subway:**
1, 9 to 66th St.; A, B, C, D to 59th St.

Metropolitan Opera House—Lincoln Center Columbus Ave. and 64th St.
(212) 362-6000. **Tickets:** $23–$200. Standing room tickets are usually
$12–$16, on sale at the Box Office Saturday mornings at 10 A.M., for Sat.–Fri.
performances. Lines start early. **Subway:** 1, 9 to 66th St.; A, B, C, D to 59th St.

New York State Theater—Lincoln Center 20 Lincoln Center Plaza
(Columbus Ave. and 63rd St.) (212) 870-5570. **Tickets:** $20–$85. **Subway:** 1,
9 to 66th St.; A, B, C, D to 59th St.

Dance

Ballet, modern dance, jazz dance, tap dance and folk groups: As the dance capital of the world, New York plays host to all. Troupes from abroad and resident
companies perform throughout the year.

The New York City Ballet and American Ballet Theater, the country's top
classical troupes, have regular seasons. Founded in 1948 by the Russian-born
choreographer George Balanchine and his American patron, Lincoln Kirstein,
New York City Ballet remains faithful to Balanchine's view of dance for
dance's sake. One-act plotless works, not story ballets, are the norm. The focus
on the company's two late resident geniuses, Balanchine and Jerome Robbins,
makes for high art. New works by Peter Martins, the current director, continue
the emphasis on distinguished composers. The company has a winter season
(including five weeks of *The Nutcracker*) and a spring season at Lincoln Center's
New York State Theater (*see section* "Lincoln Center" *earlier in this chapter*).

American Ballet Theater, founded in 1939, is more eclectic and its reputation stems from its ballets in different styles and an ability to attract great
dancers. Male virtuosity has been dazzling. The company favors 19th-century
classics and other three-act story ballets in May and June at the **Metropolitan
Opera House** (*see section* "Lincoln Center"). In the fall, a brief season at **City
Center** concentrates on one-act works, including premieres by contemporary
choreographers like Twyla Tharp.

New York has a variety of theaters and performing spaces that are hospitable
to dance. For raw cutting edge, the loftlike spaces of **The Kitchen, Dance Theater Workshop, P.S. 122** and **St. Mark's Church** are a must (*see listings below*).
Many a newcomer, including Mark Morris, had a start in these well-attended
nonproscenium theaters.

City Center of Music and Drama   MIDTOWN WEST

131 W. 55th St. (between Sixth and Seventh Aves.) (212) 581-1212. The Paul
Taylor Dance Company performs in the spring and the Alvin Ailey American
Dance Theater is here in December. Both are highly popular modern-dance
companies with brilliant dancers. Taylor's choreography ranges in mood from
light to dark and his mastery is unquestioned. Ailey died in 1989 but his troupe,
inspired by African-American heritage, is directed now by Judith Jamison, who
has brought the dancing to an even more exciting level. The company's signature work is *Revelations*, a masterpiece that Ailey set to spirituals.

Dance Theater of Harlem performs here and in other venues. It is an internationally known ballet troupe with a strong neo-Classical style. Arthur Mitchell,

once a star at New York City Ballet, used the Balanchine aesthetic as a spring-board for the company he founded in 1969 as an outlet for black ballet dancers.

The Martha Graham Dance Company appears at City Center when not at the Joyce Theater. Often compared to Picasso and Stravinsky as one of the 20th century's groundbreaking artists, Graham died in 1991 but left extraordinary works that are powerfully danced by a dedicated company. Highly dramatic pieces inspired by Greek myth share the stage with the striking spare pieces of Graham's early years. (Recent financial problems have put the company's future in doubt.)

As a different icon of American modern dance, Merce Cunningham changed the way audiences look at choreography. The Merce Cunningham Dance Company's works often resemble collages. When composing dances, Cunningham uses coin tossing or other chance procedures to decide which movement follows which and his experiments make him the pope of the avant-garde. Once a City Center regular, the company has recently appeared at Lincoln Center. **Subway:** B, D, E to 57th St.; N, Q, R, W to Seventh Ave.

Joyce Theater   CHELSEA

175 Eighth Ave. (between 18th and 19th Sts.) (212) 242-0800. The choreographer Eliot Feld created the Joyce, a former movie house, as a theater for dance and a home for his ballet company, now called Ballet Tech. Feld's quirky ballets for young dancers have a loyal following and can be seen in the spring and in August, with a brief season in December. In January, the intimate 500-seat theater produces the "Altogether Different" series that features small experimental troupes. Modern dance predominates during the year with a range wide enough to keep the viewer abreast of what is happening in more than one precinct of dance. The popular Pilobolus troupe appears in July. **Subway:** A, C, E to 14th St.; L to Eighth Ave.

Brooklyn Academy of Music   BROOKLYN

651 Fulton St. (between Rockwell and Ashland Places) (718) 636-4100. The Next Wave Festival in the fall makes the Academy the mecca of trendy and serious audiences (sometimes the two overlap). Experimental dance is at the heart of the festival. Pina Bausch, Germany's iconoclastic choreographer, and Sankai Juku, a group working in Japan's post-Hiroshima Butoh style, are staples of the series. Leading American experimental choreographers associated with the Next Wave and the Academy are more unpredictable and include Trisha Brown, Bill T. Jones, Meredith Monk, Lucinda Childs and Mark Morris. (*See section* "Brooklyn" *in chapter* **The Arts** *for BAM's full listing.*) **Subway:** Q, 2, 3, 4, 5 to Atlantic Ave.; M, N, R, W to Pacific St.

Metropolitan Opera House   UPPER WEST SIDE

Lincoln Center, Columbus Ave. and 64th St. (212) 362-6000. The Met is the way station for major ballet companies from abroad in July. You might see Russia's Kirov Ballet and Bolshoi Ballet, the Royal Ballet from England or the Paris Opera Ballet. Lincoln Center Festival uses the Met, the New York State Theater and the Center's smaller theaters for dance attractions in July. (*See section* "Lincoln Center" *earlier in this chapter for full listing.*) **Subway:** 1, 9 to 66th St.

Sylvia and Danny Kaye Playhouse at Hunter College
UPPER EAST SIDE, Hunter College, E. 68th St. (between Park and Lexington Aves.) (212) 772-4448. Modern-dance companies like the joint troupe of Alwin Nikolais and Murray Louis, mixed- media pioneers, have performed here as has the great French mime Marcel Marceau. **Subway:** 6 to 68th St.

—*Anna Kisselgoff*

Other Dance Theaters and Studios

Dance Theater Workshop—Bessie Schonberg Theater 219 W. 19th St. (between Seventh and Eighth Aves.) (212) 924-0077. A couple of flights of stairs and a few twists and turns get you to the Bessie Schonberg Theater, one of the city's best dance venues. The theater packs a lot of performances into its season, with an array of artists from the dance and the music worlds generally performing for one to three nights. Best of all, tickets tend to range from $8 to $15. **Subway:** A, C, E,1, 2, 3, 9 to 14th St.; L to Eighth Ave.

Dixon Place at Vineyard 26 309 E. 26th St. (at Second Ave.) (212) 532-1546. Choreographers, actors, writers, performance artists and musicians can present works in progress here. It remains a playground for starry-eyed wannabes and a refuge for the already established. Tickets prices range from nothing to $12, depending on the event. **Subway:** 6 to 28th St.

Fiorello H. La Guardia High School for the Performing Arts 108 Amsterdam Ave. (at 64th St.) (212) 496-0700. This high school theater presents mostly student performances, but occasionally offers dance festivals and opportunities for master classes with visiting choreographers. The level of talent is extraordinary, as displayed in the movie *Fame*. **Subway:** 1, 9 to 66th St.—Lincoln Center.

Free Range Arts 250 W. 26th St. 3rd Fl. (between Seventh and Eighth Aves.) (212) 691-4551. Free Range showcases the works of a wide variety of performers and choreographers at their spacious studio and at other locations around New York. **Subway:** C, E, 1, 9 to 23rd St.

Isadora Duncan Foundation Studio 141 W. 26th St., 3rd Fl. (between Sixth and Seventh Aves.) (212) 691-5040. This small, attractive studio seats about 50 for its occasional shows of classic Duncan works and dances from contemporary choreographers. **Subway:** F, 1, 9 to 23rd St.

Joyce SoHo 155 Mercer St. (between Houston and Prince St.) (212) 431-9233. The Joyce SoHo provides a place for experimental and new choreographers to showcase their work before they venture on to larger performance spaces like the Joyce itself in Chelsea. With 75 freestanding seats, the comfortable loft-like space has a very open feel. Thanks to the lack of columns, every seat in the house is a good one. **Subway:** F, S to Broadway–Lafayette St.; N, R to Prince St.

The Kitchen 512 W. 19th St. (between 10th and 11th Ave.) (212) 255-5793. The careers of avant-garde luminaries such as the composer Philip Glass and the performance artist Laurie Anderson began at The Kitchen. Today the the-

ater continues to present unknown artists in dance, theater, film and everything
in between in innovative ways. **Subway:** A, C, E to 14th St.; L to Eighth Ave.

La MaMa ETC 74A E. 4th St. (between Second Ave. and Bowery)
(212) 254-6468. La MaMa's four stages showcase a diverse and sometimes
bizarre program of avant-garde dance and performance from American and
international troupes. **Subway:** F to Second Ave.

Merce Cunningham Studio 55 Bethune St. (between Washington and West
Sts.) (212) 255-8240. Save yourself some embarrassment and wear socks with no
holes. No one—not even Michael Flatley, Mr. Lord of the Dance himself—is
allowed to wear shoes at the Merce Cunningham Studio; they have to be left in
the lobby to preserve the floor for the dancers. The studio is large and can easily
accommodate 200 people. **Subway:** 1, 9 to Christopher St.; A, C, E to 14th St.

Movement Research at the Judson Church 55 Washington Sq. South
(212) 477-0351. Since the 1960's, this former house of worship has hosted performances of bold and eclectic new work by experimental dance and performance artists. Movement Research continues the tradition with a free Monday-
night series. **Subway:** A, C, E, F, S to W. 4th St.

Mulberry Street Theater 70 Mulberry St. (at Bayard St.) (212) 349-0126.
Once a public school, this theater space has been transformed effectively into
two dance studios and a black-box theater. It is home to H.T. Chen and
Dancers, a company that infuses technically vigorous American modern dance
with Chinese inflections. In addition to forging ahead with Chen's aesthetic
imperative, Mulberry hosts programs that feature the work of unknown and
mid-career artists, including "Moving Word," a series devoted to choreography
inspired by poetry. **Subway:** J, M, N, Q, R, W, Z, 6 to Canal St.

St. Mark's Church in the Bowery 131 E. 10th St. (at Second Ave.)
(212) 674-6377. Following a devastating fire in 1978, the interior of the city's
second-oldest church was restructured into a versatile open space that hosts performing arts, especially dance, and religious services. **Subway:** 6 to Astor Pl.

Squid Dance Performance Space 127 Fulton St. (between Nassau and
Williams Sts.) (212) 566-8041. The Squid Dance group presents its own work
and rents out this large studio for classes, rehearsals and performances. **Subway:**
A, C, J,M, Z, 2, 3 to Fulton St.—Broadway–Nassau.

Warren Street Performance Loft 46 Warren St. (212) 732-3149. This intimate space features the improvisational work of Richard Bull Dance Theatre
and other visiting groups. **Subway:** A, C, 1, 2, 3, 9 to Chambers St.

FILM

Whether New York is watching movies or making them, there is no question
that this city is in love with film. No American city can account for more cinemas consistently screening independent and foreign movies or showing revivals
of old classics. A walk through Manhattan inevitably leads you to a block
crowded with a film crew and actors, or a cluster of New York University film

students fine tuning their craft on a downtown street corner with an old camera. With New York hosting so many up-and-coming auteurs it comes as no surprise that several greats in the movie industry— including Martin Scorsese, Woody Allen and Spike Lee—not only call New York home but also feature it prominently in their films, including *Goodfellas*, *Taxi Driver*, *Annie Hall*, *Manhattan* and *Do the Right Thing*.

So many movies show throughout the city in a single evening that it's important to learn a few essentials if you want to find what you're looking for. For starters, tickets to most standard theaters are now around $10, and if you buy your tickets in advance through Moviefone at (212) 777-3456, an additional $1.50 will be charged to your credit card. There is no surcharge for online orders at *www.moviefone.com*. Moviefone services every major movie house, and it's well worth the price hike if you're hoping to see a popular movie or a recent release. Local papers, including *The New York Times* and the *Village Voice* print times and locations.

NOTE: The serious movie buff will want to visit the American Museum of the Moving Image *(see section* "Queens" *in chapter* **Exploring New York***)*.

Movie Theaters of Note

Angelika Film Center 18 W. Houston St. (at Mercer St.) (212) 995-2000. One of New York's favorite cinemas for independent and foreign films, this six-screen theater on the border of SoHo and Greenwich Village, offers the extra bonus of midnight screenings on weekends. In addition to the concession stand, the theater's lobby cafe serves higher than standard fare to match its higher prices. It is advisable to buy tickets in advance as shows can sell out quickly. **Subway:** F, S to Broadway-Laffayette St.; N, R to Prince St.

Anthology Film Archives 32 Second Ave. (at 2nd St.) (212) 505-5181. It's no surprise that this theater has a wealth of unusual material to offer. In 1970 it began as a museum dedicated to avant-garde cinema. True to its history, the films shown here are often unknown, but in spite of their obscurity you're likely to find the best of the genre. Check listings for early works from better-known directors as well as the chance to catch a loved classic on the big screen. Tickets are available only at the box office. **Subway:** F to Second Ave.

Film Forum 209 W. Houston St. (between Sixth Ave. and Varick St.) (212) 727-8110. Film buffs throughout the city know this charming three-screen theater consistently provides some of the best cinema New York offers, ranging from recent documentaries to silent films. The concession stand offers the best movie theater popcorn in the city. Tickets are sold only at the box office and sell out quickly, especially on weekends. **Subway:** 1, 9 to Houston St.; C, E to Spring St.

Lincoln Plaza Cinemas 1886 Broadway (at 62nd St.) (212) 757-2280. This modest looking, six-screen theater on the cusp of the Upper West Side may be the best place to see foreign and independent movies uptown; but don't expect to find Snow Caps or Raisinettes at the concession stand—you're more likely to overpay for a smoked salmon sandwich. Still, devotees steadily show up for new independent releases and events such as a Fellini or Bergman retrospective. **Subway:** A, B, C, D, 1, 9 to 59th St.-Columbus Circle.

The Quad 34 W. 13th St. (between Fifth and Sixth Aves.) (212) 225-8800. If the movies at this four-theater cinema were not some of the best independent and foreign shows in town nobody would put up with watching movies on such tiny screens. But its charm as well as its selection of films keep people coming back to this Village standby. **Subway:** F, L, N, Q, R, W, 4, 5, 6 to 14th St.

The Screening Room 54 Varick St. (at Canal St.) (212) 334-2100. Found near the industrial entrance to the Holland Tunnel, this little theater redefines dinner and a movie. One part restaurant and one part cinema, the independent, foreign and classic material found in the theater beats the fare found on the dinner menu. Though the schedule changes, you can count on a regular offering of Sunday brunch followed by a showing of *Breakfast at Tiffany's*. **Subway:** 1, 9, A, C, E to Canal St.

Sony IMAX at Lincoln Center 1992 Broadway at 68th St. (212) 336-5000. At the top of the four-story monolithic movie theater on the Upper West Side is New York's only IMAX theater. The size and scope of the screen is tremendous, the seats on an alarmingly steep angle and the schedule of films range from enhanced Discovery Channel material to animation and science fiction. Some of the features require goggles in order to catch every 3-D effect while others presentations keep to the standard IMAX format, though even those might upset viewers prone to motion sickness. **Subway:** 1, 9 to 66th St.

Walter Reade Theater 70 Lincoln Center Plaza (at Columbus Avenue) (212) 875-5600. The clientele at this spacious, state-of-the-art theater located at the heart of the Lincoln Center complex is as varied and diverse as the films that are shown here. Recent festival themes have included Jewish cinema, films celebrating human rights, Iranian cinema and a "dance on camera" series. Also common are retrospectives of particular actors and directors, films by up-and-coming Independent American directors and silent movies accompanied by a live orchestra.

The best ways to keep up with what is going on are via the Film Society of Lincoln Center Web site or by phoning the box office. Alternatively, each month's schedule is available outside the theater. Inside, the atmosphere is spacious and the single screen is large. The 268 plush, comfortable seats are set on a sloping floor, which ensures that there is not a bad seat in the house. Tickets (which sell out quickly) are available only at the box office. **Subway:** 1, 9 to 66th St.

The Ziegfeld 141 W. 54th St. (at Sixth Ave.) (212) 765-7600. One of the few old-fashioned movie palaces left in New York that hasn't been renovated into a multiplex, this midtown classic with a bright red décor boasts an enormous screen, seating for nearly 1,200 people, and is the perfect place for a revival of *Gone With the Wind* or the viewing of a modern epic. **Subway:** B, D, E to Seventh Ave.; N, R, Q, W to 57th St.

Film Festivals

Name any type of film and New York probably has a festival for it. In fact, it's difficult to find a time of the year when a film festival isn't occurring somewhere in the city. The **New York Film Festival,** now starting its fifth decade, is easily the biggest and most famous of the group. Held annually in late September or early October, the festival screens around 20 independent, foreign and big studio films in a two-week run at Lincoln Center's Alice Tully Hall (*see section* "Lincoln Center"). Tickets go on sale at the box office the first Sunday after Labor Day and sell quickly. It's advisable to buy tickets early—especially for the much anticipated film that opens the event. Call (212) 875-5600 for details.

Another festival of note, **The New Directors/New Films** held at the Museum of Modern Art is one of the most celebrated cinematic events in the city. The Film Society of Lincoln Center and the Museum of Modern Art co-sponsor this March affair that hosts a series of diverse and daring projects. For the past three decades the New Directors/New Films festival has offered first glimpses at the work of directors as talented and varied as John Sayles, Steven Spielberg, Peter Greenaway and Whit Stillman. Tickets are sold at the Museum of Modern Art box office, and due to the popularity of the event it is a good idea to buy tickets well in advance.

Among the city's other film festivals is the **Margaret Mead Film Festival** held each November at the Museum of Natural History, which presents anthropological documentaries (212-769-5650). The **Independent Feature Film Market** at the Angelika Film Center in September shows films looking for distribution—but note that tickets for this event are particularly pricey (212-995-2000). The **Lesbian and Gay Film Festival** occurs each June at the Joseph Papp Public Theater in the East Village (212-924-3363). And the **First Run Festival** gives New York University's best and brightest students a chance to show off their efforts at this April event (212-924-3363).

INSTITUTES OF WORLD CULTURE

Asia Society UPPER EAST SIDE 725 Park Ave. (between 70th and 71st Sts.) (212) 517-ASIA *www.asiasociety.org.* The Asia Society was founded by John D. Rockefeller III to encourage better relations between the U.S. and Asia by introducing Americans to the cultures of Asia and the Pacific. Scholarly symposia, films, public programs and publications have long been central to its mission, with an emphasis on the arts. Today, its elegant galleries feature changing exhibitions for connoisseurs as well as for the general public. **Admission:** $7; $4, students and seniors; Fri., 6–8 P.M., free. **Hours:** Tue.–Sat., 11 A.M.–6 P.M.; Fri., 11 A.M.–8 P.M.; Sun., noon–5 P.M. **Subway:** 6 to 68th St.

China Institute in America UPPER EAST SIDE 125 E. 65th St. (between Park and Lexington Aves.) (212) 744-8181 *www.chinainstitute.org.* Housed in an elegant red-brick building on the Upper East Side, the China Institute offers Chinese language classes and hosts lectures, films and discussions. If you're fascinated by Chinese culture, but don't feel up to the daunting task of learning Mandarin, you can also sign up for calligraphy and Chinese art classes. Courses for children are also available. The institute's gallery hosts periodic shows of Chinese art. **Admission** (suggested): $3, general; $2, students and seniors; Tue., Thu. 6–8 P.M., free. Cash only. **Hours:** Mon., Wed., Fri.–Sat., 10 A.M.–5 P.M.; Tue., Thu., 10 A.M.–8 P.M.; Sun., 1 P.M.–5 P.M. **Subway:** 6 to 68th St.

French Institute and Florence Gould Hall MIDTOWN EAST 55 E. 59th St. (between Park and Madison Aves.) (212) 355-6100 *www.fiaf.org.* A cultural institute for Francophile New Yorkers and the city's French community, the French Institute/Alliance Française offers language courses as well as a variety of cultural events with French themes. Florence Gould Hall offers films, concerts and dance, while the smaller Tinker Auditorium holds lectures, receptions and cabaret performances. In 1996 a downtown branch opened at 95 Wall Street. **Hours:** Mon.–Thu., 9 A.M.–8 P.M.; Fri., 9 A.M.–6 P.M.; Sat., 9 A.M.–1:30 P.M. **Subway:** 4, 5, 6 to 59th St.

Goethe-Institut/German Cultural Center UPPER EAST SIDE 1014 Fifth Ave. (between 82nd and 83rd Sts.) (212) 439-8700. A cultural institute funded by the German government, the Goethe-Institut promotes German language and culture abroad. The New York center, one of roughly 150 branches in some 60 countries, organizes cultural events, including lectures, art exhibitions and concerts of contemporary classical music. Occupying a Beaux-Arts limestone town house that was formerly the residence of a U.S. Ambassador to Germany, the institute also collaborates with other organizations around the city in presenting events such as the annual "Recent Films from Germany" series at the Museum of Modern Art. The organization operates a lending and reference library at its Fifth Avenue headquarters, and offers language courses through New York University's Deutsches Haus. **Hours:** Tue.,Thu., 10 A.M.–7 P.M.; Wed., Fri., 10 A.M.–5 P.M.; Sat. noon–5 P.M.; closed Sun. **Subway:** 4, 5, 6 to 86th St.

Japan Society MIDTOWN EAST 333 E. 47th St. (between First and Second Aves.) (212) 832-1155. Founded in 1907, the Japan Society made its permanent home on East 47th Street in 1971. The society's mission is to promote relations between the U.S. and Japan and to bring New Yorkers a wonderful blend of the traditional and the contemporary in Japanese culture. Events include regular film series, art exhibits and live theater. If you want to learn the ins and outs of Japanese conversation, the society also offers language lessons at all levels. **Hours:** Tue.–Sun., 11 A.M.–6 P.M. **Subway:** 4, 5, 6 to 42nd St.

Museum of Jewish Heritage—A Living Memorial to the Holocaust
18 First Pl., Battery Park City (at West St.) (212) 968-1800. Strongest on the social history of European Jews and Israel, this museum on the water's edge is dedicated to living history, and to recording and preserving the memories of Holocaust survivors, rescuers and witnesses. The roof design of its impressive granite structure forms a Star of David. Opened in 1997, it is a dignified

reminder of New York's important place in Jewish history. **Price:** $7, general; $5, students and seniors; children under 5, free. **Subway:** 1, 9 to Rector St.

Ukrainian Museum 203 Second Ave. (between 12th and 13th Sts.) (212) 228-0110 *www.ukrainianmuseum.org.* The East Village is home to a small but thriving Ukrainian population. The Ukrainian Museum houses permanent and changing exhibitions of native arts and crafts, including photos, documents, coins, stamps, textiles, costumes, Easter eggs and rare books. **Admission:** $3, general; $2, students and seniors. **Subway:** L, N, Q, R, W, 4, 5, 6 to 14th St.; L to First Ave. or Third Ave.

For the latest information on restaurants, hotels, concerts, nightlife, sporting events and more, check online at New York Today, the *New York Times* Web site devoted entirely to life in New York City: www.nytoday.com.

Welcome to New York City, shoppers—you're in the big leagues now. What's most appealing about a Big Apple shopping spree is the myriad number of possibilities the city affords, from world-famous department stores to a seemingly infinite variety of boutiques. Special finds can be had at every price, whether you have $10 to spend or $10,000. Everything you've heard is true: You can buy anything here—and it's a lot more fun than surfing the Internet.

MIDTOWN & UPTOWN SHOPPING

Shopping in Manhattan above 34th Street is a little like ascending a Himalayan peak. The foot of the mountain is dense and rich with store growth, but there is a lot of undesirable vegetation. Ascend to the lofty heights of the peak and the views are spectacular, but the expenses are so steep that it might make your blood thin.

The trailhead for the expedition is **Herald Square**, home to **Macy's**, the world's largest department store, made famous by Thanksgiving parades. Navigating Macy's, which takes up an entire city block, is neither easy nor particularly satisfying. Your best bet is to stick to the subterranean floors, where bargains are most abundant.

Move up Broadway from 34th and come smack into the heart of the **Garment District**—not particularly inviting to casual shoppers, but a paradise for do-it-yourself fashionistas. Every fabric, button, feather or bit of leather trim ever imagined is available here. Shops tend to specialize in one niche or another, so if a particular shop doesn't have what you want, ask the proprietor to direct you to a store that will.

Continue walking north up Broadway and emerge at the recently cleansed and sanitized **Times Square**. The goods news is that most of the triple X pornography is gone; the bad news is that there is mostly schlock in its place. But for those who cannot leave the city without a Yankees baseball cap or a Statue of Liberty headpiece made of green Styrofoam, this is the place. Besides the innumerable trinket vendors, Disney, MTV and the World Wrestling Federation all have logo stores along Broadway. Around the corner, 42nd Street between Seventh and Eighth Avenues has been transformed into a neon-bright shopping arcade, complete with such mall standards as the Museum Company and a Hello Kitty boutique.

Style mavens with something a little classier in mind should make a quick break east, and start strolling up Fifth Avenue. As the famous sites of St.

Patrick's Cathedral and Rockefeller Center loom ahead, **Saks Fifth Avenue**, the venerable clothier to the ladies who lunch, will appear on the right.

Fifth Avenue from 50th Street to Central Park is one of the richest shopping corridors in the world (surpassed only in recent years by Madison Avenue). As you parade up the designer-clad avenue—which has been democratized of late by super-boutiques from accessible retailers such as **Banana Republic** and **Liz Claiborne**—don't miss one of the more unique offerings. Whatever you think of the clothes, the **Versace** store at 52nd Street is worth a quick stop. Remodeled to look like an 18th-century palazzo, it comes complete with a marble facade, a sweeping serpentine staircase and elaborate mosaics.

As Fifth Avenue meets Central Park, it suddenly morphs from a commercial hub into a fancy residential boulevard. But right at the corner of 59th is a landmark institution for children of all ages: **F.A.O. Schwartz**. For better or worse, every outlandish toy your child has ever dreamed of is in this huge city-block-long playland. Small people are free to mount the life-sized stuffed elephants or drive the pint-sized Porsches as they please.

Go east one block and yet another Gold Coast emerges. It seems that every upscale merchant on the planet has a store on Madison Avenue between 57th Street and 72nd. The boulevard continues its platinum march through the 70's and 80's, where it becomes a haven of luxury home décor shops.

Most shops along Madison specialize in sumptuous merchandise, but a few are particularly entertaining. **Nicole Farhi's** showcase on 60th Street off Madison is wide open, with clean lines, a muted palette and clothes ranging from simple cotton separates to orange leather shirt-coats. Nearby, Donna Karan's **DKNY** is infused with the color and energy that are the designer's hallmarks. The other must on Madison is **Barneys New York**, a dizzying display that makes a fitting conclusion to a shopping spree, Manhattan style.

—Leslie Kaufman

Garment District
Subway: A, B, C, D, E, F, N, R, S, Q, W, 1, 2, 3, 7, 9 to 42nd St.

Daytona Trimmings 251 W. 39th St. (at Eighth Ave.) (212) 354-1713

Hyman Hendler & Sons 67 W. 38th St. (at Sixth Ave.) (212) 840-8393 *www.hymanhendler.com*. The last word in ribbons.

Paron Fabrics 206 W. 40th St. (between Seventh and Eighth Aves.) (212) 768-3266 *www.paronfabrics.com*

Fifth & Madison Avenues
(See also "Jewelry" later in this chapter.)
Subway: E, F, N, R, W to Fifth Ave.; 4, 5, 6 to nearest cross street.

Banana Republic 626 Fifth Ave. (at 50th St.) (212) 974-2350 *www.bananarepublic.com*

Boutique Georgio Armani 760 Madison Ave. (at 65th St.) (212) 988-9191 *www.emporioarmani.com*. **Emporio Armani** 601 Madison Ave. (at 57th St.) (212) 317-0800.

Calvin Klein 654 Madison Ave. (at 60th St.) (212) 292-9000

Chanel 15 E. 57th St. (between Fifth and Madison Aves.) (212) 355-5050
www.chanel.com

DKNY 655 Madison Ave. (at 60th St.) (212) 223-DKNY *www.dkny.com*

F.A.O. Schwarz 767 Fifth Ave. (at 59th St.) (212) 644-9400 *www.fao.com*

Liz Claiborne 650 Fifth Ave. (at 52nd St.) (212) 956-6505
www.lizclaiborne.com

Nicole Farhi 10 E. 60th St. (between Fifth and Madison Aves.)
(212) 223-8811

Prada 724 Fifth Ave. (between 56th and 57th Sts.) (212) 664-0010
www.prada.com. Other location: 841 Madison Ave. (at 70th St.)
(212) 327-4200.

Ralph Lauren 867 & 888 Madison Ave. (at 72nd St.) (212) 626-2100 or
484-8000 *www.polo.com*

Valentino 747 Madison Ave. (at 65th St.) (212) 772-6969

Versace 647 Fifth Ave. (at 52nd St.) (212) 744-6868 *www.versace.com*. Other
location: 815 Madison Ave. (between 68th and 69th Sts.) (212) 317-0224.

DEPARTMENT STORES

Barneys New York 660 Madison Ave. (at 61st St.) (212) 826-8900
www.barneys.com. Smaller location, 225 Liberty St. (at South End Ave.)
(212) 945-1600; **Co-Op Barneys New York**, 23 W. 18th St. (at Seventh Ave.)
(212) 826-8900. Barneys continues to be the purveyor of what is hip and fash-
ion-chic. The beautiful store offers cutting-edge designer fashions, accessories,
cosmetics and wearable designs from up-and-coming visionaries, both international and homegrown. Fashionistas usually go straight for the shoe section to
pick up sharp, sexy heels. Barneys Co-Op, on 18th Street, offers casual-chic
fashions, from Daryl K jeans to Juicy Couture tees, while Liberty Street focuses
on sharp business wear for men and women. Fabulous twice-a-year warehouse
sales are held at 255 West 17th Street (between Seventh and Eighth Aves.),
where natives and tourists compete to find the perfect black Italian suit and
other ultra-hip must-haves at huge savings. The summer sale generally runs
from late August until Labor Day, the winter sale in February or March. **Subway:** 4, 5, 6 to 59th St.

Bergdorf Goodman 754 Fifth Ave. (at 58th St.) (212) 753-7300. **Bergdorf
Goodman Man** at 745 Fifth Ave. (at 58th St.). Visit Bergdorf's, a worthy neighbor of Tiffany & Co. and the Plaza, for a whiff of old New York glamour. This
purveyor of sophisticated dresses both ladies who lunch and the Park Avenue
junior socialites following in their footsteps. An ultra-refined, almost exclusive
atmosphere sets the ideal stage for haute couture fashions of Badgley Mischka,
Carolina Herrera, Dolce and Gabbana and other upscale designers. The elegant
emporium is particularly excellent in high-end housewares, handbags, jewelry

and shoes. For those unable to get to the Jo Malone flagship store downtown (*see* "Beauty" *later in this chapter*), Bergdorf's is the only other source for the exquisite scents from across the pond. **Subway:** E, F, N, R to Fifth Ave.

Bloomingdale's 1000 Third Ave. (at 59th St.) (212) 705-2000 *www.bloomingdales.com*. Many New Yorkers are devoted to Bloomingdale's for everything from beaded cocktail dresses to bridal registries. "Bloomies" attracts a diverse clientele, from trust-fund teens to stylish professionals and savvy tourists, all of whom exit with arms full of "big brown bags." The upscale selection is a step above Macy's in quality and sophistication, but more egalitarian and affordable than Saks. Great for shoes, coats, cosmetics and homewares, the store also boasts a huge men's department for the fashion-conscious who demand a stylish cut. Men's and women's selections include American classic designers Ralph Lauren and Donna Karan, plus the sexy international threads of Helmut Lang and Gucci. Regular weekend sales, which usually include designer labels, happen about once a month. **Subway:** 4, 5, 6 to 59th St.

Henri Bendel 712 Fifth Ave. (at 56th St.) (212) 247-1100. The signature brown-and-white striped Bendel bags alone are reason enough to buy something in this jewel box of a store. One of Manhattan's prettiest stores, Bendel's offers an excellent selection of both sophisticated and funky designer threads and accessories. The first floor greets you with counters of Bobbi Brown, MAC and Trish McEvoy cosmetics. A large circular staircase winds up through the entire town-house-style store, serving as its grand focal point and enabling you to spot a silk scarf on the third floor that will go perfectly with that cashmere twin set you're holding on the second. Although Bendel's does not carry menswear or shoes, it's an essential stop on any Fifth Avenue shopping jaunt. **Subway:** 4, 5, 6 to 59th St.; E, F, N, R, W to Fifth Ave.

Jeffrey New York 449 W. 14th St. (between Ninth and 10th Aves.) (212) 206-1272 *www.jeffreynewyork.com*. Too-cool-for-school Jeffrey is for the individual who shops like a fashion editor with a take-no-prisoners attitude. If you consider yourself a big-league shopper, then a trip to this cutting-edge fashion mecca in the booming Meatpacking District is sure to satisfy. Jeffrey dresses fashionistas that demand de rigueur chic from the hottest designers, from stylish favorites like Michael Kors and John Bartlett to talented upstarts like Tuleh and Veronica Branquinho. The shoe department is a standout, sharpened by the likes of Jimmy Choo, Gucci and Christian Louboutin. **Subway:** A, C, E to 14th St.; L to Eighth Ave.

Lord & Taylor 424 Fifth Ave. (between 38th and 39th Sts.) (212) 391-3344. A few blocks from Macy's, Lord & Taylor offers reasonable prices, regular sales, quality mid-priced lines and some big-name designers. Although not exactly poised at the fashion forefront, Lord & Taylor holds a certain traditional charm of shopping days past with its signature red rose logo and hand-painted glass escalators. Shoppers browse mostly for dresses, bags and work suits; think conservative, tasteful American classics. Midtown workers come in droves to buy hosiery on their lunch breaks, especially during the first-rate sales. **Subway:** B, D, F, S to 42nd St.

Macy's 151 W. 34th St. (between Broadway and Seventh Ave.) (212) 695-4400 *www.macys.com.* The world's largest department store, and the historic heart of New York shopping, Macy's celebrates its centennial in 2002. The mammoth, always-crowded store is particularly well known for its storewide one-day sales (midweek, usually Wednesdays) and great Cellar bargains on essentials for the home. The extensive first-floor cosmetics department offers all major brands, and the coat, bathing suit and shoe sections are exceptionally large. The fourth floor junior department packs a dense array of trendy gear targeted at the quintessential American teen. Try to visit during the annual Flower Show, a two-week event that marks the launch of Spring. **Subway:** B, D, F, N, R, S, Q, W, 1, 2, 3, 9 to 34th St.

Saks Fifth Avenue 611 Fifth Ave. (between 49th and 50th Sts.) (212) 753-4000 *www.saksfifthavenue.com.* Poised in a coveted location across from Rockefeller Center, Saks is a city landmark for sophistication, style and selection. Saks has served an upscale crowd for almost a century with one of the best and most extensive designer shoe departments in the city, plus excellent, well-organized apparel, accessories and cosmetics departments. Most high-end labels for both women and men are on hand, from Armani to Carolina Herrera. If you visit during the holidays, get in line to see the exquisitely decorated store windows before sweeping indoors for an early gift to yourself (a pair of Ferragamo cashmere shoes, perhaps?). **Subway:** B, D, F, S to 47th-50th St.–Rockefeller Center; E, F, N, R to Fifth Ave.

Takashimaya 693 Fifth Ave. (between 54th and 55th Sts.) (212) 350-0100. This is Zen shopping, exquisite and spare. This Japan-goes-French country store beckons customers to browse with an air of tranquility after escaping the sensory overload of Fifth Avenue. Takashimaya specializes in high-end household gifts for people with an eye for design, from subtly fragranced soaps to delicate beaded floral barrettes. Exotic flowers and elegant garden essentials fill the first floor, while the upper floors offer home, bath and fashion accessories both luxe and minimalist. **Subway:** E, F, N, R, W to Fifth Ave.; 4, 5, 6 to 59th St.

DOWNTOWN SHOPPING

The premiere shopping district of downtown Manhattan is the square mile known as **SoHo** (Houston to Grand Street, from Broadway to Sixth Avenue). This jumble of cobblestone streets and industrial-era loft buildings grew to prominence two decades ago as an artists' paradise—a place where an aspiring painter or sculptor could grab 6,000 square feet of raw space in crowded Manhattan for next to nothing. That's no longer true, of course. The artists created cachet, which in turn attracted rock stars, fashion models and then anyone with loads of cash.

The creative community has largely been driven out, but the cavernous spaces they once inhabited have been converted to galleries and lots and lots of

fabulous stores, both familiar names and one-of-a-kind boutiques. Everything
from vinyl platform boots to minimalist beige bed linens is available in this
richly varied shopping district. But fair warning: Everything costs top dollar. In
fact, like the Fifth and Madison Avenue corridors, SoHo is also couture territory, but with a downtown, left-of-center, rock-and-roll twist: Expect to find
artsy designer names like **Marc Jacobs**, **Vivienne Westwood**, **Helmut Lang** and
Vivienne Tam, plus hipped up outlets of uptown retailers like **Louis Vuitton**
and **Prada** (**Prada Sport** and **Miu Miu**).

Other better-than-garden-variety, less-than-couture-priced merchants
include **Otto Tootsie Plohound**, which offers the latest in platform footwear in
a setting more like a dance club than a shoe store. **Anthropologie** has a whimsical selection of velvet slip dresses, antiqued candlesticks and wicker furniture to
go with its mod-attic décor. Home design goes Austin Powers-mod at **Property**.
And **Kate's Paperie** is a veritable wonderland of textured and swirled papers.

Just east of SoHo is **NoLIta** (**North of Little Ita**ly), which has evolved into a
tidy, stylish neighborhood with a chic shopping scene in the last couple of years.
The unique boutiques along Mott, Mulberry and Elizabeth Streets are pricey but
wonderful, leaning toward up-and-coming clothing, jewelry and accessories
designers, plus modern home-design shops. If you have a passion for headwear,
do not miss hat designer **Kelly Christy**, who can frequently be found outside
her shop sipping coffee with friends, while French handbag designer **Jamin
Puech** is a standout for romantic French-sewn totes.

The East Village, especially along 9th Street east of Second Avenue, and the
area called NoHo around Bond Street, has become another bastion of young
designers styling one-of-a-kind wear, much of it quite affordable.

Above 14th Street, Broadway from Union Square north has become a corridor of home decorating stores. The essential stop here is **ABC Carpet & Home**,
an eclectic, expensive bazaar of luxuriant clutter, from quality furnishings to
international carpets to luxury linens.

Fashionistas looking for the newest frontier should head east to the Meatpacking District, where fabulous **Jeffrey New York** (think pony skin belts and
fur-lined stiletto heels) is accompanied by a multiplying crop of modernist
design boutiques, particularly along Gansevoort and Washington Streets.

—*Leslie Kaufman*

*(See also "Specialty Stores" later in this chapter for recommendations on outstanding
shops throughout the downtown area. See "Department Stores" for* **Jeffrey New
York** *and "Gifts & Homewares" for* **ABC Carpet & Home**.*)*

SoHo & NoLIta
Subway: F, S to Broadway–Lafayette St.; N, R to Prince St.; 6 to Spring St.
Anna Sui 113 Greene St. (between Prince and Spring Sts.) (212) 941-8406
www.annasui.com
Anthropologie 375 West Broadway (between Spring and Broome Sts.)
(212) 343-7070 *www.anthropologie.com*

Helmut Lang 80 Greene St. (between Spring and Broome Sts.)
(212) 925-7214

Jamin Puech 252 Mott St. (between Houston and Prince Sts.)
(212) 334-9730

Kate's Paperie 561 Broadway (between Prince and Spring Sts.)
(212) 941-9816 *www.katespaperie.com*

Kelly Christy 235 Elizabeth St. (between Houston and Prince Sts.)
(212) 965-0686

Louis Vuitton 116 Greene St. (between Prince and Spring Sts.)
(212) 274-9090 *www.vuitton.com*

Marc Jacobs 163 Mercer St. (between Houston and Prince Sts.)
(212) 343-1490

Miu Miu 100 Prince St. (between Mercer and Greene Sts.) (212) 334-5156
www.miumiu.it

Otto Tootsie Plohound 431 West Broadway (between Prince and Spring Sts.)
(212) 925-8931

Prada Sport 116 Wooster St. (between Prince and Spring Sts.) (212) 925-2221

Property 14 Wooster St. (between Grand and Canal Sts.) (917) 237-0123

Vivienne Tam 99 Greene St. (between Prince and Spring Sts.)
(212) 966-2398

Vivienne Westwood 71 Greene St. (between Spring and Broome Sts.)
(212) 334-5200 *www.viviennewestwood.co.uk*

Yohji Yamamoto 103 Grand St. (at Mercer St.) (212) 966-9066
www.yohjiyamamoto.co.jp

BARGAIN SHOPPING

Bargains, bargains come and get your bargains! Manhattan, even these days, is
full of hawkers.

The **Diamond District** (W. 47th St. between Fifth and Sixth Aves.) is the
place to go for bargains on diamonds, precious gems, gold and other fine jewelry.
The block is lined with dealers, most of whom are Hasidic Jews for whom diamonds are the family business. You can get an emerald ring for one-fifth the
price of a similar ring at Tiffany's—but you have to know what you're doing.
Your best bet is to prepare in advance by reading up on the kinds of gems or
jewelry you're interested in, perhaps visiting some high-end jewelers in your
area who can point out the features that speak quality in fine jewelry. You might
also read up on shopping the district at *www.47th-street.com*, which has some
frank and useful tips that will help you avoid pitfalls in the discount district,
plus a full list of reputable dealers. Once you arrive in the Diamond District, be
sure to price compare. And keep in mind that virtually all stores are only open
weekdays, usually from 10 A.M. to 5 P.M. or so.

It's not as tough to find real bargains in clothes, but you still have to know where to go. Generally speaking, stay off Madison Avenue. Instead, try stores like **Daffy's** ("Clothing Bargains for Millionaires"). It's a badly organized, slightly neurotic atmosphere, but persevere.

And without doubt, take a subway (F train to Delancey St.) to **Orchard Street**, in the heart of the Lower East Side. Hipster boutiques are raiding this historic bargain district like wildfire, but there are still plenty of deals to be had. The street has a tarnished reputation. People say the bargains are only pseudo-bargains, but check out **Ben Freedman**, an old-world cheapie paradise with sidewalk racks that feature $5 leather belts and $6 ties. Don't miss the string of leather shops, and **Joe's Fabrics** for a kaleidoscope of linens, velvets, silks and damasks. The secret on Orchard Street is haggling: Don't be afraid. You don't have to be a pro. Just try walking out. . . and see what happens. Think of what you want to pay, and just keep repeating it on your way to the door. It's fun, and you'll probably get what you want. But don't play the game if you're not serious, or you'll end up with some angry merchants! Stop in first at the **Lower East Side Visitor Center** (261 Broome St. between Orchard and Allen Sts., 212-226-9010 *www.lowereastsideny.com*) to pick up a pamphlet-sized shopping guide.

Chinatown's **Canal Street** is a blast to stroll if you're looking for inexpensive backpacks, almost-free leather belts or exotic souvenirs. Stroll east from the intersection of Canal and Broadway for the best bounty, and bargain as you go. Skip the bootleg CDs, videos and DVDs though—you will be disappointed.

If you arrive just before—or better—just after Christmas, or in mid-summer, check out the sales in the world's best boutiques and department stores. Open the daily paper once you arrive and start researching; the sales in the finest stores usually appear in the first couple of pages. Even on sale, the prices won't be cheap at stores like Hermès and Henri Bendel, but you won't find merchandise of this quality anywhere else, including the so-called premium outlet malls.

The other secret of New York City bargains is the sample sale, in which last season's designer merchandise is offered at a fraction of the price. These sales go on throughout the year. To give you an idea, take the Echo Scarf sample sale: Silk scarves that normally sell for between $60 and $90 can be found in cardboard boxes labeled $5, $10 and $15. The best places to hunt them down is in the "Check Out" section of the weekly *Time Out New York*; on the Citysearch Web site (*www.newyork.citysearch.com*; click on "Shopping"), which announces the latest sample sales on Wednesdays; and at *www.nysale.com* and *www.styleshop.com*. When you hit a sample sale, avoid the lunch-hour crowds, bring cash, and don't expect much in the way of dressing rooms, so know your size or be ready to be creative (no returns).

If you're ready to splurge on a made-to-measure suit or jacket (don't gasp, it's almost affordable), try **Saint Laurie Merchant Tailors**, a company that used to sell racks of inexpensive knock-offs downtown but now has moved to Park Avenue. The shop is fun to visit; there are tables full of bolts of fine wools and tweeds tagged along with the prices for a suit or sport coat. You can choose both your fabric and your style—fitted, like an Italian count, or baggy like a Boston Brahmin. Prices run $950 to $1,200 for a suit and around $700 for a blazer.

A raft of men's discount clothing stores dot the Flatiron District. **Moe Ginsburg** is the most famous, but the prices aren't much different from those you'd find in a suburban discount mall. Nearby, the landmark **Ladies' Mile**, along Sixth Avenue below 21st Street, is lined with familiar discount names like **T.J. Maxx, Filene's Basement** and **Bed, Bath & Beyond**. Some say that the merchandise in these stores is picked especially for chic Manhattan shoppers, and is better than what comes to the suburbs; see what you think.

While you're in the neighborhood, check out the thrift shops just around the corner. The **Housing Works Thrift Shop** is a gem for men's and women's designer hand-me-downs, shoes and, best of all, furniture, with items like a great-looking oval Biedermaier table for $200.

And if you're in town on a weekend, don't forget the indoor and outdoor flea markets that operate all year round on and near the corner of Sixth Avenue and West 26th Street *(see "Flea Markets" later in this chapter)*.

—*Tracie Rozhon*

*(See "Vintage, Thrift & Resale" in the "Clothing" section for **Housing Works Thrift Shop**, **Salvation Army** and other stores for used clothing and housewares.)*

Diamond District
Subway: B, D, F, S to 47th-50th St.–Rockefeller Center.

M Khordipour Enterprises 10 W. 47th St. (at Fifth Ave.) (212) 869-2198

Peachtree Jewelers Inc. 580 Fifth Ave. (at 47th St.) (212) 398-1758

Unusual Wedding Rings in the National Jewelers Exchange, 4 W. 47th St., booth 86 (212) 944-1713 *www.unusualweddingrings.com*

Orchard Street Bargain District
Subway: F to Delancey St.; J, M, Z to Essex St.

Altman Luggage 125 Orchard St. (between Delancey and Rivington Sts.) (212) 254-7275 *www.altmanluggage.com*

Arivel Fashions 150 Orchard St. (between Rivington and Stanton Sts.) (212) 673-8992 *www.arivel.com*. For furs and leather goods.

Ben Freedman 137 Orchard St. (between Delancey and Rivington Sts.) (212) 674-0854

Joe's Fabrics 102 Orchard St. (at Delancey St.) (212) 674-7089

Klein's of Monticello 105 Orchard St. (at Delancey St.) (212) 966-1453. High-quality businesswear.

Rita's Leather Fair 176 Orchard St. (at Houston St.) (212) 533-2756

Discount Clothing
Burlington Coat Factory 707 Sixth Ave. (at 23rd St.) (212) 229-1300 *www.coat.com*. Other location: 45 Park Pl. (between West Broadway and Church St.) (212) 571-2631. More than just coats—men's, women's and children's wear, plus housewares and luggage. **Subway:** F to 23rd St.

Canal Jean Co. 504 Broadway (between Spring and Broome Sts.)
(212) 226-1130 *www.canaljean.com*. Cheapie jeans and T's for the MTV crowd.
Subway: N, R to Prince St.; J, M, Q, W, Z, 6 to Canal St.

Daffy's 111 Fifth Ave. (at 18th St.) (212) 529-4477 *www.daffys.com*. Other
location: 1311 Broadway (at 34th St.) (212) 736-4477; check for more locations. **Subway:** L, N, Q, R, W, 4, 5, 6 to 14th St.

Filene's Basement 620 Sixth Ave. (at 18th St.) (212) 620-3100
www.filenes.com. Other location: 2222 Broadway (at 79th St.) (212) 873-8000.
Subway: F to 14th St.

Loehmann's 101 Seventh Ave. (at 16th St.) (212) 352-0856
www.loehmanns.com. The place for designer fashions at a discount. **Subway:** 1,
2, 3, 9 to 14th St.

Moe Ginsburg 162 Fifth Ave. (at 21st St.) (212) 982-5254 or 242-3482. **Subway:** F, N, R to 23rd St.

Saint Laurie Merchant Tailors 350 Park Ave. (between 51st and 52nd Sts.)
(212) 473-0100 *www.saintlaurie.com*. **Subway:** 6 to 51st St.

T.J. Maxx 620 Sixth Ave. (at 18th St.) (212) 229-0875 *www.tjmaxx.com*. **Subway:** F to 14th St.

Syms 400 Park Ave. (at 54th St.) (212) 317-8200 *www.syms.com*. Other location: 42 Trinity Pl. (at Rector St.) (212) 797-1199. Discount career wear for
men and women. **Subway:** 6 to 51st St.

ANTIQUES

New York is the largest center for antiques and collectibles in the world, a giant
bazaar stocked with period furniture, china, glassware, textiles, books, coins,
jewelry, rugs and toys from just about anywhere on earth. Collectors are either
ecstatic by the sheer abundance of antiques, or frustrated by the difficulty of
finding exactly what they seek—be it a 19th-century trotting-horse weather
vane, a Ming vase, an 18th-century desk from Versailles, a 1930's Mickey Mouse
toy or a baseball signed by Babe Ruth.

Another frustrating thing: the prices. Expect to pay top collectible dollar for
any quality find. Still, the city remains an antique hound's dream come true.

Collectors with limited time, plan ahead. If you're a serious shopper, put
together an itinerary, and let the dealers you're interested in know beforehand
about the type of pieces you wish to see. Dealers are busy, especially world-class
dealers like **James J. Lally**, a specialist in Chinese art. They travel as much as
some of their clients do in order to present scholarly exhibitions with catalogues
in their museum-style galleries.

Browsers who are not in the market for a specific piece but prefer to browse
can do well in a few select neighborhoods—most notably on the Upper East
Side, along East 59th, 60th and 61st Streets around Second Avenue, and along
Madison Avenue in the 70's. Lafayette Street north and south of Houston
Street is a good hunting ground for 20th-century finds.

New York is host to about 60 antiques fairs each year. Dealers come from throughout the world to participate in fairs, the most notable of which take place in the Park Avenue and Lexington Avenue armories. The **Asian Art Fair**, a Spring event (*www.haughton.com*), is often described as the best of the art and antiques shows in Manhattan. The preeminent dealer in Asian art, Robert H. Ellsworth, explained its success, saying, "Even if you spent a year going around the world, you would never be able to see all the fine Asian art exhibited here." At the **Triple Pier Antiques Show**, held in the passenger ship terminals on the Hudson River in March and November (212-255-0020 *www.antiqnet.com/-Stella*), more than 600 dealers sell goods spanning the centuries and collectors' budgets.

Antiques and collectibles are also sold year-round at flea markets, the most enduring of which is held on weekends at a parking lot on Sixth Avenue at 26th Street (*see "Flea Markets" later in this chapter*).   —*Rita Reif*

Barry Friedman 32 E. 67th St. (between Park and Madison Aves.) (212) 794-8950. Art Deco furniture and decorations by masters like Jean-Michel Frank, Eileen Gray and Jean Dunand, plus avant garde art. **Subway:** 6 to 68th St.

Chisolm Gallery 55 W. 17th St. (at Sixth Ave.), 6th floor (212) 243-8834 *www.vintagepostersnyc.com*. A century of collectible-quality advertising posters from around the globe. **Subway:** F to 14th St.

City Barn Antiques 269 Lafayette St. (at Prince St.) (212) 941-5757 *www.citybarnantiques.com*. One of the nation's premier specialists in mid-20th-century Heywood Wakefield furnishings. **Subway:** N, R to Prince St.

Didier Aaron 32 E. 67th St. (between Park and Madison Aves.) (212) 988-5248 *www.didieraaron.com*. Prominent Parisian dealer in French 18th-century palace-quality furniture, objects and art. **Subway:** 6 to 68th St.

Doyle & Doyle 189 Orchard St. (between Houston and Stanton Sts.) (212) 677-9991 *www.doyledoyle.com*. Fine estate and antique jewelry, including Georgian, Victorian, Edwardian, Art Deco and Art Nouveau pieces. **Subway:** F to Delancey St.; J, M, Z to Essex St.

Evergreen Antiques 1249 Third Ave. (at 72nd St.) 212-744-5664 *www.evergreenantiques.com*. Mostly 19th-century Scandinavian and Northern European furniture in the neoclassical, Biedermaier and Empire styles. **Subway:** 6 to 68th St.

Guéridon 359 Lafayette St. (between Bleecker and Bond Sts.) (212) 677-7740. French mid-century modern furnishings and accents. **Subway:** 6 to Bleecker St.; F, S to Broadway–Lafayette St.

J.J. Lally & Co. 41 E. 57th St. (at Madison Ave.) (212) 371-3380. Chinese art and antiques. **Subway:** 4, 5, 6 to 59th St.; N, R to Fifth Ave.

Kentshire Galleries 37 E. 12th St. (between University Pl. and Broadway) (212) 673-6644. Large gallery dedicated to 18th- and 19th-century English antiques, ranging from jewelry and tabletop items to formal furnishings. **Subway:** L, N, R, Q, W, 4, 5, 6 to 14th St.

Manhattan Art & Antiques Center 1050 Second Ave. (between 55th and 56th Sts.) (212) 355-4400 *www.the-maac.com*. Three-floor antiques center housing more than 100 dealers. Genres run the gamut from antiquities to fine early 20th-century collectibles. **Subway:** 4, 5, 6 to 59th St.

Skyscraper 237 E. 60th St. (between Second and Third Aves.) (212) 588-0644 *www.skyscraperny.com*. High-quality Art Deco and streamline furniture and collectibles. **Subway:** N, R, W to Lexington Ave.

WaterMoon Gallery 211 West Broadway (near Franklin St.) (212) 925-5556. Fine Chinese and Tibetan antique furniture, Tibetan carpets, and Chinese porcelain and ceramics from the Neolithic era to the Ming Dynasty, plus an extensive selection of Chinese and Miao textiles and contemporary artwork by young Chinese artists, many of whom have never been shown outside of China. **Subway:** 1, 9 to Franklin Ave.

AUCTIONS

Manhattan's world-renowned auction houses have long provided lavish forums for those who can afford to indulge their passions for collecting. If you are interested in buying, be sure to attend the sale preview and study the catalogue for price estimates before you raise your paddle and bid. For those not in the market, simply watching the ceremonious sale can be a delight. Check local publications such as *The New York Times* and *Time Out New York*, as well as the auctions' own Web sites, for dates and events.

Christie's 20 Rockefeller Plaza (49th St. between Fifth and Sixth Aves.) (212) 636-2000 *www.christies.com*. **Christie's East**, 219 E. 67th St. (between Second and Third Aves.) (212) 606-0400. This British institution boasts a history that dates back more than two centuries. Items that have graced the block at Christie's include everything from Matisse and da Vinci canvases to the Academy Award Bette Davis won for *Jezebel*. Although this house is best known for headline-making sales, it also boasts departments for wine, cars, coins and sports memorabilia. Christie's East is relatively modest. **Subway:** B, D, F, S to 47th-50th St.–Rockefeller Center.

Sotheby's 1334 York Ave. (at 72nd St.) (212) 606-7000 *www.sothebys.com*. From its humble beginnings in 1744 as a London book dealer, this house has grown into one of the world's most esteemed auction houses with branches all over the map. Auctions run the gamut, from the sale of van Gogh's "Irises" to Jacqueline Kennedy Onassis's estate. **Subway:** 6 to 68th St.

Guernsey's 108 1/2 E. 73rd St. (between Park and Lexington Aves.) (212) 794-2280 *www.guernseys.com*. One of New York's smaller auction houses, this institution is an esteemed source for modern collections, from artwork of the Soviet Union to rock-and-roll memorabilia. **Subway:** 6 to 77th St.

Swann Auction Galleries 104 E. 25th St. (between Park and Lexington Aves.) (212) 254-4710 *www.swanngalleries.com*. This specialized house devotes itself to rare books and the visual arts, including photos, vintage posters, autographs, maps and atlases, drawings and the like. **Subway:** 6 to 28th St.

Tepper Galleries 110 E. 25th St. (between Park and Lexington Aves.) (212) 677-5300 *www.teppergalleries.com*. To simply say that estates are sold off here doesn't do justice to the fine pieces that pass through this house. Offerings include antique furniture, fine silver, jewelry, carpets and fine artworks. **Subway:** 6 to 28th St.

SPECIALTY STORES
Beauty & Spa

Bath & Beauty

C.O. Bigelow 414 Sixth Ave. (between 8th and 9th Sts.) (212) 533-2700 *www.bigelowchemists.com*. This West Village spot offers a quirky mix of quality products, from the hard-to-find Biotherm skincare line to practical pillboxes. Perfect that messy "beach hair" with Kusco Murphy products, get squeaky clean with a bath treat from Katherine Memmi or Claus Porto, and give your daily regimen an international touch with an Elgydium toothbrush from Italy. **Subway:** A, C, E, F, S to W. 4th St.

Calypso Beaute 252 Mott St. (between Prince and Houston Sts.) (212) 625-0658. Year-round, Calypso Beaute makes a city girl feel sun-kissed and beachy. Sweet scents like Mimosa come in perfumes and candles, dressing body and home with island memories. The fragrance line complements the ultra-chic fashions of Calypso boutiques, bringing Euro-tropical style to the isle of Manhattan. **Subway:** F, S to Broadway–Lafayette St.; N, R to Prince St.

Creed 9 Bond St. (between Broadway and Lafayette St.) (212) 228-1940. Other locations: 660 Madison Ave. (at 61st St.) (212) 228-1940; 754 Fifth Ave. (at 57th St.) (212) 872-2729. Much like an Hermès Kelly bag, a custom-made fragrance by this two-century-old French perfumer—which has designed signature scents for such larger-than-life ladies as Audrey Hepburn and Grace Kelly—is a grand splurge. You may have to be a real princess to afford it, but what wonderful company you'll be in. **Subway:** 6 to Bleecker St.

Face Stockholm 110 Prince St. (at Greene St.) (212) 966-9110 *www.facestockholm.com*. Other locations: 226 Columbus Ave. (at 70th St.) (212) 769-1420; 687 Madison Ave. (at 61st St.) (212) 207-8833. As if lighting ceremonial candles, faithful customers stand before rows of lipsticks, glitter and nail polish, testing the wide array of hip shades, both glossy and matte. A perfect buy is one of FACE's sleek custom-filled compacts with miniature applicator. **Subway:** N, R to Prince St.

5S 98 Prince St. (between Broadway and Mercer St.) (212) 925-7880
www.five-s.com. Skincare and makeup in Shiseido's 5S line are organized by five
principles for the soul and body—purifying, calming, energizing, adoring and
nurturing—and displayed on bright island counters for testing and playing. Pick
up a Rebirth body powder of ginseng extract and chamomile for that second
shopping wind. **Subway:** N, R to Prince St.

Fresh 57 Spring St. (between Lafayette and Mulberry Sts.) (212) 925-0099
www.fresh.com. Other location: 1061 Madison Ave. (at 80th St.)
(212) 396-0344. This Boston-based line excels at bath and body treats that
come in delicious scents that are almost good enough to eat. Their popular
Sugar line comes in perfume, shower gel and lotion; cocoa, lychee, lemon, milk,
honey, soy and rose are also irresistible. Soaps are individually wrapped and tied
with wire and stone, making perfect gifts to go. **Subway:** 6 to Spring St.

Helena Rubinstein Beauty Gallery 135 Spring St. (between Greene and
Wooster Sts.) (212) 343-9966 *www.helenarubenstein.com*. This beauty oasis
offers a moment of repose in the middle of a SoHo spree. The spacious white-
on-white, gallery-like store promotes the experimentation of color. Helpful staff
will advise you on beauty products like the popular Lip Sculptor treatment,
packaged in the signature HR gold. **Subway:** N, R to Prince St.; 6 to Spring St.

Jo Malone 949 Broadway (at 23rd St.) (212) 673-2220. The new North American flagship store of London's favorite perfumery is located in the Flatiron
Building—and women across the city are celebrating the stateside arrival of Jo
Malone's lime basil and mandarin lotion. Malone's philosophy is that one can
find the perfect personal scent by experimenting with her 10 original fragrances,
so enjoy the sniffing. **Subway:** N, R to 23rd St.

Kiehl's 109 Third Ave. (at 13th St.) (212) 677-3171 *www.kiehls.com*. Long
lines at this venerable beauty landmark allow you to spot more products to add
to your basket. Models and athletes alike are devotees of such classics as the
Ultra Facial Moisturizer, Creme of Silk Groom for glossy hair and Lip Balm #1,
a ubiquitous item in many city bags. Stay calm as the knowledgeable staff
rewards you with more exceptional product samples, all in Kiehl's plain-wrap
bottles. Saks boasts a well-stocked Kiehl's counter if you can't make it downtown. **Subway:** L, N, R, Q, W, 4, 5, 6 to 14th St.

Lafco 200 Hudson St. (between Canal and Vestry Sts.) (800)362-3677.
A newer addition to New York's beautyscape, this sleek and sprawling home-
design store is the proud purveyor of the cult favorite Santa Maria Novella bath
products. These beautifully packaged soaps by the famous Italian monastery are
home accents in themselves. **Subway:** 1, 9 to Canal St.

L'Occitane 146 Spring St. (between West Broadway and Wooster St.)
(212) 343-0109 *www.loccitane.com*. Other location: 198 Columbus Ave. (at
69th St.) (212) 362-5146; check for more locations. This Provençal import is a
bath lovers' dream. The luxuriant hand cream is an epiphany. The most popular
product is the 100 percent shea butter; extracted from the fruit of the African

shea tree, it works wonders on skin, lips and hair and is an excellent treat for expectant mothers. Candles, shampoos, moisturizing soaps and fragrances are among the offerings. **Subway:** N, R to Prince St.; C, E to Spring St.

M.A.C. 113 Spring St. (between Mercer and Greene Sts.) (212) 334-4641 *www.maccosmetics.com*. Other locations: 14 Christopher St. (at Gay St.) (212) 243-4150; 1 E. 22nd St. (bet. Broadway and Fifth Ave.) (212)677-6611. M.A.C. cosmetics raise the roof with bold colors, sleek black packaging, and spokesdivas like Lil' Kim, k.d. lang and RuPaul. It's hard to resist sassy lipsticks; a purchase of one of M.A.C.'s signature Viva Glam lipsticks is also a donation to AIDS research. **Subway:** N, R to Prince St.; 6 to Spring St.

Sephora 636 Fifth Ave. (at 51st St.) (212) 245-1633 *www.sephora.com*. Other locations: 1500 Broadway (between 43rd and 44th Sts.) (212) 944-6789; 555 Broadway (between Prince and Spring Sts.) (212)625-1309; check for more locations. Sephora's black-and-white-striped columns support a dazzling beauty superstore. Gloved staff guide customers through aisles of Stila, Hard Candy, Clarins and other impressive international brands from A to Z, including its own bath line. You're invited to create your own scent at the perfume bar. **Subway:** E, F to Fifth Ave.

Shu Uemura 121 Greene St. (between Prince and Houston Sts.) (212) 979-5500. Well-lit workstations help customers identify a complexion-perfect hue from among the powders and blushes of this elegant Japanese line. With a selection of over 100 brushes, this is a great place to pick up basic makeup tools. For the perfect wink, buy the popular eyelash curler and a chic set of come-hither lashes. **Subway:** F, S to Broadway–Lafayette St.; N, R to Prince St.

Zitomer 969 Madison Ave. (between 75th and 76th Sts.) (212) 737-4480 *www.zitomer.com*. Zitomer is the upscale bath, beauty and health resource for Upper East Siders, featuring such bare necessities as DeCleor sunscreen and Chanel moisturizers. **Subway:** 6 to 77th St.

Day Spas

Avon Centre Salon & Spa Trump Tower, 725 Fifth Ave. (between 56th and 57th Sts.) (212) 755-AVON *www.avoncentre.com*. This chic uptowner is home to colorist-of-the-moment Brad Johns, king of the buttery blondes, and eyebrow doyenne Eliza Petrescu, the woman who revolutionized shaping and tweezing. Spa treatments run the gamut to cellulite-reducing endermologie to wellness counseling. Expensive, but worth the dough. **Subway:** N, R, W to Fifth Ave.

Bliss 568 Broadway (at Prince St.), 2nd floor (212) 219-8970 *www.blissspa.com*. Other location: 19 E. 57th St. (between Fifth and Madison Aves.). The Big Apple's favorite day spa is housed in stylish loft space with a funky downtown look and buckets of *Sex and the City* attitude. It may be a bit much for some, but there's no arguing with the top-notch facials and massages. Book as far in advance as possible. **Subway:** N, R to Prince St.

Carapan Urban Spa 5 W. 15th St. (at Fifth Ave.) (212) 633-6220
www.carapan.com. This candlelit, Native American-inspired spa is an oasis of
tranquility in the urban jungle. Eastern and Western techniques are combined
in the relaxing spa treatments, which run the gamut from aromatherapy facials
to reiki to sports massage, and the romantic space is a true delight. Book it
ahead if you want sauna time. **Subway:** F, L, N, Q, R, W, 4, 5, 6 to 14th St.

Ella Baché Spa 8 W. 36th St. (at Fifth Ave.) (212) 279-8562
www.ellabache.com. Women in the know have celebrated the arrival of this
Parisian skincare haven on New World shores. The spa is intimate and delightful, the signature products are first-rate, and the noninvasive imported thera-
pies—from massages to facials to body polishes to waxing—are administered
with a supremely gentle touch. **Subway:** B, D, F, N, Q, R, S, W to 34th St.

Greenhouse Spa 127 E. 57th St. (at Third Ave.) (212) 664-4449
www.greenhousespa.com. The legendary Arlington, Texas, spa has finally arrived
in New York, and the uptown set is thrilled. And for good reason: This is a
lovely, comfortable spa with a light, airy and soothing contemporary ambiance
and a full slate of relaxation and salon treatments, plus excellent service. **Subway:** 4, 5, 6 to 59th St.

Stone Spa 104 W. 14th St. (at Sixth Ave.) (212) 741-8881 *www.stonespa.com*.
This little, lovely, loft-style spa with a distinctly downtown edge isn't for everybody—but hot stone massage simply doesn't get better. All of the A-one treatments incorporate soothing hot stones in some capacity (even the marvelous
Jurlique facials), the therapists are all first-rate, and the soundtrack tends more
toward ethereal world music than the new-age standard. **Subway:** F to 14th St.

Stressless Step 115 E. 57th St. (between Lexington and Park Aves.), 5th floor
(212) 826-6222 *www.stresslessstep.com*. New Yorkers who want a first-rate massage without the trendier-than-thou spa trappings consistently head to Stressless
Step, a straightforward, utilitarian kind of place with a full treatment menu,
excellent sauna and steam rooms, and a wallet-friendly no-tipping policy that
keeps your bill down to earth. **Subway:** 4, 5, 6 to 59th St.

Bookstores

New York is Book City. While the big book chains' discount prices and huge
inventories have driven some independents out of business, the Big Apple still
shines with first-rate neighborhood and special-subject bookstores.

Major Chains

Barnes & Noble 33 E. 17th St. (at Union Square) (212) 253-0810
www.bn.com. Other locations: 105 Fifth Ave. (at 18th St.) (212) 807-0099;
1972 Broadway (at 66th St.) (212) 595-6859; 4 Astor Pl. (between Broadway
and Lafayette St.) (212) 420-1322; check for more locations. Barnes & Noble is
Manhattan's biggest book retailer with supersized stores located throughout the
city. In addition to huge selections of current and backlist titles in every genre,

you'll find extensive magazine racks, plus cafes in most locations. (The original Fifth Ave. and 18th St. store has been selling books since 1863—the pre-book-store-cum-coffeehouse days—so you can't get a latte there. Its selection is heavy on academic texts.) A chock-full events calendar includes best-selling authors reading from their latest. Check *www.bn.com* for the current author-appearances schedule, or call the stores directly. B&N events are also advertised in *The New York Times* and *Time Out New York* magazine. **Subway:** L, N, R, Q, W, 4, 5, 6 to 14th St.

Borders Books & Music 461 Park Ave. (at 57th St.) (212) 980-6785; Other locations: 550 Second Ave. (at 32nd St.) (212) 685-3938. New York's second-biggest book chain is this well-stocked retailer, which averages 150,000 book and titles per store. (The Park Avenue location is substantially larger than the Second Avenue one; both feature cafes.) Borders has a stronger emphasis on music and video than Barnes & Noble, which has largely backed out of these markets (videos and DVDs are carried only in the Park Avenue store). Call or check *www.bordersstores.com* for music, book signings, author readings and other events. **Subway:** 4, 5, 6 to 59th St.

Independent Bookstores

Coliseum Books 1771 Broadway (at 57th St.) (212) 757-8381. One of the city's best and most popular independent bookstores, this sprawling store just south of Columbus Circle offers both an extensive and highly browsable collection of fiction and nonfiction, as well as discounted remainders on last year's top titles in the basement. The knowledgeable staff is most helpful. Rumor has it that rent battles may shutter the store some time in 2002, so call first. **Subway:** N, R, Q, W to 57th St.; B, D, E to Seventh Ave.

Gotham Book Mart 41 W. 47th St. (between Fifth and Sixth Aves.) (212) 719-4448. This cramped and dusty new-and-used store has been a mecca for serious readers since it was founded in 1920 by the late Frances Steloff, who championed the works of Henry Miller, Gertrude Stein and other literary luminaries. She sold forbidden copies of James Joyce's *Ulysses*, and once hired Tennessee Williams as a clerk—then fired him for tardiness. Strong in intelligent fiction, literary criticism and poetry. It will be moving after 70-plus years. **Subway:** B, D, F, S to 47th-50th St.–Rockefeller Center.

Madison Avenue Bookshop 883 Madison Ave. (between 69th and 70th Sts.) (212) 535-6130 *www.madisonavenuebookshop.com*. An excellent general-interest bookstore with a familiar air and great customer service. Authors often stop in to sign books. **Subway:** 6 to 68th St.

Posman Books 9 Grand Central Terminal (Vanderbilt Ave. and 42nd St.) (212) 983-1111 *www.posmanbooks.com*. This pleasant shop on the main level at Grand Central offers a high-quality selection of general-interest fiction and nonfiction as well as gift books, making it an ideal stop for readers on the go. **Subway:** S, 4, 5, 6, 7 to 42nd St.

Rizzoli 31 W. 57th St. (between Fifth and Sixth Aves.) (212) 759-2424. This sophisticated bookstore has a strong emphasis on art books, but it also makes a very browsable general-interest shop with an opinionated and helpful staff. **Subway:** E, F, N, R to Fifth Ave.

Shakespeare & Co. 939 Lexington Ave. (at 69th St.) (212) 570-0201 *www.shakeandco.com*. Other locations: 137 E. 23rd St. (at Lexington Ave.) (212) 505-2021; 716 Broadway (at Washington Pl.) (212) 529-1330; 1 White-hall St. (between Bridge and Stone Sts.) (212) 742-7025; check for more locations. The emphasis at these comfortable, unpretentious neighborhood book-stores is on quality fiction, with a good selection of small-press titles in the mix. A New York favorite. **Subway:** 6 to 68th St.

St. Marks Bookshop 31 Third Ave. (at 9th St.) (212) 260-7853 *www.stmarksbookshop.com*. This winning East Villager is a prime haunt for left-of-center readers. The well-chosen and nicely displayed selection runs the gamut from avant-garde poetry and alternative fiction to Eastern philosophy to glossy photography books with an esoteric bent. **Subway:** 6 to Astor Pl.

Three Lives & Company 154 W. 10th St. (at Waverly Pl.) (212) 741-2069 *www.threelives.com*. This ultra-charming West Village landmark is a real find for those who truly delight in reading, especially fiction, biography and memoirs. Author readings are a big part of the mix. **Subway:** 1, 9 to Christopher St.

Out-of-Print, Used and Rare Books

Argosy Book Store 116 E. 59th St. (between Park and Lexington Aves.) (212) 753-4455 *www.argosybooks.com*. This wonderful, wood-paneled septuage-narian bookshop overflows with antiquarian, rare and well-cared-for used books—77,000 of them, to be exact—plus antique prints, maps and autographs. Prices run from $5 to $5,000, so there's something for everybody. **Subway:** 4, 5, 6 to 59th St.

Bauman Rare Books 535 Madison Ave. (between 54th and 55th Sts.) (212) 751-0011; smaller gallery at the Waldorf=Astoria, 301 Park Ave. (at 49th St.) (212) 759-8300 *www.baumanrarebooks.com*. Bauman, one of the most well-respected rare-book dealers in the nation, has two Big Apple galleries rife with museum-quality titles. The place to go if you're on the hunt for a rare first edi-tion, be it the first English edition of Aristotle's *Politics* or Frank Herbert's *Dune*; many are signed. Bring a well-padded wallet. **Subway:** 4, 5, 6 to 59th St.

Bookleaves 304 W. 4th St. (near Bank St.) (212) 924-5638. This cozy nook is everything a neighborhood used-book store should be. **Subway:** 1, 9 to Christo-pher St.

Gotham Book Mart (*See "Independent Bookstores" earlier in this section.*)

Gryphon Bookshop 2246 Broadway (between 80th and 81st Sts.) (212) 362-0706. This cramped store is a nightmare for some, but the wide array

of used and rare editions makes this unusual collection a bibliophile's dream
come true. **Subway:** 1, 9 to 79th St.

Housing Works Used Books Cafe 126 Crosby St. (at Houston St.)
(212) 334-3324 *www.housingworksubc.com*. This warm and wonderful wood-
paneled, library-like store sandwiched between SoHo and NoLIta is the perfect
antidote for chain-store rebels who nevertheless appreciate a good latte while
perusing the stacks. The high-quality all-used selection is particularly strong on
coffee-table books and review copies. All profits go to not-for-profit Housing
Works, which provides housing and services to homeless people living with
HIV and AIDS, so there's no better place to buy. **Subway:** F, S to
Broadway–Lafayette St.; 6 to Bleecker St.

JN Bartfield Fine Books 30 W. 57th St. (between Fifth and Sixth Aves.)
(212) 245-8890. Good, pricey selection of rare books, focusing on fine bindings.
Subway: N, R, W to Fifth Ave.

Skyline Books & Records 13 W. 18th St. (at Fifth Ave.) (212) 759-5463.
A well-chosen selection of used reads as well as jazz and blues records. **Subway:**
F, L, N, R, Q, W, 4, 5, 6 to 14th St.

The Strand 828 Broadway (at 12th St.) (212) 473-1452 *www.strandbooks.com*.
Annex, 95 Fulton St. (between William and Gold Sts.) (212) 732-6070. This
epic used bookstore—which claims to have "eight miles of books"—is heaven
for used-book hounds. You could get lost in these monolithic stacks, but
patience and time are guaranteed to turn up a stack of must-haves in any category. A good selection of new books at greatly reduced prices is usually on hand
at the smaller Fulton Street annex. **Subway:** L, N, R, Q, W, 4, 5, 6 to 14th St.

Ursus Books & Prints Carlyle hotel, 981 Madison Ave. (at 76th St.), mezzanine (212) 772-8787 *www.ursusbooks.com*. Other location: 132 W. 21st St.
(between Sixth and Seventh Aves.) (212) 627-5370. Like Bauman (listed in
this section), another stop for well-funded collectors looking for first-rate rarities. Ursus stocks art as well. **Subway:** 6 to 77th St.

SPECIALTY BOOKSTORES

New York has dozens of specialty bookstores focusing on particular fields of
interest—the arts, comics, yoga—you name it. The following list is just a sampling of stores in Manhattan. Many carry a full range of non-specialty titles as
well. The Yellow Pages lists many more, including stores that concentrate on
titles in French, German, Spanish, Russian and other languages.

Art & Architecture

Archivia 1063 Madison Ave. (between 80th and 81st Sts.) (212) 439-9194
www.archivia.com. A wonderful source for books on the decorative arts, architecture and gardening, and an eye-popping collection of coffee-table books.
Subway: 6 to 77th St.

Hacker Art Books 45 W. 57th St. (between Fifth and Sixth Aves.), 5th floor (212) 688-7600 *www.hackerartbooks.com*. A comprehensive shop for the art lover, with new, rare and out-of-print titles. **Subway:** N, R, W to Fifth Ave.

Urban Center Books Villard Houses, 457 Madison Ave. (at 51st St.) (212) 935-3592 *www.urbancenterbooks.com*. The store for both serious students and avid fans of architecture, design and urban planning. **Subway:** 6 to 51st St.

Biography

Biography Bookshop 400 Bleecker St. (at 11th St.) (212) 807-8655. The most comprehensive selection for readers fascinated with the lives of others. A small non-biography section has diversified the shelves in recent years. **Subway:** A, C, E to 14th St.; L to Eighth Ave.

Children
(See also "Toys" later in this chapter.)

Books of Wonder 16 W. 18th St. (west of Fifth Ave.) (212) 989-3270 *www.booksofwonder.com*. **Subway:** F, L, N, Q, R, W, 4, 5, 6 to 14th St.

Comics

Forbidden Planet 840 Broadway (at 13th St.) (212) 473-1576. The city's largest collection of science fiction, fantasy, comics and graphic-illustration books, plus games and toys. **Subway:** L, N, Q, R, W, 4, 5, 6 to 14th St.

St. Marks Comics 11 St. Marks Pl. (between Second and Third Aves.) (212) 598-9439 *www.stmarkscomics.com*. St. Marks boasts a huge merchandise collection and the city's largest back-issue archive. **Subway:** 6 to Astor Pl.

Cosmic Comics 36 E. 23rd St. (between Park and Madison Aves.), 2nd floor (212) 460-5322. **Subway:** 6 to 23rd St.

Cooking & Gourmet

Bonnie Slotnick Cookbooks 163 W. 10th St. (at Seventh Ave.) (212) 989-8962 *www.bonnieslotnickcookbooks.com*. This cozy Village shop is the prime source for out-of-print and antiquarian cookbooks. **Subway:** 1, 9 to Christopher St.

Kitchen Arts & Letters 1435 Lexington Ave. (between 93rd and 94th Sts.) (212) 876-5550 *www.kitchenartsandletters.com*. Food lovers from professional chefs to take-out gourmets will relish the vast collection of more than 10,000 cookbooks here, including rare, hard-to-find, out-of-print, and French-language titles. A browser's delight. **Subway:** 6 to 96th St.

Gay & Lesbian

Creative Visions 548 Hudson St. (near Charles St.) (212) 645-7573 *www.creativevisionsbooks.com*. **Subway:** 1, 9 to Christopher St.

Oscar Wilde Memorial Bookshop 15 Christopher St. (between Sixth and Seventh Aves.) (212) 255-8097 *www.oscarwildebooks.com*. **Subway:** 1, 9 to Christopher St.

Government

U. S. Government Bookstore 26 Federal Plaza (Broadway between Duane and Worth Sts.), 2nd Floor (212) 264-3825 *bookstore.gpo.gov*. Come here for a complete selection of books, pamphlets and forms from the U.S. Government Printing Office—from the Department of Interior's guide to Washington D.C. attractions to IRS bulletins and U.S. Labor Code guides. **Subway:** A, C, 1, 2,3 9 to Chambers St.

History

Chartwell Booksellers Park Avenue Plaza, 55 E. 52nd St. (212) 308-0643 *www.churchill-books.com*. Who knew an entire store could focus solely on books by, about, and with contributions from Winston Churchill and still pay the rent? Actually, a fascinating collection for rare-book collectors and history buffs. **Subway:** 6 to 51st. St.

The Liberation Bookstore 421 Lenox Ave. (at 131st St.) (212) 281-4615. This legendary bookstore dedicated to Africa and the African diaspora is under the threat of closure, so call first. **Subway:** 2, 3 to 135th St.

The Military Bookman 29 E. 93rd St. (at Madison Ave.) (212) 348-1280 *www.militarybookman.com*. The prime stop for books on military, naval and aviation history, with a focus on out-of-print and rare titles. **Subway:** 6 to 96th St.

Revolution Books 9 W. 19th St. (between Fifth and Sixth Aves.) (212) 691-3345. If you're looking for a diehard Marxist who refuses to give up the fight, this utilitarian store is for you. **Subway:** F to 14th St.

Mystery

Armchair detectives will love these three shops, all stocked from floor to ceiling with both new and used mysteries, from the classics to out-of-print titles to rare signed editions to current releases.

Murder Ink 2486 Broadway (between 92nd and 93rd Sts.) (212) 362-8905 *www.murderink.com*. **Subway:** 1, 2, 3, 9 to 96th St.

The Mysterious Bookshop 129 W. 56th St. (between Sixth and Seventh Aves.) (212) 765-0900 *www.mysteriousbookshop.com*. **Subway:** N, R, Q, W to 57th St.; B, D, E to Seventh Ave.

Partners & Crime 44 Greenwich Ave. (at Charles St.) (212) 243-0440 *www.crimepays.com*. **Subway:** 1, 9 to Christopher St.

Religion

Christian Publications 315 W. 43rd St. (between Eighth and Ninth Aves.)
(212) 582-4311 *www.christianpub.com*. The New York metropolitan area's
largest Christian bookstore also stocks music and videos. **Subway:** A, C, E to
42nd St.

J. Levine Books and Judaica 5 W. 30th St. (at Fifth Ave.) (212) 695-6888
www.levinejudaica.com. More than a bookstore—a full resource center for
Judaica. **Subway:** B, D, F, N, Q, R, S, W to 34th St.; 6 to 33rd St.

Theater

Drama Book Shop 723 Seventh Ave. (between 48th and 49th Sts.), 2nd floor
(212) 944-0595 *www.dramabookshop.com*. The resource for books on the arts of
stage and screen, including scripts and screenplays, scene and monologue books,
biographies and more. **Subway:** 1, 9 to 50th St.

Richard Stoddard Performing Arts Books 41 Union Square West (at E.
17th St.), room 937 (212) 645-9576 *www.richardstoddard.com*. Specialists in
out-of-print performing arts books. **Subway:** L, N, Q, R, W, 4, 5, 6 to 14th St.

Travel

Complete Traveller 199 Madison Ave. (at 35th St.) (212) 685-9007. As well
as a good general-interest selection, the Complete Traveller features a room
dedicated to antiquarian travelogues and guides. **Subway:** 6 to 33rd St.

Traveler's Choice 2 Wooster St. (between Grand and Canal Sts.)
(212) 941-1535. This general-interest bookstore can meet all of your travel-
guide needs. **Subway:** J, M, N, R, Q, W, Z, 6 to Canal St.

Hagstrom Map & Travel Center 57 W. 43rd St. (near Sixth Ave.)
(212) 398-1222; 125 Maiden Lane (at Water St.) (212) 785-5343. The city's
best map publisher runs these two shops, dedicated to cartography and travel
publishing. **Subway:** Midtown: B, D, F, S to 42nd St. Downtown: 2, 3 to Wall St.

Wellness & Eastern Teachings

East-West Books 78 Fifth Ave. (between 13th and 14th Sts.) (212) 243-5994.
The shelves here are stocked with books that do as the name suggests: Bring
Eastern philosophy, healing religion and literature to the West. **Subway:** F, L,
N, R, Q, W, 4, 5, 6 to 14th St.

New York Open Center 83 Spring St. (at Crosby St.) (212) 219-2527
www.opencenter.org. This center for holistic learning also features a small but
well-stocked bookshop. **Subway:** 6 to Spring St.

Quest Bookshop 240 E. 53rd St. (between Second and Third Aves.)
(212) 758-5521 *www.theosophy-ny.org*. This petite shop stocks titles ranging
from Astrology to Zoroastrianism. **Subway:** 6 to 51st St.

Cameras & Electronics

With the terrific buys available on the Web these days, New York isn't the discount electronics mecca it once was. Unless you've done your homework, stay out of the shady electronics stores that line Broadway near Times Square. Also avoid the stretch along Canal Street near East Broadway, where the hawkers will surely take advantage of your good nature given a chance.

If you are in the market for a cordless phone or VCR and don't feel like venturing downtown to J&R (below), East 86th Street between Second and Third Avenues is uptown's Electric Avenue, with **Circuit City** (232-240 E. 86th St., 212-734-1694) and **The Wiz** (1534-1536 Third Ave. at 86th St., 212-876-4400) within shouting distance.

B&H Photo-Video 420 Ninth Ave. (at 34th St.) (212) 444-6615 *www.bhphotovideo.com*. Many professional photographers wouldn't consider going anywhere else. This superstore sells everything an amateur or pro could want, from an impressive selection of cameras to dark-room equipment. Video equipment, lighting, pro audio and telescopes also fill the cavernous space, as does a decent selection of used merchandise. **Subway:** A, C, E to 34th St.

J&R Music/Computer World 23 Park Row (between Beekman and Ann Sts., across from City Hall Park) (212) 238-9000 *www.jandr.com*. J&R is New York's premier electronics store, shining for both its extensive range of merchandise and its reasonable prices. Just about anything that plugs in or uses a battery can be found here, from travel irons to Palm Pilots, cameras to iMacs. Great prices on CDs, too. **Subway:** 4, 5, 6, N, R to Brooklyn Bridge–City Hall.

Olden Camera & Lens Co. 1265 Broadway (between 31st and 32nd Sts.) (212) 725-1234. This Herald Square standard carries a full timeline of photography equipment, from the most technologically advanced to used Super 8's, with prices that are equally diverse. **Subway:** B, D, F, N, Q, R, S, W to 34th St.

Clothing

Below are just few particularly well-dressed standouts from a monster crop of clothing stores that blanket the Manhattan map. If you're in the market for couture wear, the big-name designers have one or more boutiques in one or more locations: On Fifth Avenue in the 50's, on Madison Avenue and/or in SoHo. See "Midtown & Uptown Shopping" and "Downtown Shopping" earlier in this chapter for addresses—and don't forget about the city's stellar department and discount stores, of course, also listed earlier in this chapter.

Men's & Women's

H&M 640 Fifth Ave. (at 51st St.) (212) 489-0390 *www.hm.com*. Other locations: 1328 Broadway (at 34th St.) (212) 564-9922; 558 Broadway (between Prince and Spring Sts.) (212) 343-8313. Fashion-forward wearables for men and women at low, low prices from Swedish discounter Hennes & Mauritz. The youthful looks won't outlast the season—but when it's $7 for a tiny T, who cares? Accessories are so cheap they're almost free. **Subway:** E, F to Fifth Ave.

Kenneth Cole 610 Fifth Ave. (at 48th St.) (212) 373-5800 *www.kennethcole.com*. Check for other locations. The shoewear designer has really arrived with this brand-new Rockefeller Center flagship store, which will dress you from head to toe in Kenneth Cole's modern, casually glamorous clothing as well as shoes. Stylish outerwear and accessories add the finishing touches. **Subway:** B, D, F, S to 47th-50th St.–Rockefeller Center.

Seize sur Vingt 243 Elizabeth St. (between Houston and Prince Sts.) (212) 343-0476 *www.16sur20.com*. Made-to-measure businesswear with downtown flair is the stock in trade at this marvelous NoLIta shop. Bespoke suits come in clean, slim, contemporary lines for both men and women. Divine Egyptian cotton shirts are both custom-tailored and pre-sized for men and women; sweaters and accessories are part of the picture now, too. **Subway:** F, S to Broadway–Lafayette St.; N, R to Prince St.

Thomas Pink 520 Madison Ave. (at 53rd St.) (212) 838-1928 *www.thomaspink.co.uk*. Other location: 1155 Sixth Ave. (near 44th St.) (212) 840-9663. This legendary British shirt maker has taken the Big Apple by storm with its beautifully cut, classically crafted button-downs (all made from finest quality twofold pure cotton poplin) in bold colors and patterns that add a dramatic twist to the tradition. Men's ties come in dame-catching jewel tones. **Subway:** E, F to Fifth Ave.

Women's Only

Women looking for up-and-coming designers selling unique but wearable fashions at affordable prices will do well to browse East 9th Street between Second Avenue and Avenue A, where stars include **Jill Anderson** (331 E. 9th St., 212-253-1747), who unites a retro-reminiscent sensibility and the clean lines of modernism in her distinctly feminine, trend-proof and utterly stylish clothing; don't miss her Italian widow's dress, which can go corporate or clubhopping depending on how you accessorize. Another stunner on the block is **Selia Yang** (328 E. 9th St., 212-254-9073), who specializes in stunning special-occasion sheath dresses, including beaded and bridal versions. Meghan Kinney's easy-to-wear, figure-accentuating separates are available at **Meg** (312 E. 9th St., 212-260-6329), while **Mark Montano** (434 E. 9th St., 212-505-0325, *www.markmontano.com*) defines retro glamour with Jackie O-inspired fashions.

NoLIta is another excellent neighborhood for fresh fashion looks. Check out **Mayle** (252 Elizabeth St. between Houston and Prince Sts., 212-625-0406), whose vintage-inspired looks have even made a few famous fans.

Anthropologie 85 Fifth Ave. (at 16th St.) (212) 627-5885 *www.anthropologie.com*. Other location: 375 West Broadway (between Spring and Broome Sts.) (212) 343-7070. Romantic, exotic-tinged fashions for slender women who like a feminine look. Bias cuts and fluttery fabrics are part of the picture, as are embroidered silks and delicate accessories. **Subway:** F, L, N, Q, R, W, 4, 5, 6 to 14th St.

Daryl K 21 Bond St. (at Lafayette St.) (212) 777-0713 *www.darylk.com.* Other location: 208 E. 6th St. (at Third Ave.) (212) 475-1255. Some of the city's best casually hip urban streetwear and clubwear comes out of this NoHo boutique. Women who can wear her body-hugging, bootlegged pants swear by them; her jeans, T's, and miniskirts are dynamite, too. Values abound at the East Village outlet store. **Subway:** F, S to Broadway–Lafayette St.; 6 to Bleecker St.

Diane von Furstenberg 385 W. 12th St. (at Washington St.) (646) 486-4800 *www.dvf.com.* The Me Decade's favorite designer gets serious props for understanding the fashion-forward value of a Meatpacking District location. Her slim, clingy, 70's look is back in style in a big way, and prices are reasonable considering the designer label. **Subway:** A, C, E to 14th St.

Eileen Fisher 395 West Broadway (between Spring and Broome Sts.) (212) 431-4567 *www.eileenfisher.com.* Other locations: 103 Fifth Ave. (near 18th St.) (212) 924-4777; 521 Madison Ave. (at 53rd St.) (212) 759-9888; 314 E. 9th St. (between First and Second Aves.) (212) 529-5715; check for more locations. Eileen Fisher's gorgeous clothing is for stylish, grown-up women who prefer season-transcending cuts that bespeak ease and movement over trendy look-at-me wear. The lines may be simple, but the fabrics—from crinkly silks to cashmere—rich textures and colors are stunning. The West Broadway flagship carries the full line, while the narrow 9th Street store is an outlet of sorts that's great for bargain hunters. **Subway:** N, R to Prince St.; C, E to Spring St.

Kirna Zabête 96 Greene St. (between Houston and Prince Sts.) (212) 941-9656 *www.kirnazabete.com.* Kirna Zabête is every stylish girl's new favorite SoHo shop, thanks to racks full of ultra-chic wearables from such hard-to-find designers as Alice Roi and Balenciaga; delightful accessories and home accents that surpass the SoHo standard; and fab mod décor that even includes a couple of iMacs to entertain significant others of the male persuasion who are far less enchanted than you are. **Subway:** F, S to Broadway–Lafayette St.; N, R to Prince St.

Children's

Bebe Thompson 1216 Lexington Ave. (between 82nd and 83rd Sts.) (212) 249-4740. The atmosphere here is exclusive and the prices high, but it's worth visiting for the very best in delightful, well-crafted imported European wear for infants and children up to size 16. **Subway:** 4, 5, 6 to 86th St.

Bu & the Duck 106 Franklin St. (between Church St. and West Broadway) (212) 431-9226 *www.buandtheduck.com.* It is apparent from the inviting atmosphere and quality merchandise that owner and designer Susan Lang really likes kids—and understands them. Gone are pastels and the cartoony farm animals;

instead, Lang's vintage-inspired clothing and shoes are bold and interesting, practical and playful. A real gem. **Subway:** 1, 9 to Franklin St.

Calypso Enfant 426 Broome St. (between Lafayette and Crosby Sts.) (212) 966-3234. The store for chic SoHo babies and kids (or parents who want them to be), boasting bright, offbeat togs and toys—some with a tropical flair, all with designer price tags. **Subway:** N, R to Prince St.; 6 to Spring St.

Jacadi 1281 Madison Ave. (between 91st and 92nd Sts.) (212) 369-1616. Other location: 787 Madison Ave. (at 67th St.) (212) 535-3200. Beautiful, French-designed clothing for infants and children and all the accessories to match, including shoes, tights and hats. Although the prices are high, it's a pleasure to shop here, where the air is blissfully free of the off-putting attitude found at many Madison Avenue children's boutiques. Look for the sales, often in January and June. **Subway:** 6 to 96th St.

Lilliput/Lilliput SoHo Kids 240 & 265 Lafayette St. (between Spring and Prince Sts.) (212) 965-9567 or (212) 965-9201 *www.lilliputsoho.com*. These sibling shops offer an enjoyably eclectic selection of apparel for babies and youngsters for parents who'd rather not outfit their kids in uniform Gap or Oshkosh B'Gosh. Prices on some imported labels can soar, but most are reasonable. Shoes, accessories and toys are also in the mix. **Subway:** 6 to Spring St.; N, R to Prince St.

Peanutbutter & Jane 617 Hudson St. (between 12th and Jane Sts.) (212) 620-7952. This fun store for teenagers as well as younger kids stocks clothes and accessories that brim with the imagination of youth and funky West Village style. The eclectic mix ranges from girlish party dresses to leather skirts. **Subway:** A, C, E to 14th St.; L to Eighth Ave.

Zitomer 969 Madison Ave. (between 75th and 76th Sts.) (212) 737-4480 *www.zitomer.com*. This chic Upper West Side apothecary (*see "Beauty" earlier in this chapter*) is also well known for its high-quality selection of children's clothing, especially designer-label party and flower-girl dresses, plus little-man clothing from labels like Burberry's and Tommy Hilfiger. **Subway:** 6 to 77th St.

Vintage, Thrift & Resale

Allan & Suzi 416 Amsterdam Ave. (at 80th St.) (212) 724-7445. This terrific boutique is often overlooked by thrifty shoppers who can't see beyond the Superfly-meets-Dance Fever windows. That's just fine—there's more one-of-a-kind finds for the rest of us. Most of the collection is a thoughtfully selected and well-organized 20th-century fashion timeline, from gently worn bell-bottoms to pristine couture gowns worn once and cast aside. **Subway:** 1, 9 to 79th St.

Antique Boutique 712 Broadway (between Washington Pl. and 4th St.) (212) 460-8830. This huge store offers a wealth of one-of-a-kind cheapies (and some not so cheap), with new, used and vintage apparel targeted at the youth market. Expect vibrant Hawaiian shirts from the 50's and print polyester ones from the 70's, as well as wonderfully worn Levi's and leather jackets. **Subway:** 6 to Astor Pl.; N, R to 8th St.

Foley & Corinna 108 Stanton St. (between Essex and Ludlow Sts.) (212) 529-2338. This warm and wonderful Lower East Side boutique specializes in hand-picked vintage finds, creative restructurings of vintage pieces (such as old T's with new beaded trim), and vintage-inspired new designs. **Subway:** F to Delancey St. or Second Ave.; J, M, Z to Essex St.

Housing Works Thrift Shop 143 W. 17th St. (between Sixth and Seventh Aves.) (212) 366-0820 *www.housingworks.org*. Other locations: 202 E. 77th St. (at Third Ave.) (212) 772-8461; 306 Columbus Ave. (between 74th and 75th Sts.) (212) 579-7566. Fashionable clothing, accessories, books, housewares, furniture and more. The wares are almost always excellent quality, and the proceeds benefit people living with HIV and AIDS. **Subway:** F, 1, 2, 3, 9 to 14th St.

Michael's 1041 Madison Ave. (between 79th and 80th Sts.), 2nd floor (212) 737-7273 *www.michaelsconsignment.com*. This elegant consignment boutique boasts top-shelf designer wear in like-new condition—but for a fraction of the original prices. Don't expect dated styles—society dames shed this season's Chloé, Chanel and Manolos faster than you'd think. The Bridal Salon is a savvy gal's dream come true. **Subway:** 6 to 77th St.

Resurrection 217 Mott St. (between Prince and Spring Sts.) (212) 625-1374. Other location: 123 E. 7th St. (between First Ave. and Ave. A) (212) 228-0063. Vintage wears like-new price tags here, but designer threads chosen with an artist's eye make up the coolest, most pristine collection of retro-wear in the city. Expect an emphasis on the 1960's and 70's, with such designer names as Gucci and Halston peppering the racks. **Subway:** N, R to Prince St.; 6 to Spring St.

Screaming Mimi's 382 Lafayette St. (between 4th and Great Jones Sts.) (212) 677-6464. Laura Wills's legendary store boasts a top-notch collection of vintage threads, all at reasonable prices. Every piece is something special, whether it's a vivid floral design stamped onto an A-line mini-dress or a perfect vintage suit from the 40's. Housewares, bags, shoes, lingerie, even vintage New York souvenirs are on hand, all prettily displayed. **Subway:** 6 to Bleecker St.

Tokio 7 64 E. 7th St. (between First and Second Aves.) (212) 353-8443 *www.tokio7.com*. Here's a funky designer consignment shop for the downtown set, featuring gently used couture from labels like Anna Sui, Helmut Lang and Vivienne Westwood. **Subway:** 6 to Astor Pl.

Salvation Army Thrift Store 536 W. 46th St. (between 10th and 11th Aves.) (212) 757-2311. If shopping by the pound appeals to you, then don't miss this two-level thrift emporium. An entire floor is devoted to furniture and appliances, and the clothing department is a chaotic maze with prizes for the patient bargain-hunter. **Subway:** A, C, E to 42nd St.

Flea Markets

Manhattan's flea markets offer wonderful opportunities for bargain hunters in search of antiques and collectibles. Whether your grail is pristine Lustreware, vintage velvet Elvis paintings or old opera 78's, you have a good shot at finding what you want at the **Annex Antiques Fair and Flea Market** (212-243-5343, *www.annexantiques.citysearch.com*), the city's biggest and best outdoor flea market, held in a series of adjoining parking lots on Sixth Avenue between 24th and 27th Streets every Saturday and Sunday year-round. Some of New York's finest retro merchants started out here, so you can expect top-quality finds in furnishings, clothing and jewelry. Once you're done, head over to the **Garage**, (112 W. 25th St. at Sixth Ave., 212-647-0707). At 23,000 square feet, the Garage is the city's largest indoor market, also brought to life every Saturday and Sunday.

Right around the corner, things take root a bit at the **Chelsea Antiques Building** (110 W. 25th St. between Sixth and Seventh Aves., 212-929-0909) with 12 floors of permanent stalls and prices so attractive that the city's antiques dealers come to buy here; open daily.

Food Markets

Agata & Valentina 1505 First Ave. (at 79th St.) (212) 452-0690. The focus is on the foods of Sicily at this wonderful gourmet market. You won't find a better selection of olives, oils, and Italian meats and cheeses in the city, and the prepared foods surpass the gourmet-market standard. Pricey? Yes, but the quality and service are peerless. **Subway:** 6 to 77th St.

Barney Greengrass 541 Amsterdam Ave. (between 86th and 87th Sts.) (212) 724-4707. The self-proclaimed "Sturgeon King" has been a fixture on the Upper West Side since 1929, selling caviar, smoked fish and herring since 1908 out of the sit-down deli and shop. The sturgeon is exquisitely moist and thin, as is the smoked salmon. The excellent whitefish salad, borscht and chicken livers can also be carried out or eaten in the lively diner. **Subway:** 1, 9 to 86th St.

Chelsea Market 88 10th Ave. (between 15th and 16th Sts.) (212) 243-5678. This brick-walled ex-cracker factory overflows with wonderful purveyors of gourmet goods, from bakers to butchers to professional kitchenware hawkers. You can lunch at several small restaurants inside and outside the concourse. **Subway:** A, C, E to 14th St.; L to Eighth Ave.

Citarella 2135 Broadway (at 75th St.) (212) 874-0383 *www.citarella.com*. Other location: 1313 Third Ave. (at 75th St.) (212) 874-0383. What was always the city's best seafood market has expanded in recent years to excel on all gourmet fronts. The store is bright and well organized and the prepared foods are first-rate. Choice and service like this comes at a price, but Citarella offers great value and service. **Citarella To Go** (Sixth Ave. at 49th St.) makes a great lunch stop in the Rockefeller Center area; an adjacent full-service restaurant opened in mid-2001. **Subway:** 1, 9 to 79th St.

Dean & Deluca 560 Broadway (at Prince St.) (212) 431-1691
www.dean-deluca.com. So what if prices are stratospheric? This gorgeous SoHo
grocer is New York's best. A mecca for well-heeled foodies, Dean & Deluca
offers picture-perfect produce, stunning flowers by the bunch, and dazzling
selections of pâtés, cheeses, meats, fish, baked goods and prepared foods, all
handsomely displayed, clearly labeled and knowledgeably attended. A small
selection of fine cookware and cookbooks are nestled in back. **Subway:** N, R to
Prince St.

Grace's Marketplace 1237 Third Ave. (at 71st St.) (212) 737-0600. Grace
Balducci and her husband, Joe Doria, created the marketplace a dozen years
ago. Like her family's downtown shop, **Balducci's** (424 Sixth Ave. at 9th St.,
212-673-2600), it offers fine service, stunning displays of produce, wonderful
baked goods and cheeses, quality smoked and fresh meats and fish, fresh pastas,
whole-bean coffee and everything else worth wanting in a gourmet grocery. Pre-
made sandwiches are excellent and fairly priced. **Subway:** 6 to 68th St.

Grand Central Market Grand Central Terminal, Lexington Ave. (between
42nd and 44th Sts.) *www.grandcentralterminal.com*. The crown jewel of Grand
Central's glorious renovation is this spiffy gourmet food mart, where the array of
first-rate vendors include **Koglin German Hams** (212-499-0725) for quality
cold cuts and meats; **Adriana's Caravan** (212-972-8804) for spices from around
the world; **Pescatore Seafood Company** (212-557-4466) for a first-quality
range of fresh catches; and **Li-Lac Chocolates** (212-370-4866) for old-fashioned
handcrafted sweets. **Subway:** S, 4, 5, 6, 7 to 42nd St.

Kam Man Food Products 200 Canal St. (between Mott and Mulberry Sts.)
(212) 571-0330. **Kam Kuo Foods** 7 Mott St. (on Chatham Square at Park
Row) (212) 349-3097. These two markets are New York's largest Asian grocers.
Kam Man specializes in fresh and bulk foods, including barbecued meats, fresh
water chestnuts, fresh and dried fish, pickled vegetables, dozens of soy and
hoisin sauces, a broad selection of fresh vegetables and specialties from Vietnam
and Thailand. Smaller, with fewer cooked foods and less produce, Kam Kuo carries frozen Chinese foods, a large selection of teas and cooking utensils. The
staff is generally friendly in both crowded stores. The language barrier can be
formidable, but English-language signs at Kam Kuo help matters. **Subway:** J, M,
N, Q, R, W, Z, 6 to Canal St.

Russ & Daughters 179 E. Houston St. (between Allen and Orchard Sts.)
(212) 475-4880 *www.russanddaughters.com*. Sunday morning is when Jewish
customers observe their post-sabbath ritual at the Lower East Side's premier
gourmet market—buying smoked fish, cream cheese and sturdy, old-fashioned
bagels home-made at nearby Kossar's bakery. Schmooze with the countermen,
who will tell you how to prepare the excellent herring. Prices are lower than in
most uptown stores, even for the divine caviar. **Subway:** F to Second Ave.

Vinegar Factory 431 E. 91st St. (near York Ave.) (212) 987-0885.
Eli's Manhattan 1411 Third Ave. (between 80th and 81st Sts.)
(212) 717-8100. To rival his uncles on Broadway (*see* **Zabar's** *below*) Eli Zabar

turned an old vinegar factory into a gourmet market overflowing with top-quality produce, cheese, meat, fish, prepared foods, fresh flowers, baked goods and Eli's tasty breads, as well as wines and housewares. Prices—even for tomatoes grown in the rooftop greenhouse—are not unreasonably high. A pleasant brunch is served on weekends. Eli's Manhattan offers virtually the same products and services, as well as an oyster and sushi bar and a cafe open daily (except Sat. in summer). **Subway:** 4, 5, 6 to 86th St.

Union Square Greenmarket E. 17th St. and Broadway (212) 477-3220. The city's premier greenmarket is held alfresco year-round at Union Square (Mon., Wed., Fri., Sat., 7 A.M.–6 P.M.), with the biggest markets on Saturday and Wednesday when producers from New York, New Jersey and Pennsylvania jam the area. Here you might discover crosnes (tiny snail-like vegetables that taste like Jerusalem artichokes but don't require peeling), diminutive Japanese turnips and baby Chinese cabbages, whole-foods, baked goods, exotic fresh flowers and more. Everything is fresh, lots of organics are on hand, and prices tend to be low. More important, this is the real New York: diverse, friendly and enthusiastic. Call for times and locations of other city greenmarkets. **Subway:** L, N, Q, R, W, 4, 5, 6 to 14th St.

Zabar's 2245 Broadway (at 80th St.) (212) 496-1234 *www.zabars.com*. Visiting this West Side institution is like dropping into a scene from Manhattan, complete with Woody Allen in the frame. It's particularly well known for its smoked fish and herring counter, where you can sample the goods before your smoked nova is sliced paper-thin. Other delights include hundreds of cheeses, condiments, breads, cold cuts and pâtés, kosher foods and an array of prepared foods, including divine rice and tapioca puddings (no greens, though). Service is fast and efficient. There are bargain housewares on the second floor, and a corner cafe features hot foods and sandwiches. **Subway:** 1, 9 to 79th St.

Ethnic Markets

With immigrants from virtually every country living in New York, intrepid foodies can really go around the world in a day. Be aware that some smaller markets will not take credit cards or checks; call ahead if it matters.

For the city's best Chinese, Vietnamese and Thai foodstuffs, see **Kam Man Food** and **Kam Kuo Foods**, above; for Italian goods, see **Agata & Valentina**; and for Jewish favorites, see **Barney Greengrass** and **Russ & Daughters**.

English: Myers of Keswick 634 Hudson St. (between Jane and Horatio Sts.) (212) 691-4194. **Subway:** A, C, E to 14th St.; L to Eighth Ave.

German: Schaller & Weber 1654 Second Ave. (between 85th and 86th Sts.) (212) 879-3047 *www.schallerweber.com*. **Subway:** 4, 5, 6 to 86th St.

Indian: Foods of India 121 Lexington Ave. (between 28th and 29th Sts.) (212) 683-4419. **Subway:** 6 to 28th St.

Japanese: Katagiri & Co. 224 E. 59th St. (between Second and Third Aves.) (212) 755-3566 or (212) 838-5453 (gift store) *www.katagiri.com*. **Subway:** 4, 5, 6 to 59th St.

Korean: Han Arum Market 25 W. 32nd St. (between Broadway and Fifth Ave.) (212) 695-3283. **Subway:** B, D, F, N, Q, R, S, W to 34th St.

Latin American: Mosaico 175 Madison Ave. (between 33rd and 34th Sts.) (212) 213-4700. Restaurant and grocer. **Subway:** 6 to 33rd St.

Mexican: Kitchen Market 218 Eighth Ave. (at 21st St.) (212) 243-4433. **Subway:** C, E to 23rd St.

Middle Eastern: Kalustyans 123 Lexington Ave. (between 28th and 29th Sts.) (212) 685-3451 *www.kalustyans.com.* Excellent selection of spices and beans. **Subway:** 6 to 28th St.

Polish: Kurowycky Meat Products 124 First Ave. (between 7th St. and St. Marks Pl.) (212) 477-0344. **Subway:** 6 to Astor Pl.

West African: West African Grocery 535 Ninth Ave. (between 39th and 40th Sts.) (212) 695-6215. **Subway:** A, C, E to 42nd St.

Gifts & Homewares

New York is such a home-design mecca that the list of shops below barely scratches the surface. Shoppers looking for one-of-a-kind home décor and accents can't go wrong exploring Madison Avenue in the 80's for luxury goods with a European flair. SoHo and adjacent NoLIta are best for offbeat and international looks—Lafayette Street, in particular.

The West Village is a delight for browsers. The leafy, town-house-lined streets run the style gamut. Boutiques range from **The Lively Set** (33 Bedford St. near Downing St., 212-807-8417), a charming shop overflowing with collectible-quality home and garden accents from days past, to **Flight 001** (96 Greenwich Ave. at Seventh Ave., 212-691-1001, *www.flight001.com*), for the grooviest travel-related goods, both chic and practical, around. And be sure to check out modern **Mxyplyzyk** (123 and 125 Greenwich Ave. at 13th St., 212-989-4300), a fun-filled shop offering high-design housewares, arty toys for grown-ups and the like, all at affordable prices.

Additionally, East 59th Street has blossomed into a home-design mecca of late, no doubt inspired by the arrival of the **Terence Conran Shop**, London's high-design twist on IKEA-style home décor, located in the Bridgemarket complex—worth a look in itself for its stunning architecture (407 E. 59th St. at First Ave., 212-755-9079, *www.conran.com*). Joining Sir Terence in the area are upscale boutiques such as **Extraordinary*** (below), **Royal Hut** (328 E. 59th St., 212-207-3027, *www.royalhut.com*) and the ultra-elegant domain of **Mary Vinson** (wife of Island Records king Chris Blackwell), offering stunning cross-cultural furnishings and textiles from, or inspired by, Africa and Asia.

Also, don't pass up a chance to browse **ABC Carpet & Home** (below) or ten-gorgeous **Takashimaya** (*see* "Department Stores" *earlier in this chapter*). For less pricey housewares try the massive **Bed, Bath & Beyond** (620 Sixth Ave. at 18th St., 212-225-3550; 410 E. 61st St. at First Ave. 646-215-4702; *www.bedbathandbeyond.com*). Consider **Bacarrat** and **Tiffany & Co.** for crystal and silver, Fifth Avenue style (*see* "Jewelry" *later in this chapter*).

ABC Carpet & Home 881 and 888 Broadway (at 19th St.) (212) 473-3000 *www.abccarpet.com.* Two landmark buildings house the city's crown jewel of home shopping, with 10 floors abundantly stocked with luxury home furnishings. The first floor indulges shoppers with eclectic tastes in home accessories, from baby Tiffany lamps to bead-fringed cashmere pillows. On other floors you will find a wide-ranging mix that includes Indonesian wooden chests, flat screen TVs, mid-century modern office chairs, luxury linens, imported fabrics on the bolt and much, much more. And of course, there are the rugs—a whole building, in fact, dedicated to helping you find that perfect gabbeh to place beneath your feet. **Subway:** L, N, Q, R, W, 4, 5, 6 to 14th St.

The Apartment 101 Crosby St. (between Prince and Spring Sts.) (212) 219-3066 *www.theapt.com.* This super-groovy shop, outfitted like a real New York apartment, has done a divine job of blurring the line between public and private, art and commerce: You can browse and buy the clever modern goods on display in every room, from the bed itself to the slippers half-hidden underneath. Beyond the pop value, the goods are first-rate. **Subway:** N, R to Prince St.; 6 to Spring St.

Apartment 48 48 W. 17th St. (between Fifth and Sixth Aves.) (212) 807-1391. The coolest new home store in town, which takes The Apartment concept (above) one step further, expanding the design spectrum from antique to sleek—and cozying it up substantially in the process. **Subway:** F, L, N, Q, R, W, 4, 5, 6 to 14th St.

Avventura 463 Amsterdam Ave. (at 82nd St.) (212) 769-2510 *www.forthatspecialgift.com.* This stunning Upper West Sider is two stores in one: One side is stocked with eye-catching art glass from the best Italian artisans, while the other boasts beautifully displayed Italian table settings and serveware. The Carlo Moretti glassware alone is worth a look. Prices are high, as is the quality. **Subway:** 1, 9 to 79th St.

Breukelen 69 Gansevoort St. (between Washington and Greenwich Sts.) (212) 645-2216. The Meatpacking District has come on strong of late, but funky form tends to prevail over function in the majority of just-plain-silly postmodern shops. Not so at Breukelen, a stunning shop overflowing with the finest in contemporary design, from furniture to lighting to tableware, much of it Scandinavian-inspired and designed by Brooklyn-based designers. **Subway:** A, C, E to 14th St.; L to Eighth Ave.

Chelsea Garden Center 435 Hudson St. (at Morton St.) (212) 727-7100 *www.chelseagardencenter.com.* This loftlike space is a haven of green in the concrete jungle. The marvelous store sells everything from bonsai-scale cacti to full sets of garden furniture, plus all the essentials for city gardening and gorgeous garden-inspired gifts. **Subway:** 1, 9 to Houston St.

Extraordinary* 251 E. 57th St. (at Second Ave.) (212) 223-9151 *www.extraordinaryny.com.* This warm and wonderful gallery is one of the city's best-kept secrets for gifts. The store overflows with portable home accents handcrafted around the world, including cracked eggshell bowls and vases from

Vietnam, Japanese lacquer boxes and coasters, horn-carved dishes from Madagascar and much, much more. The collection is uniformly stunning thanks to owner J.R. Sanders's museum-trained eye. Best of all, prices are shockingly low—it's easy to find a special gift for $50 or less—and hours are long (daily until 10 P.M.). **Subway:** 4, 5, 6 to 59th St.

MoMA Design Store 44 W. 53rd St. (between Fifth and Sixth Aves.) (212) 767-1050 *www.momastore.org.* The best museum shop in the city is operated by the Museum of Modern Art, and it's stylish and well stocked enough to compete in the big leagues of home décor stores. The modern goodies range from clever toys and desktop accessories to licensed reproductions of Alvar Aalto free-form vases, Eames chairs and the like. Look for a new SoHo location at (81 Spring St. at Crosby St.) to open soon. **Subway:** E, F to Fifth Ave.

Nomad Shop 110 Thompson St. (between Prince and Spring Sts.) (917) 237-1500. Come to this SoHo boutique for offbeat gifts from around the world, from African cloth table linens to sisal baskets and chopsticks in day-glo hues. **Subway:** N, R to Prince St.; C, E to Spring St.

Pearl River 277 Canal St. (at Broadway) (212) 431-4770 *www.pearlriver.com.* Other location: 200 Grand St. (between Mott and Mulberry Sts.) (212) 966-1010. These sister department stores are the best places to shop in Chinatown for exotic souvenirs, from paper lanterns to mandarin-collared silk pajamas to Hong Kong action videos. The three-floor Canal Street branch is the larger of the two. **Subway:** J, M, N, Q, R, W, Z, 6 to Canal St.

Jewelry

All of the biggest names in diamonds, gold and platinum have dazzling boutiques on Fifth Avenue in the 50's, often with a second location on Madison Avenue. Witness **Bulgari** (*www.bulgari.com*), whose bold, flashy Italian jewels can be had at 730 Fifth Avenue at 57th Street (212-315-9000), and 783 Madison Avenue between 66th and 67th Streets (212-717-2300); and **Cartier** (*www.cartier.com*), whose glamorous French designs are available at 653 Fifth Avenue at 52nd Street (212-753-0111), 725 Fifth Avenue (Trump Tower) at 56th Street (212-308-0843), and 828 Madison Avenue at 69th Street (212-472-6400). Additionally, Fifth Avenue is home to the glamorous, timeless wedding sets of **Harry Winston** (718 Fifth Ave. at 56th St., 212-245-2000, *www.harrywinston.com*), considered "King of the Diamonds"; and **Van Cleef & Arpels** (744 Fifth Ave. at 57th St., 212-644-9500, *www.vancleef.com*), with its movie-star glamorous jewels. The crystal, gold and silver pieces of **Baccarat** (625 Madison Ave. at 59th St., 212-826-4100, *www.baccarat.fr*) are surprisingly modern, while the first name in estate jewelry and Oscar baubles is **Fred Leighton** (773 Madison Ave. at 66th St. 212-288-1872).

Those looking for cutting-edge styles and lower prices will do well to browse NoLIta, where a good number of fashion-forward jewelry designers have set up shop, including **Me & Ro** (239 Elizabeth St. between Prince and Houston Sts., 917-237-9215, *www.meandrojewelry.com*), whose beautiful contemporary designs—many with Near East inspirations that lend them a gypsy feel—

appeared on Julia Roberts in *The Mexican*. **Push** (240 Mulberry St. at Spring
St., 212-965-9699, *www.pushjewelry.com*), showcases Karen Karch's rough-
hewn, nature-inspired, gem-studded jewelry. Two blocks west, **Jill Platner** (113
Crosby St. at Prince St. 212-324-1298, *www.jillplatner.com*) showcases her own
marvelous aboriginal-inspired silver collars and bracelets, many strung on
brightly colored Gortex, lending her pieces a wonderfully contrary modern feel.

For antique pieces, browse the stalls at the **Manhattan Art & Antiques
Center** (1050 Second Ave. at 55th St., 212-355-4400, *www.the-maac.com*),
where a number of dealers specialize in collectible jewelry of yore, or visit **Doyle
& Doyle** (*see* "Antiques" *earlier in this chapter*).

Fortunoff 681 Fifth Ave. (at 54th St.) (212) 758-6660 *www.fortunoff.com*.
Known for fine merchandise and competitive prices, Fortunoff boasts one of the
city's largest selections of fine jewelry, and an especially impressive selection of
silver and other bridal registry staples. Stone cuts and designs stick close to the
classics, but the discount prices are very attractive. **Subway:** E, F to Fifth Ave.

H. Stern 645 Fifth Ave. (at 51st St.) (212) 688-0300. Other location: 301 Park
Ave. (at 49th St., in the Waldorf=Astoria) (212) 753-5595. This elegant Brazilian company specializes in high-end contemporary designs, with many pieces at
the affordable end of the spectrum. Some of the pieces are crafted with unusual
semiprecious stones. **Subway:** E, F to Fifth Ave.

Mikimoto 730 Fifth Ave. (between 56th and 57th Sts.) (212) 457-4600
www.mikimotoamerica.com. This beautiful Japanese shop is known exclusively
for high-luster cultured pearls. While countless perfect strands come from Mikimoto's own farms, you can also find some of New York's most respectable South
Sea and fresh-water varieties. **Subway:** E, F, N, R, W to Fifth Ave.

Reinstein/Ross 29 E. 73rd St. (at Madison Ave.) (212) 772-1901
www.reinsteinross.com. Other location: 122 Prince St. (between Greene and
Wooster Sts.) (212) 226-4513. This fine jeweler has been a huge hit with young
brides in search of a more exotic look than mainstream jewelers offer. Expect
matte finishes, intricate detailing and unusual gems. **Subway:** 6 to 77th St.

Stuart Moore 128 Prince St. (at Wooster St.) (212) 941-1023. This futuristic
jewel box is the place to come for the sleekest, most ultra-modern designs
around in fine jewelry, including wedding sets. **Subway:** N, R to Prince St.

Tiffany & Co. 727 Fifth Ave. (at 57th St.) (212) 755-8000 *www.tiffany.com*.
Long before Holly Golightly gazed into its jewel-bedecked windows, Tiffany's
was firmly established as one of the world's premier jewelers. The collection is
remarkable, ranging from affordable silver everyday pieces in signature Tiffany
designs to nature-inspired and jewel-studded baubles soaring into the thousands.
The collection is elegantly displayed on multiple floors; don't be shy about just
stopping into browse—everybody else does. The fine china, sterling silver and
crystal are also magnificent. Small pieces—money clips, key chains and the
like—for less than $100 mean even shoppers with limited budgets can depart
with a signature blue box in tow. **Subway:** E, F, N, R, W to Fifth Ave.

Tourneau 12 E. 57th St. (between Fifth and Madison Aves.)
(212) 758-7300 *www.tourneau.com*. Other locations: 500 Madison Ave. (at
52nd St.) (212) 758-6098; 200 W. 34th St. (at Seventh Ave.) (212) 563-6880.
Hands down, the city's finest collection of watches is available at Tourneau, particularly at the large 57th Street location, called **Tourneau Time Machine**,
where brands range from Swiss Army to Rolex. **Subway:** E, F, N, R, W to Fifth
Ave.

Unusual Wedding Rings 4 W. 47th St., booth 86 (212) 944-1713
www.unusualweddingrings.com. Bill Shifrin and son-in-law Howard Rotenberg
are well known throughout New York as the "Wedding Ring Kings." Their stall
at the National Jewelers Exchange is the best place in the Diamond District to
buy beautifully designed, top-quality wedding sets in gold and platinum at
below-market prices. (*For more on bargain hunting in the* **Diamond District**, *see*
"Bargain Shopping" *earlier in this chapter.*) **Subway:** B, D, F, S to 47th-50th
St.–Rockefeller Center.

Leather, Handbags & Luggage

Altman Luggage 125 Orchard St. (between Delancey and Rivington Sts.)
(212) 254-7275 *www.altmanluggage.com*. For fairly priced utilitarian bags, brief-
cases, computer bags and luggage, head to this Lower East Side discounter with
an extensive selection that includes reliable brand names like Travelpro, Sam-
sonite and Jansport. **Subway:** F to Delancey St.; J, M, Z to Essex St.

Bottega Veneta 635 Madison Ave. (between 59th and 60th Sts.)
(212) 371-5511 *www.bottegaveneta.com*. This Gucci offshoot specializes in fine
woven leather and other chic handbags—with shoes and coats (and designer
price tags) to match. **Subway:** 4, 5, 6 to 59th St; N, R to Lexington Ave.

Coach 595 Madison Ave. (at 57th St.) (212) 754-0041 *www.coach.com*. Check
for other locations. Known for butter-soft leather and classic handbag designs,
Coach has hipped up its high-quality everyday lines of late, adding vivid colors,
21st-century fabrics, and fashion-forward backpacks, computer bags, shoes, and
travel and pet accessories to the mix. The Madison and 57th Street branches
carry the largest selections. **Subway:** 4, 5, 6 to 59th St.; N, R, W to Fifth Ave.

Gucci 685 Fifth Ave. (at 54th St.) (212) 826-2600 *www.gucci.com*. Gucci king
Tom Ford has revolutionized the gorgeous Gucci line of handbags and luggage,
reinventing the pieces in bold shapes and dressing them in sexy leathers in
addition to the traditional Gucci logo pattern. The best of couture luggage, bar
none. **Subway:** E, F to Fifth Ave.

Jutta Neumann 158 Allen St. (between Stanton and Rivington Sts.)
(212) 982-7048. German-born leather worker Jutta Neumann has crafted her
own bold-lined, brightly hued line of handbags, backpacks, wallets and sandals.
Her leather cobbling style may be retro, but her designs are entirely fashion-
forward. Not cheap, but well worth the dough. **Subway:** F to Second Ave.

kate spade 454 Broome St. (at Mercer St.). (212) 274-1991
www.katespade.com. Everybody knows about handbag and accessories maven
Kate Spade by now; her cute rectangular totes are carried by stylish, *Sex and the
City*-watching gals all around the world. Here's ground zero for her super-chic
collection, which has expanded to include accessories, pajamas, stationery and a
travel line large enough to justify its own store, **kate spade travel** (59 Thompson St. at Spring St., 212-965-8654). **Subway:** N, R to Prince St.

Louis Vuitton 116 Greene St. (between Spring and Prince Sts.)
(212) 274-9090. Other locations: 49 E. 57th St. (between Park and Madison
Aves.) (212) 371-6111; 703 Fifth Ave. (at 55th St.) (212) 758-8877. The most
instantly recognizable designer leather goods and luggage on the planet is the
perpetually chic Vuitton line. The empire has expanded to include bold fashions, shoes, outerwear, and even travel guides over the years, but the unmistak-
ably monogrammed bags—from totes to steamer trunks—are the heart of the
matter. **Subway:** N, R to Prince St.

Manhattan Portage Factory Store 333 E. 9th St. (between First and Second
Aves.) (212) 995-5490 *www.manhattanportageltd.com*. First loved for their
durable, colorful, made-in-New York messenger bags finished with a red skyline
logo, Manhattan Portage is also the place to go for those hip one-shoulder backpacks that everybody's wearing these days. **Subway:** 6 to Astor Pl.

Original Leather Store 171 W. 4th St. (between Sixth and Seventh Aves.)
(212) 675-0303 *www.originalleather.com*. Other locations: 552 La Guardia Pl.
(between Bleecker and 3rd Sts.) (212) 777-4362; 84 Seventh Ave. (between
15th and 16th Sts.) (212) 989-1120; check for more locations. Greenwich Village is well known for its collection of leather houses hawking outerwear at discount prices, but Original Leather boasts the best selection, usually without the
hard sell that's so common in this district. **Subway:** A, C, E, F, S to W. 4th St.

Village Tannery 173 Bleecker St. (between Macdougal and Sullivan Sts.)
(212) 673-5444. Other location: 742 Broadway (between Astor and Waverly
Places) (212) 979-0013. Original Leather (above) excels in the jacket department, but Village Tannery is cream of the crop when it comes to high-quality
leather handbags, backpacks and accessories. **Subway:** A, C, E, F, S to W. 4th St.

Music

Greenwich Village is a record-hunting bonanza just north of Houston Street,
mainly along Bleecker and West 3rd Streets. Between Sixth and Seventh
Avenues, the highlights include legendary **Bleecker Bob's Golden Oldies** (118
W. 3rd St. near Sixth Ave., 212-475-9677), a dirty hole of a store that's nevertheless a prime source for vinyl collectors; **Bleecker St. Records** (239 Bleecker
St. near Carmine St., 212-255-7899), a real standout for its clean and well-organized selection of CDs and vinyl, which runs the genre gamut from blues, folk
and golden oldies to 70's punk and current rock; **Vinylmania** (60 Carmine St.
near Bedford St., 212-924-7223, *www.vinylmania.com*), a prime stop for DJs as

well as hip-hop, classic funk and current dance music fans. East of Sixth Avenue, **Generation Records** (210 Thompson St. between Bleecker and W. 3rd Sts., 212-254-1100), is a bright and well-organized store specializing in hardcore sounds upstairs, plus one of the city's best used CD departments downstairs; and **Second Coming Records** (231-235 Sullivan St. near W. 3rd St., 212-228-1313), offering a good selection of new and used vinyl and CDs, from 60's soul to post-millennium drum 'n' bass. **Rebel Rebel** (319 Bleecker St. at Christopher St., 212-989-0770) is the place for U.K. imports from glam to alt-pop to techno.

In the East Village, St. Marks Place between Second and Third Avenues is another prime hunting ground, especially for used CDs. Standout shops on the street-party block are **Sounds** (20 St. Marks Pl., 212-677-3444), and **Joe's CDs** (11 St. Marks Pl., 212-673-4606), both renowned for their bargain-basement prices; **Mondo Kim's** (6 St. Marks Pl., 212-598-9985, *www.kimsvideo.com*), for anything weird on CD, DVD and video; and **13** (13 St. Marks Pl. 212-477-4376), an orderly shop boasting standout collections in rock, metal, country, blues, jazz and folk. Around the corner is **Wowsville** (125 Second Ave., 646-654-0935, *www.wowsville.net*), a hoot of a shop specializing in 60's psychedelia, Ramones-era punk, psychobilly and other underground sounds on vinyl, CD and video. Around the corner on Third Avenue is **Norman's Sound & Vision** (67 Cooper Sq., 212-473-6610), a tidy, well-stocked store with a straightforward selection of new and used CDs.

If you're in the market for musical instruments, West 48th Street between Sixth and Seventh Avenues is your neighborhood. The block's big kahuna is **Sam Ash** (160 W. 48th St., 212-719-2299, *www.samashmusic.com*), hawking everything from pro-DJ turntable systems to Les Pauls and Flying V's to the latest in accordions. **48th Street Custom Guitars** (170 W. 48th St., 212-764-1364) specializes in axes.

Academy Records & CDs 12 W. 18th St. (between Fifth and Sixth Aves.) (212) 242-3000 *www.academy-records.com*. This tidy, relaxed shop is the prime city stop for used classical, opera, jazz and soundtrack LPs and CDs. **Subway:** F, L, N, Q, R, W, 4, 5, 6 to 14th St.

Colony Music Center 1619 Broadway (at 49th St.) (212) 265-2050 *www.colonymusic.com*. Housed in the legendary Brill Building—the Tin Pan Alley of the 50's and 60's, where songwriters like Neil Diamond and Goffin and King crafted such pop classics as "I'm a Believer" and "Locomotion"—this emporium of nostalgia doesn't offer any bargains, but it does have an excellent selection of vintage vinyl and CD reissues of classic and contemporary pop vocalists and Broadway cast recordings. A wide range of sheet music is also on hand, especially if you're looking for the latest *NSync hit or Broadway score. **Subway:** N, R to 49th St.

Footlight Records 113 E. 12th St. (between Third and Fourth Aves.) (212) 533-1572 *www.footlight.com*. Serious aficionados of cast recordings, big band, pop vocalist and spoken-word collectibles should skip Colony and head straight for this collectors' favorite.**Subway:** L, N, Q, R, W, 4, 5, 6 to 14th St.

Jazz Record Center 236 W. 26th St. (between Seventh and Eighth Aves.), room 804 (212) 675-4480 *www.jazzrecordcenter.com*. Frederick Cohen's shop has the best selection of jazz, both on vinyl and CD, in New York, including a phenomenal choice of out-of-print records. A must for serious listeners. **Subway:** C, E, 1, 9 to 23rd St.

Joseph Patelson Music House 160 W. 56th St. (near Seventh Ave.) (212) 582-5840 *www.patelson.com*. Where better to house the city's finest collection of classical sheet music—some 47,000 titles—than behind Carnegie Hall? The phenomenal collection features both common and unusual scores and sheet music, even metronomes and pitch pipes. **Subway:** N, R, Q, W to 57th St.; B, D, E to Seventh Ave.

Other Music 15 E. 4th St. (between Broadway and Lafayette St.) (212) 477-8150 *www.othermusic.com*. Eclectica is treated like academia at this super-cool store, which spans the globe and expands your mind with other-worldly sounds. You can find cult classics (MC5, Holy Modal Rounders), groove and free jazz, as well as 70's Krautrockers who make Kraftwerk seem like a household name. This is also the place for the most esoteric new releases, including the farthest-out electronica, avant-garde and Japan-only releases. A perfect antidote to Tower Records across the street. **Subway:** 6 to Bleecker St.

Stern's Music 71 Warren St. (near West Broadway) (212) 964-5455 *www.sternsmusic.com*. This tri-continental cubby (with outposts in London and São Paulo) is a prime source for world music, especially African and Brazilian. **Subway:** 1, 2, 3, 9 to Chambers St.

Tower Records 692 Broadway (at 4th St.) (212) 505-1500 *www.towerrecords.com*. Other location: 1961 Broadway (at 66th St.) (212) 799-2500. The nation's best chain music retailer has a veritable compound surrounding the Greenwich Village corner of Broadway and E. 4th Street, where you'll not only find the mainstream retail outlet (including Tower's first-rate classical department) but also **Tower Books and Video** (383 Lafayette St., 212-505-1166); the adjacent **Tower Outlet** (212-228-5100, where cutouts and discontinued titles are so cheap they're practically free; and the new **Tower World Music** store (20 E. 4th St., 212-505-1500). **Subway:** 6 to Bleecker St.; F, S to Broadway–Lafayette St.

Virgin Megastore 1540 Broadway (at 45th St.) (212) 921-1020 *www.virginmega.com*. Union Square location, 52 E. 14th St. (212) 598-4666. Richard Branson's rollicking entertainment complex—complete with huge CD collection, listening posts, extensive video and DVD department, small but eclectic bookstore, cafe, even a travel agent and multiplex movie theater—is a Times Square attraction unto itself. Don't let the neon overwhelm you; the selection is excellent, new releases are usually on sale, and star-studded appearances are not uncommon. **Subway:** N, Q, R, S, W, 1, 2, 3, 7, 9 to 42nd St.

Shoes

Known for its cutting-edge fashion sense, New York has an endless supply of shoe retailers. Madison Avenue is the place to be if you're willing to pay top dollar for the biggest names, from practical **Timberland** (709 Madison Ave. at 63rd St., 212-754-0436, *www.timberland.com*), to smart sophisticates **Cole Haan** (667 Madison Ave. at 61st St., 212-421-8440, *www.cole-haan.com*) and **Bally of Switzerland** (628 Madison Ave. at 59th St., 212-751-9082, *www.ballyswiss.com*), to stiletto mavens **Stuart Weitzman** (625 Madison Ave. at 59th St., 212-750-2555, *www.stuartweitzman.com*) and **Sergio Rossi** (835 Madison Ave. near 70th St. 212-396-4814, *www.sergiorossi.it*).

SoHo and adjacent NoLIta are tops for shoe fanatics looking for top quality with a twist, be it from **Camper** (125 Prince St. at Wooster St., 212-358-1842), offering runway-hot updates on the classic bowling shoe and other smart-comfy styles; funky, punky, youth-minded **John Fluevog** (250 Mulberry St. at Prince St., 212-431-4484, *www.fluevog.ca*); strappy, sexy **Sigerson Morrison** (28 Prince St. near Elizabeth St., 212-219-3893, *www.sigersonmorrison.com*); or Prada's playful **Prada Sport** line (116 Wooster St. near Prince St., 212-925-2221).

For the latest trendy footwear at affordable prices, stroll 8th Street between Fifth and Sixth Avenues in Greenwich Village, and newly cutting-edge Orchard Street in the Lower East Side, where you'll find such outposts of hip as **alife** (178 Orchard St. near Houston St., 646-654-0628).

The major department stores also have sizable shoe departments offering a sampling of famous labels, from casual to couture. Another great place to shop for shoes is in stylish clothing boutiques that carry their own lines, such as the **Kenneth Cole** flagship store or **Jeffrey New York** (*see* "Clothing" *and* "Department Stores" *earlier in this chapter*). For athletic shoes, you can't beat **Niketown** or **Modell's** (*see* "Sporting Goods" *later in this chapter*). Also try the many jeans-and-sneakers stores along Broadway between 8th and Canal Streets.

Arche 10 Astor Pl. (between Broadway and Lafayette St.). (212) 529-4808. Check *www.arche-shoes.com* for additional locations. Women's casual shoes don't get more comfortable than these French-made sandals and slip-ons, which come in a rainbow of soft nubucks that feel like suede but wear beautifully. **Subway:** 6 to Astor Pl.

Church's English Shoes Check phone book for new location. *www.churchsshoes.com*. Thanks to top-quality leather and craftsmanship and an unwavering devotion to classic styles, Church's has been a standard bearer in men's shoes since 1873. Church's benchcrafted oxfords, monk straps and moccasins are still the height of fashion among well-dressed traditionalists. **Subway:** E, F to Fifth Ave.; 6 to 51st St.

Harry's Shoes 2299 Broadway (at 83rd St.) (212) 874-2035 *www.harrys-shoes.com*. If you prefer comfort and quality over spiked heels and flashy couture labels, head to Harry's for the biggest and best selection of shoes for the entire family. You name it, Harry's has it, from American and Euro comfort brands like Rockport, Mephisto, Ecco, Clark's and Dansko to weekend footwear by New Balance, Birkenstock and Teva to kid favorites Keds and Stride Rite. **Subway:** 1, 9 to 86th St.

Jimmy Choo 645 Fifth Ave. (entrance on 51st St.) (212) 593-0800 *www.jimmychoo.com.* These seductive designs unite bold finishes and come-hither allure with the very best materials and workmanship. The sexy women's line is what Jimmy Choo is about, but the eye-catching men's line is worth a look, too. **Subway:** E, F to Fifth Ave.

Manolo Blahnik 31 W. 54th St. (near Sixth Ave.) (212) 582–3007. The first name in ultra-sexy, ultra-luxury pumps and mules for women who firmly believe that it's better to look good than to feel good. Manolo's sultry signatures are pointy toes, narrow stiletto heels and platinum-card pricing. **Subway:** E, F to Fifth Ave.

Otto Tootsi Plohound 38 E. 57th St. (between Park and Madison Aves.) (212) 231-3199. Other locations: 137 Fifth Ave. (near 20th St.) (212) 460-8650; 413 West Broadway (near Spring St.) (212) 925-8931. Europe's funkiest, chunkiest styles for both men and women line the shelves of these whimsical boutiques. Shoes are not cheap, but no other store unites fashion-forward looks and high quality so well. **Subway:** 4, 5, 6 to 59th St.

Varda 147 Spring St. (between West Broadway and Wooster St.) (212) 941-4990. Other location: 786 Madison Ave. (between 66th and 67th Sts.) (212) 472-7552. These gorgeous styles in soft and supple Italian leather are the Manolo equivalent for the mid-priced and more practical woman. Varda's shoes are not only beautifully crafted, but they'll last—and remain in style—for years to come. **Subway:** C, E to Spring St.; N, R to Prince St.

Sporting Goods

Bicycle Habitat 244 Lafayette St. (between Prince and Spring Sts.) (212) 431-3315 *www.bicyclehabitat.com.* Downtown's most highly regarded bike shop is this friendly SoHo cubby, featuring wheels from Trek and Specialized, plus Mercian custom road frames, rentals and repairs. **Subway:** 6 to Spring St.; N, R to Prince St.

Bicycle Renaissance 430 Columbus Ave. (at 81st St.) (212) 724-2350. Selling everything from the newest mountain and racing models to custom bikes built by in-house professionals, this well-regarded shop also offers repair services. For all the expertise found here, the prices are moderate and the attitude friendly to all comers. **Subway:** 1, 9 to 79th St.

Eastern Mountain Sports 611 Broadway (near Houston St.) (212) 505-9860 *www.shopems.com.* Other location: 20 W. 61st St. (at Broadway) (212) 397-4860. If you are planning a camping trip, learning to kayak or just want the best insect repellent for a Central Park picnic, EMS can meet your needs. They sell several top labels as well as their own sturdy brand of outdoor wear and gear. **Subway:** F, S to Broadway–Lafayette St.; 6 to Bleecker St.

Modell's 200 Broadway (between Fulton and John Sts.) (212) 964-4007 *www.modells.com*. Manhattan Mall location, 901 Sixth Ave. (at 32nd St.) (212) 594-1830; call (888) 783-7790 for more locations. Family owned and operated since 1889, Modell's can't be beat for one-stop athletic wear and sporting goods shopping. A range of brand names fill the racks, from Reebok to Rollerblade to Spalding, and prices are fair. The place to come for a range of home team souvenirs, too. **Subway:** A, C to Broadway–Nassau St.; J, M, Z, 2, 3, 4, 5 Fulton St.

NBA Store 666 Fifth Ave. (at 52nd St.) (212) 515-NBA1 *www.nbastore.com*. This tri-level mega-store is a high-tech multimedia celebration of pro-basketball, both NBA and WNBA. **Subway:** E, F to Fifth Ave.

Niketown 6 E. 57th St. (between Fifth and Madison Aves.) (212) 891-6453. This high-design five-story advertorial for all things Nike carries the full line, all stunningly displayed. You'll pay full retail prices, but the shopping experience is first-class. **Subway:** N, R, W to Fifth Ave.

Paragon Sports 867 Broadway (at 18th St.) (212) 255-8036 *www.paragonsports.com*. Manhattan's definitive sporting goods store, this sprawling shop covers all the bases, from racquet sports and golf to ice skating and sailing, and equipment is top of the line. Prices can be steep, but sales are gold mines. **Subway:** L, N, Q, R, W, 4, 5, 6 to 14th St.

Patagonia 101 Wooster St. (between Prince and Spring Sts.) (212) 343-1776 *www.patagonia.com*. Other location: 426 Columbus Ave. (between 80th and 81st Sts.) (917) 441-0011. The first name in eco-friendly fleece and other nature-minded sports and adventure wear for men, women and kids (no gear, though). **Subway:** N, R to Prince St.; 6 to Spring St.

Scandinavian Ski & Sports Shop 40 W. 57th St. (between Fifth and Sixth Aves.) (212) 757-8524. Come to this cozy midtown nook before you hit the slopes to meet all your ski and board needs, from boots, goggles, parkas and poles to high-end après ski wear. **Subway:** N, R, W to Fifth Ave.

Yankees Clubhouse Shop 245 W. 42nd St. (between Seventh and Eighth Aves.) (212) 768-9555 *www.yankees.com*. Check for more locations. The Big Apple's favorite home team has its own mini-chain of boutiques where you can pick up everything from logo jerseys to home-game tickets.

   The Mets keep a similar, smaller-scale store (143 E. 54th St. near Lexington Ave., 212-888-7508), where Shea-bound fans can score tickets.
Subway: Yankees store: A, C, E, N, Q, R, S, W, 1, 2, 3, 7, 9 to 42nd St. Mets store: 6 to 51st St.

Stationery & Paper Goods

Jamie Ostrow 876 Madison Ave. (between 71st and 72nd Sts.) (212) 734-8890. There's no better stop in town for custom stationery, business cards and invitations. The emphasis is on bold fonts and contemporary looks. **Subway:** 6 to 68th St.

Kate's Paperie 561 Broadway (between Prince and Spring Sts.)
(212) 941-9816 *www.katespaperie.com*. Other locations: 8 W. 13th St. (between Fifth and Sixth Aves.) (212) 633-0570; 1282 Third Ave. (between 73rd and 74th Sts.) (212)396-3670. If you're in the market for stationery with a twist, eye-catching invitations for your next get-together or wrap that will make your gifts really pop, come to Kate's, the best paper store in New York. The selection is large and also features beautifully bound journals and albums, fountain pens, and more, including custom stationery. **Subway:** N, R to Prince St.

Ordning & Reda 253 Columbus Ave. (between 71st and 72nd Sts.)
(212) 799-0828 *www.ordning-reda.com*. Other locations: 1035 Third Ave. (between 61st and 62nd Sts.) (212) 421-8199; 1088 Madison Ave. (between 81st and 82nd Sts.) (212) 439-6355. Straight angles and Mondrian-inspired primary colors are the keynotes of this Swedish paper and design company. Bring order to your home and office with such clever solutions as the business-card filing book and the perfect desktop stapler. **Subway:** 1, 2, 3, 9 to 72nd St.

Papivore 117 Perry St. (near Hudson St.) (212) 627-6055 *www.papivore.com*. This fragrant, candlelit shop sells the simple, delicate stationery of Parisian papermaker Marie-Papier. Think simple lines and soft sherbet hues and you'll get the picture. Custom cards and invites, too. **Subway:** 1, 9 to Christopher St.

Toys

Alphaville 226 W. Houston St. (near Varick St.) (212) 675-6850 *www.alphaville.com*. Specializing in vintage toys from the 1940's through the 70's, this gallery-like shop is entirely for grown-ups—ones who may look like doctors, lawyers and investment bankers on the outside, but are nostalgic kids at heart. The collection runs the gamut from vintage Mr. Potato Heads to classic Paint-by-Numbers sets, but there's a strong emphasis on TV-themed and outerspace toys. **Subway:** 1, 9 to Houston St.

Big City Kite Company 1210 Lexington Ave. (at 82nd St.) (212) 472-2623 *www.bigcitykites.com*. This entire store is a loving ode to kites. Choices range from delicate, artful tissue-paper creations to utilitarian plastic varieties that can withstand the learning curve of first-time fliers. The wonderful staff also offers repair services. **Subway:** 4, 5, 6 to 86th St.

Classic Toys 218 Sullivan St. (between Bleecker and 3rd Sts.) (212) 674-4434. Both kids and collectors love this toy store for its wide range of old and new toys, from diecast trucks and Matchbox cars to the latest modern playthings. More than a century's worth of toy soldiers are on display, as is a fascinating collection of antique toys. **Subway:** A, C, E, F, S to W. 4th St.

Dinosaur Hill 306 E. 9th St. (near Second Ave.) (212) 473-5850. Toys from around the world can be found in this tiny, fanciful East Village space: old-fashioned American wooden blocks, Latin American masks, marbles, puppets, crafts and much more, as well as a good selection of children's literature. **Subway:** 6 to Astor Pl.

Enchanted Forest 85 Mercer St. (between Spring and Broome Sts.)
(212) 925-6677. This fantastical gallery (designed by the set designer Matthew
Jacobs) is a child's dream world actualized, from its forest of fuzzy beasts to a
Victorian room straight from C.S. Lewis's Narnia tales. The emphasis is on toys
based on the classic model meant to stimulate the imagination, rather than
video games and the like. The selection of children's books really shines. **Subway:** N, R to Prince St.; 6 to Prince St.

F.A.O. Schwarz 767 Fifth Ave. (at 59th St.) (212) 644-9400 *www.fao.com*.
Long before Tom Hanks danced down a set of piano keys here in the movie *Big*,
this toy-filled fantasyland was the number one-destination of choice for any
kid—and with good reason. The enormous store buzzes with the zaps and beeps
of toys and the squeals of delighted children. The selection is dazzling, and
whole departments are dedicated to big-name toymakers—Lego, Barbie, Nintendo, Gund, and so on. You'll find everything here but a bargain. **Subway:** N,
R to Fifth Ave; 4, 5, 6 to 59th St.

Wine Shops

New York has the best selection of wine shops in the world; no other city comes
close. Standouts include **Sherry-Lehmann**, regularly lauded as among the best
wine shops in the world; **Morrell and Co.**, boasting a sumptuous wine bar and
cafe in the adjacent storefront; **Chelsea Wine Vault** at Chelsea Market; and, on
the Upper West Side, **67 Wines & Spirits** and **Acker** and **Merrall & Condit**.
These are full service shops where the clerks are knowledgeable and always
ready to rescue the clueless—provided it's not during a busy Saturday morning
or in the middle of the frantic holiday season.

Bargain hunters often head to **Garnet Wines & Liquors**, **Best Cellars**,
Crossroads Wine & Liquor and **Astor Wines & Spirits**. The atmosphere in
these shops, particularly Garnet, can be hectic, so savvy customers try to know
what they want before they push open the doors. If business is slow, which it
rarely is, the staff can be most helpful. And prices can be appealingly low.

New York has its specialists, too. When they run short on Romanee-Conti,
Burgundy lovers head for the **Burgundy Wine Company** in the West Village,
where you usually have to ring the bell and wines are often selected from an
order book rather than samples on the very tiny floor.

Looking for a special Barolo or a little-known Chianti? Take a trip to the
Italian Wine Merchants. Some of New York's best-known restaurateurs, Mario
Batali (Babbo, Esca, Lupa) and Lydia Bastianich (Becco, Felidia), are partners
in this first-class shop. Devotees of rare old Bordeaux know they are likely to
find what they want at **Royal Wine Merchants**.

—Frank Prial

Acker, Merrall & Condit 160 W. 72nd St. (between Broadway and Columbus
Ave. (212) 787-1700 *www.ackermerrall.com*. **Subway:** 1, 2, 3, 9 to 72nd St.

Astor Wines & Spirits 12 Astor Pl. (at Lafayette St.) (212) 674-7500
www.astoruncorked.com. **Subway:** 6 to Astor Pl.

Best Cellars 1291 Lexington Ave. (at 87th St.) (212) 426-4200
www.best-cellars.com. **Subway:** 4, 5, 6 to 86th St.

Burgundy Wine Company 323 W. 11th St. (between Greenwich and Washington Sts.) (212) 691-9092. **Subway:** A, C, E, 1, 2,3, 9 to 14th St.; L to Eighth Ave.

Chelsea Wine Vault Chelsea Market, 75 Ninth Ave. (at 15th St.)
(212) 462-4244 *www.chelseawinevault.com*. **Subway:** A, C, E to 14th St.; L to Eighth Ave.

Crossroads Wine & Liquor 55 W. 14th St. (between Fifth and Sixth Aves.) (212) 924-3060. **Subway:** F to 14th St.

Garnet Wines & Liquors 929 Lexington Ave. (at 68th St.) (212) 772-3211 *www.garnetwine.com*. **Subway:** 6 to 68th St.

Italian Wine Merchants 108 E. 16th St. (near Union Square East) (212) 473-2323 *www.italianwinemerchant.com*. **Subway:** L, N, Q, R, W, 4, 5, 6 to 14th St.

Morrell and Co. 1 Rockefeller Plaza (at 49th St.) (212) 981-1106
www.morrellwine.com. **Subway:** B, D, F, S to 47th-50th St.–Rockefeller Center.

Royal Wine Merchants 25 Waterside Plaza (at the East River near 23rd St.)
(212) 689-4855 *www.royalwinemerchants.com*. **Subway:** 6 to 23rd St.

Sherry-Lehmann 679 Madison Ave. (at 61st St.) (212) 838-7500
www.sherry-lehmann.com. **Subway:** N, R to Fifth Ave.; 4, 5, 6 to 59th St.

67 Wines & Spirits 179 Columbus Ave. at 67th St. (212) 724-6767
www.67wine.com. **Subway:** 1, 9 to 66th St.

New York for Children

Most adults tend to think of New York as a less-than-hospitable place for children: all concrete and steel, with a cultural life appreciated mainly by the sophisticated. But real New Yorkers know that the city could not be more welcoming to the young. The parks system more than makes up for the lack of street-side greenery, and the Urban Park Rangers' free weekend programs demonstrate that peregrine falcons and raccoons as well as Wall Street moguls reside here. **Central Park**, which all Manhattan children regard as their personal backyard, offers playgrounds, a Swedish marionette theater, Belvedere Castle, which presents free nature workshops, and a recently refurbished children's zoo. And in the Bronx, there's the **Everett Children's Adventure Garden** at the New York Botanical Garden, a paradise of plants and interactive exhibits that invites children to learn about the flowers as well as smell them.

In addition to the **Central Park Zoo**, several other wildlife centers compete with the world-class **Bronx Zoo**. The **Queens Zoo** specializes in American species (this is where the buffalo still roam), while the **Staten Island Zoo** offers a prodigious reptile collection and a "Breakfast With the Beasts" program for children several times a year. Brooklyn is home to the alluring **New York Aquarium**, where children can observe dolphin and orca shows, get nose to nose with sharks and handle crabs and starfish in a "touch tank" (the aquatic equivalent of a petting zoo).

Indoor New York also provides a wealth of fun and learning. Almost all of the major cultural institutions have young people's programs, from the **Museum of Modern Art** to the **American Museum of Natural History**, which is New York's answer to Jurassic Park, with its magnificently redone hall of dinosaurs. In the outer boroughs, young people's attractions range from the **BAM Family** series at the Brooklyn Academy of Music to the enormous insect collection at the **Staten Island Institute of Arts and Sciences**.

But while most of New York's famous places welcome children, there are some locations that were built with them especially in mind. The following are a few of the best places and programs to visit if you're 12 or under—or love someone who is. (*For children's bookstores, clothing stores and toy stores see chapter* **Shopping in New York**.)

Six Great Places for Kids

New Victory Theater   MIDTOWN WEST
209 W. 42nd St. (between Seventh and Eighth Aves.) (646) 223-3000. If you think of children's theater as marionettes, fairy tales and clowns, you have obviously never visited the New Victory. This is not to say that its productions never use these elements, but if they do, the marionettes are likely to be life-

size, the fairy tales sometimes grim (as well as Grimm), and the clowns more like Bill Irwin than the Three Stooges. Opened in December 1995 as part of the redevelopment of Times Square, the New Victory is Broadway's first theater for families, and it is determined never to condescend to its audiences. Its season (October to May) includes the best productions worldwide, from extravaganzas like the Shanghai Circus and Circus Oz (Australia) to small, intimate productions like *Old Man River,* a one-woman play. Highlights of the 2001-2002 season include a revival of *Peter and Wendy,* a startling reinterpretation of the Peter Pan story, performed by one woman with the help of props and a marionette, and the return of the Fred Garbo Inflatable Theater Company, which takes the themes of comedy and ballooning to new dimensions. Generally geared to children 6 and older, the season also includes "Step Lively: Dance at the New Victory," a series that exposes young people to different forms of dance. Participants in the one-hour programs, which include a question-and-answer session with the audience, have ranged from Suzanne Farrell's ballet troupe to the Peter Pucci Plus Dancers. This is thinking children's theater, with family-friendly prices ($10–$30; $6–$15 for members) and a location that can't be missed: right across from *The Lion King* on 42nd Street.
Subway: A, C, E, N, Q, R, W, 1, 2, 3, 7, 9 to 42nd St.

Theaterworks/USA   CHELSEA
151 W. 26th St. (between Sixth and Seventh Aves.) (212) 647-1100
www.theaterworks.org. You don't have to spend money on Disney to take your children to a memorable musical that will send them (and you) home humming. Theaterworks/USA, founded in 1961, produces both musicals and drama that not only introduce children ages 5 and above to the theater, but also provide them with insights into history that are so entertaining that they may not realize how much they're learning. In the last several years, Theaterworks has illustrated a number of important chapters in the growth of the United States, with plays like *Gold Rush, Young Tom Edison, The Color of Justice* (about Thurgood Marshall and *Brown v. Topeka*) and *Paul Robeson, All-American.* It has also brought literary favorites to the stage, like *Swiss Family Robinson, Ramona Quimby* (based on Beverly Cleary's novels) and *A Christmas Carol.* The 17-show season of hour-long plays runs October to April, with special free productions over the summer. The best works are repeated season to season, but somehow they never get old.
Subway: 1, 9, F to 23rd St.

Children's Museum of Manhattan   UPPER WEST SIDE
212 W. 83rd St. (between Amsterdam Ave. and Broadway) (212) 721-1223
www.CMOM.org. Children are often consumed by fascinating exhibitions, but the Children's Museum of Manhattan is one of the few places where this can be literally true. At "Body Odyssey," they can enter a huge mouth, wander down a human digestive tract (it even pulsates) and shoot blasts of mock digestive juices. This combination of fun and learning is typical of the museum, which is unusual for both the breadth of its offerings and the wide age range it serves. One of its exhibitions, "Wordplay," includes places for infants to crawl, gaze at

mobiles and push buttons as their parents learn about the role of language in their babies' lives. Literacy, in fact, is one of the museum's passions. "Good Grief!," the museum's exhibition on the humor of Charles Schulz and *Peanuts* will continue through April 2002. Coming summer 2002 are two more exhibitions about reading and learning: "Blue's Clues," based on the popular Nickelodeon preschool television show, and "Peter Rabbit," about literature's favorite bad bunny. The Children's Museum is one of only two United States locations for "Peter Rabbit," which is traveling from the Victoria and Albert Museum in London.

Conveniently located on the Upper West Side, the museum also offers the Time-Warner Media Center, an actual television studio where visitors 6 and over can produce their own versions of a newscast or a talk show, and the Sussman Environmental Center, an outdoor oasis for learning about urban ecology. Currently in the midst of a major expansion, the museum will only offer more as the millennium progresses, from a renovated performance theater to a glass-enclosed rooftop garden.
Admission: $6; $3, seniors; children under 1, free. **Hours:** Tue.–Sun., 10 A.M.–5 P.M. **Subway:** 1, 9 to 86th St.

Brooklyn Children's Museum   BROOKLYN
145 Brooklyn Ave. (at St. Mark's Ave.) (718) 735-4400. City chauvinists wouldn't be surprised to learn that the world's first children's museum is in New York. They might be shocked, however, to learn that it's in Crown Heights, Brooklyn. This museum, which celebrated its centennial in 1999, pioneered the hands-on approach characteristic of contemporary children's exhibitions as early as 1904, when it began taking the objects on display out of their glass cases. That's still the philosophy at the museum, which invites children to pluck at musical instruments, handle insect models or try on shoes. Distinctive because it has a permanent collection (very few children's museums do), the Brooklyn Children's Museum has more than 27,000 objects, ranging from an elephant skeleton to Queen Elizabeth II coronation dolls. Early in 2000, the museum opened its Learning Early Gallery, an exhibition space devoted to toddlers. The museum also has a greenhouse, where children can "adopt a plant" and handle earthworms, and a live animal collection whose residents range from furry to scaly. These creatures used to be taken out only for special occasions, but in 2001 the museum opened its Animal Outpost, which puts many of them on permanent display. Children can observe species like frogs and double-crested basilisks while learning about their life cycles through displays that include animal skeletons and a microscope. After all, how many museums invite you to pet a snake?
Admission: $4. **Hours:** Mon., Wed., Thu., noon–5 P.M.; Fri., noon–6:30 P.M.; Sat., Sun., 10 A.M.–5 P.M. Closed Tue. **Subway:** 3 to Kingston Ave.; weekend shuttle bus from Brooklyn Museum and Grand Army Plaza 2/3 subway stations.

Staten Island Children's Museum   STATEN ISLAND
1000 Richmond Terrace (between Tysen St. and Snug Harbor Rd.)
(718) 273-2060. Staten Island was once famous for its landfill, but that's not all that's remarkable about the borough. Consider the Snug Harbor Cultural

Center, home to the Staten Island Children's Museum. Nestled in one of the most bucolic settings a New York institution can boast, the museum has a huge front lawn that is turned into a festival site every spring when the museum hosts its Meadowfair, an indoor-outdoor carnival. (The lawn also has a large praying mantis—or, as the museum puts it, playing mantis—sculpture that children climb on.) Indoors, it's just as enticing, with Block Harbor, an area for preschoolers that includes a pirate ship; Portia's Playhouse, which offers children costumes, props and a stage to act out their fantasies; and permanent exhibitions on irresistible subjects like water and bugs (there's an Arthropod Zoo), as well as traveling displays. Now 20,000 square feet, the museum is expanding into an adjacent turn-of-the-century barn.
Admission: $4; children under 2, free. **Hours:** Tue.–Sun., noon–5 P.M. (Opens at 11 A.M., Jul.-Aug.) **Directions:** Staten Island Ferry to S-40 bus.

New York Hall of Science   QUEENS
47–01 111th St. (at 47th Ave.), Flushing (718) 699-0005 *www.nyhallsci.org*.
Any playground is potentially a lesson in physics. But only one playground in New York is especially designed to teach children the scientific concepts that are behind every sway of the seesaw and zoom down the slide. That is the Science Playground at the New York Hall of Science in Queens, the largest (30,000 square feet) playground of its kind in the Western Hemisphere and winner of several awards since it opened in 1997. In 1999, the Hall of Science opened a companion area, the Sound Playground, which is understandably—and educationally—noisy.

   Although these special playgrounds are open only to children over 6, the Hall of Science, which began as a pavilion for the 1964–65 World's Fair, offers attractions for younger adventurers, too. The Preschool Discovery Place allows them to explore sound, color, light and simple principles of construction, while permanent displays in the Exhibition Hall offer their older siblings forays into the physical world, from the atomic level on up. Major recent additions include "Marvelous Molecules," an in-depth look at the building blocks of all life. In January 2001, the hall opened the Pfizer Foundation Biochemistry Discovery Lab, the first interactive biochemistry lab open to the public. The space invites visitors to explore the chemistry of living things by conducting any of 12 available experiments, on subjects ranging from why roses are red and violets are blue to how bees communicate. Recommended for ages 8 and up, the lab is open to the public on Saturdays and Sundays from noon to 4:45 P.M., and Thursdays and Fridays from 2 to 4:45 P.M. The city's only hands-on science and technology museum, the Hall is best summed up by its own slogan: "Where Minds Play."
Admission: $7.50; $5, children (4–16) and seniors; Thu.–Fri., 2–5 P.M., free.
Credit cards: MC/V; checks. **Hours:** Mon.–Wed., 9:30 A.M.–2 P.M.;
Thu.–Sun., 9:30 A.M.–5 P.M. **Subway:** 7 to 111th St. in Queens.

—Laurel Graeber

Circuses

Big Apple Circus (800) 922-3772 *www.bigapplecircus.org*. With its local roots, intimate one-ring big top and kid-friendly mission, the Big Apple Circus has staked out its own ground between the glitz of Ringling Brothers and the artistry of Cirque du Soleil. Shows are held in the circus's quaint big top in Damrosch Park at Lincoln Center, from late October to early January.

Cirque du Soleil Liberty State Park Park, Jersey City, New Jersey (800) 678-5440 *www.cirquedusoleil.com*. This French-Canadian troupe reaches New York with one of its touring shows about every other year. No animals here, but kids and adults won't miss them—each of the several themed shows includes an incredible variety of performers from clowns and trapeze artists to those with talents you never knew existed. The surreal humor of of these shows may be over the heads of young children, but they'll still be entranced by the spectacle.

Ringling Brothers and Barnum and Bailey Circus Madison Square Garden, Seventh Ave. (at 33rd St.) (800) 755-4000 *www.ringling.com*. The classic American three-ring circus—trapeze artists, lion tamers and all—descends on Madison Square Garden every spring, running shows in March and April.

Museums and Programs for Children

(See "Six Great Places for Kids" in this chapter for **Brooklyn Children's Museum, Children's Museum of Manhattan** *and* **Staten Island Children's Museum**.*)*

Children's Museum of the Arts 182 Lafayette St. (between Broome and Grand Sts.) (212) 941-9198. The museum's home in SoHo includes interactive installations like the ever-popular Ball Pond, a room filled with oversized rubber balls that children can crawl through, and two floors of art studios where children can participate in hands-on projects. There are also exhibits of work by children and adults. **Admission:** $5; seniors and children under 1, free. Cash only. **Hours:** Wed.–Sun., noon–5 P.M. Closed Mon., Tue. **Subway:** N, R to Prince St.

South Street Seaport Museum 207 Front St. (between South and Water Sts.) (212) 748-8600. There is a special children's center here, but all of the nautical galleries, shops and ships are meant to be family-friendly. **Admission:** $6, general; $5, seniors; $4, students. **Hours:** Apr.–Sept.: Daily, 10 A.M.–6 P.M. Oct.–Mar.: Wed.–Mon., 10 A.M.–5 P.M. **Subway:** 2, 3, 4, 5 to Fulton St.

Special Children's Programs at NYC's Top Museums

(For prices, hours and subway directions see museum listings in other chapters.)

American Museum of Natural History Central Park West (at 79th St.) (212) 769-5100. This is a can't-go-wrong trip for families. Kids and adults will find much here to enjoy together, from the Dinosaur Halls to the enormous IMAX theater to the Hall of Ocean Life, with its giant blue whale hanging from the ceiling. The museum's latest attraction for children (and curious adults) is its

new Discovery Room, which opened in June 2001. A huge, two-level space dominated by a model of an African baobab tree (with plenty of artificial creatures in
its branches), the room offers many opportunities to play zoologist, paleontologist,
geologist and anthropologist (and just about any other "ologist" you can think of).

Brooklyn Museum 200 Eastern Parkway, Prospect Park (718) 638-5000
www.brooklynmuseum.org. Kids will enjoy the largest collection of mummies
outside Egypt, as well as an excellent children's workshop.

Guggenheim Museum 1071 Fifth Ave. (at 88th St.) (212) 423-3587. If nothing else, kids will enjoy the fun, spiraling space (but remember, no strollers).
Make time for the cafe, too, and consider coming in for one of the Friday or
Saturday night Jazz sessions. Call ahead to find out about special family programs, like the Family Tour and Art Workshops: tours of current exhibits followed by a hands-on workshop for the whole family. In 2000, the Guggenheim
also introduced "Cinekids," a film program for young visitors. Occurring several
times throughout the year, the program includes not only shorts and features for
children, but by them as well.

The Jewish Museum 1109 Fifth Ave. (at 92nd St.) (212) 423-3200.
The museum offers a diverse series of family programs every Sunday, from
sing-a-longs to storytimes to art activities to theater performances.

Metropolitan Museum of Art 1000 Fifth Ave. (at 82nd St.)
(212) 535-7710. Children and adults alike will find the Met overwhelming,
so come here with a game plan. The "Museum Hunt" guides, available at
information desks, are a good place to start: they present special and permanent collections to kids through fun activities. There are a number of family
tours and workshops, like A First Look, offered Saturdays at 11 A.M. and
2:30 P.M., and Sunday at 11 A.M. These hour-and-a-half sessions introduce
adults and kids (6–12) to art via discussions and art projects. The museum
also offers family films on Saturday from 12:30–1 P.M. and 2–2:30 P.M.

Museum of Modern Art (MoMA) 11 W. 53rd St. (between Fifth and Sixth
Aves.) (212) 708-9805. MoMA offers some of the most extensive and varied
family programs around. The museum is unique in offering Tours for Tots—
introductions to painting and sculpture for kids as young as four. You can also
try the One-at-a-Time drop-in guided walks for kids 5–10, or the Two-in-a-Row
tours (held on two consecutive mornings) for the entire family. Or take a break
from walking, and enjoy MoMA's family films, generally strong in live action,
animation, documentary and fantasy. Films are introduced by a museum educa-
tor who encourages discussion and suggests related activities to pursue in the
galleries. Don't forget the **Donnell Public Library** across the street, which
houses the original Winnie the Pooh collection. **Prices:** One-at-a-Time: $5, per
family; $3, members. Two-in-a-Row: $15, per family; $10, members. Family
Films: $5, per family; members, free. **Hours:** Most family programs are held Sat-
urday mornings, and advance reservations are necessary for most talks and tours.
NOTE: MoMa will be closed for renovation from summer 2002 until 2004. Displays and children's programs will be relocated to **P.S. 1** in Queens.

The Whitney Museum 945 Madison Ave. (at 75th St.) (212) 570-7710.
The Whitney offers programs and activities in conjunction with current exhibitions, encouraging adults and children to learn about American art and culture together. In addition, families can attend a free guided tour every Saturday at 11:30 A.M. No reservations are required.

Music for Children
(For more information see chapter **The Arts***.)*

Amato Opera-in-Brief 319 Bowery (at 2nd St.) (212) 228-8200. In addition to its standard performances, this company has been doing opera for children for over 50 years. The "Brief" performances are fully costumed, abbreviated versions of classic operas, featuring interwoven narration so everyone can follow the story. All performances are only 90 minutes long (including intermission) and should be appropriate for children 5 and up. **Prices:** $15 all seats. **Schedule:** Usually six shows per year, all start at 11:30 A.M., days vary.

Carnegie Hall Family Concerts 152 W. 57th St. (at Seventh Ave.) (212) 903-9670. At these hour-long Saturday afternoon concerts, families get an introduction to music and musical instruments and concepts through a variety of demonstrations and activities led by well-known performers and groups. Kids also get a special "KidsBill," filled with musical activities and information. **Prices:** $5. **Schedule:** Held throughout the season.

Lincoln Center Children's Programs
Many people don't know about the special kids' concerts available at Lincoln Center, most of which feature the same performers as the regular season concerts. Unfortunately, there are only a few of these concerts each year, and schedules can vary from season to season; parents should call well in advance to find out when these shows will be available.

Growing Up With Opera (212) 769-7008. The Metropolitan Opera sponsors two shows each year for kids 4–6 and 6–12, often featuring question-and-answer sessions and "cast parties" with the artists afterward. **Prices:** Avg. $10.

Jazz for Young People Alice Tully Hall (212) 721-6500. Wynton Marsalis hosts and performs at these educational concerts, delving into themes like "What Is Swing Dancing?" and "What Is Afro Cuban Jazz?" Concerts are usually held three Saturdays a year. **Prices:** $15, adults; $10, children 18 and under.

Little Orchestra Society (212) 704-2100. Each season, the Society sponsors three New York Philharmonic concerts geared toward children 6–12 at Avery Fisher Hall, and nine for children 3–5 at Florence Gould Hall (55 E. 59th St.). Shows often sell out, but sometimes same-day tickets do become available.

Meet the Music Alice Tully Hall (212) 875-5788. The Chamber Music Society of Lincoln Center sponsors four concerts each year, introducing children to chamber music.

New York City Opera Family Workshops New York State Theater
(212) 870-5643. These hour-long workshops are held before select City Opera
weekend matinee performances. Children ages 6–12 can participate in musical
numbers with opera performers, as well as other educational activities.

New York Philharmonic Young People's Concerts (212) 721-6500
www.nyphilharmon.org. The Philharmonic offers four of these Saturday afternoon concerts each year, providing a fun introduction to symphonic music for
6–12 year olds. Ticket holders can also attend the one-hour "Children's Promenades" before each concert, where children can participate in music-making
activities and meet members of the orchestra. **Prices:** $6–$24.

Play Spaces

Chelsea Piers Pier 62 (West Side Hwy. and 23rd St.) (212) 336-6500.
Two gyms for kids with some designated free hours. There's also an area for
younger kids that is completely supervised at times. **Subway:** C, E to 23rd St.

Lazer Park 163 W. 46th St. (between Sixth and Seventh Aves.)
(212) 398-3060. A 5,000-square-foot laser tag arena, meant solely for older kids.
Subway: B, D, F, N, Q, R, W, 1, 2, 3, 7, 9 to 42nd St.

Playspace 2473 Broadway (at 92nd St.) (212) 769-2300. This is a bright and
clean operation, with a good cafe for parents. It will be crowded on rainy weekends. It also offers birthday parties and classes. **Subway:** 1, 2, 3, 9 to 96th St.

Rain or Shine 202 E. 29th St. (at Third Ave.) (212) 532-4420.
www.rainorshinekids.com. Everything under one roof: a playhouse, art center and
baby center. Some days they offer puppet shows and free playtime.
Subway: 6 to 28th St.

Puppets

Crowtations Bethesda Fountain, Central Park (mid-park at 72nd St.). In good
weather, this group performs between 1 and 6 P.M. on weekends. **Subway:** 1, 2,
3, 9 to 72nd St.

The Lenny Suib Puppet Playhouse 555 E. 90th St. (between York and East
End Ave.) (212) 369-8890, ext. 159. This large theater offers puppet shows,
magicians, clowns, ventriloquists and storytellers. **Subway:** 4, 5, 6 to 86th St.

Swedish Cottage Marionette Theater Central Park West Drive (at 81st St.)
(212) 988-9093. (*See section* "Central Park" *in chapter* **Exploring New York**.)

Puppetworks 338 Sixth Ave. (at 4th St.), Park Slope, Brooklyn
(718) 965-3391. This group has been performing with their hand-crafted marionettes since 1938. They generally offer three or four stories per year, with performances Saturdays and Sundays. **Subway:** F to Seventh Ave.

Science for Children

(See section "Six Great Places for Kids" earlier in this chapter for **New York Hall of Science**.*)*

Liberty Science Center 251 Phillip St. (at Communipaw Ave.), New Jersey (201) 200-1000 *www.lsc.org*. The Liberty Science Center in Jersey City is an institution that uses interactive exploration to teach visitors about science and technology. Each of the center's three floors is devoted to a specific theme: environment, health and invention. Visitors of all ages can touch starfish or giant insects at the center's many hands-on exhibits, crawl through a 100-foot "touch tunnel," play virtual basketball or see movies on the domed Imax screen. At Roach World, renowned entomologist Betty Faber will teach you everything there is to know about your unwelcome kitchen guests. There are also many temporary exhibitions and IMAX films. **Admission:** $10; $8, children and seniors. **Credit cards:** All major. **Hours:** Daily, 9:30 A.M.–5:30 P.M. **Directions:** Free shuttle buses from the Grove Street PATH train station and the Colgate Center, which is linked by ferry to the World Financial Center in Manhattan.

Sony Wonder Technology Lab 550 E. 56th St. (between Madison and Fifth Aves.) (212) 833-8100. No doubt about it: Sony Wonder Technology Lab is one of the city's coolest destinations for kids, and it's free. Greeted by a talking robot, kids get bar-coded cards that make them part of the lab's attractions. They can produce their own TV shows or remix a song by Celine Dion. At a command center, they can analyze weather data to avert disasters, cruise the Net or watch HDTV. But, keep in mind, this free public space dedicated to technology education is more specifically dedicated to Sony technology education. It just happens to be operated by Sony's retail division, and, not surprisingly, showcases only Sony products. **Admission:** Free. Reservations required. **Hours:** Tue.–Wed., Fri.–Sat., 10 A.M.–6 P.M.; Sun., noon–6 P.M.; Thu., 10 A.M.–8 P.M. **Subway:** E, F to Fifth Ave.; 4, 5, 6 to 59th St.

Theater for Children

(For the **New Victory Theater** *and* **Theaterworks/USA**, *see "Six Great Places for Kids" earlier in this chapter.)*

Arts Connection 120 W. 46th St. (between Sixth Ave. and Broadway) (212) 302-7433. Ask about the "Saturdays Alive" series of affordable performances and workshops. **Subway:** B, D, F, N, Q, R, W, 1, 2, 3, 7, 9 to 42nd St.

Grove Street Playhouse 39 Grove St. (Seventh Ave. and Bleecker St.) (212) 741-6436. This group adapts classics for children with humor for adults, and presents shows in a participatory manner: kids are encouraged to talk, move, and even shout. **Subway:** 1, 9 to Christopher St.

Henry Street Settlement—Abrons Arts Theater 466 Grand St. (at Pitt St.) (212) 598-0400. Weekly Arts for Family series, from puppetry to magic to theater. **Subway:** F to Delancey St.; J, M, Z to Essex St.

Kids 'N Comedy 34 W. 22nd St. (between Fifth and Sixth Aves.)
(212) 877-6115. Monthly children's shows and comedy workshops are offered at
the Gotham Comedy Club for kids 7-15. **Subway:** F, N, R, 1, 9 to 23rd St.

Lunt-Fontanne Theater 205 W. 46th St. (between Eighth Ave. and Broadway) (212) 575-9200. The current home of Disney's ever-popular production of
Beauty and the Beast. **Subway:** A, C, E, N, Q, R, W, 1, 2, 3, 7, 9 to 42nd St.

New Amsterdam Theater 214 W. 42nd St. (between Seventh and Eighth
Aves.) (212) 282-2900. Tickets for the theater's current and seemingly permanent attraction, *The Lion King,* are hard to come by, but Disney does offer tours
of the theater. If you can get your hands on them when Julie Taymor's life-size
animal puppets and costumes lumber down the aisles, pandemonium erupts.
Subway: A, C, E, N, Q, R, W, 1, 2, 3, 7, 9 to 42nd St.

TADA! Youth Ensemble 120 W. 28th St. (between Sixth and Seventh
Aves.) (212) 627-1733. They sell out quickly, but most kids will appreciate
these one-hour original shows performed by 6-to-17-year-old actors. The schedule runs throughout the year, and frequently includes weekday and Friday night
performances. **Subway:** 1, 9, to 28th St.

13th Street Repertory Theater 50 W. 13th St. (between Fifth and Sixth
Aves.) (212) 675-6677. Located in a Greenwich Village brownstone, this 72-
seat theater offers weekend-afternoon children's shows . **Subway:** F to 14th St.

Zoos & Wildlife Centers

Bronx Zoo (Wildlife Conservation Park) 2300 Southern Blvd. at Bronx
Park South (718) 367-1010. *(See section* "The Bronx" *in chapter* **Exploring New
York** *for full listing.)*

Central Park Zoo Fifth Ave. and 64th St. (212) 861-6030. *(See section* "Central Park" *in chapter* **Exploring New York** *for full listing.)*

New York Aquarium for Wildlife Conservation Surf Ave. and W. 8th St.,
Brooklyn (718) 265-3400. Located on a strip of coastline between Coney Island
and Brighton Beach, the aquarium may at first seem prohibitively remote. But
it's out there for a reason, and worth the trip. With more than 300 species of
marine life and an impressive collection of marine mammals, the aquarium has
narrated feedings, underwater viewing areas and up-close animal encounters.
Check out sea lion and dolphin performances in the Aquatheater, as well as the
hands-on Discovery Center. The aquarium also offers seasonal events, like the
Halloween "Sea Monsters" weekend. **Admission:** $9.75, adults; $6, children
2–12 and seniors; children under 2, free. Children under 18 must be accompanied by an adult. Special group rates are available by reservation only. Call
(718) 220-5198. **Hours:** Mon.–Fri., 10 A.M.–5 P.M.; Sat.–Sun., 10 A.M.–6
P.M. **Subway:** F, Q to W. 8th St.; take pedestrian bridge to aquarium.

Prospect Park Zoo 450 Flatbush Ave., Brooklyn (718) 399-7339. It isn't as
comprehensive as the Bronx Zoo, but this 19-acre park is still worth a trip out of

Manhattan. It's extremely kid-friendly, featuring giant lily pads and kid-size goose eggs to play with, plus a "barnyard" with assorted touchable animals. Kids will also enjoy the interactive Wildlife Center, which offers lectures and workshops throughout the year. **Admission:** $2.50, adults; $.50, children 3–12; $1.25, seniors; children under 3, free. No group rates. **Hours:** Open 365 days at 10 A.M.; close, 5 P.M., weekdays, and 5:30 P.M. weekends and holidays, (4:30 P.M. Nov.-Mar.). **Subway:** Q to Prospect Park.

Queens Zoo 111th St. (at 54th Ave.), Flushing, Queens (718) 271-1500. This 11-acre park was renovated in 1992, making it more child-oriented and interactive. Kids will enjoy the aviary, the herd of American bison, and a variety of domesticated animals in the petting zoo. The zoo runs special seasonal programs, too, including an elaborate Groundhog's Day "celebration of prognosticating rodents." **Admission:** $2.50, adults; $1.25, seniors; $.50, children, 3–12; children under 3, free. **Hours:** Open 365 days at 10 A.M.; close, 5 P.M., weekdays and 5:30 P.M., weekends and holidays, April-Oct.; close 4:30 P.M. Nov.-Mar. **Subway:** 7 to 111th St.

Staten Island Zoo 614 Broadway(at Glenwood Pl.) (718) 442-3100. Opened in 1936, the Staten Island Zoo is smaller than the zoos in the other four boroughs, but it holds its own as an educational institution by offering extensive outreach programs. The zoo houses a menagerie of more than 400 animals on its eight acres. There is also an aquarium, a children's zoo where youngsters can feed the animals, a noteworthy display of reptiles, a tropical forest exhibit and a simulation of the African savannah at twilight. **Admission:** $3, adults; $2, children, 3–11; children under 3, free. Wed. after 2 P.M., free. **Hours:** Daily, 10 A.M.–4:45 P.M.

Outdoor Attractions and Activities for Children

(See also "Prospect Park" *in chapter* **Exploring New York** *and chapter* **Sports & Recreation**.*)*

Central Park *(See section* "Central Park" *in chapter* **Exploring New York** *for more detailed information on the park).* Central Park's Children's District (mid-park, 64th–65th St.) offers a wealth of activities, from the **Carousel** and **Wollman Skating Rink** to the **Heckscher Playground.** A good place to start is **The Dairy** (mid-park at 64th St.)—originally a real dairy, now an information center with a variety of activities for children. It also offers an excellent map of the park. Perhaps the most popular children's attraction in the park lies to the east, along Fifth Avenue: the **Children's Zoo**, part of the Central Park Wildlife Conservation Center, has interesting exhibits, a petting zoo and structures (like a giant spider's web) for kids to climb.

Around 74th Street, also on the east side of the park, lies **Conservatory Water**, a popular pond where kids and adults can rent remote controlled boats in the afternoon. Nearby are the well-known statues of **Alice in Wonderland**

and **Hans Christian Andersen** (story readings Wed. and Sat., 11 A.M., at this statue during the summer). Toward the center of the park, around 79th Street, is **Belvedere Castle;** kids will love this miniature storybook castle and the **Nature Observatory** inside. You can also see a show at the **Swedish Cottage Marionette Theater,** located just to the west of the Castle.

If you find yourself above the 97th Street Transverse, you'll want to stop at the **North Meadow Recreation Center** (mid-park, around 98th St.) to borrow one of their great "field kits" for kids, packed with assorted toys and activities to try in the park. And if you're at the very top of the park, plan to spend some time around the body of water known as **Harlem Meer.** From the **Charles A. Dana Discovery Center** to **Conservatory Garden,** with its charming Secret Garden statue, to **Lasker Rink and Pool,** families will easily find a fun way to while away the afternoon.

New York Botanical Garden 200th St. (at Southern Blvd.), the Bronx (718) 817-8705. A 25-minute tram tour gives an excellent overview of the gardens. The Everett Children's Adventure Garden provides eight acres and hours of entertainment. There's a three-foot-high hedge maze that will delight small children, and the Garden's numerous workshops and activities give kids a good introduction to botany and gardening. (*See the section* "The Bronx" *in chapter* **Exploring New York** *for complete description.*)

KID-FRIENDLY RESTAURANTS

Too often taking children out to eat is more about endurance than enjoyment. But these restaurants are welcoming to families, relaxing for parents and adept at putting children at ease, making them less conscious of being on their best behavior.

Upper West Side

Avenue 520 Columbus Ave. (at 85th St.) (212) 579-3194. This informal French restaurant features a baby-food menu, including carrots with a soft but slightly chunky texture, a tasty organic pear purée and a vanilla custard that parents will finish if the baby does not. **Subway:** 1, 9 to 86th St.

Upper East Side

Barking Dog Luncheonette 1678 Third Avenue (at 94th St.) (212) 831-1800. If the children fidget while waiting for the All-American menu items or rich, bountiful desserts, distract them with the restaurant's dog tchotchkes. For families that can't get going in the morning, breakfast is served until 4 P.M. **Subway:** 6 to 96th St.

Pig Heaven 1540 Second Ave. (near 80th St.) (212) 744-4333. The staff at this terrific Chinese restaurant is friendly, efficient and especially receptive to children, who love the collection of pig decorations. They will also love the exotic desserts, like frozen praline mousse or the Peking snowball. **Subway:** 6 to 77th St.

Saigon Grill 1700 Second Ave. (at 88th St.) (212) 996-4600. This plain, bright Vietnamese restaurant is usually packed with families. Despite the volume, it manages to serve delicious, meticulously prepared dishes like green papaya salad, topped with grilled beef; cool rice noodles; and summer rolls wrapped in rice paper. **Subway:** 4, 5, 6 to 86th St.

Midtown West

John's Pizzeria 260 W. 44th St. (between Seventh and Eighth Aves.) (212) 391-7560. Housed in what used to be the Christian Alliance Gospel Tabernacle Church, this is both the largest pizzeria in New York and the most beautiful. For families, there are two important distinctions: the service is friendly, and you are likely to get a seat without waiting. **Subway:** A, C, E, N, R, Q, S, W, 1, 2, 3, 7, 9 to 42nd St.

Virgil's 152 W. 44th St. (between Broadway and Sixth Ave.) (212) 921-9494. How could parents not appreciate a restaurant that offers towels in place of napkins? Virgil's also offers uncanny reproductions of barbecue styles from North Carolina to Texas. Family favorites like pork ribs and pulled Carolina pork are top-notch. **Subway:** B, D, F, N, R, Q, S, W, 1, 2, 3, 7, 9 to 42nd St.

East Village

Cyclo 203 First Ave. (near 12th St.) (212) 673-3957. Many children love Vietnamese restaurants for chao tom, the ubiquitous appetizer of grilled shrimp paste wrapped around a stalk of sugar cane. Cyclo offers other kid-pleasing dishes like greaseless spring rolls, or chicken roasted with lemongrass and lime juice. **Subway:** L to First Ave.; L, N, Q, R, W, 4, 5, 6 to 14th St.

Little Italy

Lombardi's 32 Spring St. (near Mott St.) (212) 941-7994. The chefs at historic Lombardi's love to show off their pizza oven. If it's not too busy, they shepherd children to the rear, explain how the oven works and even allow them to toss in a chunk of coal. **Subway:** 6 to Spring St.; N, R to Prince St.

TriBeCa

Odeon 145 West Broadway (at Thomas St.) (212) 233-0507. The dining room here is unpretentious, comfortable and friendly to children. Entrees stretch from hamburgers to risotto, roast chicken and the usual pastas. A children's menu is available at all times, even 2 A.M. **Subway:** A, C, 1, 2, 3, 9 to Chambers St.

Sosa Borella 460 Greenwich St. (near Desbrosses St.) (212) 431-5093. With its open-arms policy toward children, this quiet, out-of-the-way restaurant is a natural choice for a family weekend brunch. There is an extensive list of delicious sandwiches at midday and an Argentine dinner menu. Desserts and cookies are delectable. **Subway:** 1, 9 to Canal St.

SoHo

Penang 109 Spring St. (between Mercer and Greene Sts.) (212) 274-8883. This wonderfully authentic Malaysian restaurant is popular with children for the rocky waterfall in back and for the delicious roti canai, a thin crepe served with mild coconut curry sauce. Children also like the pork ribs and the sweet, crunchy peanut pancake. **Subway:** N, R to Prince St.; 6 to Spring St.

Popular Theme Restaurants for Families

Hard Rock Café 221 W. 57th St. (at Broadway) (212) 459-9320. Don't be deterred when you see a busload of kids waiting outside. If you are on your own, they'll give you a pager that calls you from the Hard Rock souvenir store next door when your time has come. Service inside is quick and friendly. The walls are covered with memorabilia—rock stars' guitars, platinum platters, more guitars, photos, posters. **Price range:** Avg. kids meal, $6.99; adult entrees, $8–$20. **Subway:** N, R, Q, W to 57th St.

Jekyll & Hyde Club 1409 Sixth Ave. (at 57th St.) (212) 541-9505. Spooky, bizarre and famously camp, with generous helpings of food. Jekyll & Hyde packs hair-raising hourly entertainment, animated skeletons, roving actors and a conversational sphinx into a dark old four-story mansion. The best tables for seeing and interacting are on the first two floors. A voice from nowhere wishes "Happy Birthday!" to all who admit it. Waits can be long, but children are usually enchanted. Reservations are required for groups of 15 or more. **Price range:** Avg. kids meal, $8.95; adult entrees, $7.95–$19.50. **Subway:** N, R, Q, W to 57th St.

Mars 2112 1633 Broadway (at 51st St.) (212) 582-2112. It doesn't get any stranger than this multimillion-dollar theme restaurant, featuring a mock flight to Mars, where steaming lava pools greet your arrival. At the Mars Bar, you'll find everything from planetary news and weather reports to scenic views of the planet, not to mention fancifully named drinks and locally brewed "Martian" beers. Sit-down dining in one of the three dining areas in the Martian colony offers much of the same visual experience, with options ranging from Big Bang bruschetta to Ziggy Stardust spaghetti. Souvenirs, of course, are available for sale at the Martian shopping complex. **Price range:** Avg. kids meal, $8.95; adult entrees, $10–$26. **Subway:** N, R, W to 49th St.; 1, 9 to 50th St.

Nightlife

By now, most visitors (as well as the majority of residents) have grown tired of song lyrics about "the city that never sleeps"; where you "can do a half a million things, all at a quarter to three." Well, like most clichés, these are entirely true. With the possible exception of New Orleans during Mardi Gras, New York reigns as—get ready for another cliché—the nightlife capital of the world.

All platitudes aside, bar closing time *is* at 4 A.M. Dance clubs often stay open until well into the morning, but stop serving at the bar. Music venues may close after the last set or keep jumping with a DJ or jukebox until the last customer has gone home. Whichever nighttime activities are on the agenda, chances are you will be exhausted before your options are.

The distinctions among bars, lounges, clubs and music venues are blurry at best. Expect live music at bars and clubs, dancing at lounges and music venues, and DJs everywhere.

Because so many establishments feature a variety of activities, it is always important to check local listings. *The New York Times* (Friday), *www.nytoday.com* (*The New York Times'* city guide on the Web), *Time Out New York*, the *Village Voice*, *New York* magazine, *The New Yorker* and the *New York Press* all run weekly listings.

BARS & LOUNGES BY NEIGHBORHOOD

Many tourists concentrate on dance clubs and other places with music (*discussed later in this section*) when planning their evenings in the city. But while New York's clubs are essential to the city's nightlife, it's often in the pubs and lounges, the neighborhood watering holes and swank hot spots, that New York after dark can really be appreciated. From the most elegant hotel bars to the deepest of dives, New York has something for everyone—often all on one block.

The difference between bars and lounges is subtle and usually lies in the attitude—and maybe a few couches. Lounges also often have DJs, but not the cabaret license required to host legal dancing. Throughout the Giuliani administration raids were frequently conducted, but the requisite signs reading, "No dancing by order of law," are often disregarded by patrons and displayed with a wink from the management.

The following listings cover only a small fraction of the more than 1,000 bars in Manhattan. They were chosen for their historical significance, current popularity, location or other particular points of interest. For more listings go to *www.nytoday.com*. (*For Brooklyn bars see separate listings in chapter* **Exploring New York**.)

Lower Manhattan/TriBeCa

Bridge Café 279 Water St. (at Dover St.) (212) 227-3344. The Bridge Café, located in a three-story wood-framed building dating from 1794, may be the oldest continually operated eating and drinking establishment in the city. Neighborhood residents and employees of the nearby courthouses, financial district and City Hall crowd the cafe's bar stools and petite burgundy cloth-covered tables. The drink list includes more than 60 domestic wines and 30 varieties of single malt Scotch. **Subway:** J, M, Z, 2, 3, 4, 5 to Fulton St.; A, C to Broadway–Nassau St.

Bubble Lounge 228 West Broadway (between White and Franklin Sts.) (212) 431-3433. With over 290 types of champagne and sparkling wine, expensive cigars, caviar and clams on the half shell, there's no shortage of opportunities to splurge here. With plush red couches, seductive lounge music and dim lighting, this sophisticated bar is a great place to take a date if you're trying to look classier than you really are. **Subway:** 1, 9 to Franklin St.

El Teddy's 219 West Broadway (between Franklin and White Sts.) (212) 941-7070. Finding decent Mexican food and drink in this city is harder than finding a good apartment. It's no wonder, then, that El Teddy's is constantly packed to the gills, combining a schmaltzy 1980's wonderland décor with solid cocktails and dining. Its TriBeCa location means the bar is packed with after-work Wall Streeters slamming back drinks over some seriously tasty guacamole and chips. **Subway:** 1, 9 to Franklin St.

Grace 114 Franklin St. (between West Broadway and Church St.) (212) 343-4200. Grace is attractive and warm, with a narrow front area dominated by the long, deep mahogany bar, behind which friendly bartenders pour tasty drinks from an extensive collection of liquors. Bowls of plump olives keep the crowd fed until they order from the menu of light entrees. Classical light fixtures and mahogany walls complete the picture. **Subway:** 1, 9 to Franklin St.

Liquor Store 235 West Broadway (at White St.) (212) 226-7121. The laid-back locals who frequent this undersized corner bar blend congenially with the more upscale crowd that takes over on the weekend. Big windows and little attitude tempt you to kick back and watch the goings-on across the street at the Bubble Lounge and No. Moore. Summertime means a happy clutter of plastic chairs—many without tables—are scattered outside, just waiting for you to plop down and have a cool margarita. Cash only. **Subway:** 1, 9 to Franklin St.

No. Moore 234 West Broadway (at N. Moore St.) (212) 925-2595. No. Moore is the kind of place that has something for everyone. There's live music most nights. If you're hungry, you can order in and the staff will deliver your meal to you; if you're thirsty, everything from microbrews to cognac is on hand. The crowd is as far-ranging as the drink offerings. Artists and musicians come for the shows in the spacious performance space, located in the former basement, which offers table seating and its own small bar. **Subway:** 1, 9 to Franklin St.

North Star Pub 93 South St. (near Fulton Sts.) (212) 509-6757. Just a stone's throw from the South Street Seaport and all of its maritime glory is this quaint English-style pub. It's about as real as Epcot's European pavilion, but for Anglophiles and Wall Streeters it does the trick. There are more than 75 types of single-malt Scotch, a good selection of British ales and a menu of hearty pub fare. **Subway:** J, M, Z, 2, 3, 4, 5 to Fulton St.; A, C to Broadway–Nassau St.

Puffy's Tavern 81 Hudson St. (between Harrison and Jay Sts.) (212) 766-9159. On a sleepy TriBeCa corner, Puffy's offers a low-key, scene-free, classic neighborhood bar. And it may actually stay that way because it's the kind of exceptionally unexceptional place that most people won't go out of their way to get to. If they did, they'd find a beautiful, welcoming, old-fashioned place with dark wood, sultry fans and a darts alcove, frequented by locals, old-timers and folks from the nearby financial district. **Subway:** 1, 9 to Franklin St.

Walkers Restaurant 16 N. Moore St. (at Varick St.) (212) 941-0142. Walkers' enormous mahogany bar, high tin ceilings and good, uncomplicated cuisine recall old New York—right down to the red-and-white-checked table-cloths. There's plenty of history in the walls, or you can write your own in Crayolas on the white paper table covers. This is a down-to-earth holdout in a neighborhood where prices—and attitude—snake steadily heavenward. Cash only. **Subway:** 1, 9 to Franklin St.

Lower East Side

Angel 174 Orchard St. (between Houston and Stanton Sts.) (212) 780-0313. This Lower East Side lounge is long like a swimming pool with its walls painted a vibrant aquamarine and three bubble-like mirrors above the bar that conjure up portholes on a ship. Yet though there's an underwater feel to the place, the high ceilings make a visitor feel anything but claustrophobic. Angel has a second floor at the back, a platform where the main attraction is the DJ. **Subway:** F to Second Ave.

Baby Jupiter 170 Orchard St. (at Ludlow St.) (212) 982-2229. This bar and restaurant is devoted to the graffiti art of André Charles, who did the Houston Street obituary wall featuring Tupac, Princess Diana and Joe Camel, among others. The bar serves Cajun food during the day and into the night, when it opens as a full-functioning funk parlor. Bands play or DJs spin funk, soul and hip-hop in a room next to the restaurant. **Subway:** F to Second Ave.

bOb 235 Eldridge St. (between Houston and Stanton Sts.) (212) 777-0588. This living-room-sized bar attracts a gaggle of Lower East Side hipsters who'd love to groove along to bOb's numerous house, hip-hop and reggae DJs, if only they could. Once a popular (and cramped) place to dirty dance, bOb has been forced to reduce its debauchery quotient since it hasn't got a cabaret license. But it's still a great place to have a drink. **Subway:** F to Second Ave.

Idlewild 145 E. Houston St. (between First and Second Aves.)
(212) 477-5005. It's a bar, it's a plane, it's Idlewild. This lounge takes the theme bar concept to another dimension, or at least another elevation. Idlewild's front room is done up like the first-class section of a jetliner, complete with real airplane seats, and the back room resembles a sleek 1960's airport lounge. The barmen don ground-crew jumpsuits and the waitresses dress like vintage stewardesses. Drinks are pricey, but it's worth seeing. **Subway:** F to Second Ave.

Kush 183 Orchard St. (between Houston and Stanton Sts.) (212) 677-7328. Were it not for the small blackboard on the sidewalk out front, you might walk right past this oasis. Inside, all things Moroccan adorn the whitewashed walls, bathed in soft, warm lighting. On weekends, a DJ spins a variety of sensuous music for a swank crowd. The marinated olives at the bar provide a welcome change from the traditional pretzels. **Subway:** F to Second Ave.

Lansky Lounge 104 Norfolk St. (between Delancey and Rivington Sts.)
(212) 677-9489. From its subterranean alleyway entrance to its Art Deco bar lamps, Lansky Lounge goes all out in its attempt to conjure the atmosphere of a speakeasy-style swinger joint. The music is mostly non-stop Frank, with a few other swingin' tunes thrown in. It's attached to the restaurant Ratner's (they even share a coat check), but one enters Lansky through the stairway on Norfolk. On weekends, when the $5 cover kicks in, the place is bursting with downtown types—weekdays can be virtually empty. **Subway:** F to Delancey; J, M, Z to Essex St.

Ludlow Bar 165 Ludlow St. (between Houston and Stanton Sts.)
(212) 353-0536. The epicenter of Ludlow hip, this dimly lit, low-ceilinged, drinking den features cheap pours and a pool table in the back. There are a number of great weekly events that attract some of the best DJs in the city and a small, friendly (sometimes overly) dance floor. **Subway:** F to Second Ave.

Max Fish 178 Ludlow St. (between Houston and Stanton Sts.)
(212) 529-3959. One of the first venues to attract bar-goers to the burgeoning Lower East Side scene, Max Fish still draws its fair share of hipsters. Brightly lit and without downtown attitude, Max Fish is both hip and casual at the same time. Never lacking in interesting artwork, this spot also offers plenty of other attractions, including pinball, video games, a pool table and cheap beer. Cash only. **Subway:** F to Second Ave.

Welcome to the Johnsons 123 Rivington St. (between Norfolk and Essex Sts.) (212) 420-9911. Welcome to the Johnsons is a nostalgic visit to some cool kid's 70's-style basement. Everything about this bar is designed to make you feel at home (that is, someone else's retro home). The orange-and-brown furniture is covered in plastic and the place is snazzed-up with macramé curtains, trophies and houseplants. Strong mixed drinks are whipped up behind the bar, and bottles are served from a vintage, avocado-green refrigerator. Cash only. **Subway:** F to Delancey St.; J, M, Z to Essex St.

Chinatown/Little Italy to Houston

Botanica 47 E. Houston St. (between Mott and Mulberry Sts.)
(212) 343-7251. An evening in this subterranean dive is like a house party in someone's basement. The motif is Thrift Shop Eclectic: Naugahyde couches, 70's easy chairs, Formica tables, old theater seats and red lighting from Holiday Inn table lamps. The front door opens into the faintly lit bar area, and past the two unisex bathrooms is a back room. Cash only. **Subway:** F, S to Broadway–Lafayette St.; N, R to Prince St.; 6 to Bleecker St.

Double Happiness 173 Mott St. (at Broome St.) (212) 941-1282. It's easy to miss this Chinatown lounge: only the line outside gives it away. Once inside, you will be surrounded by the young and fashionable nestled comfortably into various softly lit nooks. Settle into your own corner and sip the bar's delectable martinis (including the house speciality, which adds a dash of green tea to the concoction). **Subway:** F, S to Broadway–Lafayette St.; N, R to Prince St.; 6 to Spring St.

M & R Bar 264 Elizabeth St. (between Houston and Prince Sts.)
(212) 226-0559. Any evening is a good one at M & R, where the marble bar, tin ceilings and brick wall beckon. The bar staff is never too stuffy to chat or too busy to keep you filled up. Friday nights the DJ, set up in one corner of the bar, spins Latin jazz and funk. M & R's bar area fills up fast and, unless you're eating dinner, it can be tough to get a seat. **Subway:** F, S to Broadway–Lafayette St.; N, R to Prince St.

Mare Chiaro 176 1/2 Mulberry St. (between Broome and Grand Sts.)
(212) 226-9345. At first glance, Mare Chiaro seems like the ultimate in Little Italy authenticity: old Italian men smoking cigars, a jukebox that's about 85 percent Sinatra and photos of the owner alongside Ol' Blue Eyes himself. Look more closely and you'll notice that the crowd is largely hipsters and slumming Ivy Leaguers. It's this crazy mix that makes Mare Chiaro such a good time. Cash only. **Subway:** N, R to Prince St.; 6 to Spring St.

Vig Bar 12 Spring St. (at Elizabeth St.) (212) 625-0011. A neat and richly appointed lounge with dark wood and crimson upholstery, Vig is quiet enough to enjoy well-mixed, though not inexpensive, cocktails after work. After 10 P.M. on weekends, the crowd of young professionals can get boisterous. **Subway:** N, R to Prince St.; 6 to Spring St.

SoHo

Ear Inn 326 Spring St. (between Greenwich and Washington Sts.)
(212) 226-9060. Built in the 1830's, this landmark Federal-style house once stood on the river's edge and was a favorite spot for sailors. Although landfill has pushed the shoreline a few blocks westward, the bar still sports remnants of its nautical past. In this friendly neighborhood atmosphere, you're likely to find men in pinstripe suits sharing the bar with tattooed bikers. **Subway:** C, E to Spring St.; 1, 9 to Houston St.

Fanelli 94 Prince St. (at Mercer St.) (212) 226-9412. Fanelli, an unfussy place with tiled floors, tin ceilings and a lot of old New York atmosphere (it opened in 1872), is nestled among SoHo's glitzier restaurants and stores. The bar draws a mixed clientele and can be crowded on weekends, but during the week the place caters to locals, and is always laid-back. Basic but tasty bar food is available, and there is a back room intended for those more interested in eating than imbibing. The bartenders are friendly, and the old-fashioned mugs are perfect for a frosty beer. **Subway:** F, S to Broadway–Lafayette St.; N, R to Prince St.

Merc Bar 151 Mercer St. (between Houston and Prince Sts.) (212) 966-2727. The beautiful people may have moved on from this SoHo hot spot, but the Merc Bar still offers softly lit, lounge-like surroundings, great tunes on a great sound system and bartenders who mix a good stiff drink. So if you're kicking back on the comfortable couches out front or mingling in the red room in back, drinking a $9 martini, remember that this place used to be standing room only and enjoy the fact that the crowds have gone elsewhere.
Subway: F, S to Broadway–Lafayette St.; N, R to Prince St.

Pravda 281 Lafayette St. (between Prince and Houston Sts.) (212) 226-4944. Pravda has succumbed to the inevitable condition that afflicts all hip SoHo night spots. Word of the lounge's appeal has spread to the Wall Street crowd, who now flock here, driving out the beautiful people who once actually stood in line to get in. However, the downstairs room maintains its allure, with arched, cavelike ceilings that create a feeling of intimacy.
Subway: F, S to Broadway–Lafayette St.; N, R to Prince St.

Puck Fair 298 Lafayette St. (between Houston and Prince Sts.)
(212) 431-1200. This inviting bar is massive, yet full of enough nooks and crannies that patrons can easily find an intimate corner. A popular after-work spot, there are three levels, usually filled with young professionals. The exposed beams and wooden booths on the main floor and balcony, and the dungeonlike basement effectively conjure a medieval feel.
Subway: F, S to Broadway–Lafayette St.; 6 to Spring St.

Sway Lounge 305 Spring St. (between Greenwich and Hudson Sts.)
(212) 620-5220. The neon sign outside may read McGoverns Bar, but this is no Hibernian homestead. Sway has the look and feel of a gigantic VIP room. Hand-picked by an oh-so-hip gatekeeper, those lucky enough to be let into this Moroccan-style lounge drink expensive cocktails and move to the beat of a different drum 'n' bass DJ. **Subway:** C, E to Spring St.

Void 16 Mercer St. (at Howard St.) (212) 941-6492. Like a Czech rock club in the days of Communism, Void prides itself on being difficult to locate. No obvious facade greets visitors; only a tiny sign directs patrons into an industrial loft building, down a hallway and past a heavy door. Of course, Void's clandestine overtures now seem quaint, as news of the club has spread far beyond SoHo. Cash only. **Subway:** J, M, N, Q, R W, Z, 6 to Canal St.

East Village

(See also "Dive Bars in the East Village" *later in this section.)*

Baraza 133 Ave. C (between 8th and 9th Sts.) (212) 539-0811. From the children's letter blocks that spell the bar's name on the blue front door to the cadre of DJs that spin Brazilian-tinged records and the tropical drink menu, Baraza has the perfect tone for a hip Alphabet City lounge. Inside, there's dim lighting over small tables and an enticing back corner with sofas and a metal-plated fish tank. Be sure to visit the bathroom, which is "wallpapered" with pennies. Baraza fills up on weekend nights, but it's enough out of the way to remain comfortable. Cash only. **Subway:** L to First Ave.; N, Q, R, W, 4, 5, 6 to 14th St.

Beauty Bar 231 E. 14th St. (between Second and Third Aves.) (212) 539-1389. A beauty salon for decades, it's now a bar. From the people who brought you **Barmacy** (538 E. 14th St.)—a mom-and-pop pharmacy reinvented as a hipster watering hole—comes this popular spot. You can sit beneath antique hair dryers and swill Rolling Rocks, or go whole hog and get your nails done at the bar—just don't soak 'em in your Jack Daniel's. Is it mere coincidence that many of Beauty Bar's female clientele resemble 50's pinup icon Bettie Page? **Subway:** N, Q, R, W, 4, 5, 6 to 14th St.; L to Third Ave.

d.b.a. 41 First Ave. (between 2nd and 3rd Sts.) (212) 475-5097. A chalkboard over d.b.a's long bar lists 18 draught beers, nearly 150 bottled beers, some 70 single-malt whiskies and 30 tequilas. Filled with locals and die-hard regulars, everything served here is first-rate and the staff is usually helpful in navigating you through the choices. The interior is simple and spacious, with marble-topped tables and church pews. In warmer weather, the garden out back is the perfect place to contemplate what next to imbibe on the gargantuan menu. **Subway:** F to Second Ave.

Guernica 25 Ave. B (between 2nd and 3rd Sts.) (212) 674-0984. Don't go to Guernica expecting to find a resurrected Save the Robots, the semi-legendary after-hours club that once occupied the same spot. Full more of brushed metal than of studded belts, Guernica is exactly the sort of place you expect to pop up in the eternally gentrifying East Village. The serious drinking happens downstairs in the blue-lit basement lounge. Large, convex mirrors dot the walls and a sheet of blue-tinged water runs behind the bar, while music blares from a turret-like DJ booth. **Subway:** F to Second Ave.

McSorley's Old Ale House 15 E. 7th St. (between Second and Third Aves.) (212) 473-9148. Anybody who has ever read a book by Joseph Mitchell owes himself a visit to this historic bar, though it's not as old as it pretends. Have a beer and forget the food. Cash only.
Subway: 6 to Astor Pl.; N, R to 8th St.; F to Second Ave.

288 Bar (also called Tom and Jerry's) 288 Elizabeth St. (at Houston St.) (212) 260-5045. This friendly neighborhood bar offers a relaxed atmosphere

Dive Bars in the East Village

Neighborhood bars and local holes-in-the-wall are some of the best places to see the real New York. This is particularly true in the East Village, where dives are equivalent to town hall. Hipsters, artists and colorful residents retreat to shoot pool, chat over cheap drinks or melt into a bar stool. If you find a surly bartender, the smell of stale beer, and air thick with smoke and character appealing, an East Village dive crawl is highly recommended.

Ace Bar 531 E. 5th St. (between Aves. A and B) (212) 979-8476. Ace is perfect for people with limited attention spans—pool, darts, pinball, and video games are all provided for your enjoyment, as well as a virtual museum of over 100 children's lunch boxes.

Blue and Gold Tavern 79 E. 7th St. (between First and Second Aves.) (212) 473-8918. This is a no-nonsense beer and whisky kind of a place, where many a cigarette has been smoked over a Bud in the ancient booths. On weekends the pool table can see some heated action.

Cherry Tavern 441 E. 6th St. (between First Ave. and Ave. A) (212) 777-1448. One of the hippest of the East Village dives, Cherry Tavern has seen a model or two in the crowd. Though there's a pool table and a good jukebox, the drink special—a shot of tequila and a can of Tecate beer for $4—may be Cherry's biggest attraction.

Coyote Ugly Saloon 153 First Ave. (between 9th and 10th Sts.) (212) 477-4431. It's ugly, all right, but there's something truthful—even pure—about this place, with its warped floorboards, lopsided bar stools, country jukebox and buxom bartender in her half-shirt and tight jeans.

Holiday Cocktail Lounge 75 St. Marks Pl. (between First and Second Aves.) (212) 777-9637. This classic East Village hangout is famous for its never-changing aesthetic; quilted faux-leather booths, a cigarette machine, a jukebox and video games are worn and sprinkled with a palpable seediness. Be prepared for the bar to close at the bartender's whim.

International Bar 120 First Ave. (between 7th St. and St. Marks Pl.) (212) 777-9244. Much like Johnny's S&P in the West Village, International is very local, very casual and very cheap. Though this tiny bar can get crowded on the weekends, it remains unaffected.

Joe's 20 E. 6th St. (between Aves. A and B) (212) 473-9093. The jury's still out on whether this hole-in-the-wall is a dive or a honky-tonk bar. On the dive side, it's unpretentious, homey and on the honky-tonk side, it's known for its mostly country jukebox. It attracts a neighborhood mix of old-timers and young locals.

Marz Bar 25 E. 1st St. (at Second Ave.). This punk-art bar has been around for well over a decade, and continues to revel in its downhill slide. We're talking hardcore—yet harmless. This unpretentious little dive is a breath of fresh air for those who don't associate spending money with being cool.

and more space than can normally be found in an East Village venue. There are several large, round wooden tables that allow groups to sit together, and a cavernous area in the back of the bar where you can actually talk to a group of people without the feeling that you're blocking traffic. 288 features average prices for drinks (including a decent Scotch selection) and a jukebox heavy on classic-rock tunes. Cash only.
Subway: F, S to Broadway–Lafayette St.; 6 to Bleecker St.

Temple Bar 332 Lafayette St. (between Houston and Bleecker Sts.) (212) 925-4242. The crowd inside this softly lit, wood-paneled lounge is just as refined as the drinks served—Temple Bar has 42 different varieties of vodka from 15 different countries. Bankers in expensive suits and models with expensive hair gather at the green marble-topped bar and in a second room of octagonal tables and plush banquettes. But as popular as the Temple Bar is it's been around too long to be considered hot, so you don't have to worry about too much attitude. **Subway:** F, S to Broadway–Lafayette St.; 6 to Bleecker St.

Von 3 Bleecker St. (between Elizabeth St. and Bowery) (212) 473-3039. Von is a compromise between old (Bowery grunge) and new (SoHo chic). A yuppyish crowd saunters in for after-work wines and hors d'oeuvres before giving way to a neighborhood clientele later at night. With its scuffed wooden bar and tattered leather couches, Von has the air of an upper-class saloon, and its lack of pretension and quiet location foster a desire to sit and stay for a while. The wine-and-beer-only drink menu is limited but well chosen.
Subway: F, S to Broadway–Lafayette St.; 6 to Bleecker St.

Greenwich Village/West Village

Art Bar 52 Eighth Ave. (between Jane and Horatio Sts.) (212) 727-0244. Certainly more bar than gallery, the Art Bar consists of two spaces: a front barroom with large, curvy booths and a cozy back room with a working fireplace. Candles provide intimate lighting and a jukebox plays rock music, but not so loudly as to drown out conversation. The womblike back room, with its antique couches and armchairs, is a particularly good spot for couples and small groups. **Subway:** A, C, E to 14th St.; L to Eighth Ave.; 1, 2, 3, 9 to 14th St.

Automatic Slims 733 Washington St. (between 11th and 12th Sts.) (212) 645-8660. Though exteriors can be deceiving at the isolated bars in the way-West Village, you can usually get a take on things once you walk in the door. No so with Automatic Slims; this tiny place could keep you guessing all night. The crowd consists of old barflies, a couple of investment banker types, pockets of gay men and yuppie girls. The décor is classic, modern and cozy all at once. **Subway:** A, C, E to 14th St.; L to Eighth Ave.; 1, 2, 3, 9 to 14th St.

Chumley's 86 Bedford St. (between Bleecker St. and Seventh Ave. South) (212) 675-4449. The story of Chumley's heyday as a speakeasy is as worn as its old wood tables, but it seems to keep people coming to the place in droves. The pub's three rooms are rustic, with a fireplace, sawdust on the floors and walls

hung with book jackets by famous authors who used to be regulars. F. Scott Fitzgerald allegedly wrote part of *The Great Gatsby* in a corner booth, Robert Kennedy wrote a speech here, and the place is said to be haunted by the ghost of the woman who owned it in the 30's. All lore aside though, today Chumley's resembles an upscale frat house for a clientele of young professionals swilling pints of the impressively varied beers on tap. Cash only.
Subway: 1, 9 to Christopher St.; A, C, E, F, S to W. 4th St.

Corner Bistro 331 W. 4th St. (at Jane St.) (212) 242-9502. If a simple, straightforward place to drink a beer (or something stiffer) and chomp on a top-notch burger is what you're after, then the Corner Bistro is a godsend. The front room has a worn, wooden bar and worn, wooden tables all on top of a worn, wooden floor. In back is more worn seating, and if you arrive after 7 P.M. any night of the week, be prepared to wait for a table. Cash only.
Subway: A, C, E, 1, 2, 3, 9 to 14th St.; L to Eighth Ave.

White Horse Tavern 567 Hudson St. (at 11th St.) (212) 989-3956. Located in one of the few remaining wood-framed buildings in Manhattan, the White Horse Tavern opened in 1880. The tavern was a speakeasy during Prohibition, and poet Dylan Thomas was a regular in the late 1940's. Legend has it that, in 1953, Thomas drank 18 shots of whisky, stepped outside onto the sidewalk and dropped dead. (The truth is it was about seven whiskies, and what really killed him was a misdiagnosis of his diabetes.) Though once considered a "writer's bar," the three darkly paneled sections are now populated with more former frat boys than literary types. Cash only.
Subway: A, C, E, 1, 2, 3, 9 to 14th St.; L to Eighth Ave.

WXOU Radio 558 Hudson St. (between Perry and 11th Sts.) (212) 206-0381. An unpretentious neighborhood bar, WXOU is a good place in the area for a quiet drink after a hectic day. In this simple room with white walls darkly pan-eled halfway down, a twenty-something crowd in jeans and baseball caps sits at small, wood tables lining one wall, and orders drinks from the bar lining the other. Cash only. **Subway:** A, C, E, 1, 2, 3, 9 to 14th St.; L to Eighth Ave.

Flatiron/Union Square/Murray Hill

Belmont Lounge 117 E. 15th St. (between Park Ave. and Irving Pl.) (212) 533-0009. Dark, discreet, and dripping with attitude, the Belmont Lounge has secured a permanent place in the pantheon of downtown hipster hangouts. The bar has all the requisites for downtown cool: candlelight, velvet curtains and a smattering of deep, comfy couches. The crowd is usually young and gawking, though an occasional posse of suits can be found at the bar. Most nights feature a DJ. **Subway:** L, N, Q, R, W, 4, 5, 6 to 14th St.

Nativa 5 E. 19th St. (between Fifth Ave. and Broadway) (212) 420-8636. Nativa, the Flatiron District's trendy tri-level hot spot, offers a stylish-but-sim-ple 3,000-square-foot interior, designed by a former production designer for MTV. The result is a spacious, votive-filled main floor; a stately and discussion-friendly purple-themed basement lounge; and an intriguing VIP balcony area for a private evening that only an additional reservation deserves. **Subway:** L, N, Q, R, W, 4, 5, 6 to 14th St.

Old Town Bar and Restaurant 45 E. 18th St. (between Broadway and Park Ave. South) (212) 529-6732. There are no gas-lit lamps or horse-drawn carriages on the streets outside this tavern. But inside, you feel as though you have entered a bygone era from New York's history. Built in 1892, Old Town is one of the city's oldest taverns. From the 14-foot pressed-tin ceiling to the mahogany bar and huge beveled mirrors, it's filled with details from another time. Even the booths tell a story: they were specially built during Prohibition with a hidden compartment for stowing liquor. Though Old Town was almost turned into a museum, it doesn't feel like a tourist attraction.
Subway: L, N, Q, R, W, 4, 5, 6 to 14th St.

Pete's Tavern 129 E. 18th St. (at Irving Pl.) (212) 473-7676. "Oldest Original Bar in New York City Opened 1864," reads the sign behind the worn, ornate bar—a claim that's debatable. With its cracked tile floor, tin ceilings and hanging brass lamps, it has certainly retained that old New York flavor. O. Henry reportedly wrote "The Gift of the Magi" at one of the tavern's dark wooden booths. A casual crowd and friendly bartenders make this a nice place for a drink and snack. In warmer weather, the sidewalk tables are particularly pleasant. **Subway:** L, N, Q, R, W, 4, 5, 6 to 14th St.

Tiki Room 4 W. 22nd St. (at Fifth Ave.) (646) 230-1444. Is it possible to take the kitsch out of Tiki culture? That is the concept behind Tiki Room, a sleekly modern lounge with abstract sunsets made of backlighted Plexiglas and plasma television screens playing surf videos. Instead of servers in Don Ho attire, the waitresses wear midriff-baring Hawaiian-print halter tops. The traditional massive Tiki head is still there, but its forbidding features have been smoothed away, leaving an 18-foot-tall modernist sculpture with a V.I.P. seating area inside.
Subway: F, N, R to 23rd St.

Meatpacking District/Chelsea
(For more Chelsea venues, see "Gay & Lesbian" and "Dance Clubs.")

Hogs 'n' Heifers 859 Washington St. (at 13th St.) (212) 929-0655.
Tucked away in Manhattan's meatpacking district, Hogs 'n' Heifers offers a taste of Hazard County for anyone with a hankering for Budweiser and debauchery. Here brawny bikers and yuppies ogle female bartenders dancing on the bar. If nothing else, this place is a testament to the effectiveness of hard liquor and peer pressure in convincing women to abandon their inhibitions as well as their bras. Cash only. **Subway:** A, C, E, 1, 2, 3, 9 to 14th St.; L to Eighth Ave.

Lot 61 550 W. 21st St. (between 10th and 11th Aves.) (212) 243-6555. Lot 61 is housed in a vast, converted warehouse space, cleverly divided by sliding panels and bursting with furniture straight out of Elle Décor (don't miss the rubber sofas salvaged from insane asylums). In keeping with the area's burgeoning art scene, the walls are adorned by all the right painters' works (Hirst, Landers and

Salle, to name a few). And if that weren't enough eye candy, there's always the drop-dead gorgeous staff. **Subway:** C, E to 23rd St.

Lotus 409 W. 14th St. (between Ninth and 10th Aves.) (212) 243-4420. With the no-dancing lounge scene feeling more and more tired, nightlife entrepreneurs are diversifying, creating ambitious hybrids. Lotus is a fine example, fusing a restaurant, lounge and nightclub into a single, three-level space—divided, of course, by a velvet rope or three. **Subway:** A, C, E to 14th St.

Passerby 436 W. 15th St. (between Ninth and 10th Aves.) (212) 206-6847. British gallery owner Gavin Brown has taken over the space next door to his gallery and converted it into a bar. No sign marks the space as a bar, and tinted windows obscure any activity. As a result, most of the patrons are either artists and gallery owners, or friends of Brown. Though not exactly diverse , anyone wishing to rub elbows with working artists could hardly ask for a better crowd. **Subway:** A, C, E to 14th St.

Triple Crown Ale House 330 Seventh Ave. (between 28th and 29th Sts.) (212) 736-1575. A perfect mix of Irish pub and American sports bar, the Triple Crown caters to a mostly young professional crowd during the week and post-event crowds from Madison Square Garden on the weekends. Spacious with elegant, dark-wood paneled walls, the bar goes on red alert for sporting events. Eight TVs (one of them a very, very big-screen) broadcast the action for those who care. The full menu features excellent pub fare. **Subway:** 1, 9 to 28th St.

Midtown East/Murray Hill

Bliss 256 E. 49th St. (at Second Ave.) (212) 644-8750. You can't miss Bliss— just look for the garish, blue-lit sign, just the first of several features that make this two-story bar a distinctive alternative to nearby bars. The first floor features a clean, sleek, metallic bar. Wade through the thick traffic to find a stairway to the candle-lit second floor, which has a separate lounge in the back and large windows overlooking Second Avenue. **Subway:** 4, 5, 6, 7 to 42nd St.

British Open 320 E. 59th St. (between First and Second Aves.) (212) 355-8467. Although a round of golf often requires a trip over a bridge or tunnel, Manhattan boasts a golf pub with warmth and conviviality. The bar draws a well-heeled clientele who, even if they've never picked up a golf club, appreciate the civilized tenor of the game and its associated lifestyle. In this unexpected oasis, the mood is set by easy swing music and twinkling lights tied to trees. The patrons, though not particularly aged, seem like throwbacks to another era. Imagine bachelors in their late 40's wearing ascots and ordering Brandy Alexanders for their dates.
Subway: 4, 5, 6 to 59th St.; N, R, W to Lexington Ave.

Campbell Apartment Grand Central Terminal, 15 Vanderbilt Ave. (at 42nd St.) (212) 953-0409. Between cocktails at the Campbell Apartment patrons crane their necks to take in the 30-foot wood-beam ceilings. They admire the deep blue Moroccan-inspired rug, the overstuffed couches set against stone walls and the huge steel safe installed by John Campbell, the original inhabitant of the space. Tucked away in Grand Central, it's sure to become a classic. **Subway:** 4, 5, 6, 7 to 42nd St.

Divine Bar 244 E. 51st St. (between Second and Third Aves.) (212) 319-9463. File this one under "Great First-Date Spots." Divine Bar has everything you're looking for to avoid those awkward silences: loud music, good beer and a crowd interesting enough to talk about. It might be difficult to find a quiet little corner in which to chat, but the nook you'll find will be cozy, if not downright cramped. **Subway:** 4, 5, 6, 7 to 42nd St.

Ginger Man 11 E. 36th St. (between Fifth and Madison Aves.) (212) 532-3740. Combining old-world charm with new-world overkill, the Ginger Man has the feel of a British pub—just on a larger scale, with 100 bottled beers and 66 beers on tap from around the world. A 45-foot-long oak bar dominates the spacious high-ceilinged area in the front. In the back room the atmosphere is more intimate, with comfortable couches and chairs ideal for the end-of-day unwind. The menu contains all kinds of bar food with an upscale twist. **Subway:** 6 to 33rd St.

P.J. Clarke's 915 Third Ave. (at 55th St.) (212) 759-1650. P.J. Clarke's, in a two-story brick building with a frosted glass facade, is a remnant of an older New York. There are dark wood walls, a tile floor, a bar with an altar-like, wood-carved back and hand-painted, brown-lettered signs listing the draft prices. It has the look of a Hollywood set created for a serious movie about drinking, and, in fact, scenes from the 1945 classic *The Lost Weekend* were shot here. **Subway:** 4, 5, 6 to 59th St.; N, R, W to Lexington Ave.

Midtown West

Jimmy's Corner 140 W. 44th St. (between Sixth Ave. and Broadway) (212) 944-7819. Tucked away among big Midtown hotels, is this New York gem. Covering almost every inch of wall space at this narrow spot are posters, photos and newspaper clippings about boxing. The space at front is so small that you can barely squeeze past the regulars holding court at the bar, but that's not a problem, because everyone is friendly. The crowd is happily diverse: there are scruffy slacker types and men and women in suits, construction workers and, of course, boxing enthusiasts, all clearly glad to have found this slice of authenticity in touristy Midtown. **Subway:** B, D, F, N, Q, R, W, 1, 2, 3, 7, 9 to 42nd St.

Landmark Tavern 626 11th Ave. (at 46th St.) (212) 757-8595. When it first opened in 1868, the view from the Landmark's three-story brick building was of bustling piers and a neighborhood full of longshoremen. Since then, the river's edge has moved westward, pushed back by landfill and 12th Avenue, and the docks have gone quiet. But unlike the streets around it, the Landmark Tavern has hardly changed. Not that it still serves nickel beers, but the enormous bar—turned from a single mahogany tree—and the potbellied stove in the rear dining room remain. **Subway:** A, C, E to 42nd St.

A Grand Oasis: New York's Hotel Bars

New York City is filled with unappreciated treasures. But in the world of food and drink, none are so neglected as hotel bars. Some are new additions, but many have been here for ages, planted like pillars around the city, elegantly decorated like miniatures of the grand hotels that engulf them. Perhaps that is why they tend to be overlooked by New Yorkers. But beyond the barrier of the hotel lobbies lie some of the city's most secluded oases, where you can relax over a well-mixed drink, be treated like a king or simply be as anonymous as the bars themselves.   —Amanda Hesser

(See chapter **Hotels** *for addresses and phone numbers; see also* "Cabarets and Supper Clubs" *later in this chapter for more listings.)*

Cafe Pierre—Hotel Pierre
The dark and often empty Cafe Pierre could be a French Embassy tearoom. There is piano music every evening at 8:30 P.M.

Cellar Bar—Bryant Park Hotel
This vast bar with vaulted ceilings and geometric furniture bathed in orange light is a place to see, be seen and lounge with the beautiful people.

Fifty-Seven Fifty-Seven—Four Seasons Hotel
At the top of a short set of polished stone stairs on the main floor of the Four Seasons, is in an icy space with 30-foot ceilings, enormous mirrors and hardwood floors. It attracts mainly executives with a yen for heavily made-up companions and pricey drinks.

44 Bar—Royalton Hotel
A sleek, austere corridor lobby filled with chic women. If you're really ambitious, try to snag a seat in the tiny Round Bar.

Grand Bar—SoHo Grand Hotel
The polyglot crowd at this striking, plush and expensive hotel bar creates an energetic buzz that makes you feel like you're at the center of things—much like New York itself.

Journeys Bar—Essex House Hotel
This tiny bar in the Essex House hotel has an opulent, old-money feel to it, though it has occupied the space only since 1989.

King Cole Bar—St. Regis Hotel
The very essence of swank, where even the chips are served in silver-plated dishes. The King Cole Bar also claims to have invented the Bloody Mary—though they call it the Red Snapper. Whatever you order, it's bound to be well made. The friendly bartenders know a thing or two about mixing drinks.

Mark's Bar—The Mark Hotel
The Mark Hotel is known for its relaxed elegance, a reputation that rightly

extends to its gem-like bar, which draws in European tourists and Upper East Side matrons-in-training.

Mercer Kitchen—Mercer Hotel
Cool lighting and clean lines make the bar at Mercer Kitchen feel like the set for a fashion shoot. Identification is probably not necessary, but something with a Prada tag may be.

Morgans Bar—Morgans
At the cavelike bar, calling ahead for a table is a good idea. The place can get quite crowded on weekends—or, during the summer, on Thursday, when the pre-Hamptons crowd congregates.

Oak Room and Bar—Plaza Hotel
A beer hall for men in suits. The Oak Room features live cabaret nightly.

Oasis Bar—W New York Hotel
The ambiance at the Oasis Bar at the W New York Hotel is California and casual. One day it is calm and Zen-like, the next it is filled with *Friends* cast look-alikes.

Serena—Chelsea Hotel
Though almost antithetical to the Chelsea Hotel spirit, this swank lounge that opened in 1999 quickly became a major hot spot. (Think very thin people lining up in very expensive dresses to push through Serena's heavy wrought-iron door to sip cosmopolitans under tin palm trees and lounge on plush couches).

Thom's Bar—Thompson Hotel
This bar offers a quiet little sanctuary for intimate conversation and a safe haven away from the majority of the "gotta-be-seen" SoHo bars. Minimalist in design with stark white walls, dim lighting and cozy chairs, this low-key locale is a perfect spot to catch up with friends after work or meet a date for a drink without the threat of loud music or boisterous conversation.

Villard's Bar & Lounge—New York Palace Hotel
Elegant rooms that had been offices in the Villard Houses have been restored to their rouged and gilded glory in the French Empire and Victorian styles and turned into the Villard Bar & Lounge. There are four lounges on two floors, some intimate and others grand with soaring ceilings. Fancy snacks (caviar, foie gras, oysters) are available.

Whiskey Bar—Paramount Hotel
Adjacent to the hyper-swanky Paramount (a hotel so exclusive it lacks a marquee), the Whiskey is smaller than one might expect, but just as dark and well appointed as the Paramount's lobby. The bar attracts an odd mix of business types, tourists and hipsters.

P G Kings 18 W. 33rd St. (between Fifth and Sixth Aves.) (212) 290-0080. For tourists who find themselves near the Empire State Building, this pub is an oasis. The wood-paneled front room with its tiled floor and vintage oak bar, and the hearty pub fare served in the back room, make it worth a stop. The selection of tap beers is excellent, the bartenders are genial and professional and there's a shelf full of paperbacks available for solo drinkers who forgot to bring a book. **Subway:** B, D, F, N, Q, R, W to 34th St.

P.J. Carney's 906 Seventh Ave. (between 57th and 58th Sts.) (212) 581-4138. Just a few steps from Carnegie Hall in the heart of the 57th Street tourist mecca, P.J. Carney's is an old standby for locals. The crowd fills up on shepherd's pie and 20-ounce pints of Guinness and hard cider at the bar's handful of tightly packed tables, while a grinning bartender dressed in overalls, who knows every other customer by name, glides back and forth behind a wee horseshoe-shaped bar. **Subway:** N, R, Q, W to 57th St.; B, D, E to Seventh Ave.

Revolution 611 Ninth Ave. (between 43rd and 44th Sts.) (212) 489-8451. More restaurant than bar, this spot does a terrific job of providing an inviting place to have drinks with friends. Elegantly decorated, the front of Revolution has a small lounge area with antique sofas and chairs around a fireplace. A friendly after-work crowd and weekend patrons often fill Revolution to capacity. **Subway:** A, C, E to 42nd St.

Upper East Side

Auction House 300 E. 89th St. (between First and Second Aves.) (212) 427-4458. The main room in this opulent bar has a decorative fireplace, cut-glass chandeliers, couches, oriental rugs and window seats on either side of the front door. Gilt-framed mirrors and a few oil paintings hang on the exposed brick walls. The Auction House's patrons are drawn from the neighborhood, but they tend to be older and better dressed (no baseball hats or sneakers are permitted) than at other bars in the area. **Subway:** 4, 5, 6 to 86th St.

Dorrian's Red Hand Restaurant 1616 Second Ave. (at 84th St.) (212) 772-6660. This bar may never live down its association with Robert Chambers, who met Jennifer Levin here in 1986 and then murdered her the same night in Central Park. Despite the bad publicity, Dorrian's has recovered from the heady days of the late 80's and remains a respectable neighborhood bar and restaurant with an eclectic menu and window seating at red-checkered tables. Ask the bartender about the gory legend of the "red hand." **Subway:** 4, 5, 6 to 86th St.

Elaine's 1703 Second Ave. (between 88th and 89th Sts.) (212) 534-8103. A meeting place for the older guard of New York's celebrity elite (think Joan Collins and Ivana Trump). A collage of literati memorabilia covers the walls, and *Entertainment Weekly* has been throwing its Oscar party here for years. In addition to the famous frequenters, watch for Elaine herself, who opened these doors almost 40 years ago and routinely table-hops to schmooze with her guests.

Sing, Sing a Song: Karaoke in New York

Karaoke, once considered corny by the uninitiated, has had something of a surge in popularity of late. And for good reason. There's nothing quite like belting out your favorite tune in front of a crowd, cheering you on as if you were a superstar—no matter how offensive the performance.

New York has a few karaoke options. There are karaoke lounges (often run by Japanese, Chinese or Korean Americans, but usually welcoming to all) that have karaoke every night. There are also places that rent out private rooms by the hour—a blast with a group. And then there are regular bars that have weekly or monthly karaoke nights. For more venues, check *www.murphguide.com/karaoke.htm*. If you've never done karaoke, it's about time you tried. If you have, you're probably already convinced.

Arlene Grocery 95 Stanton St. (between Ludlow and Orchard Sts.) (212) 358-1633. Come for Punk Rock/Heavy Metal Karaoke Monday nights at 10 P.M. With a live band and an enthusiastic crowd, you'll feel like a rock star, or—if you'd rather just watch—a groupie.

Asia Roma 40 Mulberry St. (between Worth and Bayard Sts.) (212) 385-1133. This small, basement karaoke lounge is good for intimate groups.

Japas 55 253 W. 55th St. (between Broadway and Eighth Ave.) (212) 765-1210. At this long skinny bar with an after-work crowd of both dilettantes and hardcore crooners, the bartenders bring you a mike where you're seated for $1 per song. Private rooms are available. Japas also has a darker downtown location where you can be practically anonymous while you're singing (11 St. Marks Pl. between Second and Third Aves., 212-473-4264).

Planet Rose 219 Ave. A (between 13th and 14th Sts.) (212) 353-9500. This wannabe-swank karaoke lounge has a steep cover charge most of the week (around $40), but Sundays are free.

Toto Music Studio 38 W. 32nd St. (between Fifth and Sixth Aves.) (212) 594-6644. Private rooms only. A good spot for groups, the bigger rooms can literally hold dozens. Bring your own alcohol.

Village Karaoke 27 Cooper Square (212) 254-0066. Private rooms, a good song list and a bring-your-own-alcohol policy make this a great place to get rowdy.

Winnie's 104 Bayard St. (bet. Mulberry and Baxter Sts.) (212) 732-2384. A regular cast of folks from Chinatown shares the space with Lower East Side hipsters, rowdily handing off the microphone for both classics and Chinese pop tunes (on most nights, one of the bartenders will also step out to belt a tune herself).

But you won't received the royal treatment if they don't know you. **Subway:** 4, 5, 6 to 86th St.

Fitzpatrick's 1641 Second Ave. (at 85th St.) (212) 988-7141. This old Irish pub—founded in 1917—came under new ownership in 1996. Completely renovated and very clean (even the bathrooms!), the pub has retained its friendly neighborhood feel, absent in many bars nowadays. From 10:30 A.M. until early evening, the older gents sitting at the mahogany bar make up a family of sorts. In the evening, and especially on weekends, Fitzpatrick's comes alive, even turning people away. **Subway:** 4, 5, 6 to 86th St.

Subway Inn 143 E. 60th St. (at Lexington Ave.) (212) 223-8929. With a worn bar, cracked red-and-white tile floor and a row of dingy, high-backed booths, the surprise in this seediest of seedy bars is a strong showing of stylishly outfitted young people found mixing with workers from the nearby hotels and stores, and students from Hunter College. Yet there's no threat of the place being overrun by beautiful people: It's still a place where they serve dollar draft beers, though only during the day. Cash only.
Subway: N, R to Lexington Ave; 4, 5, 6 to 59th St.

Upper West Side

Alligator Alley 485 Amsterdam Ave. (between 83rd and 84th Sts.) (212) 873-5810. If you long to crawl back into the undergraduate womb, you'll find a reasonable approximation at Alligator Alley. This watering hole provides school-sick twenty-somethings a haven from the cold reality of the working world, faithfully recreating the décor and ambiance of a frat-house basement lounge. The jukebox offers a selection of classic rock, alternative and top 40, and prices are reasonable. **Subway:** 1, 9 to 86th St; B, C to 81st St.

All State Cafe 250 W. 72nd St. (between Broadway and West End Ave.) (212) 874-1883. Inside this narrow, cozy, basement-level dive there's a brief stretch of bar, a jukebox and postage-stamp sized color TV, a well-trod floor and to the rear, a patch of little wooden tables where fine pub fare is served. Cash only. **Subway:** 1, 2, 3, 9 to 72nd St.

Dive 75 101 W. 75th St. (at Columbus Ave.) (212) 362-7518. Tucked away on a side street, Dive 75 merges the friendliness of a neighborhood bar with the atmosphere of a living room. A large blue aquarium separates the bar area from a small collection of tables; wooden bookshelves house a selection of board games. The bar attracts a local twenty-something crowd seeking an alternative to the neighborhood's array of swanky lounges and raucous frat bars.
Subway: 1, 2, 3, 9 to 72nd St.

420 Bar and Lounge 420 Amsterdam Ave. (at 80th St.) (212) 579-8450. Dark and smooth, 420 is part of the burgeoning Upper West Side bar scene, adding a tinge of sophistication to a neighborhood that has its share of frat parlors. Cafe tables in the main room and an intimate mezzanine enhance the ambience. Weekends here are lively when the downstairs lounge opens to accommodate the crowds, and DJs meld Top 40 with disco classics. **Subway:** 1, 2, 3, 9 to 72nd St.

Hi-Life Bar and Grill 477 Amsterdam Ave. (at 83rd St.) (212) 787-7199. The management of Hi-Life proclaims that their mission is to recreate the great restaurant-lounges of the 1930's and 40's. With its dark wood furnishings, padded black Naugahyde walls and matching banquettes, large round mirrors and curved wooden bar, it comes awfully close. The crowd is mostly professional, late 20's and up. Hi-Life offers a full-New American menu and prides itself on cocktails. **Subway:** 2, 3 to 72nd St.; 1, 9 to 79th St.

GAY & LESBIAN

The following listings are a selection of bars that cater to the gay and lesbian communities of New York. Also, many of the city's premier dance and cabaret venues are predominately gay or gay-friendly; several have gay or lesbian parties at least one night per week. (*See* "Dance Clubs" *and* "Cabarets and Supper Clubs" *later in this chapter.*) Also check Homo Xtra (HX), Next magazine, HX for Her, or Time Out New York for weekly events.

Men

Barracuda CHELSEA 275 W. 22nd St. (between Seventh and Eighth Aves.) (212) 645-8613. This popular gay bar is often described as an oasis of East Village-style nightlife in the heart of tan-and-taut Chelsea. Barracuda's décor is decidedly low-key, effecting an Alphabet City aesthetic of kitschy squalor. But don't be fooled. Despite the assumed atmosphere, aging disco-bunny muscle-queens in tank tops and skin-tight Diesel gear still abound. Cash only. **Subway:** C, E, 1, 9 to 23rd St.

Blu CHELSEA 161 W. 23rd St. (between Sixth and Seventh Aves.) (212) 633-6113. Blu is a large, comfortable spot promoting itself as a "cy-bar" for the gay Chelsea nightlife scene. With four free customer-ready computers connected to Web-TV, Blu makes it possible for drinkers to cruise for Web sites as well as other patrons. Blu attracts a mostly down-to-earth assortment of gay men who avoid the pretensions found at nearby gay bars. **Subway:** F, 1, 9 to 23rd St.

Boiler Room EAST VILLAGE 86 E. 4th St. (between First and Second Aves.) (212) 254-7536. The Boiler Room has the magnetic charm of a black hole: its dim lighting and powerful gravity draws in and compresses ever-increasing masses of darkly-clothed gay East Village guys in their 20's and early 30's. Though the crowd can approach gridlock proportions on Friday and Saturday nights, the Boiler Room retains the feel of a neighborhood bar. Cash only. **Subway:** F to Second Ave.

Chase MIDTOWN WEST 255 W. 55th St. (between Eighth Ave. and Broadway) (212) 333-3400. This attractive bar, located on the northern border of Hell's Kitchen, is a comfortable spot for locals and out-of-towners. While the actual bar can only accommodate six or seven people, there's room up front for a modest crowd, and a cozy lounge in the back. The atmosphere is best described as serene, with a tasteful array of flowers and candles, and a subdued level of background music. **Subway:** A, B, C, D, 1, 9 to 59th St.

Cleo's Ninth Ave. Saloon MIDTOWN WEST 656 Ninth Ave. (between 45th and 46th Sts.) (212) 307-1503. About the only dead giveaway to the gay and lesbian nature of this friendly, laid-back bar is the large rainbow flag that hangs on the back wall. Otherwise, distinguishing Cleo's from any other local dive would take a discerning eye. The beer is cheap (Budweiser is served in a can), the jukebox has a good selection and they serve popcorn in a basket. Cash and checks only. **Subway:** A, C, E to 42nd St.

The Cock EAST VILLAGE 188 Ave. A (at 12th St.) (212) 777-6254. A dark East Village dive, the Cock offers DJs nightly to a downtown crowd. Known more for its cruising potential than its décor, this bar is aptly located on one of the city's seedier avenues. **Subway:** L to First Ave.

East of Eighth CHELSEA 254 W. 23rd St. (at Eighth Ave.) (212) 352-0075. Join the fun at this small but spirited Chelsea bar, where a mostly gay crowd mingles to the sounds of 80's favorites. The lighting here is superb; the red bulbs and candles will make you look as though you've been on a long, restful vacation. The staff at East of Eighth is as gracious as the lighting and the service is swift. **Subway:** C, E to 23rd St.

Excelsior BROOKLYN 390 Fifth Ave. (between 6th and 7th Sts.) (718) 832-1599. This warm, inviting bar with a great garden area attracts a mellow local crowd. There's plenty of action, but it's done Brooklyn-style, without all the show. Though Excelsior is definitely for the boys, the crowd can be mixed. **Subway:** F, N, R to Fourth Ave.

G Lounge CHELSEA 223 W. 19th St. (between Seventh and Eighth Aves.) (212) 929-1085. Smart-dressed Chelsea guys line up to get into this den of chic, with a juice bar in the back and a bar in the middle of the main room to encourage smooth cruising. G also features some of the best DJs in the city. A hot spot from the day it opened. Cash only. **Subway:** C, E, 1, 9 to 23rd St.

Hell WEST VILLAGE 59 Gansevoort St. (between Washington and Greenwich Sts.) (212) 727-1666. A nice, dimly lit lounge up the street from the popular late-night diner Florent, Hell attracts a mostly gay clientele (and a classy, not overtly cruisey one at that). It's a swell place to have a cosmopolitan as long as there's a DJ spinning. Otherwise it's those same old Erasure and Everything But the Girl songs on the jukebox—always something there to remind you of an ex-boyfriend or two. **Subway:** A, C, E to 14th St.; L to Eighth Ave.

The Monster WEST VILLAGE 80 Grove St. (between W. 4th St. and Waverly Pl.) (212) 924-3557. Located on Sheridan Square (with a view of Stonewall), the Monster is one of New York's oldest gay establishments. On the main floor, there's a huge, attractive wooden bar with plenty of seating for everyone. Moving farther in, you'll hear various patrons by the piano belting out a favorite show tune (or 10). Venture downstairs and there's another large bar and a fairly spacious dance floor. Cash only. **Subway:** 1, 9 to Christopher St.

Saints UPPER WEST SIDE 992 Amsterdam Ave. (between 109th and 110th Sts.) (212) 222-2431. This is not your typical gay bar. For one thing, its location is far from the city's other gay watering holes. For another, the patrons of this neighborhood hangout are much more diverse—and far less cruisey—than one might find in Chelsea. Saints is a stone's throw from Columbia, so students often pack the bar. Cash only. **Subway:** 1, 9 to 110th St.

Splash FLATIRON/UNION SQUARE 50 W. 17th St. (between Fifth and Sixth Aves.) (212) 691-0073. Splash is a friendly, wholesome bar—except for the go-go boys, the cruisey atmosphere and the almost-exclusively male crowd. Splash keeps its customers coming back with cozy seating around the downstairs bar and a dance floor with music that ranges from disco classics to 90's dance favorites. **Subway:** F, L, N, Q, R, W, 4, 5, 6 to 14th St.

Starlight Bar & Lounge EAST VILLAGE 167 Ave. A (between 10th and 11th Sts.) (212) 475-2172. This elegant, congenial bar with a sizable gay clientele smack dab in the center of the East Village reflects the local penchant for dive-to-diva makeovers. The clean décor and dark, muted color scheme seem to be appreciated by the buff, clean-cut male (and the occasional female) crowd that frequents the place from early evening into the wee hours. Cash only. **Subway:** L to First Ave.

Stonewall WEST VILLAGE 53 Christopher St. (between Sixth and Seventh Aves.) (212) 463-0950. Get out your gay history books: Stonewall is the little hole in the wall where the famous riots started. (The brief version: The police raided the bar, a drag queen threw a bottle, purses flew and, over the course of a couple of days in the summer of 1969, the gay rights movement was born.) These days, the bar is a quieter, more open, less tumultuous neighborhood hangout. Cash only. **Subway:** 1, 9 to Christopher St.

Townhouse MIDTOWN EAST 206 E. 58th St. (between Second and Third Aves.) (212) 826-6241. A "gentleman's club" in the truest sense of the term, this classy gay bar has the old boys' atmosphere down pat. A dress code ensures that the clientele maintains the proper image at all times. Dark wood, tapestry carpeting and paintings of hunting scenes provide the perfect backdrop for the civilized meeting and greeting that goes on here. The crowd consists of older, well-polished men in suits lounging on couches or leaning suavely against walls. **Subway:** 4, 5, 6 to 59th St.; N, R, W to Lexington Ave.

View Bar CHELSEA 232 Eighth Ave. (at 22nd St.) (212) 929-2243. Living up to its name, this attractive addition to the Chelsea bar scene has a flirty gay clientele and much to recommend: friendly service, cheap drink options and comfortable spaces in which to sit or stand. In case you weren't sure this was a gay-friendly bar when you entered, flat-screen TVs on the wall display sexually explicit video art. Perhaps the best thing the View Bar has to offer, is the superb skyline view in the back room. **Subway:** C, E, 1, 9 to 23rd St.

Wonderbar EAST VILLAGE 505 E. 6th St. (between Aves. A and B)
(212) 777-9105. This is one of the coolest places to meet the man of your
dreams. The owners have created a warm, Wallpaper-style lounge complete with
low couches and an elevated DJ booth. The young, mixed crowd is fashionable
without being pretentious, cruisey without being seedy and cute without being
intimidating. Cash only. **Subway:** F to Second Ave.; L to First Ave.

The Works UPPER WEST SIDE 428 Columbus Ave. (between 80th and 81st
Sts.) (212) 799-7365. An ad for The Works proclaims: "89% have jobs, 73%
own their own apartments, the odds are in your favor. Find your new husband
here." A hint, ladies: this ad isn't aimed at you. This bar is a neighborhood fixture, and—as the ad might indicate—attracts guppies of all ages. The crowd is
friendly, and the bartender swears that the chocolate martinis are delicious.
Cash only. **Subway:** B, C to 81st St.

XL CHELSEA 357 W. 16th St. (between Eighth and Ninth Aves.)
(212) 366-9176. One of the latest hot spots, XL features cabaret on Monday
nights and a great happy hour throughout the week. Lauded for its décor and
fabulous lighting, it's a welcome addition to the Chelsea scene.
Subway: A, C, E to 14th St.; L to Eighth Ave.

Women

Cubby Hole WEST VILLAGE. 281 W. 12th St. (at W. 4th St.)
(212) 243-9041. A lack of pretension characterizes this narrow room, which
lives up to its matchbook's claim of being "the friendly neighborhood bar."
Although it caters predominantly to casually dressed, local lesbians in their 30's
and 40's, this West Village bar welcomes all. A miscellaneous collection of gen-
ders, races, ages and styles makes up the usual crowd. Cash only.
Subway: 1, 2, 3, 9 to 14th St.

Dumba Café BROOKLYN 57 Jay St. (between Front and Water Sts.)
(212) 726-2686. A raw loft space in Dumbo (Down Under Manhattan Bridge
Overpass), an artists' enclave in Brooklyn, Dumba has a riot-grrl and lesbian
bent, but welcomes all types and ages into its makeshift, artsy environs. Exceptional punk bands on the riot-grrl circuit often play semi-secret concerts here.
Cash only. **Subway:** F to York St.

Ginger's BROOKLYN 363 Fifth Ave. (between 5th and 6th Sts.). The owners of
the **Rising Café** (listed below) have expanded their domain on Park Slope's
Fifth Avenue with this casual neighborhood bar. A dimly-lit space with a
vaguely nautical theme, Ginger's provides just the right pub-like elements:
tables for two, a long wooden bar that runs the length of the front room, a pool
table, darts in the back and a greenly glowing jukebox replete with an eclectic
selection. The clientele is representative of the neighborhood: racially mixed,
straight and gay. **Subway:** F, N, R to Fourth Ave.

Henrietta Hudson WEST VILLAGE 438 Hudson St. (between Morton and Barrow Sts.) (212) 924-3347. A younger, less high-powered crowd than at

Rubyfruit. Some nights are packed, others are dead, but the service is always pleasant and friendly. The crowd ranges from locals to bridge-and-tunnel girls, seductively (they think) grinding their hips to Madonna.
Subway: 1, 9 to Christopher St.

Meow Mix LOWER EAST SIDE 269 E. Houston St. (between Aves. A and B) (212) 254-0688. The epicenter of the lesbian queercore scene, Meow Mix has been featured in several films including *All Over Me* and *Chasing Amy*. It's a tiny place with a rec-room-type basement where young lesbians can go and shoot pool, flirt and drop quarters in the Ms. Pac Man machine. There's a small stage upstairs where local bands perform and the bar's restrooms feature the most exciting graffiti in town. Although primarily lesbian there's almost always a handful of men in attendance, with no hostility toward them. Cash only.
Subway: F to Second Ave.

Rising Café BROOKLYN 186 Fifth Ave. (at Sackett St.) (718) 789-6340. Though the clientele is mainly lesbian, all are welcome at this neighborhood cafe, which serves good coffee, beer and light food. Wood floors and art on the walls give the Rising Café an air of casual elegance. This former storefront can get quite crowded during live folk, jazz and poetry performances.
Subway: R to Union St.

Rubyfruit Bar and Grill WEST VILLAGE 531 Hudson St. (between W. 10th and Charles Sts.) (212) 929-3343. A mature, friendly lesbian crowd gathers here to relax at the bar or on one of the richly upholstered settees. The tables are made of such artifacts as old-fashioned sewing machines, with pedals that still work. For added privacy, there is a step-up seating area at the back of the bar area, partially enclosed by lush draperies. **Subway:** 1, 9 to Christopher St.

DANCE CLUBS

More than any other nightlife activity in New York, dancing requires some research. Most of the city's dance clubs host several different parties each week. There is usually a cover charge that differs with each event and an occasional dress code. In addition, thanks to periodic "crackdowns," there's always a chance that a venue will be closed. It is in any club-goers best interest to call first and check local listings for details *(see **Nightlife** introduction for resources)*. Note: Clubs usually do not accept credit cards for the cover charge.

Also very popular are roving parties that change location at will, and organizations that sponsor various events. **Organic Grooves** (212-439-1147) and **Giant Step** (*www.giantstep.net*) are among the best. In warmer months, outdoor events at venues like the **Frying Pan** at Chelsea Piers and **P.S. 1** in Queens are not to be missed. And don't ignore the outer boroughs. These days some of the best parties occur in out-of-the-way spots like **Frank's Lounge** and **The Anchorage** in Brooklyn. Events can be found by picking up a *Time Out New York* or a *Flyer* magazine.

Baktun WEST VILLAGE 418 W. 14th St. (between Ninth and Washington St.) (212) 206-1590. Take a trip way west and check out the grooves at Baktun, an up-and-coming club with a chill attitude. Though the club's art-house scene is sometimes a bit heavy-handed (let's be honest: who really enjoys listening to the recorded sounds of metal grinding and children screaming?), on a good day the club can't be beat. **Subway:** A, C, E to 14th St.

Centro-Fly FLATIRON/UNION SQUARE 51 W. 21st St. (between Fifth and Sixth Aves.) (212) 627-7770. The motif at work at Centro-Fly is futurism, which from a decorative standpoint apparently means Op Art spirals, plentiful Plexiglas and a door staff dressed in orange jumpsuits. The club, which boasts a state-of-the-art DJ booth, has been a hot spot since opening in 1999, drawing big crowds of electronic music aficionados and just plain dancing fools. **Subway:** F to 23rd St.

Chaos LOWER EAST SIDE 225 E. Houston St. (at Essex St.) (212) 505-5033. The red-curtained environs of Chaos are impressive, as are its exotic sounding hideaways—the Neptune Room, the Red Salon. But the club also subscribes to the same obnoxious policy requiring the minimum order of a bottle of pricey Champagne or liquor to secure a table, and it is often beset by around-the-corner lines. **Subway:** F to Second Ave.

Cheetah FLATIRON/UNION SQUARE 12 W. 21st St. (between Fifth and Sixth Aves.) (212) 206-7770. The former Sound Factory space has changed clientele entirely; the gay crowd stays away, while the champagne-swilling European set flocks here on weekends. The venue's tacky décor leaves a lot to be desired, but Cheetah's a good space as far as midsized clubs go. There is also a mellower downstairs lounge. **Subway:** F, N, R, 1, 9 to 23rd St.

China Club MIDTOWN WEST 268 W. 47th St. (between Broadway and Eighth Ave.) (212) 398-3800. This glitzy dance spot in the theater district attracts a fair number of movie, theater and music people. Just don't ogle—the club has a reputation as a safe haven for celebrities. The massive upstairs space has three full bars, a dance floor and stage, and there's a new outdoor terrace. Weekends feature house and top-40 DJs. The cover is $20 every night except Monday, when it's $25. Closed Wednesday.
Subway: A, C, E, N, Q, R, W, 1, 2, 3, 7, 9 to 42nd St.

Club New York MIDTOWN WEST 252 W. 43rd St. (between Broadway and Eighth Ave.) (212) 997-9510. If you're looking for a comfortably mainstream crowd in a comfortably mainstream setting, you could hardly do better than Club New York. The Times Square club (yes, the one where the Puff Daddy scandal went down) targets the hotel and international tourist crowd. Most of the club's DJs spin a dance-friendly mix of accessible house and hip-hop. Be prepared to part with $20 at the door for men and $10 for women, $3 at the coatcheck and obscene sums at the bar.
Subway: A, C, E, N, Q, R, W, 1, 2, 3, 7, 9 to 42nd St.

Don Hill's TRIBECA/SOHO 511 Greenwich St. (at Spring St.) (212) 219-2850. A small bar on the fringes of SoHo that has played host to Squeezebox, Michael Schmidt's raucous party, for several years now. As popular as ever, though somewhat straighter than it once was, Squeezebox still features renegade drag queen hostesses, live acts of a proudly dubious quality and a familiar sleazy 1970's and 80's soundtrack spun by the extraordinary Bowie-obsessed drag queen Miss Guy. BeavHer is a more behaved night of disco and 80's classics for a decidedly vanilla crowd. **Subway:** 1, 9 to Canal St.; C, E to Spring St.

Exit MIDTOWN WEST 610 W. 56th St. (between 11th and 12th Aves.) (212) 582-8282. Formerly Carbon (and, before that, Mirage), Exit is one of New York's largest, least subtle clubs. With four floors and room for 5,000 partiers, Exit tries to offer everything for everyone—often at the same time. **Subway:** A, B, C, D, 1, 9 to 59th St.

Fun CHINATOWN 130 Madison St. (at Pike St.) (212) 964-0303. Nestled right under the Manhattan Bridge, Fun is one of the city's latest (and possibly greatest) super-lounge. The club's fringe location mirrors its operating philosophy, namely, unrepentantly keeping a distance from the cooler-than-thou attitude that accompanies many an A-list clubbing address. Not that Fun is lacking in pretensions—$10 martinis, a VIP room and a black-clad clientele meet that demand—but the place does have a certain frivolous, fun-house appeal. **Subway:** F to E. Broadway.

La Nueva Escuelita MIDTOWN WEST 301 W. 39th St. (at Eighth Ave.) (212) 631-0588. Transsexuals, drag queens, gay men and the women who love them, and a progressive straight crowd mix it up on the dance floor. It's one of the cheaper dance venues in town—patrons pay $5–$15 on most nights and when you add the free condoms you can score in the back from Nora Molina, a buxom brunette, it's clearly worth the price. Cash only. **Subway:** A, C, E, N, Q, R, W, 1, 2, 3, 7, 9 to 42nd St.

Nell's WEST VILLAGE 246 W. 14th St. (between Seventh and Eighth Aves.) (212) 675-1567. The old mainstay from the 80's is still kicking along, but you won't see any of the big names that made the scene—they've all had children and moved to Westchester. Nell's is mostly hip-hop these days. **Subway:** A, C, E, 1, 9 to 14th St.; L to Eighth Ave.

NV TRIBECA/SOHO 304 Hudson St. (between Spring and Vandam Sts.) (212) 929-6868. This hot spot on the western bounds of SoHo is a lounge palace. Heavy scarlet curtains cloak the main parlor and a brown-marble and copper bar curves along the length of the mezzanine. NV puts on its club face every night at 10 P.M., when the $20 cover charge kicks in and DJs meld dance tracks with hip-hop and R&B. A favorite among New York's professional athletes, NV has also seen Mariah Carey do some impromptu time in the DJ booth. **Subway:** 1, 9 to Houston St.; C, E to Spring St.

Ohm FLATIRON/UNION SQUARE 16 W. 22nd St. (at Sixth Ave.) (212) 229-2000. An ultra-swank dance and supper club that features an eclectic array of expensive food, a lounge area and a dance floor upstairs. A second lounge and DJ-driven dance area are downstairs. **Subway:** F to 23rd St.

Polly Esther's WEST VILLAGE 186 W. 4th St. (between Sixth and Seventh Aves.) (212) 924-5707. All dressed up in flammable synthetics and no place to go? Then consider Polly Esther's: With a floor-to-ceiling "fresco" of Travolta in his *Saturday Night Fever* prime, *Charlie's Angels* collages, and, of course, ABBA blaring from the speakers, the theme of this franchise (yes, this is a chain of nightclubs) is unmistakable. And that people pay the $8 cover on weekends to pack the place proves that the 70's just will not die.
Subway: A, B, C, D, E, F, Q to W. 4th St.

Roxy CHELSEA 515 W. 18th St. (between 10th and 11th Aves.)
(212) 645-5156. A cavernous Chelsea club that takes its weekend parties deep into the night (and early morning). The club draws a mixed crowd and music ranging from house to trance, depending on the night. Saturdays are mostly gay and on Wednesdays the place turns into a roller disco as it was originally. Cash only. **Subway:** A, C, E to 14th St.

Sapphire Lounge LOWER EAST SIDE 249 Eldridge St. (between Houston and Stanton Sts.) (212) 777-5153. On weekends, the $5 cover, velvet rope, hulking bouncers, pounding dance music and young, rowdy crowd spilling onto the grubby street outside the Sapphire Lounge suggest a large, exclusive club. In truth, Sapphire is a small, overstuffed bar, decorated in cheap, haphazard lounge style. DJs spin a range of house, funk and jazz, making Sapphire a good place for some weeknight dancing. Cash only. **Subway:** F to Second Ave.

Shine TRIBECA 285 West Broadway (at Canal St.) (212) 941-0900. Banquettes and booths line most of the room, creating a rather anti-social setup, and the long, well-stocked bar in the back is really too far away from the stage. Still, Shine attracts both decent musical acts (Cheryl Crow and Mono have performed here) and nightlife events, like those put on by the popular Giant Step on Thursday nights. **Subway:** A, C, E to Canal St.

XVI EAST VILLAGE 16 First Ave. (between 1st and 2nd Sts.) (212) 260-1549. Whether the evening's theme is Blaxploitation films or French strip-pop, XVI has the unique ability to adopt the character of any party—and not because it lacks its own. Long and narrow with a wall of exposed brick, XVI's main floor features a decently stocked bar and lounge in the rear. Downstairs, DJs, dancing and a Persian motif prevail. Intricately cut glass mirrors, tile work tables and tapestry wall hangings dominate the room. **Subway:** F to Second Ave.

Sound Factory MIDTOWN WEST 618 W. 46th St. (between 11th and 12th Aves.) (212) 489-0001. Closed for a short time by federal prosecutors the Sound Factory re-emerged, bloodied but unbowed. It's still a hopping late-night weekend destination that keeps the deep house pumpin' until well beyond dawn. Not quite as enthralling as the original Sound Factory, its latest incarnation nevertheless boasts an impressive sound system in addition to one of the more workable dance floors in town. Cash only. **Subway:** A, C, E to 42nd St.

Spa EAST VILLAGE 76 E. 13th St. (between Broadway and Fourth Ave.) (212) 388-1060. Spa is the direct descendant of Life, the popular Bleecker Street dance hall that recently closed. Holistic pretensions aside, Spa is all about commotion. Visitors pack its bars three deep, and the lines to the bathrooms (decorated like saunas, get it?) snake out their doors. The club also traffics in such notions as a two-bottle minimum (at $250 a bottle) for all who wish to occupy its white leather booths. Spa also has a back room, a quieter, classier space where the minimum-bottle business is less strict and the music is devoted to rhythm and blues, trance and pop. **Subway:** L, N, Q, R, W, 4, 5, 6 to 14th St.

Speeed MIDTOWN WEST 20 W. 39th St. (between Fifth and Sixth Aves.) (212) 719-9867. Speeed (a.k.a. Creation) can't help feeling like a multilevel mall. There's the VIP room on the third floor, the Moroccan Room on the first floor, the main dance floor in the basement and the Vinyl Room on the second floor (featuring a DJ spinning vinyl, as well as vinyl furniture and padded vinyl walls). Also like a mall, Speeed (which is 18-and-over for women, 21-and-over for men) is filled with wide-eyed and trendy youngsters trying to look more experienced than their parents hope they are. **Subway:** B, D, F, S to 42nd St.

13 EAST VILLAGE 35 E. 13th St. (between University Pl. and Broadway) (212) 979-6677. This cozy second-story boîte below Union Square hosts a number of weekly parties, most notably Sunday night's long-running Shout!, a glamorous but young gathering of immaculately turned-out mods, skins, soulies and ska babies, all frugging away to an eclectic 60's soundtrack. It's an Anglophile's dream. Cheap drinks, comfy seating and a small dance floor help to make 13 an off-the-beaten-path downtown gem. **Subway:** L, N, Q, R, W, 4, 5, 6 to 14th St.

True FLATIRON 28 E. 23rd St. (at Madison Ave.) (212) 254-6117. Housed in the space formerly occupied by Vanity, this two-level, relatively intimate club has a widely varying roster of events. Of particular note is Kitsch Inn, a party featuring performers and DJs that cater to a mixed crowd—straight and gay, men and women. **Subway:** N, R to 23rd St.

Twirl CHELSEA 208 W. 23rd St. (between Seventh and Eighth Aves.) (212) 691-7685. Of all the mid-size clubs to set up shop in Chelsea, Twirl may be the most high-concept. In addition to the usual squad of bouncers, visitors are greeted by an endless array of candles and a wall of televisions—a throwback to 80's-era excess. The 80's nostalgia continues throughout the club. The crowd, predictably, is young, European and energetic. DJs spin dance-friendly house and hip-hop on the main floor. In the mellow basement lounge, expect Depeche Mode and canoodling couples. **Subway:** C, E, 1, 9 to 23rd St.

Vinyl TRIBECA/SOHO 6 Hubert St. (between Hudson and Collister Sts.) (212) 343-1379. Once a rave hall for New Jersey teens, now the home to several popular parties. Vinyl's Body and Soul may be the hippest place to be on a Sunday afternoon. At Tsunami, a psychedelic trance party, dancers wear neohippy clothing in a hallucinogenic ambiance. No alcohol is served. Cash only. **Subway:** A, C, E to Canal St.; 1, 9 to Franklin St.

Webster Hall EAST VILLAGE 125 E. 11th St. (between Third and Fourth Aves.) (212) 353-1600. A cavernous, multilevel East Village club. On weekends you can't get near the place, which may be just as well; 11th Street is closed to all through-traffic. Thursday is Girls Night Out, with free admission for the ladies. Various DJs spin various sounds in various rooms.
Subway: L, N, R, 4, 5, 6 to 14th St.

POPULAR MUSIC VENUES
Rock, Folk & Country

Acme Underground EAST VILLAGE 9 Great Jones St. (between Lafayette St. and Broadway) (212) 677-6963. Located beneath Acme Bar and Grill, Acme Underground presents live rock and eclectic music most nights. (Weekend shows tend to be strictly 21 and over, while weekday age limits fluctuate.) There's room for a standing crowd of 225 and performers often mingle with the crowd as they walk to the stage, giving the place an intimate atmosphere.
Subway: F, S to Broadway–Lafayette St.; 6 to Bleecker St.

Arlene Grocery LOWER EAST SIDE 95 Stanton St. (between Ludlow and Orchard Sts.) (212) 358-1633. With its stellar sound system, relaxed atmosphere, willingness to book unknown acts and free admission, Arlene Grocery (housed in an old bodega) has quickly become an integral part of Lower East Side bar circuit. Emerging stars such as Beth Orton and Ron Sexsmith, as well as older performers like Marianne Faithful, have used the 150-person-capacity club for intimate engagements. The club has the feel of a musicians' hangout, much like CBGB in its 1970's heyday. Cash only. **Subway:** F to Second Ave.

Baggot Inn WEST VILLAGE 82 W. 3rd St. (between Thompson and Sullivan Sts.) (212) 477-0622. Formerly the Sun Mountain Cafe, the Baggot Inn continues the folk music tradition of long-gone 1960's coffeehouses on Bleecker Street. Occasionally, performers go electric among the flock of aspiring singer-songwriters. For the most part, however, the stage at the back of the club offers acoustic sounds. Poetry, comedy, open-mike nights and DJ events also take place. **Subway:** A, C, E, F to W. 4th St.

Bitter End WEST VILLAGE 147 Bleecker St. (between Thompson St. and La Guardia Place) (212) 673-7030. Bob Dylan, Joan Baez, Harry Chapin, Paul Simon and Patti Smith have graced this rickety wooden stage on their way to larger fame, and the promotional posters that line the walls give a sense of the venue's history. Opened in 1961 as an ice cream shop, the Bitter End has maintained its informal feel and continues to present aspiring folk and rock acts for a mix of curious tourists, N.Y.U. students and each band's contingent of fans. Cash only. **Subway:** A, C, E, F to W. 4th St.

The Bottom Line WEST VILLAGE 15 W. 4th St. (at Mercer St.) (212) 228-7880. Since 1974, the Bottom Line has presented singer-songwriters—a young Bruce Springsteen, an older Elvis Costello, among oth-

ers—in its spacious room. Patrons sit cabaret-style at tables, and though the seating is a bit cramped, it is more pleasant than standing, especially when the main musical fare is meant more for listening than dancing. The crowd varies according to the performer, but audiences tend to be slightly older than those at typical New York concerts. One of the best things about the Bottom Line is its willingness to book rarely heard country and bluegrass performers. Cash only.
Subway: F, S to Broadway–Lafayette St.; N, R to 8th St.

Brownies EAST VILLAGE 169 Ave. A (between 10th and 11th Sts.) (212) 420-8392. Transformed in the early 90's from a neighborhood bar to one of the best indie-rock clubs on the downtown circuit, Brownies continues to present punk-inspired, guitar-driven bands in a no-frills, music-first bar environment. Not the most comfortable of spaces, especially when the rectangular room gets crowded, Brownies redeems itself by putting together thoughtful bills of local bands with potential and touring acts that have garnered a buzz in the college-rock world. Cash only. **Subway:** L to First Ave.

Cafe Wha? WEST VILLAGE 115 Macdougal St. (between Bleecker and 3rd Sts.) (212) 254-3706. Decorated with hanging lights and wooden booths packed tightly together, this cozy basement club has been a Greenwich Village institution for more than 30 years. Cafe Wha? once hosted performances by young artists like Bob Dylan and Jimi Hendrix. The standout night nowadays is Brazilian night on Mondays—a festive, Carnaval-like party that combines the hip-shaking sounds of bossa nova, samba and Brazilian rock and jazz. Tuesday nights features the funky Slam Clinic with Mike Davis; various rock and pop musicians play on the weekends. **Subway:** A, C, E, F to W. 4th St.

CBGB LOWER EAST SIDE 315 Bowery (at Bleecker St.) (212) 982-4052. The famed CBGB's is still an ideal place to try out unknown rock bands and catch the occasional bigger name playing an intimate show. Since its heyday (the Ramones, the Talking Heads and Blondie are some of the bands that got their start here), CB's has lost some of its hold on the rock scene, but only because other similar venues have arisen. Patrons are allowed to enter and leave the club at will, giving CB's a neighborhood-hangout feel. Cash only.
Subway: 6 to Bleecker St.; F, S to Broadway–Lafayette St.

CB's 313 Gallery EAST VILLAGE 313 Bowery (at Bleecker St.) (212) 677-0455. By presenting mellow, acoustic-based sounds and monthly art exhibits in a cafe setting, CB's Gallery offers an entirely different experience from its legendary progenitor, CBGB. Here you'll find tables and candles instead of a mosh pit, spoken word and poetry instead of guitar distortion and sonic shriek. Like the original CBGB, however, the gallery makes an effort to present new and unknown talent. **Subway:** 6 to Bleecker St.; F, S to Broadway–Lafayette St.

Continental EAST VILLAGE 25 Third Ave. (between St. Marks Pl. and 9th St.) (212) 529-6924. With a dive-bar feel, four to five aspiring rock bands nightly and a blaring sound system, the sublimely sleazy Continental is the tongue-pierced stud at the mouth of St. Marks Place. Formerly known as the Continental Divide, the bar has launched many a career—from jam-band success Blues Traveler to garage-rock renovators the Pristeens. Punk legends such as Iggy Pop, Patti Smith and the late, great Joey Ramone have been known to perform unannounced sets. Cash only. **Subway:** 6 to Astor Pl.

Fez Under Time Cafe EAST VILLAGE 380 Lafayette St. (at Great Jones St.) (212) 533-2680. Two floors below the trendy Time Cafe, Fez presents indie-rockers, weekly jazz band "workshops," comedy acts and cabaret shows—all in a swank clubhouse atmosphere. It's equal parts Moroccan hashish den (hence the name), Village Vanguard-like basement jazz club and gangster hideaway. Patrons, generally a bit older than your average rock club crowd, sit at tables or in the plush leather booths that line the back wall of the room, which accommodates about 150. **Subway:** 6 to Bleecker St.; F, S to Broadway–Lafayette St.

Lakeside Lounge EAST VILLAGE 162 Ave. B (between 10th and 11th Sts.) (212) 529-8463. Enter the Lakeside Lounge and you could be in a shack on the edge of a pond deep in the country—it's trout fishing in Alphabet City. At first glance, East Village hipsters appear to dominate the front-room bar, but all are welcome. Excellent rockabilly, country and "cowpunk" bands appear most nights. Cash only. **Subway:** L to First Ave.

The Living Room LOWER EAST SIDE 84 Stanton St. (at Allen St.) (212) 533-7235. With its affordable but scrumptious vegetarian-leaning menu and its intimate folk music, the Living Room lives up to its name. The décor is makeshift but elegant. There are games for playing with friends or for breaking the ice. Rows of tables take up most of the floor space leading up to the stage. Fans of singer-songwriter folk music will enjoy the relaxed atmosphere, the sincere performances, and the casual, parlor-room feel. **Subway:** F to Second Ave.

Luna Lounge LOWER EAST SIDE 171 Ludlow St. (between Houston and Stanton Sts.) (212) 260-2323. Luna Lounge is half bar hangout, half free-music venue. Décor is minimal, but the wood bar adds a touch of elegance. The back room is an intimate space where alternative pop acts play for free each night. At the infamous Monday night comedy sessions, local pros try out their more edgy material. After the bands, a good jukebox makes Luna Lounge a quality last stop on the Ludlow Street bar circuit. Cash only. **Subway:** F to Second Ave.

Mercury Lounge LOWER EAST SIDE 217 E. Houston St. (between Essex and Ludlow Sts.) (212) 260-4700. The Mercury Lounge attracts a varied crowd that comes to listen to everything from singer-songwriters and alterna-rockers to the latest experimental electronic music practitioners. Since the back room holds only 200 people, buying tickets at the bar ahead of time is recommended when bigger names are on the bill. Inside the performance space, there are a few highly coveted tables, but most patrons stand. Be sure to bring ID; most shows are strictly 21 and over. **Subway:** F to Second Ave.

Nightingale Music Bar EAST VILLAGE 213 Second Ave. (at 13th St.) (212) 473-9398. A neighborhood dive that looks like a tomb from the outside but is warm and festive inside, Nightingale's is a prime spot for sipping a Budweiser and taking in a groovy jam. Loud and passionate live rock and funk (with occasional jazz) are presented nightly. Performers like Blues Traveler, the Spin Doctors and Joan Osborne got their start playing on the miniature stage, barely 10 feet from the bar in this small, almost windowless room. Cash only. **Subway:** L to Third Ave.; N, Q, R, W, 4, 5, 6 to 14th St.

Paddy Reilly's Music Bar MURRAY HILL 519 Second Ave. (at 29th St.) (212) 686-1210. Over the last few years, this bar has become a prime spot for all things Irish. The Irish expatriate community gathers here to catch up on gossip and news and to drink and dance, but all are welcome. The décor of the long bar, the small stage, and the adjoining billiard room strike a balance between dive-bar sublimity and aged-wood elegance. Of particular interest are the "sessi-uns," traditional Irish jam sessions where participants sit in a circle and play Celtic songs on guitar, hand drum and sometimes the uilleann pipes. Cash only. **Subway:** 6 to 28th St.

Rodeo Bar MURRAY HILL 375 Third Ave. (at 27th St.) (212) 683-6500. When it opened in 1987, the Rodeo Bar was one of the first places in New York to feature roots-rock made for and by local performers. Since then, it has expanded its booking policy to include touring roots-rockers as well. Long wooden railings and peanut shells on the floor add to the honky-tonk atmosphere. There is no music cover, making the Rodeo Bar a prime spot for savoring the flavor of long-time New York bar bands. **Subway:** 6 to 28th St.

Sidewalk Cafe EAST VILLAGE 94 Ave. A (at 6th St.) (212) 473-7373. The back of the Sidewalk Cafe is home to the Fort, where a musician who calls himself Lach books like-minded "anti-folk" singer-songwriters eager to rescue folk music from cloying sentimentality by adding a dose of punk sass. Most shows at the Fort have no cover and a one-drink minimum at tables. Performers pass the hat for donations. Pinball machines are in the front room, and a pool table is located in the basement. **Subway:** 6 to Astor Pl.; F to Second Ave.

The West End UPPER WEST SIDE 2911 Broadway (between 113th and 114th Sts.) (212) 662-8830. Jack Kerouac and Allen Ginsberg spent much of their college years as burgeoning beatniks eating and drinking at this Columbia University hangout, just as many a Columbian does today. Jazz (as well as rock and folk by student bands) still plays in the back room. What was once a dive is now a pleasant restaurant with brick and wood décor, tall ceilings and overhead fans. And maybe at one of the booths in the back, some young Columbians are creating more great American literature. **Subway:** 1, 9 to 116th St.

Jazz, Blues & Experimental

Birdland MIDTOWN WEST 315 W. 44th St. (between Eighth and Ninth Aves.) (212) 581-3080. Birdland features some of the most thoughtfully booked jazz in the city. The club pays direct homage to its namesake, the legendary original Birdland at Broadway and 52nd Street. (The only thing missing are the caged parakeets that used to slowly asphyxiate on cigarette smoke during bebop's hey-day in the 1940's and 50's.) Though it's a fully functional restaurant with a

Southern-tinged menu, Birdland's main attraction is music. Reservations are recommended for the music sets ($20–$35 and a $10 food or drink minimum). **Subway:** A, C, E to 42nd St.

Blue Note WEST VILLAGE 131 W. 3rd St. (between Sixth Ave. and Macdougal St.) (212) 475-8592. Performances by jazz heavyweights such as Tony Bennett, Oscar Peterson and Chick Corea, and exhilarating double bills are the main attractions at the Blue Note. A night at the Blue Note can easily cost you $100. Because the club's seating sometimes makes rush-hour subway trains seem cozy, reservations and early arrival are essential. Record labels use Monday nights, when it's considerably less expensive, to break in new acts—a real bargain when established musicians join in. **Subway:** A, C, E, F to W. 4th St.

Chicago B.L.U.E.S. WEST VILLAGE 73 Eighth Ave. (between 13th and 14th Sts.) (212) 924-9755. There's nothing fancy here, just a bar and a plain, brick-walled music room with a robust sound system. But the club is an outpost of the Chicago-centered Midwestern blues circuit, which yields some of the most subtle and big-hearted American music. Unlike the run of New York blues clubs, this club books not only the headliner but the whole band, which provides qualitatively different music. **Subway:** A, C, E to 14th St.; L to Eighth Ave.

Cooler WEST VILLAGE 418 W. 14th St. (between Ninth Ave. and Washington St.) (212) 645-5189. Once a meat market—literally—this former basement butchery offers some of the best edgy experimental music around. Much like the Knitting Factory, the Cooler has become a center for strange, new sounds with its booking policy based on a "downtown" aesthetic rather than a particular genre of music: everything from DJs to ska to noise-rock can be heard, sometimes all at once. The Cooler is a great place to expand one's appreciation of the sonic boundaries where music meets chaos, and dance while doing so. Cash only. **Subway:** A, C, E to 14th St.; L to Eighth Ave.

Iridium Jazz Club MIDTOWN WEST 1650 Broadway (at 51st St.) (212) 582-2121. Since it opened in 1993, this tony club has become one of the top jazz venues in the city. Success has led to a recent move and a series of "Live at the Iridium" recordings on various labels. In addition to presenting legendary guitarist Les Paul every Monday night, Iridium features both established and up-and-coming jazz stars. **Subway:** 1, 9 to 66th St.

Izzy Bar EAST VILLAGE 166 First Ave. (between 10th and 11th Sts.) (212) 228-0444. Upstairs there's a bar with fashionable club music on the speakers and fashionable young Manhattanites on the comfy chairs. The bottom floor, unexpectedly, has a music space for fairly experimental jazz and dance music; center stage seats are almost right in the bandleader's face. Bookings are a mixed lot and the cover charge is usually $10 or less. **Subway:** L to First Ave.

Knitting Factory TRIBECA 74 Leonard St. (between Broadway and Church St.) (212) 219-3055. With four spaces for live music, the Knitting Factory is host to not only the avant-garde jazz that first earned this place its reputation, but also rock, spoken word, theater, film and even children's shows. So much is going on in the Knitting Factory on any given night that there's often a bottleneck at the front door. The Main Space holds 350 patrons and can get quite crowded. The Alterknit Theater presents lesser-known acts as well as spoken word, theater and films in a space that holds 90. Free performances occur in the downstairs Tap Room, which has over 15 microbrews on tap. And the newest space, the Old Office, presents up-and-coming jazz artists in a more traditional jazz-club setting. **Subway:** 1, 9 to Franklin St.; A, C, E to Canal St.

Lenox Lounge HARLEM 288 Lenox Ave. (between 124th and 125th Sts.) (212) 427-0253. This Harlem art-deco bar is rich with musical history, including a corner banquette where Billie Holiday liked to claim a regular table. Bandleaders are mostly drawn from New York jazz's middle-aged netherworld: Musicians like Chico Freeman and James Spaulding—too old to be lions, too young to be legends. And the management doesn't rustle you out between sets; you can settle in for the evening. That's the type of peace of mind you can't buy downtown. **Subway:** 2, 3 to 125th St.

Roulette TRIBECA/SOHO 222 West Broadway (between Franklin and N. Moore Sts.) (212) 219-8242. Above boisterous young professionals drinking champagne in the Bubble Lounge, serious avant-garde music takes place in Roulette. This nonprofit performance space has a mix of elegant informality and concentrated audacity, with musicians trying all sorts of new, experimental ideas. Avant-garde saxophonist John Zorn performed some of his first "game piece" compositions at Roulette, and everyone from Oliver Lake, the esteemed jazz composer, to Thurston Moore, guitarist for the noise-rock band Sonic Youth, has appeared as part of Roulette's concert programs. Cash only. **Subway:** 1, 9 to Franklin St.

Smoke UPPER WEST SIDE 2751 Broadway (between 105th and 106th Sts.) (212) 864-6662. Smoke (formerly known as Augie's Pub) captures the spirit of legendary jazz jam joints like Minton's—where bebop was born in the 1940's. Up-and-coming jazz musicians blow and wail in the small, cozy storefront room. It can get quite packed, but the atmosphere is friendly and the music is almost always exciting. Jazz aficionados such as the authors Stanley Crouch and Albert Murray regularly show up, crowding in alongside Columbia University students. Cash only. **Subway:** 1, 9 to 103rd St.

St. Nick's Pub HARLEM 773 St. Nicholas Blvd. (at 149th St.) (212) 769-8275. A legendary Harlem jazz bar, St. Nick's still serves up live jazz six nights a week, Wednesday to Monday. Saxophonist Patience Higgins and the Sugar Hill Jazz Quartet lead a popular jam session every Monday, with musicians playing well past 1 A.M. When the band takes a booze break, the jukebox cranks up, blaring both classic jazz and R&B, as well as contemporary hip-hop. Even on a Monday, seats are difficult to come by in this tiny shoebox of a bar. Cash only. **Subway:** A, B, C, D to 145th St.

Terra Blues WEST VILLAGE 149 Bleecker St. (between Thompson St. and La Guardia Pl.) (212) 777-7776. In the heart of the Village, a flight above Bleecker Street, Terra Blues is home to both local and national blues acts. Though it's named after an obscure, rural Mississippi blues genre, Terra Blues is a modern-day urban saloon with surreal sculpture and blowzy curtains framing the small stage. Musicians like playing the club and the same performers are likely to return throughout the month. **Subway:** A, C, E, F to W. 4th St.

Tonic LOWER EAST SIDE 107 Norfolk St. (between Delancey and Rivington Sts.) (212) 358-7503. Downtown nightlife goes synergistic in a former kosher wine market next to the parking lot for Ratner's Restaurant. Tonic, which opened in early 1998, used to be a hair salon, but is now a night spot with experimental jazz, comedy nights, spoken words and occasional movie screenings. Cash only. **Subway:** F to Delancey St.; J, M, Z to Essex St.

Village Vanguard WEST VILLAGE 178 Seventh Ave. South (between W. 11th St. and Waverly Pl.) (212) 255-4037. Known for its intimacy, pristine acoustics and lack of pretense, the Village Vanguard is the one of the world's finest jazz venues. Since 1935, this basement hideaway has hosted a staggering lineup— from Barbra Streisand and Woody Allen to John Coltrane and Thelonious Monk. Over 100 albums bear the imprimatur "Recorded Live at the Village Vanguard." In 1965, the Mel Lewis-Thad Jones Orchestra began a Monday night big band tradition that endures under the moniker Vanguard Jazz Orchestra. Reservations are recommended. Cash only. **Subway:** 1, 2, 3, 9 to 14th St.

World & Latin

Bistro Latino MIDTOWN WEST 1711 Broadway (at 54th St.) (212) 956-1000. Most of the friendly, all-aged Latino crowd at the upscale Bistro Latino come for dinner and stay salsa on Fridays and Saturdays, featuring free dance lessons. You can also pay a small cover to skip dinner and go straight for the music and dancing and sip one of the Bistro's delicious, fruity cocktails made with mangoes, passion fruit, and South American specialty liquors like Chilean Muscat brandy or Brazilian sugar cane rum. **Subway:** A, B, C, D, 1, 9 to 59th St.

Copacabana MIDTOWN WEST 570 W. 34th St. (near 11th Ave.). Copacabana is both a Latin American club where the most respected salsa and merengue musicians perform and a disco where house music thunders. The crowd is predominantly Latino, but New Yorkers of all stripes mix together along with tourists from Europe, South America and Japan. Most wear formal attire and come to dance. Seasoned veterans and hot newcomers, from Eddie Palmieri to La India, perform about three days a week. Copacabana **temporarily closed** in mid-2001 after losing its lease. The new location listed above is scheduled to open in the summer of 2002. Until then, Copacabana's music has moved to **Ohm** (*see* "Dance Clubs") four nights a week. **Subway:** A, C, E to 34th St.

El Flamingo CHELSEA 547 W. 21st St. (between 10th and 11th Aves.) (212) 243-2121. A snazzy venue that plays up the Art Deco supper-club theme to the hilt. The main room has a good-sized dance floor that splits in half when the club hosts live music performances; the non-rhythmically inclined can watch from above. Various promoters use El Flamingo for shows, so keep an eye out for upcoming gigs. **Subway:** C, E to 23rd St.

Gonzalez y Gonzalez EAST VILLAGE 625 Broadway (between Bleecker and Houston Sts.) (212) 473-8787. Wednesday through Saturday bands play salsa, mambo, merengue and charanga, and DJs spin the latest Latin-tinged records in this bar's back room, the Blue Lounge. Outside, there's often a line of stylishly dressed patrons (semi-formal attire is the norm but not required) who come from far and wide for the mango or guava margaritas, scorching sounds and moderately priced Mexican food.
Subway: F, S to Broadway–Lafayette St.; 6 to Bleecker St.

S.O.B.'s TRIBECA/SOHO 200 Varick St. (at Houston St.) (212) 243-4940. The audience sways more than the palm fronds on the faux-tree, making S.O.B.'s one of the city's best clubs for Latin, Caribbean and Afropop music. Decorated in a copacabana-hut style, but with disco lights, S.O.B.'s is a dancer's heaven. The club even offers salsa and tango lessons before most weekend shows. In the best New York manner, ethnic groups mix at S.O.B.'s to produce a culture greater than that of any individual subgroup. Purchase advance tickets for popular shows. **Subway:** 1, 9 to Houston St.; C, E to Spring St.

Zinc Bar WEST VILLAGE 90 W. Houston St. (between Thompson St. and La Guardia Pl.) (212) 477-8337. The Zinc Bar is a downtown venue that manages to be sophisticated yet retain an informal atmosphere. Opened in 1993, the Zinc presents some of the best up-and-coming jazz and world sounds—especially Brazilian music—in the city. The Zinc Bar can get quite crowded, so arrive early if you want to sit. Be on the lookout for two kinds of cats at the Zinc Bar: famous jazz musicians kicking back after a gig and the two felines who fearlessly roam through the crowd. **Subway:** F, S to Broadway–Lafayette St.

CABARET

One of the singular attractions of New York City is its busy cabaret scene. The term "cabaret" applies to high-end supper clubs featuring singers who perform popular standards from the pre-rock era on. Cabaret flourishes in New York because of its proximity to Broadway. Theater stars often moonlight as cabaret performers, and a nightclub act can also be a stepping-stone to Broadway. Cabaret also intersects with the world of jazz, although these two worlds are quite distinct.

An evening of cabaret with an entertainment charge and food and drink minimum can cost quite a bit more than a Broadway show. But the kind of magical intimacy that the best cabaret has to offer is something that can only be experienced in a nightclub where the lights are low and the champagne flowing.

The city's four leading cabarets are the chic **Café Carlyle** in the Carlyle hotel, the **Oak Room** at the Algonquin Hotel, **Feinstein's at the Regency** (named after the popular singer and pianist Michael Feinstein who helps book the club and who has performed there) at the Regency Hotel and **Arci's Place** on Park Avenue South.

Café Carlyle Carlyle hotel, 981 Madison Ave. (between 76th and 77th Sts.) (212) 744-1600. The Café Carlyle, the Rolls-Royce of the city's cabarets, tends to book the same performers every year for extended engagements. Ruling the roost in the late spring and late fall is the singer and pianist Bobby Short, who has appeared there every year for more than three decades. Now in his 70's, Mr. Short is an effervescent musical bon vivant with exquisite taste in songs, who brings the urbane music of Cole Porter, Cy Coleman and others thrillingly to life in performances that have the feel of nightly parties. **Subway:** 6 to 77th St.

Oak Room The Algonquin, 59 W. 44th St. (between Fifth and Sixth Aves.) (212) 840-6800. The Oak Room of the Algonquin (the site of the famous literary Round Table in the 1920's and 30's) is the regular home of the singer and actress Andrea Marcovicci, a diehard romantic, who appears in the late fall resurrecting the Golden Age of American popular song.
Subway: B, D, F, S to 42nd St.

Feinstein's at the Regency Regency Hotel, 540 Park Ave. (at 61st St.) (212) 759-4100. Pricey and elegant, situated in the hotel's "power breakfast" room, Feinstein's at the Regency books big name talent that has run the gamut from country music (Glen Campbell) to comedy (the Smothers Brothers) to Las Vegas legends (Keely Smith). Performers who appear their regularly and have solid followings include Rosemary Clooney, John Pizzarelli and Michael Feinstein. The atmosphere might be described as "romantic library."
Subway: N, R, W to Lexington Ave.; 4, 5, 6 to 59th St.

Arci's Place 450 Park Ave. South (at 30th St.) (212) 532-4370. Among the performers who appear regularly at the up-and-coming supper club are Karen Mason, Donna McKechnie and Jim Caruso. There is an emphasis on Broadway performers (from shows like *Jekyll and Hyde*) who have put together cabaret acts. The atmosphere is warm and homey, the menu Italian. **Subway:** 6 to 33rd St.

Firebird Café 365 W. 46th St. (between Eight and Ninth Aves.) (212) 586-0244. The cafe, an adjunct of the Firebird Restaurant which serves Russian haute cuisine, has a high turnover of mid-level cabaret performers (some of them very promising) who are not yet well enough known to have extended engagements. **Subway:** A, C, E to 42nd St.

—by Stephen Holden

Other Cabarets and Supper Clubs
(See also "A Grand Oasis: New York's Hotel Bars," earlier in this chapter.)

Bemelmans Bar Carlyle hotel, 981 Madison Ave. (between 76th and 77th Sts.) (212) 744-1600. At Bemelmans, for only a $10 cover, you can hear Barbara Carroll, one of the great jazz pianists, who's in residence half the year and attracts a celebrity audience. (Tony Bennett has been known to drop in and join her for a song or two.) Peter Mintun provides the music the rest of the year. Enjoy the private, romantic booths or reserve one of the small tables for two right by the piano. **Subway:** 6 to 77th St.

Danny's Skylight Room 346 W. 46th St. (between Eighth and Ninth Aves.) (212) 265-8133. There is a skylight in Danny's Skylight Room, but don't expect

to see too much sky—or too much light, for that matter. But that's O.K., because your focus should be on the front of this rather unadorned, crowded room in the back of Danny's Grand Sea Palace, a good Thai restaurant on Restaurant Row. That's where you'll find some of the city's finest cabaret performers, from fresh upstarts to great old-timers like Blossom Dearie. As you enter Danny's, there's also a narrow piano bar, a cramped but festive spot decked out with strings of Christmas lights, where you can sing along with the theater types who've made the stools around the piano their second home.
Subway: A, C, E to 42nd St.

Delmonico Lounge Hotel Delmonico, 502 Park Ave. (at 59th St.) (212) 355-2500. A remarkably small room (seating just 38), the D Lounge is the only bar at the Hotel Delmonico, so patrons are not necessarily here for the music. But the room itself is very comfortable; especially if you can ease back into one of the cushy banquettes. The performers (usually a singer accompanied by trio or piano) are practically at one with the patrons. Shows are presented only on weekends, and the music goes on hiatus in the summer.
Subway: 4, 5, 6 to 59th St; N, R, W to Lexington Ave.

Don't Tell Mama 343 W. 46th St. (between Eighth and Ninth Aves.) (212) 757-0788. This enterprising theater district perennial is really three venues in one: two cabaret rooms and a piano bar under the same management. On weekdays, there are up to four shows a night, and on weekends, up to eight— and that's in addition to the virtually nonstop show in the bar, which features singing waiters after 9 P.M. Cover charges and minimums vary, but the piano bar has no cover. **Subway:** A, C, E to 42nd St.

The Duplex 61 Christopher St. (at Seventh Ave. South) (212) 255-5438. This Village bar and cabaret ought to be called Camp Duplex, given the nature of the crowd and many of the shows. It's the oldest continually running cabaret in the city, where many a career was launched. With three levels—a lively piano bar on the first, a lounge/game room on the second and, tucked away off to the side between the two, a small cabaret/theater—the Duplex always seems to be hopping. The cabaret has a tiny proscenium stage (an unusual feature for a cabaret) with rows of crowded cocktail tables providing the seating. Besides the standard music, there's comedy, improv, theater and drag. Cash only.
Subway: 1, 9 to Christopher St.

Joe's Pub 425 Lafayette St. (between Astor Pl. and 4th St.) (212) 539-8777. A portrait of the legendary producer Joseph Papp watches over the plush banquettes, red votives and zinc ballustrades at what is one of the latest buzz-heavy night spots. Depending on the time and the scheduled act, Joe's Pub will be a swank cabaret, a pre-theater watering hole, a place to slam poetry or a late-night drop-in center for hip, downtown laze-abouts. You'll usually find top-quality performers in this friendly, laid-back setting.
Subway: 6 to Astor Pl.; N, R to 8th St.

Judy's 169 Eighth Ave.(between 18th and 19th Sts.) (212) 929-5410.
Judy Kreston, a singer, and her husband, David Lahm, a pianist, run this
Chelsea cabaret and restaurant that attracts interesting lounge acts. Kreston and
Lahm frequently perform on Saturday nights. Cash only.
Subway: A, C, E to 14th St.

Roseland Ballroom 239 W. 52nd St. (between Broadway and Eighth Ave.)
(212) 247-0200. Arena-like rock shows, retro-big band jazz nights, occasional
salsa dancing and rhythm and blues "Rhythm Revues" are all on the program in
this legendary palace. Opened by Louis Brecker in 1951, the Ballroom moved to
its current location on 52nd Street, once occupied by the Gay Blades ice-skating rink in 1956. Inside, the gigantic dance floor (it can hold 3,200 people) fills
up for rock concerts. Arrive early, since the line to get in, complete with friskers
and multiple ticket checks, can wrap around the block. The swing and salsa
nights usually require formal or semi-formal attire. **Subway:** C, 1, 9 to 50th St.

Rose's Turn 55 Grove St. (between Bleecker St. and Seventh Ave. South)
(212) 366-5438. One of the friendliest cabaret and piano bars in the West Village, Rose's Turn attracts a mixed crowd—gay, straight, locals and tourists who
hear the music and laughter and wander in off the street. Upstairs there are
singers, comedy acts and musical revues (usually for a cover charge and a two-
drink minimum). Downstairs you can just hang out at the bar or sit by the
piano. The in-house talent varies from night to night, but none can hold a candle to the team on Saturday nights: a piano player who takes requests (anything
except Barry Manilow's "Mandy") and three warbling bartenders who sing and
tell jokes. **Subway:** 1, 9 to Christopher St.

Supper Club 240 W. 47th St. (between Broadway and Eighth Ave.)
(212) 921-1940. A historic ballroom that once served as the theater of the Edison Hotel, the Supper Club holds rock shows during the week. But the club's
heart lies in swanky ballroom dinner dances and late-night jump-swing parties,
which it presents Friday and Saturday nights. Although some rockers play the
club cabaret-style to listeners seated at tables, most perform to a standing-only
audience. Top-notch musicians play at the big-band and jump-swing shows, and
a full restaurant menu is available. The Blue Room, a space upstairs with velvet
couches, periodically features cabaret acts. **Subway:** A, C, E to 42nd St.

Torch 137 Ludlow St. (between Rivington and Stanton Sts.) (212) 228-5151.
There's no name on the facade of this addition to the Lower East Side's burgeoning scene, but it would be hard to walk by or mistake it for one of its worn-
looking neighbors. The front of 137 Ludlow is an appealing mix of brushed
steel, birch-colored wood grain and frosted glass. Inside the atmosphere recalls a
40's or 50's lounge, with a long narrow bar area at the front, semicircular booths
at the back and cabaret seating in front of a small stage. Expect fabulous torch
singers, all glammed up, filling the air with newfangled renditions of vocal jazz
classics. **Subway:** F to Second Ave.

Triad Theater 158 W. 72nd St. (between Columbus Ave. and Broadway) (212) 362-2590. The Triad Theater is usually home to a show with an open-ended run, and after 10 P.M. becomes a cabaret space. What it lacks in atmosphere it makes up in sightlines and proximity to the performers. Downstairs, in the Dark Star Lounge, an average of four performers a night keep customers satisfied. Food is served in both rooms, and downstairs, in addition to the comfortable tables near the stage, there's a friendly bar that attracts neighborhood regulars.
Subway: 1, 2, 3, 9 to 72nd St.

Wilson's Grill 201 W. 79th St. (at Amsterdam Ave.) (212) 769-0100. Occupying what used to be the ballroom of the Lucerne Hotel next door, this Upper West Side find is a sophisticated change of pace from the yuppified beer joints lining Columbus and Amsterdam Avenues. High ceilings and a deep, rich, wood interior create a regal ambiance, enjoyed by a clientele of mainly young professionals. There's live music seven nights a week with no cover. The schedule is jazz heavy, but classical, Motown and R&B groups are frequent performers. **Subway:** 1, 9 to 79th St.

COMEDY CLUBS

(Many music venues and cabarets have comedy nights, like Luna Lounge, Fez Under Time Cafe and Rose's Turn. Check local listings for schedules.)

Boston Comedy Club GREENWICH VILLAGE 82 W. 3rd St. (between Sullivan and Thompson Sts.) (212) 477-1000. This lesser-known basement club features comedy nightly, often with several acts on the bill. Monday is open-mike.
Price: Sun.–Thu., $8, two-drink minimum; Fri.–Sat., $12, two-drink minimum.
Subway: A, C, E, F to W. 4th St.

Caroline's Comedy Club MIDTOWN WEST 1626 Broadway (at 49th St.) (212) 757-4100. Just when you were afraid fun had been banished from Times Square, Caroline's comes to the rescue. In 15 years, Caroline Hirsch's club has gone from a comedy fledgling to a block-long complex where many TV stars perform, often testing new material. Save some dollars and ask about the dinner-and-show packages. **Price:** $20–$27, two-drink minimum.
Subway: N, R, W to 49th St.; C, E, 1, 9 to 50th St.

Comedy Cellar WEST VILLAGE 117 Macdougal St. (between 3rd and Bleecker Sts.) (212) 254-3480. In the more than 20 years that it has been open, Robin Williams, Stephen Wright and Jerry Seinfeld have made surprise appearances at this intimate Greenwich Village club. **Price:** Sun.–Thu., $10; Fri.–Sat., $12, two-drink minimum. **Subway:** A, C, E, F to W. 4th St.

Comic Strip Live UPPER EAST SIDE 1568 Second Ave. (between 81st and 82nd Sts.) (212) 861-9386. You'll find 24 years' worth of autographed photos on the wall of alums such as Eddie Murphy (one of the club's discoveries), Paul Reiser and Chris Rock. New comics are so eager to perform in the no-cover Monday Talent Spotlite that twice a year they line the streets to get a lottery number.

Drinks are top-dollar, but usually so are the headliners. **Price:** $10–$14, $10 drink minimum. **Subway:** 4, 5, 6 to 86th St.

Dangerfield's Comedy Club MIDTOWN EAST 1118 First Ave. (between 61st and 62nd Sts.) (212) 593-1650. Rodney Dangerfield's 30-year-old club feels like it's in a 1960's time warp with its swingin' red velvet and wood paneling. There's no drink minimum (a rarity in New York), affordable parking and a large menu. The featured acts are pros from the circuit, and Rodney himself performs when in town. **Price:** Sun.–Thu., $12.50; Fri.–Sat., $15–$20. **Subway:** N, R, W to Lexington Ave.; 4, 5, 6 to 59th St.

Gotham Comedy Club FLATIRON/UNION SQUARE 34 W. 22nd St. (between Fifth and Sixth Aves.) (212) 367-9000. With its comfortably upscale atmosphere this Flatiron oasis beckons audiences tired of divey or over-crowded clubs. Top-notch comics who regularly emcee jokingly complain that the bathrooms here are nicer than their apartments. The room is only a few years old, but name stars and TV comics perform , and there are also frequent new talent nights. **Price:** $10–$15, two-drink minimum. **Subway:** F, N, R, 1, 9 to 23rd St.

New York Comedy Club FLATIRON/UNION SQUARE 241 E. 24th St. (between Second and Third Aves.) (212) 696-5233. It's a small, divey joint that many comedians have played at least once. Despite its size, the club does pull in pros, and on a regular night, expect truly funny performances from younger comedians. **Price:** Sun.–Thu., $5, two-drink minimum; Fri.–Sat., $10, two-drink minimum. **Subway:** 6 to 23rd St.

Stand-Up New York UPPER WEST SIDE 236 W. 78th St. (between Broadway and Amsterdam Ave.) (212) 595-0850. What do Denis Leary, Jon Stewart and Comedy Central's Dr. Katz have in common? They all started at this 10-year-old club. While short on atmosphere, it's full of comedy history. There have been surprise visits from stars like Drew Carey, Robin Williams, Dennis Miller and Al Franken. **Price:** Sun.–Thu., $7, two-drink minimum; Fri.–Sat., $12, two-drink minimum. **Subway:** 1, 9 to 79th St.

Upright Citizens Brigade Theater CHELSEA 161 W. 22nd St. (between Sixth and Seventh Aves.) (212) 366-9176. The Upright Citizens Brigade, which had a series on Comedy Central, has its own 74-seat theater in Chelsea, where you can find some of the most talented performers around. They supplement their comedic arsenal with equally talented guests, like David Cross of Mr. *Show* and Janeane Garofalo. The Sunday 9:30 show is free. **Price:** $5. **Subway:** F, 1, 9 to 23rd St.

Sports & Recreation

Whether the bleachers are your milieu or you like to get your hands dirty, New York City can satisfy the most avid sports enthusiast. There are countless professional and amateur sporting events for spectators, though some tickets are easier to come by than others. And for those who want to be part of the action, there are venues throughout the city, both private and public, that offer virtually every kind of activity. According to the Parks Department, the municipal park system has more than 28,000 acres including 854 playgrounds, 700 playing fields, 500 tennis courts, 33 outdoor swimming pools, 10 indoor swimming pools, 33 recreation and senior centers, 15 miles of beach, 13 golf courses, six ice rinks, four major stadiums and four zoos. The department's Web site, *www.ci.nyc.ny.us/html/dpr,* is extremely useful with information on area parks, facilities and activities throughout the year.

PARTICIPANT SPORTS & ACTIVITIES
Basketball

Pick-up, playground basketball is one of New York's great traditions. Players of NBA caliber such as Connie Hawkins and Stephon Marbury have all honed their game on the city's blacktop courts, as have legends of more local renown such as The Goat of Amsterdam Avenue, Joe "The Destroyer" Hammond, and Pee Wee Kirkwood to name but a few.

Many of the top games are hard to join if you're not a regular, so the best places for a quick run are usually inside city gyms. The **West Side YMCA** (5 W. 63rd St. off Central Park West, $15 day pass) has one of the nicest, full-length floors, and the **Vanderbilt YMCA** offers a smaller court (47th St. between Second and Third Aves., $20 day pass). The **Harlem YMCA** (180 W. 135th St.) also offers basketball, and a day pass is only $10. The relatively new **Basketball City,** offering six hardwood courts at 24th Street and the West Side Highway also allows walk-ons ($10, 9 A.M.–3 P.M., Mon.–Fri.; weekends, $15 for half-hour sessions), as does the **Field House at Chelsea Piers** (*see section* "Chelsea Piers"*).* The **Carmine Street Recreation Center** also offers basketball, though it can be crowded, and you must purchase a year membership for $25 (which you can do on-site).

If you're determined to play outside, playgrounds where one is likely to get into a full-court game include **Riverside Park** (courts can be found at 79th, 96th and 110th Sts.), **Central Park** (just north of the Great Lawn), **Asphalt Green** (York Ave. between 91st and 92nd Sts.), **96th Street Playground** (96th St. between First Ave. and the FDR Dr.), and the courts at 37th Street and Second Avenue.

But no trip to New York is complete for the basketball enthusiast without a visit to the West 4th Street courts (at Sixth Ave.), where many tournaments featuring some of the best talent in the city are played. In the summer months—if you're lucky—you may even witness ex-Knick, Queens-native, and now hated Miami Heat forward Anthony Mason posting up hapless opponents on this hallowed ground.

Biking

Organizations and Tours

Bike New York 891 Amsterdam Ave. (at 103rd St.) (212) 932-2300. Sponsored by Hostelling International and the New York City Department of Transportation, Bike New York is a 42-mile, five-borough tour of New York City that takes place each year in early May. This unique cycling tour begins at Battery Park and then winds its way over five bridges and through the many ethnic neighborhoods of the Bronx, Queens and Brooklyn before it ends in Staten Island. The pace is comfortable, there are plenty of rest stops, and the route is entirely traffic-free. At the Tour-ending Festival at Fort Wadsworth in Gateway National Recreation Area you can relax, dance to live music, purchase lunch and eventually return to Manhattan on a free Staten Island Ferry ride.

The Fast and Fabulous Cycling Club Fast and Fab, as it is more widely known, a lesbian and gay bike club, was formed in 1994 when triathletes needed to train for Gay Games IV. Recognizing that not everyone would be able to cycle together, founder Bob Nelson drew up ride lists, one column marked "Fast" and the other—avoiding the word "slow" so as not to discourage anyone from participating— "Fabulous." Free rides for both levels begin at the boathouse in Central Park at 9 A.M. Sunday morning. For more information, call Bob Nelson (212-567-7160) or Paulette Meggoe (718-293-0885).

Time's Up! (212) 802-8222 *www.times-up.org*. Activist in spirit, Time's Up! sponsors a number of free bicycle and in-line skate tours that challenge the traffic-centered nature of New York City. The monthly "Critical Mass" ride is an attempt to defy the dominance of motor vehicles by bringing together many bikers to "raise the profile of cyclists" in the city, and assert equal rights to the road. On the other hand, many of the club-sponsored rides have no political aim at all: they're simply fun and even educational. The "Historical Ride" looks at important urban sites in Lower Manhattan and compares them to archival photographs, while the "Socrates Sculpture Ride" takes cyclists along the shores of Manhattan, Wards and Randalls Islands, and Queens to the Socrates Sculpture Park in Long Island City.

Bicycle Rentals

Larry and Jeff's Bicycles Plus 1690 Second Ave. (between 87th and 88th Sts.), (212) 722-2201. Bikes are available for $7.50 per hour or $25 per day. Credit card necessary for deposit.

Loeb Boathouse in Central Park (74th St. and East Dr.) (212) 861-4137. There are three-speed, 10-speed and tandem bikes for rent at the Boathouse, 10 A.M.–5:30 P.M. daily, $9–$15 per hour.

Metro Bicycle Stores 332 E. 14th St. (between First and Second Aves.) (212) 228-4344; 546 Sixth Ave. (at 15th St.) (212) 255-5100; 417 Canal St. (212) 334-8000; 231 W. 96th St. (between Broadway and Amsterdam Ave.) (212) 663-7531; 360 W. 47th St. (at Ninth Ave.) (212) 581-4500; 1311 Lexington Ave. (at 88th St.) (212) 427-4450. With six locations in Manhattan, Metro is one of the more convenient places to rent a bike. All stores offer bicycles at $7 per hour and $35 per day.

Pedal Pusher Bicycle Shop 1306 Second Ave. (at 68th St.) (212) 228-5592. Pedal Pusher has the best rental deal in the city, offering hybrids and mountain bikes for just $5.77 per hour and $17.32 per day. A credit card, driver's license or passport must be left at the store as security.

Sizzling Bicycle Inc. 3100 Ocean Pkwy, Brooklyn (718) 372-8985. Here there are a limited number of bikes available for $6 per hour or $30 per day, if you'd like to explore the Brooklyn waterfront or the bustling Russian community of Brighton Beach.

Toga Bike Shop 110 West End Ave. (65th Street) (212) 799-9625. Bicycles are available for $30 per day (there are no hourly rentals). Toga's convenient for exploring Manhattan's Upper West Side or Central Park only blocks away.

Billiards/Pool

Amsterdam Billiard Club West Side, 344 Amsterdam Ave. (at 77th St.) (212) 496-8180; East Side, 210 E. 86th St. (between Second and Third Aves.) (212) 570-4545. Upscale venues with plentiful, well-kept tables, full bars and amiable table-to-table waitress service. **Price:** $7.50–$10.50 per hour per person. **Credit cards:** All major. **Subway:** West Side: 1, 9 to 79th St.; East Side: 4, 5, 6 to 86th St.

Billiard Club 220 W. 19th St. (between Seventh and Eighth Aves.) (212) 206-7665. This is the place to go for an intimate game of pool in a somewhat clubby environment, with its polished pine floor, low-key atmosphere and dark wood paneling. The 42 tables are spread out over two levels. **Price:** $8–$14 per hour per table. **Credit cards:** All major. **Subway:** 1, 9 to 18th St.

Corner Billiards 85 Fourth Ave. (at 11th St.) (212) 995-1314. Corner Billiards is your only option if you want to shoot a rack in the Village (excluding the numerous bars with smaller pool tables that proliferate in the area). The 28 Brunswick Gold Crown Tables, a cafe, a microbrewery and waitress service all conspire to make this a much more civilized experience than one might expect. **Price:** $7–$12 per hour for one player, $4 per hour each additional player. **Subway:** L, N, Q, R, W, 4, 5, 6, to 14th St.

Slate 54 W. 21st St. (between Fifth and Sixth Aves.) (212) 989-0096. Named after the stone beneath the green felt on a pool table, Slate is an upscale billiards hall and restaurant where visitors can play on one of the 34 pool tables (billiards and snooker tables also available). **Price:** $5–$16 per hour per player.

SoHo Billiard Sport Center 56 E. Houston St. (between Mulberry and Mott Sts.) (212) 925-3753. Brightly lit and pleasantly spacious, this street level pool hall has a young downtown crowd. Players shoot pool on 28 tables spread out on multiple levels. **Price:** $7–$8 per hour for one player, $2–$3 per hour each additional player. **Subway:** F to Broadway–Lafayette St.; 6 to Bleecker St.; N, R to Prince St.

Boating

Downtown Boathouse West St. (between Chambers and Canal Sts.) (212) 966-1852. May through October, the Downtown Boathouse offers free kayaking between two piers on the Hudson River. A staff of volunteers will outfit you with a life jacket and a boat and give you some basic instructions. Once you have gained some experience, you can join them for longer kayaking trips. Trips are on a first-come, first-serve basis. **Subway:** 1, 9 to Canal St.

Floating the Apple Hudson River (at 44th St.) (212) 564–5412. The aim of this club is to make the waters of New York City more accessible to boating enthusiasts. They offer a series of weekly events in Manhattan, Brooklyn and the Bronx that encourage use of the area's waterways and harbor by water-sports aficionados. The Manhattan activities originate at Pier 40 (Hudson River at Houston St.) and include youth and adult rowing programs. The club also sponsors various sailing and swimming events, including the Great Hudson River Swim from the Marina at 79th Street to Chelsea Piers at 23rd Street.

Loeb Boathouse Central Park Lake (74th St. and East Drive) (212) 517-2233. For one of the most relaxing (and romantic) afternoons you'll ever experience, rent a rowboat at Central Park's Loeb Boathouse and ply the waters of one of the Park's most scenic areas. Explore the western marsh area, visit one of the gazebos or simply watch as other landlubbers try to tame their oars. Boats are available year-round, weather permitting. **Price:** $10 per hour, $30 cash deposit required. **Subway:** 6 to 77th St.

Prospect Park Brooklyn, (718) 282-7789. Get some exercise and a different view of the Park by touring the Lullwater and the Lake on a pedal boat. A great way to spend a lazy summer afternoon, pedal boats may be rented from the Wollman Center and Rink on weekends and holidays from May 15 through September. **Price:** $10 per hour. **Subway:** Q to Prospect Park or Parkside Ave.

Bowling

Bowlmor Lanes 110 University Pl. (between 12th and 13th Sts.) (212) 255-8188. Weekend nights at Bowlmor Lanes rival some of the neighboring bars and clubs for popularity—and noise. Two floors of lanes and a large bar area open until 4 A.M., complemented by a dance music soundtrack, make for a vibrant evening. Monday nights feature Nightstrike, the only DJ party with a mixture of house and techno tracks, pitchers of beer and bowling shoes. Expect to wait for a lane. **Price:** $5.95 per person per game, $6.95, evenings and weekends; $4 shoe rental. **Credit cards:** All major. **Subway:** L, N, Q, R, W, 4, 5, 6 to 14th St.

Chelsea Piers (*See section* "Chelsea Piers" *in this chapter.*)

Leisure Time Bowling 625 Eighth Ave., 2nd Fl. (at Port Authority Bus Terminal) (212) 268-6909. When Leisure Time Bowling opened its modern 30 lanes a few years ago on the second floor of the Port Authority Bus Terminal, it seemed curiously out of place. Now the alley is more popular than ever, with people of all ages trying to knock down a few on the lanes. Waits can be over two hours on weekends and when the weather is bad. **Price:** $6 per person per game; $3.50 shoe rental. **Credit cards:** All major. **Subway:** A, C, E, 1, 2, 3, 9 to 42nd St.

Golf

Perhaps surprisingly, New York City offers a number of excellent golf courses, in addition to other golf resources such as driving ranges and instruction. Listed below are some of the most noteworthy and accessible of the area links. Tee times for all New York City area golf courses can be made by calling New York Golf at (718) 225-4653. There's a $2 reservation fee per player.

Douglaston Golf Course 63-20 Marathon Pkwy., Queens (718) 224-6566. This short course will challenge you with narrow fairways, and its hilly nature will often result in uneven lies. While there is only one water hazard on the course, the many blind shots required make Douglaston relatively difficult. The course's signature hole is #18, a 550-yard, par 5, requiring an approach shot to a large, well-bunkered green. **Green Fees:** Weekdays, $25 for 18 holes and $9 for nine holes; weekends, $27.50 for 18 holes and $13 for nine holes. **Reservations:** 10 days in advance. Call (718) 225-GOLF. **Directions by car:** Long Island Expy. east to Douglaston Pkwy.; turn left, continue to 61st Ave. and make a left; turn right on Marathon; drive two blocks and course will be on the right.

Dyker Beach Seventh Ave. and 86th St., Brooklyn (718) 836-9722. This is perhaps the ultimate inner-city golfing experience. Because of the streets adjacent to the course, the sounds of the city usually follow golfers along the fairway. The course has undergone a dramatic renaissance, and is now considered one of the best maintained in the city, despite the over 80,000 rounds played here each year. **Green Fees:** Weekdays, $19 for 18 holes and $9.50 for nine holes; weekends, $21 for 18 holes and $10.50 for nine holes. **Reservations:** Seven days in advance. Call (718) 225-GOLF. **Subway:** R to 86th St.; walk along 86th Street to course or take B-64 bus or cab.

Kissena Park Golf Course 164–15 Booth Memorial Ave., Flushing, Queens (718) 939-4594. This is a short course (the back tees play only 4,727 yards), but the hilly terrain makes it a rather difficult one. Built in 1934 and redesigned in

Chelsea Piers

Since 1995, New Yorkers have enjoyed the benefits of the 40-acre **Chelsea Piers** sport complex (17th–23rd St., on the Hudson River), offering everything from basketball and batting cages to golf and gymnastics. Once the city's premier passenger terminal, it is a site steeped in history; here many immigrants first set foot on American soil, and it was the intended destination of the *Titanic* (instead, the *Carpathia* arrived with the "unsinkable" ship's 675 survivors on April 20, 1912). There may be more scenic or historic playing fields in New York, but nowhere else will you find so many activities in one location. Call (212) 336-6666 for general information, or see below for specific sports and prices.

Baseball/Softball Field House, (212) 336-6500. There are four batting cages, two for righties, one for lefties, and another that serves both. Try hitting major league heat in the fast-pitch cage, where the speed is set to about 90 mph. 10 pitches for $1.

Basketball Field House, (212) 336-6500. There are two hardwood courts in the Field House. Walk-ons are welcome, but call ahead for available hours. The cost is $7 per hour. Court rental, $110 per hour.

Bowling Chelsea Piers Bowl, (212) 835-BOWL. The avid bowler will appreciate the 40 new lanes and automatic scoring. $7 per person per game, $4.50 shoe rental charge; 9 A.M.–2 A.M. (to 4 A.M. Fri., Sat.).

Dance Field House, (212) 336-6500. The 1,400-square-foot air-conditioned dance studio features Gerstung sprung flooring and can be divided into three separate studios. Jazz, tap and modern dance classes are offered.

Golf Golf Club at Chelsea Piers, (212) 336-6400. This multitiered, year-round facility must be seen to be believed. Offering 52 heated stalls and an automatic tee-up system, the driving range is a net-enclosed, artificial turf fairway stretching 200 yards out into the Hudson River. There is also a 1,000-square-foot putting area, or call ahead to rent a sand bunker for practice. Lessons are available at the Golf Academy, where PGA professionals offer video analysis of your swing. **Rates:** $15 minimum, for 89 or 60 balls, depending on time of day; indoor sand bunker, $15 for a half hour; club rentals, $4, one club; $6, two clubs; $8, three clubs.

Gymnastics Field House, (212) 336-6500. With 23,000 square feet of floor space, Chelsea Piers Gymnastics is New York City's largest and best-equipped gymnastics training center and the only one sanctioned by USA Gymnastics for local, state and regional competitions. Call for class schedule and walk-on hours.

Health Club Sports Center, (212) 336-6000. The 150,000-square-foot Sports Center at Chelsea Piers offers two fitness studios with over 150 sports and fitness classes a week; the world's longest indoor running track (.25 mile); a 200-meter banked competition track; three wood basketball/volleyball courts; Manhattan's only indoor sand volleyball court; one of the largest and most challenging rock climbing walls in the world; a six-lane, 25-yard swimming pool; a separate Spinning Room; two outdoor sun decks overlooking the Hudson River; Manhattan's largest and most extensive cardio- and strength-training areas; a boxing ring and equipment circuit; and personal and sport-specific training. And once you're spent from all that activity, relax in the club café. You deserve it. Non-member rate is a hefty $36 per day.

Ice Hockey Sky Rink (212) 336-6100. Open ice hockey time is available daily, and follows this schedule: Mon.–Thu., noon–1:20 P.M.; Fri., noon–1:20 P.M. and 1 A.M.–2:20 A.M.; Sat. and Sun., 11:30 A.M.–12:50 P.M. It's $22 for 80 minutes. Goalies play for free.

Ice Skating Sky Rink (212) 336-6100. Sky Rink, which has been one of New York's favorite places to ice skate for more than a quarter of a century, moved to Chelsea Piers in 1995. The new twin-rink facility on Pier 61 operates 24 hours a day, seven days a week, year-round, welcoming skaters of all ages and ability levels for general skating sessions, figure skating, hockey training and league play. **Admission:** Adult, $11.50 (10-pass, $103); youth/senior, $8 (10-pass, $72); skate rental, $5; helmet rental, $3.

In-line Skating Roller Rink, (212) 336-6200. Open skating time is available on both the outdoor (weather permitting) and indoor roller rinks. There is also an outdoor skate park offering challenging ramps, rails and launch boxes that are sure to thrill the extreme athlete. **Skate Park** Mon.–Sun., 10 A.M.–6 P.M. (admission $8). **Rink rates:** $5, adults; $4, kids. **Rentals:** $13.50, adults; $8, kids. Rentals require credit card or $150/per pair for security deposit.

Soccer and Lacrosse Field House, (212) 336-6500. The Field House is the only facility in New York City with two state-of-the-art indoor playing fields built specifically for indoor soccer and lacrosse. Measuring 55-by-110 feet, the climate-controlled, artificial turf fields are surrounded by Plexiglas boards, and equipped with goals, nets and electronic scoreboards.

Rock Climbing Field House, (212) 336-6500. The 30-foot-high artificial rock surface offers a variety of routes that challenge climbers of all skill levels. Cost is $17 per person. As the schedule is seasonal, call for available times.

Roller Hockey Roller Rink, (212) 336-6200. Chelsea Piers, in addition to numerous leagues and clinics, also offers open roller hockey on the weekends. Cost is $15 for 1 1/2 hours of pick-up play.

General Information: Dining: Chelsea Brewing Company, (212) 336-6440; Famous Famiglia at Sky Rink, (212) 803-5552 (pizza); Chelsea Piers Bowl Snack Bar, (212) 835-2695; Rita's Burgers, (212) 604-0441. **Parking:** Available at Pier 62, (212) 336-6840. **Subway:** C, E, F, 1, 9 to 23rd St.

1986, the course requires a variety of shots. According to the course pro, it will require every club in your bag. **Green Fees:** Weekdays, $18 for 18 holes and $9 for nine holes; weekends, $21.50 for 18 holes and $10 for nine holes. **Reservations:** Seven days in advance. Call (718) 225-GOLF. **Subway:** 7 to Main St.–Flushing; cab from station (about 3 miles). **By car:** Long Island Expy. east to Exit 24 (Kissena Blvd.); take the service road to 164th St., turn left, go to the traffic light (Booth Memorial Ave.); turn right, you'll see the course from there.

La Tourette Golf Course 1001 Richmond Hill Rd., Staten Island (718) 351-1889. Once a private course, this verdant oasis from the city offers open, rolling fairways, plenty of bunkers and countless trees. The 1836 Greek-revival clubhouse is a landmark itself, and this venerable course is home to the annual New York City Amateur tournament. It is the only city course that offers a driving range on the property. **Green Fees:** Weekdays, $19 for 18 holes and $9.50 for nine holes; weekends, $21.50 for 18 holes and $11 for nine holes. **Reservations:** Ten days in advance. Call (718) 225-GOLF. **Directions by car:** Brooklyn-Queens Expy. (BQE) to Verrazano Bridge to the Bradley Ave. exit; at second traffic signal (Wooley Ave.), turn left and proceed past the next five traffic signals; left on Richmond Hill Rd.

Marine Park Golf Course 2880 Flatbush Ave., Brooklyn (718) 338-7113. Built in 1964, Marine Park was designed by the legendary Robert Trent Jones Sr. and its large and undulating greens are, according to regulars, the finest in the city. The signature hole is no. 15, a 467-yard, par 4, featuring a well-bunkered fairway and requiring a downhill approach shot to a sloping green. **Green Fees:** Weekdays, $24 for 18 holes or nine holes; weekends, $26 for 18 holes or nine holes.**Reservations:** Seven days in advance. Call (718) 225-GOLF. **Subway:** Q to Kings Highway; B-100 bus to course. **Directions by car:** Long Island Expy. to Brooklyn-Queens Expy. (BQE) to Belt Pkwy. east; take exit 11N (Flatbush Ave.), drive to the second traffic signal and you will see the course entrance on the left.

Mosholu Golf Course 3700 Jerome Ave., Bronx (718) 655-9164. Narrowly avoiding demolition last year, Mosholu is another classic inner city course, with tenements rising above the many trees to provide a uniquely urban backdrop. Built in 1904, it is one of the oldest in the city. Nine holes were lost some years ago to the addition of parkways to the area, but it is a difficult course nonetheless: the tree-lined fairways are narrow, the medium-sized greens are fast, and there are several blind fairways in the design. Easy to get to via public transportation. **Green Fees:** Weekdays, $17 for nine holes; weekends, $19.50 for nine holes. **Reservations:** Two days in advance. Call (718) 225-GOLF. **Subway:** 4 to Woodlawn (last stop).

Pelham Bay/Split Rock 870 Shore Rd., Bronx (718) 885-1258. Pelham Bay Park offers two excellent 18-hole courses in a bucolic setting: it is not unusual to have pheasant, wild turkey and deer cross your path as you traverse either of these courses. The Pelham Bay Course offers a links-style design, and it the easier of the two. Its signature hole is no. 9, a 433-yard, par 4, requiring a shot to an extremely undulating green that is well bunkered. The Split Rock Course is more difficult because it is very wooded and has tight fairways. A creek comes into play on four holes, and the terrain is rolling. The signature hole on the Split Rock Course is no. 18, a 392-yard, par 4, requiring an approach shot around what may be America's oldest living White Oak tree. **Green Fees:** Weekdays, $25 for 18 or nine holes; weekends, $27.50 for 18 or nine holes. **Reservations:** Ten days in advance. Call (718) 225-GOLF. **Subway:** 6 to Pelham Bay Park (last stop); W-45 or M-45 bus or cab to course (as this is quite a long trip, driving is preferable). **By car:** FDR Dr. to Triborough Bridge, exit toward Bronx; take 95 going North (New England Thruway); get off at Exit 8B; the course is one mile away, look for the course entrance off Shore Rd.

Silver Lake Park 915 Victory Blvd., Staten Island (718) 447-5686. This course is well manicured and located within a tight wooded area. The design includes several sloping, tight fairways, two water hazards and many trees lining the fairways. **Green Fees:** Weekdays, $19 for 18 holes or nine holes; weekends, $21.50 for 18 or nine holes. **Reservations:** 11 days in advance. Call (718) 225-GOLF. **Directions by car:** Brooklyn-Queens Expy. (BQE) to Verrazano Bridge; stay on the Staten Island Expy., get off at the Clove Rd.–Victory Blvd. exit, turn right on Clove Rd.; proceed on to Victory Blvd., travel one mile, the course is on the left.

South Shore Golf Course 200 Huguenot Ave., Staten Island (718) 984-0101. This very scenic and picturesque course was built on hilly terrain and seems to have been cut out of the forest itself. Designed by Alfred H. Tull in 1927, the course challenges golfers with narrow fairways and large, fast greens. **Green Fees:** Weekdays, $25 for 18 or nine holes; weekends, $27.50 for 18 or nine holes. **Reservations:** 11 days in advance. Call (718) 225-GOLF. **Directions by car:** Brooklyn-Queens Expy. (BQE) to Verrazano Bridge; stay on the Staten Island Expy., get off at exit 5–Rte. 440 South/West Shore Expy. exit; take Rte. 440 south to exit 4; make a left onto Arthur Kill Rd.; stay straight to Huguenot Ave.

Van Cortlandt Golf Course Van Cortlandt Park S. and Bailey Ave., Bronx (718)543-4595. The granddaddy of New York City courses and the nation's oldest public course, designed by Tom Bendelow and built in 1885. Van Cortlandt is well maintained, and there is a nice mix of long par 5s and short par 4s, with a few difficult par 3s thrown in for good measure. While you might drive the green on no. 6, a 292-yard par 4, watch out for no. 2, the signature 620-yard par 5 and the par 3 no. 13 that requires a shot over water to a large, undulating green. The final four holes are extremely hilly and offer a challenging end to this scenic course. In 2001 a new irrigation system was installed, which promises to improve conditions on a course that sees over 63,000 rounds played per year. **Green Fees:** Weekdays, $25 for 18 or nine holes; weekends, $27.50 for 18 or nine holes. **Reservations:** 10 days in advance. Call (718) 225-GOLF. **Subway:** 1, 9 to Van Cortlandt Park (last stop).

Gyms & Health Clubs

Most of the hundreds of health clubs around the city offer one-day passes. You'll save time and money if your bring your own lock, though most will rent you one and nearly all (even the Y's) will provide a towel. Make sure to bring a picture ID with you too, as most require one for their records.

Health Clubs

Asphalt Green 555 E. 90th St. (between York Ave. and 91st St.) (212) 369-8890. A wave-shaped building constructed in 1993 on the site of the city's former asphalt plant. What really separates this from other gyms are the full-size Astroturf soccer field and Olympic-sized pool with a hydraulic floor that adjusts the water depth for children and those learning to swim. Day passes are $20. **Subway:** 4, 5, 6 to 86th St.

Crunch Fitness *www.crunchfitness.com,* or check Yellow Pages for nearest location. This self-styled alternative gym offers seven locations in Manhattan. A day pass at any of Crunch's gyms is $23.

New York Sports Club (800) 796-NYSC, for nearest location *www.nysc.com.* This chain, with its 28 Manhattan locations, is about as common a sight on New York streets as pizzerias and Chinese restaurants. Day passes are $25.

World Gym 232 Mercer St. (between Bleecker and 3rd Sts.) (212) 780-7407; 1926 Broadway (between 64th and 65th Sts.) (212) 874-0942 *www.worldgym.com.* These gyms are generally peaceful, with natural light flowing through large windows, wood surfaces and warm lighting. They are rarely crowded, and music is isolated to certain areas of the facilities. Day passes are $25.

YMCAs

New York City's YMCAs offer an affordable alternative to the health club scene, though the gyms can often be quite crowded.

Harlem YMCA 180 W. 135th St. (at Seventh Ave.) (212) 281-4100. **Day pass:** $12. **Subway:** 2, 3 to 135th St.

Vanderbilt YMCA 224 E. 47th St. (between Second and Third Aves.) (212) 756-9600. **Day pass:** $25. **Subway:** 6 to 51st St.

West Side YMCA 5 W. 63rd St. (between Broadway and Central Park West) (212) 875-4100. **Day pass:** $15. **Subway:** A, B, C, D, 1, 9 to 59th St.; 1, 9 to 66th St.

Horseback Riding

Claremont Riding Academy 175 W. 89th St. (between Amsterdam and Columbus Aves.) (212) 724-5100. Built in 1892, Claremont is the oldest stable in the country. Experienced equestrians (who can walk, trot and canter comfortably) can hire horses by the hour to ride on the six miles of bridle paths in nearby Central Park. Lessons are available and there is an indoor arena for beginners. **Price:** $45 per hour. **Credit cards:** MC/V. **Subway:** 1, 9 to 86th St.

Kensington Stables 51 Caton Pl., Brooklyn (718) 972-4588. Horses can be hired here for leisurely guided rides on Prospect Park's trails. Lessons are also available. **Price:** $25 per hour. **Subway:** F to Ft. Hamilton Pkwy.

Ice Skating

Central Park—Lasker Rink Central Park at 106th St. (212) 396-0388. Located just below the scenic Harlem Meer, the Lasker Rink is open for ice skating during the winter season (it serves as Central Park's only swimming pool in the summer months). **Subway:** 6 to E. 103rd St.; B, C to W. 103rd St.

Central Park—Wollman Memorial Rink Enter park at Sixth Ave. and Central Park South (212) 396-1010. To appreciate the beauty and calm of Central Park, head to the 33,000-square-foot Wollman Rink. Wollman offers a spacious skating area and an unparalleled view of the Duck Pond framed by landmark buildings like the Plaza Hotel. **Admission:** $7, adults; $3.50, children and seniors. **Skate Rental:** $3.50 **Subway:** N, R, W to Fifth Ave.

Chelsea Piers (*See section* "Chelsea Piers" *in this chapter.*)

Prospect Park—Wollman Rink (718) 287-6431. Kate Wollman Center and Rink is located near the Lincoln Road entrance of the Park and is open for ice skating from November until March. An especially nice feature of this rink is the "early bird" session from 8:30–10:30 A.M. on weekdays. If you're an avid skater who hates the crowds at most public rinks, this is the place for you. **Admission:** $4. **Skate rental:** $3.50. **Subway:** Q to Parkside Ave.

Rink at Rockefeller Plaza 601 Fifth Ave. (between 49th and 50th Sts.) (212) 332-7654. Throughout the holiday season, music plays as skaters waltz around the rink under the glow of the awe-inspiring Rockefeller Center Christmas tree. While the rink is cramped and often crowded, the thrill of skating at the epicenter of the city's holiday spirit is unrivaled. Visit earlier or later in the season for a less crowded (but no less enjoyable) experience. Call ahead for available dates and times. **Admission:** $14, general; $10, children under 12 (admission varies, so call ahead). **Skate rental:** (figure skates only) $6. **Credit cards:** Cash only. **Subway:** B, D, F, S to 47th-50th St.–Rockefeller Center.

In-Line Skating

Popular street skating spots include "the cube" at **Astor Place** in the East Village, "the banks" under the **Brooklyn Bridge** (Manhattan side) and **Union Square**. **Central Park** is full of great places to skate outside the Wollman Rink (listed below), especially the main drives throughout the park, the open plaza at the north end of the Mall and the closed driveway west of the Mall. Skating in the **Riverside Park** grounds near 108th Street, which is permitted in the warmer months, requires a helmet, signing of a waiver and a $3 fee. Wrist and kneepads are essential, and elbow pads are recommended (212-408-0239 for info). (*See also section* "Chelsea Piers" *in this chapter.*)

Central Park—Wollman Memorial Rink Enter park at Sixth Ave. and Central Park South (212) 396-1010. During the summer months, Rollerblades replace ice skates at Wollman Rink. The rink also offers classes and guided skating tours around the park. Compared to the skating lanes in the park, the rink is fairly uncrowded, leaving plenty of room for New Yorkers to strut their stuff. **Admission:** $7, adults; $3.50, children and seniors. **Rental:** Rollerblades and safety equipment (state law requires children 14 and under to wear helmets and pads) can be rented for rink use ($6) or for park use ($15 with a $100 deposit). **Subway:** N, R, W to Fifth Ave.

Empire Skate Club of New York (212) 774-1774 *www.empireskate.org.* The Empire Skate Club of New York is a non-profit organization of in-line skaters dedicated to having fun and improving the skating environment in New York. The Club organizes social skates and get-togethers in the city, trips around the eastern seaboard and farther afield, clinics, seminars, parties and skate advocacy. A year's membership is $25.

Other places to rent skates: **Time's Up** (*see section* "Biking" *in this chapter*); **Blades,** 160 E. 86th St. (between Third and Lexington Aves.) (212) 996-1644, or 120 W. 72nd St. (between Amsterdam and Columbus Aves.) (212) 787-3911; **Peck & Goodie,** 919 Eighth Ave. (at 55th St.) (212) 246-6123.

Running

While out-of-towners may think of New York City as a concrete jungle with few safe places to run, there are actually many excellent—even tree-lined and relatively bucolic—routes right in Manhattan. **East River Park** is a favorite of those living downtown, offering a scenic course that stretches along the river just across from downtown Brooklyn. The **Battery Park Promenade** is also well suited for those who enjoy sightseeing as they work out: the Statue of Liberty is visible from this route, as is Ellis Island. Farther north, **Riverside Park**—which stretches with some interruptions from 72nd Street to the George Washington Bridge on Manhattan's Upper West Side—offers some excellent courses, both pavement and dirt.

But the crown jewel of the NYC runner's kingdom is **Central Park,** unofficial home of the **New York Road Runners Club** (212-860-4455). The club sponsors many races throughout the year, usually along the Park's main Loop, the most famous race being the **New York City Marathon**, finishing at Tavern on the Green on the west side. You don't have to be a member to run in club-sponsored events (though there's usually a small fee), and an excellent place to find out about upcoming races is the Road Runners Club Web site, *www.nyrrc.org.*

The length of the entire Central Park Loop—the road that follows a circular route through the interior of the park—is 6.1 miles. This road is closed to cars 10 A.M.–4 P.M., and then again 7 P.M.–dusk. During the hours when vehicular traffic is permitted, there is a runner's lane that is open for use, though it is unprotected. Good short courses include the 3.5-mile route used by Chase's Corporate Challenge race, which begins at the Puppet Theater (roughly W. 70th St.), follows the Loop to the 102nd Street transverse, rejoins the Loop on the east side, and ends at the Rumsey Playground (where SummerStage events are held) at about East 70th Street. A popular 5K course (3.1 miles) begins at the East Drive (Loop) and 86th Street, proceeds north and across the 102nd Street transverse, back onto the Drive and finishes at the Engineer's Gate (90th St. and Fifth Ave.). The Reservoir run is one of the most popular courses in the city. The cinder track offers a level run of 1.6 miles and offers great views of the Manhattan skyline at virtually every step. In spring it is especially pleasant as flowering trees line the eastern side of the course. Enter the park at 86th St. on the east or west side. **Don't run in the park at night.**

In the Bronx, try **Van Cortlandt Park** (242nd St. and Broadway). As well as regular roads there are hilly 2.5-mile, 5-kilometer (3.1-mile) and 5-mile trails. Van Cortlandt Park Track Club stages weekly runs. No parking is allowed within the park. Nonmembers are welcome (718-796-0736).

The best spot for a run in Brooklyn is definitely **Prospect Park.** There is a dirt path, roughly three miles, on the inside of the roadway (3.5 miles) circling the park grounds, along with other isolated trails. Prospect Park Track Club has Sunday morning runs at 8 A.M. Meet at the Park Circle, Railroad Avenue and Prospect Park Southwest. Nonmembers are welcome (718-224-5814).

Swimming

(See section "Gyms & Health Clubs" for YMCAs and private gyms with pools.)

Public Pools

Asphalt Green 555 E. 90th St. (between York Ave. and 91st St.)
(212) 369-8890. Asphalt Green has one of the biggest and newest public pools in the city. The 50-by-20-meter indoor pool is heated to an even 80 degrees. While nonmembers can purchase a day pass to swim, some lap swimming lanes are always reserved for members only. Day passes are $20 for adults and $8 for children. **Subway:** 4, 5, 6 to 86th St.

Lasker Pool Central Park, East Drive and 106th St. Swimming in Lasker Pool is by far one of the favorite activities for kids visiting Central Park. During the summer months, Lasker is open for community swimming, racing and lessons. At less than four feet deep, the pool is ideal for kids. You can't beat the cost either—free. Swimmers must wear a swimsuit (no denim shorts or t-shirts), and while lockers are available, swimmers must bring their own lock. **Subway:** 6 to E. 103rd St.; B, C to W. 103rd St.

Riverbank State Park Pool 679 Riverside Dr. (at 145th St.)
(212) 694-3666. This is one of the most recently built pools in Manhattan, located in Riverbank State Park, built atop a sewage treatment center on the Hudson. It's not as grim as it sounds: the park is very attractive, and offers many other sports in addition to swimming. The view along the Hudson on a clear day is quite spectacular.

Sheraton Manhattan Hotel 790 Seventh Ave. (between 51st and 52nd Sts.)
(212) 581-3300. This midtown hotel offers an indoor swimming pool and an adjacent outdoor sun deck. Nonguests are allowed to use the facilities for a fee.

Municipal Pools

New York City's municipal pools require a year's membership, but it's only $25 and can be paid on the spot. If you're planning on returning to the Big Apple in the next 12 months, this might be your best option.

East 54th St. Recreation Center 348 E. 54th St. (212) 397-3154 Midtown

59th Street Recreation Center 533 W. 59th St. (212) 397-3159 West Side

Asser Levy Park 23rd St. and Asser Levy Pl. (212) 447-2020 Gramercy Park

Carmine Street Recreation Center 1 Clarkson St. (212) 242-5228 Greenwich Village

Dry Dock Swimming Pool 408 E. 10th St. (212) 677-4481 East Village

Hamilton Fish Recreation Center Pool 128 Pitt St. (212) 387-7687 Downtown

John Jay Swimming Pool 77th St. and Cherokee Pl. (212) 794-6566 Upper East Side

Lenox Hill Neighborhood House 331 E. 70th St. (212) 744-5022 Upper East Side

Tennis

Public Courts

The Har-tru public courts at Central Park's venerable **Tennis Center** (mid-park, 94th-96th Sts.) are among the nicest in the city, but half of the 24 courts are booked in advance, and the rest are usually reserved on a first-come, first-serve basis early each morning. Plus, you have to put up with a lot of attitude on the part of regulars who treat the Center as their own private club. But if you can handle these obstacles, playing amidst the trees of the park is a real treat. The Center also offers a pro shop, a locker room with showers, and a snack bar. Call (212) 360-8133 for information.

Other less crowded courts include those at **Riverside Park,** which boasts beautiful red-clay courts at the western end of 96th Street (no reservations) and recently restored hard-surface courts at 118th Street. **East River Park** (East River at Broome St.) also offers 12 hard-surface courts, and these are perhaps the least crowded in Manhattan. If you can make it to Brooklyn, **Prospect Park Tennis Center** provides 10 Har-tru courts, located at the southwest corner of the park, near the Park Circle. From mid-October through the end of April, a bubble structure covers these courts, and a private company rents them by the hour (call one day ahead to make reservations). Also in Brooklyn are the six excellent hard-surface courts at **Fort Greene Park.** These are among the least-used in the city, and, while there is a core group of regulars, it's relatively easy to walk on and play. Use of all city tennis courts requires either a season pass ($50) or a day pass ($5), which can be purchased either at the Tennis Center or Paragon Sporting Goods (867 Broadway at 18th St.). Permits are less apt to be checked at the courts at Riverside and 118th and Fort Greene Park. The season is Apr.-Nov., 7 A.M.–8 P.M. (light permitting). Call for information on individual courts.

Private Courts

Crosstown Tennis Club 14 W. 31st St. (212) 947-5780. The Crosstown facility, just steps from the Empire State Building, offers four Championship Deco-Turf tennis courts, each with an 18-foot back-court area and 40-foot ceilings. **Price:** $35–$55 per hour. **Credit cards:** All major. **Subway:** B, D, F, N, Q, R, S, W. 34th St.

Midtown Tennis Club 341 Eighth Ave. (27th St.) (212) 989-8572. When it opened in 1965, the Midtown Tennis Club was the first indoor club in Manhattan, and it's still one of the largest and most accessible tennis sites in the city. Air-conditioned, with eight tournament Har-Tru courts, and full locker-room facilities, the club offers tennis in a comfortable and relaxed atmosphere at low rates. **Price:** $27–$70 per hour. **Credit cards:** All major. **Subway:** 1, 9 to 28th St.; C, E to 23rd St.

New York Health and Racquet Club (HRC) Tennis Piers 13 and 14 (at Wall St.) (212) 422-9300; 110 University Pl. (at 13th St.) (212) 989-2300. HRC offers two climate-controlled facilities in the city, offering members a total of eight Har-Tru courts and two Supreme courts. Nonmembers can reserve courts too, though the price might make you seek out a municipal alternative. **Price:** $50–$100 per hour. **Credit cards:** All major.

USTA National Tennis Center (718) 760-6200 ext. 6213, ask for the program office. The USTA National Tennis Center, site of the U.S. Open, is the largest public tennis facility in the world, offering nine indoor courts, 18 practice courts and 18 tournament courts. All courts are open to the public year round except for August and September, during the U.S. Open itself. They reopen for public play one week after the last day of the Open. **Price:** $14–$40 per hour. **Credit cards:** All major. **Subway:** 7 to Willets Point—Shea Stadium.

BEACHES

From the heart of Manhattan, it's easy to forget that New York is actually a coastal town. But believe it or not, beyond the wall of skyscrapers, are the Atlantic Ocean and miles and miles of beach. There are city beaches in Brooklyn, Queens and the Bronx, as well as some very accessible spots on Long Island. If the temperature hits 90 degrees on a summer weekend, expect crowds. For millions of New Yorkers, the Atlantic provides the only chance of relief from the heat.

Brooklyn

Coney Island at Surf and Stillwell Aves. (718) 946-1350. (*See section* "Brooklyn" *in chapter* **Exploring New York** *for full entry.*) Though this is by far the most famous of the Brooklyn beaches, you may also want to try **Brighton Beach** right next door or **Manhattan Beach** next to that. **Subway:** F, N, Q to Stillwell Ave.–Coney Island

---

The Urban Jungle Gym, All Within a Metrocard Ride

New York, with its diverse geographical terrain, tidal channels, deep harbor and rocky outcrops can compete recreationally with any city on the planet. Outdoor enthusiasts may want to try one of these activities.

Canoeing At Pier 63 (23rd St. and 12th Ave.) **New York Outrigger** (212-684-0812) offers canoe clinics and half-day excursions for $50 per hour per person. The **Parks Department** also has six sites where the public can launch canoes and kayaks throughout the city. Call (212) 360-8134 for locations and information. *(See also "Boating" in this chapter.)*

Mountain Biking Trail biking is allowed on the abandoned Old Putnam railroad track bed in **Van Cortlandt Park** (Bronx). Elsewhere in city parks, mountain bikes are allowed on paved roads and paths only.

Rock Climbing To find **Rat Rock,** a popular boulder in Central Park enter at 63rd Street and Central Park West. Walk east toward the Heckscher Playground. The boulder is to the right of the ballfields. You'll know it by the chalk marks left by climbers who powder their fingers for a good grip. Other small outcrops are scattered throughout the park. The **Parks Department** offers rock climbing at other locations. Call (212) 348-4867 for information on classes. There are also artificial climbing walls at **Chelsea Piers** *(see section "Chelsea Piers" in this chapter)* and **Extravertical Climbing Center,** (212) 586-5718, where day passes and equipment rental are available.

Bronx

Orchard Beach Long Island Sound (between Park Dr. and Bartow Circle) (718) 885-2275. At the turn of the century, this was a popular bathing spot for the affluent residents of Pelham Manor. A large, luxurious stand of trees skirts the beach, giving the place a feeling of anti-urban festivity. From the vantage point of a patio between the two halves of the old bathhouse, one can gaze over the entire expanse of sand at the people, umbrellas and bathers dotting the shore, as idyllic as a picture postcard. **Subway:** 6 to Pelham Bay Park; BX 12 bus to Orchard Beach.

Queens

Rockaway Beach at Beach 1st and Beach 149th Sts. (718) 318-4000. Unlike most of the city's other public beaches, Rockaway has no distinctive New York flavor; its plain plank boardwalk, pale arc of sand and high-rise condos are welcoming enough, but they could just as easily belong to Long Island, Virginia or any other point on the East Coast. That's not to say it's without character. The beautiful old buildings, nearby hotels and ornate subway station have a kind of wind-swept, sunburned grandeur, and the fact that it's accessible only by bridge gives it the aura of adventure and isolation. **Riis Park**, a beach that is often overcrowded in the summer, is just west. **Subway:** A to Rockaway Park.

Long Island

Fire Island (516) 852-5200. Fire Island is a barefoot society, car-free and care-free. A barrier island, it stretches across 32 miles between the end of **Robert Moses State Park** (best bet for day-trippers) and Moriches Inlet, where the Hamptons begin. Despite an influx of tourist attention, the island has changed little in the last century. The concrete walks (rustically wooden in some communities) are still lined with cedar-shingled cottages hemmed in by pines and bayberry, and bicycle and walking paths are still the transportation arteries of choice. **Directions:** From Penn Station, take the Long Island Railroad to Babylon. Take Suffolk Buses, or taxi to ferries (total price, $10–$15 one way).

Jones Beach (516) 785-1600. Jones Beach is the single most popular site in the entire state park system, averaging nearly seven million visitors a year—more than Niagara Falls. The swimming and sunbathing crowds for which Jones Beach is famous are only a part of the action. Elsewhere in the 2,413-acre park, people fly kites and determined joggers, bikers and skaters swoosh along their designated paths. In the bushes birdwatchers and other nature lovers stalk their prey. Surf-casters think bluefish, while anglers on the four bay piers are after fluke. The park is open 365 days a year. The truly faithful visit even in winter, by the thousands. **Directions:** From Penn Station, take the Long Island Railroad to Freeport. Buses run every half hour from the train station to the beach ($11, includes shuttle bus). If you go by car, go early. Parking lots fill quickly.

Long Beach In recent years, this seaside city—once the playground of the wealthy, then a dumping ground for the elderly poor and the mentally ill—has made a remarkable comeback. Smart, new high-rise oceanfront buildings have emerged, and young families, attracted by the Atlantic Ocean beaches and the 53-minute commute by train to Manhattan, are moving here in droves. For the weekend visitor, the best reason to trek to Long Beach is its boardwalk. At a little more than two miles in length, it is Long Island's longest, and its 60-foot width is double that of Jones Beach's. Open 24 hours a day, the boardwalk features a block of stores and eateries. **Directions:** From Penn Station, take the Long Island Railroad to Long Beach ($11 round-trip package).

SPECTATOR SPORTS
Baseball

New York Yankees—Yankee Stadium 161st St. (at River Ave.), Bronx (718) 293-4300. Like Fenway Park in Boston and Wrigley Field in Chicago, Yankee Stadium is steeped in history, a place where it's easy to remember that, once upon a time, baseball truly was America's favorite pastime. While the 75-year-old park was remodeled in the mid-70's, the reminders of a bygone era are everywhere: the decorative white colonnade above the outfield (Mickey Mantle hit the one above right field with a monster blast in 1965), the plaques in Monument Park, the "Bronx cheers" that still greet hapless opponents. This is, after all, home to some of the game's most legendary ballplayers: Babe Ruth, Lou Gehrig, Joe DiMaggio, Roger Maris and Reggie Jackson to name a few. And with three consecutive World Series titles under their belts, the current Yankee squad—with stars such as Derek Jeter, Bernie Williams and Roger Clemens—boasts one of the strongest lineups in the team's long and storied history. **Price:** $8–$65. **Credit cards:** All major; checks. **Subway:** 4, B, D to 161st St.—Yankee Stadium.

New York Mets—Shea Stadium 123–01 Roosevelt Ave. (between Grand Central Pkwy. and Van Wyck Expy.), Flushing, Queens (718) 507-6387. While the Mets can't compete with the Yankees in terms of history—or World Series titles (the Yankees have appeared in the Fall Classic almost as many years as the Mets have been in existence)—the team has certainly had its share of colorful moments. The Amazins' first season was in 1962 when the likes of Marvelous Marv Throneberry made them the most inept team in the history of the game: 40 wins and a whopping 120 losses. Shea Stadium opened amidst the bustle of the adjacent World's Fair in 1964, and things finally got better when the Mets completed an improbable championship run in 1969, defeating the Orioles four games to one. They appeared in the series again in 1973 (losing to the A's in seven games) and won their second championship in 1986 (who can forget their game six come-from-behind, 10th-inning victory over the Boston Red Sox?). In 2000, Mike Piazza & Co. lost to the Yankees in the first "subway series" since 1956, reinforcing the Mets' status as New York's also-ran baseball team. And with the departure of pitcher Mike Hampton and injuries to some key players, the 2001 season looked sadly familiar to loyal Mets fans. **Price:** $12–$43. **Credit cards:** All major. **Subway:** 7 to Willets Point—Shea Stadium. **Long Island Railroad:** Stops at stadium on game days (from Penn Station, peak $5.50, off-peak $3.75, one way).

Brooklyn Cyclones—Keyspan Park 1904 Surf Ave. (between W. 17th and W. 19th Sts.) (718) 449-8497. "Baseball returns to Brooklyn!" So read many of the tabloid headlines when the first pitch was thrown at Keyspan Park on June 18, 2001. The Cyclones, a Mets minor league affiliate, are the first professional team to play in Brooklyn since the departure of the Dodgers for Los Angeles in 1958, and baseball couldn't ask for a better venue. Located on Surf Avenue in legendary Coney Island, fans can enjoy a relaxing day at the ballpark, as well as an ocean view. And if the baseball isn't exciting enough, why not ride the famed Cyclone roller coaster before making your way home? **Price:** $5–$10. **Subway:** F, N, Q to Stillwell Ave.–Coney Island.

Staten Island Yankees—Richmond County Bank Ballpark at St. George, 75 Richmond Terrace (718) 720-9265. While the Cyclones may be getting all the press, a Yankees minor league squad plays their games in New York City too. Also opening in 2001, the 6,500-seat stadium is home to the Staten Island Yankees. With eight games against their Brooklyn counterparts scheduled in the first season, a new New York rivalry has been born. **Directions:** 1, 9 to South Ferry; exit Staten Island Ferry from the lower deck; the ballpark is on the right.

Barton Silverman/The New York Times

Yankee Stadium

Basketball

New York Knicks—Madison Square Garden 2 Penn Plaza (at 33rd St. and Seventh Ave.) (212) 465-6727. Madison Square Garden is the world's most famous arena—according to the public address system that welcomes the crowd to Knicks games. It is true that the Garden has more than its share of memories, from prize fights to championship basketball and hockey. Few basketball fans will forget Willis Reed's heroic, limping entrance onto the court for game seven of the 1970 finals, in which the Knicks defeated Wilt Chamberlain's L.A. Lakers for their first NBA title. Until his move to Seattle before the 2000-2001 season, Patrick Ewing held court here, though some of the most vivid memories in recent years have been of defeat rather than victory: Reggie Miller's astounding 25 points in the fourth quarter of a 1994 semi-finals game, Michael Jordan lighting up the Knicks for 55 points soon after his return from minor league baseball, Charles Smith missing four put-backs in the final seconds, any one of which would have advanced the Knicks to the 1993 finals. But the Knicks made it to the championship series in 1999 with the new, up-tempo game of Latrell Sprewell, Allan Houston and Marcus Camby. Though tickets are hard, if not impossible, to come by and often obscenely expensive, a night at the Garden with the Knicks is a must for any die-hard hoops fan. **Price:** $20–$1,500. **Tickets:** Ticketmaster; for ticket info call (212) 465-JUMP. **Credit cards:** All major. **Subway:** A, B, C, D, E, F, N, Q, R, W, 1, 2, 3, 9 to 34th St.

New Jersey Nets—Continental Airlines Arena (Meadowlands) 50 Rte. 120 (at Rte. 3), East Rutherford, NJ (201) 935-3900. When the Nets played on Long Island with Julius Erving running the show, they were the best in the old ABA. Alas, things haven't gone quite so well since their admission into the

NBA in 1977. Since moving to New Jersey the following year, the Nets have only made it past the first round of the playoffs once. The biggest news recently was the 2001 trade of Brooklyn-born Stephon Marbury for Jason Kidd of the Phoenix Suns, whom many consider the best all-around point guard in the NBA. **Tickets:** Ticketmaster, $10-$600. **Credit cards:** MC/V. **Directions:** Bus service for all events at the Meadowlands Sports Complex from Port Authority ($6.50 round trip). **By car:** New Jersey Turnpike to exit 16W to Complex. Or Garden State Pkwy. south to exit 153 (153N if you're northbound), Rte. 3 east.

New York Liberty—Madison Square Garden The Liberty squad is a bona fide power in the WNBA, having advanced to the finals three times in the league's first four years. And they've built quite a fan base, one that Liberty die-hards proudly describe as noncorporate, unlike the clientele of their male counterparts. Also unlike Knicks games, it's easy to get good seats that won't cost you a second mortgage. **Price:** $8–$62.50. **Credit cards:** All major. **Subway:** See New York Knicks entry.

Boxing

Madison Square Garden Madison Square Garden has a long and storied history of boxing, a tradition that began inside its first, 19th-century building in Madison Square at 23rd Street (built in 1879, this roofless arena was also the site of chariot races) and continuing through to its present and fourth location. On March 8, 1971, one of the most anticipated sporting events of the 20th century took place when Joe Frazier defeated Muhammad Ali in a 15-round decision for the heavyweight title. In a pale imitation of that bout in March 1999, Evander Holyfield battled Lennox Lewis to a draw in a 15-round fight. Your best hope for exciting (and affordable) boxing is the annual **Golden Gloves tournament** (April) where kids from around the city battle for top honors in all weight divisions. **Subway:** See New York Knicks entry.

Church Street Boxing Gym 25 Park Pl. (between Church St. and Broadway) (212) 571-1333. This is New York City's premiere boxing training facility, with over 10,000 square feet of gym space located in the heart of downtown Manhattan. The well-known gym has showcased many up-and-coming professional boxers, kickboxers and Thai-boxers and has worked on site with such marquee names as Evander Holyfield, Larry Holmes and Mike Tyson. Call for a fight schedule. **Subway:** 4, 5, 6 to Brooklyn Bridge; 2, 3 to Park Pl.

Cricket

Because of the concentration of recent immigrants from cricket-playing countries (mainly from India, Pakistan and the West Indies), it's not surprising that the New York metropolitan area is considered the mecca of cricket in North America. There are 12 leagues comprising over 200 clubs, and play can be watched in a number of area parks. **Bronx:** Van Cortlandt Park, Ferry Point Park, Randall's Island, Soundview. **Queens:** Flushing Meadow Park, Baisley Park, Kissena Park, Edgemere. **Brooklyn:** Marine Park, Seaview.

Football

New York Giants—Giants Stadium (Meadowlands) 59 Rte 120 (at Rte. 3), East Rutherford, NJ (201) 935-3900. The Giants moved to their 77,716-seat home in 1976, having played throughout most of their history in Yankee Stadium. And good luck getting tickets: the waiting list for season tickets goes all the way back to their first year in the Meadowlands stadium. The Giants have won two championships since moving across the Hudson, years when Lawrence Taylor struck fear in the hearts of visiting quarterbacks. While LT has moved to the Hall of Fame, the tailgate parties are still in high gear: during the season, a hoard of die-hard tailgaters sporting kielbasa, burgers and Budweiser claim the stadium's 25,000 parking spots. **Price:** $40–$45, available by subscription only. **Credit cards:** All major. **Directions:** See New Jersey Nets entry.

New York Jets—Giants Stadium The Jets were lured to the Meadowlands after the 1983 season, so both metropolitan-area NFL franchises are actually New Jersey teams, despite what it says on their helmets. While the Jets won the Super Bowl in 1969 under the flashy guidance of Joe Namath (an event that directly led to the merging of the AFL with the NFL), wins have been hard to come by since. Things were looking up in the late 90's—the team fell just short of reaching the Super Bowl in 1999—but after Bill Parcells left coaching for the front office and Keyshawn Johnson left for Tampa Bay, the Jets have found themselves in the familiar position of rebuilding. It's almost as hard to get a ticket for a Jets game as it is for those of their co-tenants: the waiting list for season tickets is currently 12 years. **Price:** From $35, if available. **Credit cards:** All major. **Directions:** See New Jersey Nets entry.

Hockey

New York Rangers—Madison Square Garden One of the "Original Six" NHL teams, the Rangers have a long tradition, yet only two championships. Until their successful Stanley Cup run in 1994—led by captain Mark Messier—the last time the Cup had been held aloft on Garden ice was 54 years and two buildings before. But win or lose, the Rangers have some of the most loyal—and vociferous—fans in the league, and games at the Garden, if you can find tickets, are not for the faint of heart. **Price:** $22–$675. **Credit cards:** All major. **Subway:** See New York Knicks entry.

New York Islanders—Nassau Veterans Memorial Coliseum 1255 Hempstead Tpke., Uniondale, Long Island (516) 794-9300. When the Islanders came back in the 1975 playoffs to defeat the Pittsburgh Penguins in seven games after falling behind 3–0 in the series, the fortunes of the franchise were on a meteoric rise. They won four successive Stanley Cups in the first years of the 80's and were the team to beat until the advent of Wayne Gretsky and his Edmonton Oilers. Islanders fans think back fondly on those years: the team hasn't qualified for the playoffs since the Rangers made quick work of them in a series sweep en route to the 1994 title. **Price:** $14–$85. **Tickets:** Ticketmaster. **Credit cards:** All major. **Directions:** Long Island Railroad to Hempstead (peak $6.25, off-peak $4.25); walk one block to the Hempstead Bus Terminal and take N 70, N 71 or N 72 bus to Coliseum. **By car:** Midtown Tunnel to Long Island Expy. (495) east to exit 38; Northern State Pkwy. to exit 31A; Meadowbrook Pkwy. south to exit M4, Nassau Coliseum. Parking is $6.

New Jersey Devils—Continental Airlines Arena 50 Rte. 120 (at Rte. 3), East Rutherford, NJ (201) 935-3900. Transplanted from Colorado in 1982, the Devils have risen from depths of the Patrick Division to become one of the better teams in the NHL and a perennial playoff contender. While rabid Rangers fans had to wait over five decades for the return of the Stanley Cup to New York, the wait in Jersey was only 13 years: in 1995, a year after their cross-river rivals won hockey's ultimate honor, the Devils captured their first league championship. The Devils took the Cup again in 2000, but lost a hard-fought seven-game series defending their title against the Colorado Avalanche in 2001. **Tickets:** Ticketmaster. **Credit cards:** MC/V. **Directions:** See New Jersey Nets entry.

Horse Racing

Aqueduct Racetrack 110th St. (at Rockaway Blvd.), Ozone Park, Queens (718) 641-4700. The old Aqueduct, which opened in 1894, was replaced by the new "Big A" in 1959. In 1975 the inner track was constructed, allowing for winter racing. On July 4, 1972, Aqueduct was the scene of Secretariat's first event, a 5.5 furlong maiden race. **Hours:** Gates open at 11 A.M. **Admission:** Grandstand, $1; Clubhouse, $3; Skyline Club, $4; children under 12, free. **Subway:** A to Aqueduct Racetrack; courtesy bus service to admission gate. **By car:** Midtown Tunnel to Long Island Expy. east, to Van Wyck Expy. south to exit 3, Linden Blvd.; right on Linden to track. General parking $1.

Belmont Park 2150 Hempstead Tpke. (at Plainfield Ave), Elmont, Long Island (718) 641-4700. In addition to hosting the Belmont Stakes each year, the final leg of the Triple Crown, Belmont Park has been the scene of many other historic events. One of America's oldest and most beautiful tracks, Belmont opened on May 4, 1905, and it was here that the Wright brothers supervised an international aerial tournament before 150,000 spectators in 1910. It was also the site of the first American airmail service (1918) between New York and Washington, D.C. But most important, of course, is its glorious racing past. It was here in 1973 that Secretariat won the Triple Crown, engaging Sham out of the gate in a six-furlong duel, which at 1:09 4/5 was the fastest in Belmont history (and a speed that finished Sham, who never raced again). Secretariat cruised to a 1:59 flat finish, winning the race by an astonishing 31 lengths. **Hours:** Doors open at 11 A.M.; races are 1 P.M.–5 P.M. Closed Mon., Tue except holiday weekends (closed Wed.). Season is May–Jul., and Sept.–mid-Oct. **Admission** Grandstand, $2; Clubhouse, $4. **Directions:** Long Island Railroad, round-trip package from Penn Station that includes $1 off racetrack admission. **By car:** Cross Island Pkwy. to exit 26D. General parking is $2.

Meadowlands Racetrack Rte. 3, East Rutherford, NJ (201) 935-8500. Harness and thoroughbred horse racing are the staples at this one-mile oval track next to Giants Stadium. The 40,000-person-capacity racetrack was built in 1976 and christened in high style when horseman Anthony Abbatiello rode across the George Washington Bridge to the Meadowlands. **Hours:** Gates open at 6 P.M. **Price:** Grandstand,$1; Clubhouse, $3; Pegasus (Dining Floor), $5. **Credit cards:** Cash only. **Directions:** See New Jersey Nets entry.

Yonkers Raceway Central Ave., Yonkers (718) 562-9500. Although the history of the modern Yonkers Raceway dates from only 1950, the Westchester oval's impressive past actually dates back to the 19th century, when it was founded as a replacement for Fleetwood Park, a Grand Circuit stop in the Bronx. The facility reopened as Yonkers Raceway and had its inaugural meet on April 27, 1950. **Hours:** 8 P.M. with 12:30 P.M. matinees. **Price:** Grandstand, $2.25; Empire Terrace Floor, $4.25. **Credit cards:** Cash only. **Subway:** 4 to Woodlawn; B, D to Bedford Park Blvd.; 5 to 238th St.; 1, 9 to 242nd St. Take express buses from stations to track. **By car:** New York Thruway I-87 to exit 2 North, exit 4 South; Bronx River Pkwy. to Oak St., Mt. Vernon exit; Saw Mill River Pkwy. to Cross County Pkwy. to Yonkers or Central Ave. exit).

Soccer

New York/New Jersey MetroStars—Continental Airlines Arena Major League Soccer began in 1996 amidst the enthusiasm generated by the World Cup, held in this country for the first time in its long history. Certainly the best soccer in America is being played in MLS venues, and with the recent ban of the game-deciding shootout in favor of overtime, league officials are trying to make this a more exciting game for purists. Europe, take note.**Tickets:** (888) 4METROTIX. **Credit cards:** MC/V. **Directions:** See New Jersey Nets entry.

Tennis

Chase Championships—Madison Square Garden Taking place in Madison Square Garden every November, the Chase Championships is one of the last events on the Women's Tennis Association Tour. It is also one of the most prestigious tournaments, featuring a singles field limited to the top 16 point-earners on the tour, and a similar field of eight doubles teams. The tennis is top-notch, and the Garden ambiance is, as always, electric. **Price:** $10–$125. **Tickets:** Ticketmaster. **Credit cards:** All major. **Subway:** See New York Knicks entry.

U.S. Open—USTA National Tennis Center Flushing Meadows—Corona Park, Queens (718) 760–6200. The oldest American tournament is held at the National Tennis Center, built on the site of the 1939 and 1964 World's Fairs. The best tennis players converge on the city each September, hoping to play for the championship in the spacious Arthur Ashe Stadium. Fans can pay top dollar to see the showcased matches, or purchase grounds admission, which entitles them to wander from one early-round match to another. **Tickets:** Tele-charge, 888) OPEN-TIX. **Grounds Admission:** $25–$35. **Credit cards:** All major. **Subway:** 7 to Willets Point—Shea Stadium. **Long Island Railroad:** Stops at stadium during the Open (from Penn Station, peak $5.50, off-peak $3.75).

Hotels, Inns, and B & B's

New York's new status as safe, clean and family-friendly means that it's more popular than ever as a tourist destination. A record 37.4 million folks visited the Big Apple in 2000—and everybody expects 2001 numbers to slightly exceed that almost unfathomable figure, despite a worldwide economic slowdown and shrinking consumer confidence.

On one hand, that's great. The city has responded to the flood of visitors with an ambience that's fresh, vital and welcoming. It's simply a great time to be in New York City. On the other hand, it's not. Increased occupancy over the past few years has caused rates to respond accordingly. The average room rate in the city is now a sky-high $227, giving New York the less-than-admirable distinction of being the most expensive hotel city in the United States.

The good news for price-watchers is that things seem to be loosening up. The intersection of the economic downturn (and a commensurate slowdown of expense-account travel), plateauing tourism numbers (the projected increase this year is only 1 percent), and a glut of new hotel development—more than 3,000 new hotel rooms were added to the market in 2000 alone, with 1,700 more coming by the end of 2001—has caused occupancy rates to dip, and hoteliers to panic.

What does that mean for a visitor? More bargaining power. Hotels are now slashing prices and formulating value-added packages when necessary to lure guests and their hard-earned dollars. Don't expect a bargain anytime soon, but resurrect your negotiating skills, especially if visiting between January and August when hoteliers compete hardest for visitors. During autumn and holiday time, you're probably still going to have to reconcile yourself to paying close to full price. There are some insider tips worth noting even in these seasons. For instance, hotels in Midtown West charge higher-than-usual rates for Thanksgiving, especially along the Macy's parade route; however, deals can often be had on the east side of town and downtown. And bargains abound in Financial District hotels during the holiday season, and over just about any weekend.

One more important thing you need to know: Room size is almost invariably smaller here than in most other cities. Sure, more money will usually buy you more space, but not always. Bathrooms and closets tend to be on the small side even at the luxury level. Space limitations (as well as hotels that are generous with space) are noted in the reviews, but if you require extra space, be sure to make specific inquiries when you book.

It is easy to spend a fortune for the privilege to a sleep in Manhattan, but it's not necessary to do so. The city boasts many great places to stay for (relatively)

reasonable rates. The best way to find them is to forsake a prime Midtown location for another part of the city. Consider staying in one of Manhattan's hip
downtown neighborhoods, or in quiet Murray Hill, or in the family-friendly
Upper West Side instead, where you'll almost always get more hotel room for
your money. And don't worry about convenience. Each of these neighborhoods
is well-connected to Midtown by mass transit, which can have you to the Theater District inside 15 minutes—and with more money to spend on yourself.

Getting the Best Rate

All hotels have official "rack rates"—sometimes published, sometimes unpub-
lished—which they'll often discount to get you in the door. In the listings in
this section, we have included dollar signs that reflect the average daily rate for
a double room at each given hotel:

$	under $150
$$	$150–$249
$$$	$250–$375
$$$$	$375 and over

However, keep in mind that rates vary dramatically depending on dates and
availability. Also remember that every hotel room is subject to a hotel tax of
13.25 percent plus $2 per night.

Don't accept the first rate you're quoted; always see if they can do better.
Ask about special packages, discounts for seniors or AAA members, or whatever else might score you a savings.

You might also check with the following hotel reservation agencies, which
buy up blocks of rooms in advance and offer them to buyers at discounted rates
(much like airline consolidators do). Among the most reliable agencies are:

Quickbook (800) 789-9887, (212) 779-7666 *www.quickbook.com*
Hotel ConXions (800) 522-9991 or (212) 840-8686 *www.hotelconxions.com*
Hotel Reservations Network (800) 715-7666 *www.180096hotel.com* or
www.hoteldiscount.com

Members of the American Automobile Association should also try the AAA
Travel Agency, which often can reward members with seriously discounted rates
(*www.aaa.com*, or dial the number listed on the back of your membership card).

Never just book a room through a reservation agency without shopping
around; otherwise, you may end up paying more, not less. Compare the rate to
what your travel agent can do, or what you can get by booking directly through
the hotel; often, you can score a better rate by calling or surfing the Internet on
your own.

DOWNTOWN

Abingdon Guest House   GOOD $$
13 Eighth Ave. (between W. 12th and Jane Sts.), West Village
www.abingdonguesthouse.com   Phone: (212) 243-5384   Fax: (212) 807-7473

Two historic town homes and two professional owners, both with artistic vision
and unimpeachable taste, add up to one of New York's most charming guest-
houses. Located in the brownstone-lined, boutique-dotted West Village, the
Abingdon boasts an inviting residential ambiance that combines an authentic
neighborhood vibe with all the modern comforts. Since there's no resident
innkeeper, the guesthouse is best for independent-minded guests who prefer
artistic, one-of-a-kind accommodations and genuine New York ambiance over a
generic Midtown hotel. If that's you, you'll love the Abingdon.

   Each room has a private bath, cable TV, air conditioning and ceiling fans, a
private phone with answering machine, fluffy bathrobes and bold, beautiful
décor; the Ambassador Room has a wet-bar-style kitchenette and a VCR. Maid
service is a daily feature on all but major holidays (not a given in Big Apple
B & B's). On the downside, there's no elevator, so overpackers and travelers
with mobility issues should stay elsewhere. What's more, while the windows are
double-paned, Eighth Avenue can be noisy; choose a back room if you want
maximum quiet (located at patio level, the Garden Room is a good choice).

Rooms: Nine; four floors; all nonsmoking rooms. **Hotel amenities:** None. **Food
services:** Coffee bar at street level. **Cancellation:** Four days prior to arrival (10
days during holiday season). **Wheelchair access:** None. **Note:** Not for children.
Subway: A, C, E, 1, 2, 3, 9 to 14th St.

Best Western Seaport Inn   BASIC $$
33 Peck Slip (at Front St., two blocks north of Fulton St.), South Street Seaport
www.bestwestern.com/seaportinn
Phone: (212) 766-6600, (800) 468-3569   Fax: (212) 766-6615

Behind a beautifully restored red-brick 1852 facade lies a perfectly unremarkable but comfortable hotel. Outfitted in green and beige, the motel-goes-tradi-
tional rooms are generic but do the trick; all have VCRs, and some have sleeper
sofas, others steam or jetted baths. Corner rooms are largest; ask for one with a
terrace and a harbor view. Experienced with visiting Wall Streeters who consider this their home away from home, the staff is quite attentive. The historic
seaport is steps away.

Rooms: 72; seven floors; designated nonsmoking rooms. **Hotel amenities:**
None. **Food services:** Rates include continental breakfast. **Cancellation:** 4 P.M.
day of arrival. **Wheelchair access:** ADA compliant. **Subway:** J, M, Z, 2, 3, 4, 5
to Fulton St.; A, C to Broadway–Nassau St.

Cosmopolitan Hotel—TriBeCa   GOOD **$**
95 West Broadway (at Chambers St.), TriBeCa   *www.cosmohotel.com*
Phone: (212) 566-1900, (888) 895-9400   Fax: (212) 566-6909

In the heart of hip TriBeCa is one of Manhattan's best cheap hotels. Make no
mistake—rooms are little and appointments are strictly budget, but everything
is very nice. A pleasant lobby area and elevator leads to well-maintained rooms
furnished in a pleasant modern IKEA-ish style, and each has its own tiny but
pristine black-and-white-tiled bathroom. Linens and towels are of good quality,
and mattresses are firm. All rooms have a work desk and TV, and most have an
armoire (a few have wall racks instead). For a few extra dollars, you can have a
sitting area with a love seat, or a two-level mini-loft.

This neighborhood is one of the hippest on the island of Manhattan. And
with the Chambers Street express subway stop out the front door—ready to
whisk you to Times Square in five minutes—and a wealth of first-rate restaurants at every price point within walking distance, the location is a practical
choice, too. Services are nonexistent—but at these prices, who cares?

Rooms: 105; seven floors; designated nonsmoking rooms. **Hotel amenities:**
None. **Food services:** None. **Cancellation:** 4 P.M. day of arrival. **Wheelchair
access:** Not accessible. **Subway:** A, C, 1, 2, 3, 9 to Chambers St.

Embassy Suites New York   EXCELLENT **$$$**
102 North End Ave. (between Vesey and Murray Sts.), Battery Park City
www.embassysuites.com
Phone: (212) 945-0100, (800) 362-2779 (EMBASSY)   Fax: (212) 945-3012

Note: This hotel suffered substantial damage during the September 11, 2001
plane crashes that destroyed the World Trade Center. It may not be operational
by the time you plan your visit.

This brand-new all-suite chain hotel heralds the arrival of the new Lower Man-
hattan—one that mixes families and fun with the world of finance. Next to the
World Financial Center, the hotel is well-situated for business, and there's no
arguing with the terrific facilities for corporate travelers. But magnificent mod-
ern art throughout (the collection was curated by the Public Art Fund), Hudson
River views, proximity to waterside parks and Statue of Liberty ferries, two
restaurants from acclaimed chef Larry Forgione and a wealth of open space lend
the hotel a relaxed, artistic air that elevates it well above the business standard.
While the warmly contemporary décor isn't exactly cutting edge, the hotel has
substantially more designer panache than most of its peers do—without sacrific-
ing comfort.

Best of all is the space. Open hallways overlook a soaring, light-filled atrium
and lead to extra-large, all-new suites, which range from a whopping 450 to a
cavernous 850 square feet. Each has a living room with dining area and pullout
sofa; a wet-bar kitchenette with microwave and coffee maker; two TVs with on-
screen Web access; high-speed Internet access for laptop toters; and nice bath-
rooms with generous counter space. (Executive suites also have fax, VCR, CD

player and an extra-large dining/meeting table.) Rates are expense-account-targeted on weekdays, but substantial weekend discounts and slow-season packages are a steal for families. In fact, considering what you get for your money—including full cooked-to-order breakfast—everyone gets a big bang for their buck here.

Rooms: 463; 14 floors; designated nonsmoking floors. **Hotel amenities:** Concierge, dry-cleaning and laundry service, coin-operated laundry, health club, business center, full conference center, executive suites for small meetings, adjacent 16-screen movie theater. **Food services:** Steak house with martini bar, more casual seafood bar and grill, plus additional restaurants in building; room service; rates include full breakfast. **Cancellation:** 24 hours prior to arrival. **Wheelchair access:** Fully accessible. **Subway:** N, R, 1, 9 to Cortlandt St.

Holiday Inn Downtown/SoHo   BASIC $$
138 Lafayette St. (between Canal and Howard Sts.), Chinatown
www.holiday-inn.com
Phone: (212) 966-8898, (800) 465-4329 (HOLIDAY)   Fax: (212) 966-3933

This chain-standard hotel overlooking Chinatown is nothing to write home about. However, shoppers in search of a SoHo location for half of what the luxury hotels charge will consider this a find, since the boutique-lined streets of SoHo and NoLIta are just a stroll away. Rooms are utterly unremarkable, and many are quite small, but they're clean and comfortable in a completely reliable Holiday Inn way. A good number of government contractors are among the guests, so the place feels like a business hotel, but Asian accents add a neighborhood flair to the décor. Chinatown is fun for those who enjoy the exotica and bustle (not to mention the food), but ask for a room at the back of the hotel if you're a light sleeper.

Rooms: 227; 14 floors; designated nonsmoking floors. **Hotel amenities:** Concierge, dry cleaning and laundry service, meeting room. **Food services:** Chinese restaurant, bar, room service. **Cancellation:** 24 hours before arrival. **Wheelchair access:** Accessible. **Subway:** J, M, N, Q, R, W, Z, 6 to Canal St.

Holiday Inn Wall Street   EXCELLENT $$$
15 Gold St. (at Platt St.), Lower Manhattan
www.holidayinnwsd.com or *www.holiday-inn.com*
Phone: (212) 232-7800, (800) 465-4329 (HOLIDAY)   Fax: (212) 269-9569

Forget your motel expectations—this new-in-1999 Holiday Inn is a first-rate hotel. In fact, it's Manhattan's most technologically advanced hotel. The high-tech toys greet you in the small but pleasant lobby, where you can choose to bypass the professionally staffed front desk in favor of an ATM-style machine where you can check in with one touch; you can also download city information to your PDA at the mobile concierge or print out city info from a PC.

Rooms are very comfortable and boast conveniences galore for the traveling executive, or anybody who just likes toys. The eight-foot L-shaped workstation

boasts its own T1-connected PC with a 14-inch flat-screen monitor, MS Word
and Office applications, and full Internet access ($9.95 per day); desk-level
"Plug and Play" high-speed ethernet input for laptop toters; an ergonomic chair;
dual-line cordless phone with direct-dial number; and the kind of supplies you
never bring but always need, like paper clips, Liquid Paper, and a Webster's the-
saurus. For after-work time, there's a CD player, TV with on-screen Internet
access, and Nintendo. SMART rooms feature laptop computers with carrying
cases and wireless aircards (for mobile Internet access), fax/copier/printers and
other upgraded amenities.

Furnishings are surprisingly nice, if not particularly stylish, and everything is
brand-new. The staff prides itself on service, even anticipating needs by providing an amenity station on each floor stocked with everything from toothpaste to
extra blankets.

Rooms: 138; 18 floors; designated nonsmoking floors. **Hotel amenities:**
Concierge, dry cleaning and laundry service, coin-operated laundry, exercise
room, business center, state-of-the-art executive boardroom, CD library. **Food
services:** Italian restaurant, bar, room service, plated delivery from a range of
restaurants. **Cancellation:** 24 hours before arrival. **Wheelchair access:** Fully
accessible. **Subway:** 2, 3 to Wall St.

Larchmont Hotel   GOOD $
27 W. 11th St.(between Fifth and Sixth Aves.), West Village
www.larchmonthotel.com   Phone: (212) 989-9333   Fax: (212) 989-9496

New York could use a dozen more Larchmonts. This cheerful European-style
hotel is an excellent value for those who don't mind sharing hall bathrooms
with fellow guests in exchange for a very low rate. You'll feel the warm and welcoming vibe the instant you enter the butter-yellow lobby, where you'll be
greeted by the professional staff. Each bright room is prettily furnished in rattan,
with a writing desk and a wash basin, plus a TV and telephone (not a given in
this price range), a ceiling fan, a library of books and a nice cotton robe and
slippers that allow you to comfortably pad down the hall to the older but spotless shared bathrooms. The hotel's leafy brownstone-lined street brims with old
New York charm, and a wealth of subway lines are a short walk away. Loyal
guests keep this jewel booked, so reserve as far in advance as possible.

Rooms: 58 (all with shared bathrooms); six floors; smoking allowed. **Hotel
amenities:** Fax service, common kitchens. **Food services:** Rates include continental breakfast. **Cancellation:** Two days prior to arrival. **Wheelchair access:**
Not accessible. **Subway:** F, L, N, Q, R, W, 4, 5, 6 to 14th St.

The Mercer   EXCELLENT $$$$
147 Mercer St. (at Prince St.), SoHo   *www.mercerhotel.com*
Phone: (212) 966-6060, (888) 918-6060   Fax: (212) 965-3838

The Mercer is so cool that it's downright frosty. Still, modern design buffs will
love the stunning Christian Liagre-designed interiors, which are brazenly angu-

lar but comfortable nonetheless; gorgeous textured fabrics and rich African woods soften the look and add character. The high-ceilinged guest rooms are spacious and practical with extra-large work desks that double as generous dining tables. Steel carts add extra storage in the big and beautiful architecturally impressive bathrooms, which boast either an oversized shower or a tub for two. VCRs and CD players are on hand to keep you entertained (if the beautiful-people clientele isn't enough).

No other chic SoHo hotel is so well located, and no other hotelier knows how to run a luxury boutique hotel like Andre Balazs (also the power behind L.A.'s legendary Chateau Marmont). The air is more regal and exclusive than that at party scenes like Schrager's Royalton or the W hotels. The chic restaurant is the domain of superstar chef Jean-Georges Vongerichten (of four-star Jean Georges).

Rooms: 75; six floors; smoking allowed. **Hotel amenities:** 24-hour concierge, laundry and dry-cleaning service, business services, video and CD libraries. **Food services:** Restaurant and bar (The Mercer Kitchen), lobby cafe and bar, 24-hour room service. **Cancellation:** 48 hours prior to arrival. **Wheelchair access:** Fully accessible. **Subway:** N, R to Prince St.

Millenium Hilton   GOOD $$$

55 Church St. (between Fulton and Dey Sts.), Financial District
www.newyorkmillenium.hilton.com
Phone: (212) 693-2001, (800) 445-8667   Fax: (212) 571-2316

Note: This hotel suffered substantial damage during the September 11, 2001 plane crashes that destroyed the World Trade Center. It may not be operational by the time you plan your visit.

This freestanding glass tower across from the former site of the World Trade Center makes a smart choice for visiting bulls and bears—and heavily discounted weekend rates make it a relative bargain for leisure travelers, too. The focus is on corporate business, so don't expect anything in the way of personality; still, the comfort level is high. The rooms are light and bright on every floor, but the Lower Manhattan and bay views become more and more thrilling as you go up. The accommodations are very comfortable, with platform beds fitted with cushioned quilts, firm mattresses and down pillows. Other appealing in-room features include well-designed built-ins that maximize work and storage space, big bathrooms with lots of counter space, fax/printer/copiers and cushy bathrobes. An enclosed top-floor swimming pool is an extra perk for fitness-minded visitors.

Rooms: 561; 58 floors; designated nonsmoking floors. **Hotel amenities:** Concierge, business center, laundry and dry-cleaning service, health club, swimming pool, business center, meeting rooms. **Food services:** Restaurant and bar, more casual bar and grill, room service. **Cancellation:** One day prior to arrival. **Wheelchair access:** Fully accessible. **Subway:** N, R, 1, 9 to Cortlandt St.

New York Marriott Financial Center   GOOD $$$
85 West St. (at Carlisle St.), Financial District   *www.marriott.com*
Phone: (212) 385-4900, (888) 236-2427   Fax: (212) 227-8136

Note: This hotel suffered substantial damage during the September 11, 2001 plane crashes that destroyed the World Trade Center. It may not be operational by the time you plan your visit.

Rooms are utterly unremarkable at this nondescript but perfectly comfortable business hotel just steps from Wall Street. Some rooms have appealing views of the southern tip of the island. On site is good, tropical-accented Roy's New York, the first eastern U.S. restaurant from venerable Hawaiian chef Roy Yamaguchi. Weekend rates drop substantially, and all of Lower Manhattan's attractions are just a walk away.

Rooms: 515; 38 floors; designated nonsmoking rooms. **Hotel amenities:** Concierge, laundry and dry-cleaning service, health club with sauna and swimming pool, good business center, meeting rooms, valet parking. **Food services:** Roy's New York restaurant and bar, casual tavern-style restaurant, room service, complimentary coffee in lobby. **Cancellation:** 6 P.M. day of arrival. **Wheelchair access:** Fully accessible. **Subway:** N, R, 1, 9 to Rector St.

Regent Wall Street   EXTRAORDINARY $$$$
55 Wall St. (at William St.), Financial District   *www.regenthotels.com*
Phone: (212) 845-8600, (800) 545-4000   Fax: (212) 845-8601

The Regent isn't just the Financial District's finest hotel—it's one of the finest hotels in the city. The stunning 1842 Greek Revival building originally served as the New York Mercantile Exchange, then the U.S. Customs House; the legendary architectural firm of McKim, Mead and White remade the grand interiors in Italian Renaissance style in 1907. Its overarching neo-classical grandeur has been both beautifully preserved and smartly updated to meet its new purpose as a grand luxury hotel for a discerning expense-account audience.

The huge rooms are done in an elegant style and muted palette that bespeaks refinement and tranquility, yet isn't too stiff or formal. The décor seamlessly fuses neoclassical details and contemporary luxury. First-class appointments include monster marble bathrooms with his-and-hers vanities and extra-large soaking tubs, 34-inch TVs, DVD players, executive-size work desks with printer/fax/copier and cordless phones. Facilities include an intimate but excellent full-service spa. There's simply no better choice for visiting CEOs. Visit over a weekend or holiday, when promotional and special deals cut rates by half or more—sometimes as low as $200—and you don't have to be a platinum-card-toting executive to bask in the luxury of the Regent.

Rooms: 144; nine floors; designated nonsmoking floors. **Hotel amenities:** 24-hour concierge, excellent full-service health club and spa, business center, laundry and dry-cleaning service, spectacular Wedgwood-ceilinged ballroom, meeting rooms, DVD and CD libraries, valet parking. **Food services:** Restaurants with open-air terrace, lounge, 24-hour room service. **Cancellation:** 24 hours prior to arrival. **Wheelchair access:** Fully accessible. **Subway:** 2, 3 to Wall St.

Ritz-Carlton New York, Battery Park   EXCELLENT $$$$
2 West St., Battery Park City   *www.ritzcarlton.com*
Phone: (212) 344-0800, (800) 241-3333   Fax: (212) 877-6465

Note: This hotel suffered substantial damage during the September 11, 2001 plane crashes that destroyed the World Trade Center. It may not be operational by the time you plan your visit.

The reliably refined Ritz-Carlton chain unveiled Manhattan's first-ever water-side luxury hotel in October 2001. The shiny new glass-and-brick Battery Park City tower stands like a modern sentry over the Hudson River, just a shout from Wall Street, so it's no surprise that the hotel is geared towards high-level business travelers. But you don't have to be a CEO or senior VP to appreciate the amenity-laden rooms, which combine Ritz-Carlton's classic European style with 1920's-inspired Art Deco style. Appointments emphasize luxury (think Frette linens, feather beds, the works), cutting-edge technology (including high-speed Internet access and technology butler service), and sweeping skyline and/or harbor views; harbor-view rooms even feature telescopes so you can enjoy close-ups of Lady Liberty. In consistent Ritz-Carlton fashion, the ultimate in luxury is reserved for the club-level floors, where additional perks include DVD/CD players with surround sound, dedicated concierge, and private lounge with complimentary food service throughout the day. Expect impeccable service throughout.

Rooms: 298; 39 floors (hotel occupies first 14 floors); designated nonsmoking floors. **Hotel amenities:** Concierge, fitness center, spa, state-of-the-art business center with secretarial services, laundry and dry-cleaning service, conference and meeting/function rooms. **Food services:** Two restaurants, bar and lounge with afternoon tea service, 24-hour room service. **Cancellation:** 24 hours prior to arrival. **Wheelchair access:** Fully accessible. **Subway:** 4, 5 to Bowling Green.

Second Home on Second Ave.   GOOD $-$$
221 Second Ave. (between 13th and 14th Sts.), East Village
www.secondhome.citysearch.com   Phone/Fax: (212) 677-3161

Friendly innkeeper Carlos Delfin runs this comfortable and well-located guesthouse. The exterior promises little—but as soon as you walk up the flight of stairs to the first level of guest rooms, you'll know that you have stumbled onto a nifty secret. The pleasant rooms are large enough to accommodate two double beds in most, and the terrific suite has a pullout sofa as well. Each is tastefully outfitted, usually on a loose theme (tribal, modern, Caribbean and so on). Each room has its own phone, and big TV with VCR and CD player, both uncommon extras in this price category. The two priciest rooms have private baths, while the others share.

It wouldn't be a second home without a kitchen; this one is clean, modern, and well-stocked with the basics: pots, pans, dishes and silverware. There's no elevator and no resident innkeeper (Carlos lives off-site), so the guesthouse isn't suitable for heavy packers, those with limited mobility or travelers who need personal guidance. But if you're an intrepid type who will like easy access to the East Village's hip restaurants, bars and clubs, Second Home is a good choice.

If you're in need of shoestring accommodations, inquire with Carlos about his fun and funky Alphabet City guesthouse, **East Village Bed & Coffee**—another great value.

Rooms: Seven (five with shared bathroom); four floors; smoking allowed. **Hotel amenities:** Common kitchen. **Food services:** None. **Cancellation:** Seven days prior to arrival. **Wheelchair access:** Not accessible. **Subway:** L to First or Third Ave.; N, Q, R, W, 4, 5, 6 to 14th St.

60 Thompson   VERY GOOD $$$$
60 Thompson St. (between Spring and Broome Sts.), SoHo
www.60thompson.com   Phone: (212) 431-0400   Fax: (212) 431-0200

Despite its chic modernist lines and sky-high hip factor, this super-cool SoHo newcomer gets the restful residential tone just right. The entrance alone sets the tone: The facade is set back from the street, behind a courtyard of birch trees and blending easily with the surrounding cast-iron buildings and brownstones. Thomas O'Brien of Aero Studios hit all the right notes with the modernism-goes-domestic interiors. Public spaces are designed for easy lounging, and guest rooms, done in a soothing celadon-and-mahogany palette, are plush, comfortable and sexy without feeling faddish. While not large, they are well-equipped, with DVD and CD players, high-speed Internet access, comfortable seating areas and marble baths that are the most beautiful in town. O'Brien's signature low-slung, wing-backed Thompson chair makes the perfect reading cradle, while the abstract photography of Laura Resen adds artistic accents.

The restaurant, Thom, has already made a splash with its edgy Asian-fusion fare. One of the best things about 60 Thompson is its wealth of alfresco spaces, including Thom's outside dining room and a patio off the bar/breakfast room; a rooftop terrace bar and street-side cafe are coming soon.

Rooms: 100; 10 floors; designated non-smoking floors. **Hotel amenities:** 24-hour concierge, dry-cleaning and laundry service, breakfast room and lounge with open-air terrace. **Food services:** Thom restaurant and bar, room service. **Cancellation:** 24 hours prior to arrival. **Wheelchair access:** Fully accessible. **Subway:** C, E to Spring St.

SoHo Grand Hotel   EXCELLENT $$$$
310 West Broadway (between Grand and Canal Sts.), SoHo
www.sohogrand.com
Phone: (212) 965-3000, (800) 965-3000   Fax: (212) 965-3244

Although built only seven years ago, this designer hotel harkens back to SoHo's 19th-century cast-iron past with Industrial Age details (including Edison light bulbs), retro-minded furnishings with a strong Arts-and-Crafts influence, and gorgeous William Morris fabrics. Still, the overall effect is wholly modern, and comforts are 21st-century luxurious. The grand staircase that ascends from the ground floor to the lobby sets the tone from the start, as urban-industrial hardware gives way to 24-foot ceilings and two-story windows.

The understated but lovely guest rooms boast a studied Arts-and-Crafts ambiance with an Asian slant. Custom furnishings include saddle-stitched leather headboards and large, functional desks that resemble artists' drafting tables. The natural tones are warm and soothing, textiles are plush, and soft lighting abounds. CD players and VCRs add to the luxury. The building's T shape gives many rooms entrancing views (including one north to Midtown that is worth the price of admission), but bathrooms are generally small. The chic clientele includes more than a few celebrities, who prefer the slightly more relaxed vibe of this hotel over the party scene at sister hotel the TriBeCa Grand (below). The comfortable bar and lounge remains a stylish hangout. Owned by Hartz Mountain, the hotel welcomes pets, who even have their own room-service menu.

Rooms: 369; 17 floors; designated nonsmoking floors. **Hotel amenities:** Concierge, fitness center, laundry and dry cleaning, meeting and function rooms. **Food services:** Restaurant, bar, lounge, 24-hour room service, butler's pantry with coffee, tea and hot chocolate on every floor. **Cancellation:** 24 hours prior to arrival. **Wheelchair access:** Fully accessible. **Subway:** A, C, E, 1, 9 to Canal St.

St. Mark's Hotel   BASIC $

2 St. Marks Pl. (at Third Ave.), East Village   *www.stmarkshotel.qpg.com*
Phone: (212) 674-2192   Fax: (212) 420-0854

In a city where ancient carpet and dingy walls are the norm in budget hotels, this bright and clean hotel offers welcome relief. It is housed in a freshly renovated four-story walkup on St. Marks Place, the heart of the rock-and-roll East Village, lined with used record stores, cheap-eats restaurants and bars and a never-ending parade of pierced, tattooed youth. Travelers in search of silent nights or grown-up pursuits will hate the location, but those attracted to New York's funky side will love it.

From the second-floor reception area, bright oak-and-marble hallways lead to sparsely furnished but relatively spacious guest rooms (most painted a pretty butter yellow) with tiny, freshly tiled bathrooms. Everything is strictly budget-basic, but even the smallest room features new kelly-green carpet, a firm bed, a new TV and a phone (with voice mail); nicely framed prints brighten things up a bit. Expect nothing in the way of service or amenities, but there's just about anything you could want within blocks.

Rooms: 70; four floors; smoking allowed. **Hotel amenities:** None. **Food services:** None. **Cancellation:** No charge. **Wheelchair access:** None. **Note:** No credit cards accepted. **Subway:** 6 to Astor Pl.; N, R to Eighth St.

Tribeca Grand Hotel   EXCELLENT **$$$$**
2 Sixth Ave. (at White and Church Sts.), TriBeCa   *www.tribecagrand.com*
Phone: (212) 519-6600, (877) 519-6600   Fax: (212) 519-6700

This chic sister to the highly successful SoHo Grand (reviewed above) is another winner in the downtown luxury category. The brick-and-cast-iron exterior is right at home in the historic neighborhood—but inside, an unabashedly modern world awaits. Designer Larry Bogdanow has styled a dramatic eight-story atrium lobby—which gives the hotel an air of luxury that only open space can bestow—in one of the best public areas that any city hotel has to offer. The Church Lounge allows for socializing in an open, fluid restaurant-and-bar area, with luxurious leather-and-velvet seating nooks. It's a hugely popular hangout with a designer-clad downtown crowd.

Set along open, atrium-facing corridors, the guest rooms feature similar smart-meets-luxe modern design, although they've been deservedly criticized for emphasizing utilitarianism over leisure. An extra-long built-in, L-shaped work desk dominates the room, as does cutting-edge technology that includes a TV with wireless Internet access and VCR, a CD player, high-speed connectivity, fax/printer/copier and a cordless phone, plus a second TV in the gorgeous bath. A warm gold-and-red palette, sumptuous velvet, and soft, glowing light soften the look and add luxury-level comfort. The most beautiful staff in town adds to the downtown appeal, and their professionalism is welcome relief from the chic-boutique standard. Pets are warmly welcomed by owner Hartz Mountain.

Rooms: 203; eight floors; designated nonsmoking floors. **Hotel amenities:** 24-hour concierge, fitness center, business center with PC workstations, laundry and dry-cleaning service, video and CD libraries, screening room, coffee/tea/cocoa bar on each floor. **Food services:** Restaurant, lounge, 24-hour room service. **Cancellation:** 24 hours prior to arrival. **Wheelchair access:** Fully accessible. **Subway:** 1, 9 to Franklin St.

Union Square Inn   GOOD **$**
209 East 14th St. (between Second and Third Aves.), East Village
www.unionsquareinn.com   Phone: (212) 614-0500   Fax: (212) 614-0512

This newcomer a few blocks east of Union Square is a first-rate find for discerning budget travelers who want standard comforts at an affordable rate. There's no elevator, no facilities, no services to speak of, and rooms are small and lack anything resembling a view. But brand-new pillow-top mattresses, good-quality linens, contemporary redwood furniture, cheery autumn-hued prints and art, and brand-new bathrooms tiled in pretty Italian ceramic add up to comforts that are far superior to most hotels in this price category.

Rooms: 40; five floors; designated nonsmoking rooms. **Hotel amenities:** None. **Food services:** Rates include a basic continental breakfast. **Cancellation:** 48 hours prior to arrival. **Wheelchair access:** Not accessible. **Subway:** L, N, Q, R, W, 4, 5, 6 to 14th St.

Wall Street Inn
VERY GOOD $$$

9 South William St. (at Mill Lane), Financial District *www.thewallstreetinn.com*
Phone: (212) 747-1500   Fax: (212) 747-1900

This serene and welcoming small hotel offers an excellent alternative for business travelers (and leisure visitors looking for a downtown perch) who prefer intimate inns over anonymous corporate hotels. This is a boutique hotel in the true rather than trendy sense; management has done everything right here, paying close attention to the fundamentals and staying away from showy gimmicks. The plush Americana-style interiors are the perfect match for the historic building. Rooms are not overly large, but the décor is extremely attractive, the bedding is very high quality, and bathrooms are spacious and pretty. Windows are double-paned and filled with argon gas for extra noise abatement. Seventh-floor rooms are best, as the bathrooms have extra counter space and jetted tubs. The staff excels at offering individualized service and a personal touch. A terrific choice on every front—and heavily discounted weekend rates make it a veritable steal for weekenders.

Rooms: 46; seven floors; designated nonsmoking rooms. **Hotel amenities:** Concierge, fitness room with steam and sauna, business center, meeting room, laundry and dry-cleaning service, video library. **Food services:** Rates include continental breakfast. **Cancellation:** 24 prior to arrival. **Wheelchair access:** Accessible. **Subway:** 2, 3 to Wall St.; J, M, Z to Broad St.; N, R to Whitehall St.

Washington Square Hotel
BASIC $$

103 Waverly Pl. (between Macdougal and Waverly Sts.), West Village
www.wshotel.com
Phone: (212) 777-9515, (800) 222-0418   Fax: (212) 979-8373

This budget-minded hotel overlooking Washington Square Park, in the heart of N.Y.U. territory, has been in the Paul family for more than two decades. A surprisingly luxurious marble-and-brass lobby leads to teensy rooms that are little more than budget-basic, but each is clean and boasts its own private bathroom. A recent upgrade in décor improved their attractiveness appreciably, adding sponged sea-green walls, firm mattresses and new furniture. Unfortunately, rates increased commensurately. Ceilings are high, but closet space is nil. Still, the Washington Square is a perfectly good choice if you want a bustling village location convenient to good restaurants, bars and live music venues. In fact, you don't even have to leave the building for a good meal or a martini, since the hotel's own C3 attracts locals in its own right, especially for Sunday jazz brunch.

Rooms: 170; nine floors; smoking allowed. **Hotel amenities:** Exercise room, laundry and dry-cleaning service. **Food services:** C3 Restaurant and lounge; rates include continental breakfast. **Cancellation:** 48 hours prior to arrival. **Wheelchair access:** Not accessible.

CHELSEA/FLATIRON/
GRAMERCY PARK

Chelsea Inn
BASIC $–$$

46 W. 17th St. (between Fifth and Sixth Aves.)   *www.chelseainn.com*
Phone: (212) 645-8989, (800) 640-6469   Fax: (212) 645-1903

A hotel with a lot of heart and a lot of stairs, the Chelsea Inn offers friendly, simple and spotlessly clean lodging. Two 19th-century brownstones have been merged to form an eclectic mix of rooms and suites. Don't expect much in the way of décor; the rule of thumb is mix-and-match thrift-store furnishings, faded textiles, and mattresses that range from decent to mushy, all of which make the place feel more like a genuine New York City tenement than a hotel. Still, everything is neat as a pin. The ceilings are remarkably high, which adds to the feeling of space. Closets are big, bathrooms are fine and all rooms feature a hot plate, minifridge, coffee maker, a cheap set of cups and utensils, a safe and free coffee; those without private bathroom have their own sink, too. Shoestring travelers saddled with a shared-bath room, take heart: You'll only have to share with one other room. The front desk isn't staffed 24 hours, but guests are given keys to the front door, and phones have voice mail. Internet specials are a regular feature, and the reservations staff is usually willing to negotiate in all but the busiest seasons, so be sure to give it a shot.

Rooms: 26 (eight with shared bathrooms); five floors; smoking allowed. **Hotel amenities:** None. **Food services:** None. **Cancellation:** 48 hours prior to arrival. **Wheelchair access:** Not accessible. **Subway:** F, L, N, Q, R, W, 4, 5, 6 to 14th St.

Chelsea Lodge/Chelsea Lodge Suites
VERY GOOD $–$$

318 W. 20th St. (between Eighth and Ninth Aves.)
www.chelsealodge.com, www.chelsealodgesuites.com
Phone: (212) 243-4499   Fax: (212) 243-7852

This absolute gem of a hotel offers two kinds of lodging for discriminating budget travelers who want spotless accommodations, a dash of style and a location in the heart of the Chelsea Historic District surrounded by excellent restaurants and night spots. All rooms in the original brownstone are petite but delightful doubles with a unique semi-private bath situation: Each room has a sink and a stall shower, so guests only have to share toilets. The entire building has been gorgeously renovated, and both public spaces and guest rooms overflow with country-in-the-city charm. Rooms are small but superior comforts include high-quality bedding, smartly refinished vintage furniture, TVs and lovely little touches like Hershey's Kisses on the fluffy pillows. Everything is like new and impeccably kept. High ceilings make the first-floor rooms feel a bit larger.

The lodge has been such a success—as it should be!—that the innkeepers now let four additional studio-style suites in a nearby brownstone. Each features a queen bed, a brand-new marble bathroom, a fully outfitted kitchenette and a sitting area with TV/VCR and pullout sleeper sofa that allows the suites to accommodate up to four. Free local phone calls and daily maid service are included, and two suites even share a private garden. An excellent value.

Rooms: 22 doubles with semiprivate bathrooms, four studios; three floors; all nonsmoking. **Hotel amenities:** None. **Food services:** None. **Cancellation:** 72 hours prior to arrival. **Wheelchair access:** Not accessible. **Subway:** C, E, 1, 9 to 23rd St.

Chelsea Pines Inn   GOOD $–$$
317 W. 14th St. (between Eighth and Ninth Aves.)   *www.chelseapinesinn.com*
Phone: (212) 929-1023   Fax: (212) 620-5646

This delightful walk-up on a very busy street in the heart of gay New York—is targeted at gay and lesbian travelers, but all are welcome. The spotlessly kept rooms are attractively and wittily appointed. Each is named for a Golden Age film star—Susan Hayward, Rock Hudson, Paul Newman and so on—and features vintage poster art from the star's classic filmography (hence the groovy kitten-with-a-whip poster in the Ann-Margret room). Otherwise, décor is very comfortable, everything is like-new, and floral-print textiles create a pleasant homey feeling. All rooms have minifridges and a phone with answering machine; most have queen beds and daybeds for extra seating/sleeping. A half-dozen have breakfast areas with cafe tables and microwaves. Private bathrooms are bright and freshly renovated; rooms that share baths have private showers and sinks, so you budget-minded guests only have to share a hall toilet. Service is smart, professional and friendly, and the generous breakfast spread includes fresh Krispy Kreme doughnuts.

Rooms: 24 (9 with shared bathroom); 5 floors; smoking allowed. **Hotel amenities:** Fax service, greenhouse-style breakfast/sitting room, back garden. **Food services:** Rates include continental breakfast. **Cancellation:** 7 days prior to arrival; $50 cancellation fee. **Wheelchair access:** Not accessible. **Note:** Not for children. **Subway:** A, C, E to 14th St.

Chelsea Savoy Hotel   GOOD $$
204 W. 23rd St. (at Seventh Ave.)
www.chelseasavoy.qpg.com, www.chelseasavoy.citysearch.com
Phone: (212) 929-9353   Fax: 212-741-6309

This modern hotel has won a committed clientele with generic but consistent comforts. Locals love to hate the boxy modern structure, but it's blessedly free of the quirks that most mid-priced hotels shoulder: hallways are wide, elevators swift and quiet, rooms are pleasant and good-sized, and bathrooms are spacious and well-endowed with counter space. Those with two doubles are big enough for small families and budget-minded shares. This isn't Chelsea's prettiest corner, but the neighborhood has definitely arrived; restaurants and nightlife abound in the surrounding blocks, the city's best weekend flea markets are a block over on Sixth Avenue, and the 1 and 9 trains are just out the front door, ready to whisk you to the Theater District inside five minutes. Front rooms are brightest but overlook either 23rd Street or Seventh Avenue, both of which can be bothersome for light sleepers; ask for a darker back-facing room if you need total quiet.

Rooms: 90; six floors; designated nonsmoking floors. **Hotel amenities:** None. **Food services:** Rates include continental breakfast (restaurants in the works). **Cancellation:** 24 hours prior to check-in. **Wheelchair access:** Fully accessible. **Subway:** 1, 9 to 23rd St.

Colonial House Inn   GOOD $
318 W. 22nd St. (between Eighth and Ninth Aves.)   *www.colonialhouseinn.com*
Phone: (212) 243-9669, (800) 689-3779   Fax: (212) 633-1612

This lovely brownstone on a leafy Chelsea block was the first permanent home of the Gay Men's Health Crisis (GMHC). It's now an attractive and comfortable bed-and-breakfast that caters largely to a gay crowd but welcomes everybody. Rooms are small and simple but very nice. Almost half have private baths, and a few in the deluxe category (those with private baths) have working fireplaces and refrigerators. All have TV, phone, radio and a comfortable bed. Everything is well tended, including the shared baths. A surprisingly terrific collection of original abstract art (the work of owner and activist Mel Cheren) fills the public spaces, breakfast room and guest rooms, adding a thoughtful, creative air to the place. The staff is professional and friendly, and the expanded continental breakfast is bounteous with fresh baked goods. There's also a clothing-optional rooftop sun deck. All in all, an excellent choice. Book well in advance, especially for weekend stays.

Rooms: 20 (12 with shared bathrooms); 4 floors; smoking allowed. **Hotel amenities:** None. **Food services:** Rates include continental breakfast. **Cancellation:** Two weeks prior to arrival. **Wheelchair access:** None. **Subway:** C, E to 23rd St.

Gramercy Park Hotel   GOOD $$
2 Lexington Ave. (at 21st St.)   *www.gramercyparkhotel.com*
Phone: (212) 475-4320, (800) 221-4083   Fax: (212) 505-0535

This old-world hotel overlooking the lovely square-block that is Gramercy Park, boasts huge rooms and an appealing good-old-days ambiance (Babe Ruth and Humphrey Bogart are two of many famous-name former guests). Going strong since 1924, this privately owned hotel is stuck in the past with interiors that tout history over high design. Space makes up for a lot in New York, though; even standard doubles, which come with a king or two double beds, are large enough for families. Suites are mammoth, with a sleeper sofa in the living room and a kitchenette. (Park-view doubles also have small kitchenettes; request one when booking.) Furnishings are older—TVs are refugees from the *Starsky and Hutch* days—but everything is traditionally styled, relatively attractive and comfortable. Bathrooms are dated, but they're universally large, too.

   One of the best things about staying at this hotel is that guests have access to gated Gramercy Park, which feels like an elite London square. The park is off-limits to almost everyone (for area residents to qualify for a key, their windows have to overlook the park), so hotel guests beat out locals on this score.

Rooms: 509; 18 floors; designated nonsmoking rooms. **Hotel amenities:** Laundry and dry-cleaning service, meeting and function rooms (including roof deck), access to gated Gramercy Park. **Food services:** Continental-style restaurant, piano bar, room service. **Cancellation:** 72 hours prior to arrival. **Wheelchair access:** Fully accessible. **Subway:** 6 to 23rd St.

Hotel Chelsea GOOD $$

222 West 23rd St. (between Seventh and Eighth Aves.) *www.hotelchelsea.com*
Phone: (212) 243-3700 Fax: (212) 675-5531

Dozens of legendary writers, artists, actors and other creative types, ranging from William Burroughs to Sid Vicious, have stayed at or lived in this hotel since it opened in 1884. Artwork from tenants (often offered in lieu of rent in decades past) fills the lobby, enlivening every available space. The hotel is still largely occupied by residents with an artistic bent, but about 100 rooms are available to short-term visitors with a bohemian spirit. Rooms are large and eccentrically outfitted with generally older fixtures and furnishings, but usually comfortably so. The hotel is generally well-kept, but the ghosts hovering in every corner of this landmark see to it that nothing is obsessively clean. Needless to say, travelers in search of predictable comforts should stay elsewhere. Still, you get more space than in most New York hotels; most rooms have good light, many have kitchenettes, some have hand-carved marble fireplaces, and walls are famously thick. The staff is offbeat but quite attentive.

Rooms: 400 (usually about 100 available to travelers, some with shared bathroom); 12 floors; smoking allowed. **Hotel amenities:** Bell service (will send out dry-cleaning, pick up take-out food and so on). **Food services:** El Quijote restaurant, hip bar Serena. **Cancellation:** Three days prior to arrival. **Wheelchair access:** Accessible. **Subway:** C, E, 1, 9 to 23rd St.

Hotel Giraffe VERY GOOD $$$–$$$$

365 Park Ave. South (at 26th St.) *www.hotelgiraffe.com*
Phone: (212) 685-7700, (877) 296-0009 Fax: 212-685-7701

Designed from the ground up by supremely talented husband-and-wife team Stephen B. Jacobs (the architect) and Andi Pepper (the designer), this Flatiron District boutique beauty brims with Art Moderne-inspired elegance. Rooms aren't huge, but 10-foot ceilings create an open feeling, and honey-hued built-ins that include generous granite-topped work desks use the available space beautifully, giving both business and leisure travelers the necessary room to move in, spread out and reside in real comfort. Amenities include CD players, cordless phones and windows that shut out virtually all street noise, plus gorgeous granite bathrooms. Deluxe rooms have French doors opening onto a juliet balcony, while suites add a separate living room with a smartly designed long-legged coffee table that doubles beautifully for dining. Franco-Asian fusion restaurant Chinoiserie provides a reason to dine in, but the stylish neighborhood brims with good restaurants.

Rooms: 73; 12 floors; dedicated nonsmoking floors. **Hotel amenities:** Concierge, business services, laundry and dry-cleaning service, video and CD libraries, rooftop garden, 1,000-square-foot penthouse suite with terrace for events. **Food services:** Restaurant, bar, room service; rates include continental breakfast and all-day cappuccino and snacks. **Cancellation:** 24 hours prior to arrival. **Wheelchair access:** Fully accessible. **Subway:** 6 to 28th St.

The Inn at Irving Place   EXCELLENT $$$$
56 Irving Pl. (between 17th and 18th Sts.)   *www.innatirving.com*
Phone: (212) 533-4600, (800) 685-1447   Fax: (212) 533-4611

Romance is the rule at this impeccably run, supremely elegant bed-and-breakfast inn, housed in adjoining 1834 Greek Revival brownstones on a lovely cafe-dotted Gramercy Park block. Each guest room has its own layout, design and theme, usually a literary allusion (the Madame Olenska room, the Else deWolf suite, and so on). No matter which one you choose, you can expect lavish high Victorian appointments that include well-chosen antiques and art, a grand non-working fireplace, Oriental rugs, luxurious fabrics and a supremely comfortable Frette-made queen bed. The cream-and-white-tiled bathrooms are brand-new and beautiful. Modern-day luxuries include a TV with VCR (hidden in an armoire so as not to disturb the mood) and a CD player. Deluxe rooms feature a small seating area, and the ultra-luxurious suites are larger than most Manhattan apartments, but standard rooms are sufficiently conducive to romance. The elegant staff is trained not to say no, and they usually don't. Lady Mendl's Tea Salon is a dream come true for ladies who like high tea—it doesn't get any better than this. Avoid rooms that overlook the basement-level restaurant's back-garden patio. And beware—there's no elevator. Otherwise, B & B fans looking for a special-occasion splurge should be thrilled; only Inn New York City comes close *(see section "Uptown" later in this chapter)*.

Rooms: 12; 3 floors; no smoking allowed. **Hotel amenities:** Business services, laundry and dry-cleaning service, light shopping service. **Food services:** American bistro (Irving on Irving), elegant tearoom (Lady Mendl's), cocktail lounge (Cibar), room service; rates include continental breakfast. **Cancellation:** 48 hours prior to arrival. **Wheelchair access:** Not accessible. *Note: Not appropriate for children under 12. **Subway:** L, N, Q, R, W, 4, 5, 6 to 14th St.

The Inn on 23rd St.   VERY GOOD $$
131 W. 23rd St. (between Sixth and Seventh Aves.)
www.bbonline.com/ny/innon23rd
Phone: (212) 463-0330, (877) 387-2323   Fax: (212) 463-0302

This marvelous full-service bed-and-breakfast offers a perfect blend of genuine B & B charm and real-hotel amenities. Innkeepers Annette and Barry Fisherman renovated this spacious 19th-century town house in the heart of Chelsea, and got everything exactly right in the process. The beautifully outfitted rooms and one suite have been outfitted by Annette with an eye to both style and function. Every room is themed, but in a classy, not kitschy, way: The 40's room is outfitted in Heywood-Wakefield and vintage bark cloth, while the Bamboo Room is elegantly Zen. The Loft Room has a loft bed at skylight level that the sleeper reaches via a ship's ladder, and Ken's Cabin is a large, lodgey brick-walled room outfitted in wonderfully worn leather and delightful Americana accents, from Navajo rugs to vintage license plates. Appointments are first-class all the way. One of the great things about the Inn on 23rd is that it's child-friendly and fully wheelchair accessible—yes, the Fishermans even installed an elevator, and a number of rooms feature pullout sofas or Murphy beds to accommodate extra travelers.

Rooms: 11; five floors; no smoking allowed. **Hotel amenities:** Business services, living room-style library. **Food services:** Rates include continental breakfast. **Cancellation:** One week prior to arrival. **Wheelchair access:** Fully accessible.

The Marcel   VERY GOOD $$
201 E. 24th St. (at Third Ave.)   www.nychotels.com
Phone: (212) 696-3800, (888) 66-HOTEL (664-6835)   Fax: (212) 696-0077

Generally the Amsterdam Hospitality Group's hotels are nothing to rave about, but this one is a standout for budget-minded travelers who nevertheless like a strong dash of style in their accommodations. This Gramercy Park newcomer brings high design to the people, with fabulous faux 60's Scandinavian stylings and bold geometric patterns. A teak lobby with abstract murals, mod leather furniture, and a surprisingly beautiful powder blue and chocolate color scheme gives way to guest rooms where smart blond-wood built-ins make terrific use of space. Extras include writing desks, marble baths, VCRs and CD players.

One of the strongest appeals of the Marcel is Spread, a stylish hybrid restaurant/lounge. Chef Michael Navarro's innovative small-plates and sushi menu is so terrific that it's drawing in throngs of locals. Low-slung interiors, inspired cocktails and a savvy DJ add to the lounge-style allure.

Rooms: 97; eight floors; two designated smoking floors. **Hotel amenities:** Laundry and dry-cleaning service, meeting room. **Food services:** Spread restaurant and lounge, 24-hour cappuccino bar, room service; rates include continental breakfast. **Cancellation:** 24 hours prior to arrival. **Wheelchair access:** ADA compliant.

W Union Square   VERY GOOD $$$$
201 Park Ave. South (at 17th St. and Union Sq. East)   www.whotels.com
Phone: (212) 253-9119, (877) 946-8357 (W-HOTELS)   Fax: 212-253-9229

The magnificent 1911 Beaux-Arts Guardian Life building boasts great bones and a terrific location, overlooking leafy, lively Union Square, the hub of New York's new media frenzy. Architect David Rockwell has done an excellent job of shepherding the transformation from office building to luxury hotel for the boutique-chic arm of Starwood Hotels (the folks behind such famous-name hotel brands as Sheraton, Westin and St. Regis), successfully fusing original architectural details with chic, clean-lined modernism. Due to its smaller size, the bright, comfortable, high-ceilinged lounge-like lobby isn't quite the scene that the original W New York is—which many will consider a benefit. It's also cozier and warmer, with the W chain's signature wheat grass in planters used to great effect. Off the lobby is celebrity chef Todd English's Olives, which serves up very good Mediterranean-inspired nouveau fare.

Guest rooms are done in dark, angular woods and gorgeous muted tones, with plush fabrics and aubergine-purple accents, divinely inspired beds with leather-cushioned headboards, large worktables, full-length mirrors and excellent bathrooms with luminous mother-of-pearl countertops. Suites have fax machines and corner views overlooking Union Square Park. Service is a beneficial fusion of boutique intimacy and chain-standard reliability.

Look for yet another W—the W Times Square—to debut in the Big Apple in late 2001/early 2002.

Rooms: 286; 21 floors; designated non-smoking floors. **Hotel amenities:** Concierge, laundry and dry-cleaning service, exercise room, stunning ballroom, state-of-the-art meeting space. **Food services:** Noted restaurant, living room-style lounge, stylish subterranean UnderBar, 24-hour room service. **Cancellation:** 4 P.M. day before arrival. **Wheelchair access:** Fully accessible. **Subway:** L, N, Q, R, W, 4, 5, 6 to 14th St.

MIDTOWN EAST & MURRAY HILL

The Benjamin   EXCELLENT $$$
125 E. 50th St. (at Lexington Ave.)   *www.thebenjamin.com*
Phone: (212) 715-2500, (888) 4-BENJAMIN (423-6526) Fax: (212) 715-2525

The gorgeous, low-key Benjamin is the flagship of the Manhattan East Suites group, and it's a real winner. Housed within a stunning 1927 Emery Roth-designed building, the Benjamin boasts all the hallmarks of a boutique hotel, including a gracious staff. The magnificent lobby sets the tone with a tranquil silver-and-taupe palette, beautifully preserved architectural details, Venetian mirrors and a sweeping staircase leading to the mezzanine-level lounge.

The beautifully outfitted guest rooms are some of the best in town, especially for the money. They're gorgeously decorated in a sophisticated neoclassical-meets-modern style, wearing rich textiles (chenille, mohair, linen) and champagne hues. But the real story is the appointments—the custom-designed Serta mattresses dressed in Frette linens and down-filled duvets, with cushioned headboards and a choice of 11 pillow types; the best kitchenettes in town, featuring microwaves and coffee makers, and stocked with china and gourmet goodies; oversized work desks wired for high-tech travelers, with fax/printer/copiers, high-speed connectivity and outlets at desk level, ergonomic executive chairs, task lighting, cordless phones and pullout table leaves that are ideal for in-room dining; and Web TV and video games on 27-inch TVs. Service is excellent, and double-paned windows keep rooms blissfully free of street noise. The white marble bathrooms are on the small side, but use space beautifully. Suites add a divine sitting room and a CD player, plus terraces in some.

Rooms: 209; 26 floors; dedicated nonsmoking floors. **Hotel amenities:** Concierge, full-service Woodstock Spa & Wellness Center with gym, laundry and dry-cleaning service, business services, executive boardroom and function rooms. **Food services:** Excellent New American restaurant, Larry Forgione's An American Place; lounge; 24-hour room service. **Cancellation:** 3 P.M. day of arrival. **Wheelchair access:** Fully accessible. **Subway:** 6 to 51st St.

Crowne Plaza at the United Nations   VERY GOOD $$$
304 E. 42nd St. (near Second Ave.)   www.crowneplaza-un.com
Phone: (212) 986-8800, (800) 879-8836   Fax: (212) 297-3440

A striking neo-Tudor building houses one of Manhattan's best chain hotels, located and designed to appeal to discerning diplomats. It also makes sense for visitors who want to be near Midtown, but not in the thick of it. Rooms are outfitted in a very comfortable and surprisingly high-quality traditional style. Italian marble baths and bedside controls for climate and lighting, and well-chosen belle époque poster art and vintage black-and-white New York scenes add to the feeling of luxury. Triple-paned windows shut out street noise entirely. High-speed connectivity is a plus for laptop toters. Club-level rooms include whirlpool tubs, pullout sofas or love seats, and free access to the club lounge, where complimentary continental breakfast and cocktails make the extra charge a good value. Dining and service surpass chain expectations, as they should in a hotel that caters to the U.N. clientele. Weekend rates can be a coup for leisure travelers.

Rooms: 300; 20 floors; designated nonsmoking rooms. **Hotel amenities:** Concierge, fitness center with sauna, business center, laundry and dry-cleaning service, meeting and function rooms. **Food services:** American bistro-style restaurant and bar, lounge for afternoon tea and cocktails, room service. **Cancellation:** 6 P.M. day of arrival. **Wheelchair access:** Fully accessible. **Subway:** S, 4, 5, 6, 7 to 42nd St.

Doral Park Avenue Hotel   GOOD $$–$$$
70 Park Ave. (at 38th St.)   www.doralparkavenue.com
Phone: (212) 973-2500, (877) 99-DORAL   Fax: (212) 973-2440

The big draw at this pleasant Park Avenue hotel is the value-laden packages, smartly designed to draw in travelers with a wealth of fun and money-saving extras. The most recent slate of packages included theater-and-dining packages with tickets to *Cabaret*; a "Girl's Getaway" package with a personal training session, a massage, and a manicure and pedicure, plus shopping discounts; and a golf package including lessons and drive time at the Golf Club at Chelsea Piers. Substantially discounted weekend and slow-season rates are a big attraction.

   On its own, the Doral Park Avenue isn't particularly special. Rooms are pleasant but largely nondescript with marble baths, older TVs, a small work desk with fax machine, decent-sized closets with Frette bathrobes and umbrellas for rainy days. A smart new design adds a contemporary accent to the 1920's neoclassical lobby, while a brand-new, seafood-heavy grill restaurant boasts a wholly modern look and sidewalk cafe tables overlooking Park Avenue. A big plus for workout buffs is the free access to the full-service, excellently equipped Doral Fitness Center, one block away; all you have to do is bring your sneakers, and they'll supply you with workout clothes. The location, just four blocks from Grand Central, is another plus.

Rooms: 188; 17 floors; designated nonsmoking rooms. **Hotel amenities:** Concierge, full-service Doral Fitness Center one block away, laundry and dry-cleaning service, secretarial services, meeting and function rooms. **Food services:** Restaurant with sidewalk dining, bar, room service. **Cancellation:** 24 hours prior to arrival. **Wheelchair access:** ADA compliant. **Subway:** S, 4, 5, 6, 7 to 42nd St.

Fitzpatrick Grand Central Hotel   VERY GOOD $$–$$$
141 E. 44th St. (at Lexington Ave.)   *www.fitzpatrickhotels.com*
Phone: (212) 351-6800, (800) 367-7701   Fax: (212) 818-1747

This lovely hotel from the Dublin-based Fitzpatrick hotel group is notable for its distinctive Emerald Isle personality, its warm hospitality and its excellent location, just steps from Grand Central Terminal. Kelly-green-carpeted hallways lead from the small but welcoming lobby to elegant guest rooms that far surpass the business-hotel standard with elegant half-canopied beds, luxury fabrics and colors, very pleasing and spacious navy-and-white baths, a fridge stocked with complimentary Irish spring water, a coffee maker, fax machine, high-speed Internet access and plush terry robes. The junior suites also have VCRs, CD players and extra TVs (including one in the giant bathroom, which also has a soaking tub), but they're more suitable for couples or executives than families, since the sitting-room sofa isn't a sleeper model. The Liam Neeson penthouse offers Waterford-and-marble-adorned ultra-luxury, including many imported-from-Ireland amenities. The Garden Suites may not be quite so luxurious, but outdoor patios and big, beautifully tiled baths make them a worthwhile splurge. Check for value-added special packages and heavily discounted Internet rates, especially for weekend stays.

Rooms: 155; 10 floors; designated nonsmoking rooms. **Hotel amenities:** Concierge, exercise room, laundry and dry-cleaning service, meeting room. **Food services:** Wheeltapper Irish pub, 24-hour room service. **Cancellation:** 24 hours prior to arrival. **Wheelchair access:** Fully accessible. **Subway:** S, 4, 5, 6, 7 to 42nd St.

Four Seasons Hotel New York   EXCELLENT $$$$
57 E. 57th St. (between Park and Madison Aves.)   *www.fourseasons.com*
Phone: (212) 758-5700, (800) 819-5053   Fax: (212) 758-5711

This ultra-modern, I.M. Pei-designed hotel is a haven of ultra-luxury for international CEOs and superstars. Pei's sleek 52-story limestone tower is the tallest hotel in Manhattan and rife with 1930's-meets-21st-century glamour. The combination of stunning spaces, first-class amenities and impeccable Four Seasons service makes this one of the city's most outstanding places to stay. Come with your platinum card in hand, though, because this shockingly expensive hotel is one of Manhattan's priciest.

The money-is-no-object ostentation begins the moment you step into the soaring, streamlined lobby with its reflective marble floors and backlit onyx ceiling. All but the cheapest rooms are large—500 to 600 square feet, 800 in suites—and sumptuously designed in a lovely cream-on-white style that harkens back to the Golden Age of Hollywood. Standout features include lustrous silks, warm English sycamore furnishings that include an oversized dining/work table, spacious dressing areas, massive Florentine marble baths with soaking tubs that fill in 60 seconds, fax/printer/copiers and high-speed connectivity for business folks, video and CD players for in-room entertainment, and floor-to-ceiling windows framing breathtaking views (plus bedside controlled window treatments if you prefer to shut them out). The custom Frette-dressed, Sealy Posture-Lux mattresses offer a night's sleep so legendary that many guests purchase them as a big-ticket souvenirs for back home.

Rooms: 370; 52 floors; designated nonsmoking floors. **Hotel amenities:** 24-hour concierge; full-service spa and fitness center with steam, whirlpool and sauna; full-service business center; laundry and dry-cleaning service; health club; extensive meeting and conference space. **Food services:** *New York Times* three-star Fifty Seven Fifty Seven restaurant and martini bar, Lobby Lounge for afternoon tea and cocktails; 24-hour room service. **Cancellation:** 24 hours prior to arrival. **Wheelchair access:** Fully accessible. **Subway:** 4, 5, 6 to 59th St.

The Helmsley Middletowne   GOOD $$
148 E. 48th St. (between Lexington and Third Aves.)   *www.helmsleyhotels.com*
Phone: (212) 755-3000, (800) 221-4982   Fax: (212) 832-0261

A converted apartment building that still feels like one, the Middletowne doesn't have room service, an exercise room or even much of a lobby. What it does have are large, relatively affordable rooms and suites (both junior suites and full one- and two-bedrooms). Every room has a refrigerator (most have wet bars, too), two-line phones, older but nice tile bathrooms and generous closet space. Furnishings are older and lack anything called style, but mattresses are fresh and firm, and carpets, textiles and linens are like-new. The one- and two-bedroom suites are big enough to call home, and full galley kitchenettes make it so (cabinets are without dishware, though); some also have terraces and/or fireplaces. The location is pleasant and convenient, and the long-employed staff is friendly and strives to meet your needs.

Rooms: 192 (includes 42 suites); 18 floors; designated nonsmoking floors.
Hotel amenities: Laundry and dry-cleaning service, meeting room. **Food services:** Rates include continental breakfast. **Cancellation:** 4 P.M. day before arrival. **Wheelchair access:** Fully accessible. **Subway:** 6 to 51st St.

Hotel Bedford   BASIC $$
118 E. 40th St. (between Park and Lexington Aves.)   *www.bedfordhotel.com*
Phone: (212) 697-4800, (800) 221-6881   Fax: (212) 697-1093

The Bedford offers comfortable, no-style lodging in a great location, just two blocks from Grand Central Terminal. Owner Hy Arbesfeld really cares about giving guests a good experience and value for their dollar. There are generously sized studios and suites with generic Levitz-style furnishings, serving pantries with microwaves and coffee makers, hair dryers in the standard bathrooms and little else, but everything is neat and clean. The good space and safe neighborhood makes this a reasonable choice for wallet-watching families. The best value is available during the heavily discounted off-season.

Rooms: 136; 17 floors; designated nonsmoking rooms. **Hotel amenities:** Laundry and dry-cleaning service. **Food services:** Restaurant, room service; rates include continental breakfast. **Cancellation:** 24 hours prior to arrival. **Wheelchair access:** Not accessible. **Subway:** S, 4, 5, 6, 7 to 42nd St.

Hotel Elysée

VERY GOOD $$$

60 E. 54th St. (between Park and Madison Aves.)   *www.elyseehotel.com*
Phone: (212) 753-1066, (800) 535-9733   Fax: (212) 980-9278

Built in 1926, this charming and intimate hotel makes a lovely choice for travelers who want a boutique hotel without pretensions. Styled like a small European hotel, rooms and suites are generously sized and traditionally decorated in dark woods and soft, pretty pastels. Entry halls and vestibules make the rooms feel more residential and buffer guests from hallway noise (as do the thick walls). All accommodations have nice, firm beds, well-maintained marble baths, good closet space, VCRs and terry robes. A handful of junior suites have nonworking fireplaces, while two deluxe rooms and a suite have much coveted terraces. Rooms with two doubles are especially large and suitable for families and shares; suites also have sleeper sofas. Complimentary breakfast, all-day coffee and cookies, and weekday afternoon wine and cheese is served in the supremely comfortable, Euro-elegant sitting room, which recalls the French Empire with its rich velvets and reds and golds. The service is intimate and attentive, and the location is the very best part of Midtown—and there's no denying the value of all that free food.

Rooms: 101; 15 floors; designated nonsmoking rooms. **Hotel amenities:** Laundry and dry-cleaning service, sitting room, clubby library with flat-screen PC with free Internet access, free access to nearby health club. **Food services:** Monkey Bar restaurant and bar, room service; rates include continental breakfast and daytime snacks. **Cancellation:** 24 hours prior to arrival. **Wheelchair access:** ADA compliant. **Subway:** E, F to Lexington Ave.

Kimberly Hotel

VERY GOOD $$$

145 E. 50th St. (between Lexington and Third Aves.)   *www.kimberlyhotel.com*
Phone: (212) 755-0400, (800) 683-0400   Fax: (212) 486-6915

This low-profile hotel was conceived in the mid-1980's as an apartment building but, during construction, was reconceived as a hotel. The practical effect of this quick-change is plenty of room for guests. The very pleasing hotel boasts mostly apartment-style one-bedroom and two-bedroom/two-bath suites featuring all the comforts of home, including a fully outfitted kitchen with full-size appliances; a fully furnished living room with a dining area and Oriental rugs; marble bathrooms; and large, well-appointed rooms. One-bedroom suites run about 600 square feet, two-bedroom suites a whopping 1200 square feet, making them perfect for families and business travelers looking to stay awhile. Video games are on hand to please the kids and fax machines are en suite for business travelers. A number of attractive and comfortable standard doubles with especially nice bathrooms and deep soaking tubs are also available, but the best values are clearly the suites. The generally traditional décor isn't what you'd call stylish, but the comfort level is very high. Service is refined and attentive. The Kimberly's ongoing promotions and package rates are excellent; almost no one pays full rack rate here, so be sure to mine for discounts.

Rooms: 186 (mostly suites); 30 floors; designated nonsmoking floors. **Hotel amenities:** Concierge, laundry and dry-cleaning service, business center, meeting suite, free access to nearby health club with swimming pool. **Food services:** Two restaurants, two bars, room service. **Cancellation:** 24 hours prior to arrival. **Wheelchair access:** Fully accessible. **Subway:** 6 to 51st St.

The Kitano New York   EXCELLENT $$$$
66 Park Ave. (at 38th St.)   *www.kitano.com, www.summithotels.com*
Phone: (212) 885-7000, (800) KITANO-NY (548-2666)   Fax: (212) 885-7100

Reopened in 1995 after a three-year, $55 million reconstruction, this elegant Japanese-owned hotel is a sea of tranquility in the bustle and chaos of New York City. Botero's voluptuous bronze sculpture "Dog" greets you at the entrance— and the art collection only gets better from there. The clean-lined lobby exudes luxury in the high quality of the materials—deep-grained mahogany, rich suede-upholstered sofas and fabulous, mostly modern art. The overall feeling is one of warmth, sophistication and Zen-like repose.

The modern guest rooms and suites are clean-lined, natural-hued havens of Japanese luxury. The building's corner situation grants impressive cityscape views to most. Though the windows do open, they seem to hermetically seal each room from street noise, so a good night's sleep is practically guaranteed. Other luxury extras include large work desks with fax machines, heated towel racks, bathrobes and umbrellas for borrowing. If you're the adventurous sort in the mood for something special, book New York's only authentic Tatami Suite, which boasts its own Japanese tea ceremony room. Nadaman Hakubai, the hotel's elegant kaiseki restaurant, is exceptional, and the largely Japanese staff specializes in flawless service. Weekend packages are the way to go for vacationers in search of a Far Eastern-flavored getaway.

Rooms: 149; 19 floors; designated nonsmoking rooms. **Hotel amenities:** Concierge, business services, laundry and dry-cleaning service, rooftop meeting rooms, free access to nearby health club. **Food services:** Nadaman Hakubai restaurant, continental cafe, lounge, room service. **Cancellation:** 24 hours prior to arrival. **Wheelchair access:** Fully accessible. **Subway:** S, 4, 5, 6, 7 to 42nd St.

Library Hotel   VERY GOOD $$$

299 Madison Ave. (at 41st St.)   *www.libraryhotel.com*
Phone: (212) 983-4500, (877) 793-7323   Fax: (212) 499-9099

One of the best among the bevy of new boutique hotels is this biblio-themed charmer, located just a stone's throw from the New York Public Library, the hotel's inspiration. The Library Hotel is intimate and beautifully outfitted in a classic-goes-contemporary style; the clear and consistent unifying theme establishes a tone of both residential-tinged luxury and joyful discovery. The floors are categorized by the Dewey Decimal system, with each room's "subject" reflected in the framed photography and books within: Romance Languages, Ethics, Botany, Fairy Tales, Erotic Literature, African Religion and so on. Would-be astronauts might like the Astronomy room (Neil Armstrong did), while those with a penchant for the past might prefer the Twentieth Century room (on the History floor) or the Dinosaurs room (Math and Science). The Love room (on the Philosophy floor) is a must for romancing couples, who can read Shakespeare's sonnets to one another (or sex tips, if they prefer). Fiction and nonfiction books covering a range of subjects also fill the cozy penthouse-level library; overall, the hotel's collection numbers more than 6,000 titles.

The guest rooms themselves are an understated but beautiful haven of smart design dressed in a rich and restful natural palette. Mahogany built-ins provide a wealth of work and storage space; bathrooms aren't very big, but they're beautifully and smartly designed. Amenities include VCRs and CD players (the full library of the American Film Institute's top 100 films is on hand for you to borrow, as is a music library), cordless phones and bathrobes. Considering the quality, prices are reasonable, and all-day food service makes it more so.

Rooms: 60; 14 floors; designated nonsmoking rooms. **Hotel amenities:** Laundry and dry-cleaning service, business center, penthouse-level conference room, library lounge with fireplace, penthouse-level terrace, video and CD libraries. **Food services:** Italian restaurant Vigneti with sidewalk dining in warm weather, room service; rates include continental breakfast, all-day cappuccino and cookies, weekday wine and cheese. **Cancellation:** 24 hours prior to arrival. **Wheelchair access:** ADA compliant. **Subway:** S, 4, 5, 6, 7 to 42nd St.

The Lombardy   EXCELLENT $$$

111 E. 56th St. (between Park and Lexington Aves.)   *www.lombardyhotel.com*
Phone: (212) 753-8600, (800) 223-5254   Fax: (212) 754-5683

Built in 1926, the Lombardy is a marvelous vestige of old New York, one of its last genuine apartment hotels. The Lombardy is a co-op residence made up of individually owned apartments—75 one-bedrooms and 40 studios—that are let as hotel rooms, along with a full spectrum of hotel services. The superior products here are the huge one-bedroom suites, which average 850 square feet. Décor varies dramatically since they're individually owned, but almost all have been beautifully renovated, some remarkably so. Studios, which average about 450 square feet, are a bit of a crapshoot décor-wise, but owners are held to a high standard, and you still get a lot for your money. All units have fully equipped kitchenettes in separate rooms; all have fridges and microwaves, most have coffee makers, and many have stovetops and/or dishwashers. Bathrooms are usually marble and always pleasant, but not large; on the other hand, most New Yorkers would kill to have this much closet space. Other common features include dining areas and work desks; maid service is also a part of the package. A standout is no. 402, a glorious one-bedroom outfitted with marble floors, two glorious marble baths, a new kitchen and a museum-worthy collection of mid-century and modern furnishings and art.

The hotel runs like a well-oiled machine: The entire place is immaculately kept, the fiercely loyal staff is equally solicitous to residents and hotel guests alike, and management is striving to always improve an already-stellar property. Smoking is allowed in all rooms (unless the owner prohibits it), but the hotel is so well maintained that it's hard to smell a whiff anywhere in the hotel.

Rooms: 115 (mostly suites); 14 floors; smoking allowed. **Hotel amenities:** Concierge, day spa and salon, laundry and dry-cleaning service, exercise room. **Food services:** Etoile restaurant and lounge, room service. **Cancellation:** 24–48 hours prior to arrival, depending on season. **Wheelchair access:** Fully accessible. **Note:** Children under 12 not accepted. **Subway:** 4, 5, 6 to 59th St.

Metropolitan Hotel   GOOD $$–$$$
569 Lexington Ave. (at 51st St.)   *www.metropolitanhotelnyc.com*
Phone: (212) 752-7000, (866) METRO-NY (638-7669)   Fax: (212) 752-3817

The formerly staid but completely reliable Loews New York is still undergoing transformation into the moderately stylish Metropolitan Hotel, still under Loews management. Once the renovation is complete, the Metropolitan will surely qualify for a "Very Good" rating; room renovations will be ongoing until September 2002. The good news is that the current room décor is still in great shape, so even unremodeled rooms are a good value. Renovations will take place floor by floor, so construction should not be very intrusive.

The new design of the public spaces, already in place, takes its cues from the Morris Lapidus's curvilinear 1961 architecture. Pottery Barn-style furnishings, good lighting and a stylish contemporary palette (sand, ochre, olive and cardamom) replaces a dark and dated corporate look. Large rooms with two double beds and junior suites with queen sleeper sofas and bathroom access from both bedroom and living area are a big hit with families, as is the Loews chain's corporate-wide warm welcome for kids and pets. Complimentary food service (including continental breakfast, all-day snacks, evening wine and hors d'oeuvres) presented in a lovely, freshly remodeled lounge with wraparound terrace and excellent city views makes concierge-level rooms an excellent value (they're usually about $40 extra).

Rooms: 722; 20 floors; designated nonsmoking floors. **Hotel amenities:** Concierge, business center, exercise room, laundry and dry-cleaning service, salon, excellent concierge-level lounge with open-air desk, meeting and function rooms. **Food services:** Restaurant, bar, cyber cafe, room service. **Cancellation:** 24 hours prior to arrival. **Wheelchair access:** Fully accessible. **Subway:** 6 to 51st St.

Morgans   VERY GOOD $$$

237 Madison Ave. (between 37th and 38th Sts.)   *www.ianschragerhotels.com*
Phone: (212) 686-0300, (800) 334-3408   Fax: (212) 779-8352

Ian Schrager's first boutique hotel opened in 1984 as a low-profile "anti-hotel" without a sign or a staff member experienced in hotel management. There's still little to give away its quiet Murray Hill location except for the limos occasionally dropping off some high-profile type, but today the staff is experienced and competent. Andrée Putman's interiors eschew the over-the-top, hotel-as-theater elements of Schrager's other Philippe Starck-designed hotels in favor of a low-key, grown-up sensibility. Hotel restaurants don't get more popular than the perennially hot Asia de Cuba, but tucked away with a separate entrance, the scene doesn't intrude on the tranquil domestic tone of the hotel itself.

Rooms are not huge, but low-to-the-ground furnishings and beautiful maple-eye built-ins—including cushioned window seats for both lounging and out-of-sight luggage storage—make them feel spacious, and the taupe-and-black colors are serene and restful. The beds are luxuriously comfy, with down comforters, Scottish wool blankets, and suede headboards. Other pleasing extras include VCRs, CD players and spacious work desks. The small bathrooms are a Putman signature, with black-and-white checkered tile and stainless-steel sinks; most have double-wide stall showers, so request a tub when booking if you want one.

Rooms: 113; 19 floors; designated nonsmoking rooms. **Hotel amenities:** Concierge, business services, dry-cleaning and laundry service, meeting space. **Food services:** Asia de Cuba restaurant, Morgans Bar, 24-hour room service; rates include continental breakfast. **Cancellation:** One day prior to arrival. **Wheelchair access:** ADA compliant. **Subway:** S, 4, 5, 6, 7 to 42nd St.

Murray Hill Inn   BASIC $

143 E. 30th St. (between Lexington and Third Aves.)   *www.murrayhillinn.com*
Phone: (212) 683-6900   Fax: (212) 545-0103

Rooms are small, spare and as stylish as your great-aunt Erma's house, but so what? This well-managed walk-up hotel, sister to the Union Square Inn (Downtown) and the Amsterdam Inn (Uptown), makes an excellent choice for travelers on a strict budget. Most rooms are tiny, outfitted with a single bed, bunks or a double bed; a TV; a phone; a wall rack for hanging clothes; and a cheap set of drawers. Guests share like-new bathrooms that are substantially nicer than those in most shared-bath budget hotels. There are some rooms with private bathrooms that are quite nice, and most have sleeper sofas. Facilities and services are virtually nonexistent, as is standard for New York's cheapest hotels.

Rooms: 50 (39 with shared bathrooms); five floors; designated nonsmoking rooms. **Hotel amenities:** None. **Food services:** None. **Cancellation:** Two days prior to arrival. **Wheelchair access:** Not accessible. **Subway:** 6 to 33rd St.

Omni Berkshire Place

EXCELLENT $$$

21 E. 52nd St. (at Madison Ave.)
www.omnihotels.com
Phone: (212) 753-5800, (800) THE-OMNI (843-6664)   Fax: (212) 754-5018

Omni may not have as high a profile as some hotels in the city, but this tranquil and refined luxury hotel is first-rate on all fronts, from the comfortably traditional décor to the impeccable service. Built by internationally renowned architectural firm Warren & Wetmore in 1926, the hotel underwent a complete $70 million renovation in 1995 that went so far as to redesign floor plans. Thus, the guest rooms are freshly appointed from top to bottom, and the rose-hued marble-and-granite bathrooms are substantially larger than those in most other historic luxury hotels. Even standard rooms are large, and luxury appointments include silken gros-grain duvets, TVs with Internet access and Nintendo, fax machines, robes and umbrellas, plus a bedside superphone that controls the lights, TV, music and more; suites also have CD stereos. A serene air pervades all of the public spaces and guest floors, and double-glazed windows mean that even the second-floor meeting rooms on the Madison Avenue side are ultra-quiet.

Management is first-class and Omni corporate (which manages just 38 hotels) keeps a tight rein, so service is first-rate. Extensive business facilities mean that corporate travelers are well served, and the neighborhood is prime hunting ground for shoppers.

Rooms: 396; 21 floors; one designated smoking floor. **Hotel amenities:** Concierge, full-service business center, good fitness center with sun deck, laundry and dry-cleaning service (including quick service upon request), extensive meeting and function space (including executive boardroom). **Food services:** Restaurant, bar, lounge for afternoon tea and light fare, 24-hour room service. **Cancellation:** 24 hours prior to arrival. **Wheelchair access:** Fully accessible. **Subway:** 6 to 51st St.; E, F to Fifth Ave.

The Roger Smith

GOOD $$$

501 Lexington Ave. (at 47th St.)
www.rogersmith.com
Phone: (212) 755-1400, (800) 445-0277   Fax: (212) 758-4061

The Roger Smith manages to be frumpy, eccentric, hip and reliable, all at the same time. Owner/sculptor James Knowles has infused his hotel with a wide-ranging art collection and a truly independent spirit; frankly, it's a welcome relief from the standard East Side stuffiness. Knowles's own bronzes stand sentry at the entrance, for which he hand-casted the main door pulls. The art collection that fills the hotel stands in amusingly quirky contrast to the grandma-reminiscent Americana-style décor. Appointments aren't perfect, street noise can be an issue, and most bathrooms are older, but rooms are quite large and amenities include fridges, coffee makers, writing desks and free local calls, plus sleeper sofas and pantries with microwaves in suites; VIP rooms have newish granite bathrooms with whirlpool tubs. The regular client base consists of Swedish businessmen, European honeymooners, tennis pros and low-key touring rockers who

like the easygoing vibe and midline rates. There's nothing offbeat about the terrific location, however. Definitely not for everybody, but a good choice for travelers who delight in a few funky twists. Check for seriously discounted off-season rates.

Rooms: 130; 16 floors; designated nonsmoking rooms. **Hotel amenities:** Laundry and dry-cleaning service, iMac for email access, meeting rooms, video
library, art gallery. **Food services:** Restaurant, bar; rates include continental
breakfast. **Cancellation:** 4 P.M. day prior to arrival. **Wheelchair access:** ADA
compliant. **Subway:** S, 4, 5, 6, 7 to 42nd St.

The Roger Williams   VERY GOOD $$$
131 Madison Ave. (at 31st St.)   www.rogerwilliamshotel.com
Phone: (212) 448-7000, (888) 448-7788   Fax: (212) 448-7007

This pleasing hotel presides over lower Madison Avenue like a temple of sleek
modern design. The two-story lobby sets a tranquil tone that's carried into the
compact but smartly designed guest rooms. Architect Rafael Viñoly has used
space very well, with blond Scandinavian-inspired built-ins that include platform beds, entertainment centers, and user-friendly worktables; task lighting,
shoji-like window coverings and white-on-white Belgian linens enhance the
bright, clean-line look. Many guests prefer the hunter green-and-white-tiled
baths with the double shower stalls over the tub/shower combos. Additional
perks include VCRs, CD players and complimentary bottled water; in addition,
kings and penthouse-level rooms have plush robes and "sound therapy"
machines that set an ocean, rainforest or babbling-brook mood. Penthouse
rooms also have semi-private terraces with memorable views of Midtown.

Rates are slashed during slow periods, but some type of discount or value-
added theater or dining package is almost always available, so be sure to ask.

Rooms: 183; 16 floors; designated nonsmoking rooms. **Hotel amenities:**
Concierge, laundry and dry-cleaning service, exercise room, business center,
mezzanine-level guest lounge, CD and video libraries. **Food services:** Cookies
and self-serve cappuccino; room service; rates include continental breakfast.
Cancellation: Day prior to arrival. **Wheelchair access:** Fully accessible; ADA
compliant. **Subway:** 6 to 33rd St.

The St. Regis, New York   EXTRAORDINARY $$$$
2 E. 55th St. (at Fifth Ave.)   www.stregis.com
Phone: (212) 753-4500, (800) 325-3589, (800) 759-7550 Fax: (212) 787-3447

Commissioned by industrialist John Jacob Astor and opened in 1904 when 55th
Street was still considered the suburbs, the St. Regis still reigns supreme as the
pinnacle of Gilded Age wealth, grace and civility. This Beaux Arts landmark is
a monument to Industrial Age conspicuous consumption with 22K gold leaf,
Italian marble, Louis XVI antiques and Waterford crystal covering every square
inch (apparently, even the walls of the boiler room are marble). A complete
restoration in 1991 insured thoroughly modern conveniences, but the style
remains unabashedly, ostentatiously Old World.

After checking in, guests are escorted to their floor, where they are greeted by a butler to meet their every need during the course of the stay. Even the smallest guest room is at least 430 square feet, and brims with luxury features: high ceilings, silk wall coverings, king beds dressed in 300-thread-count Egyptian cotton sheets, bedside controls, VCRs, executive work desks with fax machines, and glamorous bathrooms with double sinks and ultra-plush bathrobes. Formal French dining doesn't get any better than Lespinasse, one of only a fistful of *New York Times* four-star winners; with its Maxfield Parrish mural and legendary bar nuts, the King Cole Bar is the most well-heeled of Midtown watering holes; and the St. Regis Rooftop is one of New York's most sought-after spaces for society weddings and other once-in-a-lifetime events.

Rooms: 315; 18 floors; designated nonsmoking rooms. **Hotel amenities:** Concierge, Maitre d'Etage butler service, business center, fitness center with saunas, barber shop/salon, laundry and dry-cleaning service, extensive meeting and function space. **Food services:** Lespinasse restaurant, King Cole Bar, Astor Court tea lounge, 24-hour room service. **Cancellation:** 3 P.M. day prior to arrival. **Wheelchair access:** Fully accessible. **Subway:** E, F to Fifth Ave.

Sheraton Russell Hotel   EXCELLENT $$$$
45 Park Ave. (at 37th St.)   *www.sheraton.com*
Phone: (212) 685-7676, (800) 325-3535   Fax: (212) 889-3193

This serene and intimate hotel is richly residential in feeling and exceptionally well run. Don't let the chain-hotel name fool you: Offering accommodations under the Sheraton brand since the 1940's, the Russell is intertwined with New York history (in fact, the property originally belonged to the family for which the surrounding Murray Hill neighborhood is named) and has its own independent spirit—not to mention a comforting sense of permanence in a city where hotels change owners and names like hats.

The civilized tone is set in the mahogany-paneled lobby, off of which sits a gorgeous living room with cozy sofas, shelves of books for borrowing and a gas fireplace that adds toast and crackle in cool weather. The spacious, high-ceilinged rooms are comfortably and traditionally decorated, with swagged drapes and dark furnishings, but the tones are light and the atmosphere inviting. Features include Bose Wave radios, coffee makers, decent closet space, terry robes, full-length mirrors, soundproofing that successfully banishes street noise and some of the best work desks in the city with swiveling ergonomic chairs, fax/printer/copiers, desk-level inputs and a leaf that pulls out for more workspace or in-room dining. Suites also have queen sleeper sofas, cordless phones, and second TVs. First-rate service includes two Clefs d'Or concierges; not surprisingly, the regular clientele is fiercely loyal.

Rooms: 146; 10 floors; designated nonsmoking floors. **Hotel amenities:** Clefs d'Or concierge, living room-style lounge, fitness room, business center, laundry and dry-cleaning service, boardroom. **Food services:** Breakfast room, cocktail lounge serving complimentary hors d'oeuvres (weekdays 5-7 P.M.) and a light dinner menu, room service; continental buffet breakfast included in some rates (otherwise $20.95 per person). **Cancellation:** 24 hours prior to arrival. **Wheelchair access:** Fully accessible. **Subway:** 6 to 33rd St.

Swissôtel New York-The Drake   EXTRAORDINARY $$$–$$$$
440 Park Ave. (at. 56th St.)   *www.swissotel.com*
Phone: (212) 421-0900, (888) 737-9477   Fax: (212) 371-4190

A brand-new lobby in mid-2001 put the finishing touch on a total facelift that has transformed the 1929-vintage Drake from Depression-era dowager into the most stylish roost on Park Avenue. That brand-new lobby sets the tone with a contemporary European look of warm woods, blown Italian glass vases, light-diffusing parchment sconces and a massive grip of orchids that heighten the modern elegance. The high-ceilinged guest rooms wear a smart Regency-goes-contemporary style, with bold-lined furnishings and art, and textiles in rich coffee tones, ethnic-inspired patterns and splashes of vibrant color. Amenities include triple-paned windows, an oversized work desk with fax machine, a club chair or other seating area, coffee maker, bathrobes and an umbrella for rainy days. More than 100 rooms are one- or two-bedroom suites with wet bar and fridge; the larger ones have VCRs and CD players, and some of the Park Avenue suites feature terraces and/or nonworking fireplaces.

Terrific accommodations aside, the Drake is worth a stay alone for its superior facilities. The brand-new Q56 restaurant is designed to attract a stylish foodie crowd with a smart contemporary interior.

Rooms: 495; 21 floors; designated nonsmoking floors. **Hotel amenities:** Concierge, full-service Park Avenue Spa & Fitness Center, salon, full-service business and conference center, laundry and dry-cleaning service, extensive meeting and function space. **Food services:** Q56 restaurant and bar, Fauchon Salon de The for afternoon tea, 24-hour room service. **Cancellation:** 4 P.M. day prior to arrival. **Wheelchair access:** Fully accessible. **Subway:** 4, 5, 6 to 59th St.

Thirty Thirty   GOOD $
30 E. 30th St. (between Park and Madison Aves.)   *www.thirtythirty-nyc.com*
Phone: (212) 689-1900, (800) 804-4480   Fax: (212) 689-0023

The former home of the Martha Washington women's hotel (model for the Tom Hanks and Peter Scolari roost in vintage sitcom *Bosom Buddies*) and legendary nightclub, Danceteria (where Madonna launched her career), has been transformed into a sleek modern hotel that is ideal for budget travelers who want a great value and a dash of panache. An industrial-chic lobby leads to smallish but quite comfortable rooms that boast a hip khaki look and brand-new everything; even the hallways have a smart modern look. Nice features include cushioned headboards, firm mattresses, good bedside lighting, roman shades on the windows, built-in wardrobes and nicely tiled baths that are pretty spacious considering the low price tag. Most rooms are either queens or twin-bedded rooms, and a few larger rooms have kitchenettes. A handful of brand-new suites were are in the works. A terrific addition to the affordable hotel scene.

Rooms: 240; 12 floors; one designated smoking floor. **Hotel amenities:** Concierge, dry-cleaning and laundry service. **Food services:** Restaurant scheduled for construction. **Cancellation:** 24 hours prior to arrival. **Wheelchair access:** Fully accessible. **Subway:** 6 to 33rd St.

W New York—The Court — VERY GOOD $$$

130 E. 39th St. (at Lexington Ave.) *www.whotels.com*
Phone: (212) 685-1100, (877) W-HOTELS (946-8357) Fax: (212) 889-0287

W New York—The Tuscany — VERY GOOD $$$

120 E. 39th St. (between Lexington and Park Aves.) *www.whotels.com*
Phone: (212) 686-1600, (877) W-HOTELS (946-8357) Fax: (212) 779-7822

Like the new W Union Square, these side-by-side sister hotels are superior to their uptown counterpart, the original W New York on Lexington Avenue. The beautifully designed rooms are both substantially larger and significantly improved in both form and function. The cosmopolitan-chic look features sumptuous textiles in a restful taupe palette interrupted by just a few sexy red accents; pillowtop mattresses dressed in gorgeous linens with a cozy thermal throw; a plush chaise for before-bed lounging; and big, bold, angular furnishings that include an oversized worktable. Rooms look the same at both properties, but the Tuscany gives you a bit more space in both bedroom and bath for your money. In-room luxuries include CD players, cordless phones and bathrobes.

It used to be that the Court was the trendy crowd's activity hub, with the highly-praised restaurant Icon from Drew Nieperont (Tribeca Grill, Nobu) and the hot Wetbar in residence. But the recent addition of the W Cafe in the Tuscany's living room-style lobby as well as Cherry, a bar that serves food, has upped the volume of the scene at the Tuscany, too. Come to these hotels if you want a party scene; for a more restful ambiance, try the W Union Square.

Rooms: 198 at the Court, 122 at the Tuscany; 16 floors; designated nonsmoking rooms. **Hotel amenities:** Concierge, fitness center, laundry and dry-cleaning service, meeting rooms. **Food services:** Icon New York restaurant, Wetbar at the Court; W Cafe, Cherry bar with food service at the Tuscany; room service. **Cancellation:** 4 P.M. day before to arrival. **Wheelchair access:** Fully accessible. **Subway:** S, 4, 5, 6, 7 to 42nd St.

Waldorf=Astoria, A Hilton Hotel — EXCELLENT $$$–$$$$

301 Park Ave. (between 49th and 50th sts.) *www.waldorfastoria.com*
Phone: (212) 355-3000, (800) WALDORF (925-3673), (800) 774-1500
Fax: (212) 872-4799

Waldorf Towers, A Conrad Hotel — EXCELLENT $$$$

100 E. 50th St. (at Park Ave.) *www.waldorf-towers.com, www.conradhotels.com*
Phone: (212) 355-3100, (888) WA-TOWER (928-6937), (800) 774-1500
Fax: (212) 872-7272

Sure, everybody loves to experience the legend that is the Plaza—but we prefer this grande dame over that tourist magnet any day of the week. This mammoth block-square hotel is now in the capable hands of the Hilton Hotels group, and it is as glamorous as ever. Rates are actually rather reasonable in the main hotel, considering the old New York pedigree, well-appointed rooms, and first-class dining and amenities. No two rooms are alike, but you can expect a high-ceilinged room or suite that's extra-large by city standards, outfitted in a hybrid deco-traditional style and very comfortable. Marble bathrooms are the norm, and 21st-century touches include fax/printer/copiers for laptop toters. Don't expect anything resembling personal attention in a hotel of this size, but the place runs remarkably smoothly considering that it's practically big enough to occupy its own ZIP code.

Now operated under the Conrad Hotels flag (Hilton's new ultra-luxury brand), the exclusive Waldorf Towers occupies floors 28 through 42. This is where globetrotting celebrities and world leaders stay (including every president from Herbert Hoover to Bill Clinton), ushered in through a separate entrance and attended by butlers around the clock. With themes ranging from French Provincial to opulent Asian, these elegant rooms and suites boast original art and antiques, crystal chandeliers and the like, plus full dining rooms, kitchens and maid's quarters in many. The ultimate in residential hotel living—which is why legends ranging from the Duke of Windsor and wife Wallis Simpson to Frank Sinatra called the Towers home for so many years.

Rooms: 1,246 in the Astoria, 181 in the Towers; 42 floors; designated non-smoking floors. **Hotel amenities:** Concierge, theater desk, Plus One fitness center with massage services, laundry and dry-cleaning service, newly renovated Starlight Ballrooms and extensive meeting space; butler service and Clefs d'Or concierge in Towers. **Food services:** Four restaurants: Peacock Alley for classic French, Bull & Bear for steaks and chops, Oscar's for American brasserie food, Inagiku for nouveau Japanese; Cocktail Terrace for afternoon tea and cocktails; Sir Harry's Bar and bar at the Bull & Bear; 24-hour room service. **Cancellation:** Day prior to arrival. **Wheelchair access:** Fully accessible. **Subway:** 6 to 51st St.

MIDTOWN WEST

The Algonquin
EXCELLENT $$$
59 W. 44th St. (between Fifth and Sixth Aves.)
www.algonquinhotel.com
Phone: (212) 840-6800, (800) 555-8000
Fax: (212) 944-1419

Birthplace of *The New Yorker* and *My Fair Lady*, home to Dorothy Parker's literary "Round Table" of the 1920's, this legendary hotel has been stunningly restored to its full glory, making it one of Midtown's most evocative and enjoyable hotels. The oak-paneled lobby is as splendid as ever, and the perfect place to linger over afternoon tea or a cocktail. Hallways delightfully wallpapered with a century's worth of *New Yorker* cartoons lead to guest rooms that are not large, but fresh-feeling and exceedingly comfortable; leisure travelers out on the town all day will like them better than business travelers who need space to spread out. Boasting short but deep soaking tubs, bathrooms have been beautifully updated without losing their period vibe. Terry robes are another nice touch, and rooms with window seats set into bay windows are especially charming. For the ultimate in historic appeal, book one of the delightfully and individually outfitted literary-themed suites. Off the glorious mahogany-paneled lobby is the Oak Room, still one of the city's premier cabaret rooms. Be sure to check out the rotating collection of Hirschfield drawings in the equally atmospheric Blue Bar with its clubby, pubby appeal.

Rooms: 165; 12 floors; designated nonsmoking floors. **Hotel amenities:** Concierge, exercise room, business center, laundry and dry-cleaning service, meeting and function rooms. **Food services:** American/Continental restaurant, lobby lounge for light meals and cocktails, Blue Bar pub, room service. **Cancellation:** Day prior to arrival, September-December three days prior to arrival. **Wheelchair access:** ADA compliant. **Subway:** B, D, F, S to 42nd St.

Americana Inn   BASIC $
69 W. 38th St. (at Sixth Ave.)   www.newyorkhotel.com
Phone: (212) 840-6700   Fax: (212) 840-1830

Shoestring accommodations convenient to the Theater District don't get better than the Americana, run by the same reliable hotel group behind Midtown's Travel Inn and the Upper West Side's Lucerne (both highly recommended in this chapter). Linoleum floors and fluorescent lighting lend the small property an institutional feel, but rooms and shared bathrooms are bright and spotless, beds are quite comfortable, service is professional and an elevator (uncommon in many budget-basic hotels) makes luggage-toting easy. Every room has bulk-purchased but like-new furniture, a TV, and a sink. The Garment District location is central, but ask for in the back to avoid street noise.

Rooms: 50 (all with shared bathroom); 5 floors; designated nonsmoking rooms. **Hotel amenities:** None. **Food services:** Common kitchen with fridge and microwave. **Cancellation:** 24 hours prior to arrival. **Wheelchair access:** Wheelchair accessible. **Subway:** B, D, F, S to 42nd St.

The Ameritania   BASIC $$
230 W. 54th St. (at Broadway)   www.nycityhotels.com
Phone: (212) 247-5000, (888) 66-HOTEL (664-6835)   Fax: (212) 247-3313

A member of the Amsterdam Hospitality Group (the folks behind the Upper East Side's Bentley and Gramercy Park's Marcel) sells itself as a high-style hotel, but its best feature is really its location just north of Times Square, adjacent to the *Late Show with David Letterman* theater. The décor does have some modern flair, rooms are quite sizable considering the Midtown location, and CD players and velvet pillows add a touch of luxe. On the downside, amenities pretty much end there, the marble is cheaply laid in the small bathrooms (some of which have showers only), and the smallest rooms have no closets. Stay here only for cheap rates and a central location.

Rooms: 208; 12 floors; designated nonsmoking floors. **Hotel amenities:** Laundry and dry-cleaning service. **Food services:** Restaurant, Twist Lounge. **Cancellation:** 3 P.M. day prior to arrival. **Wheelchair access:** Not accessible. **Subway:** B, D, E to Seventh Ave. St.; N, R, Q, W to 57th St.

Broadway Inn   VERY GOOD $$

264 W. 46th St. (at Eighth Ave.)   www.broadwayinn.com
Phone: (212) 997-9200, (800) 826-6300   Fax: (212) 768-2807

Here's a find for folks who want bed-and-breakfast comforts and charm without
sacrificing a Theater District location. Part full-service hotel, the Broadway Inn
is a haven of tranquility and good taste just off garish, neon-lit Times Square.
The big draw is the phenomenal service—some of the best the city has to offer
in this price range—and the charming ambiance. Rooms are impeccably maintained and tastefully decorated with an Art Deco flair, but are otherwise pretty
simple; still, beds are firm, linens are of good quality, and bathrooms are nice.
Boasting a sleeper sofa, microwave, minifridge and lots of closet space, the suites
are a good bet for longer stays or shares. Continental breakfast is served in the
charming sitting room/lobby, where brick walls, book-lined shelves, an overstuffed sofa and classical music set a restful, homey tone. Children are welcome
(a nice change from the B & B norm). Rates are a bit high in fall, but reasonable the rest of the year, especially considering the quality and location. An A+
for cleanliness, reliability and service. Keep in mind that this is a walk-up, however, so stay elsewhere if you require an elevator. And while windows are double
paned and rooms are relatively quiet, this is a noisy corner of the city; ask for a
back-facing room if you want to insure quiet.

Rooms: 41; four floors; designated nonsmoking rooms. **Hotel amenities:** Fax
and copy services. **Food services:** Rates include continental breakfast. **Cancellation:** 24 hours prior to arrival. **Wheelchair access:** Not accessible. **Subway:**
A, C, E to 42nd St.

Bryant Park Hotel   EXCELLENT $$$$

40 W. 40th St. (between Fifth and Sixth Aves.)   www.bryantparkhotel.com
Phone: (212) 642-2200, (877) 640-9300   Fax: (212) 869-4446

Situated directly across from lovely Bryant Park, one of the city's most civilized
squares, this brand-new boutique hotel is a stunner. It's housed in the majestic
1924 American Radiator Building (immortalized by Georgia O'Keefe during her
New York years), whose breathtaking gilt-edged facade has been impeccably
restored. As a result, entering the unapologetically modern-minimalist lobby
comes as something of a shock, but a pleasant one.

Extra-high ceilings, super-white walls and blond-wood floors give the large
and airy rooms and suites the look of finished luxury lofts. Furnishings are bold
and angular, softened by ultra-luxury textiles—cashmere-covered goose-down,
color-block Tibetan rugs, phenomenal 400-thread-count Egyptian linen—and
bold, autumn-inspired accent colors. Bathrooms are luxurious in an equally
clean-lined, high-quality way, with a beautiful blend of stainless steel and teak
furnishings, plus the most beautiful sinks to occupy any hotel bathroom. Unparalleled amenities include 24-hour butler service, high-speed Internet access,
VCRs, Bose CD players, digitally downloadable movies, cordless phones and fax
machines.

Sexy, subterranean Cellar Bar, and chef Rick Laakkonen's delightfully innovative restaurant, Ilo, multiply Bryant Park's appeal. Expect your fellow guests to be a well-heeled mix of fashion and media folks.

Rooms: 151; 22 floors; designated nonsmoking floors. **Hotel amenities:** 24-hour butler service and butler's pantry on each floor, state-of-the-art fitness center, laundry and dry-cleaning service, boardroom, 70-seat screening room. **Food services:** Ilo restaurant, Lobby Bar, Cellar Bar, 24-hour room service. **Cancellation:** 48 hours prior to arrival. **Wheelchair access:** Fully accessible. **Subway:** B, D, F, S to 42nd St.

Chambers   EXCELLENT $$$$

15 W. 56th St. (between Fifth and Sixth Aves.)
www.chambers-ahotel.com, www.designhotels.com
Phone: (212) 974-5656, (800) 337-4685

Celebrity architect David Rockwell envisioned this new boutique hotel as an uptown version of a downtown loft—and he largely succeeded. Unfinished concrete and a phenomenal (and somewhat controversial) modern art collection set a SoHo tone, while luxe fabrics and furniture, as well as faultless service, add Fifth Avenue polish. The cutting-edge hotel has already made such an impression among the power crowd that comedian Chris Rock recently quipped, "The Four Seasons is a nice place to stay if Chambers is booked."

The lobby of the hotel is streamlined and fairly straightforward; the magnificent art collection starts on the mezzanine-level lounge. Each guest-floor hallway wears a specially commissioned artwork or installation by a noted or up-and-coming contemporary artist, including Katerina Grosse, Sheila Pepe and filmmaker John Waters; some simply installed a piece, while others actually used the entire hallway as their tableau.

Each of the guest rooms is modeled after an artist's loft. Each has carefully chosen furniture and objects that emphasize the cutting edge, plus at least four original artworks. The result is a stimulating combination of rough-hewn and luxurious. Turkish rugs, mohair, faux furs and hand-painted velvet soften the look, but some may consider the exposed concrete slabs, hand-troweled walls and unfinished base moldings to be a bit much. Iridescent tiles, rainwater-style showerheads and deep soaking tubs add luxury to the monolithic concrete bathrooms. Technology includes high-speed connectivity, cordless phones and CD/DVD players.

Another notable feature is Geoffrey Zakarian's exciting restaurant Town, already a *New York Times* three-star winner.

Rooms: 77; 15 floors; two designated smoking floors. **Hotel amenities:** Concierge, fitness room, laundry and dry-cleaning service, CD and DVD libraries. **Food services:** Town restaurant with bar, 24-hour room service. **Cancellation:** 24 hours prior to arrival. **Wheelchair access:** Fully accessible. **Subway:** B, D, E to Seventh Ave. St.; N, R, Q, W to 57th St.

Comfort Inn Midtown   GOOD $–$$

129 W. 46th St. (between Sixth Ave. and Broadway)
www.comfortinn.com, www.applecorehotels.com
Phone: (212) 221-2600, (800) 567-7720   Fax: (212) 790-2760, (212) 764-7481

As of August 1, 2001, this Theater District hotel has officially declared itself a
nonsmoking hotel, eliminating all smoking rooms. It's yet another reason to
recommend this modest but comfortable hotel (run by the same team that manages the very good Red Roof Inn, see below), which underwent a $2 million
renovation a few years back. A marble-and-mahogany lobby leads to petite but
pleasant guest rooms that wear cheerful Shaker-style décor and boast coffee
makers and nice marble-and-tile bathrooms (some of which only have showers).
Facilities, which include a self-serve business center and an exercise room, are
better than most in this price category. Rates swing wildly by season, so price-
compare by calling the toll-free number and checking the Web site (rates are
often more attractive there). Complimentary continental breakfast adds value.

Rooms: 79; nine floors; no smoking allowed. **Hotel amenities:** Fitness room,
business room, laundry and dry-cleaning service, meeting room. **Food services:**
Rates include continental breakfast. **Cancellation:** 24 hours prior to arrival.
Wheelchair access: Not accessible. **Subway:** B, D, F, N, Q, R, S, W, 1, 2, 3, 7, 9
to 42nd St.

Crowne Plaza Manhattan   GOOD $$$

1605 Broadway (between 48th and 49th Sts.)   *www.crowneplaza.com*
Phone: (212) 977-4000, (800) 243-6969   Fax: (212) 333-7393

Towering over revitalized Times Square is the international flagship of Holiday
Inn's upscale brand. Style-setting designer Adam Tihany infused the public
spaces with new zest in 1999, but they're still more chain-generic than bou-
tique-stylish. Expect anonymous but comfortable accommodations outfitted
with standard comforts like coffee makers and work desks. Sightlines are one of
the towering glass monolith's best assets; no guest rooms are located below the
16th floor, so most are well endowed with views and quiet. There's no better
perch for watching the Thanksgiving Day parade float by or the New Year's Eve
ball drop. Another excellent attraction is the massive New York Sports Club fitness center, which features a 50-foot skylit lap pool. On the downside, the hotel
always bustles with convention and group business, and its huge size can make
the service slow and chaotic at times.

Rooms: 770; 46 floors; designated nonsmoking floors. **Hotel amenities:**
Concierge, tour desk, business center, secretarial services, 29,000-square-foot
New York Sports Club with swimming pool, laundry and dry cleaning, 29,000
square feet of meeting and function space. **Food services:** Two restaurant/bars,
24-hour room service. **Cancellation:** 24 hours prior to arrival. **Wheelchair
access:** Fully accessible. **Subway:** 1, 9 to 50th St.; N, R, W to 49th St.

Doubletree Guest Suites   VERY GOOD $$$

1568 Broadway (at 47th St. and Seventh Ave.)   *www.nyc.doubletreehotels.com*
Phone: (212) 719-1600, (800) 222-TREE (222-8733)   Fax: (212) 921-5212

This all-suite hotel's central location at the neon heart of Times Square and its
extensive amenities make it a good choice for families, business travelers, and
theater lovers alike. Don't expect much in the way of personality, of course, but
suites are spacious, attractive and contemporary. The suites are remarkably
quiet, given the location, and the ceilings are low but you don't feel cramped.
Each suite has a separate bedroom, a living room with a sleeper sofa (great for
the kids), a table that does double duty for dining and working, a wet bar with
microwave and coffee maker, and two TVs with Sony Playstation. For business
travelers, a dozen conference suites are ideal for getting the job done, since
they're set up for small meetings (for up to eight) and feature good workstations.
A floor of childproof suites cater to families, as do a range of special amenities,
including a well-outfitted playroom, a children's room-service menu, and a staff
well-practiced in catering to the needs of families. Theatergoers will appreciate
the connected concierge; those who want half-price tickets need only step out
the front door to reach the TKTS discount ticket booth. All in all, a terrific
choice, especially for those who want their space and a heart-of-it-all location.

Rooms: 460 (all suites); 43 floors; designated nonsmoking floors. **Hotel amenities:** Concierge, tour desk, business center, secretarial services, fitness center,
laundry and dry-cleaning service, coin-operated laundry, meeting and function
rooms. **Food services:** Restaurant, lounge, room service. **Cancellation:** 4 P.M.
day of arrival. **Wheelchair access:** Fully accessible. **Subway:** 1, 9 to 50th St.; N,
R, W to 49th St.

Essex House, A Westin Hotel   EXCELLENT $$$$

160 Central Park South (between Sixth and Seventh Aves.)   *www.westin.com*
Phone: (212) 247-0300, (800) 937-8461 (WESTIN-1)   Fax: (212) 315-1839

Now operated under the Westin flag, the ornate and legendary Essex House is as
glamorous as ever. The splendid Art Deco lobby gives way to two hotels in one:
the main hotel, whose rooms are situated on the lower floors and wear a blue-
and-silver palette; and the tony, exclusive St. Regis Club, offering an extra layer
of luxury that includes private check-in, concierge-style butler service and more
opulent gold-toned rooms that feature Bose CD stereos and cordless phones.
Frankly, unless you feel you must, there's no need to splurge on the pricier level.
The reason to stay (besides the old New York ambiance, of course, and easy
access to Central Park) is the Westin Heavenly Bed, touted as "ten layers of
heaven" and offering a genuinely celestial sleeping experience in every room.
Otherwise, rooms vary in size from small to spacious, but they're generally well
outfitted in period style and have decent-sized bathrooms.

Top-quality dining is another advantage to this glamorous address. Celebrated chef Alain Ducasse keeps his phenomenally pricey French restaurant
here; those unwilling to foot the bill can enjoy a fabulous brunch at elegant,
garden-like Café Botanica.

Rooms: 501, plus 104 St. Regis Club rooms; 40 floors; designated nonsmoking floors. **Hotel amenities:** Clef d'Or concierge, full-service, business center, fitness center and spa, laundry and dry-cleaning service (overnight service available), extensive meeting and function space, including Grand Salon ballroom; English-style butler service at St. Regis Club. **Food services:** Alain Ducasse's classic French restaurant; Café Botanica restaurant; clubby Journeys lounge, 24-hour room service. **Cancellation:** 3 P.M. day prior to arrival. **Wheelchair access:** ADA compliant. **Note:** Pets permitted with advance approval. **Subway:** N, R, Q, W to 57th St.

Flatotel International   VERY GOOD $$$$
135 W. 52nd St. (between Sixth and Seventh Aves.)   *www.flatotel.com*
Phone: (212) 887-9400, (800) 352-8683   Fax: (212) 887-9442

In 2002, it is most probable that the Flatotel's rating will be upgraded from "Very Good" to "Excellent," when renovations are complete.

Flatotel was born as a condo development, so rooms and suites are extra-large. The deluxe renovated rooms are massive by city standards and outfitted in a modern Scandinavian-reminiscent style in soothing grays and naturals. Each features beautifully designed walnut furnishings (including a cushioned bench with under-drawers for storage, an extremely clever piece of hotel furniture), a gorgeous platform bed, a comfortable lounging area with a Sony flat-screen TV and VCR, a CD player, high-speed connectivity, an oversized full-length mirror, and a wet bar with fridge, microwave and coffee maker. The spacious bathrooms wear beautiful Bulgarian limestone and opalescent glass tiles; most are windowed, which is very rare in New York. Unfinished rooms and suites won't get you nearly as much in the style department, but furnishings are decent and spaces are huge.

Rooms: 268; 46 floors; designated nonsmoking floors. **Hotel amenities:** Concierge, staffed business center, fitness room, laundry and dry-cleaning service. **Food services:** Moda restaurant (with alfresco dining) and bar. **Cancellation:** 48 hours prior to arrival. **Wheelchair access:** Fully accessible. **Subway:** B, D, E to Seventh Ave.

The Gorham   GOOD $$$
136 W. 55th St. (between Sixth and Seventh Aves.)   *www.gorhamhotel.com*
Phone: (212) 245-1800, (800) 735-0710   Fax: (212) 582-8332

The Gorham is far from the sexiest hotel in Midtown. But its top-notch location, impeccable maintenance and first-rate package deals—which can often save you big bucks and/or score you hard-to-get theater tickets for shows like *The Lion King*—make it very appealing. Rooms are currently undergoing a freshening—new textiles, new furniture and the like—that makes them a bit smarter-looking, but even the unrenovated rooms are spacious and comfortable. Every one has a king or two doubles, plus a fully outfitted kitchenette with microwave and coffee maker, high-speed Internet access and a roomy marble bath with plush terry robes. Junior suites also have a pullout sofa tucked away in a "nanny nook" with a second TV, making them a great choice for those travel-ing with kids.

The simple but pleasant lobby is most notable for its terrific concierge, who is so adept at acquiring theater tickets that she regularly scores more-precious-than-gold *Producers* tickets for guests. Management is exceedingly family-friendly and is happy to supply strollers and the like.

Rooms: 115; 17 floors; designated nonsmoking floors. **Hotel amenities:** Concierge, business services, PC in lobby with free Internet access, fitness room, laundry and dry-cleaning service, meeting room. **Food services:** Breakfast room with buffet spread ($8.50-$11.50 per person), restaurant, room service. **Cancellation:** 24 hours prior to arrival. **Wheelchair access:** Fully accessible. **Subway:** B, D, E to Seventh Ave.; N, R, Q, W to 57th St.

Hilton New York   GOOD $$$
1335 Sixth Ave. (between 53rd and 54th Sts.   *www.newyorktowers.hilton.com*
Phone: (212) 586-7000, (800) HILTONS (445-8667)   Fax: (212) 315-1374

The largest hotel in New York is a virtual city unto itself, with traffic congestion in the lobby, guests from all over the globe, a staff that speaks 30 languages, even a 24-hour foreign currency exchange office. Rooms are small, as are bath-rooms, but the Hilton name guarantees reliable mid-level comforts—and you'll find them here. A $90 million renovation has left things feeling fresh and sophisticated, and the Rockefeller Center location suits business and leisure travelers alike. The brand-new Times Square sister hotel (described below) is preferable, but this is by no means a bad choice—as long as you don't mind crowds and conventioneers. The hotel plays host to countless business and soci-ety functions in its whopping four floors of ballroom and meeting space.

The hotel's hallways are incredibly long, so expect a hike from your room to the nearest elevator. Standard rooms come with either a queen, a king or two double beds. You may find it worthwhile to spend a few dollars extra on an Executive-Floor room, which allows you to bypass the throngs with private check-in and awards you with slightly more handsome décor, a dedicated concierge, and complimentary breakfast, all-day snacks and evening hors d'oeu-vres in the Executive Lounge.

Rooms: 2,041; 46 floors; designated nonsmoking rooms. **Hotel amenities:** Concierge, theater desk, full-service business center, fitness center and full-ser-vice day spa, laundry and dry-cleaning service, meeting and function rooms. **Food Services:** Two restaurants, two bars, room service. **Cancellation:** 24 hours prior to arrival. **Wheelchair access:** Fully accessible. **Subway:** B, D, E to Seventh Ave.

Hilton Times Square   EXCELLENT $$$
234 W. 42nd St. (between Broadway and Eighth Ave.)
www.timessquare.hilton.com
Phone: (212) 840-8222, (800) HILTONS (445-8667)   Fax: (212) 840-5516

This brand-new Hilton is a prime symbol of the new Times Square. It sits mid-block on 42nd Street between Broadway and Eighth Avenue, on what used to be the heart of the peep-show-and-porn district—and what's now the most family-friendly strip in the city, complete with Broadway theaters, two movieplexes, mall-familiar shopping and dining and the new Madame Tussaud's wax museum. But the Hilton gracefully rises above it all, thanks to clever design that puts all guest rooms above the 22nd floor. As a result, even the cheapest room is peacefully quiet and with a great view.

As soon as you enter the 21st-story Sky Lobby, you'll realize that this isn't just another Hilton. Co-opted from the pervasive boutique-hotel movement is a living-room-style lobby with extra-high ceilings, cozy seating nooks, original contemporary art, a chic open bar, a stylish restaurant (above) from celebrity chef Larry Forgione and a pervasive air of sophistication. Guest accommodations surpass their chain-hotel status with larger-than-standard room sizes that host a king or two double beds, smart décor featuring blond wood furnishings and an attractive natural palette, attractive original art on the walls, an easy chair with ottoman, a generous work desk, expansive marble counters in the spacious bathrooms, and in-the-moment technology that includes high-speed connectivity, desk-level inputs and TVs with on-screen Web access and video games. Suites are especially comfortable and stylish, and make a worthy splurge.

Rooms: 444; 44 floors (hotel on floors 21-44); designated nonsmoking floors. **Hotel amenities:** Concierge, business center, secretarial services, fitness room, laundry and dry-cleaning service, meeting and function space. **Food services:** Larry Forgione's restaurant Above, Pinnacle lobby bar, 24-hour room service. **Cancellation:** 24 hours prior to arrival. **Wheelchair access:** Fully accessible. **Subway:** A, C, E, N, Q, R, S, W, 1, 2, 3, 7, 9 to 42nd St.

Hotel Casablanca   VERY GOOD $$$
147 W. 43rd St. (between Sixth Ave. and Broadway)   *www.casablancahotel.com*
Phone: (212) 869-1212, (888) 922-7225   Fax: (212) 391-7585

Thanks to a designer with a deft touch and an eye for style, this Moroccan-spiced hotel avoids the kitsch in favor of a sexy, exotic look that's downright enchanting. In fact, the Casablanca is such a welcoming and tranquil spot that it's hard to believe that it's situated in the eye of the Times Square storm. Rooms are not large, but high-quality details—including polished rattan furnishings, Murano glass light fixtures, gorgeous Andalusian tile in the bathrooms (which have either a tub or an oversized shower), North African art, VCRs and ceiling fans—speak to the care that has gone into this place. While spaces aren't overly generous, they're just fine for two—and the Casablanca suits a romantic mood.

The second floor is home to an extremely inviting lounge with a serve-yourself cappuccino machine, a roaring fireplace in winter and a small alfresco patio in warmer months. You also won't encounter many warmer hotel staffs. Book well ahead, because loyal fans keep this place busy.

Rooms: 48; six floors; designated nonsmoking floors. **Hotel amenities:** Rick's Cafe, business center, complimentary use of nearby New York Sports Club, laundry and dry-cleaning service, conference room, video library. **Food services:** Rates include continental breakfast, all-day cappuccino and weekday wine and cheese. **Cancellation:** 24 hours prior to arrival. **Wheelchair access:** ADA compliant. **Subway:** B, D, F, N, Q, R, S, W, 1, 2, 3, 7, 9 to 42nd St.

Hotel Edison   BASIC $$
228 W. 47th St. (between Broadway and Eighth Ave.)   *www.edisonhotelnyc.com*
Phone: (212) 840-5000, (800) 637-7070   Fax: (212) 596-6850

Located in the heart of the Theater District since it opened in 1931, the Edison has long been a beacon for budget-minded travelers looking for a central location. Unfortunately, popularity seems to have gone to its head—this mammoth hotel has raised its rates substantially in the last handful of years. Still, it continues to be a good choice for travelers who want to be in the heart of it all. Rooms don't even register on the personality meter—think run-of-the-mill motor lodge and you'll get the picture—but they're reasonably comfortable and very well kept. Most double rooms feature two twins or a full bed, but there are some queens; request one at booking and show up early in the day for your best shot at one. Quad rooms suit families well. Off the grand, block-long, Art Deco-muraled lobby is the perennially popular—and perennially cheap—Cafe Edison, a Polish deli and de facto canteen for up-and-coming theater types. Service is virtually nonexistent, so don't expect much.

Rooms: 850; 22 floors; designated nonsmoking rooms. **Hotel amenities:** Theater/transportation desk, salon, laundry and dry-cleaning service. **Food services:** Two restaurants, bar. **Cancellation:** 24 hours prior to arrival. **Wheelchair access:** Fully accessible. **Subway:** A, C, E, N, Q, R, S, W, 1, 2, 3, 7, 9 to 42nd St.

Hotel Metro   VERY GOOD $$
45 W. 35th St. (between Fifth and Sixth Aves.)   *www.hotelmetronyc.com*
Phone: (212) 947-2500, (800) 356-3870   Fax: (212) 279-1310

The Metro is Midtown's best mid-priced hotel. The entire hotel brims with bright and jaunty Art Deco style, and rooms are larger and better-outfitted than others at this price point. First-quality comforts include attractive neo-Deco furniture, fluffy pillows and towels, and small but beautifully appointed marble bathrooms, most with an oversized shower stall (junior suites have whirlpool tubs). Everything is spotless, and beautifully framed black-and-white photos add a touch of glamour. The Metro comes to the rescue of moderate-income families with the clever family room, a two-room suite that has a second bedroom in lieu of a sitting area. Rooms with two doubles do the trick for families on a budget.

The lobby lounge is especially comfortable and inviting, as is the library-style back lounge. Be sure to head up to the rooftop terrace on pleasant days, where you can enjoy one of the most breathtaking perspectives of the Empire State Building. The Metro Grill restaurant is surprisingly stylish and good. Despite the low rates, the hotel is very popular with the fashion and media crowds, who know a good value when they see one.

Rooms: 179; 13 floors; designated nonsmoking rooms. **Hotel amenities:** Fitness room, library lounge, rooftop terrace with Empire State Building views, laundry and dry-cleaning service, meeting room. **Food services:** Restaurant and bar, room service. **Cancellation:** 4 P.M. day prior to arrival. **Wheelchair access:** Accessible. **Subway:** B, D, F, N, Q, R, S, W to 34th St.

Hudson   VERY GOOD $$
356 W. 58th St. (between Eighth and Ninth Aves.)
www.hudsonhotel.com, www.ianschragerhotels.com
Phone: (212) 554-6000 (800) 444-4786   Fax: (212) 554-6001

Many love the Hudson, but it is definitely not for everybody. The newest creation from the trend-busting team of Ian Schrager (owner, and the man behind the entire boutique hotel movement) Philippe Starck (the designer) is less about service and all about scene.

With the Hudson, Schrager has transformed an unhip block of 58th Street into Scene Central, attracting star-studded events and premier parties to its wealth of riotously designed public spaces. Impressive areas include the ivy-draped lobby, the second-level Private Park deck (one of the best alfresco spaces in the city) and the white-hot Hudson Bar with its glowing floor and Francesco Clemente-frescoed ceiling. These spaces often overflow with revelers, so you must love a party to enjoy the Hudson.

Schrager made big news by pricing the smallest guest rooms at just $95. These tiny doubles are so small that they look like they could've been airlifted from a cruise ship, or Tokyo. In fact, even the pricier doubles are small, so if you're a heavy packer or need space to spread out, again, stay elsewhere. But style hounds will prize the beauty and efficiency of Starck's design. Rooms were modeled on the retro-romantic idea of the early 20th-century oceanliner, with rich detailing that includes African Makore paneling, hardwood floors, white-leather steamer trunk upholstery, white-on-white beds and tiny white-marble baths. The mini technology area includes a TV with DVD/CD player. Expect zero in the way of service and you won't be disappointed.

Rooms: 1000; 24 floors; designated nonsmoking rooms. **Hotel amenities:** 24-hour concierge service, fitness center, business center, laundry and dry-cleaning service, indoor and outdoor event space, video and CD libraries; full-service spa in the works. **Food services:** Hudson Cafeteria restaurant, two bars, 24-hour room service. **Cancellation:** 3 P.M. day prior to arrival. **Wheelchair access:** Not accessible. **Subway:** A, B, C, D, 1, 9 to 59th St.

The Iroquois New York   GOOD $$$
49 W. 44th St. (between Fifth and Sixth Aves.)   *www.iroquoisny.com*
Phone: (212) 840-3080, (800) 332-7220   Fax: (212) 398-1754, (212) 719-0006

For those of you who like the intimacy a boutique hotel can offer but prefer to pass on the highbrow modernism that seems to go hand-in-hand with the concept these days, there's the Iroquois. This understated hotel is a favorite among business and leisure travelers beccause of its domestic, clubby ambiance.

The Iroquois' rooms and suites are outfitted in a traditional French townhouse style, in a soft color scheme of celadon, taupe, rose and cream. Nice touches include jacquard textiles, Frette linens and robes, CD player, TV with

VCR and video games, and Italian marble bath. Our biggest complaint is size—
we think the rooms are too small for the money, even in the deluxe category.
About half of the rooms have an executive-size work desk with desk-level jacks,
so request one when booking if it matters.

The cozy James Dean Lounge, named for the hotels most famous resident
(1950-53) makes a great place to kick back with a cocktail. Dinner at intimate,
elegant Triomphe, chef Steven Zobel's *New York Times* two-star winner, is a must.

Rooms: 123; 12 floors; designated nonsmoking floors. **Hotel amenities:** 24-hour
concierge, fitness room with Finnish sauna, business center, two library-style
lounges (one with PC with free Internet access), laundry and dry-cleaning service, meeting and function rooms, video library. **Food services:** Triomphe
restaurant, James Dean Lounge, room service. **Cancellation:** 3 P.M. day prior to
arrival. **Wheelchair access:** ADA compliant. **Subway:** B, D, F, S to 42nd St.

Le Parker Meridien   EXCELLENT $$$$
118 W. 57th St. (between Sixth and Seventh Aves.)   *www.parkermeridien.com*
Phone: (212) 245-5000, (800) 543-4300   Fax: (212) 307-1776

After a massive, multiyear, multimillion-dollar makeover, this formerly stuffy
French luxury hotel emerged a couple of years back with an unmistakable new
energy and sleek new look embodied in their tagline: "Uptown. Not Uptight."
The new attitude is immediately apparent in the soaring neoclassical lobby, now
a stage set for classic modern furnishings, pinwheel art from Brit bad-boy artist
Damien Hirst and a hip monochromatic-clad staff.

The Parker may be the most successful hotel in New York at fusing chic
modern style with classic, full-service functionality. This hotel overflows with
top-notch facilities, including a massive 17,000-square-foot health club and spa,
a glass-enclosed penthouse-level swimming pool, two terrific restaurants—high-
design Norma's for American and all-day gourmet breakfast, charming Seppi's
for Alsatian French, both worthy of attention in their own right—and a Jet-
sons-inspired cocktail lounge. Two concierges on staff have Clef d'Or designa-
tion, so service is first rate, and the Parker is legendary for being the most pet-
friendly hotel in town.

Rooms are spacious and outfitted in the latest Scandinavian-modern style,
in blond woods and warm blue and ecru textiles. Features include extra-large
worktables with ergonomically correct (and beautiful) Aeron chairs and desk-
level inputs, plus a wealth of technology that includes a 32-inch TV with video
games and Web TV, DVD/CD player and VCR, cordless phones, and high-
speed connectivity. Bathrooms wear warm slate-gray tile and good mirrors.
Junior suites are beautifully configured for work and play, with a cozy seating
area with pullout sofa, extra work space and a swivel entertainment center that
caters to both living area and bedroom. The only quibble is that the platform
beds may be a mite too firm for some.

Rooms: 730; 41 floors; designated nonsmoking floors. **Hotel amenities:** Clefs
d'Or concierge, full-service business center, 15,000-square-foot Gravity fitness
center and spa, penthouse-level pool, laundry and dry-cleaning service, meeting

and function rooms, complimentary weekday transportation to Wall St. **Food services:** Two restaurants, Jack's cocktail lounge, 24-hour room service. **Cancellation:** 3 P.M. day before arrival. **Wheelchair access:** Fully accessible. **Subway:** N, R, Q, W to 57th St.

The Mansfield   GOOD $$$
12 W. 44th St. (between Fifth and Sixth Aves.)   *www.mansfieldhotel.com*
Phone: (212) 944-6050, (877) 847-4444, (800) 255-5167
Fax: (212) 894-5220, (212) 764-4477

The Mansfield exemplifies how distinctive a small hotel can be. This 1905 hotel beautifully fuses romance and modernism in rooms that are very inviting despite their small size. The public spaces are dressed mainly in period style, with their original terrazzo floors and mahogany balustrades beautifully maintained. A more heavily modern fusion look takes over in the guest rooms, where natural-fiber rugs cover ebony-stained floors, contemporary metal-mesh sleigh beds wear gorgeous Belgian linens, and bathrooms are stylishly updated with limestone and stainless steel, while framed prints and wood Venetian blinds keep a nostalgic cast.

A lovely fireplace-lit library doubles as a breakfast room and all-day lounge for serve-yourself cappuccino and tea. Stylish M Bar makes a romantic cocktail spot. Management is thoughtful and keeps the place in excellent shape. As with most hotels in the Boutique Hotel Group (including the Shoreham, also in Midtown West, and Murray Hill's Roger Williams), rack rates are high but discounts are often available, so always ask.

Rooms: 124; 12 floors; designated nonsmoking floors. **Hotel amenities:** Fax service, laundry and dry cleaning, small meeting room, video and CD libraries. **Food services:** M Bar with light menu, lounge with continental breakfast ($14 per person) and complimentary serve-yourself cappuccino, tea, and cookies. **Cancellation:** 24 hours prior to arrival. **Wheelchair access:** Not accessible. **Subway:** B, D, F, S to 42nd St.

Mayfair New York   GOOD $$
242 W. 49th St. (between Broadway and Eighth Ave.) *www.mayfairnewyork.com*
Phone: (212) 586-0300, (800) 556-2932   Fax: (212) 307-5226

The Mayfair is one of the nicest budget hotels in the Theater District, but there are two things you need to know about it: rooms are tiny, and rates are way too high in the autumn and holiday high season. Still, service is exceedingly friendly, and the location is prime. Rooms are not particularly stylish but appointments are pleasant, as are the smallish black-and-white-tiled bathrooms. An ongoing renovation should make things even more appealing.

Rooms: 77; seven floors; no smoking allowed. **Hotel amenities:** Concierge. **Food services:** None. **Cancellation:** 24 hours prior to arrival. **Wheelchair access:** Not accessible. **Subway:** N, R, W to 49th St.; C, E to 50th St.

Millennium Broadway   VERY GOOD $$$$

145 W. 44th St. (between Broadway and Sixth Ave.) *www.millennium-hotels.com*
Phone: (212) 768-4400, (800) 622-5569   Fax: (212) 768-0847

The Millennium is built for business, but it's ideal for any visitor who wants an
attractive, well-mannered hotel in the heart of the Theater District. A vast,
mahogany-and-marble lobby leads to the original Millennium rooms, in the
main building. They are large and outfitted in a smart Art Deco style, with rich
red mahogany and black lacquer furnishings, good-quality mattresses and textiles, comfy streamlined club chairs, and spacious marble baths.

But the real perks come in the Premier tower, built from scratch in 1999.
These designer rooms manage to combine sleek design, coziness and 21st-cen-
tury technology in one beautiful package. White sycamore predominates, giving
the rooms a feeling of openness and light, accented by green glass and natural-
fiber textiles. The Premier tower is not as tall as the Millennium, so the views
are not as good, and some of the closets are too small—but bathrooms are big
and beautiful, and the custom bedding is heaven-sent. Premier guests also have
access to their own lounge with dedicated concierge and food service, plus a
flat-screen TV.

Rack rates are high at the Millennium, but one of its greatest appeals are terrific package rates—especially on weekends—so be sure to inquire.

Rooms: 750; 52 floors (22 floors in Premier tower); designated nonsmoking
floors. **Hotel amenities:** Concierge, fitness center with sauna, business center,
secretarial services, laundry and dry-cleaning service, Millennium Conference
Center with meeting and function rooms, video library. **Food services:** Well-
regarded Restaurant Charlotte, bar, room service. **Cancellation:** 24 hours prior
to arrival. **Wheelchair access:** Fully accessible. **Subway:** B, D, F, N, Q, R, S, W,
1, 2, 3, 7, 9 to 42nd St.

The Muse   VERY GOOD $$$

130 W. 46th St. (between Fifth and Sixth Aves.)   *www.themusehotel.com*
Phone: (212) 485-2400, (877) THE-MUSE (843-6873)

With its emphasis on both comfort and functionality, the Muse is ideal for travelers who want the tone and service boutique hotels can offer but find no appeal
in their often steely and unwelcoming modern design (and attitude). A modern
exterior gives way to a warm, wood-paneled lobby where management has done
away with the traditional front desk in favor of full concierge service that makes
everyone feel like a VIP. After a welcoming hassle-free check-in, you'll be led to
your inviting room, which features modern furnishings in warm woods with
lines reminiscent of classic pieces. Bathrooms are handsome and well-outfitted.
Perks include plump feather beds and duvets, CD players, high-speed Internet
access, cordless phones, coffee makers and business cards personalized with your
in-house direct-dial line.

The Muse's most distinctive keynote is anticipatory service, embodied in the
concept of the midnight pantry, open to all to raid when the after-hours
munchies hit. For more refined dining, don't miss the gorgeous, David Rock-

well-designed District, a stellar New American brasserie. Pets are warmly welcomed (in the hotel, not the restaurant). All in all, a terrific addition to the Theater District.

Rooms: 200; 19 floors; three designated smoking floors. **Hotel amenities:** Concierge, business services, midnight pantry, in-room spa services, laundry and dry-cleaning service, meeting rooms. **Food services:** District restaurant, room service. **Cancellation:** 24 hours prior to arrival. **Wheelchair access:** Fully accessible. **Subway:** B, D, F, N, Q, R, S, W, 1, 2, 3, 7, 9 to 42nd St.

New York Marriott Marquis   VERY GOOD $$$
1535 Broadway (between 45th and 46th Sts.)   *www.marriott.com*
Phone: (212) 398-1900, (800) 843-4898   Fax: (212) 704-8930

This hulking monolith has a look somewhere between a convention hall and a parking garage. It takes a good 10 minutes to ascend a variety of escalators and always-packed elevators from street level to your room. But once you get there, your room will be surprisingly spacious (by New York standards, anyway) and decently outfitted. Rooms are especially well designed for business travelers, with good work space; an executive floor is available for those who need extra attention. (Request a room with high-speed connectivity if you need it.) Generic is the overarching theme—and service is less than attentive at a hotel of this size, of course—but the location couldn't be better for theatergoers. Skyline views are stellar from the revolving rooftop lounge.

Rooms: 1,946; 50 floors; designated nonsmoking floors. **Hotel amenities:** Concierge, tour desk, full-service business center, health club with sauna, laundry and dry-cleaning service, guest laundry, meeting and function rooms. **Food services:** Three restaurants (one American, one steakhouse, one sushi bar), rooftop revolving restaurant and lounge, two additional bars, coffee bar, 24-hour room service. **Cancellation:** 24 hours prior to arrival. **Wheelchair access:** Fully accessible. **Subway:** N, Q, R, S, W, 1, 2, 3, 7, 9 to 42nd St.

Paramount   GOOD $$$
235 W. 46th St. (between Broadway and Eighth Ave.)
www.ianschragerhotels.com
Phone: (212) 764-5500, (800) 225-7474   Fax: (212) 354-5237

Style over square footage is the mantra at Ian Schrager's first entry into the high design/low price hotel market, a decade before the now stylish Hudson (see above). The miniscule rooms are all whites and grays, with compact stainless-steel bath, a cartoonish cafe table and chairs, a swiveling armoire hiding a small TV and VCR, and a low-slung platform bed with a silk-screen version of Vermeer's "The Lacemaker" or another gilt-framed classic work doubling as art and headboard; CD players are available upon request. Be prepared, because it's a tight fit—you'll need an extra room if there's more than two of you, or a suite if you can't manage to pack light. These rooms are only for visitors who really value style over space; otherwise, you're much better off elsewhere. While rack rates have skyrocketed, weekend and off-season deals are often a very good value, sometimes even in the high $100's (don't pay $300 or more for one of these rooms!). The Art Deco-meets-industrial lobby isn't the buzzy scene that the Royalton's lobby is, but it's still a good perch for people-watching.

Rooms: 618; 19 floors; designated nonsmoking floors. **Hotel amenities:** Concierge, business center, fitness room, laundry and dry-cleaning service, meeting room, video library. **Food services:** Restaurant, Whiskey Bar, Dean & Deluca coffee bar, 24-hour room service. **Cancellation:** 24 hours prior to arrival. **Wheelchair access:** Not accessible. **Subway:** A, C, E, N, Q, R, S, W, 1, 2, 3, 7, 9 to 42nd St.

The Peninsula New York   EXTRAORDINARY $$$$
700 Fifth Ave. (at 55th St.)   *www.peninsula.com*
Phone: (212) 956-2888, (800) 262-9467   Fax: (212) 903-3949

In a stunning neoclassical building, renovated to the tune of $45 million in 1998, is one of New York's best ultra-luxury hotels. The lobby largely retained its longstanding Beaux Arts grandeur, but guest rooms were completely gutted and laid out afresh to allow for extra-large room configurations, monster-size marble bathrooms and state-of-the-art wiring. No other hotel so successfully fuses old New York style with 21st-century luxury.

The décor is exquisite, a dramatic but sublimely comfortable fusion of art nouveau lines, elegant Asian accents and contemporary art. Mahogany is polished to a high sheen and silks are lustrous. A wealth of beautifully designed storage space and a CEO-sized work desk with desk-level outlets and ethernet connectivity, a leather executive chair and fax/printer/copier adds a practical edge to the elegance. But the technology isn't limited to business travelers: In the bathroom, a tub-level panel lets you to control the room-wide sound system, answer the phone and even watch TV (in all but the cheapest rooms) as you soak. Bedside, touch-screen console controls the lights, climate, TV, "Do Not Disturb" sign—in short, does everything but tuck you in. There's even an outside climate display next to the door so you know how to dress or whether to tote an umbrella.

The spectacular tri-level spa is a big asset, offering a full range of services, a complete health club and a swimming pool with panoramic skyline views. Service is flawless, and small pets are welcome.

Rooms: 241; 23 floors; designated nonsmoking rooms. **Hotel amenities:** 24-hour concierge; penthouse-level fitness center and spa with heated pool, whirlpool, sauna and sun deck; business center; laundry and dry-cleaning service; meeting and function rooms. **Food services:** Two restaurants, library-style lounge for tea and cocktails, indoor/outdoor rooftop bar, 24-hour room service. **Cancellation:** 48 hours prior to arrival. **Wheelchair access:** Fully accessible.

The Plaza   VERY GOOD $$$$
768 Fifth Ave. (at Central Park South and 59th St.)   *www.fairmont.com*
Phone: (212) 759-3000, (800) 441-1414   Fax: (212) 546-5324

If ever a hotel has earned the right to be officially declared a landmark, it is the Plaza. Designed and built by Henry J. Hardenbergh, the stately French Renaissance hotel—which sits at one of the world's most glamorous intersections—has hosted countless famous names and events since 1907, from the visits of Mark Twain and "Diamond" Jim Brady to the recent nuptials of Michael Douglas and Catherine Zeta-Jones. No doubt you already know what the Plaza looks like, thanks to films such as *North by Northwest*, *Funny Girl*, *Crocodile Dundee*, and *Home Alone 2*.

Now under the guiding hand of the terrific Fairmont hotels group, the Plaza is looking pretty fabulous these days. While some suites still wear a garish red and gold, most accommodations have been redone in soft and sophisticated corals, yellows and blues, with luxury touches like pillowtop mattresses and big leather-top desks with fax machines. Even the smallest room is a reasonable size, and the building's U-shape means that every one gets a measure of fresh air and sunlight. After a stylish culinary and design reinvention, the dated Edwardian Room has been reinvented as OneCPS, but other dining-and-cocktail options, including the gilded Palm Court for tea and the justifiably legendary Oak Bar, remain pleasingly old world. A new spa—with a full-service menu, a state-of-the-art gym and his-and-hers tiled Jacuzzis—is a marvelous addition. Unfortunately, hordes of tourists in the public spaces often undermine the elegance.

Rooms: 805; 18 floors; designated nonsmoking rooms. **Hotel amenities:** Concierge, theater desk, full-service spa and fitness center with Jacuzzi, full-service business center, laundry and dry-cleaning service, extensive meeting and function space, including the Grand Ballroom. **Food services:** OneCPS restaurant, Oyster Bar pub, Palm Court for tea, Oak Bar for cocktails, 24-hour room service. **Cancellation:** 24 hours prior to arrival. **Wheelchair access:** Fully accessible. **Subway:** N, R, W to Fifth Ave.; 4, 5, 6 to 59th St.

Red Roof Inn   VERY GOOD $–$$
6 W. 32nd St. (between Fifth and Sixth Aves.)
www.redroof.com, www.applecorehotels.com
Phone: (212) 643-7100, (800) 567-7720, (800) RED-ROOF (733-7663)
Fax: (212) 790-2760, (212) 643-7101

The first Big Apple outpost of one of Middle America's favorite motel chains has been a red-hot success thanks to comfortable, freshly outfitted rooms, better-than-budget lobby and amenities, and professional service. Don't expect anything in the way of style or luxury comforts; Red Roof earns its "Very Good" rating with reliable middle-of-the-road comforts, including relatively spacious bedroom and bathroom configurations; all-new appointments; in-room features that include coffee makers and Web TV for on-screen Internet access; and pleasant public spaces that include a mezzanine-level lounge, a business center and an exercise room. Lined with affordable Korean restaurants and other mid-priced hotels, the bright, safe and bustling block is also well-located, just a stone's throw from Macy's, the Empire State Building and a clutch of subway lines. Rates swing wildly by season, so be sure to price-compare by calling both toll-free numbers (one is local management, one Red Roof central reservation) and checking the Web site.

Rooms: 172; 17 floors; designated nonsmoking floors. **Hotel amenities:**
Concierge, mezzanine-level lounge, exercise room, business center, laundry and
dry-cleaning service, meeting room. **Food services:** Rates include continental
breakfast. **Cancellation:** 24 hours prior to arrival. **Wheelchair access:** Accessible. **Subway:** B, D, F, N, Q, R, S, W to 34th St.

Royalton   EXCELLENT $$$$
44 W. 44th St. (between Fifth and Sixth Aves.)   www.ianschragerhotels.com
Phone: (212) 869-4400, (800) 635-9013   Fax: (212) 869-8965

This super-stylish hotel may be the best effort from bad-boy boutique-hotel pioneers Ian Schrager and Philippe Starck. Guest rooms are gorgeously designed
after ocean-liner cabins, with rich mahogany, low-slung furniture covered in
white cotton duck, dove gray carpet, porthole-reminiscent windows and slate
floors in the exceptionally appealing bathrooms, which feature either a five-foot
round tub or a oversize shower stall. Bedding is simple but luxurious, and the
overall effect is cool and uncluttered. A perennially popular and relentlessly
fashionable lounge scene occupies the lobby and adjoining restaurant.

   The hotel was set to begin a major renovation in autumn 2001, which
should only improve matters. It will remain open throughout the process, but
inquire about the current status when booking.

Rooms: 205; 12 floors; designated nonsmoking rooms. **Hotel amenities:** 24-
hour concierge, exercise room, laundry and dry-cleaning service, meeting room,
video library. **Food services:** Restaurant, bar, 24-hour room service. **Cancellation:** 3 P.M. day prior to arrival. **Wheelchair access:** Accessible.
Subway: B, D, F, S to 42nd St.

Sheraton Manhattan   GOOD $$$
790 Seventh Ave. (at 52nd St.)   www.sheraton.com
Phone: (212) 581-3300, (800) 325-3535   Fax: (212) 541-9219

Sheraton New York Hotel & Towers   GOOD $$$
811 Seventh Ave. (between 52nd and 53rd Sts.)   www.sheraton.com
Phone: (212) 581-1000, (800) 325-3535   Fax: (212) 262-4400

Situated on opposite corners, these sister Sheratons are sold as separate hotels.
Even so, it makes sense to think of them as a single mega-property, since they
fundamentally feature the same monster-chain-hotel ambiance; cater to the
same corporate convention and group business; and guests at both hotels can
use the Towers' business center and the Manhattan's indoor pool and sun deck.

   The Sheraton Manhattan is extra-large, the New York jumbo economy size.
Rooms, however, are tight squeezes. The look is chain standard—mostly light
golds and earth tones—but everything is good quality and comfortable. Corporate Club and top-tier Towers rooms are outfitted for business travelers with
oversized work desks with printer/fax/copiers, ergonomic chairs, plus free breakfast and afternoon hors d'oeuvres weekdays in the club-level lounge. The Rockefeller Center location is terrific for leisure and business guests alike.

Sheraton Manhattan: Rooms: 654; 22 floors; designated nonsmoking floors. **Hotel amenities:** Concierge, fitness room, heated swimming pool and sun deck, laundry and dry-cleaning service. **Food services:** Russo's Steak & Pasta, 24-hour room service. **Cancellation:** 6 P.M. day prior to arrival. **Wheelchair access:** Fully accessible. **Subway:** B, D, E to Seventh Ave.

Sheraton New York Hotel & Towers: Rooms: 1,750; 50 floors; designated nonsmoking floors. **Hotel amenities:** Concierge, theater desk, good health club with steam and sauna, full-service business center, laundry and dry-cleaning service, 55,000 square feet of state-of-the-art meeting and function space. **Food services:** Restaurant, bar and grill, lobby bar, 24-hour room service. **Cancellation:** 6 P.M. day prior to arrival. **Wheelchair access:** Fully accessible. **Subway:** B, D, E to Seventh Ave.

The Shoreham   GOOD $$$
33 W. 55th St. (between Fifth and Sixth Aves.)   *www.shorehamhotel.com*
Phone: (212) 247-6700, (800) 553-3347, (877) 847-4444   Fax: (212) 765-9741

Just off the prime Fifth Avenue shopping area, four blocks from Central Park and surrounded by excellent dining options, the Shoreham boasts an excellent location. Its smart modern style features clean lines and a warm natural palette; luxury finishes include very comfortable white-on-white beds dressed in Belgian linens, plus VCRs, CD players and complimentary bottled water. Over half of the rooms were brand-new in 1999, so try to score one of these. Unfortunately, some rooms and bathrooms are too small relative to the high rates. Always query for discounts, which regularly deflate the puffed-up rack rates.

Rooms: 176; 11 floors; designated nonsmoking floors. **Hotel amenities:** Fax service, free access to nearby health club, in-room spa services, laundry and dry-cleaning service, meeting room, video and CD libraries. **Food services:** Shoreham Restaurant & Bar (Franco-Asian); noted French restaurant La Caravelle; complimentary cappuccino, tea and cookies. **Cancellation:** Day prior to arrival. **Wheelchair access:** ADA compliant. **Subway:** N, R, W to Fifth Ave.

Sofitel New York   EXCELLENT $$$$
45 W. 44th St. (between Fifth and Sixth Aves.)   *www.sofitel.com*
Phone: (212) 354-8844, (800) SOFITEL (763-4835)   Fax: (212) 354-2480

This sophisticated French import is the best among a large crop of new luxury hotels. The good impressions begin with the brand-new curvilinear tower, which occupies a narrow but block-deep lot on Hotel Row (the block of W. 44th St. also home to the Algonquin and the Royalton, among other hotels). Once you enter the stunning lobby, with its soaring ceilings, fluted columns and streamlined Art Moderne club chairs, its clear that this is one handsome hotel.

The Sofitel is beautifully run, too. The front desk is at the far end of the ballroom-sized lobby, tucked away to the side, which gives the entrance a wonderfully serene quality. The bilingual staff (they are required to speak both English and French, at minimum) is thoughtful, efficient and attentive. Filled with well-chosen and beautifully displayed Parisian- or New York-themed gifts—Guy

Buffet china, Lenôtre chocolates, coffee-table books on the Big Apple—even the boutique is something special.

Sofitel's thoroughly French perspective also adds a fashionable flair to the guest rooms, where dramatic design seamlessly blends Art Deco and contemporary elements. Amenities include first-rate soundproofing, desk-level inputs with ethernet connectivity, CD players, Web TV and plush robes. The spacious bathrooms are done in honey-hued marble with separate tub and shower, plus a beautifully lit beveled mirror. The only miscalculation is the decision to make all standard rooms queen-sized; king beds are only available in suites.

The stylish, Roaring Twenties-themed Gaby brasserie is overseen by executive chef Eric Fraudeau, who earned his toque in the kitchens of Joël Robuchon and Alain Ducasse. Plan to dine in at least once during your stay.

Rooms: 398; 30 floors; designated nonsmoking floors. **Hotel amenities:** Concierge, business center, laundry and dry-cleaning service, ballroom, state-of-the-art meeting and function space. **Food services:** Gaby brasserie and piano bar, 24-hour room service. **Cancellation:** 24 hours prior to arrival. **Wheelchair access:** Fully accessible. **Subway:** B, D, F, S to 42nd St.

The Time   GOOD $$$
224 W. 49th St. (between Broadway and Eighth Ave.)   *www.thetimeny.com*
Phone: (212) 320-2900, (877) TIME-NYC (846-3692)   Fax: (212) 320-2926

This fashion-forward hotel, the first to be designed by Adam Tihany (most famous for colorful, big-ticket restaurant design), is a study in Mondrian-like modernism. All clean lines and straight angles, the guest rooms are decorated in white, black and gray with vivid accents of primary color in either fire-engine red, canary yellow or electric blue. Appointments are attractive and remarkably efficient—big worktables, soft backlighting, coffee maker caddies, custom valets and cubbies in the bathrooms—but some rooms remain uncomfortably petite nonetheless. VCRs, Bose radios, fax/printer/copiers and terry robes are nice additions (CD players are available upon request), but closets are small and sometimes enclosed only by a drape rather than a door. Rates are high but discounts are common, so be sure to ask.

Rooms: 200; 16 floors; designated nonsmoking rooms. **Hotel amenities:** Concierge, exercise room, laundry and dry-cleaning service, meeting room, video library. **Food services:** Coco Pazzo Teatro restaurant, lounge, room service. **Cancellation:** 24 hours prior to arrival. **Wheelchair access:** Not accessible. **Subway:** N, R, W to 49th St.; C, E to 50th St.

Travel Inn   GOOD $$
515 W. 42nd St. (between 10th and 11th Aves.)   *www.newyorkhotel.com*
Phone: (212) 695-7171, (800) 869-4630, (888) HOTEL58 (468-3558)
Fax: (212) 967-5025

Now that far-west Midtown is rife with chic restaurants and resident yuppies, this agreeable motor inn isn't so far removed anymore. The recently renovated rooms are universally large, clean, bright and comfortable, if nondescript. Even the smallest room is spacious and has a good-sized bathroom; those with two double beds make well-priced shares for families. In-room perks include TVs with video games and on-screen Internet access.

But the best reason to stay here is the free parking, since virtually every other hotel in town charges anywhere from $20 to $45 a day. The rooftop outdoor pool and well-furnished sun deck—another otherwise-nonexistent perk in the Big Apple—is a refreshing summertime treat that makes the Travel Inn a worthwhile choice even for those who don't have their own wheels. The Javits convention center is just three blocks away. What's more, Internet and other specials often drop prices.

Rooms: 160; seven floors; designated nonsmoking rooms. **Hotel amenities:** Exercise room, outdoor rooftop swimming pool and sun deck, laundry and dry-cleaning service, meeting room, Gray Line tour desk. **Food services:** Coffee shop, 24-hour room service. **Cancellation:** 48 hours prior to arrival. **Wheelchair access:** Not accessible. **Subway:** A, C, E to 42nd St.

The Warwick   GOOD $$$
65 W. 54th St. (at Sixth Ave.)   *www.warwickhotels.com*
Phone: (212) 247-2700, (800) 223-4099   Fax: (212) 713-1751

The formerly dowdy Warwick was reinvented in the late 1990's, given renovated rooms, marble and palms in the lobby, and the overarching air of a smallish European hotel despite its rather large size. This hotel always had good bones, not to mention a few celebrity associations: It was built in 1927 by William Randolph Hearst for his mistress Marion Davies, the Beatles often stayed here when they were in the Big Apple, and Cary Grant lived in one of the apartment-style suites (no. 2706, to be exact) for 12 years.

You're less likely to find a star in residence these days, but you will find liberally sized rooms decorated in a light and pleasant traditional style. Features include mahogany furnishings, large marble bathrooms, good closet space and double-glazed windows to restrict street noise. Suites, some of which have wraparound terraces, are downright massive, making them a very good deal for the money. Randolph's Bar is ideal for a sophisticated tipple, and lovely, elegantly muraled Ciao Europa serves surprisingly good Northern Italian cuisine.

Rooms: 495; 33 floors; designated nonsmoking floors. **Hotel amenities:** Concierge, business center, exercise room, laundry and dry-cleaning service, meeting and function rooms. **Food services:** Ciao Europa restaurant, Randolph's Bar, room service. **Cancellation:** 24 hours before arrival. **Wheelchair access:** Fully accessible. **Subway:** B, D, E to Seventh Ave.

UPTOWN

Amsterdam Inn   BASIC **$**
340 Amsterdam Ave. (at 76th St.)   *www.amsterdaminn.com*
Phone: (212) 579-7500   Fax: (212) 579-6127

This sister property to the Murray Hill Inn (earlier in this chapter) is a similarly wallet-friendly choice for budget travelers. The narrow rooms are outfitted with little more than a bed, a wall rack for hanging clothes and a cheap set of drawers; only a small TV and a telephone make them more luxurious than monk's quarters. About half the rooms have private baths, and the rest share; all of the like-new bathrooms are the nicest available in this under-$100 price range. Visitors opting for a double with private bathroom will find slightly nicer rooms at the Murray Hill Inn (where they take credit cards), but the Amsterdam is a fine option, too, and the upscale residential neighborhood is terrific. Note, however, that some "doubles" have single beds with a pull-out trundle rather than a real bed for two, so find out exactly what you're reserving. Facilities and service are virtually nonexistent, as in most of New York's cheapest hotels.

Rooms: 25 (12 with shared bathrooms); four floors; smoking allowed. **Hotel amenities:** None. **Food services:** None. **Cancellation:** No charge. **Wheelchair access:** Not accessible. **Note:** Cash and traveler's checks only. **Subway:** 1, 2, 3, 9 to 72nd St.

The Barbizon, A Melrose Hotel   VERY GOOD **$$$**
140 E. 63rd St. (at Lexington Ave.)   *www.thebarbizon.com*
Phone: (212) 838-5700, (800) 223-1020   Fax: (212) 223-3287

A literary landmark thanks to poet Sylvia Plath's memoir of tormented youth, *The Bell Jar*, the Barbizon is now under the guiding hand of the Dallas-based Melrose Hotel group, who expect to add the finishing touches by early 2002 that will transform it into the flagship of their burgeoning domestic mini-chain. At the southern end of the residential Upper East Side, just three blocks from Bloomingdale's, location is a prime asset. The hotel was refurbished to the tune of $40 million just four years ago, so it's in very good shape. Rooms are very comfortably outfitted with firm beds, soft pastels (mostly blues and greens), and distinctive wrought-iron furnishings, nice baths and CD players. On the downside, many are small. Still, rooms are light and bright, and housekeeping is immaculate. Deluxe rooms buy you more space and a foldout love seat.

The top-of-the-line Tower Suites are worth a special note. Located on the 18th and 19th floors, the hotel's Moorish architecture is in evidence, particularly the intricate detailing and Romanesque arches of the generous, nicely furnished terraces attached to about half of these rooms and suites. Views are stunning, décor is slightly more luxurious, and Jacuzzi tubs and Dolby surround-sound stereos are among the extras. All in all, the Barbizon is a good value, one that should only get better in the coming months.

Rooms: 306; 22 floors; designated nonsmoking floors. **Hotel amenities:** Concierge, first-rate Equinox gym on site ($18 charge), laundry and dry-cleaning service, CD library. **Food services:** Breakfast room, room service; restaurant, lobby bar in planning stages. **Cancellation:** 24 hours prior to arrival. **Wheelchair access:** Fully accessible. **Subway:** N, R, W to Lexington Ave.; 4, 5, 6 to 59th St.

The Bentley   VERY GOOD $$
500 E. 62nd St. (at York Ave.)   *www.nychotels.com*
Phone: (212) 644-6000, (888) 66-HOTEL (664-6835)   Fax: (212) 207-4800

There's no denying the Bentley's out-of-the-way location on the far East Side, but it has three main selling points: great East River views from three sides; cheap on-site valet parking for visitors with cars ($20 a night); and low rates, considering the space and stylishness of the accommodations. From the outside, the Bentley still looks like an office building; in fact, it was once the NAACP headquarters. Inside, the corporate look gives way to fluid modern style that stars warm khaki tones and natural elements (including fresh flowers in wall-mounted bud vases in the halls and river-rock wall accents in the rooms); the look is attractive and contemporary rather than coldly modern. Good room layouts accommodate two doubles or a king. The platform beds fall short of ideally comfortable in all Amsterdam Hospitality Group hotels (including Gramercy Park's Marcel and the Theater District's Ameritania), but they're not bad. Nice amenities include decent work desks, marble baths, good bedside lighting, roman shades, comfortable chenille chairs for reading and pullout sofas in the suites. Corner rooms are most spacious, and views of the 59th Street Bridge are spectacular.

Rooms: 208; 21 floors; designated nonsmoking floor. **Hotel amenities:** Laundry and dry-cleaning service. **Food services:** Penthouse B restaurant and bar; room service; sitting room with self-serve 24-hour cappuccino, tea and cookies. **Cancellation:** 24 hours prior to arrival. **Wheelchair access:** Accessible. **Subway:** N, R, W to Lexington Ave.; 4, 5, 6 to 59th St.

The Carlyle   EXTRAORDINARY $$$$
35 E. 76th St. (at Madison Ave.)
Phone: (212) 744-1600, (800) 227-5737   Fax: (212) 717-4682

The discreet and elegant Carlyle epitomizes Upper East Side glamour. About half of the hotel is occupied by permanent residents, while the other half is made up of rooms and multibedroom suites available to short-term guests with deep pockets. The softly lit lobby is distinctly un-public, which heightens the exclusive residential feel. Generations of famous faces and power brokers have been attracted by this low-profile ambiance, as well as the impeccable attention to detail and the unmatched service.

Individually decorated rooms and suites are luxuriously appointed, but not in the gilded, big-money way of luxury palaces like the St. Regis. Think understated, traditional, rare, and you'll get the picture: Chintz, satin, antiques, oils, Oriental rugs over wood floors. There is a full roster of amenities you have every right to expect at this price level, including jetted tubs, plus many less common luxuries, such as terraces and/or full kitchens. Many regulars prefer the high-floor tower rooms; they're not large, but the light and the views—particularly those overlooking Central Park—are enthralling.

Cafe Carlyle is New York's premier cabaret room, and still the domain of the legendary Bobby Short and other big-ticket song stylists; Woody Allen is usually in the house on Monday, swinging on clarinet with the Eddy Davis New Orleans Jazz Band. Jazz vocalist Barbara Carroll often entertains a well-heeled crowd at Bemelmans Bar (named for the author/illustrator of the Madeline children's books, who also painted the murals here).

Rooms: 180; 33 floors; designated nonsmoking rooms. **Hotel amenities:** Concierge; attractive fitness center with whirlpool, sauna and spa services; business services; laundry and dry-cleaning service; meeting and function rooms. **Food services:** Two restaurants, Bemelmans Bar, Café Carlyle supper club, Gallery for afternoon tea, 24-hour room service. **Cancellation:** 24 hours prior to arrival. **Wheelchair access:** Fully accessible. **Subway:** 6 to 77th St.

Comfort Inn Central Park West   GOOD $$
31 W. 71st St. (between Columbus Ave. and Central Park West)
www.comfortinn.com, www.bestnyhotels.com
Phone: (212) 721-4770, (877)-727-5236 (PARKCEN)   Fax: (212) 579-8544

This nicely renovated chain hotel is so unassuming that most locals don't even realize it's here. All of the rooms are small, so if limited space is a deal-breaker, look elsewhere. But if you want an A-one location in a prime residential neighborhood just steps from Central Park, this Comfort Inn makes a terrific choice. An attractive modern lobby leads to the generic but comfortable guest rooms; smart layout, good-quality bedding and furniture, and like-new bathrooms make up for the lack of space. Executive rooms boast much-better-than-chain-standard contemporary furnishings in rich mahogany. Facilities are good, but don't expect much in the way of service.

Rates swing wildly from one end of the spectrum to the other, depending on the season, but can be an excellent value when discounts kick in, which happens quite often.

Rooms: 96; 14 floors; four designated nonsmoking floors. **Hotel amenities:** Business center, exercise room, laundry and dry-cleaning service. **Food services:** Rates include continental breakfast. **Cancellation:** 4 P.M. two days prior to arrival. **Wheelchair access:** ADA compliant. **Subway:** 1, 2, 3, 9 to 72nd St.

Country Inn the City   VERY GOOD $$
270 W. 77th St. (between Broadway and West End Ave.)
www.countryinnthecity.com   Phone: (212) 580-4183   Fax: (212) 874-3981

This beautifully outfitted guesthouse is a true delight, offering both amenity-laden accommodations and a true taste of New York living to discerning visitors who want more personality than your average hotel offers. Tucked away on a leafy block just off Broadway, this 1891 limestone town house features four spacious and impeccable studio suites, each outfitted by innkeepers with an eye for design and a nose for practicality. Apartments are bright and elegant, and homey features include wood floors covered with Oriental rugs, a beautifully dressed queen bed (two are four-posters, one a romantic canopy bed) with a high-quality mattress, a cozy sitting area facing a nonworking fireplace, and bright colors, original art and well-chosen collectibles that heighten the domestic air. Modern appointments include a fully equipped galley kitchen, a cafe-style dining table for two and a private phone with answering machine and free local calls.

There are a few downsides that you should be aware of before you book. There is no resident innkeeper, so the inn is best for independent types who don't need anything in the way of personal service. And while each kitchen comes stocked with coffee and basic breakfast fixings, you're likely to have to stock up on your own if you're staying beyond the three-night minimum. Lastly, there is no daily maid service, so be prepared to pick up after yourself and make your own bed.

Rooms: Four; five floors; smoking not allowed. **Hotel amenities:** None. **Food services:** Stocked breakfast pantry. **Cancellation:** 30 days prior to arrival; $30 cancellation fee. **Wheelchair access:** Not accessible. **Note:** Limit two per apartment; no children under 12; credit cards not accepted.
Subway: 1, 2, 3, 9 to 72nd St.

Excelsior Hotel   VERY GOOD $$
45 W. 81st St. (between Columbus Ave. and Central Park West)
www.excelsiorhotelny.com
Phone: (212) 362-9200, (800) 368-4575   Fax: (212) 721-9224

This recently renovated hotel has a lot going for it, most notably an amazing location: It sits across the street from the American Museum of Natural History's new Rose Center for Earth & Space, on a block of regal apartment buildings, with a prime entrance to Central Park in one direction, boutique- and restaurant-lined Columbus Avenue in the other. This is the very best residential territory the Upper West Side has to offer.

But the appeal doesn't end with the address. A richly wood-paneled lobby that looks like it belongs on a far more expensive hotel leads to freshly outfitted, traditionally styled guest rooms and suites that are good-sized, comfortable and well outfitted with good-quality bedding and textiles, white-tiled bathrooms with floral accent tiles, thick terry robes, a fax/copier/printer on the work desk, and complimentary bottled water. The plush library-style lounge—with gorgeous leather seating nooks, fireplace, books and games, and a large flat-screen TV with VCR and DVD player—is additional value-added attraction.

Rooms: 196; 16 floors; designated nonsmoking rooms. **Hotel amenities:** Concierge, exercise room, entertainment room/library, laundry and dry-cleaning service, conference room. **Food services:** Breakfast buffet served in library ($18 for full breakfast, $14 for continental). **Cancellation:** 4 P.M. day prior to arrival. **Wheelchair access:** Not accessible. **Subway:** 1, 9 to 79th St.

Holmes Bed & Breakfast

VERY GOOD $

W. 91st St. (off Amsterdam Ave.)

www.holmesnyc.com

Phone: (917) 838-480

Fax: (518) 854-7148

A nicely maintained traditional brownstone on a pretty tree-lined residential block houses this little-known but excellent-quality budget B & B. Four guest rooms are available on two floors, two with private bath and two that share a bath, all value priced. Owner Marguerite Holmes is an accomplished artist; not only do her terrific multi-genre paintings (which run the gamut from pastoral scenes to impressive abstracts) fill the hallways and guest rooms, but her creative eye has turned what could be very basic accommodations into something really special. Each clean and well-maintained room has a TV with cable (some have VCRs); a direct-dial phone; a fridge, coffee maker, microwave, and toaster oven (the shared-bath rooms also share a pantry kitchenette); a well-chosen mix of vintage furnishings and original art; and good-quality bedding. The Cranberry Room is the best of the bunch, with its own very nice marble bath with shower, generous closet space, and terrace.

There's no formal breakfast serving, but a cupboard is stocked with morning foodstuffs. As with most B & B's, the Holmes house is best for independent-minded travelers, but the young and friendly resident innkeeper (also an artist) is on hand and glad to help if you need advice or assistance. All in all, an excellent choice for budget travelers who prefer offbeat, home-style accommodations.

Rooms: Four; three floors; smoking not allowed. **Hotel amenities:** None. **Food services:** Cupboard with breakfast items. **Cancellation:** 14 days prior to arrival; $50 processing fee. **Wheelchair access:** None. **Subway:** 1, 2, 3, 9 to 96th St.

Hotel Beacon

VERY GOOD $$

2130 Broadway (at 75th St.)

www.beaconhotel.com

Phone: (212) 787-1100, (800) 572-4969

Fax: (212) 724-0839

The focus at the Beacon isn't on amenities or service but on room size and value for dollar—and on those counts, it scores extremely well. Built in 1929 for permanent residents, the Beacon has grown into an Upper West Side staple since becoming a full-fledged hotel a dozen or so years ago. Almost half of the rooms are apartment-sized suites, but even the standard configurations can easily accommodate four in two double beds. Every room and suite features a modern kitchenette with cooktop, coffee maker, minifridge, microwave and a full complement of cookware and dishes; and a new marble bathroom; plus a pullout sleeper sofa in suites. The generic décor isn't likely to win any ardent fans, but there's no arguing with the comfort level. Front, Broadway-facing rooms can't avoid street noise, so ask for a back unit or a high floor.

Rooms: 236; 25 floors; designated nonsmoking rooms. **Hotel amenities:** Concierge, laundry and dry-cleaning service, coin-operated laundry, fax service, meeting room. **Food services:** 24-hour coffee shop. **Cancellation:** 24 hours prior to arrival. **Wheelchair access:** Fully accessible. **Subway:** 1, 2, 3, 9 to 72nd St.

Hotel Olcott   GOOD $

27 W. 72nd St. (between Central Park West and Columbus Ave.)
www.hotelolcott.com
Phone: (212) 877-4200   Fax: (212) 580-0511

This old-world apartment house is spectacularly located in first-class Upper
West Side residential territory, just steps from the legendary Dakota (where
John Lennon once lived, and Yoko still does) as well as the absolute best part of
Central Park. The cheaply appointed apartments—more than half of which are
one- and two-bedroom suites—are as stylish as a discount furniture store in the
Nixon era, but they're clean, monster-sized and bargain-priced. Each has a
kitchenette, a large bathroom, roomy closets, a dining table and double-paned
windows for noise reduction; otherwise, expect low tech and you won't be disappointed. Most kitchenettes and bathrooms have been recently renovated
with all-new, bright-white tile and fixtures. Sofas aren't sleepers, but most bed-
rooms are so enormous that they hold two queens, and the friendly management will be happy to lend you a cot. Discounts on weekly stays make the
already-attractive rates an even better bargain. The hotel's affordable barbecue
restaurant serves decent ribs and bathtub margaritas, and a world of dining
options exist in the surrounding neighborhood.

Rooms: 150; 16 floors; smoking allowed. **Hotel amenities:** None. **Food services:** Dallas BBQ restaurant and bar. **Cancellation:** Seven days prior to arrival.
Wheelchair access: Fully accessible. **Subway:** 1, 2, 3, 9 to 72nd St.

Hotel Wales   GOOD $$$

1295 Madison Ave. (between 92nd and 93rd Sts.)   *www.waleshotel.com*
Phone: (212) 876-6000, (877) 847-4444   Fax: (212) 894-5220, (212) 860-7000

Built in 1901, this freshly renovated but still-quirky Victorian-style hotel offers
relatively affordable accommodations in a shopping and museum-convenient
corner of the extremely civilized Upper East Side called Carnegie Hill. Most
guest rooms are not large; luckily, almost half are suites and ample amenities—
including pillowy beds beautifully dressed in Belgian linens, Frette robes, VCRs
and CD players—up the appeal substantially. The new look mixes contemporary touches with turn-of-the-century Victorian details for a pleasing look: Original woodwork is beautifully refinished, walls wear warm and pretty cream and
mint hues, furnishing accents the heritage without adding frill. In addition, the
Victorian lobby, a generous breakfast buffet and all-day snacks laid out in a
sunny lounge and wonderful home-style-chic Sarabeth's restaurant contribute a
lot to making the Wales makes a pleasing place to stay. Be aware, however, that
the nearest subway stop is a good 10-minute hike from the hotel.

Rooms: 87; 10 floors; one designated smoking floor. **Hotel amenities:** Lounge,
rooftop terrace, exercise room, in-room spa treatments, laundry and dry-cleaning service, fax service, video and CD library. **Food services:** Sarabeth's restaurant, a New American bistro, room service; rates include access to help-yourself
cappuccino, tea and cookies. **Cancellation:** 3 P.M. day prior to arrival. **Wheelchair access:** Not accessible. **Subway:** 6 to 96th St.

Inn New York City
EXCELLENT $$$$

266 W. 71st St. (between Broadway and West End Ave.)
www.innnewyorkcity.com   Phone: (212) 580-1900   Fax: (212) 580-4437

This one-of-a-kind, four-suite luxury inn just may be the most romantic place to stay in the city. Its only peer is the Inn on Irving Place, but this place has an air of private luxury and personalized hospitality that's unparalleled. There are no public spaces whatsoever—no front desk, no concierge, no lobby—so upon entering the beautifully restored brownstone you'll feel like you're the treasured guest of a doting, and very rich, friend with impeccable taste. Each of the four suites takes up an entire floor, so space is in abundance, and you may not even ever see your fellow guests.

Each suite has a unique theme and tailored amenities, plus 12-foot ceilings, a fully equipped gourmet kitchenette, sumptuously outfitted sleeping quarters, a terrific bathroom, beautifully chosen antiques and only the plushest textiles. On the grand parlor-floor the Opera Suite has a baby grand piano, a working fireplace in the bedroom, a Jacuzzi tub in the bath and French doors leading to a private terrace. One entire room of the ultra-romantic, Victorian-style spa suite is dedicated to the art of bathing, with a monster Jacuzzi tub (big enough for a party), a fireplace, a glass-block shower and a cedar-lined sauna, plus a vintage barber chair for character. The skylit, somewhat masculine and extremely handsome Library Suite is ideal for small families or shares, since pocket doors can convert the mammoth living room into a second bedroom. The duplex Vermont Suite is also available for month-long stays.

The discreet service is impeccable; the innkeepers will leave you entirely alone if you prefer, or will be at your service in a flash with the push of a button. Inn New York City is very expensive, but simply stunning—you will get your money's worth here.

Rooms: Four suites; four floors; smoking not allowed. **Hotel amenities:** Copy and fax services, dry-cleaning service, washer/dryers in three suites (maid will do laundry for Opera Suite guests). **Food services:** Stocked breakfast cupboard in each suite. **Cancellation:** 14 days prior to arrival, $50 cancellation fee. **Wheelchair access:** Not accessible. **Note:** Best for children over 12. **Subway:** 1, 2, 3, 9 to 72nd St.

The Lowell
EXCELLENT $$$$

28 E. 63rd St. (between Madison and Park Aves.)   *www.lhw.com*
Phone: (212) 838-1400, (800) 221-4444   Fax: (212) 319-4230

The low-profile Lowell is the hidden jewel of the Upper East Side—small, quiet, private, elegant and service oriented. Even though it's well located at the Midtown end of the Upper East Side, it feels like a secret hideaway from the moment you enter the intimate, deco-influenced French Empire lobby. Two-thirds of the accommodations are suites; each has a well-equipped kitchenette but is otherwise unique, with individual appointments ranging from wood-burning fireplaces to an in-suite gym (a result of a request from Madonna while in residence some years ago). Chintzed to the max, the Lowell Suites are just right for honeymoons and other special occasions. The Hollywood Suite has a 41-inch TV, a full selection of Hollywood classics on video and a delightful collection of movie paraphernalia, while the Garden Suite boasts not one but two ultra-romantic terraces. Expect a full slate of luxuries in any accommodation. Warmth is the order of the day from the first-rate staff.

Rooms: 67; 17 floors; designated nonsmoking rooms. **Hotel amenities:** 24-hour concierge, good fitness center, secretarial services, laundry and dry-cleaning service, meeting and function rooms, video library. **Food services:** Post House steakhouse, Pembroke Room for continental cuisine and afternoon tea, 24-hour room service. **Cancellation:** 48 hours prior to arrival. **Wheelchair access:** Accessible. **Subway:** N, R, W to Lexington Ave.; 4, 5, 6 to 59th St.

The Lucerne
VERY GOOD $$–$$$
201 W. 79th St. (at Amsterdam Ave.) www.newyorkhotel.com
Phone: (212) 875-1000, (800) 492-8122 Fax: (212) 579-2408

A landmark 1903 terra-cotta building houses one of the city's best mid-priced hotels. The bright and comfortably furnished marble lobby leads to extremely well-maintained rooms that are outfitted in a comfortable and attractive colonial Americana style. Rooms are generally spacious; even the standards are large enough to accommodate a king or queen bed, or two doubles for shares or small families. All rooms have TVs with Nintendo and Web TV, coffee maker and an attractive bathroom with spacious travertine counters. One-bedroom suites have granite-counter wet-bar kitchenettes with microwave, plus sleeper sofas, extra sitting-room TVs and terry bathrobes; the deluxe king suite also has a Jacuzzi tub. Corner units are especially light and bright. Management is fanatical about excellent service, so you can count on it. A stylish bar and grill hosts live jazz and blues three or four nights a week. Rack rates are too high in the height of the season, but discounts are often available.

Rooms: 250; 14 floors; designated nonsmoking floors. **Hotel amenities:** Laundry and dry-cleaning service, fitness room, penthouse meeting space. **Food services:** Bar and grill, room service; rates include continental breakfast, served in the penthouse-level breakfast room; second restaurant in the works. **Cancellation:** 24 hours prior to arrival. **Wheelchair access:** Fully accessible. **Subway:** 1, 9 to 79th St.

The Mark
EXCELLENT $$$$
25 E. 77th St. (at Madison Ave.) www.mandarinoriental.com
Phone: (212) 744-4300, (800) THE-MARK (843-6275) Fax: (212) 744-2749

This Big Apple representative of the world-renowned Mandarin Oriental hotel group is the Carlyle's chief neighborhood rival for the deepest-pocketed travelers. Boasting an intricate Art Deco facade and outfitted in an elegant English-Italian neoclassical style, the Mark is nevertheless lighter and more contemporary in feeling than the Carlyle and most other hotels in the super-luxury category. Guest rooms are a comfortable mix of classic and contemporary design, with luxuriant textiles; pillowy king-sized beds dressed in Belgian and

Frette linens; a stylish, oversized and well-lit bathroom, most with separate tub
and shower; plus modern features like VCRs, fax machines, and phones with
cordless handsets. About three-quarters of the rooms and suites have full
kitchens or kitchenettes. Service is beyond reproach, and Mark's is one of the
city's best hotel restaurants. An excellent choice on all counts. Prime your plastic, shoppers, because the location is in prime platinum-card spending territory.

Rooms: 177; 15 floors; designated nonsmoking floors. **Hotel amenities:** Clefs
d'Or concierge, fitness center, full business services, laundry and dry-cleaning
service, meeting and function rooms, complimentary weekday-morning shuttle
to Wall Street. **Food services:** Mark's Restaurant, intimate Mark's Bar, 24-hour
room service. **Cancellation:** 4 P.M. day of arrival. **Wheelchair access:** Fully
accessible. **Subway:** 6 to 77th St.

Mayflower Hotel on the Park   GOOD $$–$$$
15 Central Park West (at 61st St.)   www.mayflowerhotel.com
Phone: (212) 265-0060, (800) 223-4164   Fax: (212) 265-0227

Extra-large rooms and an A-one location—in an upscale residential neighborhood at the southwest corner of Central Park, just a stone's throw from both
Lincoln Center and the Theater District—are the best reasons to stay at this
perfectly fine but otherwise undistinctive hotel. Accommodations, about half of
which are suites, are extra-large, traditionally styled and comfortable with good-
sized bathrooms and closets; most also have pantries with mini-fridges. The
hotel has a pleasant lived-in feel to it, but don't expect anything approaching
modern style or quality service—but that front-row seat on the park has a timeless appeal. What's more, your pick of subway lines is out the front door.

Rooms: 365; 17 floors; designated nonsmoking floors. **Hotel amenities:** Fitness
center, laundry and dry-cleaning service, meeting and function rooms, complimentary shuttle service to Javits Center for major trade shows. **Food services:**
Restaurant and bar with park views, room service; complimentary morning coffee (6–7 A.M.). **Cancellation:** 4 P.M. day before arrival. **Wheelchair access:**
Accessible. **Subway:** A, B, C, D, 1, 9 to 59th St.

On The Ave   GOOD $$–$$$
2178 Broadway (at 77th St.)   www.ontheave-nyc.com
Phone: (212) 362-1100, (800) 509-7598   Fax: (212) 787-9521

Travelers with mid-range budgets and an eye for modern design will appreciate
this sleekly styled hotel, a recent reinvention of a down-at-the-heels residence
hotel. Rooms feature Scandinavian-style modular furniture, earth tones, and
attractive modern art specially commissioned for the hotel. Bathrooms are marble, with slate floors and custom-designed stainless sinks; some have showers
only, so request one with a tub if it matters to you. Spaces are not huge, especially at the cheapest price point, furnishings should be a bit more practical and
beds a bit more comfortable, but rooms are rather comfortable overall. Those in
the deluxe category offers the best space-for-money ratio. Penthouse rooms and
suites are an incredible bargain considering their large alfresco terraces and ter-

rific views. Request a nonsmoking room if you want one, because rooms seem to hold on to the cigarette smell. Services are minimal, but the terrific residential neighborhood abounds with good restaurants, and slow-season pricing can be a phenomenal deal.

Rooms: 251; 15 floors; designated nonsmoking rooms. **Hotel amenities:** Concierge, fax service, laundry and dry-cleaning service. **Food services:** None. **Cancellation:** 24 hours prior to arrival. **Wheelchair access:** ADA compliant. **Subway:** 1, 2, 3, 9 to 72nd St.

The Pierre   EXCELLENT $$$$
2 E. 61st St. (at Fifth Ave.)   *www.fourseasons.com/pierre*
Phone: (212) 838-8000, (800) 332-3442   Fax: (212) 826-0319

This old-world, well-mannered, very European-style residential hotel is enormously appealing. A stay in the beautifully restored 1930s Georgian-style building will make you feel regal. The old-world ambiance is extremely formal—with doormen worthy of the Queen's Guard and white-gloved elevator operators—but not uninvitingly so. Opulent, almost museum-like public spaces give way to guest rooms that are individually appointed in a supremely elegant classical style featuring chintzes and dark woods polished to a high sheen. Ceilings are high, so even the smaller rooms feel light, airy and spacious. The rooms are less about business and technology (things like VCRs and fax machines are mostly on request) and more about supreme comforts and superbly fluid service—the staff will graciously fulfill any request. Services include elevators staffed around the clock; anytime laundry, dry cleaning, and pressing; packing and unpacking service; even special menus and amenities for well-heeled kids. Grand suites are apartment-like and uniquely appointed, but many include full dining rooms, park views and/or terraces. The most thrilling rooms are those with views over Central Park, which is just across the street, and north over Manhattan. For a memorable experience, take tea in the distinctive Rotunda room, with its trompe l'oeil murals by Edward Melcarth. Keep in mind, though, that this is the kind of hotel where you must be willing to dress the well-heeled part, or you will feel out of place.

Rooms: 202; 41 floors; designated nonsmoking rooms. **Hotel amenities:** Concierge and theater desk, full-service business center, fitness center, two salons (one with spa services), 24-hour laundry and dry-cleaning service, Grand Ballroom and extensive meeting and function space, courtesy car to Theater District. **Food services:** Cafe Pierre for contemporary-classic French dining; Rotunda for breakfast, light fare, and afternoon tea; 24-hour room service. **Cancellation:** 6 P.M. day of arrival. **Wheelchair access:** Fully accessible; ADA compliant. **Subway:** N, R to Fifth Ave.

The Regency Hotel   EXCELLENT $$$$
540 Park Ave. (at 61st St.)   *www.loewshotels.com*
Phone: (212) 759-4100, (800) 23-LOEWS (235-6397)
Fax: (212) 688-2898, (212) 826-5674

The Regency has new polish, grace and energy following a major $35 million remake in 1999 under the direction of designer Connie Beale. She has done fine work infusing ornate spaces both public and private with warmth and a comfortable feeling of contemporary luxury; this is a Park Avenue address where you can feel comfortable putting your feet up. Plush materials—rich mahogany, deep-hued leather, silks and velvets—do much of the work. A strong lineup of amenities helps, too. Traveling executives and leisure travelers alike love that the rooms have large granite-top work desks with ergonomic chairs and fax/printer/copiers, kitchenettes with microwaves and fridges, four-line phones, CD and video players, beds dressed in Frette linens and goose-down-filled duvets, fluffy terry robes and extra TVs in the bathrooms. Though well equipped, the bathrooms are quite small.

Under the guiding hand of the Loews hotel chain, the Regency just may be the best choice in the luxury category for visiting families. Extensive children's services and amenities include a dedicated "kid concierge," who will do everything from play soccer in the hallways on rainy days to read bedtime stories. Dog-walking and other pet-friendly services also make the Regency ideal for travelers with Rover in tow. Feinstein's at the Regency has quickly evolved into one of the city's top cabaret rooms.

Rooms: 351; 21 floors; designated nonsmoking floors. **Hotel amenities:** Concierge, full-service Casa at the Regency fitness center (with personal training and massage), full-service business center, laundry and dry-cleaning service (including overnight service), meeting and function rooms. **Food services:** 540 Park Avenue restaurant, Feinstein's at the Regency supper club, Library lounge, 24-hour room service. **Cancellation:** Day prior to arrival. **Wheelchair access:** Fully accessible. **Subway:** N, R, W to Lexington Ave.; 4, 5, 6 to 59th St.

The Stanhope, Park Hyatt New York

EXCELLENT $$$$

995 Fifth Ave. (at 81st St.)																	*www.parkhyatt.com*

Phone: (212) 774-1234, (800) 233-1234																	Fax: (212) 988-7439

This bright and elegant member of the posh Park Hyatt chain is ideal for museum lovers, since the Metropolitan Museum of Art is just across tony Fifth Avenue, and the Frick, the Guggenheim, the Whitney and other Museum Mile institutions are within easy walking distance. That's enough reason to stay, but the Stanhope offers many additional incentives, too—most notably, a feeling of privacy and accessible Old World luxury. The Versailles-inspired lobby displays Louis XIV antiques and museum-quality tapestries, while the rooms are done in a very pleasing peach-and-gold-tone French Empire style with Chinoiserie accents. The impressive list of amenities include CD players, VCRs, fax machines and plush robes, plus small but well-outfitted bathrooms. The location keeps the clientele pleasantly mixed between business travelers and vacationers. Sidewalk cafe seating in warm weather is another appeal.

Rooms: 185; 17 floors; designated nonsmoking floors. **Hotel amenities:** Concierge, fitness room, business services, laundry and dry-cleaning service, meeting and function rooms, personal shopping service, complimentary transportation to Midtown and the Theater District. **Food services:** Restaurant, bar, 24-hour room service. **Cancellation:** 48 hours prior to arrival. **Wheelchair access:** Fully accessible. **Subway:** 6 to 77th St.

Surrey Hotel
VERY GOOD $$$–$$$$

20 E. 76th St. (at Madison Ave.)   *www.mesuite.com*
Phone: (212) 288-3700, (800) ME-SUITE (637-8483)   Fax: (212) 628-1549

This all-suite hotel has two prime draws: a tony Upper East Side address for less than most neighborhood hotels charge and room service from Daniel Boulud's Cafe Boulud, a *New York Times* three-star restaurant. Done in 18th-century English parlor style, the lobby has a slightly faded air, and the hallways upstairs could do with some gentler lighting. But spacious Old World suites—studios, one- and two-bedrooms—offer unsexy but solidly reliable accommodations. Rooms and closets are large, black-and-white-tiled bathrooms are spacious and pleasant, and thick walls keep things quiet. Every one has a fully equipped kitchen and a dining area—and the staff will even do your shopping for you.

Rooms: 130 (all suites); 17 floors; designated nonsmoking floors. **Hotel amenities:** Concierge, exercise room, business services, fitness room, laundry and dry-cleaning service, guest laundry, meeting room, grocery shopping service. **Food services:** Cafe Boulud, bar, room service. **Cancellation:** 3 P.M. day of arrival. **Wheelchair access:** Fully accessible. **Subway:** 6 to 77th St.

Trump International Hotel & Tower
EXTRAORDINARY $$$$

1 Central Park West (at Columbus Circle)   *www.trumpintl.com*
Phone: (212) 299-1000, (888) 44-TRUMP (448-7867)   Fax: (212) 299-1150

Trump International may be considered a diamond with a curse. Controversial real-estate developer and Page Six favorite Donald Trump is something less than universally beloved by New Yorkers. Even so, it is hard to imagine anybody finding fault with the jewel of a hotel that bears his name. It is simply spectacular.

The hotel is housed in a smoking mirrored tower at Columbus Circle, overlooking Central Park; park views are most prized, of course, but the tower's freestanding situation awards all rooms with light, and three sides offer at least a glimpse of the green. Rooms with city views over Broadway lose a bit of the magic but retain their status as an unreserved cocoon of contemporary luxury.

About three-quarters of the accommodations are suites. High ceilings, floor-to-ceiling windows, and smart design maximize space. The look is definitely sumptuous, but in a restrained, meditative way with warm beiges and honey hues predominating. Appointments include TV with VCR and video games, CD stereo, high-speed connectivity and fax for business-minded travelers (PCs and printers on request), plush bathrobes and slippers, a Jacuzzi tub in the marble bath and a telescope for taking in the thrilling views. Most rooms and all suites also have a top-of-the-line Euro-style kitchens stocked with Limoges china and crystal. If you don't feel like relying on run-of-the-mill room service or hiking all the way down to the lobby level to dine at *New York Times* four-star winner Jean Georges, one of Jean-Georges Vongerichten's sous-chefs will prepare your meal en suite. What's more, each guest is assigned a personal concierge for the course of their stay, making service unparalleled.

Rooms: 167; 52 floors (hotel rooms housed on floors 3 through 17); designated nonsmoking rooms. **Hotel amenities:** Concierge; Trump Attaché butler service; 6,000-square-foot health club with spa services, swimming pool, steam and sauna; full-service business center; laundry and dry cleaning; meeting and function rooms; CD library. **Food services:** Jean Georges restaurant, 24-hour room service. **Cancellation:** 4 P.M. day prior to arrival. **Wheelchair access:** Fully accessible. **Subway:** A, B, C, D, 1, 9 to 59th St.

B & B BOOKING AGENTS AND SHORT-TERM APARTMENT RENTALS

Independent-minded travelers who are looking for home-style accommodations and a high value-to-dollar ratio can often do well by booking a bed-and-breakfast room (either hosted or unhosted) or a private apartment through a rental agency. Accommodations can run the gamut from spartan to splendid, from studios to multi-bedroom homes (which makes this a great option for families), and always come fully equipped. You don't have to be coming to the city for the long term to take advantage of these kinds of accommodations; many agencies require just a 2-, 3-, or 4-night minimum, and rates on full studio apartments can start as cheaply as $90 or $100 a night.

Another advantage to booking an accommodation through a booking agency rather than a formal hotel is that taxes are often lower, usually just 8.25 percent, instead of the standard 13.25 percent plus $2 per night hotel tax. Sometimes, tax is eliminated altogether on longer stays, thanks to a loophole in the tax laws; ask for the details on sales tax when you book.

If you opt to book an accommodation in this manner, be prepared to be largely on your own. You won't have the services that a hotel offers, like maid service. In fact, many accommodations that call themselves bed-and-breakfasts don't even offer breakfast as part of the package ("guesthouse" would be a better term), so ask. In fact, get all promises in writing and an exact total up front to avoid any misunderstandings. And try to pay by credit card if you can, so you can dispute payment if the agency fails to live up to its promises. The following agencies are usually reliable bets:

Abode Apartment Rentals (212) 472-2000, (800) 835-8880, *www.abodenyc.com*

A Hospitality Company (212) 965-1102, (800) 987-1235, *www.hospitalityco.com*

Assured Accommodations (212) 431-0569, *www.assurednyc.com*

Homestay New York (718) 434-2071, *www.homestayny.com*

Manhattan Getaways (212) 956-2010, *www.manhattangetaways.com*

Manhattan Lodgings (212) 677-7616, *www.manhattanlodgings.com*

Urban Ventures (212) 594-5650, *www.nyurbanventures.com*

West Village Reservations (212) 614-3034, *www.citysonnet.com*

BEYOND MANHATTAN
THE BRONX

Le Refuge Inn   GOOD $
620 City Island Ave. (between Sutherland and Cross Sts.), City Island
www.lerefugeinn.com   Phone: (718) 885-2478   Fax: (718) 885-1519

This pleasant old 19th-century sea captain's house on the main strip of enjoyably funky City Island in the far reaches of the Bronx, makes for a pleasant
country-in-the-city-style getaway. The warmth of the welcome, the delightful
French meals prepared by Normandy-born innkeeper and chef Pierre Saint-
Denis (who also presides over Le Refuge Restaurant on the Upper East Side),
and the chamber concerts on Sunday afternoons are the best reasons to visit the
inn. M. Saint-Denis imbues the inn with the genuine ambiance of his homeland. The backyard faces the water, offering delightful views.

Rooms: Nine (some with shared bathrooms); three floors; no smoking allowed.
Hotel amenities: None. **Food services:** Rates include breakfast; prix-fixe dinner
$45, Sunday brunch $19.50. **Cancellation:** Five days prior to arrival. **Wheelchair access:** Not accessible. **Directions:** 6 to Pelham Bay Park (last stop); then
transfer to City Island Bus No. 29 towards City Island (third stop).

BROOKLYN

Bed & Breakfast on the Park   VERY GOOD $$–$$$
113 Prospect Park West (between 6th and 7th Sts.), Park Slope *www.bbnyc.com*
Phone: (718) 499-6115   Fax: (718) 499-1385

A beautifully restored town house built in 1895 situated right across the street
from Prospect Park now houses Brooklyn's best bed-and-breakfast inn, and one
of the finest the entire city. The house is enchantingly and lavishly outfitted out
with antiques, oriental rugs, fine oil paintings and stained glass. The rooms are
individually appointed, but each is ultra-romantic in its own way; the most
sumptuously outfitted suites stumble into the $$$ price category. Breakfast is
vast and satisfying. A real jewel.

Rooms: Eight (two with shared bathroom); four floors; no smoking allowed.
Hotel amenities: None. **Food services:** Rates include full breakfast. **Cancella-
tion:** 10 days prior to arrival, subject to cancellation fee. **Wheelchair access:**
Not accessible. **Subway:** F to Seventh Ave.

New York Marriott   VERY GOOD $$
333 Adams St. (between Tillary and Willoughby Sts.), Downtown Brooklyn
www.marriott.com
Phone: (718) 246-7000, (888) 436-3759   Fax: (718) 246-0563

Unveiled in the heart of downtown Brooklyn in 1998, this brand-new Marriott occupying seven floors of a big office tower is the first full-service hotel Brooklyn has had in over 50 years. It's an attractive and well-outfitted hotel with nods to its home borough that pulls it out of the chain-generic doldrums. Behind the front desk is a mural of the Brooklyn Bridge, and artwork and photos of Brooklyn or by Brooklyn artists adorn the walls throughout the hotel.

Once you reach your room, it's strictly Marriott, but all the bases are well covered. Even though the hotel is built over busy Adams Street, the rooms are tranquil. Quite a few subway lines converge in this area, so citywide access is easy, and you can be in Manhattan inside 10 minutes.

Rooms: 376; seven floors; designated nonsmoking floors. **Hotel amenities:** Concierge, business center, health club with lap pool, laundry and dry-cleaning service, meeting and function rooms, valet parking. **Food services:** Restaurant, cocktail lounge, room service. **Cancellation:** 6 P.M. day of arrival. **Wheelchair access:** Fully accessible. **Subway:** M, N, R to Court St.; 2, 3, 4, 5 to Borough Hall; A, C, F to Jay St.–Borough Hall.

STATEN ISLAND

Harbor House   GOOD $
1 Hylan Blvd.(at Edgewater St.)   www.nyharborhouse.com
Phone: (718) 876-0056   Fax: (718) 420-9940

Built in 1890, the Harbor House is not luxurious in any way, but it does have wonderful views over the harbor to Manhattan, taking in the Verrazano Bridge and Lady Liberty as well. One smart man rented the whole place for the Fourth of July and had his family there to watch the fireworks. The house feels more like a beach house than anything else, and you can lie in bed and look out to the water. Rooms tend to be large, with a TV, dresser, armoire and ceiling fan, but no phone.

Rooms: 11 (six with shared bathroom); three floors; no smoking allowed. **Hotel amenities:** None. **Food services:** Rates include continental breakfast. **Cancellation:** 10 days prior to arrival, $20 cancellation fee. **Wheelchair access:** Not accessible. **Directions:** Staten Island Ferry to S-51 bus to Hylan and Bay Street; walk across Bay Street and down one block.

AIRPORTS
*(For directions to airports see chapter **Visiting New York**.)*

La Guardia Airport
Crowne Plaza Hotel La Guardia   GOOD $$
104-04 Ditmars Blvd. (at 23rd Ave.), East Elmhurst
www.crowneplaza.com, www.crowneplazalaguardia.com
Phone: (718) 457-6300, (800) 692-5429   Fax: (718) 899-9768

This recently renovated airport hotel features classic-contemporary rooms that have ample amenities. Closets aren't large and ceilings are low but the sound-proofing is very good. A few dollars extra will garner you a club-level room, which comes with access to a complimentary full American breakfast buffet, evening hors d'oeuvres and slightly improved accommodations. An airline screen shows up-to-date flight information.

Rooms: 358; seven floors; designated nonsmoking rooms. **Hotel amenities:** Concierge; full-service business center; fitness center with swimming pool, sauna and whirlpool; laundry and dry-cleaning service, guest laundry; meeting rooms. **Food services:** Restaurant, bar, room service. **Cancellation:** 6 P.M. day of arrival. **Wheelchair access:** Fully accessible.

La Guardia Marriott   GOOD $$
102-05 Ditmars Blvd. (at 23rd Ave.), East Elmhurst   *www.marriott.com*
Phone: (718) 565-8900, (800) 228-9290   Fax: (718) 898-4955

Here's a competent and comfortable, if not particularly colorful, hotel near La Guardia's terminal, which keeps the noise-level down (runway-close hotels are much noisier). All of the familiar Marriott and airport-hotel trappings are here, including a executive concierge level and an airline monitor.

Rooms: 436; nine floors; designated nonsmoking floors. **Hotel amenities:** Concierge; full-service business center; fitness center with swimming pool, sauna and whirlpool; laundry and dry-cleaning service; meeting and function rooms. **Food services:** Restaurant, coffee shop, bar, room service. **Cancellation:** 6 P.M. day of arrival. **Wheelchair access:** Fully accessible.

J.F.K. Airport

Holiday Inn New York—J.F.K. Airport   GOOD $$
144-02 135th Ave. (Van Wyck Expressway, exit 2), Jamaica
www.holidayinnjfk.com
Phone: (718) 659-0200, (800) 692-5350   Fax: (718) 322-2533

Situated on the airport's periphery, this Holiday Inn offers some serenity. It has quiet rooms, a pleasant pool area and even a Japanese garden. In fact, if you have a room facing away from the airport, you'd hardly know you were there. Rooms aren't exactly charming, but they are clean, comfortable and decently sized; bedding is quite comfortable, and bathrooms are plain but adequate.

Rooms: 360; 12 floors; designated nonsmoking rooms. **Hotel amenities:** Concierge; business center; health club with indoor/outdoor pool, sauna, and whirlpool; laundry and dry-cleaning, and guest laundry facilities; meeting and function rooms. **Food services:** Two restaurants, bar, room service. **Cancellation:** 6 P.M. day of arrival. **Wheelchair access:** Fully accessible.

Radisson Hotel J.F.K. Airport   GOOD $$
135-30 140th St., Jamaica   *www.radisson.com*
Phone: (718) 322-2300, (800) 333-3333   Fax: (718) 322-5569

Opened in 1998, this Radisson is the newest of J.F.K.'s airport hotels. Rooms are traditionally decorated and moderately attractive; mattresses are good, but your sleep may be undermined by noise from the Belt Parkway just outside. The hotel's biggest selling point is that it's the only area hotel to have a 24-hour restaurant.

Rooms: 386; 12 floors; designated nonsmoking floors. **Hotel amenities:** Business center, fitness room, laundry and dry-cleaning service, meeting and function rooms. **Food services:** Restaurant, bar, 24-hour room service. **Cancellation:** 4 P.M. day of arrival. **Wheelchair access:** Fully accessible.

Newark International Airport, Newark NJ

Newark Airport Marriott   GOOD $$$

Newark International Airport   *www.marriotthotels.com/ewrap*
Phone: (973) 623-0006, (800) 882-1037   Fax: (973) 623-7618

The only hotel on Newark Airport property, this Marriott has the company's familiar combination of comforts and corporate-traveler-friendly amenities. Most importantly, the windows offer virtually complete soundproofing against airplane noise. Rooms aren't particularly spacious, but they're perfectly adequate and feature in-room coffee makers.

Concierge-level rooms have additional amenities and use of a separate lounge serving complimentary continental breakfast and evening hors d'oeuvres. A telescope helps you keep track of the air traffic, and an airline monitor in the lobby helps you keep track of flight schedules.

Rooms: 597; 10 floors; designated nonsmoking floors. **Hotel amenities:** Concierge; business center; health club with swimming pool, sauna and whirlpool; laundry and dry-cleaning service, and guest laundry facilities; meeting and function rooms. **Food services:** Two restaurants, lounge, cigar bar, 24-hour room service. **Cancellation:** 6 P.M. day prior to arrival. **Wheelchair access:** Fully accessible.

HOTELS BY PRICE

$$$$ Very Expensive

Bryant Park Hotel	Midtown West	EXCELLENT
The Carlyle	Upper East Side	EXTRAORDINARY
Chambers	Midtown West	EXCELLENT
Essex House, A Westin Hotel	Midtown West	EXCELLENT
Four Seasons Hotel New York	Midtown East	EXCELLENT
The Inn at Irving Place	Gramercy Park	EXCELLENT
Inn New York City	Upper West Side	EXCELLENT
The Kitano New York	Murray Hill	EXCELLENT
Le Parker Meridien	Midtown West	EXCELLENT
The Lowell	Upper East Side	EXCELLENT
The Mercer	SoHo	EXCELLENT
Millennium Broadway	Times Square	VERY GOOD
The Mark	Upper East Side	EXCELLENT

The Peninsula New York	Midtown West	EXTRAORDINARY
The Pierre	Upper East Side	EXCELLENT
The Plaza	Midtown West	VERY GOOD
The Regency Hotel	Upper East Side	EXCELLENT
Regent Wall Street	Financial District	EXTRAORDINARY
Ritz-Carlton New York, Battery Park	Battery Park	EXCELLENT
Royalton	Midtown West	VERY GOOD
60 Thompson	SoHo	VERY GOOD
Sheraton Russell Hotel	Murray Hill	EXCELLENT
Sofitel New York	Midtown West	EXCELLENT
SoHo Grand Hotel	SoHo	EXCELLENT
The Stanhope, Park Hyatt New York	Upper East Side	EXCELLENT
The St. Regis New York	Midtown East	EXTRAORDINARY
Tribeca Grand Hotel	TriBeCa	EXCELLENT
Trump International Hotel & Tower	Upper West Side	EXTRAORDINARY
W Union Square	Union Square	VERY GOOD
Waldorf Towers, A Conrad Hotel	Midtown East	EXCELLENT

$$$–$$$$

Hotel Giraffe	Flatiron District	VERY GOOD
Surrey Hotel	Upper East Side	EXCELLENT
Swissôtel New York-The Drake	Midtown East	EXTRAORDINARY
Waldorf=Astoria, A Hilton Hotel	Midtown East	EXCELLENT

$$$ Expensive

The Algonquin	Times Square	EXCELLENT
The Barbizon, A Melrose Hotel	Upper East Side	VERY GOOD
The Benjamin	Midtown East	EXCELLENT
Crowne Plaza at the United Nations	Midtown East	VERY GOOD
Crowne Plaza Manhattan	Times Square	GOOD
Doubletree Guest Suites	Times Square	VERY GOOD
Embassy Suites New York	Battery Park City	EXCELLENT
The Gorham	Midtown West	GOOD
Hilton New York	Midtown West	GOOD
Hilton Times Square	Times Square	EXCELLENT
Holiday Inn Wall Street	Financial District	EXCELLENT
Hotel Casablanca	Times Square	VERY GOOD
Hotel Elysée	Midtown East	VERY GOOD
Hotel Wales	Upper East Side	GOOD
The Iroquois New York	Times Square	GOOD
Kimberly Hotel	Midtown East	VERY GOOD
Library Hotel	Midtown East	VERY GOOD
The Lombardy	Midtown East	EXCELLENT
The Mansfield	Midtown West	GOOD
Millenium Hilton	Financial District	GOOD

Morgans	Murray Hill	VERY GOOD
The Muse	Midtown West	VERY GOOD
Newark Airport Marriott	Newark	GOOD
New York Marriott Brooklyn	Brooklyn	VERY GOOD
New York Marriott Financial Center	Financial District	GOOD
New York Marriott Marquis	Times Square	GOOD
Omni Berkshire Place	Midtown East	EXCELLENT
Paramount	Times Square	GOOD
The Roger Smith	Midtown East	GOOD
The Roger Williams	Midtown East	VERY GOOD
Sheraton Manhattan	Midtown West	GOOD
Sheraton New York Hotel & Towers	Midtown West	GOOD
The Shoreham	Midtown West	GOOD
The Time	Times Square	GOOD
Wall Street Inn	Financial District	VERY GOOD
W New York--The Court	Midtown East	VERY GOOD
W New York--The Tuscany	Midtown East	VERY GOOD
The Warwick	Midtown West	GOOD

$$–$$$

Bed & Breakfast on the Park	Brooklyn	VERY GOOD
Doral Park Avenue Hotel	Murray Hill	GOOD
Fitzgerald Grand Central Hotel	Midtown East	VERY GOOD
The Lucerne	Upper West Side	VERY GOOD
Mayflower Hotel on the Park	Upper West Side	GOOD
Metropolitan Hotel	Midtown East	GOOD
On the Ave	Upper West Side	GOOD

$$ Moderate

Abingdon Guest House	West Village	GOOD
The Ameritania	Times Square	BASIC
The Bentley	Upper East Side	VERY GOOD
Best Western Seaport Inn	South Street Seaport	BASIC
Broadway Inn	Midtown West	VERY GOOD
Chelsea Lodge Suites	Chelsea	VERY GOOD
Chelsea Savoy Hotel	Chelsea	GOOD
Comfort Inn Central Park West	Upper West Side	GOOD
Country Inn the City	Upper West Side	VERY GOOD
Crowne Plaza Hotel La Guardia	Queens	GOOD
Excelsior Hotel	Upper West Side	VERY GOOD
Gramercy Park Hotel	Gramercy Park	GOOD
The Helmsley Middletowne	Midtown East	GOOD
Holiday Inn Downtown/Soho	Chinatown	BASIC
Holiday Inn New York—J.F.K. Airport	Queens	GOOD
Hotel Beacon	Upper West Side	VERY GOOD

Hotel Bedford	Midtown East	BASIC
Hotel Chelsea	Chelsea	GOOD
Hotel Edison	Times Square	BASIC
Hotel Metro	Midtown West	VERY GOOD
Hudson	Midtown West	VERY GOOD
The Inn on 23rd St.	Chelsea	VERY GOOD
La Guardia Marriott	Queens	GOOD
The Marcel	Gramercy Park	VERY GOOD
Mayfair New York	Times Square	GOOD
Radisson Hotel J.F.K. Airport	Queens	GOOD
Travel Inn	Midtown West	GOOD
Washington Square Hotel	East Village	BASIC

$–$$

Chelsea Inn	Flatiron District	BASIC
Chelsea Pines Inn	Chelsea	GOOD
Comfort Inn Midtown	Midtown West	GOOD
Red Roof Inn	Midtown West	VERY GOOD
Second Home on Second Ave.	East Village	GOOD

$ Inexpensive

Americana Inn	Midtown West	BASIC
Amsterdam Inn	Upper West Side	BASIC
Chelsea Lodge	Chelsea	VERY GOOD
Colonial House Inn	Chelsea	GOOD
Cosmopolitan Hotel—Tribeca	Tribeca	GOOD
Harbor House	Staten Island	GOOD
Holmes Bed & Breakfast	Upper West Side	VERY GOOD
Hotel Olcott	Upper West Side	GOOD
Larchmont Hotel	West Village	GOOD
Le Refuge Inn	The Bronx	GOOD
Murray Hill Inn	Murray Hill	BASIC
St. Mark's Hotel	East Village	BASIC
Thirty Thirty	Murray Hill	GOOD
Union Square Inn	East Village	GOOD

Restaurants in New York City

According to *New York Times* food critic, William Grimes, "The quality, range and sheer number of the city's restaurants has made New York the world's most exciting place to eat. Paris may have more French restaurants, and Rome more trattorias, but no city on earth offers the adventurous eater more variety and depth than New York at the present moment," says *New York Times* food critic William Grimes.

For more than 30 years, New Yorkers have been relying on restaurant reviews in the *Times* for the most trustworthy advice about where to eat in their hometown. The 300 or so restaurants included here have all been reviewed by the major food critics of the *Times*: William Grimes, Eric Asimov and Ruth Reichl. Since 1992 Eric Asimov has been responsible for finding those quintessential New York restaurants that serve high quality food at reasonable prices (his reviews are clearly identified by the term **"$25 & Under"** which appears at the top of the review). Restaurants with stars have been reviewed by Mr. Grimes since 1999 and by Ms. Reichl before then. Her original reviews have been updated in the "Eating Out" and "Good Eating" columns that appear weekly in the newspaper and those changes are reflected here. In addition, Mr. Grimes and Mr. Asimov have done recent updates for this *Guide*.

(Note: The best restaurants in Brooklyn, Queens and the other boroughs can be found in the appropriate sections.)

Using This Guide

What the Stars Mean:

☆ ☆ ☆ ☆	Extraordinary
☆ ☆ ☆	Excellent
☆ ☆	Very Good
☆	Good

Price Range: The dollar signs that appear at the top of each review are based on the cost of a three-course dinner and a 15 percent tip (but not drinks).

$	$25 and under
$$	$25 to $40
$$$	$40 to $55
$$$$	$55 and over

$25 & Under: At these restaurants you can get a complete meal, exclusive of drinks and tip, for $25 or less; recently, as a concession to inflation, some restaurants have been included where only an appetizer and main course total $25.

Abbreviations: Meals: B = Breakfast, Br = Brunch, L = Lunch, D = Dinner. LN = Late Night (restaurants open till midnight or later). Credit cards: AE = American Express; DC = Diner's Club; D = Discover; MC = Master Card; V = Visa; if there is no credit card information it means that at least three of these cards are accepted.

The Best Restaurants in New York City

☆ ☆ ☆ ☆—EXTRAORDINARY

Bouley Bakery
Daniel
Jean Georges
Le Bernardin
Lespinasse

☆ ☆ ☆—EXCELLENT

Alain Ducasse	Honmura An	Park Bistro
Atlas	Ilo	Patria
Aquavit	JoJo	Patroon
AZ	Judson Grill	Peacock Alley
Babbo	Kuruma Zushi	Periyali
Café Boulud	La Caravelle	Picholine
Cello	La Côte Basque	Pico
Chanterelle	La Grenouille	San Domenico
Craft	Le Cirque 2000	Sushi Hatsu
Danube	March	Sushi Yasuda
Felidia	Molyvos	Tabla
Fifty Seven Fifty Seven	Montrachet	Town
The Four Seasons	Next Door Nobu	Union Pacific
Gotham Bar and Grill	Nobu	Veritas
Gramercy Tavern	Oceana	

☆ ☆—VERY GOOD

Ada	Bayard's	Chez Josephine
Alison on Dominick	Beacon	Chicama
An American Place	Beppe	Cho Dang Gol
Aquagrill	Bice	Chola
Arqua	Blue Ribbon Sushi	Christer's
Artisanal	Blue Hill	Churrascaria Plataforma
Aureole	Brasserie	Circus
Balthazar	Campagna	City Eatery
Bambou	Chelsea Bistro & Bar	City Hall

D'Artagnan
Destinée
The Dining Room
Eight Mile Creek
Eleven Madison Park
Esca
Estiatorio Milos
Etats-Unis
F.Illi Ponte
Firebird
Fleur de Sel
Fresco By Scotto
Gabriel's
Grill Room
Guastavino's
Hangawi
Hatsuhana
Heartbeat
Hudson River Club
Icon
Il Valentino
I Trulli
Joe's Shanghai
Kang Suh
L'Actuel
Layla
Le Colonial

Le Perigord
Little Dove
Lutèce
Manhattan Ocean Club
Maya
Meigas
Mercer Kitchen
Mesa Grill
Michael Jordan's
Michael's
Mi Cocina
Nadaman Hakubai
New York Noodle Town
Nick & Toni's Cafe
Nicole's
Odeon
Orsay
Osteria Del Circo
Otabe
Ouest
Paola's
Parioli Romanissimo
Park Avenue Cafe
Park View at the
    Boathouse
Payard Patisserie
Petrossian

Ping's Seafood
Remi
Rosa Mexicano
Ruby Foo's
Salaam Bombay
Savoy
Screening Room
Sea Grill
71 Clinton Fresh Food
Shun Lee Palace
Smith & Wollensky
Solera
Sono
Surya
Tamarind
Thalia
Tocqueville
The Tonic
Tribeca Grill
Triomphe
21 Club
27 Standard
Union Square Café
Zarela

☆ —GOOD

Abajour
Aleutia
Asia de Cuba
Atlantic Grill
Avra
Baldoria
Barrio
Blue Water Grill
Bouterin
Calle Ocho
Chinghalle
Coup
Dawat
Della Femina
Delmonico's
District

Dim Sum Go Go
Dock's Oyster Bar
Frank's
Goody's
Jack Rose
Jane
La Nonna
Lentini
Le Zinc
Maritime
NL
Olives
One If By Land
Papillon
Pastis
Peasant

Pop
Provence
Red Bar Restaurant
The Red Cat
Redeye Grill
Scalini Fedeli
Strip House
Tappo
The Tasting Room
Tavern on the Green
Verbena
Viceversa
Virot
West 63rd Street
    Steak House

Quick Guide to the
Best Inexpensive Manhattan Restaurants

Selected by Eric Asimov

Bali Nusah Indah
Bar Pitti
Bright Food Shop
Café La Grolla
Carnegie Deli
Congee Village
Cooke's Corner
Cookies and Couscous
Cyclo
Da Ciro
Dakshin
El Cid
El Presidente
Flor's Kitchen
Funky Broome
Gennaro
Grand Sichuan Int'l
Han Bat
Holy Basil
'ino
Jean Claude
Jewel Bako
Katsu-Hama

Katz's Deli
Komodo
Kori
La Fonda Boricua
La Palapa
Lavagna
Le Tableau
Le Zie
Lombardi's
Los Dos Rancheros
   Mexicanos
Luca
Lupa
Mama's Food Shop
Mavalli Palace
Mexicana Mama
Mirchi
Moustache
National Cafe
New Green Bo
Nha Trang
Our Place Shanghai
   Tea Garden

Pao
Pearl Oyster Bar
Pepolino
Po
Pongal
Prune
Royal Siam
Sabor
Snack
Soba Nippon
Soba-Ya
SoHo Steak
Taco Taco
The Sultan
Topaz Thai
Turkuaz
Vatan
Velli
Wu Liang Ye
Xunta

MANHATTAN RESTAURANTS, A-Z

Abajour ☆ **$$$**   BISTRO/FRENCH
1134 First Ave. (at 62nd St.)   (212) 644-9757
A respectable neighborhood bistro with pleasing décor, an attractive menu and
some well-priced wines. Abajour's interior has a bright, summery look, and the
menu fits the tone, with enough smart little twists to lift Abajour above the
standardized steak frites competition. Fish and frites, the cheapest of the
entrees, may be plain, but it makes a very good showing. Even better is a grilled
prime sirloin steak smothered in roasted-garlic herb butter, an incredibly juicy,
flavorful piece of meat. **Price range:** Entrees, $15–$29. **Meals:** D, LN. **Subway:**
N, R, W to Lexington Ave.

Acquario **$25 & Under**   MEDITERRANEAN
5 Bleecker St. (near Bowery)   (212) 260-4666
With its candles, brick walls and casual service, Acquario is a small, warm place
straight out of the Village's bohemian past. A couple of Acquario's large appetiz-
ers can easily make a light meal. Try the fresh sardines, which have a strong,
briny aroma but a mild, wonderfully nutty flavor and are served with a small
green salad. Fennel salad is also wonderful, though it's hard to find a more allur-
ing dish than the Portuguese fish stew. **Price range:** Entrees, $12–$18. Cash
only. **Meals:** D. Closed Sun. **Subway:** 6 to Bleecker St.

Ada ☆☆ **$$$$**   INDIAN
208 E. 58th St. (between Second and Third Aves.)   (212) 371-6060
Ada aims to elevate the status of Indian cuisine in New York. The décor steers
clear of Indian fabrics, ornate brass plates and beaded curtains; the owner is
intent on giving the food an upgrade as well. One of the best appetizers is a
slow-grilled white-pea and potato cake accented with garam masala, fennel and
cilantro, and surrounded by caramelized bananas coated with crème fraîche.
Spices are used with great delicacy in most dishes, and they penetrate every
fiber of tandoori-cooked meats, which arrive in a state of melting tenderness.
The dessert menu uses a few Indian ingredients strategically, with some success,
as in the coconut panna cotta with a firm layer of coconut-cardamom rice.
Price range: Three-course prix fixe, $55 or $65. **Meals:** L, D. **Subway:** 4, 5, 6 to
59th St.

Alain Ducasse ☆☆☆ **$$$$**   FRENCH
155 W. 58th St. (between Sixth and Seventh Aves.)   (212) 265-7300
At Alain Ducasse at the Essex House, the outlines of a great restaurant can be
seen. The prices still make Ducasse far more expensive than any other restau-
rant in the city, and the service can seem overproduced and cluttered in the
restaurant's confined space. But the waiters have worked out the dance steps,
and what could be an overbearing formality is tempered by warmth. Most
important, the food is coming into sharp focus. One outstanding example is a
simple chicken breast, accessorized with white truffles and swathed in an inso-

lently retrograde Albufera sauce, a chicken veloute that Mr. Ducasse has quietly upgraded with foie gras butter and a blend of Madeira, Cognac and port. This is the kind of food that disarms criticism. You raise your eyes and give thanks. A bargain is a relative thing, and in the rarefied world of Alain Ducasse, the $65 three-course lunch (called the menu salad) counts as a supersaver discount. **Price range:** Menu salad, $65; prix fixe, $145-$160, higher for special menus. **Meals:** L (Thu.–Fri.), D (Mon.–Fri.). **Subway:** N, R, Q, W to 57th St.

Aleutia ☆ $$$$ NEW AMERICAN
220 Park Ave. (at 18th St.)   (212) 529-3111
When out-of-towners dream of an up-to-the-minute Manhattan restaurant, Aleutia is just the sort of place they want to be beamed into. The style starts at the door, where L.C.D. panels seductively flash the menu. There's a lot more style in the retro lounge, and in a dining room suspended over the main floor. The food is fresh and contemporary, with a sly way of interweaving Asian ingredients with down-home American favorites. It is often very good, but just as often things go awry. But venison loin, smoked like the salmon over a birch wood fire, trembles at the threshold of greatness. **Price range:** Entrees, $25–$32. **Meals:** L, D. **Subway:** L, N, Q, R, W, 4, 5, 6 to 14th St.

Alison on Dominick ☆☆ $$$$ FRENCH
38 Dominick St. (between Varick and Hudson Sts.)   (212) 727-1188
This is one of the city's most surprisingly romantic restaurants. The light here is so soft and dim that everybody looks good, and the music is loud enough to hear yet low enough not to intrude. The design is so simple it seems unplanned, but it has an easy, offhand elegance. The food and wine list are primarily French and overwhelmingly wonderful. **Price range:** Entrees, $27–$33. **Meals:** D. **Subway:** 1, 9 to Canal St.

Alley's End $25 & Under   BISTRO/NEW AMERICAN
311 W. 17th St. (between Eighth and Ninth Aves.)   (212) 627-8899
Enter a portal and traverse a passageway, and you leave the workaday Chelsea world for Alley's End, a lovely network of dining rooms and gardens that feels as pastoral and isolated as an oasis. The brief menu manages to match the romantic draw of the interior. **Price range:** Entrees, $14–$22. **Meals:** D. **Subway:** A, C, E to 14th St.; L to Eighth Ave.

Alouette $25 & Under   BISTRO/FRENCH
2588 Broadway (near 97th St.)   (212) 222-6808
Dishes at Alouette are cleverly conceived, beautifully presented and moderately priced; each item promises excitement. Service has its ups and downs, and the second floor is rather warm and stuffy. **Price range:** Entrees, $15–$18.50. **Meals:** Br, D. **Subway:** 1, 2, 3, 9 to 96th St.

Amy Ruth's $25 & Under   SOUTHERN
113 W. 116th St. (between Lenox and Seventh Aves.)   (212) 280-8779
Amy Ruth's presents Southern food that is up-to-date without sacrificing time-
honored traditions. Chicken is served with crisp yet fluffy waffles, a common
pairing, but you can also order whole-grain waffles, and they're all served with
real maple syrup. The real stars of the menu include short ribs that are falling-
off-the-bone tender in an earthy, oniony brown gravy, and deliciously spicy
shrimp, perfect over fluffy white rice, and baked spareribs served in a sweet barbecue sauce. Many of Amy Ruth's side dishes shine, like buttery string beans
and eggy potato salad. Deep-dish sweet potato pie and pineapple-coconut cake
are terrific. **Price range:** Dinner, $7.95–$17.95. **Meals:** B, L, D. **Subway:** 2, 3 to
116th St.

An American Place   ☆☆ $$$$ NEW AMERICAN
565 Lexington Ave. (between 50th and 51st Sts.)   (212) 888-5650
The name is as simple as Main Street, and like Main Street it has been around
long enough that it seems almost timeless, expressing a vision of American cuisine as an infinitely renewable resource. The food has the right blend of bold-
ness and subtlety. The pot-roasted short ribs do not require a lot of fuss and
bother; this signature dish is served with whipped potatoes that cut the richness of the meat with a sharp horseradish edge and fresh herbs. The cedar-
planked salmon has a nice, crisp char, and the rich, pillow-soft dollop of corn
pudding on the side cannot be beat. The wisest course for dessert is to order
the double chocolate pudding, a satisfyingly regressive treat served with
Schrafft's sugar cookies. **Price range:** Entrees, $26–$32. **Meals:** B, Br, L, D.
Subway: 6 to 51st St.

Aquagrill   ☆☆ $$$ SEAFOOD
210 Spring St. (at Sixth Ave.)   (212) 274-0505
Aquagrill has the comfortable air of a neighborhood place, the sort of restaurant
that ought to be serving burgers and beer. Instead there's an oyster bar in front
and the menu is refreshingly original. Devoted almost entirely to fish, it offers
unusual dishes like "snail-snaps" (bite-size popovers with a single snail) and
salmon in falafel crust. Soups are also satisfying. All the fish is well prepared and
some with imagination. **Price range:** Entrees, $18.50–$26. **Meals:** Br, L, D.
Closed Mon. **Subway:** C, E to Spring St.

Aquavit   ☆☆☆ $$$$ SWEDISH
13 W. 54th St. (between Fifth and Sixth Aves.)   (212) 307-7311
Marcus Samuelsson, Aquavit's restlessly inventive executive chef, is not the for-
mula type. Although he is young, he is a fully mature artist with a distinctive
style in which precisely defined flavors talk back and forth to each other rather
than blending into a single smooth harmonic effect. The menu sparkles with
bright thoughts. Foie gras ganache is a light duck-liver pudding that releases a
rich, liquid livery ooze when pierced with a fork. Herring, of course, remains on

the menu, a reminder that, to the Swedes, this fish is a form of cultural expression that is part of the genetic code. Mr. Samuelsson's pièce de résistance is his pellucid arctic char, pinkish orange and delicately smoked. A waiter pours a steaming mushroom consommé, or possibly a spring-onion broth, over the fish. **Price range:** Pre-theater menu, $39; prix fixe and tasting menus, $67–$110. **Meals:** L, D. **Subway:** B, D, E to Seventh Ave.

Arqua ☆☆ $$ ITALIAN
281 Church St. (at White St.)   (212) 334-1888
The setting of this restaurant named for a village in northern Italy, is alluring, but the noise can be deafening when all the chairs are occupied at night. Lunch is a more tranquil time, and the rustic fare is unfailingly good. Starters include grilled chicken and mushroom sausage on a warm lentil salad; fresh pickled sardines with sweet and sour onions; a soup of the day; and several homemade pastas. Some recommended main dishes are pan-seared tuna loin with ginger sauce; baked duck breast with a sauce of black currant and cassis; and braised rabbit with white wine and herbs. Before the espresso, try a ricotta cheesecake or a poached pear with caramel sauce and ice cream. **Price range:** Entrees, $16–$22. **Meals:** L, D. **Subway:** 1, 9 to Franklin St.

Artisanal ☆☆ $$$$ BISTRO
2 Park Ave. (at 32nd St.)   (212) 725-8585
Artisanal is a big, very good-looking brasserie with more varieties of cheese (nearly 200) than most human beings will encounter in a lifetime. About half the menu at Artisanal is honest bistro cooking. The other half shows some genuinely inspired flashes, like rabbit in riesling sauce. After the entrees comes the moment of truth. You will have plenty of help putting together a good cheese plate, and Artisanal makes all of its 140 or so wines available by the glass, so no cheese need be eaten without the mathematically precise wine pairing. **Price range:** Entrees, $16–$36. **Meals:** L, D, LN. **Subway:** 6 to 33rd St.

Asia de Cuba ☆ $$$ ASIAN/LATIN AMERICAN
237 Madison Ave. (near 37th St.)   (212) 726-7755
You won't eat very well at Asia de Cuba. But the manic energy of the place makes every night feel like a party. There aren't many main dishes to recommend. But who can think about all that when desserts are exploding all over the room? Guava Dynamite is just guava mousse wrapped in a chocolate tuile, but the sparkler on top is seductive. **Price range:** Entrees, $22–$34. **Meals:** L, D, LN. **Subway:** 6 to 33rd St.

Atlantic Grill ☆ $$ SEAFOOD
1341 Third Ave. (near 77th St.)   (212) 988-9200
This appealing, affordable restaurant with its bustling but surprisingly quiet dining room and attentive service will rarely let you down. The cold seafood platter with four sauces, which serves four, is fresh and tasty; a better appetizer is the sweet, smoky, hickory-roasted sea bass with cucumber and ginger salsa. Simplicity is the key to the best main dishes: fish served with rice and vegeta-

bles is perfectly grilled to order and makes a satisfying meal. And the red Thai curry is an absolute delight. **Price range:** Entrees, $14.50–$19.95. **Meals:** Br, L, D. **Subway:** 6 to 77th St.

Atlas ☆ ☆ ☆ $$$$ FRENCH/BRITISH
40 Central Park South (between Fifth and Sixth Aves.)   (212) 759-7968
This is one of the most exciting restaurants in the city. The starting point is French, but the animating principle is a determination to create friction by rubbing opposites together, or giving high-class treatment to low-status foods. One fixture at Atlas is an ovoid dollop of green-apple and wasabi sorbet nestled in a baby abalone shell and sprinkled with a few crunchy grains of Maldon salt. A waiter pours a drizzle of olive oil over the sorbet, and the combination is magic. The main courses at Atlas pull back from the edge just a bit. But cannon of lamb with braised artichokes in a coffee-cardamom fumet is not exactly conservative. Roasted beef fillet, fork-tender and exceptionally flavorful, takes a direct route, surrounded by a purée of roasted carrots and horseradish, baby onions poached in a cumin-accented broth and a wonderfully clear, intense jus. **Price range:** Three-course prix fixe, $68. Pre-theater, 5:30–6:15, $48. **Meals:** D. Closed Sun. **Subway:** N, R, W to Fifth Ave.

Aureole ☆ ☆ $$$$ FRENCH/NEW AMERICAN
34 E. 61st St. (between Madison and Park Aves.)   (212) 319-1660
Aureole is one of the city's most popular and revered restaurants, serving appealing food in stylish surroundings, with polished service and a warm atmosphere. When chef Charlie Palmer pulls it all together, his food has an unfussy, direct appeal that makes other chefs seem neurotic. The best entrees, like panseared quail with sautéed foie gras, cornbread and chanterelles, have a winning simplicity to them. The flavors are direct and concentrated, and there's an imaginative twist that adds intrigue to what otherwise might be a plodder. **Price range:** three-course prix fixe, $65; tasting menu, $85. **Meals:** L, D. **Subway:** N, R, W to Lexington Ave.

Avenue $25 & Under   BISTRO/FRENCH
520 Columbus Ave. (at 85th St.)   (212) 579-3194
This informal corner restaurant (with an unexpectedly French atmosphere and efficient service) serves breakfasts and light meals by day and full dinners at night. Smoked pork loin, sliced lamb and sliced steak are excellent. At brunch, try the hot chocolate, which is thick as pudding and rich as a chocolate truffle. From the terrific food to the daylong service and the good values, Avenue is a formula that works. **Price range:** Entrees, $13.95–$16.95. **Meals:** B, Br, L, D, LN. **Subway:** 4, 5, 6 to 86th St.

Avra ☆ $$$ GREEK/SEAFOOD
141 E. 48th St. (between Third and Lexington Aves.)   (212) 759-8550
Greek cuisine is a modest thing, a fairly limited catalog of simple pleasures, and Avra gives it honest, honorable representation. Fresh fish, barely touched, is the selling point here. In the open kitchen, a ball of fire blasts each side of a sea bass

or red snapper imprisoned in a grilling basket; the fish gets a squirt of lemon, a drizzling of olive oil and a sprinkling of herbs, then heads to the table. The seafood counter offers about a dozen fish. Lamb loin chops, served with lemon potatoes and okra, are tender and flavorful, and grilled chicken is served with string beans, in a zesty stewed tomato sauce. Avra's spanakopita is a flawless layering of good feta, firm spinach and leeks, with crackling-fresh leaves of phyllo dough. **Price range:** Entrees, $18.50–$26. **Meals:** L, D. **Subway:** S, 4, 5, 6, 7 to 42nd St.

AZ ☆☆☆ $$$$ FUSION
21 W. 17th St. (between Fifth and Sixth Aves.)   (212) 691-8888
AZ is gorgeous, an improbable but enchanting blend of strict Asian geometry, Western Art Nouveau and turn-of-the century Viennese craft influences. The décor, in other words, matches the menu. When the food arrives, however, Patricia Yeo's highly inventive, extroverted and wildly successful brand of fusion cooking holds center stage. Duck schnitzel sounds like a joke. The laughter stops when the rich duck meat, wrapped in a paper-thin crunchy layer of breading, makes contact with brown butter, specks of hazelnut and an intervention of sweet and bitter flavors provided by sliced golden beets. Ms. Yeo also works wonders with Asian teas. Chicken smoked in Lapsang souchong leaves absorbs the dusky perfume of the tea, which is nicely offset by a scallion pancake and a thick fig chutney. Two non-Asian desserts make the strongest impression, a fig tarte Tatin with fromage blanc ice cream, and a small coconut financier. **Price range:** Three-course prix fixe, $52; six-course tasting menu, $75. **Meals:** Br, L, D. **Subway:** F to 14th St.

Babbo ☆☆☆ $$$$ ITALIAN
110 Waverly Pl. (bet.. Sixth Ave. and Washington Sq. Park)   (212) 777-0303
The menu here is loaded with dishes Americans are not supposed to like: fresh anchovies and warm testa (head cheese) are among the appetizers, and pastas include bucatini with octopus, and ravioli filled with beef cheeks and topped with crushed squab livers. One of the best pastas is made with calf's brains wrapped in tender sheets and sprinkled with fragrant sage and thyme flowers; there is also a pasta tasting menu: five different pastas followed by two desserts. But a meal at Babbo is not complete without spicy, robust calamari. Wine is served by quartinos (250 milliliters, or a third of a bottle); if you don't like one, the kitchen will take it back. The best ending to a meal here is saffron panna cotta with poached peaches. The upstairs room is small, spare and intimate with warm golden light. Downstairs the bar is crowded and lively but the tables are uncomfortable. **Price range:** entrees, $15–$35; tasting menus, $59–$65. **Meals:** D. **Subway:** A, C, E, F, S to W. 4th St.

Baldoria ☆ $$$ ITALIAN
249 W. 49th St. (between Seventh and Eighth Aves.)   (212) 582-0460
Baldoria (meaning "rollicking good time") is a big slice of neighborhood Italian, New York style. They serve feel-good food in a feel-good atmosphere that inclines diners to overlook shortcomings. When it's good, Baldoria is quite good.

The greens and the tomatoes are always fresh and flavorful. Pastas, too, perform strongly, especially trenette with prosciutto, peas and onions in a light cream sauce. Standard appetizers are respectable, as are main courses like sweet sausages with pepper and onions. Get the costata di manzo, a thuggish-looking hunk of charred rib chop, weighing in at 54 ounces; it's an incredibly flavorful piece of beef, juicy, tender and perfectly cooked. **Price range:** Entrees, $18–$32. **Meals:** D. Closed Sun. **Subway:** C, E, 1, 9 to 50th St.

Bali Nusa Indah $25 & Under   INDONESIAN
651 Ninth Ave. (near 45th St.)   (212) 765-6500
Bali Nusa Indah offers fresh and lively Indonesian dishes in a tranquil and pretty setting. Most of the food is forcefully spiced, yet respectful of the flavors of each dish. Among the dishes worth trying are Javanese fisherman's soup; corn fritters gently flavored with shrimp; nasi goreng, the wonderful Indonesian version of fried rice; and sea bass broiled in a banana leaf. There are exceptional desserts as well. **Price range:** Entrees, $6–$13.50. **Meals:** L, D. **Subway:** A, C, E to 42nd St.

Balthazar   ☆☆ $$$ BISTRO, FRENCH
80 Spring St. (between Lafayette St. and Broadway)   (212) 965-1785
Dinner at midnight? If you don't have the private number for this oh-so-trendy SoHo French brasserie, that is probably what you'll be offered, so book weeks in advance. Try going for breakfast or lunch; the room is still beautiful, the affordable food still delicious. The Balthazar salad is a fine mix of asparagus, haricots verts, fennel and ricotta salata in a truffle vinaigrette. Sautéed foie gras is excellent, as is an appetizer of grilled mackerel with a warm potato salad. The short ribs are awesome: rich and meaty, they are accompanied by fat-soaked carrots and buttery mashed potatoes. Lighter dishes are also attractive, like seared salmon served over soft polenta. **Price range:** Entrees, $16–32. **Meals:** B, L, D, LN. **Subway:** 6 to Spring St.; N, R to Prince St.

Bambou   ☆☆ $$$ CARIBBEAN
243 E. 14th St. (between Second and Third Aves.)   (212) 505-1180
The best Caribbean food in the city is served in a room with such cozy elegance, it feels as if a warm breeze is blowing through it. There is no better way to begin a meal here than with the eggplant soup, a thick dark liquid with the scent of curry and the deep, intoxicating taste of coconut. Bambou shrimp, each encrusted in coconut, are sweet and tasty, an appetizer that could almost be a dessert. The tropical fruit plate glows with color and the coconut crème brûlée is fabulous. **Price range:** Entrees, $18–$26. **Meals:** D. **Subway:** L to Third Ave.; N, Q, R, W, 4, 5, 6 to 14th St.

Bandol $25 & Under   FRENCH
181 E. 78th St. (between Third and Lexington Aves.)   (212) 744-1800
Bandol, named for a fine Provençal wine, offers dreamy Mediterranean flavors. The food is very good, the atmosphere warm and neighborly. Even the overly familiar dishes like lamb shank, salmon and scallops have clear, direct flavors

that convey their appeal rather than their popularity. Among the appetizers, the pissaladiére, a tart of onions, olives and anchovies, is so good that you could eat two and call it a meal. While the main courses don't have the consistency of the appetizers, they are still satisfying. Coq au vin is lighter than usual, grilled steak is juicy and flavorful, and the tender lamb shank offers primal enjoyment. The mostly French wine list is long but not very exciting. **Price range:** Entrees, $16–$22. AE only. **Meals:** Br, L, D. **Subway:** 6 to 77th St.

Barking Dog Luncheonette $25 & Under   DINER
1678 Third Ave. (at 94th St.)   (212) 831-1800
1453 York Ave. (between 77th and 78th Sts.)   (212) 861-3600
With its dark wood paneling, comfortable booths, bookshelves and low-key lighting, the Barking Dog looks more like a library than a luncheonette. That, in part, explains its appeal to adults, along with its up-to-date American menu, which ranges from hamburgers, fried chicken and meatloaf to leg of lamb and roasted trout. If the children begin to fidget while waiting for the rich, bountiful desserts, distract them with the restaurant's dog tchotchkes, which can be a parent's best friend. **Price range:** Entrees, $11. Cash only. **Meals:** B, Br, L, D, LN. **Subway:** Third Ave.: 6 to 96th St. York Ave.: 6 to 77th St.

Bar Pitti $25 & Under   ITALIAN
268 Sixth Ave. (near Houston St.)   (212) 982-3300
This casual cafe offers superbly simple Tuscan fare and draws a fashion-conscious crowd. Bar Pitti's ease with people and with food is what makes it seem so Italian; its atmosphere of jangly controlled frenzy makes it a wonderful New York experience. Outdoor seating on Sixth Avenue is remarkably pleasant. The menu is small and familiar, and almost all the main courses are superb. **Price range:** Entrees, $10.50–$19. Cash only. **Meals:** L, D, LN. **Subway:** A, C, E, F, S to W. 4th St.

Barrio   ☆ $$$ BISTRO
99 Stanton St. (at Ludlow St.)   (212) 533-9212
Barrio's round-the-clock, seven-day schedule makes it a cross between a diner and a bistro. That means the food needs to be sharp and hip, but not so clever that it scares away local residents hankering for a quick bite. The lunch menu is mostly given over to soup, sandwiches and salads. But the soup could be a thick, silken blend of rutabaga and parsley root, sneakily spiced with cayenne and ginger, and the sandwiches outperform their bargain price. The prix-fixe makes it possible to enjoy lunch with substantial main courses like braised veal cheeks on a sweet-sour bed of marinated beet greens. **Price range:** Entrees, $13–$27. **Meals:** Open 24 hours. **Subway:** F to Second Ave.

Bayard's   ☆☆ $$$$ FRENCH
1 Hanover Sq. (between Pearl and Stone Sts.)   (212) 514-9454
Bayard's may be the most distinctive, romantic dining room in Manhattan, and the food suits the surroundings. Chef Eberhard Müller grows his own produce, and it features prominently on the menu. When this approach works, it works

spectacularly. Steamed savoy cabbage encases a breast of chicken folded over a slice of foie gras, sitting in a shallow pool of chicken-vegetable broth; you would have to search far and wide for a better chicken dish. The knockout wine list is a lengthy document, peppered with bargains, that many restaurants would kill for. The solid dessert list offers classics as well as highly inventive desserts like a Moroccan citrus soup with Lillet granite. **Price range:** Entrees, $29–$38. **Meals:** D. Closed Sun. **Subway:** 2, 3 to Wall St.

Bayou $25 & Under   CAJUN/SOUTHERN
308 Lenox Ave. (between 125th and 126th Sts.)   (212) 426-3800
Bayou, a handsome Creole restaurant in Harlem, would do any New Orleans native proud. With its brick walls, retro brass lamps and woody touches, Bayou looks like countless other neighborhood bars and grills, but its big picture windows and second-floor setting offer an unusual New York panorama, unimpeded by tall buildings. The menu is short, but includes standout appetizers like earthy chicken livers in a rich port wine sauce, and shrimp rémoulade, piquant with mustard and hot pepper and served with deviled eggs. The rich turtle soup is thick with bits of turtle meat and smoky andouille sausage, spiked with sherry and lemon. The sautéed snapper Alexandria, sprinkled with roasted pecans and drenched with lemon butter, is moist and altogether delicious. For dessert, both a bread pudding with a vanilla-whiskey sauce and a fudgy, wedge-shaped pecan brownie topped with peppermint ice cream and chocolate sauce are excellent. **Price range:** Entrees, $12.95–$21.95. **Meals:** L, D. **Subway:** 2, 3 to 125th St.

Beacon   ☆☆ $$$ NEW AMERICAN
25 W. 56th St. (between Fifth and Sixth Aves.)   (212) 332-0500
This classy looking midtown restaurant offers civilized dining in a beautiful setting. Organized around an open kitchen and a huge wood-burning oven, it delivers uncomplicated big-flavored food emphasizing fresh, seasonal ingredients. Meat and fish pick up a smoky tang from the oven, roasted vegetables are served with entrees and even desserts feature roasted fruits. Two of the best entrees are triple lamb chops, rubbed with cumin and pureed picholine olives, and a plain trout roasted over high heat with a bright vinaigrette of chervil, parsley, cilantro and shallots. For dessert soufflés are a point of pride but it's the carmelized apple pancake that grabs the brass ring. **Price range:** Entrees, $19–$32. **Meals:** L, D. Closed Sun. **Subway:** N, R, W to Fifth Ave.

Beppe   ☆☆ $$$ ITALIAN
45 E. 22nd St. (between Broadway and Park Ave. South)   (212) 982-8422
Beppe, named for Chef Cesare Casella's grandfather, is worth a detour. The comfortable rustic Tuscan room has exposed brick walls, wood beams, antique wooden floors and a wood-burning fireplace that is damped down in the summer. Mr. Casella is at his very best with the Tuscan dishes: Order anything made with farro, the nutty whole grain, which is served in soup and a risotto-style dish. The fried chicken would make a cook of the Deep South proud, and the 11-herb pasta is filled with flavor. For dessert, try a Tuscan riff on ice cream sandwiches, made with toasted buccellati, the Tuscan version of panettone.

(*Marian Burros*) **Price range:** Pasta, $16–$20; Entrees, $23–$29. **Meals:** L, D. Closed Sun. **Subway:** 6 to 23rd St.

Bice ☆☆ $$$ ITALIAN

7 E. 54th St. (between Fifth and Madison Aves.)   (212) 688-1999

With a main dining room done in beige and wood with brass sconces and indirect lighting, Bice is the handsomest Italian restaurant in town. If you have lots of money, good ears and a desire to see the fast and the fashionable, this offshoot of a Milanese restaurant is for you. The food is predictable but good. Fresh pastas, risotto, and the essentially uncomplicated main courses—veal chop, chicken paillard and duck breast with mango—are all recommended. The mostly Italian wine list is well chosen. **Price range:** Avg. Entree, $24–$31. **Meals:** L, D, LN. **Subway:** E, F to Fifth Ave.

Big Wong $ CHINESE

67 Mott St. (between Canal and Bayard Sts.)   (212) 964-0540

This bright, bare-bones Chinatown restaurant serves excellent barbecued meats and congee. At lunch, it is packed with jurors from the courthouse nearby and local residents drinking tea from water glasses. **Price range:** Entrees, $5–$10. Cash only. **Meals:** B, Br, L, D. **Subway:** J, M, N, Q, R, W, Z, 6 to Canal St.

Bistro le Steak $25 & Under   BISTRO/STEAK

1309 Third Ave. (at 75th St.)   (212) 517-3800

Bistro le Steak hardly strikes a false note. It does look Parisian. The friendly staff conveys warmth and informality, and the food is both good and an excellent value. Steak is the specialty, but other simple bistro specialties are consistently satisfying and desserts are terrific. **Price range:** Entrees, $15–$30. **Meals:** L, D. **Subway:** 6 to 77th St.

Blue Hill ☆☆ $$ FRENCH

75 Washington Pl. (at Sixth Ave.)   (212) 539-1776

A few steps below sidewalk level, Blue Hill almost shrinks from notice. But the quiet, adult setting admirably suits a style of cooking that is both inventive and highly assured. There are dull spots on the menu, but the overall standard is high enough to make up for the excruciating banquette seating. Poached duck deserves to be the restaurant's signature: a skinned duck breast, poached in beurre blanc and duck stock, is paired with leg meat done as a confit, then crisped at the last minute and placed over puréed artichokes. For dessert, chocolate bread pudding is a conversation-stopper. **Price range:** Entrees, $18–$23. **Meals:** D / Closed Sun. **Subway:** A, C, E, F, S to W. 4th St.

Blue Ribbon Sushi ☆☆ $$$ JAPANESE/SUSHI

119 Sullivan St. (between Prince and Spring Sts.)   (212) 343-0404

Blue Ribbon Sushi has good fish and an awesome list of sakes, but beyond that it has very little in common with a classic Japanese sushi bar. If you have ever felt like a clumsy foreigner and worried about doing the wrong thing, this is the sushi bar for you. The menu is enormous, and almost everything is good, from a pretty seaweed salad to broiled yellowtail collar. But the high point of the meal is always sushi and sashimi. The sushi chefs are at their best when inventing interesting specials. And unfettered by tradition, they create unusual special platters filled with whatever happens to be best that day. Just name the price you are willing to pay and let them amaze you. **Price range:** Entrees, $11.75–$27.50. **Meals:** D, LN. Closed Mon. **Subway:** C, E to Spring St.; N, R to Prince St.

Blue Water Grill ☆ $$ SEAFOOD
31 Union Sq. W. (at 16th St.)   (212) 675-9500
Built as a bank in 1904, this is a big, breezy room with a sidewalk cafe and a casual air. Along with pleasant service, large portions and reasonable prices can come large crowds and long waits. Shrimp and oysters are good choices; so is the grilled fish. Desserts are not among the happy surprises, but the brownie sundae would make most people very happy. **Price range:** Entrees, $18–28. **Meals:** Br, L, D, LN. **Subway:** L, N, Q, R, W, 4, 5, 6 to 14th St.

Boca Chica Restaurant $25 & Under   LATIN AMERICAN
13 First Ave. (at 1st St.)   (212) 473-0108
Many cuisines are juxtaposed on the enticing menu of this little pan-Latin restaurant. Top choices include camarones chipotle, shrimp in a tomato, chili and cilantro sauce; crisp, tangy chicharrones de pollo, the classic Dominican dish of chicken pieces marinated in lime, soy and spices; and pinones, sweet plantains stuffed with ground beef and pork. **Price range:** Entrees, $6.50–$15.95. **Meals:** L, D. **Subway:** F to Second Ave.

Bongo $25 & Under   SEAFOOD
299 10th Ave. (near 28th St.)   (212) 947-3654.
On any given day, Bongo serves half a dozen kinds of oysters, from Fanny Bays, which have a flavor shockingly like cucumbers, to Pemaquids, which are impressively salty, to Wellfleets, which have a pronounced mineral tang. With no more than a squirt of lemon, and they are always impeccably fresh and gloriously sensual. The decadent allure of the oysters makes an amusing contrast to the style of the room, a quirky replica of 1950's living rooms. The limited menu has a few other highlights, like wonderful, meaty lobster rolls and an excellent smoked trout salad **Price range:** Oysters, $1.50–$2.25 each. MC/V only. **Meals:** D, LN

Bouley Bakery ☆☆☆☆ $$$$ FRENCH
120 West Broadway (at Duane St.)   (212) 964-2525
This restaurant crackles with energy, and Mr. Bouley turns out food that is nothing less than inspired. It is stunningly good, and consistently ascends to the highest level. As a chef, Mr. Bouley has it all—elegance, finesse and flair. His flavors are extraordinarily clear and exquisitely balanced; his use of seasoning is so deft as to be insidious. Even his most complex creations have a classical simplicity to them. Despite the fireworks in the kitchen, Bouley Bakery retains the feel of a small neighborhood restaurant. Diners feel comfortable showing up in shirtsleeves, and the staff shrewdly maintains a delicate balance between infor-

mality and the more disciplined level of service implicit in the food and décor. The intensity of the service at Bouley Bakery is also remarkable in New York. The waiters seem passionate about the food and deeply concerned that diners enjoy it to the full. **Price range:** Entrees, $27–$38. **Meals:** L, D. **Subway:** A, C, 1, 2, 3, 9 to Chambers St.

Bouterin   ☆ $$$$ FRENCH
420 E. 59th St. (between First Ave. and Sutton Pl.)   (212) 758-0323
Serving Provençal food in a Provençal atmosphere, this restaurant can be charming. The best dishes are the chef's old family recipes, like the hearty vegetable soupe au pistou, which tastes the way it might if had been made on a wood-burning oven on a Provençal farm, the tarte a la Provençale, the rack of lamb wrapped in a herbal crust, and sea bass in a bold bouillabaisse sauce. The daube of beef, too, is delicious, the beef slowly stewed in red wine and garlic. **Price range:** Entrees, $20–$32. **Meals:** D. **Subway:** 4, 5, 6 to 59th St.; N, R to Lexington Ave.

Brasserie   ☆☆ $$$ BISTRO/FRENCH
100 E. 53rd St. (at Lexington Ave.)   (212) 751-4840
The old Brasserie (which closed in 1995 after a kitchen fire) was a part of the city's fabric. When patrons enter the newly-renovated restaurant, their jaws drop. The staircase down to the dining room has been transformed into a gentle slope of translucent steps. In futuristic booths along the side of the room, the tables are slabs of translucent lime-green acrylic. The Brasserie is ready for a new life, and Chef Luc Dimnet delivers sensible, well-executed food with up-to-date touches but not too many neurotic kinks. For dessert try the chocolate beignets: each powdered morsel, oozing with a perfectly measured mouthful of molten chocolate, reaffirms the genius of the doughnut concept. **Price range:** Entrees, $14–$28. **Meals:** B, Br, L, D, LN. **Subway:** 6 to 51st St.

Brasserie 8 1/2   ☆ $$$ BRASSERIE/FRENCH
9 W. 57th St. (between Fifth & Sixth Aves.)   (212) 829-0812
Visually, Brasserie 8 1/2 is a knockout. The dining room could be a galactic mess hall, with a white terrazzo tile floor and black leather booths. The traditional brasserie menu can be seen in a mostly standard raw bar selection, an iced seafood platter and a weekly rotation of specials like bouillabaisse on Fridays and confit of suckling pig on Thursdays. For dessert try the arresting milk–chocolate crème brûlée, iced with a rose marmalade and surrounded by candied rose petals. **Price range:** Entrees, $18–$30. **Meals:** B, Br, L, D, LN. **Subway:** N, R to Fifth Ave.

Bright Food Shop $25 & Under   NEW AMERICAN
216 Eighth Ave. (at 21st St.)   (212) 243-4433
This spare, minimalist former luncheonette serves an exciting blend of Asian and Southwestern ingredients. The menu changes frequently and may include dishes like a tart green chili pozole; smoked trout and red peppers wrapped in

rice and seaweed; or bluefish salpicon, in which the fish is chopped and pickled with vinegar and chilies and served in corn tortillas. **Price range:** Entrees, $11.75–$17.25. Cash only. **Meals:** Br, D. **Subway:** C, E to 23rd St.

Café Boulud   ☆ ☆ ☆ $$$$ FRENCH
20 E. 76th St. (near Madison Ave.)   (212) 772-2600
Café Boulud is sleek and easy; this is your opportunity to find out what happens when a great chef at the top of his form stretches out and takes chances. The menu, which changes frequently, is divided into four sections: La Tradition (classic country cooking), La Saison (seasonal dishes), Le Potager (vegetarian choices), and Le Voyage (world cuisine). What that really means is, anything goes. Most days there are 30 or more dishes, and none are ordinary. The most satisfying sections are La Saison and La Tradition. Soup is another sure thing. The same willingness to take risks can be found on the wine list, which explores little-known vineyards. **Price range:** Entrees, $24–$32. **Meals:** L, D. **Subway:** 6 to 77th St.

Café de Bruxelles $$ BELGIAN
118 Greenwich Ave. (between Seventh and Eighth Aves.)   (212) 206-1830
The little zinc-topped bar at this cozy Belgian café is a warm and welcoming stop. The frites, served in silver cones with dishes of mayonnaise, go beautifully with the unusual Belgian beers, while mussel dishes and heartier Belgian stews are all very good. The small tables near the battered zinc bar are good for solo diners. **Price range:** $13.75–$19.50. **Meals:** Br, L, D. **Subway:** A, C, E, 1, 2, 3, 9 to 14th St.; L to Eighth Ave.

Café des Artistes $$$ CONTINENTAL
1 W. 67th St. (between Central Park W. and Columbus Ave.)   (212) 877-3500
Its signature murals, leaded-glass windows and paneled wood walls contribute to the genteel impression at this grand cafe. The main room is more neighborly and louder than the intimate tables that ring the bar on the second level. The continental food, however, is surprisingly old-fashioned. Best for grazing before or after a concert. **Price range:** Entrees, $22–$40. **Meals:** Br, L, D. **Subway:** 1, 9 to 66th St.

Cafe La Grolla $25 & Under   ITALIAN
411A Amsterdam Ave. (near 80th St.)   (212) 579-9200
This cafe is tiny, holding no more than 30 people. The lighting is a little too bright, the walls a little too plain, but almost everything on the menu is delicious and it is anything but generic Italian. Salads are excellent and individual pizzas are superb. Agnolotti is rich and warming, delicate ravioli squares filled with veal in a velvety sage-scented reduction of beef broth. Fish are treated with the utmost respect at Cafe La Grolla, and meat dishes like calf's liver and roasted pork tenderloin have a nice vinegary edge. Even desserts are very good, especially a carefully constructed berry tart in a light marzipan crust. **Price range:** Entrees, $9–$20. **Meals:** D. **Subway:** 1, 9 to 79th St.

Café Loup $$ BISTRO
105 W. 13th St. (between Sixth and Seventh Aves.)   (212) 255-4746
Every neighborhood should have a place like easy, comfortable Café Loup,
where you can effortlessly feel like a regular. The menu of traditional bistro
favorites doesn't challenge, but the restaurant does well by the standards, and
that's really the point. **Price range:** Entrees, $13.50. **Meals:** Br, L, D. **Subway:**
F, 1, 2, 3, 9 to 14th St.

Calle Ocho   ☆ $$ SPANISH/DINER
446 Columbus Ave. (between 81st and 82nd Sts.)   (212) 873-5025
At this homage to South American cooking, the kitchen makes food with
authority, like complicated ceviches and seductive shrimp chowders. It is hard
to resist the beauty of camarones, big shrimp brushed with rum and beautifully
arranged around a heap of fried seaweed, or crisp chicken cooked in lime. The
dining room is handsomely decorated, and the big, separate bar in front has
turned into a singles scene where people sip rum, lime juice and mint mojitos
while they listen to soft mambo music. **Price range:** Entrees, $16–$24. **Meals:**
Br, D. **Subway:** B, C to 81st St.; 1, 9 to 79th St.

Campagna   ☆☆ $$$ ITALIAN
24 E. 21st St. (between Broadway and Park Ave. South)   (212) 460-0900
The rustic charm of the setting befits the bold, alluring cooking at this popular
restaurant. It's an unbeatable combination: big portions and a big scene. To begin
there is grilled sausage (made on premises) set over broccoli rabe, and grilled cala-
mari adorned with arugula and marinated tomatoes. Pastas include spaghetti in
white baby clam sauce and goat cheese tortellini mixed with fava beans, aspara-
gus, peas and prosciutto. For main courses, try grilled pork chop, aromatic of
lemon and thyme, served with roasted fennel; and salmon baked with olives,
capers and sun-dried tomatoes. **Price range:** Entrees, $17–$35. **Meals:** L, D.
Subway: 6 to 23rd St.

Carnegie Deli $$ DELI
854 Seventh Ave. (at 55th St.)   (212) 757-2245
A quintessential New York City experience, from pickles to pastrami.
Carnegie's sandwiches are legendarily enormous, big enough to feed you and a
friend and still provide lunch for tomorrow. That doesn't stop people from trying to eat the whole thing, a sight that must gratify the notoriously crabby waiters. The pastrami is wonderful, of course, but so are the cheese blintzes with sour
cream, which are only slightly more modest. **Price range:** Entrees, $10–$20.
Cash only. **Meals:** B, L, D, LN. **Subway:** N, R, Q, W to 57th St.

Casa Mexicana $25 & Under   MEXICAN
133 Ludlow St. (at Rivington St.)   (212) 473-4100
The most surprising thing about the menu here is how little it resembles the
usual array of Mexican street foods. The main courses include four steak dishes,
duck breast, sea bass, halibut and scallops, along with a couple of chicken dishes
and a single pork dish. The Azteca steak and the sirloin Tampiquena are both

fine pieces of beef. Pellizcadas, little disks of fried cornmeal with toppings like chorizo, chicken or crisp bits of pork, are always lively. The best dessert is a warm chocolate cake with a liquid center, topped with raspberry sauce and vanilla ice cream. **Price range:** Entrees, $13–$21. **Meals:** L, D, LN. **Subway:** F to Delancey St.; J, M, Z to Essex St.

Cello ☆☆☆ $$$ FRENCH
53 E. 77th St. (at Madison Ave.)   (212) 517-1200
Cello's minuscule, cocoonlike dining room provides a neutral backdrop for thrilling food. The owner and chef have conspired brilliantly to create a top-class French fish restaurant. Entrees show remarkable refinement. Grilled Alaskan black cod, a monumental chunk of ideally moist fish, floats serenely in a lightweight but intense morel bouillon that diners can thicken with the garlic-parsley purée that's served on the side. In a special menu, the chef does variations on a single theme, a two-and-a-half-pound lobster. Desserts are top-notch. **Price range:** three-course prix-fixe, $75; lobster prix-fixe, $97. **Meals:** L, D. **Subway:** 6 to 77th St.

Chanterelle ☆☆☆ $$$$ FRENCH
2 Harrison St. (at Hudson St.)   (212) 966-6960
Few restaurants are as welcoming or comfortable to enter as Chanterelle, and there's a soft, casual edge to the atmosphere and the service. Chef David Waltuck favors an opulent style. His strong suits are depth and intensity of flavor, and he doesn't shy away from thick, rich sauces in his quest to ravish the palate. The menu changes every four weeks and includes splendid dishes like a simple, pristine beef fillet, drenched in a red wine and shallot sauce with more layers of flavor than a complex Burgundy. There are always some thrilling desserts like a courageously bitter chocolate tart, served with a pastry ice-cream cone filled with banana malt ice cream. The room itself looks as though it should be serene and hushed, but the acoustics are poor. **Price range:** Three-course prix-fixe, $75; five-course tasting menu, $89 or $139 with matching wines. **Meals:** L, D. Closed Sun. **Subway:** 1, 9 to Franklin St.

Chat 'n Chew $25 & Under   NEW AMERICAN
10 E. 16th St. (between Fifth Ave. and Union Sq. West) (212) 243-1616
Middle American farm dishes and homespun décor set the tone at this restaurant, which could lead you to believe it was off a small-town courthouse square rather than off Union Square. Portions are huge, desserts are luscious and the place is particularly appealing to children. **Price range:** Entrees, $7–$14. **Meals:** Br, L, D. **Subway:** L, N, Q, R, W, 4, 5, 6 to 14th St.

Chelsea Bistro & Bar ☆☆ $$$ BISTRO/FRENCH
358 W. 23rd St. (between Eighth and Ninth Aves.)   (212) 727-2026
With a cozy fireplace, a great wine list and really good French bistro food, this is a find in the neighborhood. If the first thing you eat here is the fabulous mussel and clam soup, you will be hooked forever. The fricassee of lobster and sea scallops is almost as good. The hanger steak is fine and rare, with a dense red-wine

sauce. The restaurant serves predictable and good classic New York bistro desserts. The bread pudding is slightly less conventional, if only because it is enlivened with a shot of rum. **Price range:** entrees, $17.95–$27; pre-theater prix-fixe, $28.50. **Meals:** D, LN. **Subway:** C, E to 23rd St.

Chez Josephine   ☆☆ $$$ BISTRO/FRENCH
414 W. 42nd St. (between Ninth and 10th Aves.)   (212) 594-1925
This Theater Row pioneer has been entertaining us with its colorful parade of musicians, singers and dancers for more than a decade and is still going strong. Its reliably pleasing bistro fare and attentive service add to the charm. Highlights among starters include the endive salad topped with crumbled Roquefort and crushed walnuts and the subtle goat-cheese ravioli in a delicate veal broth scented with fresh dill. Favorite entrees include lobster cassoulet; sautéed calf's liver with honey mustard sauce and grilled onions; and grilled salmon with a coulis of fine herbs. **Price range:** Avg. entree, $19. **Meals:** D, LN. Closed Sun. **Subway:** A, C, E to 42nd St.

Chicama   ☆☆ $$$ LATIN AMERICAN
35 E. 18th St. (at Broadway)   (212) 505-2233
Hung with Peruvian rugs and decorated with Peruvian religious statues, this restaurant has a eucalyptus-burning wood oven and a big ceviche bar. The chef generates a special brand of excitement that somehow becomes part of the food, cooking in an exuberant, often flashy style that can be overwhelming, with plate-filling dishes that seem like the culinary equivalent of a carnival float. Alio chicken is a half chicken, smoky tasting after roasting over eucalyptus wood, served on a hash made from malanga root and suffused with a truffle mushroom mojo. Supporting the ceviche menu is a long list of serious beers, but the dessert list is short and almost chaste. Vanilla flan infused with bay leaf may be, in a mild way, the most striking dessert on the menu. **Price range:** Entrees, $19–$39. **Meals:** L, D, LN. **Subway:** L, N, Q, R, W, 4, 5, 6 to 14th St.

Chimichurri Grill $$ LATIN AMERICAN/ARGENTINE
606 Ninth Ave. (between 43rd and 44th St.)   (212) 586-8655
This is a good, casual place for dinner before or after the theater. Simultaneously sophisticated and homelike, it combines all the elements that make the food of Argentina so appealing: great grilled beef, a few Italian pasta dishes and some pure home cooking, like the tortilla, a frittata filled with potatoes, chorizo and onions. The empanadas are excellent, crisp little turnovers filled with a mixture of ground beef and olives. **Price range:** Entrees, $14–$24. **Meals:** L, D. Closed Mon. **Subway:** A, C, E to 42nd St.

Chinghalle   ☆ $ BRASSERIE/DINER
50 Gansevoort St. (between Greenwich and Washington Sts.)   (212) 242-3200
The interior of Chingalle, an idiosyncratic rendering of the Italian word for wild boar, reflects the local dining culture flawlessly, which is to say, most of the effort has gone into the visuals. Still, there are pleasures to be had. Homemade

waffle potato chips have a pleasingly chewy heft to them, and the zucchini chips, fried in a thin tempura batter, are outstanding. The boar sausage with baked beans works, thanks to the foursquare, chunky sausage, flavorful beans and syrupy sauce, and Cornish hen, cooked coq au vin style, is the sort of unpretentious, full-flavored bistro dish that one could eat with pleasure five nights a week. **Price range:** Entrees, $15–$19. **Meals:** D, LN. **Subway:** A, C, E to 14th St.; L to Eighth Ave.

Cho Dang Gol ☆☆ **$$**   KOREAN
55 W. 35th St. (between Fifth and Sixth Aves.)   (212) 695-8222
Cho Dang Gol serves uniquely rustic food that is very different from what is available at other Korean restaurants in the surrounding blocks. The specialty here is fresh soybean curd, made daily at the restaurant. The kitchen makes each dish with extreme care, but for the uninitiated, searching out the best dishes is not easy. Try cho-dang-gol jung-sik. It arrives in three bowls: one with rice dotted with beans, another with "bean-curd dregs" (which hardly conveys its utter deliciousness) and the third with a pungent soup-stew containing pork, seafood, onions and chilies. Also excellent is chung-kook-jang, soybean-paste stew with an elemental flavor, and doo-boo doo-roo-chi-gi, a combination of pork, pan-fried kimchi, clear vermicelli and big triangles of bean curd. **Price range:** Entrees, $6.95–$17.95. **Meals:** L, D, LN. **Subway:** B, D, F, N, Q, R, S, W to 34th St.

Chola ☆☆ **$$**   INDIAN
232 E. 58th St. (between Second and Third Aves.)   (212) 688-4619
The menu at this modest, crowded restaurant roams across the Subcontinent, offering special dishes from the Jews of Calcutta, fiery dishes beloved by the English and wonderful vegetarian dishes like dosa from South India. Start with Mysore masala dosa, a thin, crisp, lacy crepe stuffed with a hot and fragrant potato mixture. Uthappam is a scallion-laced vegetable pancake that is among the great pancakes of the world. Having started in southern India, continue with a fine dish from Kerala, konju pappas, shrimp in a chili-laden sauce. Among the excellent desserts are kulfi, a grainy frozen dessert flavored with nuts and saffron, and rasmalai, an addictive, sweet sort of homemade cheese. Best of all is the extraordinary Indian coffee: strong, milky and sweet. **Price range:** Entrees, $10.95–$24.95. **Meals:** L, D. **Subway:** 4, 5, 6 to 59th St.; N, R, W to Lexington Ave.

Christer's ☆☆ **$$$$**   SCANDINAVIAN
145 W. 55th St. (between Sixth and Seventh Aves.)   (212) 974-7224
This relaxed, upscale Scandinavian restaurant shows how a fine chef translates his love for American ingredients and ideas into traditional dishes. The chef and owner specializes in seafood, salmon in particular. Everything he makes from salmon is good, from seared smoked salmon with black beans, corn, avocado and tomatillo salsa—more Southwestern than Scandinavian—to gentle citrus-glazed salmon. His smorgasbord is wonderful, while his fricadelles, Swedish meatballs made of veal, are hearty and comforting. Desserts like

Pavlova, an airy confection of ice cream, fruit and meringue, and a tart of poached apples are perfect endings. **Price range:** Entrees, $18–$26. **Meals:** L, D. **Subway:** B, D, E to Seventh Ave.; N, R, Q, W to 57th St.

Churrascaria Plataforma ☆ ☆ $$$ LATIN AMERICAN/STEAKHOUSE
316 W. 49th St. (between Eighth and Ninth Aves.)   (212) 245-0505
Two things are required to truly appreciate this all-you-can-eat Brazilian restaurant: a large appetite to keep you eating and a large group to cheer you on. The salad bar is extraordinary, a long two-sided affair anchored at the corners by four hot casseroles. Go easy: This is only the appetizer. The waiters will entice you with ham, sausage, lamb, wonderfully crisp and juicy chicken legs, pork ribs, even the occasional side of salmon, which is delicious in its caper sauce. But it is beef that has pride of place: sirloin, baby beef, top round, skirt steak, brisket, short ribs, special top round. **Price range:** All-you-can-eat rodizio meal, $38.95; children under 10, $19.50. **Meals:** L, D, LN. **Subway:** C, E to 50th St.

Circus Restaurant ☆ ☆ $$$ BRAZILIAN
808 Lexington Ave. (near 62nd St.)   (212) 223-2965
An upscale Brazilian restaurant that turns into a party every night. Circus serves the food your mother might cook if you were raised in São Paulo or Bahia. It is a warm and cozy place, usually packed with Brazilians eager for a taste of home. The camarao na moranga is excellent, a heap of tiny, tender rock shrimp sautéed with fresh corn, hearts of palm, shallots, peas and coconut milk, mixed with cheese and baked in an acorn squash. Another satisfying dish is an appetizer, bolo de milho e rabada, little polenta cakes baked with Manchego cheese and served with a robust oxtail sauce. Among the sweet, tropical desserts, the best is caramelized bananas with ice cream. **Price range:** Entrees, $15–$23. **Meals:** L, D, LN. **Subway:** N, R, W to Lexington Ave.; 4, 5, 6 to 59th St.

City Eatery ☆ ☆ $$$ ITALIAN
316 Bowery (at Bleecker St.)   (212) 253-8644
The name, as plain as a brass doorknob, doesn't offer a clue as to what the kitchen might be serving. Neither does the spare, even severe, décor. The food does the talking. The chef turns a grilled double rib steak into the juicy underpinnings for a messy-looking platter of sliced meat buried under an avalanche of truffles, mushrooms, shallots and Parmesan. Roasted free-range kid, so tender it barely holds a shape, is piled high on a bed of potatoes, pristine peas and shallots, a country dish that the downtown city folk seem to have made the restaurant's signature, and for good reason. **Price range:** Entrees, $11–$25. **Meals:** Br, D, LN. **Subway:** 6 to Bleecker St.

City Hall ☆ ☆ $$$ AMERICAN
131 Duane St. (near Church St.)   (212) 227-7777
The cavernous dining room has the spare quality of an old steakhouse; the clean details, loud music and hip clientele give it an up-to-date air. The menu includes all the old classics, from iceberg lettuce to baked Alaska, but there is more to City Hall than old-fashioned fare. The plateau de fruits de mer, which

feeds six to eight, is a behemoth so impressive that people invariably gasp as it is carried across the room. You also can't go wrong with oysters at City Hall, raw or cooked. Among the meat dishes there is a huge double steak, still on the bone and served for two. For dessert, the apple bread pudding made with brioche is very, very good. **Price range:** Entrees, $18–$32. **Meals:** L, D. Closed Sun. **Subway:** A, C, 1, 2, 3, 9 to Chambers St.

Cocina Cuzco $25 & Under   PERUVIAN
55 Ave. A (at 4th St.)   (212) 529-3469
Cocina's Peruvian cuisine is a melting pot of Asian, European, African and ancient American influences. There are half a dozen ceviches, including some excellent choices like ceviche de concha, clams marinated in lime and served on the half shell, covered with cilantro and tiny cubes of pickled onions and peppers. Main courses demonstrate many sides of Peruvian cuisine. Lomo saltado is stir-fried beef flavored with soy and onions and served over rice and French fries, and red snapper is crusted in thin slices of sweet potatoes, making it crisp on the outside and moist within. Other fine main courses include juicy chicken and chewy, flavorful skirt steak. Desserts are delicious, like bread pudding flavored with dulce de leche. **Price range:** Entrees, $8.95–$13.95. Cash only. **Meals:** L, D, LN. **Subway:** F to Second Ave.

Congee Village $25 & Under   CHINESE
100 Orchard St. (between Delancey and Broome Sts.)   (212) 941-1818
1848 Second Ave. (near 95th St.)
The best congee in New York is in these friendly restaurants. Congee, also known as jook, is nothing more than Chinese hot cereal, a milky rice porridge. More than two dozen versions of congee are served here, some with additions as exotic as fish maws or frog. At the uptown location, most of the rest of the menu is devoted to generic sweet and crispy Chinese-American dishes and a selection of surf-and-turf meals. The downtown restaurant offers excellent Cantonese and Hong Kong dishes. **Price range:** Congee, $2.50–$4.75; entrees, $5.50–$16.95. **Meals:** L, D, LN. **Subway:** Downtown: F to Second Ave. Uptown: 6 to 96th St.

Cooke's Corner $25 & Under   EUROPEAN/AMERICAN
618 Amsterdam Ave. (at 90th St.)   (212) 712-2872
This charmingly subdued little restaurant, with its small, well-designed menu and intelligent wine list, caters to grown-ups and makes no apologies for it. The menu is quietly satisfying with attention to details. Mixed field greens is a superb selection of gently dressed lettuces that balances texture, flavor and color, accented with sweet grape tomatoes and stuffed grape leaves. Main courses include a juicy, flavorful roast chicken served over polenta with a mushroom stew. Beef, braised for four hours until remarkably tender, has a lively Eastern European scent of caraway and coriander seeds and comes with buttery spaetzle. **Note:** Some daily specials are priced at $25, far more than the regular menu items. **Price range:** Entrees, $12–$25. AE only. **Meals:** D. Closed Mon. **Subway:** 1, 9 to 86th St.

Cookies and Couscous $25 & Under   MOROCCAN
230 Thompson St. (at 3rd St.)   (212) 477-6562
This small, bright restaurant has more going for it than the peculiar name might suggest. The short menu emphasizes flavorful seasonal ingredients. Soups and salads are all tasty but almost unnecessary because all the main courses are so big. Most are made with couscous and they too are excellent, whether served with vegetables alone or with meat as well. As for the cookies, they are all very good but not as interesting as the house-made sorbets and ice creams in subtle flavors like tart plum-anise, and soothing cinnamon-apple. **Price range:** Entrees, $10–$19. Cash only. **Meals:** L, D. **Subway:** A, C, E, F, S to W. 4th St.

Coup   ☆ $$ FRENCH/NEW AMERICAN
509 E. 6th St. (between Aves. A and B)   (212) 979-2815
Like the rest of the East Village, Coup takes an ascetic stand on visual stimulation. Somehow, this sensory deprivation induces a feeling of tranquility. Beneath the cloak of mystery lies a deceptively normal neighborhood restaurant, one that fits stylistically with the blocks around it. The food does not aim too high, but what it aims at, it hits. It's the kind of place that always seems like a good idea. The roast Cornish hen takes some beating. Brown as a berry and pleasingly plump, it's packed with chunks of coarse-grained sourdough bread and Michigan cherries. The stuffing is beyond praise. Coup also has a deeply limey Key lime pie and an honest, homey pineapple upside-down cake. **Price range:** Entrees, $16–$21. **Meals:** D. **Subway:** F to Second Ave.; L to First Ave.

Craft   ☆ ☆ ☆ $$$$ NEW AMERICAN
43 E. 19th St. (between Broadway and Park Ave. South)   (212) 780-0880
This is a handsome restaurant, with a clean, vaguely Mission-influenced look that supports the culinary theme. Craft offers a vision of food heaven, a land of strong, pure flavors and back-to-basics cooking techniques. But Craft is also one of the most baroque dining experiences in New York: diners build their own meals here, with side dishes and even sauces presented as options. The saving grace is the high quality of the ingredients and their masterly handling by the kitchen. Nothing at the restaurant sounds like much, but every bite is a revelation. The oysters sparkle. The veal, a humble cut of meat wrapped around some simple roast vegetables, has an honesty and a depth of flavor that will stop you cold. And in a city famous for steak worship, the frighteningly large porterhouse ranks as one of the finest large-scale hunks of beef you'll encounter. For dessert, try a light, chiffonlike steamed lemon pudding or the custardy pain perdu, which can easily handle anything thrown at it. **Price range:** Entrees, $22–$36. **Meals:** L, D. **Subway:** L, N, Q, R, W, 4, 5, 6 to 14th St.

Cuba Libre $25 & Under   LATIN AMERICAN
200 Eighth Ave. (at 20th St.)   (212) 206-0038
The volume here is enough to make you want to scream, but you may give up on talking entirely: while the food is not always consistent, some dishes are so good that you simply want to eat and sigh. Oysters, coated in blue cornmeal and

fried, are perched on smoky collard greens and served with a mildly spicy salsa. The resulting combination is superb. Among the main courses, the best is the pork tenderloin. **Price range:** Entrees, $14.95–$18.95. **Meals:** Br, L, D. **Subway:** C, E to 23rd St.

Cyclo $25 & Under   VIETNAMESE

203 First Ave. (at 12th St.)   (212) 673-3957

This stylish little East Village restaurant serves some of the best Vietnamese food in New York City: It is inventive, impeccably fresh and meticulously prepared, while service is friendly and informative. Try cha gio, crisp and delicate spring rolls, and chao tom, grilled shrimp paste wrapped around sugar cane. Don't hesitate to order fruit for dessert, like cubes of wonderfully fresh mango that are the perfect end to a stellar meal. **Price range:** Entrees, $10–$15. **Meals:** D, LN. **Subway:** L to First Ave.

Da Ciro $25 & Under   ITALIAN

229 Lexington Ave. (near 33rd St.)   (212) 532-1636

An excellent, often overlooked little Italian restaurant. Specialties, cooked in a wood-burning oven, include terrific pizzas. Also excellent is a casserole of wild mushrooms baked in a crock with arugula, goat cheese, olives, tomatoes and mozzarella. The pastas are simple but lively, and full-flavored desserts like bitter chocolate mousse cake and hazelnut semifreddo more than hold their own. **Price range:** Entrees, $15.50–$28. **Meals:** L, D. **Subway:** 6 to 33rd St.

Dakshin $25 & Under   INDIAN

1713 First Ave. (near 89th St.)   (212) 987-9839

Much Indian food in Manhattan is bland, so it is a great pleasure to find lively spicing in more than a few dishes at Dakshin, like jhinga jal toori, small but flavorful shrimp in a sauce of tomatoes and onions made tangy by mustard greens and enhanced by the nutty, slightly bitter aroma of curry leaves. Dakshin's breads are excellent, especially mint paratha and garlic nan, made smoky in the clay oven. Among the meat main courses, try the chicken Chettinad, with the chicken in a thick sauce made lively by black pepper and curry leaves. Dakshin's vegetable dishes also excel. **Price range:** Entrees, $7–$17. **Meals:** L, D. **Subway:** 4, 5, 6 to 86th St.

Daniel   ☆ ☆ ☆ ☆ $$$$ FRENCH

Mayfair Hotel, 60 E. 65th St. (between Madison and Park Aves.)

(212) 288-0033

This is a top-flight French restaurant, sumptuous and rather grand, but still very much the personal expression of its chef and owner, Daniel Boulud. His menu is overwhelming, with a dozen appetizers and ten main courses supplemented by a daily list of specials and assorted tasting menus. The influences come from all over the Mediterranean, and as far afield as Japan and India, pulled in and made French with total assurance. There are lots of pleasant surprises at Daniel, culminating in a dessert menu remarkable for its elegance and restraint. It is also

highly advisable to study the cheese trolley when it rolls around. The selection
is well organized, the cheeses superb. It is possible to spend lavishly on wine, but
there is also a strong selection of half bottles, wines by the glass and modestly
priced bottles. Service, confident and expert, goes a long way to explain the
neighborhood's love affair with Daniel. Diners feel well cared for. The tone is
pitch-perfect, and as a result, patrons feel at ease. **Price range:** Prix-fixe and
tasting menus, $78–$140. **Meals:** L, D / Closed Sun. **Subway:** 6 to 68th St.

Danube   ☆☆☆ $$$$ AUSTRIAN
30 Hudson St. (at Duane St.)   (212) 791-3771
David Bouley does not do things in a small way. Using fin-de-siécle Vienna as a
culinary source, and a repository of romantic images, he has created Danube,
the most enchanting restaurant New York has seen in decades. This is an opiate
dream of lush fabrics, deeply saturated decadent colors and lustrous glazed surfaces. If ever a restaurant was made for a four-hour meal, Danube is it. After
anchoring the menu with a handful of classics, he has conjured up his own private Austria or, in some cases, taken leave of the country altogether with
impressive appetizers like a delicate, complexly orchestrated dish of raw tuna
and shrimp. More typically, Mr. Bouley has lightened, modernized and personalized traditional dishes, or invented new ones using traditional ingredients, often
with stunning results. Two traditional desserts are both impeccable: a Czech
palacsintak, or crêpe, and a Salzburger nockerl, a mound-shaped soufflé dusted
in confectioners' sugar and served with raspberries. **Price range:** Entrees,
$29–$35. **Meals:** L, D. **Subway:** A, C, 1, 2, 3, 9 to Chambers St.

D'Artagnan   ☆☆ $$$$ FRENCH
152 E. 46th St. (between Lexington and Third Aves.)   (212) 687-0300
D'Artagnan has so much personality it could sell it by the pound. The food is
Gascon, from France's legendary region of foie gras, duck, Armagnac and
prunes, and owner Ariane Daguin has turned D'Artagnan into a "Three Muske-
teers" theme park. The food is authentic, robust, earthy and powerfully flavored,
enlivened by a whimsical sense of humor. Foie gras appears in many guises, the
most seductive of which is the simple foie gras terrine, with a deep, dark, gamy
tinge. Cassoulet is a religion in Gascony, and the one served at D'Artagnan is
excellent. Fish, however, doesn't have a chance. The cheese course is small but
pleasing, but for the most part, the desserts seem like a distraction before the
important business of pouring the aged Armagnac. **Price range:** Entrees,
$19–$26. **Meals:** L, D. Closed Sun. **Subway:** S, 4, 5, 6, 7 to 42nd St.

Dawat   ☆ $$$ INDIAN
210 E. 58th St. (between Second and Third Aves.)   (212) 355-7555
Most of the vegetable dishes here—the small baked eggplant with tamarind
sauce, the potatoes mixed with ginger and tomatoes, the homemade cheese in
spinach sauce—are excellent. The set lunches are a bargain. Cornish hen with
green chilies offers heat balanced by the sweet and sour flavor of tamarind. And

sarson ka sag, a sour, spicy, buttery purée of mustard greens, is extremely flavorful. Bhaja are also impressive: Whole leaves of spinach, battered so lightly that the green glows through the coating, are paired with light little potato-skin fritters. **Price range:** Entrees, $15.95–$23.95. **Meals:** L, D. **Subway:** 4, 5, 6 to 59th St.; N, R to Lexington Ave.

DB Bistro Moderne   ☆ ☆ $$$$ BISTRO
55 W. 44th St. (between Fifth and Sixth Aves.)   (212) 391-2400
Daniel Boulud's newest venture is a lively, even raucous restaurant that tries to pass for a bistro but can't quite disguise its high-class leanings. The cooking, although simplified to suit the bistro concept and even countrified on occasion, plays to Mr. Boulud's strength, his refined rusticity. He simply shows that rock-solid technique, good ingredients and a sound idea translate into gustatory bliss. There's nothing fancy about his tarte Tatin, but a perfect buttery crust and flavorful tomatoes make it a little miracle. Gazpacho is clean, crisp and clear, and roasted duck breast has great depth of flavor. Years of catering to an Upper East Side clientele have also given Mr. Boulud a supernatural hand with salads and spa fare. Cristina Aliberti makes excellent light desserts, as well as richer ones like her clafoutis tout chocolat, a small round chocolate cake, runny in the center, that could win over the most hardened chocolate skeptic. **Price range:** Entrees, $28–$32. **Meals:** L, D. Closed Sun. **Subway:** B, D, F, S to 42nd St.

Della Femina   ☆ $$$$ NEW AMERICAN
131 E. 54th St. (between Madison and Lexington Aves.)   (212) 752-0111
Della Femina attracts a tony Upper East Side clientele. With its cool, restrained, Yankeefied setting straight out of Martha Stewart, it looks like a television commercial for the good life, late 1990's style. The cooking is usually described as American with international accents: perfectly poached, unusually flavorful chunks of lobster stand out in a cool salad of young greens, herbs and mango, dressed with a basil-caviar vinaigrette. Roasted turbot, rich and firm, gets just the right support from spring-fresh green peas, morels and a tomato-tarragon essence. There can be inconsistencies but when the kitchen is on its game, Della Femina is very good indeed. Desserts, however, are consistently outstanding, especially the steamed lemon pudding. **Price range:** Entrees, $26–$42. **Meals:** L, D. Closed Sun. **Subway:** 6 to 51st St.; E, F to Lexington Ave.

Delmonico's   ☆ $$$ ITALIAN/NEW AMERICAN
56 Beaver St. (at Williams St.)   (212) 509-1144
Opulent, old-fashioned and dignified, the huge rooms at this American icon are rich with stained wood and soft upholstery, and the tables are swathed in oceans of white linen. The best dishes are in the section headed "Pasta, Risotti." Linguine with clams is a classic that is very well done. Ricotta and spinach ravioli may lack delicacy, but they are generous little pockets topped with clarified butter and fresh sage, and they make a satisfying meal. The rib-eye may not have

the pedigree of a porterhouse or Delmonico, but it is big, tasty and perfectly
cooked. **Price range:** Entrees, $21–$34. **Meals:** L, D. **Subway:** 2, 3 to Wall St.;
4, 5 to Bowling Green; J, M, Z to Broad St.

Destinée   ☆☆ $$$$ FRENCH
134 E. 61st St. (between Lexington and Park Aves.)   (212) 888-1220
Fancy French food, an intimate room, relatively reasonable prices: no wonder
this small restaurant has been such a hit. This is food so decorative that each
plate makes you gasp. The chartreuse of herring, with dots of concentrated beet
that sparkle like garnets, looks like an intricate piece of jewelry. Calamari are
gorgeous too, quickly seared and set on a green tangle of herbed pasta. Some
main dishes feel fussy, but many are excellent, like the sea bass served in a crust
of shellfish and capers richly scented with Indian spices. For dessert, the apricot
tarte tatin is another jewel. **Price range:** Entrees, $14–$23. **Meals:** L, D. **Subway:** N, R, W to Lexington Ave.; 4, 5, 6 to 59th St.

Dim Sum Go Go   ☆ $$ CHINESE
5 E. Broadway (at Chatham Sq.)   (212) 732-0797
Dim Sum Go Go is a bright, happy extrovert clinging to the edge of Chinatown
like a goofy sidekick. There's a sameness to the dim sum lineup that's hard to
ignore; the better, more inventive food can be found on a larger menu abound-
ing in pleasant surprises. Bean curd skin is one of them, stuffed with bits of
black mushroom and chopped spinach, then folded like a crepe and fried. In
another, swiss chard is used to wrap crunchy julienned vegetables, arranged
around a tangle of frilly white fungus, supple yet crunchy, which the Chinese
often use in medicinal soups. The restaurant's interior design has a clean,
streamlined look, with perforated steel chairs, bright red screens and a clever
wall pattern taken from medieval scrolls with dining scenes. **Price range:**
Entrees $8.95–$16.95. **Meals:** L, D. **Subway:** J, M, N, R, Q, W, 6 to Canal St.

The Dining Room   ☆☆ $$$ NEW AMERICAN
154 E. 79th St. (at Lexington Ave.)   (212) 327-2500
The Dining Room is sincere and unassuming, an attractive setting for attractive, intelligently conceived food. The menu, like the restaurant, is small, but it
works some intriguing variations on familiar ingredients. An appetizer of seared
foie gras with sauteed peach slices is a perfectly pleasant start to the meal, but
bits of semisweet pickled watermelon rind really kick-start the dish. The chef
seems to have all sorts of ideas like that in his repertory. There is a small raw
bar, whose spirit is nicely expressed in a three-dish sampler plate. The excitement subsides a little in the main courses, which are perfectly satisfying, but not
quite as clever as the starters. Good ingredients carry most of the load, notably
in the powerfully flavored lamb and a he-man portion of prime rib. Two desserts
fly right off the charts: a column of bread pudding, soaked in coconut milk, and
a chocolate caramel icebox cake. **Price range:** Entrees, $19–$28. **Meals:** D.
Subway: 6 to 77th St.

District ☆ **$$$$**　　　　　　　　　　　　　NEW AMERICAN
130 W. 46th St. (between Sixth and Seventh Aves.)　　　(212) 485-2999
There's a theatrical aspect to dining at District. The walls look like flats, and
ropes behind the banquettes create the illusion that the scenery might be raised
at any moment. It is witty, sophisticated and surprisingly cozy, especially if you
land one of the wraparound booths. When the kitchen hits the marks, it's worth
the ticket. The food is over the top and, when it works, irresistible in a way that
makes you feel vaguely guilty. The main courses sing at top volume, especially
the fearsome chicken cannelloni, two buckwheat-pasta wrappers the size of
Christmas crackers that are filled with ricotta and chicken, balanced atop a
crisped chicken leg done as a confit, outfitted with a hefty serving of roasted
squash and surrounded by a sage and brown butter sauce. For dessert, a tall, fluffy
cheesecake with huckleberry compote scores a direct hit.
Price range: Entrees, $21–$37.50. **Meals:** B, L, D. **Subway:** B, D, F, N, Q, R, S,
W, 1, 2, 3, 7, 9 to 42nd St.

Dock's Oyster Bar ☆ **$$**　　　　　　　　　　　　　SEAFOOD
633 Third Ave. (at 40th St.)　　　　　　　　　　　　(212) 986-8080
2427 Broadway (at 89th St.)　　　　　　　　　　　　(212) 724-5588
These bustling fish houses are crowded fish emporiums that give you your
money's worth, with sparkling shellfish bars from which to choose shrimp or lob-
ster cocktails or oysters and clams on the half shell. Favorites among starters are
the Docks clam chowder, Maryland crab cakes and steamers in beer broth.
Engaging entrees include grilled red snapper with coleslaw and rice, grilled
salmon steak with coleslaw and steamed potatoes and Caesar salad with grilled
tuna. Steamed lobsters come in one- to two-pound sizes, and there is a New Eng-
land clambake on Sunday and Monday nights. **Price range:** Entrees, $15–$22.
Meals: Br, L, D, LN. **Subway:** Midtown: 4, 5, 6, 7, S to 42nd St. Uptown: 1, 9
to 86th St.

Do Hwa **$$**　　　　　　　　　　　　　　　　　　KOREAN
55 Carmine St. (at Bedford St.)　　　　　　　　　　　(212) 414-2815.
Do Hwa one of a new breed of Korean restaurants trying to win converts by
making their food more understandable to curious Americans. Entrees include
kalbi jiim (stewed chunks of beef rib and potatoes) and kimchi chigae (pork and
kimchi soup). All entrees come with panchan, the traditional palate-provoking
condiments like kimchi, pickled radish or salted shrimp. It sounds like home
cooking, and it is. The executive chef is the owner's mother. With a lively bar
scene, Do Hwa is also a great place in the area for a drink.
Price range: $12–$21. **Meals:** L, D. Closed Sun. **Subway:** 1, 9 to Houston St.;
A, C, E, F, S to W. 4th St.

Eight Mile Creek ☆☆ **$$$**　　　　　　　　　　　　AUSTRALIAN
240 Mulberry St. (at Prince St.)　　　　　　　　　　　(212) 431-4635
When a restaurant announces that it will be serving Australian cuisine, you
expect good comic material, not good food. The joke stops when the kangaroo

salad arrives: large cubes of the tender, richly flavored loin languish in a marinade
flavored with coriander seed, smoked paprika and poached garlic, and then are
seared and served on lettuce-leaf wrappers. The menu is short, but the chef makes
every dish count. Oyster pie is a pastry-wrapped stew of precisely cooked oysters,
still plump and juicy, suspended in a cream sauce chunky with salsify and leeks.
Australia without lamb is an impossibility, and the chef merely braises a whopping
big shank and surrounding it with parsnips, chanterelles and roasted apple. **Price
range:** Entrees, $17–$23. **Meals:** D. **Subway:** N, R to Prince St.

El Cid $25 & Under   SPANISH
322 W. 15th St. (between Eighth and Ninth Aves.)   (212) 929-9332
El Cid is delightful, with delicious food and a professional staff that handles any
problem with élan. Tapas are a highlight, and you can make a meal of dishes
like grilled shrimp that are still freshly briny; tender white asparagus served cool
in a delicate vinaigrette; robustly flavorful peppers; tiny smelt fillets marinated
in vinegar and spices; and chunks of savory marinated pork with french fries.
The paella is exceptional. This is not a restaurant for quiet heart-to-heart talks.
The simple décor features hard surfaces that amplify noise, producing a rollicking party atmosphere as the room gets crowded. And it does get crowded. **Price
range:** Entrees, $14.95–$27.95. AE/D only. **Meals:** L, D. Closed Mon. **Subway:**
A, C, E to 14th St.; L to Eighth Ave.

Eleven Madison Park   ☆☆ $$$ CONTINENTAL
11 Madison Ave. (at 24th St.)   (212) 889-0905
Eleven Madison Park occupies the stately ground floor of a grand Art Deco building near the Flatiron building. The restaurant is an homage to the area's past, and
the menu is a thoughtful return to Continental cuisine. The best main courses are
skate grenobloise and the choucroute of salmon and trout. Sweetbreads are spectacular, too. Desserts are irresistible. **Price range:** Entrees, $19–$32. **Meals:** L, D.
Subway: 6 to 23rd St.

El Fogon $25 & Under   SPANISH/PUERTO RICAN
183 E. 111th St. (between Lexington and Third Aves.)   (212) 426-4844
The Puerto Rican specialties are fabulous at this friendly neighborhood hangout, which generally offers two interesting main courses each day. Corned beef
is ground fine and served in a rich sauce with olives, squash, peppers and
onions, enhancing its briny, smoky flavor. Roasted pork is moist and garlicky
and chicken fricassee is a beautifully flavored stew. Each dish comes with white
rice and plump red beans; for an extra $1, try a remarkably flaky and crisp
pastelillo, the Puerto Rican version of empanadas. **Price range:** Avg. entree, $6.
Cash only. **Meals:** L, D. Closed Sun. **Subway:** 6 to 110th St.

El Paso Taqueria $25 & Under   MEXICAN
1642 Lexington Ave. (at 104th St.)   (212) 831-9831
This bustling little corner spot is one of the best restaurants in El Barrio. Tacos
are doubled up in authentic Mexican style to contain fillings like tangy mari-

nated pork, spicy crumbled chorizo sausage and grilled beef, which stretch them to the bursting point. Flautas are corn tortillas filled with a variety of stuffings, wrapped into flutelike cylinders and deep-fried. But the highlights at El Paso are the daily specials, which might include puerco adobo, tender, vinegary pork served on the bone in a spicy tomato sauce, or cecina asada, a huge thin cut of beef that has been dried, salted and spiced, with sautéed chilies and cactus pads. **Price range:** Entrees, $5–$10. Cash only. **Meals:** B, L, D. **Subway:** 6 to 103rd St.

El Presidente $25 & Under   CARIBBEAN/PAN-LATIN
3938 Broadway (between 164th and 165th Sts.)   (212) 927-7011
This small, bright restaurant specializes in the foods of the Hispanic Caribbean —Cuba, Puerto Rico and the Dominican Republic — where flavors are powered by garlic, bell peppers and annatto rather than the heat of chilies. Pernil, or roast pork, is simple but wonderfully satisfying. El Presidente also serves an excellent charcoal-broiled skirt steak, with grilled onions and peppers, well-charred around the edges yet still juicy. **Price range:** Entrees, $5.50–$14.75. **Meals:** B, L, D, LN. **Subway:** A, C, 1, 9 to 168th St.–Washington Heights.

Emily's $25 & Under   SOUTHERN
1325 Fifth Ave. (at 111th St.)   (212) 996-1212
This pleasant but institutional restaurant offers a diverse Southern menu and draws an integrated crowd. If you go, go for the meaty, tender baby back pork ribs, subtly smoky and bathed in tangy barbecue sauce, or the big plate of chopped pork barbecue. The best sides include savory rice and peas (actually red beans) and peppery stuffing, and all dishes come with a basket of fine corn bread. Sweet potato pie is the traditional dessert, and Emily's version is nice and nutmeggy. **Price range:** Entrees, $10–$25. **Meals:** Br, L, D, LN. **Subway:** 6 to 110th St.

Emo's $25 & Under   KOREAN
1564 Second Ave. (near 81st St.)   (212) 628-8699
Emo's pulls few punches, offering robust, spicy, authentic fare that is full of flavor. The highlights here are the superb main courses, like oh jing uh gui, wonderfully tender cylinders of barbecued squid scored to resemble pale pine cones and touched with hot sauce. A variation of this is jae yook gui, barbecued pork in a delectable smoky, spicy sauce. An American-style bar lines the entryway to the spare, narrow but airy dining room. **Price range:** Entrees, $11–$18. **Meals:** L, D. **Subway:** 6 to 77th St.

Empire Diner $$ DINER
210 10th Ave. (at 22nd St.)   (212) 243-2736
One of the early entries in the modern revival of America's love affair with diners was this campy Art Deco gem that attracted a hip late-night crowd in the 1980's. Nowadays, the Empire is a tourist destination. The up-to-date diner basics with some Mediterranean touches are not bad at all—better than at most diners, in fact—which is reflected in the prices. **Price range:** Entrees, $10–$17. **Meals:** B, Br, L, D, LN. **Subway:** C, E to 23rd St.

Esca ☆☆ **$$$**   ITALIAN/SEAFOOD
402 W. 43rd St. (at Ninth Ave.)   (212) 564-7272
At Esca—the name means "bait"—the most important word in the Italian lan-
guage is *crudo*. It means raw, and that's the way the fish comes to the table in a
dazzling array of appetizers that could be thought of as Italian sushi. The *crudo*
appetizers at Esca are the freshest, most exciting thing to happen to Italian food
in recent memory. By changing olive oils, adding a bitter green, or throwing in a
scattering of minced chilies, the chef works thrilling variations on a very simple
theme. The menu changes daily depending on what comes out of the sea. Look
hard enough, and you can find a dish like guinea hen or roast chicken, but it
seems perverse to order anything but seafood. The lemon-yellow walls and sea-
green tiles give it a bright, cool look, and the solid wooden table in the center
of the dining room, loaded down with vegetable side dishes, strikes a rustic note
while communicating the food philosophy: fresh from the market, and prepared
without fuss. **Price range:** Entrees, $17—$26. **Meals:** L, D / Closed Sun.
Subway: A, C, E to 42nd St.

Esperanto **$25 & Under**   PAN-LATIN
145 Ave. C (at 9th St.)   (212) 505-6559
This is a warm and welcoming place with Latin food that can be surprisingly
subtle and delicate. Bolinho de peixe, deep-fried balls of codfish, are exception-
ally light, crisp and flavorful, with a terrific dipping sauce galvanized by spicy
mustard. Esperanto's main courses are sturdy and hard to mess up, like a good
and beefy steak bathed in chimichurri, the Argentine condiment of garlic and
parsley. Esperanto serves potent caipirinhas or mojitos, a sort of Cuban mint
julep—and don't miss the stellar coconut flan. **Price range:** Entrees, $9 to $14.
AE only. **Meals:** D, LN. **Subway:** L to First Ave.

Estiatorio Milos ☆☆ **$$$$**   GREEK/SEAFOOD
125 W. 55th St. (between Sixth and Seventh Aves.)   (212) 245-7400
The restaurant is clean, spare, blindingly white, and the entire focus is on the
display of gorgeous fish by the open kitchen. Choose one and it is grilled sim-
ply and brought to the table. If you like big fish, like striped bass, bring a
crowd. All the fish are cooked whole. And the lamb chops, a concession to
meat eaters, are excellent. Appetizers are wonderful, too. The octopus, charred
and sliced, mixed with onions, capers and peppers, is truly delicious. Thick
homemade yogurt is the ideal way to end these meals. **Price range:** fish for
main courses is sold whole and by weight, from $25–$34 a pound. **Meals:** L, D,
LN. Closed Sun. **Subway:** B, D, E to Seventh Ave.; N, Q, R, W to 57th St.

Etats-Unis ☆☆ **$$$**   NEW AMERICAN
242 E. 81st St. (between Second and Third Aves.)   (212) 517-8826
This tiny family-run restaurant serves terrific, eclectic food. The menu is handwritten each day and comes wrapped up in one of the quirkiest, most personal
wine lists in the city. The food is astonishingly exuberant, yet it also has the
appealingly rustic character of the best home cooking. Entrees might include

homemade gnocchi, so light they literally seem to float off the plate into your mouth, or slow-cooked pork, so tender that it falls apart at the approach of a fork. Desserts wear their plainness with pride: an apple pie that tastes as if it has just won a blue ribbon at a county fair and a rich, warm and fabulous chocolate soufflé. **Price range:** Entrees, $24–34. **Meals:** D. **Subway:** 6 to 77th St.

Evergreen Shanghai $25 & Under   CHINESE
63 Mott St. (near Bayard St.)   (212) 571-3339
10 E. 38th St. (between Fifth and Madison Aves.)   (212) 448-1199
Concentrate on the long menu's Shanghai specialties, like cold appetizers of aromatic beef, a Chinese version of barbecued brisket, and smoked fish, sweet with light, smoky notes and hints of star anise. Great main courses include bean curd with crab sauce and yellowfish with seaweed. The staff is friendly, with enough English speakers to help with the selections. **Price range:** Entrees, $5.95–$24. Cash only at Mott St. **Meals:** L, D, LN. **Subway:** Downtown: J, M, N, Q, R, W, Z, 6 to Canal St.; Midtown: 6 to 33rd St.; 7 to Fifth Ave.

Felidia   ☆☆☆   **$$$$**   NORTHERN ITALIAN
243 E. 58th St. (between Second and Third Aves.)   (212) 758-1479
Felidia is an old-fashioned restaurant, comfortable and rustic, and largely oblivious to food fashions. The seasonal menu concentrates on the foods of Italy's northeast: Friuli, the Veneto as well as Istria, now part of Croatia, and the home of owners Felice and Lidia Bastinich. This is robust food served in generous portions, revolving around game, organ meats, and slow-cooked sauces. The plate of venison osso buco is piled high with quince, cranberries and spatzle so soft and light they seem to float off your plate into your mouth. This is not to say you can't eat lightly. Felidia serves lots of seafood, including lobster and crab-meat salad, and an impressive octopus and potato salad.
Price range: Entrees, $27–$35. **Meals:** L, D. Closed Sun. **Subway:** 4, 5, 6 to 59th St.; N, R to Lexington Ave.

Fifty Seven Fifty Seven   ☆☆☆   **$$$$**   AMERICAN
Four Seasons Hotel, 57 E. 57th St. (between Park and Madison Aves.)
                                                          (212) 758-5757
With its solicitous service in a memorable public space, Fifty Seven Fifty Seven sets a new standard for an old tradition. The menu changes frequently, but it still offers something for absolutely every taste. The food is decidedly American with a modern bent. Vegetarians will find many choices; dieters will find starred offerings low in fat and salt. And those with an appetite for meat and potatoes have many options, from rack of veal in a red wine sauce to grilled beef tenderloin with rosemary cream potato pie. One of the finest dishes, offered on occasion, is cured swordfish, sliced very thin and served with asparagus, greens and cherries. The visually restrained desserts are rich in flavor and texture, but the chocolate desserts are the greatest triumph. **Price range:** Entrees, $25–32. **Meals:** B, L, D. **Subway:** 4, 5, 6 to 59th St.; N, R to Lexington Ave.

F.Illi Ponte   ☆☆ $$$$ ITALIAN
39 Desbrosses St. (between Washington St. and West Side Hwy.)

(212) 226-4621

This is a great, rustic room with bare brick walls, beamed ceilings and a fabulous
view of the Hudson. The menu features admirable Italian fare and fine spicy
lobster. The porchetta, spit-roasted baby pig, is superb. Fried calamari are sweet,
crisp, irresistible. Shrimp cocktail is just about perfect. There is an excellent
veal chop and good (if expensive) broccoli rape. Even if the menu were not
filled with excellent dishes, it would be worth going to F.illi Ponte for the sheer
pleasure of sitting in that beautiful old room watching the light fade over the
Hudson River and to bask in the extraordinary service. **Price range:** Entrees,
$17–$35. **Meals:** L, D. Closed Sun. **Subway:** 1, 9 to Canal St.

Firebird   ☆☆ $$$ RUSSIAN
365 W. 46th St. (between Eighth and Ninth Aves.)   (212) 586-0244
This jewel box of a restaurant boasts a dining room as ornate and luxurious as a
Fabergé egg, and a staff so polished, it really does seem that you have entered
some more serene and lavish era. The caviar arrives with its own private waiter
who turns the service into a performance, pouring hot butter onto the plate,
spooning on the caviar and then delicately twirling the blini around the roe.
Firebird continues to offer imaginatively updated Russian classics, like chicken
tabaka with plum sauce, and grilled sturgeon with sorrel-potato purée. Desserts,
once a weak point, have improved greatly . **Price range:** Entrees, $26–$38.
Meals: L, D. **Subway:** A, C, E to 42nd St.

First $25 & Under   NEW AMERICAN
87 First Ave. (between 5th and 6th Sts.)   (212) 674-3823
Ambitious, creative contemporary American fare at relatively modest prices,
served late into the night. First also offers an intelligently chosen list of wines
and beers and worthwhile weekly specials, like its Sunday night pig roast.
Price range: Avg. entree, $17. **Meals:** D, LN. **Subway:** F to Second Ave.

Fleur de Sel   ☆☆ $$$$ FRENCH
5 E. 20th St. (between Fifth Ave. and Broadway)   (212) 460-9100
Who doesn't pine for that little neighborhood restaurant, tucked away on a side
street, where the lighting is subdued, the chef is French and the food is terrific?
Well, here it is. The fixed-price menu is perfectly calibrated to the small room,
and the chef knows in a quiet sort of way how to create excitement on the
plate. It might be an unfamiliar ingredient, or an unexpected flavor combina-
tion, like a purée of rose water and apricots which seems to coax extra richness
and depth from seared foie gras. Large ravioli stuffed with bits of sweetbread and
cepes also do the trick, each package containing a rich, meaty ooze. The rasp-
berry feuillete is a disarmingly simple-looking thing, two rectangular pastry
leaves, some fat fruit and a blob of white-chocolate caramel ganache, but the
pastry melts on the tongue, and the ganache is almost criminally delicious.
Price range: Three courses, $52. **Meals:** L, D. **Subway:** N, R to 23rd St.

Flor's Kitchen $25 & Under   VENEZUELAN
149 First Ave. (near 9th St.)   (212) 387-8949

Tiny, bright and colorful, this new Venezuelan restaurant offers many snacking foods like empanadas criollas, smooth, crisp pastries with fillings like savory shredded beef or pureed chicken. The arepas—corncakes with varied fillings—include a wonderful chicken and avocado salada. Two sauces—one made with avocado, lemon juice and oil; the second, a hot sauce—make dishes like chachapas (corn pancakes with ham and cheese) taste even better. Soups are superb, and desserts are rich and homespun. **Price range:** Entrees, $4–$9. **Meals:** L, D, LN. **Subway:** F to Second Ave.; L to First Ave.

The Four Seasons   ☆☆☆ $$$$ NEW AMERICAN
99 E. 52nd St. (between Park and Lexington Aves.)   (212) 754-9494

Designed by legendary architect Philip Johnson, The Four Seasons is a gracious reminder that restaurants can still be comfortable and relaxing. The Grill room is still the power lunch place for those who count in fashion, finance and publishing. At lunch the menu is straightforward: begin with a big baked potato, served with its own bottle of olive oil, followed by meaty crab cakes or the bunless burger with creamed spinach and crisp onions. The Pool Room is at its best with unfussy food like broiled dover sole or rack of lamb and the perfect steak tartare. Wherever you are seated, it is hard to eat at the Four Seasons without luxuriating in an extraordinary sense of privilege. **Price range:** Entrees, $34–$55. **Meals:** L, D. Closed Sun. **Subway:** E, F to Lexington Ave.; 6 to 51st St.

Frank $25 &   Under   ITALIAN
88 Second Ave. (near 5th St.)   (212) 420-0202

This sweet, unpretentious restaurant, with its crowded, ragtag dining room, has been packed from the moment it opened. Start with an order of insalata Caprese, ripe tomatoes and mozzarella di bufala, and you may forget the tight surroundings. Among the entrees, try the polpettone, a savory meatloaf, with a classic, slow-cooked gravy, and orecchiette with fennel and pecorino Toscano. If you go early, you can expect special touches, like a free plate of tiny potato croquettes, or a dish of olive oil flavored with orange rind with your bread. **Price range:** Entrees, $6.95–$14.95.Cash only. **Meals:** Br, L, D, LN. **Subway:** F to Second Ave.

Frank's   ☆ $$$ STEAKHOUSE
85 10th Ave. (at 15th St.)   (212) 243-1349

A paradise for carnivores and smokers. The bare brick walls and long bar announce this as a restaurant whose only desire is to serve big portions to hungry people. Three or four shrimp in a cocktail would probably provide enough protein for an average person: they are giant creatures of the sea, and absolutely delicious. The T-bone steak has the fine, funky flavor of meat that has been dry-aged for a long time and the steak fries are long and thick. The same family has been running Frank's since 1912; they will make you feel at home. **Price range:** Entrees, $18–$30. **Meals:** L, D. **Subway:** A, C, E to 14th St.; L to Eighth Ave.

Fresco By Scotto   ☆☆   **$$$**   ITALIAN
34 E. 52nd St. (between Park and Madison Aves.)   (212) 935-3434
At this political hangout in the middle of midtown, power lunchers eat grilled
pizza and great Tuscan food. Fresco is an entirely new take on the old Italian
mom-and-pop place. The heart and generosity of the red-sauce restaurants
have been blended with the sophistication of a new generation. The grilled
pizza is irresistible; so are most of the appetizers. But it's the pasta that you find
yourself remembering. All are served in staggering portions. Entrees are equally
massive. **Price range:** Avg. $45–$60 per person. **Meals:** L, D. Closed Sun.
Subway: 6 to 51st St.; E, F to Lexington Ave.

Funky Broome   **$25 & Under**   CHINESE
176 Mott St. (between Broome and Kenmare Sts.)   (212) 941-8628
From its odd name to its brightly colored interior, Funky Broome suggests youth
and energy rather than conformity. Though the menu is largely Cantonese and
Hong Kong, Funky Broome has stirred it up a bit with some Thai touches and
by making mini-woks centerpieces. Some of the dishes are unusual and good,
like plump and flavorful oysters stuffed with green onions and steamed in a red
wine sauce. Seafood dishes are excellent, and Funky Broome can breathe new
life into hoary old dishes like crisp and tender beef with broccoli. **Price range:**
Entrees, $6.95-$15.95. **Meals:** L, D, LN. **Subway:** 6 to Spring St.

Gabriela's   **$25 & Under**   MEXICAN
685 Amsterdam Ave. (at 93rd St.)   (212) 961-0574
311 Amsterdam Ave. (at 75th St.)
There really is a Gabriela, and she makes terrific, authentic Mexican dishes.
Taquitos al pastor, tiny corn tortillas topped with vinegary roast pork, pineapple
salsa and cilantro, are a wonderful Mexican street dish. Gabriela's pozole, the
traditional Mexican soup made with hominy, is an entire meal in itself, served
in a huge bowl with chunks of tender pork or chicken. Entrees all come with
tortillas so fragrant that the aroma of corn rises with the steam. Gabriela's also
offers superb desserts, including capirotada, a buttery bread pudding with lots of
honey. **Price range:** Entrees, $5.95–$14.95. **Meals:** B, L, D. **Subway:** 93rd St.:
1, 2, 3, 9 to 96th St.; 75th St.: 1, 2, 3, 9 to 72nd St.

Gabriel's ☆☆ **$$$**   ITALIAN
11 W. 60th St. (between Broadway and Columbus Ave.)   (212) 956-4600
This clubby and comfortable restaurant offers great big portions and fabulous
friendly service. Although the food is called Tuscan, it is far too American for
that, too original. The dish on almost every table is an earthy and seductive
buckwheat polenta. None of the pastas are ordinary, either. The real winner
here is homemade gnocchi, little dumplings so light they float into your mouth
and down your throat. Among the entrees, the best dish is the sea bass cooked
in a terra cotta casserole. Desserts, with the exception of the wonderful sorbets
and gelatos, are not very exciting. **Price range:** Entrees, $18–$32. **Meals:** L, D.
Closed Sun. **Subway:** A, B, C, D, E, 1, 9 to 59th St.

Gennaro $25 & Under   ITALIAN/MEDITERRANEAN
665 Amsterdam Ave. (near 93rd St.)   (212) 665-5348
This tiny, simply decorated Italian restaurant is one of the best things to happen
to the Upper West Side in years, serving wonderful dishes like an awesome osso
bucco and terrific pastas. Appetizer specials are satisfying, like ribbolita, the
classic Tuscan vegetable and bean soup. Cornish hen roasted with lemon is also
excellent. Gennaro serves its own pear tart, flaky and delicious, and a rich flour-
less chocolate cake. **Price range:** Entrees, $8.50–$14.95. Cash only. **Meals:** D.
Subway: 1, 2, 3, 9 to 96th St.

Good $25 & Under   LATIN AMERICAN
89 Greenwich Ave. (at Bank St.)   (212) 691-8080
It's possible to eat unusually, eclectically and very well here. Crisp peanut
chicken is a welcome old dish, while grilled calamari, a newcomer, takes its cue
from Asia, arriving in a lime-and-mint dressing. Also good are the grilled flank
steak with parsley-garlic sauce and sauteed rock shrimp, flavored with garlic
and served over gloriously mushy grits with corn relish. The service is warm
and professional. The signature dessert, house-made doughnuts, are rather dry
and tasteless, although the demitasse of Oaxacan chocolate served with them
is delicious. **Price range:** Entrees, $10–$17. **Meals:** L, D. Closed Mon. **Subway:**
1, 2, 3, 9 to 14th St.

Good World Bar and Grill $25 & Under   SCANDINAVIAN
3 Orchard St. (at Division St.)   (212) 925-9975
Good World Bar and Grill beckons because it's a bar in an old barbershop near
Chinatown that serves Scandinavian food. It offers a spirit of adventure, a
departure from the routine, that makes Good World's world a good world
indeed. Basic dishes like Swedish meatballs and potato pancakes can be unpredictable; Good World is on far firmer ground with seafood. Skagen is shrimp
with créme fraîche and dill, served on toast. It's a nice prelude for the tender
and tasty sautéed squid, or the fabulous fish soup, a bisque that tastes like the
essence of the sea. **Price range:** Medium and large plates, $8 to $16. **Meals:** D,
LN. **Subway:** F to East Broadway.

Goody's   ☆ $ CHINESE
1 East Broadway (at Chatham Sq.)   (212) 577-2922
Goody's pride is the crab meat version of soup dumplings, xiao long bao,
tinted pink by the seafood that glows through the sheer, silky skin. But there
are other unusual dishes, like fabulous turnip pastries, yellowfish fingers in
seaweed batter, and braised pork shoulder, a kind of candied meat. This dish is
so rich that it must be eaten in small bites. Goody's kitchen also works magic
with bean curd, mixed with crab meat so it becomes rich and delicious. **Price
range:** $15–$20. **Meals:** L, D. **Subway:** J, M, N, Q, R, W, Z, 6 to Canal St.

Gotham Bar and Grill   ☆☆☆   **$$$$**   NEW AMERICAN
12 E. 12th St. (between Fifth and University Pl.)   (212) 620-4020
Gotham Bar and Grill is a cheerful, welcoming restaurant in an open, high-
ceilinged room with a lively bar along one side. Waiters take their cues from
the customer—anticipating their every wish and making diners feel remarkably well cared for. And then there's the food. The chef works with an architecture of flavor, composing his dishes so that each element contributes something vital. His food seems modern but is almost classic in its balance. His
signature dish is seafood salad, a spiral of scallops, squid, octopus, lobster and
avocado that swirls onto the plate like a mini-tornado. Main courses are more
straightforward, like rosy slices of duck breast set off by a single caramelized
endive and a sweet potato purée. Desserts, like the wonderful chocolate cake,
are intense and very American. **Price range:** Entrees, $28–$38. **Meals:** L, D.
Subway: F, L, N, Q, R, W, 4, 5, 6 to 14th St.

Gradisca   **$25 & Under**   ITALIAN
126 W. 13th St. (between Sixth and Seventh Aves.)   (212) 691-4886
Gradisca epitomizes the local trattoria, downtown style. The dining room is rustic, but the waiters conform to a more modern stereotype: young, hip and lanky
in tight black T-shirts. The menu offers simple, delicious flavors, like piadinas,
round, unleavened flatbreads, cooked on a griddle and then stuffed with things
like prosciutto and fresh mozzarella (a marvelously nutty combination), or
spinach and pecorino. There are two superb main courses: sliced leg of lamb in a
red wine sauce, and a big pork chop under a cloud of crisp leeks. Dessert standouts include a deliciously dense, bittersweet chocolate torte and a satisfying
amaretto semifreddo. **Price range:** Entrees, $12–$20. Cash only. **Meals:** D.
Subway: F, 1, 2, 3, 9 to 14th St.

Gramercy Tavern   ☆☆☆   **$$$$**   NEW AMERICAN
42 E. 20th St. (between Broadway and Park Ave. South)   (212) 477-0777
The large and lively tavern has redefined grand dining in New York. Chef Tom
Colicchio cooks with extraordinary confidence, creating dishes characterized by
bold flavors and unusual harmonies. Marinated hamachi is brushed with lemon
and olive oil; roast beets and herbs are scattered across the top. Salmon is baked
in salt until the flesh has the texture of velvet. A silky, just-cooked breast of
chicken with truffles stuffed under the skin in a lively broth perfumed with rosemary is chicken soup raised to an entirely new level. To experience Mr. Colicchio's cooking at its best, consider the chef's extraordinary market menu. It is
expensive, but perfect for special occasions. For a less expensive alternative, the
handsome bar in front offers a casual but excellent menu. **Price range:** Prix-fixe
and tasting menus, $65–$90. **Meals:** L, D. **Subway:** N, R, 6 to 23rd St.

Grand Sichuan   **$25 & Under**   CHINESE
229 Ninth Ave. (at 24th St.)   (212) 620-5200
The owner of this terrific restaurant hands out a 27-page pamphlet that explains
five Chinese regional cuisines and describes dozens of dishes the restaurant

serves. The eating is as interesting as the reading, with wonderful dishes like sour stringbeans with minced pork and tea-smoked duck. While Sichuan food is indeed spicy, that is only part of the story, as you see when you taste a fabulous cold dish like sliced conch with wild pepper sauce, coated with ground Sichuan peppercorns, which are not hot but bright, effervescent and almost refreshing. **Price range:** Entrees, $5.95–$16.95. **Meals:** L, D. **Subway:** C, E to 23rd St.

Grange Hall $25 & Under   AMERICAN
50 Commerce St. (at Barrow St.)   (212) 924-5246
Grange Hall celebrates Depression-era American food of the Midwest with flair, from fat little loaves of white bread to succotash, pork chops and lake fish. The food is usually pretty good, the décor is inspiring and the all-American wine and beer list is appealing. **Price range:** Entrees, $10.50–$21. AE only. **Meals:** Br, L, D. **Subway:** A, C, E, F, S to W. 4th St.

Grill Room   ☆☆ $$$ NEW AMERICAN/SEAFOOD
2 World Financial Center   (212) 945-9400
Wall Street has changed, and the Grill Room means to feed modern traders with up-to-date appetites. The menu is straightforward American fare with no exotic ingredients. Meals begin with warm biscuits so rich and crumbly they're impossible to stop eating. Many of the first courses are spectacular. Crab cakes wrapped into a spring roll are light and perfectly right. The dense chowder is the essence of corn, beautifully swirled with vegetable purees. The American theme continues with the main courses, which are heavy on protein. Of all the meats, pot-roasted short ribs are the best. The desserts are rich and wonderful. **Price range:** Entrees, $15–$29. **Meals:** L, D. **Subway:** N, R, 1, 9 to Cortlandt St.

Guastavino's   ☆☆ $$$$ ENGLISH/FRENCH
409 E. 59th St. (between First and York Aves.)   (212) 980-2455
This dazzling transformation of the Queensboro Bridge vaults gives New Yorkers a glimpse of a swaggering international restaurant style where the scenes are loud, lively and up to the minute, and the food often runs second to the design. Guastavino's fits the pattern. The raw, almost brutal granite blocks that make up the caissons of the bridge have been left exposed. But the overall design is as sleek and international as the Concorde. It's not so much a restaurant as an opportunity to live, for two or three hours, a certain mood, and a certain sense of style, that suits every time zone and speaks every language. A long, low-slung bar on the main level pulls a large Upper East Side crowd. Guastavino Restaurant, on the first floor, is a 300-seat brasserie, clamorous and casual, with a glorious brasserie-style shellfish display in front of the kitchen. Up a curved marble staircase, the more formal and intimate Club Guastavino, which seats 100, hangs over the first floor like a giant balcony. Guastavino's two kitchens feed a lot of people out there, and they do a more than respectable job. At its best, these are well-conceived, well-executed dishes that really can compete with the surroundings. **Price range:** Guastavino

Restaurant: $14–$30. Club Guastavino: Dinner, three courses, $65. **Meals:** L, D. **Subway:** 4, 5, 6 to 59th St.; N, R to Lexington Ave.

Gus's Figs Bistro and Bar $25 & Under   MEDITERRANEAN
250 W. 27th St. (between Seventh and Eighth Aves.)   (212) 352-8822
This restaurant captures the dreamy, generous, sun-soaked aura that makes the Mediterranean so endlessly appealing. The chef excels at blending flavors and textures in main courses like moist, flavorful chicken, braised in a clay pot and served over creamy polenta. Top dishes include tender pieces of lamb served over a soft bread pudding made savory with goat cheese and pine nuts and sweetened with figs; and pan-roasted cod with grilled leeks, orange sections and pomegranate vinaigrette. **Price range:** Entrees, $13–$19.50.
Meals: L, D, LN. **Subway:** C, E, 1, 9 to 28th St.

The Half King $25 & Under   PUB/AMERICAN
505 W. 23rd St. (between 10th and 11th Aves.)   (212) 462-4300
Owner by Sebastian Junger, author of *The Perfect Storm*, this unconventional writers' bar serves Irish pub grub, skillfully elevated from its proletarian moorings while retaining its heartiness and simplicity. Excellent starters include a light cake constructed of potatoes and goat cheese, wrapped in excellent smoked salmon. Main courses include a superbly flavorful pork roast and a surprisingly delicate fillet of sole. The shepherd's pie, made with chopped beef, is ample and excellent. Desserts are good and rustic, like a rough-hewn berry, peach and apple crumble. A small garden in the rear is pleasant at lunch or at breakfast. **Price range:** Entrees, $9–$16. **Meals:** B, L, D.
Subway: C, E to 23rd St.

Han Bat $25 & Under   KOREAN
53 W. 35th St. (between Fifth and Sixth Aves.)   (212) 629-5588
This spare, clean, round-the-clock restaurant specializes in the country dishes of southern Korea. Typical Korean dishes, like scallion and seafood pancakes, fiery stir-fried baby octopus and bibimbab, are all excellent. Meals here are served family style and include several little appetizers; almost all dishes are served with rice and crocks of the rich beef soup, full of noodles and scallions.
Price range: Entrees, $6.95–$15.95. **Meals:** L, D. Open 24 hours.
Subway: B, D, F, N, Q, R, S, W to 34th St.

Hangawi ☆☆ $$ KOREAN/VEGETARIAN
12 E. 32nd St. (between Fifth and Madison Aves.)   (212) 213-0077
Hangawi leaves you feeling cleansed and refreshed, as if you had come from a spa instead of a vegetarian Korean restaurant. Eating in this calm, elegant space with its smooth wooden bowls and heavy ceramic cups is utterly peaceful. Diners remove their shoes on entering and sit at low tables with their feet dangling comfortably into the sunken space beneath them. They are surrounded by unearthly Korean music, wonderful objects and people who move with deliberate grace. Many of the exotic greens, porridges and mountain roots on the menu can be sampled by ordering the emperor's meal, which

includes a tray of nine kinds of mountain greens surrounded by 10 side dishes.
Price range: Entrees, $14.95–$24.95. **Meals:** L, D. **Subway:** 6 to 33rd St.

Hatsuhana   ☆☆ $$$ JAPANESE/SUSHI
17 E. 48th St. (between Fifth and Madison Aves.)   (212) 355-3345
237 Park Ave. (at 46th St.)   (212) 661-3400
Of all the city's sushi bars, Hatsuhana is the one that best bridges the gap
between East and West. It is a comfortable and welcoming restaurant where you
can depend on being served high-quality sushi whether you speak Japanese or
not. Real connoisseurs sit at the downstairs sushi bar and enjoy extraordinary
chu toro, tuna that is richer than maguro but less rich than toro, and ika uni,
pure white squid cut into long strips as thin as spaghetti. The quality of the
cooked food is excellent, too. The Park Avenue location is not nearly as good as
the 48th Street location. **Price range:** Avg. entree, $30. **Meals:** L, D. Closed
Sun. **Subway:** S, 4, 5, 6, 7 to 42nd St.

Havana NY $25 & Under   LATIN AMERICAN
27 W. 38th St. (between Fifth and Sixth Aves.)   (212) 944-0990
There's little not to like about this bustling Cuban restaurant, a lunchtime hot
spot serving tasty, inexpensive food in pleasant surroundings. The food is typically robust, flavored with lusty doses of garlic and lime, yet it can be delicate,
too, as in an octopus salad, which is marinated in citrus until tender like a
ceviche. Chilean sea bass, is moist and subtly flavored, not the sort of dish that
would succeed in an assembly-line kitchen, and grilled skirt steak is excellent.
All the main courses are enormous, served with rice, beans and sweet plantains—so appetizers are usually unnecessary. Service is swift and likable. **Price
range:** Entrees, $8.95–$12.95. **Meals:** L, D. Closed Sat., Sun. **Subway:** B, D, F,
N, Q, R, S, W to 34th St.

Heartbeat   ☆☆ $$$ NEW AMERICAN
149 E. 49th St. (at Lexington Ave.)   (212) 407-2900
New York's hippest spa food brings models to mingle with moguls in a slick setting. You could describe Heartbeat that way, but it would be doing the restaurant
a disservice; this is a very comfortable, crowded and surprisingly quiet room with
good service and good food. This approach works best when the food is simply
left alone. Try the simple grills, the good meats and the Japanese-accented
dishes. **Price range:** Entrees, $18–$30. **Meals:** B, Br, L, D. **Subway:** 6 to 51st
St.; E, F to Lexington Ave.

Hell's Kitchen $25 & Under   MEXICAN
679 Ninth Ave. (near 47th St.)   (212) 977-1588
This restaurant makes creative use of Mexican flavorings and cooking techniques, adding ingredients and dishes from the global palette of contemporary
American cooking. Head directly for the interpretations of Mexican dishes. The
appetizer of tuna tostadas is brilliant. Part of the menu is devoted to quesadillas;
in size, they are like small main courses; in spirit, they succeed because they
retain their Mexican identity even with creative enhancements. The best main

course is a pork loin flavored with chili. For dessert try the intense fruit sorbets, served over fruit with a surprising touch of chili. The loud music and hopping bar suggest that conversations will be difficult, but once you sit down the acoustics are surprisingly good. **Price range:** Entrees, $13—$18. **Meals:** D, LN. **Subway:** C, E to 50th St.

Henry's Evergreen $25 & Under   CHINESE
1288 First Ave. (near 70th St.)   (212) 744-3266
This bright and appealing restaurant follows the decorating scheme of many other Chinese restaurants, but adds a surprising wine list strong in California reds, midlevel zinfandels, pinot noirs and whites that go brilliantly with the food. For the most part, the menu will not surprise you but many of the dishes are fresh and appealing. The real excitement is discovering how good the wine and food combinations can be. Dim sum and appetizers tend to be the best part of Henry's menu; main courses are much less consistent. **Price range:** Entrees, $7.95–$27.50. **Meals:** L, D. **Subway:** 6 to 68th St.

Hog Pit $25 & Under   SOUTHERN
22 Ninth Ave. (at 13th St.)   (212) 604-0092
Nothing remarkable about this small bar in the meat-packing district, except that the kitchen unexpectedly turns out fine Southern food. The baby back ribs are terrific, meaty, and bathed in a peppery sauce sweetened by molasses and brown sugar. Hush puppies are the real thing, and the tart fried green tomatoes come with a crisp, greaseless cornmeal crust. The staff is friendly, the jukebox is loud, the room is smoky and the beer is cold. **Price range:** Entrees, $6.25–$12.95. **Meals:** D, LN. Closed Mon. **Subway:** A, C, E to 14th St.; L to Eighth Ave.

Holy Basil $25 & Under   THAI
149 Second Ave. (between 9th and 10th Sts.)   (212) 460-5557
This is one of the best Thai restaurants in the city, turning out highly spiced, beautifully balanced dishes like green papaya salad, elegant curries and delicious noodles. The dining room looks more like a beautiful church than a restaurant, jazz usually plays in the background and the wine list offers terrific choices. **Price range:** Entrees, $8–$16. **Meals:** D, LN. **Subway:** F to Second Ave.; L to First or Third Ave.

Honmura An   ☆☆☆ $$$ JAPANESE/NOODLES
170 Mercer St. (between Houston and Prince Sts.)   (212) 334-5253
Making the buckwheat noodles known as soba is not easy, but the soba chefs at Honmura An have clearly put in their time—the soba in this spare, soothing space is wonderful and worth the high price. Many appetizers, as well as good tempura, are worth trying here, but nothing is remotely on a par with the noodles. To appreciate how fine they are, you must eat them cold. The noodles are earthy and elastic, and when you dip them into the briny bowl of dashi (dipping sauce), land and sea come, briefly, together. Honmura An also makes excellent

udon, fat wheat noodles. Served hot, in the dish called nabeyaki, they virtually redefine the dish. **Price range:** entrees, $13–$22. **Meals:** L, D. Closed Mon. **Subway:** N, R to Prince St.; F, S to Broadway–Lafayette St.

Hudson River Club ☆☆ **$$$$**   NEW AMERICAN
250 Vesey St., 4 World Financial Center   (212) 786-1500
Note: This restaurant suffered substantial damage during the September 11, 2001 plane crashes that destroyed the World Trade Center. It may not be operational by the time you plan your visit.

This very sedate, very expensive restaurant has upscale American food, a dazzling view of the river, a largely male clientele and a great bar. Despite its spectacular setting, Hudson River Club is not a romantic restaurant. Everything about the place makes it a perfect place for a business meeting. It is also one of the few waterfront restaurants in which seafood is not the main draw. The kitchen makes some delicious hearty stews. Or try one of the dishes from the game menu. **Price range:** Entrees, $29–$36. **Meals:** Br, L, D. **Subway:** N, R, 1, 9 to Cortlandt St.

Icon ☆☆ **$$**   NEW AMERICAN
130 E. 39th St. (between Lexington and Park Aves.)   (212) 592-8888
Icon has a mildly lurid décor and a lighting philosophy perfectly designed for illegal trysts and furtive meetings. It is attached to the W Court Hotel, ensuring a steady flow of youngish, stylish diners. Visually, it is soothing to the nerves. Aurally, it's touch and go. As the evening progresses, a thumping rock soundtrack forces diners to shout across the table, and the noise from Wet Bar across the lobby becomes intrusive. The food at Icon is better than the setting might suggest. Desserts are not flashy; quiet good taste is more the style. **Price range:** Entrees, $19–$25. **Meals:** B, Br, L, D. **Subway:** S, 4, 5, 6, 7 to 42nd St.

Il Mulino **$$$$**   ITALIAN
86 W. 3rd St. (between Sullivan and Thompson Sts.)   (212) 673-3783
Big portions, long waits, a halcyon atmosphere. No wonder New Yorkers are so enthralled with this garlic haven. While the portions are large, so are the prices. Dinner might begin with a dish of shrimp fricassee with garlic; bresaola of beef served over mixed greens tossed in a well-seasoned vinaigrette, or aromatic baked clams oreganato. The pasta roster includes fettuccine Alfredo; spaghettini in a robust Bolognese sauce; trenette tossed in pesto sauce; and capellini all'arrabbiata, or in a spicy tomato sauce. The menu carries a dozen veal preparations, along with beef tenderloin in a shallot, white wine and sage sauce; and broiled sirloin. **Price range:** Entrees, $24 and up. **Meals:** L, D, LN. Closed Sun. **Subway:** A, C, E, F, S to W. 4th St.

Ilo ☆☆☆ **$$$$**   NEW AMERICAN
Bryant Park Hotel, 40 W. 40th St. (between Fifth and Sixth Aves.)
                                                           (212) 642-2255
At Ilo, a Finnish word meaning something like "bliss," Chef Rick Laakkonen creates complex dishes that seem simple. He knows how to coax pure flavors

from his ingredients, and how to keep those flavors clear and distinct. Grilled quail, as meaty and tender as any in recent memory, stand out heroically from their busy tableau, where a feather-light cheese flan is surrounded by spicy minced peppers, chilies, coriander and lime. Ilo's rabbit is done country style, pan-roasted with olives and accented with oregano and preserved lemon. Tasting menu portions are mercifully calibrated to a normal appetite. Don't miss the chilled apricot soup, a regular on the dessert menu. And it's worth waving over the sommelier, because the 250 or so wines on the list include many unusual grapes and lesser known regions. **Price range:** Entrees $26–$38; beef tasting menu, $85 ($120 with wines); seven-course vegetarian tasting menu, $65; eight-course chef's tasting menu, $110 ($165 with wines). **Meals:** L, D. **Subway:** B, D, F, S to 42nd St.

Il Valentino   ☆☆ $ $ ITALIAN

Sutton Hotel, 330 E. 56th St. (between First and Second Aves.) (212) 355-0001
In a city where purely pleasant restaurants have become increasingly rare, Il Valentino feels like an oasis. The food is reliable, you don't have to wait for your table and you know you will be able to hear your friends when they talk. The timbered ceiling and terra cotta floor give the room a cool rustic feeling, and the food is simple, tasty Tuscan fare. The artichoke salad is delicious, and the Caesar salad impressive. But it is the pastas that really shine. Marinated grilled lamb chops in a mustard seed sauce and osso buco are also excellent. **Price range:** entrees, $16–$25. **Meals:** L, D. **Subway:** 4, 5, 6 to 59th St.; N, R to Lexington Ave.

'ino $25 & Under   ITALIAN/SANDWICHES

21 Bedford St. (between Sixth Ave. and Downing St.)   (212) 989-5769
This inviting little Italian sandwich shop and wine bar offers intensely satisfying variations on three types of sandwich: panini, sandwiches made with crusty toasted ciabatta; tramezzini, made with untoasted white bread, crusts removed and cut into triangles, and bruschetta, in which ingredients are simply placed atop a slice of toasted bread. One dish that doesn't fall into any category but is nonetheless wonderful is truffled egg toast, a soft cooked egg served on top of toasted ciabatta with sliced asparagus and drizzled with truffle oil. It's like warm, delicious baby food. **Price range:** Entrees, $2–$10. Cash only. **Meals:** B, Br, L, D. **Subway:** 1, 9 to Houston St.

Inside $25 & Under   NEW AMERICAN

9 Jones St. (between 4th and Bleecker Sts.)   (212) 229-9999
The handsome wood bar in front and the professional greeting bespeak the comfort of a more expensive restaurant, yet the almost bare white walls make the dining room feel airy and streamlined. With dishes based on no more than three seasonal and simple ingredients, Inside can keep prices gentle. The best appetizer is a handful of shrimp with a light, crisp salt-and-pepper crust, topped with a tangy grapefruit confit. Almost as good is a salad of cubed beets, endive and peanuts, a perfect blend of sweet, bitter and crunchy. Main courses are simi-

larly streamlined. Newport steak is thick and beefy, and tender braised lamb with cinnamon and olives achieves an almost Moroccan balance of savory and sweet. For dessert, try the panna cotta or a steamed chocolate pudding with rhubarb. **Price range:** Entrees, $13–$18. **Meals:** Br, D. **Subway:** 6 to Bleecker St.

Irving on Irving $25 & Under   NEW AMERICAN
52 Irving Pl. (at 17th St.)   (212) 358-1300

This plainly-named little corner restaurant offers counter service for breakfast and lunch. By night, waiters and waitresses come out, and it becomes a real restaurant. The chef has put together a menu of uncomplicated ingredients, prepared simply. Appetizers show off their humble origins, like garlicky peasant sausage on a bed of warm, vinegary lentils, and excellent codfish cakes, savory, meaty and crisp outside. While main courses are not exactly made of humble ingredients, they are resolutely plain, with the possible exception of the peppery grilled swordfish, which is finely textured and full of flavor. The best dessert is the cinnamon doughnuts, made to order and served hot and airy in a brown lunch bag. **Price range:** Entrees, $10.50–$16.75. **Meals:** B, L, D. **Subway:** L, N, Q, R, W, 4, 5, 6 to 14th St.

Island Spice $25 & Under   CARIBBEAN
402 W. 44th St. (between Ninth and 10th Aves.)   (212) 765-1737

This little storefront offers refined Caribbean cooking to a steady stream of show business types. Little beef patties, gently spiced bits of ground beef encased in half-moons of flaky dough, are a savory way to begin, and earthy red bean soup has a long, lingering, slightly smoky flavor. Island Spice's jerk barbecue (pork or chicken) is excellent. Island Spice serves beer and wine as well as Caribbean concoctions like sorrell, a tart, refreshing deep-red beverage made from hibiscus. **Price range:** Entrees, $8.95–$21.95. **Meals:** L, D. **Subway:** A, C, E to 42nd St.

Isola $25 & Under   ITALIAN
485 Columbus Ave. (between 83rd and 84th Sts.)   (212) 362-7400

When Isola is crowded, its dining room, full of hard surfaces, can be unbearably loud, but the restaurant offers some of the best Italian food on the Upper West Side, with lively pastas like spaghetti in a purée of black olives and oregano, and fettuccine with crumbled sausages and porcini mushrooms. The wine list is nicely chosen. **Price range:** Entrees, $9.95–$18. **Meals:** Br, L, D. **Subway:** B, C to 81st St.

I Trulli   ☆☆ $$$ ITALIAN
122 E. 27th St. (between Lexington Ave. and Park Ave. South)   (212) 481-7372

This is New York City's best and most attractive restaurant dedicated to the cooking of Apulia. It serves interesting, unusual food in an understated room that is both elegant and warm; there is also a beautiful garden for outdoor dining. The rustic food from Italy's heel does not have the subtle charm of northern Italian food or the tomato-and-garlic heartiness of Neapolitan cuisine. The menu relies on bitter greens (arugula, dandelions, broccoli rape) and many foods that Americans rarely eat. The pastas have a basic earthy quality; orechi-

ette are a house staple made by the owner. **Price range:** Entrees, $18–$32.
Meals: L, D. Closed Sun. **Subway:** 6 to 28th St.

Jack Rose ☆ $$$ NEW AMERICAN/STEAKHOUSE
771 Eighth Ave. (at 47th St.)   (212) 247-7518
Jack Rose is an artful exercise in nostalgia, an all-American joint that specializes in seafood, steaks, chops and no funny stuff. Although Jack Rose reserves a
lot of room on the menu for steaks, they make a pretty feeble impression on the
palate. But the kitchen can still win you over. It might be the oysters Rockefeller, topped with lovely fresh cress and piqued with just the right touch of
Pernod, or it could be a plump, moist roasted chicken. The best desserts are
bread pudding and crème brûlée. **Price range:** Entrees, $10.95—$28.50.
Meals: L, D. **Subway:** C, E to 50th St.

Jane ☆ $$ NEW AMERICAN/BISTRO
100 W. Houston St. (at Thompson St.)   (212) 254-7000
Jane is a restaurant with the soul of a cafe. It sets itself modest goals, and for the
most part it delivers, at a fair price. Grease-free fried clams come with a hot-
cold accompaniment of sweet-corn "dip," a cool, creamy slush that nicely offsets
a pungent rice-wine vinegar dipping sauce steeped in habañero peppers. Entrees
do not, on balance, live up to the appetizers. An exception is the dark, richly
gamy hanger steak, swimming in a red wine sauce and onion marmalade. At
dessert time the bias is toward American flavors, but with a little twist here and
there, like the lemon-thyme sauce that brightens a dense cylinder-shaped
cheesecake. **Price range:** Entrees, $17–$21. **Meals:** D. **Subway:** C, E to Spring
St.; N, R to Prince St.; F, S to Broadway–Lafayette St.

Jean Claude $25 & Under   BISTRO/FRENCH
137 Sullivan St. (between Prince and Houston Sts.)   (212) 475-9232
The dining room is authentically Parisian, with the scent of Gitanes and the
sound of French in the air. For these low prices you don't expect to find appetizers like seared sea scallops with roasted beets or main courses like roasted monkfish with savoy cabbage, olives and onions. **Price range:** Entrees, $12–$16.
Cash only. **Meals:** D. **Subway:** C, E to Spring St.; N, R to Prince St.; F, S to
Broadway–Lafayette St.

Jean Georges ☆☆☆☆ $$$$ NEW AMERICAN
Trump Hotel, 1 Central Park West (at 60th St.)   (212) 299-3900
Chef and co-owner Jean-Georges Vongerichten has created an entirely new
kind of four-star restaurant. He has examined all the details that make dining
luxurious, and refined them for an American audience. Most important, he has
returned the focus to the food. And he is at the top of his form. The austerity of
the design of the restaurant, on Central Park West, also puts the focus on food.
And while some restaurants are more concerned with who is in the room than
what is on the plate, the people at Jean Georges neither fawn nor intimidate.
This is no celebrity restaurant; all over the dining room, waiters bend over the

food, carving or pouring, intent only on their guests' pleasure.
Price range: Prix-fixe and tasting menus, $45-$115. **Meals:** L, D. Closed Sun.
Subway: A, B, C, D, 1, 9 to 59th St.

Jewel Bako $25 & Under   SUSHI
239 E. 5th St. (between Second and Third Aves.)   (212) 979-1012
The first taste at Jewel Bako, a sparkling new Japanese restaurant in the East
Village, will leave no doubt that here is great sushi. Add the welcoming charm
of the owners and the warmth of the chef, and you come close to the ideal for a
neighborhood sushi bar. The chef focuses on the freshest and best ingredients;
order à la carte, allowing him to guide you. Each piece of sushi seems an almost
perfect unit of rice and fish, often with a dot of complementary flavoring, like
an almost smoky vinegar jelly, a touch of hot chili or a breezy hint of shiso.
There is a refreshing dessert of stewed mission figs, served cool in a sweetened
white wine and shiso broth. **Price range:** Sushi and sashimi selections,
$12–$29; à la carte, $3–$4.50 a piece; some specials higher.
Meals: D / Closed Sun. **Subway:** F to Second Ave.

Joe Allen $$ NEW AMERICAN
326 W. 46th St. (between Eighth and Ninth Aves.)   (212) 581-6464
Chili and celebrities in the heart of Broadway. The food's not great, but it's not
expensive either. If you're looking for safe, unpretentious American food in the
high-rent Restaurant Row, this is the place. You need to reserve both before and
after the theater. **Price range:** Entrees, $9–$19.50. **Meals:** Br, L, D. **Subway:** A,
C, E to 42nd St.

Joe's Shanghai   ☆☆ $ CHINESE
24 W. 56th St. (between Fifth and Sixth Aves.)   (212) 333-3868
9 Pell St. (between Mott St. and Bowery)   (212) 233-8888
These spartan restaurants serve awesome xiao lung bao—Shanghai soup
dumplings, modestly listed on the menu as "steamed buns". The chef has per-
fected the art of wrapping hot liquid in pastry: the filling is rich, light and swimming in hot soup. Everybody orders them, but there are many other wonderful
dishes, including smoked fish, strongly flavored with star anise, vegetarian
duck, thin sheets of braised tofu folded like skin over mushrooms, and drunken
crabs, raw marinated blue crabs with a musty, fruity flavor that is powerful and
unforgettable. **Price range:** A la carte $9.50 and up. **Meals:** L, D. **Subway:**
Downtown: J, M, N, Q, R, Z, 6 to Canal St. Midtown: N, R, W to Fifth Ave.

Jo Jo   ☆☆☆ $$$$ FRENCH
160 E. 64th St. (between Lexington and Third Aves.)   (212) 223-5656
Jo Jo's alluring décor, in a handsome townhouse setting, is the perfect background for Jean Georges Vongerichten's sophisticated, beguiling cuisine. The
restaurant is not new, but the dishes, which change frequently, still taste fresh
and exciting. And though Mr. Vongerichten made his reputation with light

dishes and Asian accents, his Alsatian roots show up from time to time. **Price range:** Entrees, $19–$36. **Meals:** L, D. Closed Sun. **Subway:** 6 to 68th St.; N, R to Lexington Ave.

Josie's $25 & Under   NEW AMERICAN
300 Amsterdam Ave. (at 74th St.)   (212) 769-1212
565 Third Ave. (at 37th St.)   (212) 490-1558
Much of the food at Josie's is billed as organically raised; the surprise is that so much of the food is so good, with highlights like light potato dumplings served in a lively tomato coulis spiked with chipotle pepper, ravioli stuffed with sweet potato purée, superb grilled tuna with a wasabi glaze and wonderful gazpacho. Josie's offers many reasonably priced wines, some organic beers and freshly squeezed juices, including tart blueberry lemonade. Even the organic hot dogs are good. **Price range:** Entrees, $9.50–$16. **Meals:** L, D, LN. **Subway:** 1, 2, 3, 9 to 72nd St.; 6 to 33rd St., S, 4, 5, 6, 7 to 42nd St.

Jubilee $25 & Under   FRENCH
347 E. 54th St. (between First and Second Aves.)   (212) 888-3569
Small, crowded and exuberant, this is a great East Side find. It offers simple and good bistro food, like steak frites and roast chicken. The restaurant makes something of a specialty of mussels, offering them in five guises with terrific french fries or a green salad, all for reasonable prices. **Price range:** Entrees, $13.50–$24. **Meals:** L, D. **Subway:** E, F to Lexington Ave.; 6 to 51st St.

Judson Grill   ☆☆☆ $$$$ NEW AMERICAN
152 W. 52nd St. (bet Sixth and Seventh Aves.)   (212) 582-5252
Judson Grill is big, bright and utterly urban, a mature restaurant with none of the irritating glitches of a new establishment. Its lighting is right, they've got the service down pat, and the wine list has had time to develop its own quirky personality. In the skillful hands of the chef, Bill Telepan, the food is unassuming but extremely eloquent, so roaring with flavor that the minute you finish one bite you instantly want another. The organically grown meats are especially impressive. Desserts include the restaurant's Jack Daniel's ice cream soda and its chocolate sampler. **Price range:** Entrees, $22–$35. **Meals:** L, D. Closed Sun. **Subway:** 1, 9 to 50th St.; N, R to 49th St.

Kang Suh   ☆☆ $$ KOREAN
1250 Broadway (at 32nd St.)   (212) 564-6845
This is the most accessible of the Korean restaurants in the small Koreatown locally known as Sam Ship Iga (32nd St.). Downstairs is a sushi bar, upstairs a huge menu of Korean dishes. Two things make this special: it's open 24 hours and you can grill your own food over live charcoal at the table. **Price range:** Entrees, $6.99–$30. **Meals:** Open 24 hours. **Subway:** B, D, F, N, Q, S, R to 34th St.

Katsu-Hama $25 & Under   JAPANESE
11 E. 47th St. (between Madison and Fifth Aves.)   (212) 758-5909
Katsu-Hama doesn't offer much in the way of atmosphere or creature comforts,

but it is an authentic Japanese experience. To enter it, you need to walk through a takeout sushi restaurant (Sushi-Tei) and pass through a curtain divider; there, you encounter an almost entirely Japanese crowd who've come for the restaurant's specialty: tonkatsu, or deep-fried pork cutlets. The best variation is unadorned, dipped into a special condiment that resembles freshly made Worcestershire sauce blended with sesame seeds. **Price range:** $8.95–$13.95, including soup and rice. **Meals:** L, D. **Subway:** S, 4, 5, 6, 7 to 42nd St.

Katz's Deli $ DELI
205 E. Houston St. (at Ludlow St.)   (212) 254-2246
A wonderful Lower East Side artifact and originator of the World War II slogan, "Send a salami to your boy in the Army." It is one of the very few delis that still carves pastrami and corned beef by hand, which makes for delicious sandwiches. **Price range:** Entrees, $5–$10.95. **Meals:** B, Br, L, D, LN.
Subway: F to Second Ave.

Komodo $25 & Under   JAPANESE/LATIN AMERICAN
186 Ave. A (between 11th and 12th Sts.)   (212) 529-2658
With a shared taste for ingredients like cilantro, chilies and rice, Mexico and Asia have more grounds for compatibility than most. Komodo's small storefront dining room is clean, simple and cool; the food never seems forced or needlessly flamboyant. A simple appetizer like beef satay is rubbed with ground ancho chilies and served with peanut sauce, a combination that seems effortlessly natural. Even better are Asian guacamole rolls, flavored with ginger and wasabi and combined with sweet potato and cumin. Grilled sirloin topped with oysters tempura and crisp fried leeks is excellent, and good dessert choices include a rich chocolate pot de créme flavored with black litchi tea, and an apple empanada. **Price range:** Entrees, $10–$16. **Meals:** D. Closed Mon. **Subway:** L to First Ave.

Kori $25 & Under   KOREAN
253 Church St. (near Leonard St.)   (212) 334-0908
Kori succeeds in merging East and West, old and new. It seems a wholly personal expression of its owner and chef, Kori Kim: up-to-date and appealing to Americans but tied to Korean traditions. She learned to cook in a big, traditional Korean family in Seoul, but it is hard to imagine Ms. Kim serving food at home as polished as her dubu sobegi, a tofu croquette stuffed with savory ground Asian mushrooms and beautifully presented like a rectangular gift box. Galbi jim is a wonderful stew of short ribs with sweet dates, chestnuts and turnips. **Price range:** Entrees, $12.95–$21. **Meals:** L, D, LN. **Subway:** 1, 9 to Franklin St.

Kuruma Zushi   ☆ ☆ ☆ $$$$ SUSHI
7 E. 47th St. (between Fifth and Madison Aves.)   (212) 317-2802
Few restaurants are more welcoming to diners who do not speak Japanese, and few chefs are better at introducing people to sushi than Toshiro Uezu, proprietor of Kuruma Zushi. One of New York City's most venerable sushi bars, it serves only sushi and sashimi and is, admittedly, expensive. But after eating at

Kuruma Zushi it is very hard to go back to ordinary fish.
Price range: Entrees, $25–$100. **Meals:** L, D. Closed Sun.
Subway: S, 4, 5, 6, 7 to 42nd St.

La Caravelle   ☆☆☆ $$$$ FRENCH
33 W. 55th St (between Fifth and Sixth Aves.)   (212) 586-4252
La Caravelle is a French restaurant of the old school, a great social stage
where people go to look at one another. The pretty murals and flattering
lighting make everyone look good, and the captains are skilled at making
their customers feel as good as they look. No restaurant in New York does a
better job at guarding tradition while honoring the present. If you are searching for solid French cooking, you will find it here. Nobody does classic dishes
like roasted chicken with Champagne sauce or canard a l'orange better. But
that is just one part of the menu. New inventions are scattered among these old
dishes, and the food changes with the seasons. For dessert, the marquise au
chocolat is intense enough to make a chocaholic swoon and soufflés are excellent. **Price range:** Prix-fixe and tasting menus, $68–110.
Meals: L, D. Closed Sun. **Subway:** E, F, N, R to Fifth Ave.

La Côte Basque   ☆☆☆ $$$$ FRENCH
60 W. 55th St. (between Fifth and Sixth Aves.)   (212) 688-6525
For 36 years La Côte Basque was a bastion of civility on East 55th Street. After
settling gracefully into intimate new quarters, the food is still well-prepared and
well-presented, but rarely so unmannerly as to call undue attention to itself.
Similarly, the menu is smaller, more modern and easier to read than the one in
the old restaurant. The most exciting entree is cassoulet, a splendid pile of
white beans cooked with pork loin, duck confit and fat chunks of garlic sausage
until each bean bursts with fat and flavor. Dover sole, a frequent special, is the
best of the fish. The fillet of black bass is a close second. These dishes are
extremely well executed, and each plate is piled with food. **Price range:** Prix-
fixe dinner $68, with supplements. **Meals:** L, D. **Subway:** E, F, N, R to Fifth Ave.

L'Actuel   ☆☆ $$$ FRENCH
145 E. 50th St. (between Lexington and Third Aves.)   (212) 583-0001
This restaurant is up-to-the-minute in a very French way, which is to say that it
is pointedly international, while hanging on for dear life to the essential quali-
ties that define a brasserie. It has an Alsatian choucroute, of course, but also a
tapas menu—French tapas, like marinated grilled zucchini stuffed with goat
cheese. There are plates of fruits de mer, but you get a superior American cock-
tail sauce along with the mignonette, not to mention chewy, saline seaweed
bread. The chef makes a place on his menu for tartes flambées, the thin-crust
pizzas of his native Alsace, but he offers a wild-card tart topped with wasabi and
bluefin tuna. Fish dishes are impressive; desserts are intriguing, including an

excellent apple tart and warm chocolate cake with a molten center. **Price range:** Entrees, $17–$24. **Meals:** B, Br, L, D. Closed Sun. **Subway:** 6 to 51st St.; E, F to Lexington Ave.

La Fonda Boricua $ LATIN AMERICAN

169 E. 106th St. (between Third and Lexington Aves.)   (212) 410-7292

Everything seems to move to a beat at La Fonda, a friendly place where the food is hearty and satisfying, particularly the beef stew, tender meat teamed with peppers and onions; arroz con pollo, smoky baked chicken with a mass of yellow rice; a chewy octopus salad made with onions, green peppers and olives; and pernil, peppery roast pork. All are served with a selection of three beans: white, pink or red. **Price range:** Entrees, $4.50–$9. Cash only. **Meals:** B, L, D. **Subway:** 6 to 103rd St.

La Grenouille   ☆☆☆ $$$$ FRENCH

3 E. 52nd St. (near Fifth Ave.)   (212) 752-1495

La Grenouille is the most frustrating restaurant in New York. This is not because the food is bad or the service unpleasant. Just the opposite, in fact, the restaurant displays such flashes of brilliance that each failure is a deep disappointment. It is also one of the few New York restaurants that still serves many of the French classics, including quenelles de brochette, perfectly grilled Dover sole and the best souffles in New York. La Grenouille could so easily be a four-star establishment with its golden light, magnificent floral displays and professional and caring staff. Each meal offers moments of joyful excellence, but many dishes are entirely forgettable. You can count on a good meal at La Grenouille. If you're lucky, however, you may get a great one. **Price range:** Three course prix-fixe dinner $80; lunch $45, Tasting menu $100. **Meals:** L, D. Closed Sun., Mon. **Subway:** E, F to Fifth Ave.

La Locanda $25 & Under   ITALIAN

737 Ninth Ave. (near 50th St.)   (212) 258-2900

La Locanda serves pastas and meat dishes that stand out for their simplicity and flavor, and offers an enticing and unusually arranged wine list. Start with the basket of bread and focaccia, freshly baked at La Locanda's bakery. Second, try one of the large and alluring salads, like insalata rifredda, essentially an Italian version of the frisée salad. Pastas can be excellent, either as a shared appetizer or as a main course. Sliced leg of lamb, served like all the main courses with roasted potatoes and sauted broccoli rape, is past the point of pink, but the sauce, simply lamb juices and herbs, imbues the meat with flavor. The same is true of veal shoulder, aromatic and delicious in its sauce of herbs, white wine and veal juices. La Locanda also makes its own desserts, some of which are quite good, especially the rustic blueberry tart or the compact French-style strawberry tart. **Price range:** Pastas and entrees, $11—$21.50. **Meals:** L, D. **Subway:** C, E to 50th St.

La Nonna   ☆ $$$ ITALIAN

133 W. 13th St. (between Sixth and Seventh Aves.)   (212) 741-3663

La Nonna is a warm, inviting place with a no-nonsense menu of thoroughly traditional Tuscan dishes, with an emphasis on meat and fish roasted or grilled in a wood-burning oven. A moist and tender marinated Cornish hen makes the best advertisement for the oven, but pasta turns out to be the most dependable category on the menu. A standout is strozzapreti, slightly sticky dumplings of Swiss chard and spinach firmed up with ricotta and Parmesan cheese, then doused with butter and sage. **Price range:** Entrees, $16.50–$24.50. **Meals:** L, D. **Subway:** F, 1, 2, 3, 9 to 14th St.

La Palapa $25 & Under   MEXICAN

77 St. Marks Pl. (at First Ave.)   (212) 777-2537

This bright and cheerful restaurant shows off the regional glories of Mexico rather than the familiar one-dimensional margarita-fueled Tex-Mex dishes. A moist cod fillet is served in pipian verde, a sauce based on ground pumpkin seeds, given its color by cilantro and extra taste by a mild chili. Tacos are authentically Mexican, made with soft corn tortillas, and are also artful, with fillings like chili-rubbed chicken, shrimp in adobo sauce or mild poblano chili with epazote and onions. The real excitement comes with the main courses, like thin slices of duck breast, fanned out in a wonderful sesame mole, or chicken enchiladas in a soupy tomatillo sauce that is very spicy. For dessert, try rich Mexican chocolate ice cream and a spicy chili-laced peach sorbet. **Price range:** Entrees, $11.95–$18.95. **Meals:** L, D, LN. **Subway:** 6 to Astor Pl.

L'Ardoise $25 & Under   FRENCH

1207 First Ave. (between 65th and 66th Sts.)   (212) 744-4752

This unfashionable little restaurant is not much to look at, but the well-prepared traditional French food and the quirky charm of the proprietor more than make up for this. Bistro favorites like warm frisée salad with lardons, steamed mussels, duck confit and steak frites are all good bets. **Price range:** Entrees, $6.50–$7.95. **Meals:** L, D. **Subway:** 6 to 68th St.

Lavagna $25 & Under   MEDITERRANEAN

545 E. 5th St. (at Ave. B)   (212) 979-1005

Lavagna's food is fresh and generous, with honest, straightforward flavors. The simple rectangular dining room is casual and inviting, but can get loud when it's crowded. Pastas are best, both simple dishes like rigatoni with crumbled fennel sausage, peas, tomatoes and cream, and more complicated ones like fresh pappardelle with rabbit stew. Cacciucco, the Tuscan fish soup scented with saffron and anise, and served with mussels, cockles and chunks of fish, is a great value. **Price range:** Entrees, $11–$16.50. Cash only. **Meals:** D, LN. Closed Sun. **Subway:** F to Second Ave.

Layla   ☆☆ $$$ MIDDLE EASTERN

211 West Broadway (at Franklin St.)   (212) 431-0700

Layla is a hip downtown setting for the Arabian nights, complete with broken pottery shards on the wall and a belly dancer twirling through the room after 9 P.M. The restaurant is tasty and lots of fun, featuring good Middle Eastern food from a wood-burning oven. The phyllo-wrapped sardines are fabulous. The lobster pastilla is one of those sweet, spicy Moroccan dishes that everybody loves. Desserts are original and delicious, especially the eggy orange blossom crème brûlée. **Price range:** Entrees, $20–$29. **Meals:** L, D. **Subway:** 1, 9 to Franklin St.

Le Bernardin ☆☆☆☆ $$$$ FRENCH/SEAFOOD
155 W. 51st St. (between Sixth and Seventh Aves.) (212) 489-1515
Most restaurants grow into their stars. Not Le Bernardin: at the ripe old age of three months, it had all four stars bestowed upon it. The restaurant has been in the spotlight ever since. Its hallmark is impeccably fresh fish cooked with respect and simplicity. Most of the problems that plague other great establishments are solved here: there are no rude reservations takers, no endless waits for tables, no overcrowding in the dining room. The waiters know their jobs and keep their distance. Dinners are appropriately paced. When you reserve a table at Le Bernardin, you can count on being seated promptly, served beautifully and fed fabulously. Le Bernardin once showed New York how to eat fish; now it is showing the city how a four-star restaurant should behave. **Price range:** Dinner prix-fixe, $77; tasting menu, $95–$125. **Meals:** L, D. Closed Sun. **Subway:** B, D, F, S to 42nd St. **Meals:** L, D. **Subway:** N, R to 49th St.; 1, 9 to 50th St.

Le Cirque 2000 ☆☆☆ $$$$ FRENCH/ITALIAN
New York Palace Hotel, 455 Madison Ave. (between 50th and 51st Sts.)
(212) 303-7788
As pure spectacle, there is nothing in New York like Le Cirque. It is more and less than a restaurant. First and foremost, it is a social institution and an emblem of status. Diners check in, have their self-esteem validated by Sirio Maccioni and settle in for a sumptuous evening surrounded by their own kind. More than any restaurant, Le Cirque is a one-man show. Diners put themselves in Mr. Maccioni's practiced hands, not the kitchen's. But food was never the most important thing about Le Cirque, and at the moment, it may not even be the second or third thing. The menu moves back and forth between two poles: an almost rustic simplicity and sometimes heavy, lavishly presented fancy food. One of Le Cirque's signature dishes, black sea bass wrapped in sheets of crisp, paper-thin potato and lavished with Barolo sauce, is still excellent, and simpler dishes deliver, like beef short ribs, a mighty cube of savory meat in a rich reduction sauce. At dessert time, ridiculous sugar sculptures and chocolate trees make their way to tables where diners grin like kids at a birthday party. **Price range:** Entrees, $28–$39. **Meals:** L, D. **Subway:** 6 to 51st St.; E, F to Lexington Ave.

Le Colonial ☆☆ $$ VIETNAMESE
149 E. 57th St. (between Lexington and Third Aves.) (212) 752-0808.
Vietnamese cuisine, as interpreted here, is sedate Asian fare that is more delicate than Chinese food, less spicy than Thai and notable mostly for its abundance of vegetables and its absence of grease. Spring rolls at Le Colonial are so delicate you

tend to forget that they are fried. The beef salad, the only really spicy dish here, is excellent. **Price range:** Entrees, $14–$23. **Meals:** L, D. **Subway:** 4, 5, 6 to 59th St.; N, R, W to Lexington Ave.

Le Gigot $25 & Under   FRENCH
18 Cornelia St. (between 4th and Bleecker Sts.)   (212) 627-3737
This little restaurant pulses with the welcoming spirit of a Parisian hangout. The Provence-inflected food adds to the illusion, with excellent bistro fare like leg of lamb in a red wine reduction; lamb stew; endive salad with apples, walnuts and Roquefort, and rounds of baguette smeared with goat cheese and smoky tapenade. The best desserts are the sweet, moist, caramelized tarte Tatin, the excellent bananas flambé, and the great little cheese course, not usually available in a restaurant like this. **Price range:** Entrees, $12–$17. AE only. **Meals:** Br, L, D. Closed Mon. **Subway:** A, C, E, F, S to W. 4th St.

Lentini   ☆ $$$ ITALIAN
1562 Second Avenue (81st Street)   (212) 628-3131
Location and atmosphere make this a neighborhood restaurant. Some of the dishes do, too. But look more closely at the menu, scan the ambitious wine list and its equally ambitious prices, and it becomes clear that Chef Giuseppe Lentini wants to be more than a nice little local standby. Pastas are a very good bet. Some are made on the premises, some are not, but either way they tend to be the highlight of the meal. Tomato sauces can be light or so concentrated that you can almost slice them like terrine. The comma-shaped gramegna has a medium weight to suit a light tomato sauce with little cubes of swordfish and eggplant. The swordfish, miraculously, comes out perfectly moist. For dessert, try cassata, a dense, even sludgy mass of sweetened ricotta and spongecake topped with loose marzipan, then iced and festively decorated with candied fruit. **Price range:** Entrees, $18—$30. **Meals:** D. **Subway:** 4, 5, 6 to 86th St.

Le Périgord   ☆ ☆ $$$$ FRENCH
405 E. 52nd St. (at First Ave.)   (212) 755-6244
Le Perigord is a French restaurant the way French restaurants used to be. The waiters, well on in years, wear white jackets. The even more senior captains wear tuxedos. On the dessert trolley you know with dead certainty that you will find floating island, chocolate mousse and tarte Tatin. A new chef brought a new spark to the kitchen, most notably in a stunning turbot with a crust of bread crumbs and Comte cheese, and a glorious overlay of pungent, hazel-nutty flavor sharpened with the faintest possible touch of mustard. If only the chef could remake the staff. Some nights, the restaurant can seem like a cross between Fawlty Towers and Katz's Delicatessen. The diners do not seem to mind. Inside Le Perigord, they can swaddle themselves in a quietly civilized atmosphere, a million miles removed from the tumult of the city outside. **Price range:** Three-course prix-fixe, $57. **Meals:** L, D. **Subway:** 6 to 51st St.; E, F to Lexington Ave.

Lespinasse ☆☆☆☆ $$$$ FRENCH

St. Regis Hotel, 2 E. 55th St. (near Fifth Ave.) (212) 339-6719

Open the door and be dazzled by the golden light of chandeliers and intoxicated by the aroma of white truffles. Flowers from lavish bouquets bend to caress your shoulders as you pass. Numerous servers hover nearby, eager to anticipate every wish. In this rarefied atmosphere, the butter never gets warm and no glass is ever empty. As you might expect, the menu descriptions are elaborate, the prices stratospheric. The only strategy is to abandon yourself to the experience and pretend, if only for a few hours, that money has no meaning. The combination of the food, the quiet setting and the solicitous service create an experience so opulent and old-fashioned that it can be a serious shock to walk outside and find no coach waiting to take you home. **Price range:** entrees, $34–$46. **Meals:** D. Closed Sun., Mon. **Subway:** E, F, N, R to Fifth Ave.

Le Tableau $25 & Under MEDITERRANEAN

511 E. 5th St. (between Aves. A and B) (212) 260-1333

This simple storefront restaurant turns out superb Mediterranean fare. Unconventional dishes stimulate the mouth with new flavors and textures, like a spicy calamari tagine that incorporates anchovies, hummus and olive purée. Main courses are familiar, yet they are presented in inventive ways. Desserts can be excellent, like a mellow pumpkin bread pudding, a honey-nut tart and an apple tajine. The dining room is dimly lighted with candles and can become noisy, especially when a jazz trio begins playing in the late evening. **Price range:** Entrees, $9.50–$14.75. Cash only. **Meals:** Br, D. Closed Mon. **Subway:** F to Second Ave.

Le Zie $25 & Under ITALIAN

172 Seventh Ave. (at 20th St.) (212) 206-8686

This modest, often crowded little trattoria offers some terrific Venetian dishes, like an inspired salad that features pliant octopus and soft potatoes acting in precise textural counterpoint. The chef has a sure hand with pastas like rigatoni with rosemary, served al dente in a perfectly proportioned sauce. Risotto with squid is also superbly cooked. Striped bass fillet with fennel and white beans is moist and wonderfully flavorful. Desserts are a weak point. **Price range:** Entrees, $8.50–$16.95. Cash only. **Meals:** L, D. **Subway:** 1, 9 to 23rd St.

Le Zinc ☆ $$ BISTRO

139 Duane St. (between Church St. and West Broadway) (212) 513-0001

Le Zinc was recently opened by the people who own the highly-rated Chanterelle. The low-key bistro menu, with an Asian accent here and a down-home touch there, qualifies as upmarket Manhattan comfort food. It's solid, reliable and reassuring, served in portions so abundant that appetizers often seem like entrees in training. And the price is right. Le Zinc offers a menu-within-a-menu of charcuterie, and there's no doubt about it, the terrines here are superior. Main courses make the usual bistro stops, with competently executed

dishes like skirt steak in a red wine reduction and skate with brown butter and
capers. **Note well:** Le Zinc takes no reservations. **Price range:** Entrees, $12–
$19. **Meals:** Br, L, D, LN. **Subway:** 1, 9 to Franklin St.

Le Zoo $25 & Under   BISTRO/FRENCH
314 W. 11th St. (at Greenwich St.)   (212) 620-0393
This popular little restaurant can get crowded, loud and zoolike, but the food is
good and often creative. Where you might reasonably expect to find steak
frites, roast chicken and pâté de campagne, there are instead such combinations as monkfish with honey and lime sauce, or wonderfully flavorful sliced
scallops served in puff pastry with a leek-and-chive coulis. The dessert selection is small and classically French, offering satisfying choices. The restaurant
does not take reservations, but once you are seated, the atmosphere becomes
relaxed, casual and unrushed, though not quiet. **Price range:** Entrees, $12.50–
$16. **Meals:** D, LN. **Subway:** 1, 9 to Christopher St.

Little Basil $25 & Under   THAI
39 Greenwich Ave. (at Charles St.)   (212) 645-8965
Little Basil serves dishes with exquisite balance, Western touches and a beautiful presentation. Dishes like lamb shank draped in herbs and delicate steamed
dumplings strewn with dried shrimp are not exactly Thai home cooking, yet the
food remains true to the essence of Thai cuisine. **Price range:** Entrees, $9–$16.
Meals: D. **Subway:** 1, 9 to Christopher St.

Little Dove   ☆ ☆ $$$ NEW AMERICAN
200 E. 60th St. (at Third Ave.)   (212) 751-8616
The tiny dining room here looks like a cross between an antiques store and the
drawing room of a dotty old aunt, but it has a civilized charm and genuine
character. The menu is a brief document but each dish counts. It stresses high-
quality ingredients and simple, strong, clearly defined flavors. The crust on an
unassuming lemon tart with pineapple meringue is thick and flaky, the filling
tartly voluptuous, the meringue lighter than air. **Price range:** Entrees, $22–$32.
Meals: L, D. **Subway:** N, R, W to Lexington Ave.; 4, 5, 6 to 59th St.

Lombardi's $25 & Under   PIZZA
32 Spring St. (between Mulberry and Mott Sts.)   (212) 941-7994
The dining room reeks of history at this reincarnation of the original Lombardi's, which is often credited with introducing pizza to New York City. The
old-fashioned coal-oven pizza is terrific, with a light, thin, crisp and gloriously
smoky crust topped with fine mozzarella and tomatoes. The garlicky clam pizza
is exceptional. **Price range:** Pizzas, $10.50–$20. Cash only. **Meals:** L, D, LN.
Subway: 6 to Spring St.

Los Dos Rancheros $25 & Under   MEXICAN
507 Ninth Ave. (at 38th St.)   (212) 868-7780
The dining room may be bare-bones (unpretentious is an understatement), but

the restaurant serves authentic, delicious Mexican fare, like pollo con pipián, chicken with a fiery green sauce made of ground pumpkin seeds, and excellent soft tacos with fillings ranging from chicken to braised pork to tongue and goat. **Price range:** Entrees, $2–$7.50. Cash only. **Meals:** B, L, D. **Subway:** A, C, E to 42nd St.

Luca $25 & Under   ITALIAN
1712 First Ave. (near 89th St.)   (212) 987-9260
This superb neighborhood Italian restaurant is spare but good-looking, with beige walls and rustic floor tiles. The menu offers dishes skillfully cooked to order that emphasize lusty flavors. The antipasto for two is very generous and very good. Pastas, like bigoli with a buttery shrimp-and-radicchio sauce, are terrific, as are main courses like grilled calamari and crisp grilled Cornish hen. **Price range:** Entrees, $8.50–$19.95. **Meals:** D. **Subway:** 4, 5, 6 to 86th St.

Lupa $25 & Under   ITALIAN
170 Thompson St. (near Houston St.)   (212) 982-5089.
Crowded and clamorous, Lupa serves intensely delicious Roman trattoria food. Appetizers range from the classic to the bizarre: Prosciutto di Parma arrives in thin, nutty slices, a reminder of why this combination became popular in the first place. Pastas are simple and tasty, and saltimbocca, thin slices of veal layered with prosciutto, is good and juicy. The resident wine expert takes great delight in directing you to the perfect choice on Lupa's 130-bottle wine list, and the best dessert choice is something from the cheese tray. **Price range:** Entrees, $9–$15. **Meals:** L, D. Closed Mon. **Subway:** F, S to Broadway–Lafayette St.

Lutèce ☆ ☆ $$$$ FRENCH
249 E. 50th St. (between Second and Third Aves.)   (212) 752-2225
Lutèce tries to project a fresh, contemporary image while retaining an old-fashioned sense of luxury and formality. The service remains an anachronism, but chef David Féau brings a youthful touch to a classic French style, with respectful innovations that never violate good taste. Certain dishes convince you that Lutèce has found the right chef to bring it back to the first rank, especially a gently cooked John Dory with a subtle peppermint jus and pommes soufflées, and sautéed black bass with a rich vanilla jus and wilted spinach. Mr. Féau also integrates Asian spices and ingredients with a fine hand. Among the desserts, a superior pistachio soufflé with sour cherries and a tart cherry sorbet stands head and shoulders above its confrères.   **Price range:** Three-course prix fixe, $72. **Meals:** L, D. **Subway:** 6 to 51st St.; E, F to Lexington Ave.

Luzia's $25 & Under   PORTUGUESE
429 Amsterdam Ave. (between 80th and 81st Sts.)   (212) 595-2000
Luzia's began life as a takeout place. Then the neighborhood fell in love with the cozy restaurant and started staying for dinner. Luzia's serves wonderful Portuguese comfort food, like caldo verde, shrimp pie and cataplana, the soupy stew of pork and clams. It also produces remarkably delicious non-Portuguese dishes,

like beef brisket that is tender and peppery. Luzia's has a great flan, and a nice list of Portuguese wines. **Price range:** $20–$25. **Meals:** Br, L, D. Closed Mon. **Subway:** 1, 9 to 79th St.

Mama's Food Shop $25 & Under   AMERICAN
200 E. 3rd St. (between Aves. A and B)   (212) 777-4425
A simple takeout shop and restaurant where you point at what you want and they dish it up. But the food is outstanding: grilled salmon, fried chicken and meatloaf. Vegetable side dishes are especially good, like brussels sprouts, carrots, beets and mashed potatoes. **Price range:** Entrees, $7–$8.50. Cash only. **Meals:** L, D. Closed Sun. **Subway:** F to Second Ave.

Mandoo Bar $25 & Under   KOREAN
2 W. 32nd St. (near Fifth Ave.)   (212) 279-3075
Mandoo (pronounced MAHN-do) is the Korean word for dumplings, the specialty of the house. Start with a platter of baby mandoo, bite-size half-moons stuffed with beef, pork and leeks and notable for a wrapper so sheer that it is almost transparent. Boiled dumplings are fine and steamed meat-and-cabbage dumplings are very good, but some of the best selections are not dumplings at all. Slender rectangles of fried tofu make an excellent appetizer, and bibimbop, a casserole of rice, vegetables and ground beef served in a stone crock, is fresh, light and delicate. The dining room is spare and handsome, service is swift and courteous, and food arrives quickly. **Price range:** Entrees, $6–$24. **Meals:** L, D. **Subway:** 6 to 33rd St.; B, D, F, N, Q, R, S, W to 34th St.

Manhattan Ocean Club   ☆☆ $$$$ SEAFOOD
57 W. 58th St. (between Fifth and Sixth Aves.)   (212) 371-7777
Tony, comfortable and trim as a luxury yacht, this is the steakhouse of fish restaurants. Eating here is an indulgence, and the prices are high. Soups like the creamy clam chowder are less expensive but no less delicious. Simple preparations are the most appealing but one of the best dishes is the oysters buried in tiny morels covered with cream and baked in the shell. The dish is an edible definition of luxury. Desserts are almost all big and sweet. **Price range:** Entrees, $22.50–$31. **Meals:** L, D. **Subway:** N, R, W to Fifth Ave.

March   ☆☆☆ $$$$ NEW AMERICAN
405 E. 58th St. (near First Ave.)   (212) 754-6272
When everything is clicking, there are few places better than this cozy, antique-filled town house. The usual three-course restaurant menu is replaced with one that allows you to choose either four or seven smaller courses. At March, no dish is more than a few bites, but those are so pretty and powerful that you are almost always satisfied. The most popular items are Beggars' purses, diminutive dumplings filled with caviar, truffles or foie gras. **Price range:** Prix-fixe, $72–126 (with specially selected wines, $116–203). **Meals:** D. **Subway:** 4, 5, 6 to 59th St.; N, R to Lexington Ave.

Maritime ☆ $$$ SEAFOOD
1251 Sixth Ave. (at W. 49th St.)   (212) 354-1717

As a piece of design, Maritime is one slippery fish: gleaming white wall tiles suggest an urban fish market, but the dark, solid wood wainscoting and cabinets feel more like a men's club. The menu is not easy to get a handle on, either. A fair number of the dishes are overthought and overwrought, but some results can be terrific. The oysters are straightforward enough; so is a crowd-pleasing shrimp cocktail. Lobster in a Portuguese tomato sauce is plump and flavorful. Two desserts break out of the pack: the Southwestern banana split and a florid apple crisp. **Price range:** Entrees, $16–$25. **Meals:** L, D. **Subway:** B, D, F, S to 47th-50th St.–Rockefeller Center.

Marumi $25 & Under   JAPANESE/SUSHI
546 La Guardia Pl. (between 3rd and Bleecker Sts.)   (212) 979-7055

This versatile, reliable Japanese restaurant near N.Y.U. offers a cross-section of casual Japanese dining. The service is swift, efficient and charming and will even go the extra mile in preventing bad choices. It's rare that you get such an interesting assortment of sushi at an inexpensive restaurant, like mirugai, or geoduck clam. Other worthwhile dishes are broiled eel, noodle soups and the economic bento box meals. **Price range:** Entrees, $9–$15. **Meals:** L, D. **Subway:** A, C, E, F, S to W. 4th St.

Mavalli Palace $25 & Under   INDIAN/VEGETARIAN
46 E. 29th St. (between Park and Madison Aves.)   (212) 679-5535

This low-key Indian restaurant turns out terrific vegetarian fare that is exciting and full of flavor, like rasa vada, savory lentil doughnuts in a spicy broth, and baingan bharta, a fiery blend of eggplant and peas. Mavalli means mother goddess, and the restaurant's symbol is a goddess figure, hand out, waiting to serve. The staff, though merely mortal, takes orders efficiently and brings food out swiftly. **Price range:** $4.25–$16.75. **Meals:** L, D. Closed Mon. **Subway:** 6 to 28th St.

Max $25 & Under   ITALIAN
51 Ave. B (near 4th St.)   (212) 539-0111

Max's draw is exactly what has always attracted people to neighborhood Italian restaurants: well-prepared food, served with warmth. Best of all, Max is cheap. Fettuccine al sugo Toscano has a wonderfully mellow meat sauce with layers of flavor that unfold in the mouth, while rigatoni Napoletano is served southern Italian style, with meatballs and sausages left intact in the sauce. Order the sauce on the side of the Neopolitan-style meatloaf, because the meatloaf is fascinating, stuffed with mozzarella, hard-boiled egg and prosciutto, making for a savory, moist and delicious combination. Max has a brief list of wines under $25 and desserts include a good tiramisu and an excellent caramel panna cotta. **Price range:** Entrees, $8.95–$14.95. Cash only. **Meals:** L, D, LN. **Subway:** F to Second Ave.

Maya ☆☆ $$$ MEXICAN/TEX-MEX

1191 First Ave. (between 64th and 65th Sts.) (212) 585-1818

Some of New York's most interesting Mexican food is served in this bright, festive but often noisy room. Although you can stick to margaritas and guacamole, you'll miss the best part if you don't try some of the more unusual dishes, like rock shrimp ceviche, seafood salad, and roasted corn soup with huitlacoche dumpling. The most impressive main courses are chicken mole (the dark sauce is truly complex) and pipian de puerco, grilled pork marinated in tamarind and served on a bed of puréed roasted corn. Desserts are not impressive. **Price range:** Entrees, $18.50–$24.50. **Meals:** D. **Subway:** 6 to 68th St.

McHale's $$ BAR SNACKS/HAMBURGERS

750 Eighth Ave. (at 46th St.) (212) 246-8948

This neighborhood bar has a single specialty: great hamburgers that are big and juicy. There's really no point in ordering anything else, except maybe a beer or two. A nice place in which to be a regular. **Price range:** Entrees, $10–$18. Cash only. **Meals:** L, D, LN. **Subway:** A, C, E to 42nd St.

Mee Noodle Shop $25 & Under CHINESE

219 First Ave. (at 13th St.) (212) 995-0333

547 Second Ave. (between 30th and 31st Sts.) (212) 779-1596

922 Second Ave. (at 49th St.) (212) 888-0027

795 Ninth Ave. (at 53rd St.) (212) 765-2929

A little chain of Chinese restaurants that is a cut above takeout, with huge portions of cheap, tasty noodles. Ingredients are fresh, and dishes like lo mein with roast pork and mee fun with chicken are carefully prepared. Mee offers seven kinds of noodles. The portions are huge—complete meals in themselves—and delicious. **Price range:** $3.75–$12. AE only. **Meals:** L, D.

Meigas ☆☆ $$$ SPANISH

350 Hudson St. (between King and Charlton Sts.) (212) 627-5800

Meigas (may-EEH-gus) is Galician for sorceresses, and one appears in a mural at the back of this large restaurant, a spooky figure who conjures from the sea an enormous table, laden with savory dishes. Chef Luis Bollo, a Basque, cultivates homey virtues here, with judiciously applied modern touches. It's possible to order something as simple as baby squid cooked in its own ink, a traditional Basque specialty, or giant prawns grilled on a wood plank and served with lemon and olive oil. An exceptionally fruity Caroliva olive oil transforms humble fillets of grilled mackerel into a memorable, two-fisted dish, enlivened with garlic and a sharp, tingling dose of chili and Rioja vinegar. The pastry chef does some brilliant work, especially with his bread pudding, crunchy at the edges with baked sugar, and topped with a wonderfully dense, sourish ice cream. **Price range:** Entrees, $17–$27. **Meals:** L, D. Closed Sat., Sun. **Subway:** 1, 9 to Houston St.

Meltemi $25 & Under GREEK/SEAFOOD

905 First Ave. (at 51st St.) (212) 355-4040

This attractive neighborhood Greek restaurant offers big portions of simply pre-

pared seafood, like grilled octopus with oil and lemon, and typical Greek offerings like grilled whole porgy and red mullet. Appetizers are generous, and two
portions can easily feed four people. Grilled seafood is the centerpiece here. The
enthusiastic staff adds to Meltemi's enjoyable atmosphere. **Price range:** Entrees,
$14.95–$28.95. **Meals:** L, D. **Subway:** 6 to 51st St.; E, F to Lexington Ave.

Mercer Kitchen ☆☆ $$$$ FRENCH

Mercer Hotel, 99 Prince St. (at Mercer St.) (212) 966-5454
Jean-Georges Vongerichten strikes again in this chic SoHo restaurant filled
with models and movie stars. The space is so mysteriously beautiful it makes
each vegetable shimmer like a jewel in the dark. The food is equally innovative.
The kitchen occasionally spins out of control, but desserts are simple and
appealing, especially the fruit terrines and the rich and fascinating custard with
a slice of carmelized pineapple. **Price range:** Entrees, $19–$35.
Meals: Br, L, D, LN. **Subway:** N, R to Prince St.

Merge $25 & Under NEW AMERICAN

142 W. 10th St. (between Greenwich St. and Waverly Pl.) (212) 691-7757
The music here is too loud and the dining area close to the bar is too smoky, but
the service is friendly and efficient, and the food is not only delicious but also a
great value. Sushi fruit salad, a combination of coconut and mango with Asian
coleslaw and thin slices of tuna and salmon, is an extraordinary blend of flavors
and textures. A grilled paillard of guinea hen is given an earthy boost by a plum
and foie gras sauce, and hanger steak is juicy and beefy. Desserts also include
some winners, like a sweet potato panna cotta with a caramel sauce. **Price
range:** Entrees, $15–$20. AE only. **Meals:** D. **Subway:** 1, 9 to Christopher St.

Mesa Grill ☆☆ $$$$ SOUTHWESTERN

102 Fifth Ave. (between 15th and 16th Sts.) (212) 807-7400
Mesa Grill is a downtown favorite, crowded and clamorous at lunch, and even
more crowded and clamorous at night. Two things set chef-owner Bobby Flay
apart. First, he goes after big flavors and he knows how to get them. Second, he
uses chilies and spices for flavor, not for heat. Sixteen-spice chicken sounds like
a tongue-scorcher. It turns out to be a subtly handled, tingling orchestration of
flavors, with an off-sweet sauce of caramelized mangos and garlic. New arrivals
keep the menu fresh. The margarita list is an inspirational document, with a list
of fine tequilas that can either be sipped on their own or used to upgrade a standard margarita. **Price range:** Entrees, $24–$39. **Meals:** Br, L, D.
Subway: F, L, N, Q, R, W, 4, 5, 6 to 14th St.

Metsovo $25 & Under GREEK

65 W. 70th St. (near Columbus Ave.) (212) 873-2300
Instead of seafood, this romantic restaurant, named after a town in northwest-
ern Greece, specializes in hearty stews, roasts and savory pies from the hills
that form a spine through the region. Try the delicious Epirus mountain pies,
which are offered with different fillings each day. Tender chunks of baby lamb

and a mellow stew of robust goat blended with thick yogurt and rice are also
very good. Once you get through the house specialties, though, you're back in
familiar territory. You may never receive the same selection of desserts twice,
so hope for the luscious fig compote, or the wonderfully thick and fresh
yogurt. **Price range:** Entrees, $10.50–$23.95. **Meals:** D. **Subway:** 1, 2, 3, 9 to
72nd St.

Mexicana Mama $25 & Under   MEXICAN
525 Hudson St. (at W. 10th St.)   (212) 924-4119
While this colorful restaurant's small menu doesn't register high on a scale of
authenticity, the food succeeds in a more important measure: it tastes good.
Rather than using the traditional mutton or goat, for example, a dish like barba-
coa is made with beef, braised and then cooked slowly in a corn husk until it is
fall-away tender, like pot roast. Authentic? No. Tasty? Definitely. Other worthy
dishes include pollo con mole, a boneless chicken breast that is surprisingly
juicy, with a terrific reddish-brown mole. **Price range:** Entrees, $8–$17. Cash
only. **Meals:** L, D. **Subway:** 1, 9 to Christopher St.

Michael Jordan's Steak House   ☆☆ $$$$ STEAKHOUSE
23 Vanderbilt Ave. (in Grand Central Terminal)   (212) 655-2300
Despite a celebrity owner and a big-deal designer (David Rockwell), the real
star of this place is Grand Central Terminal. You sit in comfort on the balcony
gazing at the starry ceiling while harried commuters dash madly through the
marble halls below. The menu is what you would expect, but the food, for the
most part, is equal to the space. Shrimp cocktail is excellent, the meat robust,
prime, aged and old-fashioned. All the standard cuts are available, but the flavorful rib eye steak is best. The hamburger, made from chopped prime sirloin, is
absurd; it's so enormous it looks more like an inflated basketball. Desserts are
not inspiring. **Price range:** Entrees, $18–$34. **Meals:** L, D.
Subway: S, 4, 5, 6, 7 to 42nd St.

Michael's   ☆☆ $$$$ NEW AMERICAN
24 W. 55th St. (between Fifth and Sixth Aves.)   (212) 767-0555
Home of the power lunch. All of publishing goes to Michael's because the
room is attractive and filled with good art. The menu offers one of the city's
finest selections of fancy salads (some large enough to feed a small nation).
The best food on the menu is unabashedly American, including grilled
chicken, grilled lobster, good steaks and chops, and California cuisine. There
are several daily fish selections. For dessert, the classic collection of tarts and
cakes is very enticing. **Price range:** Entrees, $22–$34. **Meals:** B, L, D. Closed
Sun. **Subway:** N, R, W to Fifth Ave.

Mi Cocina   ☆☆ $$ MEXICAN
57 Jane St. (at Hudson St.)   (212) 627-8273
If you're looking for real Mexican food, you can't do better than this small

Greenwich Village storefront. Floor-to-ceiling windows open up the slender rectangular space of the restaurant, with its sparkling kitchen framed in colorful tiles. A superior starter is the empanaditas de picadillo: little turnovers filled with shredded beef, raisins and olives. Main courses include chicken enchiladas and fajitas, made with grilled skirt steak or breast of chicken, onions, peppers, guacamole, black beans and salsa. Desserts include white almond flan, chocolate mousse cake and crepes filled with brandied raisins and walnuts. **Price range:** Entrees, $16–$25. **Meals:** L, D. **Subway:** A, C, E, 1, 2, 3, 9 to 14th St.; L to Eighth Ave.

Mirchi $25 & Under   INDIAN
29 Seventh Ave. (near Morton St.)   (212) 414-0931
A vast majority of Indian restaurants in Manhattan settle for a dreary sameness; Mirchi tries to break the imprisoning mold, and it succeeds often enough for its failures to be forgiven. The clean and simple design, casual service and loud music suggest other youth-oriented restaurants with bar crowds, yet the food is strictly Indian, with not even a hint of fusion. Portions are quite large and spicing is forceful, with occasionally very high heat (the word mirchi means hot, as in chilies). Chicken tak-a-tak, shredded chicken essentially stir-fried, is exceptional. Among the main courses jaipuri lal maas is a fabulous and subtle lamb dish, made, the menu says, with 30 red chilies. **Price range:** Entrees, $9–$19. **Meals:** L, D. **Subway:** 1, 9 to Houston St.

Miss Maude's Spoonbread Too $25 & Under   SOUTHERN
547 Lenox Ave. (near 137th St.)   (212) 690-3100
This bright restaurant celebrates the virtues of family meals without childish nostalgia. The generous portions of Southern dishes are not only robust and hearty, but also sometimes subtle. Meals begin with a basket of mildly spicy corn bread, grainy and not too sweet, and are served Southern style, with large portions of two sides. The smothered pork chops are thin but flavorful enough to stand up to the peppery brown gravy. Close behind are the excellent fried shrimp with traces of cornmeal in the delectable crust. Side dishes are all excellent. **Price range:** Dinners, $9.95–$12.95. **Meals:** Br, L, D.
Subway: 2, 3 to 135th St.

Molyvos   ☆☆☆ $$$ GREEK
871 Seventh Ave. (near 55th St.)   (212) 582-7500
Casual, hospitable and lively as a Greek taverna, Molyvos offers food by people who passionately want you to love it. The friendly, caring service begins with mezedes, little tastes that captivate with the intensity of their flavors. The large menu includes fine dishes from all the Greek islands. Marinated lamb shank, braised in wine with orzo and tomatoes, is soft, savory and delicious. Even Greek standards like moussaka and pastitsio are impressive. Portions are huge, and much of this food is straightforward, relying primarily on good ingredients. Fresh fish are simply grilled whole over wood. Desserts are as good (and as big)

as everything else. **Price range:** Entrees, $18.50–$27.50. **Meals:** L, D. **Subway:**
N, R, Q, W to 57th St.; B, D, E to Seventh Ave.

Montrachet   ☆ ☆ ☆ $$$$ FRENCH
239 West Broadway (near White St.)   (212) 219-2777
TriBeCa's first serious restaurant has achieved a pleasant patina of age without
losing its casual charm and thoughtful service. Montrachet is more Gallic than
ever, with muscular French cooking that seems just right for the small bistro-
like dining rooms. Try the memorable roast chicken served with a rich potato
purée and a robust garlic sauce. Then, of course, some cheese, and perhaps a
subtle tart Tatin made with seasonal fruits. Main dishes tend to be straightforward, relying on excellence of execution rather than originality. **Price range:**
Entrees, $23–$34. **Meals:** L (Fri. only), D (Mon.–Sat.). Closed Sun.
Subway: 1, 9 to Franklin St.

Moustache $25 & Under   MIDDLE EASTERN
90 Bedford St. (between Grove and Barrow Sts.)   (212) 229-2220
265 E. 10th St. (between First Ave. and Ave. A)   (212) 228-2022
These small, excellent Middle Eastern restaurants specialize in "pitzas," exceptional pizzalike dishes made with pita dough, including lahmajun, the Turkish specialty with a savory layer of ground lamb on crisp crust, and zaatar, a crisp individual pizza topped with a smoky, aromatic combination of olive oil, thyme, sesame
seeds and sumac. A sandwich of sliced lamb in pita bread with onion and tomato
is brought to life by a minty lemon mayonnaise. **Price range:** $3–$12. Cash only.
Meals: L, D, LN. **Subway:** Bedford St.: 1, 9 to Houston St. E. 10th St.: L to
First Ave.

Mughlai $25 & Under   INDIAN
320 Columbus Ave. (at 71st St.)   (212) 724-6363
Mughlai offers tantalizing glimpses of the pleasures of Indian food. Its menu offers
the litany of familiar dishes, yet it also invites diners to try uncommon regional
dishes, which are almost always better. Dal papri, potatoes and chickpeas blended
in a tangy tamarind-and-yogurt sauce and served cool, is a superb appetizer. Pepper chicken, a dish from the southwestern state of Kerala, is another adventure.
Also excellent are baghare baigan, small eggplants in an aromatic sauce of ground
peanuts, sesame, tamarind and coconut. **Price range:** Entrees, $6.95–$18.95.
Meals: L, D. **Subway:** 1, 2, 3, 9 to 72nd St.

Nadaman Hakubai   ☆ ☆ $$$$ JAPANESE
Kitano Hotel, 66 Park Ave. (at 38th St.)   (212) 885-7111
A visit to this restaurant is like a quick trip to Japan. Kaiseki cuisine, associated
with the tea ceremony, is food for the soul as well as the body, meant to feed the
eye with its beauty and the spirit with its meaning. The courses follow a strict
order and each is intended to introduce the coming season. The way to enjoy
this is to abandon yourself to the experience, appreciating the peace, the subtlety of the flavors and the sense that you are being pampered as never before.

Unless you are an extremely adventurous eater, you will probably not like every dish, but an evening in one of the private tatami rooms can be immensely rewarding. Kaiseki dinners in the main restaurant are not particularly recommended. **Price range:** $100 minimum per person, for a minimum of four people. **Meals:** B, L, D. **Subway:** S, 4, 5, 6, 7 to 42nd St.

National Cafe $25 & Under   CUBAN/LATIN AMERICAN
210 First Ave. (near 13th St.)   (212) 473-9354
If you order a roast pork sandwich at this tiny Cuban restaurant, you can watch its construction. The server picks up a leg of pork and carefully carves pieces of the tender meat, piling them high on a hero roll. Then she places a chicharrón (a crisp piece of fried pork skin) on top. The result is delicious and filling, like almost everything else on the menu. **Price range:** Entrees, $6.50–$9. **Meals:** L, D. **Subway:** L to First Ave.

New Green Bo $ CHINESE
66 Bayard St., Chinatown   (212) 625-2359
This bright, plain restaurant in Chinatown looks like many other bright, plain restaurants in the neighborhood, except that it offers delicious Shanghai specialties like soup dumplings, smoked fish and eel with chives.
Price range: Entrees, $2.75–$24. Cash only. **Meals:** L, D, LN. **Subway:** J, M, N, Q, R, W, Z, 6 to Canal St.

New York Noodle Town   ☆☆ $ CHINESE
28 1/2 Bowery (near Bayard St.), Chinatown   (212) 349-0923
With its bustle and clatter, its shared tables and its chefs wreathed in billows of steam rising from the cauldrons of soup in the front of the restaurant, New York Noodle Town is as close as you can get to Hong Kong without leaving Manhattan. It serves Chinatown's most delicious food. Everything is good, from the superb roast suckling pig to the superlative deep-fried soft-shell crabs. All the noodle dishes are wonderful, and the roasted meats are also amazing. No meal at Noodle Town is complete without one of the salt-baked specialties.
Price range: Entrees, $4–$20. Cash only. **Meals:** B, L, D, LN. **Subway:** J, M, N, Q, R, W, Z, 6 to Canal St.

Next Door Nobu   ☆☆☆ $$$$ JAPANESE
105 Hudson St. (near Franklin St.)   (212) 334-4445
Slightly more casual than Nobu, Next Door Nobu takes no reservations and does not serve lunch. To dine here, come early: later arrivals may wait up to 90 minutes for a table. But the food is as accomplished (and as expensive) as Nobu's. It strives for its own identity, with an emphasis on raw shellfish, whole fish served for an entire table, noodles, and texture. The few meat dishes on the menu are memorable. Mochi ice cream balls are the most appealing way to end a meal. Mochi, the pounded rice candy of Japan, is stretchy and sticky when warm, but hardens into a cold tackiness when frozen. **Price range:** Noodle

dishes, $10–$15; hot dishes, $8–$32; sushi and sashimi, $3–$8 a piece. **Meals:** D, LN. **Subway:** 1, 9 to Franklin St.

Nha Trang $25 & Under   VIETNAMESE
87 Baxter St. (between Canal and Bayard Sts.)   (212) 233-5948
148 Centre St. (at Walker St.)   (212) 941-9292
Nha Trang was one of the pioneering Vietnamese restaurants in Chinatown, and it's still one of the best. Spring rolls are perfectly fried, while steamed ravioli, glistening paper-thin rice noodle crepes wrapped around minced pork and ground mushrooms and served with slices of smooth, mild Vietnamese pork sausage, is another excellent appetizer. Vietnamese rice noodle soups like pho tai, a huge bowl of noodles and tender slices of beef in a coriander-scented broth, are big enough to be an entire meal. **Price range:** Entrees, $5–$11. Cash only. **Meals:** B, Br, L, D. **Subway:** J, M, N, Q, R, W, Z, 6 to Canal St. (for both locations).

Nick & Toni's   ☆☆ $$$ MEDITERRANEAN
100 W. 67th St. (between Broadway and Columbus)   (212) 496-4000
Nick & Toni's is a lot like the neighborhood it serves: casual, crowded and noisy. But there is one thing that sets it apart from most of the neighborhood's restaurants: the food is really delicious. Nick & Toni's starts with good ingredients and leaves them alone. The menu changes constantly, but there are a few perennials, like the mussels and the impeccable Caesar salad. Often there is a fine pasta with just the right number of baby clams. Desserts are simple and seasonal. **Price range:** Entrees, $11–$28. **Meals:** L, D. **Subway:** 1, 9 to 66th St.

Nicole's   ☆☆ $$$ ENGLISH
10 E. 60th St. (near Fifth Ave., in the Nicole Farhi store)   (212) 223-2288
At lunch Nicole's hums and buzzes. It's filled with stylish, well-heeled diners, nearly all of them women. At night, the store closes, shadows descend, and Nicole's light and airy downstairs dining room takes on a somber tinge. The chef has developed a bright, appealing menu with a shrewd minimalist touch and just the right English notes. Nicole's does not go in for big, flashy effects. It's happy with clever little touches. The Moroccan cumin and lemon chicken is also irresistible. Nicole's also wisely steers toward simple, homey sweets like lemon pudding, and also offers cheeses from Neal's Yard Dairy in London. **Price range:** Entrees, $20 to $32. **Meals:** L, D. **Subway:** N, R, W to Fifth Ave.

NL   ☆ $$$ DUTCH/INDONESIAN
169 Sullivan St. (near Houston St.)   (212) 387-8801
A Dutch restaurant seems like an inside joke. But NL, which is short for Netherlands, has the last laugh, serving a clever mix of beloved Dutch standbys, Indonesian dishes that have gained honorary Dutch citizenship and invented dishes that use homey Dutch ingredients like herring, potatoes, cheese and the yogurt cream known as hangop. Sauerkraut risotto sounds forbidding, but it turns out to be one of the best things on the menu: the sauerkraut, distributed in fine threads, adds piquancy without bullying the dish. For dessert, try poffert-

jes, soft, puffy mini-pancakes sprinkled with powdered anise and served with a scoop of vanilla butter. **Price range:** Entrees, $18–$25. **Meals:** D. **Subway:** 1, 9 to Houston St.

Nobu ☆☆☆ $$$$ JAPANESE
105 Hudson St. (at Franklin St.) (212) 219-0500
Chic, casual and pulsing with energy, Nobu cannot be compared with any other restaurant. The kitchen incorporates new ingredients into old dishes and retools traditional recipes; the result is something that seems like a Japanese dish but is not. The best time to eat at Nobu is lunchtime. Order an Omakase meal and let the chefs choose your meal for you. If dishes like Funazushi, a freshwater trout buried in rice for a year, do not appeal to you, just tell the waiter the foods you do not eat. A finicky child could eat happily at Nobu, munching skewers of grilled chicken, beautifully rendered fried tempura and toro, the richest of tuna. No kitchen turns out a more spectacular plate of sushi. Desserts include a warm chocolate soufflé cake with siso syrup and green tea ice cream that comes in a bento box. **Price range:** Avg. $60–$75 per person. **Meals:** L, D.
Subway: 1, 9 to Franklin St.

Oceana ☆☆☆ $$$$ SEAFOOD
55 E. 54th St. (between Park and Madison Aves.) (212) 759-5941
Oceana's downstairs dining room is small and pretty, with an old-fashioned air. The intimate upstairs dining room is as handsome and luxurious as the dining room on a private yacht. Service is excellent, and you feel that you are about to set sail on a special voyage. Oceana's viewpoint is global—dishes are inspired by a wide variety of cuisines—while firmly rooted in an American idiom. What's more, the menu changes daily as the chef continues to experiment with new combinations. His careful spicing and the extremely intelligent use of ethnic accents brings out the essential nature of the fish. In summer, there is a huge variety of fruit desserts. One of the winter standards is sticky toffee pudding with vanilla ice cream. **Price range:** Prix-fixe-and tasting menus, $65–$105 ($170 with wines). **Meals:** L, D. Closed Sun.
Subway: E, F to Lexington Ave.; 6 to 51st St.

Odeon ☆☆ $$ BISTRO/NEW AMERICAN
145 West Broadway (at Thomas St.) (212) 233-0507
TriBeCa's first great American bistro is still cooking after all these years. The neighborhood has certainly changed, but time has stood still in the dining room. It is still unpretentious and comfortable, and it still feels as if it is filled with artists. It's great for burgers, omelets, pasta and roast chicken in a slightly funky setting; it's even greater for a martini. And it's still a destination until 3 A.M.
Price range: Avg. entree, $18. **Meals:** Br, L, D, LN.
Subway: A, C, 1, 2, 3, 9 to Chambers St.

Olives ☆ $$$ MEDITERRANEAN
281 Park Ave. S., in the W Union Square Hotel (at 17th St.) (212) 353-8345

The food here is easy to like but hard to respect. Do not look for light, because you won't find it, not even hidden under a cheese shaving. But it's hard to beat chef Todd English for sheer palate-engulfing flavor. Both venison and veal feature prominently in two of the better pastas, chestnut ravioli in a venison Bolognese sauce with creamy spinach, and mezzaluna, or pasta half-moons, stuffed with artichokes and blanketed under a ragu of braised veal breast and roasted tomatoes. Desserts are the kind that make diners feel pleasantly guilty. The Napoleon, filled with layers of caramel and loaded up with hazelnuts, banana cream and a scoop of chocolate sorbet, seems halfway between a French pastry and an old-fashioned banana split. **Price range:** Entrees,$18–$30. **Meals:** B, Br, L, D. **Subway:** L, N, Q, R, W, 4, 5, 6 to 14th St.

One If By Land, Two If By Sea $$$$ CONTINENTAL
17 Barrow St. (between W. 4th St. and Seventh Ave. South)   (212) 255-8649
Considered by many to be the most romantic restaurant in New York, it is almost always booked. The lights are low, the gas fireplaces burn even in the summer and a pianist serenades you with music. Known mainly for the 1950's specialty Beef Wellington, the food has grown more ambitious of late. The seared tuna is fresh and rosy, and the lightly smoked and roasted rack of lamb is a fine piece of meat. **Price range:** Prix-fixe, $64–75. **Meals:** D. **Subway:** 1, 9 to Christopher St.

Orsay   ☆☆ $$$ FRENCH/BRASSERIE
1057 Lexington Ave. (at 75th St.)   (212) 517-6400
Orsay looks as if it was ordered from a kit, with a lot of shiny brass, pristine leather banquettes and authentic French waiter costumes. But the cuisine has a fresh, wayward bent and an international style. A dish labeled "le Britannique," with a shocking list of ingredients that includes Stilton, walnuts and Yorkshire pudding, is a triumph, its ingredients delicately interwoven to create a lovely interplay of unexpected flavors. Another area of the menu worth lingering over showcases Orsay's hickory-chip smoker, which gives a dark, woodsy bite to salmon and to a dense, deeply flavored duck sausage. Oddly enough in this traditional setting, it's the traditional brasserie and bistro dishes that disappoint, but the restrained raspberry napoleon, with just a few pastry layers defining the form, is a perfectly executed classic.   **Price range:** Entrees, $15–$26. **Meals:** Br, L, D. **Subway:** 6 to 77th St.

Osteria Del Circo   ☆☆ $$$ ITALIAN
120 W. 55th St. (between Sixth and Seventh Aves.)   (212) 265-3636
Circo (pronounced CHEER-co) means "circus" in Italian, and the atmosphere is always festive. The key to ordering from its menu is to look for the name Egidiana, sometimes shortened to Egi, who is the owner's mother. Every dish attributed to her is superb, including her zuppa alla frantoiana, a thick, flavorful purée of 30 vegetables, and cacciucco, a Tuscan fish soup. Among the main courses, try the tender roast squab, a simple rotisserie chicken, red snapper

served with capers, onions and artichokes and the expertly made risottos. Should there be the special chocolate polenta cake, don't miss it; it is just the thing to send you off with a smile. **Price range:** Entrees, $22–$29. **Meals:** L, D. **Subway:** N, R, Q, W to 57th St.; B, D, E to Seventh Ave.

Otabe ☆☆ $$$ JAPANESE
68 E. 56th St. (between Park and Madison Aves.)   (212) 223-7575
Two separate dining rooms offer two different dining experiences. In the back room it is a very upscale Benihana; the elegant front dining room serves kaiseki-like cuisine. The kaiseki dinner is a lovely and accessible introduction to the most poetic food of Japan, a ceremonial cuisine that is traditionally served in many small courses meant to reflect the season. Less ambitious eaters might want to sample fewer dishes. Desserts are the big surprise at Otabe; more French than Japanese, they are original, beautiful and very delicious. The teppan room has a separate menu, and each course is cooked before your eyes by your personal chef. **Price range:** Entrees, $14.50–$65. **Meals:** L, D. **Subway:** 4, 5, 6 to 59th St.; E, F, N, R to Lexington Ave.

Ouest ☆☆ $$$ NEW AMERICAN/BISTRO
2315 Broadway (at 84th St.)   (212) 580-8700
This place looks good and it feels good. Long before the food arrives, Ouest (pronounced WEST), with disarming confidence, has most diners eating out of the palm of its hand. Pray for a booth, however, because the upstairs balcony seating is dark, cramped and loud. The cooking has a sane, rooted quality that makes it appropriate for what is, when all is said and done, a neighborhood restaurant. Main courses drift toward the comfort zone. Roast halibut with fava bean purée and mushroom broth has a solid, uncomplicated appeal, and the same can be said of the special section of the menu devoted to simple grilled meats. For dessert try the rhubarb crisp with strawberry juice, classic and all-American. **Price range:** Entrees, $16–$27. **Meals:** D. **Subway:** 1, 9 to 86th St.

Our Place Shanghai Tea Garden $25 & Under   CHINESE
141 E. 55th St. (at Third Ave.)   (212) 753-3900
With its elevated service, the ornate birds carved out of radish and turnip that adorn serving plates, and the thick linens, Our Place has the feel of a fine yet informal banquet. The Shanghai dishes are rich and satisfying, beautifully rendered, yet accessible to Americans, who make up most of the clientele. The waiters are supremely attentive, dividing portions onto plates, putting umbrellas into drinks for young children and generally offering to do anything short of feeding you. Silver-dollar-size steamed soup dumplings are well-seasoned and nicely textured. The kitchen excels at tofu dishes, and noodle dishes are superb. **Price range:** Entrees, $9.95–$24.95. **Meals:** L, D. **Subway:** E, F to Lexington Ave.; 6 to 51st St.

Palm $$$$ STEAKHOUSE
837 Second Ave. (between 44th and 45th Sts.)   (212) 687-2953

250 W. 50th St. (between Broadway and Eighth Ave.)   (212) 333-7256
Great steak, rude waiters, high prices and the world's best hash brown potatoes.
The walls are covered with caricatures, the floor is covered with sawdust and if
you want to experience the real New York rush, this is the place for you.
Price range: Entrees, $16–$35. **Meals:** L, D. **Subway:** Second Ave.: S, 4, 5, 6, 7
to 42nd St. W. 50th St: C, E, 1, 9 to 50th St.

Pam Real Thai Food $25 & Under   THAI
404 W. 49th St. (at Ninth Ave.)   (212) 333-7500
At this sweet little restaurant, your palate will revel in the kitchen's sure-
handed spicing. Shredded green papaya salad, for instance, is not only both
tangy and sweet but fiery as well, strewn with chewy dried shrimp and tiny red
chilies, with a faint sense of pungent fish sauce in the background. Pam's curries
are superb: try chu chee curry with pork, with its underlying flavor of coconut
milk laced with chili heat, or pad kra prow with beef, which has plenty of basil
flavor, balanced by garlic and chilies. **Price range:** Entrees, $7–$14. Cash only.
Meals: L, D. **Subway:** C, E to 50th St.

Panaché $25 & Under   BISTRO/FRENCH
470 Sixth Ave. (near 12th St.)   (212) 243-2222.
Panaché is an unpretentious place with a wood floor, leather banquettes and
brass lighting fixtures. With little flash, the food is the thing at Panaché, and
the chef has put together a menu that is generally down to earth and well-
anchored in bistro traditions. Appetizers are pretty and delicious, like potatoes
lyonnaise, flecked with smoky bacon and red wine vinegar. Main courses
include a satisfying roast chicken with pearl onions, mushrooms and mashed
potatoes and salmon, cooked perfectly and enlivened by a heady horseradish
sauce. Crème brûlée is excellent. **Price range:** Entrees, $12–$27.50. **Meals:** L,
D, LN. **Subway:** F to 14th St.

Pão $25 & Under   PORTUGUESE
322 Spring St. (at Greenwich St.)   (212) 334-5464
The small menu in this small restaurant offers traditional Portuguese cuisine
with a contemporary touch. To begin, try roasted quail on cabbage braised with
mild Portuguese sausage and black grapes. Main dishes include pork and clams
in a roasted-red-pepper sauce, and grilled shrimp served with a clam-and-
shrimp-studded lemony bread pudding. Desserts are not to be missed, particularly the pudding with port-and-prune sauce and the rice pudding with citrus,
nutmeg and cinnamon. **Price range:** Entrees, $13.95–$16.95. **Meals:** L, D, LN.
Subway: C, E to Spring St.

Paola's   ☆☆ $$ ITALIAN
245 E. 84th St. (between Second and Third Aves.)   (212) 794-1890
Everybody in New York seems to be looking for the perfect neighborhood
restaurant. This may be it. Paola's is one of the city's best and least-known Italian restaurants. It makes some of the city's finest pasta, and the wine list is wonderful. No regular would even consider starting a meal here without an order of

carciofi alla giudea, a fine version of baby artichokes fried in the style of the
Roman ghetto. But pastas are the soul of the menu. Filled pastas such as cazun-
zei and pansotti are wonderful. Desserts, except the ricotta cake, seem like an
afterthought. **Price range:** Pastas, $12.95–$14.95; entrees, $16.95–$26.95.
Meals: L, D. **Subway:** 4, 5, 6 to 86th St.

Papillon ☆ $$ BISTRO/FRENCH
575 Hudson St. (near Bank St.)   (646) 638-2900
Papillon looks like a neighborhood saloon, but it delivers twice the quality at
two-thirds the price of many Manhattan bistros. The short menu bristles with
happy combinations, mildly offbeat ideas and clearly expressed flavors. The
soups are superior. The French-sounding lamb confit is a round knob of lamb
braised for several hours, then wrapped in caul fat and given a final touch-up in
duck fat. It becomes meltingly tender and moist, almost like a firm pudding.
The menu includes a vegetarian department. **Price range:** Entrees,
$16–$23. AE only. **Meals:** Br, D, LN. **Subway:** 1, 9 to Christopher St.

Parioli Romanissimo ☆☆ $$$$ ITALIAN
24 E. 81st St. (between Fifth and Madison Aves.)   (212) 288-2391
One of New York City's most civilized restaurants, Parioli Romanissimo offers
stunningly expensive Italian food in an elegant town house. The old-fashioned
table-side cooking sends seductive aromas into the air. The rack of lamb is spectacularly good. The chef clearly cooks each risotto to order, and each one,
whether it is asparagus, seafood or a simple Milanese, is perfect. Pastas are also
exemplary. But finding a good bottle of wine at a reasonable price is extremely
difficult. **Price range:** Entrees, $28–$38. **Meals:** D. Closed Sun.
Subway: 6 to 77th St.

Park Avenue Cafe ☆☆ $$$$ NEW AMERICAN
100 E. 63rd St. (near Park Ave.)   (212) 644-1900
After a decade, the restaurant feels a little past its prime. But Upper East Siders
still treat it as a beloved neighborhood fixture where they can relax and eat
sanely reinterpreted, high-spirited American food. Pastas are among the best
dishes on the menu, but the most sinfully indulgent experience is the formidable terrine of foie gras, served folksy style in a glass jar with fig jam smeared on
the hinged lid. The signature "swordchop" still holds its place on the menu, a
mighty slab of swordfish attached to the collarbone. It is juicy and big-flavored.
For dessert, try the cherry tart or the beautifully realized chocolate cube.
Price range: Entrees, $19.50–$42. **Meals:** L, D. **Subway:** N, R, W to Lexington
Ave.; 4, 5, 6 to 59th St.

Park Bistro ☆☆☆ $$$ BISTRO/FRENCH
414 Park Ave. South (between 28th and 29th Sts.)   (212) 689-1360
A classic French bistro, this restaurant offers seductive Gallic fare, good wines
at reasonable prices and a cozy setting. Among the entrees are grilled escalope
of salmon, veal medallion, roasted and caramelized shoulder of pork with carrots
and fennel, and a daube of beef with potato gnocchi. There is a daily selection

of imported cheeses, and to top off the meal, thin warm apple tart with Arma-
gnac and vanilla ice cream; fresh roasted fig tart, or the ubiquitous crème brûlée.
There is a large and interesting selection of tea in addition to several coffees.
Price range: Avg. entree, $16–$30. **Meals:** L, D. **Subway:** 6 to 28th St.

Park View at the Boathouse   ☆☆ $$$ NEW AMERICAN
Loeb Boathouse, Central Park, E. 72nd St. entrance   (212) 517-2233
Is this Manhattan's most romantic spot? Very possibly. Situated in the Loeb
Boathouse next to Central Park's prettiest lake, it combines country charm with
views of skyscrapers peeking over the trees. There is interesting, eclectic food
and a good wine list here. The setting is so swell that you feel lucky to be there.
Live jazz at the adjacent café is a real bonus. **Price range:** Entrees, $18–$30.
Meals: Br, L, D. **Subway:** B, C, 1, 2, 7, 9 to 72nd St.

Pastis   ☆ $$$ BISTRO/FRENCH
9 Ninth Ave. (at Little W. 12th St.)   (212) 929-4844
Virtually every dish here could qualify for protection by the French Ministry of
Culture. And all are good. It's a deliberate invitation to simple pleasures. Pastis
needs to work on its steak frites, but rabbit pappardelle is a pleasant surprise, a
superior plate of firm pasta with a sweetly meaty sauce. For dessert, the crêpes
suzette rise up in glory, and the floating island floats, a cloud with just enough
substance to support its light custardy sauce. **Price range:** Entrees, $14–$17.
Meals: L, D, LN. **Subway:** A, C, E to 14th St.; L to Eighth Ave.

Patria   ☆☆☆ $$$ LATIN AMERICAN
250 Park Ave. South (at 20th St.)   (212) 777-6211
With its colorful food and boisterous atmosphere, Patria feels like a party every
night. The menu offers exuberant, outrageous nuevo Latino combinations with
names like Honduran fire and ice, an extravagant tuna ceviche marinated with
chilies, ginger and coconut milk. Each dish explodes in the mouth with a rich
variety of tastes. The main dishes are no less interesting than the appetizers.
Guatemalan chicken is a gorgeous combination of grilled white meat and deep
fried leg on a bed of green rice decorated with dots of mole sauce and an avocado salad. Rib-eye steak is so deeply smoked the taste seems to fill the mouth.
Sweets are visually restrained but each has a surprising intensity of flavor. **Price
range:** Three-course prix-fixe, $54. **Meals:** L, D. **Subway:** 6 to 23rd St.

Patroon   ☆☆☆ $$$$ NEW AMERICAN
160 E. 46th St. (between Lexington and Third Aves.)   (212) 883-7373
When Patroon opened, it was intended to be a contemporary "21," with a luxurious clubhouse atmosphere, low lights, neutral colors and smooth textures, and
extremely professional service. Many gourmets, however, found the food predictable. A change in chefs brought a few truly brilliant dishes to the menu:
Duck a l'orange Patroon, served as an appetizer, is a stunning rendition of an old
standard. There is a similarly innovative take on lamb breast, cooked into a rich
terrine enlivened with accents of mango and tomato. It, too, makes an ideal
appetizer. The menu is remarkably smart, American without being hokey, rich

without being fussy. **Price range:** Entrees, $23–$38. **Meals:** L, D. Closed Sun.
Subway: S, 4, 5, 6, 7 to 42nd St.

Payard Pâtisserie   ☆☆ $$$ BISTRO/FRENCH
1032 Lexington Ave. (at 73rd St.)   (212) 717-5252
This is the ultimate Upper East Side bistro, a whimsical cafe and pastry shop,
complete with mirrors, mahogany and hand-blown lamps. Just about everything here is extraordinary, from the inventive bistro menu to the amazing
pastries sold in the bakery. A recent visit showed that chef Philippe
Bertineau is still going strong, with inventive, impeccably executed dishes
like a twice baked cheese soufflé with Parmesan cream sauce, sardines stuffed
with quince chutney, and a simple sirloin steak with four-peppercorn sauce.
Price range: Entrees, $17–$25. **Meals:** Br, L, D. Closed Sun.
Subway: 6 to 77th St.

Peacock Alley   ☆☆☆ $$$$ FRENCH
Waldorf=Astoria Hotel, 301 Park Ave. (at 50th St.)   (212) 872-4895
Chef Laurent Gras does not try to dazzle you with exotic ingredients and no
Asian accents find their way into his dishes. Dishes here change frequently—
not only with the seasons, but weekly—sometimes even daily—allowing Mr.
Gras to offer diners a varied menu. The wine list, which once offered only high-
priced selections, has been expanded to include affordable bottles. The quiet,
comfortable—even serene—dining room has little character but the staff has
been invigorated, and everyone seems intent on providing diners with an extraordinary experience. **Price range:** Avg. entree, $32; 6-course tasting menu, $80.
Meals: B, Br, D, LN. **Subway:** 6 to 51st St.; E, F to Lexington Ave.

Pearl Oyster Bar $25 & Under   SEAFOOD
18 Cornelia St. (between Bleecker and W. 4th St.)   (212) 691-8211
It's just a marble counter with a few small tables, but Pearl has won over its
neighborhood with its casual charm and Maine-inspired seafood. The restaurant
is modeled on the Swan Oyster Depot in San Francisco, and when packed
exudes a Barbary Coast rakishness. The menu changes seasonally, but grilled
pompano was sweet and delicious, while scallop chowder was unusual and satisfying. Lobster rolls are big and delicious, and blueberry pie is sensational. Don't
forget the oysters. **Price range:** Entrees, $17–$25. MC/V only. **Meals:** L, D.
Closed Sun. **Subway:** A, C, E, F, S to W. 4th St.

Peasant   ☆ $$$ ITALIAN
194 Elizabeth St. (between Prince and Spring Sts.)   (212) 965-9511
Peasant has built a following by sticking to some very simple premises. Keep the
food simple, rustic and Italian. Cook it over a wood fire. Serve abundant portions. Be nice. That's about it. When the formula works, Peasant sends out
highly satisfying food, with the rich tanginess that wood smoke imparts. It adds
a sublime crunch to the excellent crust of Peasant's little pizzas. The pasta at
Peasant is good, not great. The desserts include a few surprises. The best choices
are vanilla-soaked bread pudding and a heroically proportioned peach pie with

a rough lattice crust. **Price range:** Dinner, Entrees, $19–$24. **Meals:** D. Closed
Mon. **Subway:** N, R to Prince St.; 6 to Spring St.

Pepe Verde $25 & Under   ITALIAN
559 Hudson St. (near Perry St.)   (212) 255-2221
Pepe Verde is a slightly larger version of Pepe Rosso to Go, the excellent takeout shop in SoHo. It has tables where you can sit comfortably, but the idea is
the same: freshly prepared Italian food several notches above the typical takeout
fare, including excellent boneless chicken breasts, marinated in lemon and
grilled; rigatoni with deliciously earthy meat sauce, and a rustic, enjoyable
pear tart. **Price range:** Entrees, $4.95–$10.95. Cash only. **Meals:** L, D.
Subway: 1, 9 to Christopher St.

Pepolino $25 & Under   ITALIAN
281 West Broadway (near Lispenard St.)   (212) 966-9983
The small, cheerful dining room seems to glow with warmth, the greeting is
friendly, and the service is good-natured. The gnocchi at Pepolino are ethereal,
as light as miniature clouds, making up with intense flavor what they lack in
mass. Whether as malfatti, gnocchi made with spinach and served in a simple
sauce of butter and sage, or in their more common potato incarnation, they are
meltingly good. The chef also makes a glorious pappa al pomodoro, the Tuscan
specialty of ripe tomatoes, shreds of stale bread and fragrant olive oil, cooked
into a delicious mush. Pastas are marvelous, and one dessert stands out: a dense
chocolate cake, intensely flavored with coffee. **Price range:** Entrees, $11–$19.
AE only. **Meals:** L, D, LN. **Subway:** 1, 9 to Franklin St.; A, C, E to Canal St.

Periyali ☆☆☆ $$$ GREEK
35 W. 20th St. (between Fifth and Sixth Aves.)   (212) 463-7890
Periyali used to be the best Greek restaurant in the city, and even now with so
much new competition it is still a great place to go. The atmosphere is rustic,
and the food is made with good ingredients. Recommended starters are the
avgolemono soup (a rich chicken soup smoothed with lemon, egg and
semolina), and especially the tender and fresh octopus marinated in red wine
and grilled over charcoal. Grilled lamb chops with fresh rosemary and garides
Santorini—baked shrimp with tomato, scallions, brandy and feta cheese—are
some of the entrees. For dessert, try the creamy, lemon-scented rice pudding,
the moist orange semolina cake, walnut cake, or the deep-fried pastry twists
called thiples. **Price range:** Entrees, $17–$25. **Meals:** L, D. Closed Sun.
Subway: F, N, R to 23rd St.

Petrossian ☆☆ $$$$ NEW AMERICAN/RUSSIAN
182 W. 58th St. (at Seventh Ave.)   (212) 245-2214
Nobody in New York City serves better caviar, and nobody does it with more
style. The dark room is covered with Art Deco splendor, the waiters wear blue
blazers and an obsequious air, and the caviar arrives with warm toast, blini and
beautiful little spoons. Vodka is served in icy little flutes that make it taste

somehow better. Should you desire something else, the food is good and surprisingly affordable. **Price range:** Entrees, $24–$34. **Meals:** Br, L, D.
Subway: N, R, Q, W to 57th St.

Picholine ☆ ☆ ☆ $$$$ MEDITERRANEAN/FRENCH
35 W. 64th St. (between Broadway and Central Park West) (212) 724-8585
Picholine, named after a Mediterranean olive, focuses on the food of southern France, Italy, Greece and Morocco. Meals begin with good house-made breads, bowls of the tiny olives and olive oil. Salmon in horseradish crust is a signature dish and it is excellent. But there are also robust dishes from the north, like daube of beef short ribs with a horseradish potato purée, and a hearty cassoulet. The kitchen also has a way with game. Homey dishes—chestnut and fennel soup dotted with sausage, cassoulet rich with duck confit—are all wonderful. Don't miss the wonderfully extravagant cheese cart, worth considering if only to hear the lovingly detailed descriptions of each cheese. **Price range:** Entrees, $26–$36; prix-fixe, $58; four-course tasting menu, $70 ($90 for seven courses). **Meals:** L, D. Closed Sun. **Subway:** 6 to 66th St.

Pico ☆ ☆ ☆ $$$ PORTUGUESE
349 Greenwich St. (at Harrison St.) (212) 343-0700
Pico is named after an island in the Azores, but it's a romantic reference, rather than a specific culinary source. Chef John Villa remains faithful to the simplicity of his source material while elevating it just enough to make it memorable and exciting. Salt cod, or bacalhau, is to Portugal what the potato is to Ireland, the hero with a thousand faces. The chef whips up a brandade of cod, potato and olive oil gently sparked with piri-piri, shaping it into a cake and frying it until it's crisp outside, creamy inside. Suckling pig can be almost cloyingly rich, but Mr. Villa knows how to handle this Portuguese favorite, applying a honey-citrus glaze that leaves the skin crunchier than the surface of a good créme brûlée. The star dessert at Pico is a heaped plate of cinnamon-dusted puffs of dough meant to be dipped in molten bittersweet chocolate or warm raspberry jam. **Price range:** Entrees, $24–$34. **Meals:** L, D. Closed Sun.
Subway: A, C, 1, 2, 3, 9 to Chambers St.

Pig Heaven $25 & Under CHINESE
1540 Second Ave. (near 80th St.) (212) 744-4333
Pig Heaven has a new, sleekly modern look, with a handsome bar, almond-shaped hanging lamps and a table of ceramic and carved decorative pigs. Its terrific Chinese-American food is spiced and presented in ways that please westerners, yet it is fresh and prepared with finesse. The best place to start is the pork selection, particularly roasted Cantonese dishes like suckling pig, strips of juicy meat under a layer of moist fat and wafer-thin, deliciously crisp skin. Most of the supposedly spicy Sichuan dishes here are good, but actually quite mild, and dumplings are excellent. **Price range:** Entrees, $7.95 to $18.95.
Meals: L, D. **Subway:** 6 to 77th St.

Ping's Seafood ☆☆ **$$**   CHINESE
22 Mott St. (between Worth and Mosco Sts.)   (212) 602-9988
Near the door, a high-rise of stacked fish tanks offers the menu headliners, a stel-
lar cast that includes but is by no means limited to lobsters, eels, scallops, sea bass
and shrimp. The preparations are minimal—a ginger-garlic sauce for the lobster,
for example, or black bean sauce for the eel—and the results are maximal.
Shrimp in the shell, crackling crisp and salty, come to the table piping hot,
exhaling a delicate, fragrant steam. For the adventurous eater, the quirky and
often experimental food of Hong Kong always stands as a welcome challenge.
One of the house signatures, a rather simple stir-fry of squid cut into long strands
woven together with dried fish and crunchy matchsticks of jicama and celery is a
winner. One of the more appealing rituals at Ping's is winter melon soup. You
must call a day ahead, since the melon, which flourishes in the summer despite
its name, has to steam for six hours. It is the perfect emblem for Ping's, an exotic
package with thrilling secrets inside. **Price range:** Entrees, $6.95-$30. **Meals:**
Br, L, D. **Subway:** J, M, N, Q, R, W, Z, 6 to Canal St.

Po **$25 & Under**   ITALIAN
31 Cornelia St. (near Bleecker St.)   (212) 645-2189
At this small, vivacious, reasonably priced trattoria, the parade of lush flavors
begins with the bruschetta offered at the start of each meal, a slice of toasted
Italian bread piled high with tender Tuscan white beans. Appetizers are a strong
point, with unusual combinations like delicate marinated anchovies draped
over a delicious heap of faro, a barleylike grain. Salads, too, are exceptional.
Pasta standouts include rigatoni with cauliflower, cooked in white wine until
soft, and seasoned with Parmesan, mint, sage and parsley. A paillard of lamb, as
long as a skirt steak, is almost beefy, daubed with aioli and served over sweet
grape tomatoes. Desserts include a sublimely dense terrine of dark chocolate
with a core of rich marzipan.   **Price range:** Entrees, $12.50–$16. AE only.
Meals: L, D / Closed Mon. **Subway:** A, C, E, F, S to W. 4th St.

Pongal **$25 & Under**   INDIAN/KOSHER/VEGETARIAN
110 Lexington Ave. (near 27th St.)   (212) 696-9458
The delectable vegetarian cuisine of South India is the specialty at Pongal, where
the food is kosher as well. The centerpiece dishes are the daunting dosai, huge
crepes made of various fermented batters that are stuffed and rolled into cylinders
that can stretch two-and-a-half feet. But they are light and delicious, filled with
spiced mixtures of potatoes and onions. Pongal also serves a wonderful shrikhand,
a dessert made of yogurt custard flavored with nutmeg, cardamom and saffron.
Price range: Entrees, $7.95–$13.95. **Meals:** L, D. **Subway:** 6 to 28th St.

Pop ☆ **$$$**   PAN-ASIAN/BISTRO
127 Fourth Ave. (12th St.)   (212) 767-1800
Pop is a bright, happy place with a noncommittal, nonemotive décor and a
crowd-pleasing menu that hips and hops from one culinary source to another.

The result is toe-tapping food. Pop feels just right, within fairly narrow limits, like an episode of "Friends." Chef Brian Young sprinkles his plates with little surprises—fun, palate-pleasing footnotes like the ingenious slaw of fine-shaved brussels sprouts that comes with a thick, juicy veal chop in quince and pomegranate sauce. For dessert, try the caramel bread pudding and the strawberry cream cake, an all-out assault on the pleasure zones. **Price range:** Entrees, $24 to $36. **Meals:** D. **Subway:** L, N, Q, R, W, 4, 5, 6 to 14th St.

Provence   ☆ $$$ FRENCH
38 Macdougal St. (near Prince St.)   (212) 475-7500
A crowded French café straight out of the French countryside, but while the atmosphere is charming and rustic, the food feels tired. Mussels gratinées, baked on the half shell and sprinkled with almonds and garlic, are very tasty. Bourride, a pale fish soup, is thickened with aioli; don't miss it. Pot au feu, a sometime special, is also a fine example of hearty country cooking, and the bouillabaisse, served only on Fridays, is superb. **Price range:** Entrees, $15.50–$26. AE only. **Meals:** L, D. **Subway:** N, R to Prince St.

Prune $25 & Under   ECLECTIC
54 E. 1st St. (near First Ave.)   (212) 677-6221.
The idiosyncratic name (the chef and owner's childhood nickname) is perfect for this unconventional little place. You could describe the food as homey, or as faintly European. Thin slices of duck breast taste deliciously of smoke, vinegar and black pepper, and are served with a small omelet flavored with rye. Roasted capon is as conventional a dish as Prune offers, yet it is marvelously juicy, served over a slice of toast imbued with garlic. Desserts are terrific, like cornmeal poundcake drenched in a rosemary syrup, with a poached pear. **Price range:** Entrees, $10–$17. **Meals:** D. Closed Mon. **Subway:** F to Second Ave.

Red Bar Restaurant   ☆ $$$ AMERICAN/BISTRO
339 E. 75th St. (between First and Second Aves.)   (212) 472-7577
In an area aswarm with taco and sushi take-away joints, Red Bar offers warmth, style and good, unpretentious food. It has limited aims, and a menu that refuses to strain for effect. Much of the menu is devoted to bistro standards, some presented very straightforwardly, others with a grace note or two. Good ingredients make the simpler dishes shine in a modest way and lend support to more adventurous excursions. For dessert, try a dense frozen parfait made with three chocolates. **Price range:** Entrees, $19–$29. **Meals:** D. **Subway:** 6 to 77th St.

The Red Cat   ☆ $$ BISTRO/AMERICAN
227 10th Ave. (near 23rd St.)   (212) 242-1122
A lot of restaurants make a big noise about being warm, welcoming and accessible. The Red Cat, with little ado, manages to be all three. It is stylish, but not snooty, cool but relaxed. The menu reflects the spirit of the place with a lineup of solid, well-executed American bistro dishes, with a little trick or twist on each plate. The

obligatory steak dish comes with a ragout of roasted shallots, tomatoes and cracked olives. The short dessert list does not disappoint. **Price range:** entrees, $15–$24. **Meals:** D, LN. **Subway:** C, E to 23rd St.

Redeye Grill   ☆ $$$ NEW AMERICAN
890 Seventh Ave. (at 56th St.)   (212) 541-9000
The boisterous room seems as big as Grand Central Terminal and is lively at almost any hour. There's something for everyone on the vast menu, from smoked fish to raw clams, Chinese chicken, pasta, even a hamburger—late into the night. The small grilled lobster, served with a little potato cake and pristine haricots verts, is lovely. The steak of choice here would be the hanger steak, tender slices piled onto a biscuit. The plain Jane cream-cheese bundt cake is usually the best of the desserts. **Price range:** Entrees, $18–$29.
Meals: Br, L, D, LN. **Subway:** N, R, Q, W to 57th St.

Remi   ☆☆ $$$ ITALIAN
145 W. 53rd St. (between Sixth and Seventh Aves.)   (212) 581-4242
Remi's stunning Gothic interior and the kitchen's enticing and inventive Northern Italian fare make it easy to understand its continued popularity. The diverse menu includes excellent pastas and main courses like garganelli blended with Coho salmon in balsamic sauce; veal-and-spinach-filled cannelloni in rosemary sauce; and salmon in a horseradish crust, finished with red wine sauce.
Price range: Entrees, $16–$28. **Meals:** L, D. **Subway:** B, D, E to Seventh Ave.

Rinconcito Mexicano $ MEXICAN/TEX-MEX
307 W. 39th St. (between Eighth and Ninth Aves.)   (212) 268-1704
This tiny restaurant is little more than a smoky aisle in the garment center. English is barely spoken, but the food needs no translation: soft tacos with the freshest and most authentic ingredients, like sautéed pork, calf's tongue, goat, chorizo and pork skin. The aroma of corn rises from the steamed tacos, and the refried beans are still pleasantly grainy. **Price range:** Avg. entree, $8.
Meals: L, D. Closed Sat., Sun. **Subway:** A, C, E to 42nd St.

Risa $25 & Under   PIZZA/ITALIAN
47 E. Houston St. (near Mulberry St.)   (212) 625-1712
Risa's pizzas taste as good as they look. The crust is thin and light, with a gentle, crisp snap. The cheese and tomato pie is impeccably fresh, and other toppings only enhance. Designer pies, like one made with speck (a smoked ham), arugula and mascarpone, are notable for their subtlety. Even truffle oil, a domineering ingredient that often crowds out other flavors, is used lightly. Beyond pizzas, Risa offers pastas that are fine if not especially unusual. Appetizers are a weak link, although calamari is full of flavor and texture, and an arugula and fennel salad is appropriately refreshing. **Price range:** Pizzas, $9–$12; entrees, $8.50–$19.50. **Meals:** L, D, LN. **Subway:** F, S to Broadway–Lafayette St.

Rocking Horse   **$25 & Under**   MEXICAN

182 Eighth Ave. (near 19th St.)   (212) 463-9511

A renovation has expanded and brightened the dining room, but while the food is still inspired by Mexico, the careful and complex seasonings are now muffled. Occasionally, a dish's Mexican identity manages to peek out. Well-charred yet flavorful chicken enchiladas are the best main course, and skewers of grilled shrimp are first-rate. Desserts are highlights, with winners like a tart and refreshing Key lime custard and a dense, fudgy tart with bananas and cherimoya sorbet. Rocking Horse offers an excellent lineup of tequilas and cocktails, and an inspired list of wines that prove how well wine can go with Mexican flavors. **Price range:** Entrees, $14.95–$21.95. **Meals:** L, D. **Subway:** C, E to 23rd St.

Rosa Mexicano   ☆☆   **$$$**   MEXICAN/TEX-MEX

1063 First Ave. (at 58th St.)   (212) 753-7407

The East Side Rosa Mexicano has been one of the city's reigning Mexican restaurants for more than a decade. It's also one of the most expensive, but Rosa is also a proud proponent of Mexico's place among the world's leading cuisines. Rosa's renowned guacamole is prepared at tableside, and other top-flight dishes include sautéed marinated shrimp, taquitos de moronga, in which blood sausage is served in corn tortillas with coriander, and pozole, the soothing, earthy soup. Menudo, an earthy tripe stew, and prawns sautéed with garlic and parsley are also winners. **Price range:** Entrees, $16–$26. **Meals:** D, LN. **Subway:** 4, 5, 6 to 59th St.; N, R, W to Lexington Ave.

Rosa Mexicano   **$$$**   MEXICAN

61 Columbus Ave. (at 62nd St.)   (212) 977-7700

The cooking at Rosa Mexicano on the West Side is Latin without passion or flair, but with enough bright spots along the way to offer hope. As with the East Side location, when a guacamole cart comes rolling by, hail it. The cart superintendent will construct a superlative avocado experience. It would be tempting, but a mistake, to order ceviche next. Seafood can wind up either too tough or mushy. For whatever reason, the kitchen seems most successful with deep, earthy flavors, as in a small appetizer casserole of sauteed mushrooms, tomatoes and onions, flavored with garlic, serrano chilies and the pungent herb epazote. David Rockwell's design has a splashy exuberance that's missing from the food, featuring a glittering blue tile wall with water running over its two-story surface. **Price range:** Entrees, $17.50–$28. **Meals:** Br, L, D. **Subway:** A, B, C, D, 1, 9 to 59th St.

Royal Siam   **$25 & Under**   THAI

240 Eighth Ave. (between 22nd and 23rd Sts.)   (212) 741-1732

Royal Siam's generic décor of mirrored walls, Thai posters and glass-topped tables belie some of the most flavorful and attractively prepared Thai cooking around. Dishes to look for include tom yum koong, or shrimp and mushroom soup in a lemony seafood broth; tod mun pla, fish cakes paired with a bright peanut sauce; and nuur yunk namtok, or grilled steak served sliced on a bed of mixed greens with cucumber and tomato. **Price range:** Entrees, $8.95–$14.95. **Subway:** C, E to 23rd St.

Ruby Foo's ☆☆ $$ PAN-ASIAN

1626 Broadway (between 49th and 50th Sts.) (212) 489-5600
2182 Broadway (at 77th St.) (212) 724-6700

The Upper West Side branch has everything it takes to make the neighborhood happy: fabulous décor, interesting pan-Asian food and the sort of atmosphere that appeals to families with children as well as singles on the prowl. The new location in Times Square, cheek by jowl with cartoon operations like the World Wrestling Federation restaurant, fits right into the area, with a décor that suggests the mysterious East as imagined by a 1940's B-movie producer. The menu offers everything from dim sum to sushi with side trips through Thailand, tailored to American tastes. With the exception of dim sum, the weakest link in the menu, the Chinese food is seductive. A memorable Japanese dish is the miso-glazed black cod. But it is the Southeast Asian dishes that really sing. The green curry chicken has a fiery coconut-based sauce that is irresistible. Desserts are purely American and purely wonderful, especially the raspberry-passion fruit parfait. **Price range:** Entrees, $9.50–$19.50. **Meals:** Br, L, D, LN.
Subway: Midtown: 1, 9 to 50th St. Uptown: 1, 9 to 79th St.

Russian Tea Room $$$$ RUSSIAN

150 W. 57th St. (between Sixth and Seventh Aves.) (212) 974-2111

The Russian Tea Room of old is no more. The downstairs looks much the same, although much brighter and shinier. But upstairs, the room is meant to conjure up the glittering halls of the Peterhof Palace and the magic world of Afanasyev's fairy tales. It feels more like a pinball machine. More than ever, the Russian Tea Room is not about the food. Still, some of the charms of Russian cuisine are on display here, notably in a thick, no-holds-barred borscht, packed with braised meats, fragrant with dill (and oddly enough, cilantro) and outfitted with horse-radish dumplings. Siberian veal and beef dumplings, or pelmeni, are nicely done, and Pozharsky cutlets combine minced veal and chicken in a soft, ovoid slab perked up with puréed beets. The caviar, a fail-safe choice, makes a luscious appetizer, swaddled in buckwheat blini and smothered in sour cream and butter. **Price range:** Entrees, $20–$33. **Meals:** L, D. **Subway:** N, R, Q, W to 57th St.

Sabor $25 & Under TAPAS/PAN-LATIN

462 Amsterdam Ave. (near 82nd St.) (212) 579-2929

The menu here has enough subdivisions to keep a law student busy for hours, including ceviches, empanadas, cheeses, charcuterie, skewers, salads, a raw bar, side dishes and tapas grandes, mercifully translated as "main courses." Certain things stand out immediately among the main courses, like a fine, beefy grilled skirt steak or an impressive braised lamb shank, served off the bone over mildly sweet mashed boniato with a luscious red-wine sauce. Sabor's paella takes liberties but is delicious and beautifully presented. Also try the delightful tapas. The standout dessert is a creamy dulce de leche cheesecake.   **Price range:** Tapas, $4.50–$9.95; entrees, $10.95–$15.95. **Meals:** L (weekends only), D. **Subway:** 1, 9 to 79th St.

Salaam Bombay Indian Cuisine   ☆☆ $$ INDIAN
317 Greenwich St. (near Duane St.)   (212) 226-9400
Salaam Bombay looks much like every other upscale Indian restaurant in New York City, large and pleasant. But it departs from tradition and showcases the richness of regional Indian cooking. At lunch there's a big, affordable buffet. At dinner an interesting assortment of vegetable dishes is where this kitchen really shines. The best is ringna bataka nu shaak, a Gujarati eggplant and potato dish cooked with curry leaves and lots of spices. Also try kadhai jhinge, shrimp stir-fried with tomatoes, onions and lots of fresh and fragrant spices. For dessert, shrikhand, a dreamy, custardlike dessert, has a mysterious flavor that imparts a certain sense of wonder. **Price range:** entrees, $9.95–$19.95. **Meals:** L, D. **Subway:** A, C, 1, 2, 3, 9 to Chambers St.

San Domenico   ☆☆☆ $$$$ ITALIAN
240 Central Park South (between Broadway and Seventh Ave.) (212) 265-5959
This dignified and comfortable spot is one of a handful of American restaurants trying to showcase the cooking of the aristocratic northern Italian kitchen, the cuisine known as alta cucina. Give this staid restaurant a chance and it will manage to capture your heart. Most of the appetizers are so seductive that you will eat every meal in a flush of joyful anticipation. The restaurant's signature dish is uovo in ravioli con burro nocciola tartufato: a single large puff filled with ricotta and spinach perfumed with truffle butter. Snuggled inside is an egg that spurts golden yolk as you begin to eat. But the kitchen does not need luxury ingredients to show its stuff. You could come to San Domenico and treat it like a trattoria, choosing only simple dishes and enjoying the care with which they are cooked.
Meals: L, D. **Subway:** A, B, C, D, 1, 9 to 59th St.

Savoy   ☆☆ $$$ NEW AMERICAN
70 Prince St. (at Crosby St.)   (212) 219-8570
Savoy looks like a funky old aluminum-sided diner. But the upstairs dining room, where cooking is done right in the fireplace, is one of the city's coziest rooms. The menu dances around the globe, borrowing where it will. The results can be wildly uneven but are usually charming. If you are unlucky you may end up with one of the occasionally gummy risottos or doughy pastas. Order a salad, however, and you will instantly be seduced. Desserts are excellent and change with the market. If you have an adventurous spirit, you will discover a sense of fun that is missing in most modern restaurants. **Price range:** Entrees, $19–$26. **Meals:** L, D. **Subway:** N, R to Prince St.; F, S to Broadway–Lafayette St.

Scalini Fedeli   ☆   **$$$$**   ITALIAN
165 Duane St. (Hudson St.)   (212) 528-0400
Scalini Fedeli (which means "steps of faith") has no edge. What it has, instead,
is old-fashioned grace. The dining room is as soothing as a massage. The pleasing food rarely takes flight, and when it does, the dish is likely to be disarmingly
simple. The pappardelle with a sauce of Scottish hare and venison is a small
feast of gloriously rich, dark meats finished off with cream and truffles. The
main courses are satisfying, decorous and rather unassuming. A good-size fillet
of roasted Chilean sea bass, for example, finds an ideal matchup in a sauce of
sun-dried tomatoes and Sicilian and Greek olives, and saddle of rabbit, swaddled in pancetta and served with a black olive sauce, makes a simple, pleasing
entrée. For dessert, the panna cotta takes a back seat to the dense chocolate
tart, and to the clever miniature cannoli, filled with espresso-flavored mascarpone cream. **Price range:** Dinner, three courses, $60. **Meals:** L, D.
Subway: A, C, 1, 2, 3, 9 to Chambers St.

Screening Room   ☆ ☆   **$$$**   NEW AMERICAN
54 Varick St. (below Canal St.)   (212) 334-2100
It's a bar. It's a restaurant. It's a movie theater. The slightly funky bar serves
appealing snacks like lobster rolls, onion rings and Philadelphia cheese steaks.
The restaurant offers serious American food on the order of grilled duck and
spectacular desserts. The best appetizer is the pan-fried artichokes, served on
lemony greens topped with shavings of Parmesan cheese. The simplest entrees
are the most impressive. The pastry chef does not have a loser on the list, but
the best desserts are lemon icebox cake and toasted angel food cake. **Price
range:** Entrees, $13–$22. **Meals:** Br, L, D. **Subway:** A, C, E, 1, 9 to Canal St.

Sea Grill   ☆ ☆   **$$$**   SEAFOOD
19 W. 49th St. (in Rockefeller Center)   (212) 332-7610
During the winter the main draw here is a view of the Rockefeller Center skating rink. In warm weather, the skating rink becomes an outdoor extension of
the restaurant, with canvas umbrellas and potted shrubs. Much of the menu has
a brasserie feel to it, with a changing daily menu of day-boat fish that are simply
grilled, sauteed or seared. A fresh breeze blows over the rest of the menu as well,
with the accent on vibrant flavors and simple preparations. The crab cake is
justly renowned: a lumpy-looking thing, more ball than patty, displaying the
rough-hewn virtues that distinguish a real crab cake from a thousand prettified
pretenders. **Price range:** Entrees, $21–$29. **Meals:** L, D. Closed Sun.
Subway: B, D, F, S to 47th-50th St.–Rockefeller Center.

71 Clinton Fresh Food   ☆ ☆   **$$**   BISTRO/NEW AMERICAN
71 Clinton St. (near Rivington St.)   (212) 614-6960
Cool, understated and hip, this makes every other restaurant in New York
look as if it's trying too hard. Chef Wylie Dufresne starts with wonderful
ingredients, and when manipulating them, he shows a purist's respect for
clean flavors and harmonious combinations. He has a fresh, original take
on every dish, but an innate sense of rigor tells him when enough is

enough. And he excels at striking visual presentations. The menu is tiny. Diners can choose from six appetizers, seven entrees and four desserts, with a special or two thrown in from time to time. The wine list, too, is short. But then the restaurant itself is tiny. Desserts are simple, like a straightforward warm pineapple tart with coconut ice cream. **Price range:** Entrees, $15–$22. **Meals:** D. Closed Sun. **Subway:** F to Delancey St.; J, M, Z to Essex St.

Shun Lee Palace   ☆☆ $$$ CHINESE

155 E. 55th St. (between Lexington and Third Aves.)   (212) 371-8844

No restaurant in New York City can produce better Chinese food. And no restaurant in New York City does it so rarely. Shun Lee is a New York institution, with a cool opulence that is almost a caricature of a Chinese-American palace. Regular customers are so pampered that first-timers look on enviously as they are shunted off to a table in the far less luxurious bar area. The spareribs are long, meaty, almost fat-free and perfectly cooked. The chefs do impressive things with whole fish, and the restaurant's owner likes to appear at the table with live fish and suggest various ways the kitchen might prepare them. **Price range:** Entrees, $8.75–$29.95. **Meals:** L, D. **Subway:** E, F to Lexington Ave.; 6 to 51st St.

Shun Lee West $$$ CHINESE

43 W. 65th St. (at Columbus Ave.)   (212) 595-8895

A cavernous Chinese restaurant near Lincoln Center that is always packed. The kitchen can do great things, but they are rarely produced for a clientele that sticks mostly to the familiar. If you want the best food, call ahead and discuss the menu. Good Peking duck. **Price range:** Avg. entree, $19. **Meals:** Br, L, D, LN. **Subway:** 1, 9 to 66th St.

Silver Swan $25 & Under   GERMAN

41 E. 20th St. (between Broadway and Park Ave. South)   (212) 254-3611

The excellent selection of more than 75 beers and ales is reason enough to enjoy Silver Swan's solid German fare in a friendly atmosphere. Rauchbier, or smoked beer, made with smoked malt, goes perfectly with kassler rippchen, smoked pork chops served with vinegary sauerkraut, while any of more than a dozen Bavarian wheat beers are just right with weisswurst, mild veal sausage, or bratwurst, juicy pork sausage. This is not the place to eat if you are longing for vegetables; meat is another matter, however, starting with five varieties of schnitzel and ending with a satisfying sauerbraten. **Price range:** Entrees, $14–$27. **Meals:** L, D, LN. **Subway:** 6 to 23rd St.

Smith & Wollensky   ☆☆ $$$$ STEAKHOUSE

797 Third Ave. (at 49th St.)   (212) 753-1530

This is a place for two-fisted eating. It is also one of the few steakhouses that never lets you down: the service is swell, the steaks are consistently very, very good (if rarely great) and the portions are huge. The sirloins are aged for around two weeks to intensify the flavor and give the meat a dry edge. Beyond that, if you have noncarnivores to feed, the restaurant knows how to do it. The lobsters, clams, oysters and chicken are excellent too. Desserts, unfortunately, leave a great deal to be desired. **Price range:** Entrees, $18.50–$65. **Meals:** L, D, LN. **Subway:** 6 to 51st St.; E, F to Lexington Ave.

Snack $25 & Under   GREEK
105 Thompson St. (at Prince St.)   (212) 925-1040
This is one of Manhattan's smallest restaurants. But taste the stifado, a delicately spiced stew of braised lamb, and you know right away that Snack is worth squeezing into. Start with the impeccable cold appetizers: hummus, melitzanes salata, taramosalata, tzatziki and skordalia. Other gems among the small selection of main courses include keftedes, or savory veal meatballs, and juicy roast chicken. Desserts are simple and satisfying. **Price range:** Entrees, $8–$13. Cash only. **Meals:** L, D. **Subway:** N, R to Prince St.

Soba Nippon $25 & Under   JAPANESE/SUSHI
19 W. 52nd St. (between Fifth and Sixth Aves.)   (212) 489-2525
Few things induce serenity like a bowl of cold Japanese soba noodles, and few places make better noodles than Soba Nippon. The owner has his own buckwheat farm and soba noodles are made daily at the restaurant. Try the cold soba noodles served plain, on a flat basket with a dipping sauce of fish stock and soy. Eventually, a small, simmering pot of liquid is placed on the table: this is the broth in which the noodles were boiled. Pour the broth into the dipping sauce, add the scallions and wasabi, and drink. It's marvelous. One fine alternative to soba is cold inaniwa udon noodles, as thin as spaghetti, with a pure, clean flavor. Soba Nippon's hot soba soups are excellent as well. **Price range:** Entrees, $8–$17. **Meals:** L, D. **Subway:** E, F to Fifth Ave.

Soba-Ya $25 & Under   JAPANESE/NOODLES
229 E. 9th St. (between Second and Third Aves.)   (212) 533-6966
Noodles are the focus at this bright, handsome little Japanese restaurant. The soba noodles — buckwheat, pale tan and smooth — are served hot in soups or cold, a better bet for appreciating their lightness and clear flavors. Appetizers are excellent, differing night to night but sometimes including cooked marinated spinach, rice with shreds of marinated sardines and fried squares of marvelously fresh tofu. **Price range:** Noodles and rice bowls, $6.50–$14. **Meals:** L, D. **Subway:** 6 to Astor Pl.; N, R to 8th St.

Soho Steak $25 & Under   BISTRO/FRENCH
90 Thompson St. (near Spring St.)   (212) 226-0602
This thoroughly French little restaurant, drawing a young, good-looking crowd, emphasizes meat but is no simple steakhouse. It is a cleverly conceived, bustling bistro that serves creative dishes for lower prices than you might imagine. Steak frites, of course, is top-notch. Few places offer this much value for this kind of

money. **Price range:** Entrees, $14–$16. Cash only. **Meals:** Br, D.
Subway: C, E to Spring St.

Solera ☆☆ $$$ SPANISH

216 E. 53rd St. (between Second and Third Aves.)   (212) 644-1166
Solera looks so cozy it is almost impossible not to be drawn into the long room, with its terra-cotta tiles and romantic lighting. Pull up a chair and prepare to be seduced by the food and wine of Spain. The appetizers are all fine, but the octopus with paprika and olive oil is consistently amazing—it is as tender as marrow. There are several versions of paella, all delicious but the seafood is the most impressive. Best of all are the crisp little lamb chops served with a ragout of beans and polenta laced with cheese. **Price range:** Entrees, $25–$35; tapas, $3–$9.50. **Meals:** L, D, LN. Closed Sun.
Subway: E, F to Lexington Ave.; 6 to 51st St.

Sono ☆☆ $$$$ JAPANESE/FRENCH

106 E. 57th St. (at Lexington Ave.)   (212) 752-4411
Sono—which means "garden enhanced by man"—is a showcase for Tadashi Ono's idiosyncratic, very persuasive blend of French and Japanese cooking. There is a disarming simplicity to the menu. The excitement comes from unexpected pairings, or the sheer, inexhaustible pleasure of directly communicated taste sensations, or arresting visual presentations. The chef's assortment, an appetizer, offers a whirlwind tour through Mr. Ono's mind. The lineup varies from day to day, but it's always a carousel of tastes and textures. It's enough that Mr. Ono has given the world his roasted squab smeared with a paste of kaffir lime, a kind of hollandaise made with sake and white miso. It has a counterpart on the dessert menu, an impressively tall cheesecake made with kabocha squash (Japan's favorite pumpkin) and coconut.
Price range: Dinner, three courses, $52; seven course tasting menu, $78.
Meals: L, D. **Subway:** 4, 5, 6 to 59th St.; N, R, W to Lexington Ave.

Stella $25 & Under NEW AMERICAN

58 Macdougal St. (between W. Houston and Prince Sts.)   (212) 674-4968
For SoHo, Stella is a rare combination of elements — good food, good wine, good atmosphere, good value. The best appetizers include a rich, buttery pea risotto and a wonderful salad of leeks, radishes, sweet cantaloupe and tender little radish sprouts all topped with warm, earthy goat cheese. Some of the main courses seem conceptually flawed, but the tender, meaty Cornish hen, served in a bowl with braised prunes, olives and capers, and a thick Newport steak covered in a salad of cherry tomatoes, arugula and capers are very pleasing. There is an excellent list of New World wines. Stella's desserts are not flashy, but you'll love the humble strawberry shortcake and the sedate chocolate bread pudding.
Price range: Entrees, $13.50–$18.50, with one at $25.50. AE only.
Meals: Br, D. **Subway:** C, E to Spring St.; 1, 9 to Houston St.

Strip House   ☆   **$$$**   STEAKHOUSE
13 E. 12th St. (between Fifth Ave. and University Pl.)   (212) 328-0000
Strip House is not so much a steakhouse as a catalog of hip references to the
idea of a steakhouse. It has a cheery, comfortable atmosphere, with none of the
backslapping locker-room style of the old-line steakhouses. The filet mignon
and New York strip steaks are perfectly acceptable, but the swaggering porter-
house comes through in a big way, seared aggressively to achieve a deep crunch,
all rubescent tender meat within. The rest of the menu, however, shows a more
playful side, like the three-way lamb dish listed on the menu as Ménage à Trois.
The time-honored side dishes are reinterpreted a bit, and new ones have been
added. Desserts bring mixed results, but the caramelized apple tart with mascar-
pone ice cream and brown sugar hard sauce is as good as it sounds. **Price range:**
Entrees, $22–$32. **Meals:** D. **Subway:** F, L, N, Q, R, W, 4, 5, 6 to 14th St.

The Sultan   **$25 & Under**   TURKISH
1435 Second Ave. (near 74th St.)   (212) 861-2828
This friendly storefront restaurant offers mainstream Turkish dishes that are
notable for their fresh, lively flavors. Meals begin with a basket of puffy house-
made bread studded with tiny black sesame seeds, and a dish of tahini blended
with pekmez, a thick grape syrup. Kebabs are universally good here, especially
the lamb yogurt kebab, and whole trout is grilled perfectly, then filleted at the
table. The dessert menu is predictable yet well prepared. **Price range:** Entrees,
$11.95–$16.95. **Meals:** L, D. **Subway:** 6 to 77th St.

Surya   ☆☆   **$$**   INDIAN
302 Bleecker St. (between Seventh Ave. South and Grove St.) (212) 807-7770
The restaurant named for the sun (in Tamil) actually has a small garden in
the back along with a sleek interior. Its menu features mostly south Indian
dishes, often filtered through the technique of France. The main courses
have a bold freshness. But what is most splendid about Surya is the entirely
meatless side of the menu. It is, in fact, difficult to come up with a more
exciting place to eat vegetables in New York City. Don't eat a meal at Surya
without ordering the okra, sautéed in a thick mixture of tomatoes, onion,
garlic and kokum (a sour Indian fruit). Try the dosai, too, and the exceptional desserts. **Price range:** Entrees, $11–$24. **Meals:** Br, D.
Subway: 1, 9 to Christopher St.

Sushi Hatsu   ☆☆☆   **$$$$**   JAPANESE/SUSHI
1143 First Ave. (near 62nd St.)   (212) 371-0238
With a modest sushi bar in front, and a few tables in the rear, Sushi Hatsu serves
breathtakingly good fish of an astonishing purity. It is so light, you feel you
could go on eating forever. The bill will be huge; good sushi is never cheap. But
if you've got the money, they've got the fish. **Price range:** $30 minimum at the
sushi bar, but expect to spend $75 to $100 a person. AE/Diner's only. **Meals:** D,
LN. Closed Mon. **Subway:** N, R to Lexington Ave.; 4, 5, 6 to 59th St.

Sushi Yasuda   ☆☆☆   **$$$**   JAPANESE/SUSHI
204 E. 43rd St. (between Second and Third Aves.)   (212) 972-1001
In one of the city's dreariest restaurant neighborhoods, Sushi Yasuda glows like a
strange mineral, with a cool, celery-green façade. Inside, the mood is quiet, con-
templative, austere. But Sushi Yasuda has a lot of downtown in its soul. The
manager and the waitresses are young. The exemplary service has an open,
friendly quality to it. At the same time, the menu is dead serious, a purist's par-
adise of multiple choices among fish species—nearly 30, a startling number for a
small restaurant—and elegantly presented appetizers and side dishes. But sushi
is only half the story. The daily menu includes a small sheet of special appetiz-
ers, and they are worth jumping for. **Price range:** Sushi, $3–$6.50 a piece.
Meals: L, D. Closed Sun. **Subway:** S, 4, 5, 6, 7 to 42nd St.

Sylvia's   **$**   SOUTHERN
328 Lenox Ave. (between 126th and 127th Sts.)   (212) 996-0660.
Tour buses pull up in front for a sanitized taste of Harlem. The food's not fabu-
lous, but it offers everything you expect: fried chicken, collard greens and sweet
potato pie. Best for the gospel brunch on Sunday. **Price range:** Entrees,
$8.95–$13; gospel brunch: $15.95. **Meals:** Br, L, D. **Subway:** 2, 3 to 125th St.

Tabla   ☆☆☆   **$$$$**   AMERICAN-ASIAN FUSION
11 Madison Ave. (near 25th St.)   (212) 889-0667
The newest of Danny Meyer's restaurants, Tabla vibrates with sound and sizzles
with color. At the bar downstairs, cooks grill roti and naan in odd and interest-
ing flavors. Upstairs, the dining room is darkly sensuous with walls stained in
shades of jade and coral. Then the food arrives—American food, viewed
through a kaleidoscope of Indian spices. The powerful, original and unexpected
flavors evoke intense emotions. Those who do not like Tabla tend to dislike it
with a passion. Ignore them and abandon yourself to the joys of a fine restau-
rant. **Price range:** Three-course prix-fixe dinner, $52 (plus a few supplements).
Meals: L, D. Closed Sun. **Subway:** 6 to 23rd St.

Taco Taco   **$**   MEXICAN/TEX-MEX
1726 Second Ave. (between 89th and 90th Sts.)   (212) 289-8226
Every neighborhood should have a Mexican restaurant like this where the
atmosphere is casual and pleasant but the food is serious. Tacos, naturally, are
the mainstay, with fillings like pork with sautéed cabbage, tongue and crumbled
chorizo. More ambitious dishes include tender pork marinated with smoky
chipotle chilies and grilled. Even nachos are made with unusual care. **Price
range:** Entrees, $9–$12. Cash only. **Meals:** L, D. **Subway:** 4, 5, 6 to 86th St.

Tagine   **$25 & Under**   MOROCCAN
537 Ninth Ave. (near 40th St.)   (212) 564-7292
Tagine is, in the true bohemian spirit, a low-budget operation. The dim, alluring
dining room seems a blizzard of colors and styles and the languorous service may

lead you to believe that food is not the focus here, but you'll relax when the
food arrives. Zaalouk, an eggplant purée rich with the dusky aroma of cumin, is
wonderful on freshly baked bread. The restaurant's signature tagines, fragrant
stews served in traditional earthenware vessels with conical lids, are the least
satisfying of the main courses, though the chicken tagine and lamb shank are
quite good. Desserts can be excellent, like semolina cake soaked in orange blossom water. **Price range:** Entrees, $13–$19.50. **Meals:** L, D, LN.
Subway: A, C, E to 42nd St.

Tamarind   ☆☆ $$ INDIAN
41-43 E. 22nd St. (between Broadway and Park Ave. South)   (212) 674-7400
Tamarind, named for the sweet-and-sour fruit, looks and feels fresh. It is stylishly decorated, and the menu treats Indian cuisine as a genuine culinary language, like French, able to assimilate nontraditional ingredients and techniques.
Quality varies on the extensive dinner menu, but on balance, the winners out-
number the losers by about 3 to 1. For whatever reason, anything involving
shrimp succeeds wildly, like shrimp balchau, an exotic shrimp cocktail with a
smoothly fiery chili-masala sauce wrapped around tiny chunks of firm tomato.
Vegetarian dishes also seem to bring out the best at Tamarind. The tandoor does
not perform flawlessly, though some dishes emerge moist and succulent from the
oven, like noorani kebab, chunks of spiced chicken flavored with saffron. The
lunch menu at Tamarind is ingenious, with five set menus, each representing a
coherent Indian meal. **Price range:** Entrees, $15–$26. **Meals:** L, D.
Subway: 6 to 23rd St.

Tappo   ☆ $$ MEDITERRANEAN
403 E. 12th St. (at First Ave.)   (212) 505-0001
A really good neighborhood restaurant can be hard to find, but Tappo hits the
mark. The food is simple and fresh; the setting feels like a farmhouse kitchen.
The menu has a long, unchanging list of appetizers that mixes traditional Italian starters with less predictable Spanish and Middle Eastern dishes, but the
best of them, regardless of origins, have the sparkle that can only come from
fresh ingredients. Baby chicken sautéed in herbs and white wine is a fine,
unpretentious dish, and the kitchen turns out a superior roasted branzino, firm-
fleshed and moist, The pastas can be excellent, and the standout dessert is a
dense panna cotta drizzled with sweetly pungent 25-year-old balsamic vinegar.
Price range: Entrees, $15–$26. **Meals:** D, LN. **Subway:** L to First Ave.

The Tasting Room   ☆ $$$ NEW AMERICAN
72 E. 1st St. (between First and Second Aves.)   (212) 358-7831
When the Tasting Room is not caught up in its own spell, it does the honorable
work of serving good food at a moderate price in a pleasant atmosphere, with a
clever format. What sets the restaurant apart is its ferociously ambitious, nicely-
priced wine list. The menu allows diners to combine several tasting portions
into a meal or to order the usual appetizer and main course. At the Tasting

Room, bolder is better. Try rabbit or a simple pan-roasted sea bass. For dessert, Renée's Mother's Cheesecake is a cheesecake to die for, lighter than air, with a barely-there crust and a restrained sweetness level. In comparison, the menu is a mere footnote. **Price range:** Entrees, $13–$29. **Meals:** D. Closed Sun. **Subway:** F to Second Ave.

Tavern on the Green ☆ $$$$ NEW AMERICAN
Central Park West (at 67th St.) (212) 873-3200
This is America's largest-grossing restaurant, a wonderland of lights, flowers, chandeliers and balloons that can make a child out of the most cynical adult. Patrick Clark, who died in February 1998, was a terrific chef, and he's left a culinary legacy for his successors to follow. But even he was not able to overcome the tavern's unaccountably rude and lax service. Even so, the people keep coming for the glittery setting. **Price range:** Entrees, $21.75–$34. **Meals:** Br, L, D. **Subway:** 6 to 66th St.

Thalia ☆☆ $$$ NEW AMERICAN
828 Eighth Ave. (at 50th St.) (212) 399-4444
Thalia is the Muse of comedy, and also a confusing name for a serious restaurant. Executive chef Michael Otsuka practices an intelligent form of fusion cooking, with a strong Asian influence. He has faith in the power of simple ingredients and flavors, and the wit to use them in inventive ways. A spoonful of wasabi granita, cold and crunchy, with a piercing heat, sets off Kumamoto oysters brilliantly. Foie gras fatigue disappears the moment you lay eyes on foie gras mousse, sprinkled with chopped pistachio and accompanied by figs drenched in port. It looks like dessert but it's twice as rich—damnation on a small plate. **Price range:** Entrees, $17–$29. **Meals:** L, D. **Subway:** C, E to 50th St.

Tocqueville ☆☆ $$$ FRENCH
15 E. 15th St. (between Fifth Ave. and Union Sq. West) (212) 647-1515
Tocqueville is a quiet haven of good taste, good food and good service. Although tiny, Tocqueville never feels cramped. The spacing between tables is generous, given the floor space, and the service, which could easily feel intrusive and hovering, achieves a laudable transparency. Billy Bi soup, the oddly named classic from France's Atlantic coast, is beyond praise. The roasted rack of lamb is surrounded by braised artichokes, mushrooms and fava beans in a red-wine reduction. Desserts also do honor to the menu, especially the upside-down banana tart, a small palisade of fat banana chunks encircling a disk of almond shortbread, teamed up with a ball of brown-sugar ice cream. **Price range:** Entrees, $22–$28. **Meals:** L, D. Closed Sun. **Subway:** L, N, Q, R, W, 4, 5, 6 to 14th St.

The Tonic ☆☆ $$$ NEW AMERICAN
108 W. 18 St. (between Sixth and Seventh Aves.) (212) 929-9755
Tonic has a raucous, old-fashioned tavern in front, and in back a tranquil

restaurant filled with beautiful light that makes all the patrons look lovely. Excellent waiters serve robust American food like a wonderful pumpkin bisque, ravioli filled with sweetbreads and salsify, and scallop velouté. And who could resist sautéed fois gras set on chestnut purée? Not me. The menu changes seasonally. **Price range:** Entrees, $25–$28. **Meals:** L, D. Closed Sun. **Subway:** F, 1, 2, 3, 9 to 14th St.

Topaz Thai $25 & Under   THAI
127 W. 56th St. (between Sixth and Seventh Aves.)   (212) 957-8020
This restaurant offers fine Thai cooking. Soups, like the delicious tom kha gai, made with chicken stock, coconut milk, chili peppers and lime, are particularly good, as are spicy dishes like the soupy jungle curry made with scallops and green beans. The restaurant has a peculiar nautical theme courtesy of a previous tenant—Art Deco paneling, triangular sconces and wooden captain's chairs. **Price range:** Entrees, $8–$18. **Meals:** L, D. **Subway:** N, R, Q, W to 57th St.

Town   ☆ ☆ ☆ $$$ NEW AMERICAN
15 W. 56th St., in the Chambers Hotel (between Fifth and Sixth Aves.)
                                                           (212) 582-4445
Town has an unmistakable sense of style. It's a civilized, very adult setting that suits the chef's elegant, clean cooking. He manages to enliven his dishes with just the half twist that makes them distinctive, as in a simple roasted skate served with three sorbet-shaped quenelles: pea-peppermint, apple-miso, and eggplant with hazelnut oil and quatre-épices. Some dishes are simplicity itself. A risotto of escargots doused with black truffle broth seems unfair. How can it fail? It's like having the chef write you a large check. The dessert list is strong, and one is a showstopper: it starts with a basket of sugar-powdered beignets filled with molten chocolate. Then comes a perfect frozen dome with a matte-brown cocoa surface, a chilled version of café brûlot, a flaming liqueur-laced coffee. **Price range:** Entrees, $21–$29. **Meals:** L, D. **Subway:** N, R, Q, W to 57th St.

Tribeca Grill   ☆ ☆ $$$ NEW AMERICAN
375 Greenwich St. (at Franklin St.)   (212) 941-3900
Robert De Niro's first venture into the restaurant business in what the neighbors sometimes call Bob Row is a cool, casual outpost of modern American cuisine with an almost constant flow of celebrity guests. And the food's good. The big, airy space with exposed bricks, colorful banquettes and comfortable tables centers on a massive handsome mahogany bar. The beguiling fare remains a steady lure. **Price range:** Entrees, $12–$29. **Meals:** Br, L, D. **Subway:** 1, 9 to Franklin St.

Triomphe   ☆ ☆ $$$ FRENCH/NEW AMERICAN
Iroquois Hotel, 49 W. 44th St. (between Fifth and Sixth Aves.) (212) 453-4233
In a city with flash to spare, this restaurant has a rare commodity: charm. And the food, simple and understated, matches the room. Again and again, Triom-phe quietly strikes the right note, as with a subtle herb broth that nicely under-

lines the natural sweetness of acorn-squash wontons covered in shavings of
Parmesan cheese. When the main ingredient calls for more, the chef opens up
the flavors. A hefty rib-eye steak comes with fat grilled cepes and a muscular
brandy demi-glace, and a thick slab of salmon gets the works: a caviar-dotted
beurre blanc, a scattering of grilled shrimp and parsnip whipped potatoes.
Price range: Entrees, $23–$32. **Meals:** B, L, D. **Subway:** B, D, F, S to 42nd St.

Turkuaz $25 & Under   TURKISH/MIDDLE EASTERN
2637 Broadway (at 100th St.)   (212) 665-9541
The dining room here is draped in billowy fabric so that it resembles an
Ottoman tent. Seat covers give standard restaurant chairs a lush appearance,
and the staff is adorned in traditional Turkish costumes. Cold appetizers are
excellent, and main courses tend to be simple and elementally satisfying, like
beyti kebab, spicy chopped lamb charcoal-grilled with herbs and garlic. Desserts
include a neat variation on rice pudding, served with the top caramelized like
crème brûlée. **Price range:** Entrees, $8.50–$18.50. **Meals:** D.
Subway: 1, 9 to 103rd St.

"21" Club   ☆☆ $$$$ AMERICAN
21 W. 52nd St. (between Fifth and Sixth Aves.)   (212) 582-7200
Of all the restaurants in New York City, none has a richer history. American
royalty has been entertaining at "21" for most of this century. The restaurant
continues to be operated like a club where unknowns are led to the farthest dining room as the more favored clients are pampered and petted. Nothing much
else has changed either: the tablecloths are still red and white checked, the toys
are still hanging from the ceiling, and it still looks like the speak-easy it once
was. The menu has been modernized but with mixed results. The basics are still
superb, however. Great steak, rack of lamb, Dover sole, and the "21" burger, and
several traditional desserts such as rice pudding and crème brûlée are all worthwhile. **Price range:** Entrees, $24–$39. **Meals:** L, D. Closed Sun.
Subway: E, F to Fifth Ave.

27 Standard   ☆☆ $$ NEW AMERICAN
116 E. 27th St. (between Park and Lexington Aves.)   (212) 576-2232
27 Standard is large and airy, with an interesting wine list and unusual, tasty
American food. Salads are superb and main courses imaginative. Don't miss
the roasted oysters with braised leeks and chives. The large Black Angus sirloin
steak is bathed in a fine red wine sauce and served on a lively watercress and
onion relish. Desserts are the most ornate section of the menu. **Price range:**
Entrees, $16–$27. **Meals:** L, D. Closed Sun. **Subway:** 6 to 28th St.

26 Seats $25 & Under   FRENCH
168 Ave. B. (11th St.)   (212) 677-4787
This sweet little French restaurant is intimate yet relatively comfortable, and
the waitresses are friendly and kind to children. The menu's French country

offerings are both satisfying and a good value, like the pissaladière, a flat, wafer-thin crusted tart of caramelized onions, made pungent with anchovy fillets and olives, or the savory garlic sausage paired with boiled potato and hard-boiled eggs, all dressed in a balsamic vinaigrette. The main courses are well-executed versions of familiar recipes, with the occasional pleasing twist. The nutty flavor of a perfectly grilled fillet of striped bass, for example, is matched well with a soft cake of sweet corn, while a coating of mustard and ginger gives life to a grilled chicken breast. For dessert, a wedge of apple tart is the best choice. **Price range:** Entrees, $11–$16.50. AE only **Meals:** D. Closed Mon. **Subway:** L to First Ave.

Union Pacific ☆ ☆ ☆ **$$$$**   FRENCH/ASIAN
111 E. 22nd St. (near Park Ave. South)   (212) 995-8500
This is one of the most beautiful, comfortable and soothing environments in Manhattan. A curtain of falling water at the entrance has the cool, calm look of Japan. Service is professional and enthusiastic, and chef Rocco di Spirito has invented an exciting menu. Despite Asian touches in the main part of the menu, the focus here is largely French. The unusual wine list adds another dimension. Desserts are as interesting as entrees. **Price range:** Prix-fixe and tast-ing menus, $65–$135, with supplements. **Meals:** L, D. Closed Sun. **Subway:** 6 to 23rd St.

Union Square Café ☆ ☆ **$$$**   NEW AMERICAN
21 E. 16th St. (between Fifth Ave. and Union Sq. West)   (212) 243-4020
Union Square's pioneering fusion of fine food and wine, casual atmosphere and stellar service has made it the most influential restaurant of its time in the city, certainly one of the most popular, and a top destination for tourists. The wine list is still outstanding and still full of bargains. Don't miss the signature fried calamari, golden brown, perfectly cooked outside and inside, and nicely comple-mented with an incisive, creamy anchovy mayonnaise. Although there are sev-eral foreign accents heard on the menu, Italian dominates, especially in the pasta dishes, which put many Italian restaurants to shame. Desserts aim for an artful blend of homey and exotic, most memorably in the banana tart with a caramel shellac, a Union Square standby. **Price range:** Entrees, $18.50–$28. **Meals:** L, D. **Subway:** L, N, Q, R, W, 4, 5, 6 to 14th St.

Uskudar   **$25 & Under**   TURKISH
1405 Second Ave. (near 73rd St.)   (212) 988-2641
This restaurant is the very model of a successful neighborhood institution, and it has achieved that status without the burgers, pastas and steaks that form the default menu of most local hangouts. The selection of appetizers includes two excellent Middle Eastern spreads: patlican, smoky eggplant mashed with garlic, sesame paste and herbs; and ezme, a blend of tomatoes, onions, parsley and wal-nuts. Uskudar's kebabs are uncommonly juicy, but the best dishes are the stews, like hunkar begendi, a hearty lamb stew. Uskudar makes excellent desserts, especially kadayif, shredded wheat crowned with ground walnuts and drenched

in honey. **Price range:** Entrees, $12.95–$15.95. **Meals:** L, D.
Subway: 6 to 77th St.

Vatan $25 & Under   INDIAN/VEGETARIAN
409 Third Ave. (at 29th St.)   (212) 689-5666
This astounding Indian restaurant transports you to a bright, animated Indian
village with thatched roofs and artificial banyan trees. Vatan specializes in the
rich, spicy yet subtle vegetarian cuisine of Gujarat. For one price, a parade of little dishes is served, which might include khaman, a delicious fluffy steamed
cake of lentil flour with black mustard seeds; delicate little samosas; patrel, taro
leaves layered with spicy chickpea paste and steamed, and much more.
Price range: $19.95. **Meals:** D, LN. Closed Mon. **Subway:** 6 to 28th St.

Velli $25 & Under   ITALIAN
132 W. Houston St. (near Sullivan St.)   (212) 979-7614
The newest of Jean-Claude Iacovelli's group of sophisticated, casually lively,
moderately priced restaurants is a French bistro disguised as a trattoria. It is
filled with people who have come to enjoy good food and good talk. Yes, the
menu is Italian, but the vibe is decidedly French. The philosophy is clear: keep
the menu and wine list short, the ingredients top quality and the prices reasonable. Appetizers are exceptional. **Price range:** Entrees, $12–$15. Cash only.
Meals: Br, L, LN. **Subway:** 1, 9 to Houston St.; F, S to Broadway–Lafayette St.

Verbena   ☆ $$$ NEW AMERICAN
54 Irving Pl. (near 17th St.)   (212) 260-5454
The newly remodeled Verbena looks attractive. The tight dining room retains
its very adult sense of calm and style, and a cool, breezy and secluded courtyard
garden has been created in the back. But dishes take a long time to arrive at the
table, and what arrives does not always thrill. The bolder dishes sometimes hit
and sometimes miss. The sirloin steak is a remarkably rich, tender cut, beautifully charred outside. At the start of the meal, your waiter will ask if you are
interested in the baked-to-order Bing cherry upside-down cake. Say yes. **Price
range:** Entrees, $14.50–$28. **Meals:** Br, D.
Subway: L, N, Q, R, W, 4, 5, 6 to 14th St.

Veritas   ☆ ☆ ☆ $$$$ NEW AMERICAN
43 E. 20th St. (near Park Ave. South)   (212) 353-3700
Small, spare and elegant, Veritas could be called a wine cellar with a restaurant
attached, because at Veritas, the wine is more important than the food. The
1,300 entries on its wine list include many rarities at extremely reasonable
prices. The room often seems overcrowded, but Veritas offers clean and unfussy
food that works well with its wine. Main courses, to suit the powerful wines, are
robust, powerful and simple—with surprisingly little red meat on the menu. The
intensity does not abate with desserts. Try a startlingly delicious praline parfait

with a polished reduction of clementines. **Price range:** Prix-fixe dinner, $62.
Meals: L, D. Closed Sun. **Subway:** 6 to 23rd St.

Viceversa   ☆ $$ ITALIAN
325 W. 51st St. (Between Eighth and Ninth Aves.)   (212) 399-9265
With its crisp earth-colored awnings and gleaming façade, Viceversa (pronounced VEE-chey-VAIR-suh) stands out on one of Manhattan's grungier
blocks like a Versace suit. The menu is honest and unpretentious, a solid lineup
of mostly northern Italian dishes presented in a perfectly straightforward manner. Casoncelli alla bergamasca deserves star billing in Viceversa's strong ensemble cast of pastas: it is a ravioli filled with chopped veal, crushed amaretti,
raisins and Parmesan, then topped with butter, crisped sage leaves and crunchy
bits of fried pancetta. **Price range:** Entrees, $16.50–$22.50. **Meals:** L, D.
Subway: C, E to 50th St.

Virgil's Real BBQ $25 & Under   BARBECUE
152 W. 44th St. (between Broadway and Sixth Ave.)   (212) 921-9494
Virgil's is a wildly popular shrine to barbecue joints around the country. If the
food isn't quite authentic, the formula comes close enough and it works. And
the place smells great, as any barbecue place should. Highlights on the menu
include hush puppies served with a maple syrup butter; smoked Texas links with
mustard slaw; barbecued shrimp and Texas red chili with corn bread. For main
fare, big barbecue platters carry enticing selections of Owensboro lamb, Mary-
land ham, Carolina pork shoulder, Texas beef brisket and more.
Price range: Entrees, $10.95–$18.95. **Meals:** L, D, LN.
Subway: B, D, F, N, Q, R, S, W, 1, 2, 3, 7, 9 to 42nd St.

Virot   ☆☆ $$$ FRENCH
Dylan Hotel, 52 E. 41st St. (between Madison and Park Aves.)   (646) 658-0266
Diners will not leave Virot feeling that they've had an ordinary meal. Chef
Didier Virot starts with a main ingredient and treats it like a star. He has an
admirable sense of proportion, never letting his supporting cast of flavors and
ingredients take over the stage. In a minor miracle, big, fat shrimp, cooked to a
light outer crisp on a skewer with some basil leaves and a light saffron- mustard
dressing, remind you of what shrimp used to taste like. A cake of basmati rice
accompanies a magnificent lobster sautéed with cardamom and bathed with a
caramel ginger sauce. For dessert, try the demure, flawless flat cake made from
ricotta cheese and roasted pineapple, with a scoop of tart, concentrated pineapple sorbet. Service is a little hushed and reverential at Virot, and the style can
be traced directly to the chill, formal room, which canfeel like the waiting room
in a grand old train station. Upstairs a treasure awaits, the balcony lounge. It's
dark and intimate and feels like a secret hideaway. **Price range:** Prix fixe and
tasting menus, $49–$75. **Meals:** L, D. **Subway:** S, 4, 5, 6, 7 to 42nd St.

West 63rd Street Steak House   ☆ $$$$ STEAKHOUSE
44 W. 63rd St. (near Broadway)   (212) 246-6363

This restaurant turns the New York steakhouse experience on its head. It is quiet and restful, and the service is solicitous. As plush and comfortable as a rich man's library, it has an attractive view of Lincoln Center and serves big potent drinks and excellent shrimp cocktail. Unfortunately the steaks aren't always very good. The porterhouse and T-bone are sometimes aged to perfection, sometimes not; you just can't count on them. The veal chop, however, is a fine piece of meat and the roasted baby chicken is flavorful. Among the many side dishes the french fries are excellent, and so is the nutmeg-free creamed spinach, but the home fries are unimpressive. **Price range:** Entrees, $21–$30. **Meals:** D. Closed Sun. **Subway:** 6 to 66th St.

Wu Liang Ye $25 & Under   CHINESE
338 Lexington Ave. (between 39th and 40th Sts.)   (212) 370-9647
215 E. 86th St. (at Third Ave.)   (212) 534-8899
36 W. 48th St. (between Fifth and Sixth Aves.)   (212) 398-2308

Though each of these branches of a Chinese restaurant chain differs slightly in menu and atmosphere, they all specialize in lively, robust Sichuan dishes, notable for their meticulous preparation. Sliced conch is one of their more unusual dishes, firm, chewy and nutty, served with spicy red oil. Four kinds of dumplings are all delicate and flavorful. **Price range:** $7.50–$20. **Meals:** L, D, LN. **Subway:** Call for directions to each location.

Xunta $25 & Under   SPANISH/TAPAS
174 First Ave. (near 11th St.)   (212) 614-0620

Xunta (pronounced SHOON-tuh) has the authentic feeling of a Spanish tapas bar. It's informal, crowded, smoky and loud, with dozens of tapas. The selection of Spanish wines and sherries is just right. **Price range:** Tapas, $2.75–$16.25. **Meals:** D, LN. **Subway:** L to First Ave.

Yakiniku JuJu $25 & Under   JAPANESE
157 E. 28th St. (between Third and Lexington Aves.)   (212) 684-7830

This small and friendly restaurant specializes in cook-it-yourself shabu-shabu, sukiyaki and Japanese barbecue. Try an appetizer of "salted squid guts," chewy and salty squid cut into cylinders the size of small anchovies and immersed in a pasty liquid; or takoyaki, croquettes stuffed with pieces of octopus and flavored with dried seaweed, ginger and a fruity sauce. The large main courses include yakiniku, in which you cook pieces of meat and vegetables directly on the grill; shabu-shabu, in which you swish the meat and vegetables through boiling broth; and sukiyaki, the traditional Japanese stew. **Price range:** Dinner for two, $30–$46; for four, up to $80. **Meals:** D. **Subway:** 6 to 28th St.

Zarela   ☆☆ $$ MEXICAN/TEX-MEX
953 Second Ave. (between 50th and 51st Sts.)   (212) 644-6740

Bright, bold and raucous as a party, the sort of place that looks like a typical

---

Mexican taquería. Happily, it is not. Zarela Martinez has written several excellent Mexican cookbooks, and she serves some of the city's most exciting and authentic Mexican food. Among the best dishes are a fiery snapper hash, crisp flautas, tamales and fajitas. Good side dishes include creamy rice baked with sour cream, cheddar cheese, corn and poblano chilies, and pozole guisado, in which hominy kernels are sautéed with tomatoes, onions, garlic and jalapeño peppers. **Price range:** Avg. entree, $22. **Meals:** L, D.
Subway: 6 to 51st St.; E, F to Lexington Ave.

Zum Schneider $25 & Under   GERMAN
107 Ave. C (at 7th St.)   (212) 598-1098
Essentially an indoor beer garden, Zum Schneider packs young people in nightly. The simple menu hews closely to the Bavarian formula of wurst, pork and cabbage, but it has accomplished the unlikely feat of making a German place cool. Try the pfannkuchen soup, literally pancake soup, a mild beef broth seasoned only with parsley and a bit of salt and containing slender strips of egg pancakes, the equivalent of light dumplings. The best of the main courses is a plump, rosy smoked pork chop. The bar offers a dozen excellent seasonal draft beers, all German, and 10 more in bottles.   **Price range:** Entrees, $7–$12, with $3 and $6 appetizer portions. Cash only. **Meals:** L, D.
Subway: F to Second Ave.; L to First Ave.

Zuni $25 & Under   SOUTHWESTERN
598 Ninth Ave. (at 43rd St.)   (212) 765-7626
The original focus at this appealing little restaurant was Southwestern, and the atmosphere still reflects this, but the current menu is all over the map, with Southwestern dishes like chili-rubbed rib-eye steak, New Orleans specialties like jambalaya and geographically indecipherable offerings like sesame-crusted salmon with mango-and-black-bean salsa and basmati rice. If it's too confusing, settle for meatloaf and garlic mashed potatoes. It's usually all pretty good. **Price range:** Entrees, $8–$16.95. **Meals:** Br, L, D, LN. **Subway:** A, C, E to 42nd St.

A Guide to Restaurants by Cuisine

AMERICAN
An American
    Place ☆☆
City Hall ☆☆
Fifty Seven
    Fifty Seven ☆☆☆
Grange Hall
The Half King
"21" Club ☆☆

ARGENTINE
Chimichurri Grill

AUSTRALIAN
Eight Mile Creek ☆☆

AUSTRIAN
Danube ☆☆☆

BARBECUE
Virgil's Real BBQ

BELGIAN
Cafe de Bruxelles

CAJUN
Bayou

CARIBBEAN
Bambou ☆☆
Island Spice

CHINESE
Big Wong
Congee Village
Dim Sum Go Go ☆
Evergreen Shanghai
Funky Broome
Goody's
Grand Sichuan
Henry's Evergreen

Joe's Shanghai ☆☆
Mee Noodle Shop
New Green Bo
New York Noodle
    Town ☆☆
Our Place
Pig Heaven
Ping's Seafood ☆☆
Shun Lee Palace ☆☆
Shun Lee West
Wu Liang Ye

CONTINENTAL
Cafe des Artistes
Eleven Madison
    Park ☆☆
One if By Land

DELI
Carnegie Deli
Katz's Deli

DINER
Barking Dog
Empire Diner

DUTCH
NL ☆

EAST EUROPEAN
Danube ☆☆☆

FRENCH
Abajour ☆
Alain Ducasse ☆☆☆
Alison on
    Dominick ☆☆
Alley's End
Alouette
Artisanal ☆☆
Balthazar ☆☆

Bandol
Barrio ☆
Bayard's ☆☆
Blue Hill ☆☆
Bouley
    Bakery ☆☆☆☆
Bouterin ☆
Brasserie ☆☆
Café Boulud ☆☆☆
Café Loup
Cello ☆☆☆
Chanterelle ☆☆☆
Chelsea Bistro
    & Bar ☆☆
Chez Josephine ☆☆
Coup ☆
Daniel ☆☆☆☆
D'Artagnan ☆☆
DB Bistro Moderne ☆☆
Destinée ☆☆
Fleur de Sel ☆☆
Guastavino's ☆☆
Jean Claude
Jean Georges ☆☆☆☆
JoJo ☆☆☆
Jubilee
La Caravelle ☆☆☆
La Côte Basque ☆☆☆
L'Actuel ☆☆
La Grenouille ☆☆☆
L'Ardoise
Le Bernardin ☆☆☆☆
Le Cirque 2000 ☆☆☆
Le Gigot
Le Périgord
Lespinasse ☆☆☆☆
Le Tableau
Le Zinc ☆
Le Zoo
Lutèce ☆☆
Mercer Kitchen ☆☆

Note: Restaurants in **boldface italics** are Eric Asimov's choices for the best inexpensive restaurants in New York.

Montrachet ☆☆☆
Orsay ☆☆
Panaché
Papillon ☆
Park Bistro ☆☆☆
Pastis ☆
Payard Pâtisserie ☆☆
Peacock Alley ☆☆☆
Picholine ☆☆☆
Provence ☆
Sono ☆☆
Tocqueville ☆☆
Triomphe ☆☆
Union Pacific ☆☆☆
Virot ☆

GERMAN
Silver Swan
Zum Schneider

GREEK
Avra ☆
Estiatorio Milos ☆☆
Meltemi
Metsovo
Molyvos ☆☆☆
Periyali ☆☆☆
Snack

HAMBURGERS
McHale's

INDIAN
Ada ☆☆
Chola ☆☆
Dakshin
Dawat ☆
Mavalli Palace
Mirchi
Mughlai
Pongal
Salaam Bombay ☆☆
Surya ☆☆
Tabla ☆☆☆
Tamarind ☆☆

Vatan
INDONESIAN
Bali Nusa Indah
NL ☆

ITALIAN
Arqua ☆☆
Babbo ☆☆☆
Baldoria ☆
Bar Pitti
Beppe ☆☆
Bice ☆☆
Cafe La Grolla
Campagna ☆☆
City Eatery ☆☆
Delmonico's ☆
Esca ☆☆
F.Illi Ponte ☆☆
Felidia ☆☆☆
Frank
Fresco By Scotto ☆☆
Gabriel's ☆☆
Gradisca
Il Valentino ☆☆
Il Mulino
'ino
Isola
I Trulli ☆☆
La Locanda
La Nonna ☆
Lentini ☆
Le Cirque 2000 ☆☆☆
Le Zie
Lupa
Max
Osteria Del Circo
  ☆☆
Palio ☆☆
Paola's ☆☆
Parioli
  Romanissimo ☆☆
Peasant ☆
Pepe Verde
Pepolino
Po

Remi ☆☆
Risa
San Domenico
  ☆☆☆
Scalini Fedeli ☆
Velli
Viceversa ☆

JAPANESE
Blue Ribbon Sushi ☆☆
Hatsuhana ☆☆
Honmura An ☆☆☆
Jewel Bako
Katsu-Hama
Komodo
Kuruma Zushi ☆☆☆
Marumi
Nadaman
  Hakubai ☆☆
Next Door Nobu
  ☆☆☆
Nobu ☆☆☆
Otabe ☆☆
Soba Nippon
Sono ☆☆
Sushi Hatsu ☆☆
Sushi Yasuda ☆☆☆
Yakiniku JuJu

KOREAN
Cho Dang Gol ☆☆
Do Hwa
Emo's
Han Bat
Han Sung Garden
Hangawi ☆☆
Kang Suh ☆☆
Kori
Mandoo Bar

LATIN AMERICAN
Asia de Cuba ☆
Boca Chica
Calle Ocho ☆
Chicama ☆☆

Chimichurri Grill
Churrascaria
 Plataforma ☆☆
Circus ☆☆
Cocina Cuzco
Cuba Libre
El Fogon
Esperanto
Flor's Kitchen
Good
Havana NY
Komodo
La Fonda Boricua
National Cafe
Patria ☆☆☆

MEDITERRANEAN
Acquario
Gus's Figs Bistro & Bar
Lavagna
Nick & Toni's ☆☆
Olives ☆
Picholine ☆☆☆
Savoy ☆☆
Tappo ☆

MEXICAN/TEX-MEX
Café Frida
Casa Mexicana
El Paso Taqueria
Gabriela's
Hell's Kitchen
Los Dos Rancheros
La Palapa
Maya ☆☆
Mesa Grill ☆☆
Mexicana Mama
Mi Cocina ☆☆
Rinconcito Mexicano
Rocking Horse
Rosa Mexicano ☆☆
Taco Taco
Zarela ☆☆

MIDDLE EASTERN
Cookies and Couscous
Layla ☆☆
Moustache
Tagine
Turkuaz

NEW AMERICAN
Aleutia ☆
Alley's End
An American
 Place ☆☆
Atlas ☆☆☆
Aureole ☆☆
Beacon ☆☆
Bright Food Shop
Chat 'n Chew
City Hall ☆☆
Cooke's Corner
Coup ☆
Craft ☆☆☆
Della Femina ☆
Delmonico's ☆
The Dining Room ☆☆
District ☆
Etats-Unis ☆☆
First
The Four
 Seasons ☆☆☆
Gotham Bar
 and Grill ☆☆☆
Gramercy
 Tavern ☆☆☆
Heartbeat ☆☆
Hudson River
 Club ☆☆
Icon ☆☆
Ilo ☆☆☆
Inside
Irving on Irving
Jack Rose ☆
Jane ☆

Jean Georges ☆☆☆☆
Joe Allen
Josie's
Judson Grill ☆☆☆
Little Dove ☆☆
March ☆☆☆
Merge
Michael's ☆☆
Odeon ☆☆
Ouest ☆☆
Park Ave. Cafe ☆☆
Park View ☆☆
Patroon ☆☆☆
Red Bar Restaurant ☆
The Red Cat ☆
Redeye Grill ☆
Savoy ☆☆
Screening Room ☆☆
71 Clinton Fresh
 Food ☆☆
Stella
The Tasting Room ☆
Tavern on the Green ☆
Thalia ☆☆
The Tonic ☆☆
Town ☆☆☆
Tribeca Grill ☆☆
Triomphe ☆☆
21 Club ☆☆
27 Standard ☆☆
Union Square
 Cafe ☆☆
Verbena ☆
Veritas ☆☆☆

PAN-ASIAN
Asia de Cuba ☆
Pop ☆
Ruby Foo's ☆☆
Tabla ☆☆☆

PAN-LATIN
Boca Chica

Note: Restaurants in **boldface italics** are Eric Asimov's choices for the best inexpensive restaurants in New York.

Bolivar ☆☆
Calle Ocho ☆
Esperanto
Patria ☆☆☆
Sabor

PORTUGUESE
Luzia's
Pao
Pico ☆☆☆

RUSSIAN
Firebird ☆☆
Petrossian ☆☆
Russian Tea Room

SCANDINAVIAN
Aquavit ☆☆☆
Christer's ☆☆
Good World Bar & Grill

SEAFOOD
Aquagrill ☆☆
Atlantic Grill ☆
Avra ☆
Blue Water Grill ☆
Bongo
Cello ☆☆☆
Dock's ☆
Esca ☆☆
Estiatorio Milos ☆☆
Grill Room ☆☆
Le Bernardin ☆☆☆☆
Manhattan Ocean
   Club ☆☆
Maritime ☆
Meltemi
Oceana ☆☆☆

Sea Grill ☆☆
SOUTHERN
Amy Ruth's
Bayou
Emily's
Hog Pit
Miss Maude's
Sylvia's

SOUTHWESTERN
Mesa Grill ☆☆
Zuni

SPANISH
El Cid
El Fogon
Meigas ☆☆
Solera ☆☆
Xunta

STEAKHOUSE
Bistro Le Steak
Churrascaria
   Plataforma ☆☆
Frank's ☆
Jack Rose ☆
Michael Jordan's ☆☆
Palm
Smith &
   Wollensky ☆☆
Soho Steak
Strip House ☆
West 63rd Street ☆

SUSHI
Blue Ribbon Sushi ☆☆
Hatsuhana ☆☆
Inagiku ☆☆

Jewel Bako
Kuruma Zushi ☆☆☆
Marumi
Sugiyama ☆☆
Sushi Hatsu ☆☆
Sushi Yasuda ☆☆☆

THAI
Holy Basil
Little Basil
Pam Real Thai Food
Royal Siam
Topaz Thai

TURKISH
The Sultan
Turkuaz
Uskudar

VEGETARIAN
Hangawi ☆☆
Mavalli Palace
Pongal
Tiffin

VIETNAMESE
Cyclo
Le Colonial ☆☆
Nha Trang

Index